GABRIEL'S PALACE

BY HOWARD SCHWARTZ

Poetry
Vessels
Gathering the Sparks
Sleepwalking Beneath the Stars

Fiction
A Blessing Over Ashes
Midrashim
The Captive Soul of the Messiah
Rooms of the Soul
Adam's Soul

Editor
Imperial Messages: One Hundred Modern Parables
Voices Within the Ark: The Modern Jewish Poets
Gates to the New City: A Treasury of Modern Jewish Tales
The Dream Assembly: Tales of Rabbi Zalman Schachter-Shalomi
Elijah's Violin & Other Jewish Fairy Tales
Miriam's Tambourine: Jewish Tales from Around the World
Lilith's Cave: Jewish Tales of the Supernatural
Gabriel's Palace: Jewish Mystical Tales

Children's Books
The Diamond Tree
The Sabbath Lion

GABRIEL'S PALACE

Jewish Mystical Tales

Selected and Retold by

HOWARD SCHWARTZ

New York Oxford
OXFORD UNIVERSITY PRESS
1993

Oxford University Press

Oxford   New York   Toronto
Delhi   Bombay   Calcutta   Madras   Karachi
Kuala Lumpur   Singapore   Hong Kong   Tokyo
Nairobi   Dar es Salaam   Cape Town
Melbourne   Auckland   Madrid

and associated companies in
Berlin   Ibadan

Published by Oxford University Press, Inc.
200 Madison Avenue, New York, New York 10016

Oxford is a registered trademark of Oxford University Press, Inc.

Library of Congress Cataloging-in-Publication Data
Schwartz, Howard, 1945-
Gabriel's palace : Jewish mystical tales /
selected and retold by Howard Schwartz.
p.   cm.
Includes bibliographical references and index.
ISBN 0–19–506292–2
1. Legends, Jewish.   2. Cabala.
3. Mysticism—Judaism.   4. Hasidim—Legends.
5. Tales.   6. Jews—Folklore.
I. Title.   BM530.S465   1993   296.1'9—dc20   92–28722

Some of these tales have previously been published in
the following newspapers and journals:
The Forward, Parabola,
The Sagarin Review, The St. Louis Jewish Light,
The St. Louis Post-Dispatch,
The St. Louis Post-Dispatch Magazine,
and Tikkun.
Some of these tales are also included in the
anthology The Ways of Religion:
An Introduction to the Major Traditions,
edited by Roger Eastman.

1 3 5 7 9 8 6 4 2

Printed in the United States of America
on acid-free paper

For Rabbi Zalman Schachter-Shalomi

The Mysteries in these books are clothed in stories.
Betzalel Joshua of Glaina
Tosefta Lemidrash Pinhas

ACKNOWLEDGMENTS

I am grateful to the following people for their assistance in the editing of this book: Cynthia Read, my editor, for her patience, insight and clear vision; my wife, Tsila Schwartz, whose help was essential at every stage; Arielle North Olson and Y. David Shulman for their fine editorial assistance; Marc Bregman, for inspiration and advice, and Ellen Levine and Diana Finch of the Ellen Levine Literary Agency; as well as Tracy Armer, Rabbi James Bennett, Theresa Blackburn, Rabbi Tsvi Blanchard, James Bogan, Rabbi Jonathan Case, Michael Castro, Joseph Dan, Lawrence Davis, Paul Corby Finney, Jeremy Garber, Stanley George, Robin Goldberg, Peter Grant, Avraham Greenbaum, Helen Greenberg, Rabbi James Stone Goodman, Edna Hechal, Brenda Jaeger, Rabbi Yosef Landa, Charles Larson, Pier Marton, Lila Neel, Dov Noy, E. Terrence Jones, Rabbi Abraham Ezra Millgram, Eugene Murray, Peter Ohlin, Clarence Olson, Virginia Perrin, Barbara Raznick, Amy Roberts, Deborah Rosenbaum, Robert Rosenfeld, Steven Rowan, Barbara Rush, Steve Sanfield, Marc Saperstein, Gershom Scholem, Charles Schwartz, Maury Schwartz, Rabbi Zalman Schachter-Shalomi, Alan Segal, Laya Firestone-Seghi, Dan Sharon, Susan Stone, Byron Sherwin, Aliza Shenhar, Morton Smith, Ida Stack, David Stern, Katrina Stierholz, Rabbi Jeffrey Stiffman, T. J. Stiles, Susan Stone, Michael Swartz, Rabbi Susan Talve, David Tran, Sarita Varma, Yehuda Yaari, Eli Yassif, Gerhson Winkler, and Mary B. Zettwock.

Howard Schwartz

CONTENTS

Introduction, 3

I RABBINIC TALES

1 The Golden Dove, 41
2 An Appointment with Death, 42
3 Isaac's Ascent, 43
4 The Magic Flock, 44
5 The Ascent of Moses, 45
6 The Chronicle of Serah bat Asher, 47
7 Mysteries of the Chariot, 50
8 The Four Who Entered Paradise, 51
9 Rabbi Ishmael's Ascent, 52
10 The Waters of the Abyss, 54
11 The Vision of the High Priest, 55
12 The Keys of the Temple, 56
13 The Spirit of Idolatry, 56
14 The Angel of Conception, 57
15 The Golden Table, 58
16 The *Tzohar*, 59
17 The Gates of Eden, 62
18 The Law Is Not in Heaven, 63
19 The Voice in the Attic, 64
20 Forcing the End, 65

II KABBALISTIC TALES

The Circle of Shimon bar Yohai

21 The Cave of Shimon bar Yohai, 69
22 The Decree, 70
23 The Curtain of Fire, 71
24 A Saint from the Other World, 72

25 The Golden Scepter, 73
26 The Book of Adam, 74
27 Rabbi Gadiel the Child, 75
28 The Celestial Academy, 76
29 The Book of Flying Letters, 77
30 Candles in the Synagogue, 78
31 A Kiss from the Master, 79

The Circle of the Ari

32 The Pillar of Cloud, 80
33 The Angel of Forgetfulness, 81
34 The Dancing of the Ari, 83
35 The Blessing of the *Kohanim*, 84
36 The Journey to Jerusalem, 86
37 The Precious Prayer, 86
38 A Vision at the Wailing Wall, 87
39 Reading the Lips of the Ari, 89
40 The Speaking Flame, 90
41 Greeting the Sabbath Queen, 93
42 Gathering Sparks, 94
43 Delivering a Message, 95
44 A Stone in the Wall, 97
45 The Widow of Safed, 98
46 The Body of Moses, 100
47 A Visit to the City of the Dead, 101
48 The Angel in the Mirror, 102
49 The Handwriting of the Messiah, 103

Other Kabbalistic Tales

50 The Palace of Vanities, 104
51 The Chains of the Messiah, 106
52 The *Tzaddik* of the Forest, 109
53 The Angel of the Mishnah, 112
54 A New Lease on Life, 114
55 Redemption of the Lost Souls, 115
56 Repairing Souls, 116
57 The *Tefillin* of the Or Hayim, 117

III MYSTICAL FOLKTALES

58 Gabriel's Palace, 121
59 The Cottage of Candles, 124
60 Rabbi Shimon's Escape, 126
61 The Boy Who Blew the Shofar, 127

62 The Enchanted Inn, 130
63 Leaves from the Garden of Eden, 134
64 The Tenth Man, 135
65 The Ram Whose Horns Reached to Heaven, 137
66 The Cave of King David, 139
67 The Shining Robe, 141
68 The Evil Angel, 143
69 The Young Man without a Soul, 145
70 Asenath's Dove, 148
71 The Tale of the Kiddush Cup, 149
72 The Miracle in the Sukkah, 151
73 Rabbi Naftali's Trance, 152
74 Interpreting the Zohar, 154
75 The Secrets of Kabbalah, 155
76 The Flying Letters, 156
77 The Curse, 157
78 The Miracle of the Ring, 158
79 The Angel's Daughter, 160
80 The Bridegroom and the Angel of Death, 162
81 The Cave to the Holy Land, 164
82 The Cave of Temptations, 166
83 The Hollow of the Sling, 168
84 How Rabbi Judah the Pious Became a Great Scholar, 170
85 The Words in the Sand, 171
86 The Count Who Wanted to Study Kabbalah, 172
87 The Dream Question of the Maharal, 174
88 The Ruin, 175
89 The Voice in the Tree, 177
90 A Vision in the Cemetery, 178
91 The Spirit of Hagigah, 179

IV HASIDIC TALES

The Circle of the Baal Shem Tov

92 The Book in the Cave, 183
93 The Prince of Fire, 187
94 The Angel's Sword, 189
95 The Ladder of Prayers, 191
96 The Tree of Life, 192
97 A Crown of Shoes, 194
98 The Flaming Tree, 195
99 A Visitor from the Other World, 196
100 The Master Key, 198
101 The Enchanted Island, 199

102 The Circle of Fire, 202
103 The Tale of the Frog, 203
104 The Field of Souls, 204
105 Unlocking the Gates of Heaven, 205
106 The Healing Spring, 207
107 Lighting a Fire, 209

The Circle of Reb Pinhas of Koretz

108 Opening a Verse, 210
109 The Angel of the Zohar, 212
110 The Angel of Friendship, 213
111 The Underground Forest, 214
112 Reb Pinhas and the Angel of Death, 219

The Circle of Reb Elimelech of Lizensk

113 The Woman in the Forest, 221
114 A Bowl of Soup, 222
115 The Wine of Paradise, 223
116 The Young Magician, 224
117 Reb Shmelke's Whip, 226
118 Three Stars, 227
119 The Shadow on the Wall, 228
120 The Garden of the Torah, 229

The Circle of Reb Nachman of Bratslav

121 A Vision of Light, 231
122 The Scribe, 232
123 The Sabbath Fish, 233
124 The Sword of the Messiah, 234
125 The Souls of Trees, 236
126 Divining from the Zohar, 237
127 The Angel of Losses, 238
128 The Book That Was Burned, 239
129 A Letter from the Beyond, 240
130 Reb Nachman's Chair, 241
131 Reb Nachman's Tomb, 242
132 The Soul of Reb Nachman, 244

Other Hasidic Masters

133 A Vision of the Bride, 245
134 The Flaming Letters, 247
135 The Saba Kadisha in the Upper World, 248
136 The Wandering Well, 250
137 The Sabbath Guests, 251

Contents

138 From the Beyond, 253
139 The Prayer Leader, 254
140 The Pact, 256
141 The Clock of the Seer of Lublin, 257
142 The Soul of the Ari, 258
143 The Blind Angel, 259
144 The Cave of Mattathias, 261
145 A New Soul, 263
146 A Vision, 264
147 The Tale of the Etrog, 265
148 A Wandering Soul, 266
149 Trying to Pray, 267
150 The Tale of the Kugel, 268

V SOURCES AND COMMENTARY

Sources and Commentary, 275

Appendix, 357
Glossary, 367
Bibliography, 377
Index, 393

GABRIEL'S PALACE

Introduction

The writings of mystical circles are almost always accompanied by tales recounting the mystical experiences of the key religious figures. This is true of the tales about Zen and Sufi masters, as well as those of Jewish and Christian mystics such as Rabbi Isaac Luria or St. John of the Cross. Some kind of direct experience or revelation of the Divine is often found in these tales. So too do they define the range of mystical experience. At the same time, such tales bring with them the power of the story, making them far more accessible than most mystical texts.[1]

One of the most famous Jewish mystical tales tells of four sages who somehow entered Paradise. One lost his life there; another lost his mind; the third became an apostate. Only Rabbi Akiba "ascended and descended in peace."[2] Generations of rabbis have debated what caused the downfall of the three sages and have used the story of "The Four Who Entered Paradise" as a warning tale about the dangers of mystical contemplation. Nevertheless, there was also an ancient Jewish sect that created texts describing such heavenly journeys in great detail. These writings, known as "Hekhaloth texts," seem to have served as guidebooks for ascent, much as the Tibetan Book of the Dead was intended to guide the soul of one who journeyed from this world to the next. Thus the story of the four who entered Paradise served a key role from the perspective of both those who understood it as a warning tale and those who saw it as a model for ascent.

This account of the four sages, of talmudic origin, represents a kind of tale, based on a mystical theme, that constitutes a genre of its own. And like fairy tales, tales of the supernatural, parables, and fables, these mystical tales are found in every phase of Jewish literature.

This unexpectedly rich tradition of Jewish mystical tales abounds in postbiblical sources, not only in sacred texts but in secular ones as well. These sacred texts include kabbalistic and Hasidic sources, where such tales are most likely to be found, as well as the earlier pseudepigraphal and rabbinical texts, while the secular texts are

3

drawn from a remarkable body of mystical folktales in medieval Jewish folklore.

These mystical tales constitute the legendary dimension of the Jewish mystical tradition. They accompany and in many ways comple-
ment a body of complex mystical teachings that can be broadly defined
as "kabbalistic," when that term is used to refer to an esoteric mystical
tradition that has its origins in biblical accounts of creation and the
vision of Ezekiel,[3] and is found in every subsequent phase of sacred
Jewish literature.[4]

The tales in this book cover a range of mystical experiences, virtually all presented as true accounts, not only of mystical union but of
visions, dreams, soul travel, encounters with angels and demons, possession by both good and evil spirits, miracles, and experiences out of
body and out of time. Yet, despite these disparate themes, virtually all
of them have in common some kind of revelation or interaction with
the Divine realm, and as such can be properly defined as mystical. For
the imprint of the Divine is deeply reflected in these tales.

Just as the account of the four sages who entered Paradise serves as
the model for mystical tales of heavenly ascent, so the models for most
of the primary types of mystical tales can be found in the Talmud.
The primary repositories of rabbinic legend are the two Talmuds,
finally edited or "redacted" in Babylonia and in the Land of Israel in
about the fifth century, and the vast midrashic literature, which was
produced well into the middle ages, up until at least the twelfth century. These include tales about mystical visions ("Mysteries of the
Chariot"), visions of God ("The Vision of the High Priest), divine
miracles ("The Golden Table"), and attempts to hasten the coming of
the Messiah ("Forcing the End"). Indeed, virtually all of the major
mystical themes are found in the early rabbinic tales. However, the
tales, as they have been preserved, tend to be concise. There is little of
the narrative embellishment found in later tales, especially those of
folk origin. In many cases, including that of the four who entered
Paradise, the tales are fragmentary, and only the bare bones of what
was clearly a more extensive tradition have survived. For example, the
legend of the four who entered Paradise and the accompanying legends in tractate Hagigah of the Talmud resemble fragments of a
Hekhaloth text, some of which were either contemporaneous with the
Talmud or older. So too is the influence of these early rabbinic tales on
the subsequent literary tradition immense. Indeed, many kabbalistic
and Hasidic tales seem to seek out rabbinic models intentionally in
order to draw a parallel between the earlier rabbis and those of their
own era.

There are several early kabbalistic works, in addition to the Hekhaloth texts, such as *Sefer Yetsirah* and *Sefer Bahir*, that clearly demonstrate a developing mystical consciousness in Judaism. But it is not until the appearance of the Zohar, the central text of Jewish mysticism, in the thirteenth century that the kabbalistic era begins. This period, which is usually dated between the thirteenth and seventeenth centuries, encompasses the writing of the Zohar by Moshe de Leon in the thirteenth century and the emergence of the teachings and tales of the Ari and the other sages of Safed in the sixteenth century, as well as the school of Rabbi Shalom Sharabi in Jerusalem and the messianic movement of the false messiah Shabbatai Zevi in the seventeenth century.

Some of the most important mystical tales emerged out of this kabbalistic period. The Zohar itself is one of the richest sources of both mythic and legendary material. It contains many anecdotes about the talmudic sage Rabbi Shimon bar Yohai, known by the acronym Rashbi, who lived in the second century and who is reputed to be the author of the Zohar. However, as Gershom Scholem and other scholars have documented, the actual author was almost certainly Moshe de Leon, who lived in Guadalajara, Spain, in the thirteenth century. De Leon presented the text of the Zohar as a manuscript he had found.[5] But until the work of modern scholars cast doubt on de Leon's claim of discovery, it was considered authentic, and the Zohar was soon identified as a sacred text. Even today many Orthodox Jewish circles continue to assert that Rabbi Shimon bar Yohai is the true author of the Zohar, rejecting the scholarship in the same way that they reject any suggestion that God did not literally dictate the Torah to Moses at Mount Sinai. But for scholar and believer alike, the Zohar remains the central text of the Kabbalah.

Because of their influence on the subsequent development of the mystical tale, the tales found in the classic kabbalistic texts, especially the Zohar, and certain key legends, such as that about Joseph della Reina, who sought to force the coming of the Messiah, as well as the tales about the Ari, constitute the core of Jewish mystical tales. At the same time, these tales are largely a continuation of the earlier rabbinic traditions, just as the Zohar presents itself as the mystical account of the life and teachings of a talmudic sage, Rabbi Shimon bar Yohai. Thus it is important to distinguish the term "mystical" from the narrower term "kabbalistic." In a general sense, "Kabbalah" refers to the entire field of Jewish mysticism. But in a more technical sense, it refers specifically to the period of the thirteenth to seventeenth centuries.

The kabbalistic period concludes with the trauma of the messianic movement of Shabbatai Zevi in the seventeenth century.[6] Since kabbalistic concepts were the underpinning of the teachings of Shabbatai Zevi, his apostasy resulted in renewed efforts to limit access to the kabbalistic texts and to keep the entire study esoteric.

Nor does the mystical tale end after the failure of the Sabbatian movement. It reemerges during the Hasidic period, beginning in the eighteenth century, and achieves a flowering that dwarfs all other periods, including the kabbalistic. Here are found an abundance of tales about the Hasidic rabbis resembling those of the Zen and Sufi masters. Certain rabbis, in particular, such as the Baal Shem Tov, Reb Pinhas of Koretz, Reb Elimelech of Lizensk, and Reb Nachman of Bratslav, demonstrate great mystical powers. But evidence of these powers is also found in tales linked with many other Hasidic rabbis, such as Reb Levi Yitzhak of Berditchev, Reb Eizek of Kallo, or the Maid of Ludomir, one of the only women recognized as a rebbe.[7] While each of these masters follows his or her own path, it is apparent that the models of the master in these tales are drawn from the legends of Rabbi Shimon bar Yohai, Rabbi Isaac Luria, and the Baal Shem Tov.

Although the Jewish mystical tale is primarily found in sacred texts, there are also secular expressions of these mystical tales in collections of medieval Jewish folklore and among the rich treasury of oral tales collected by enthnologists from both Eastern European and Middle Eastern Jewish communities. These tales are primarily collected in two archives: the YIVO archives of Eastern European folklore, originally of Vilna, now of New York, and the Israel Folktale Archives (IFA) in Haifa, which has collected tales of virtually every Jewish ethnic community in the world.

The majority of these tales are about key mystical masters. Certain patriarchs, prophets, and rabbis were depicted as drawing on knowledge of the divine realm to fulfill some kind of mystical purpose. Some were described as seeking personal enlightenment, others knowledge of the divine mysteries; some as seeking to have heaven intercede to protect the Jewish community from one danger or another; still others as seeking to hasten the coming of the Messiah. Thus these masters function as shamans, going into trances, communing with angels and spirits of the dead, confronting evil spirits, and, in general, demonstrating their mastery of all the spiritual and physical realms.

The stories about these mystical masters often form cycles of tales. There are major cycles involving biblical figures such as Enoch, Moses, and Elijah; talmudic sages such as Rabbi Akiba, Rabbi Shimon bar Yohai, and Rabbi Ishmael the High Priest; medieval figures such as Judah the Pious, Rabbi Isaac Luria, and Rabbi Judah Loew; and, among Hasidic masters, the Baal Shem Tov, in particular, as well as many others. In addition, there are scattered mystical tales about many other rabbis and hidden saints. Each of the scattered Jewish communities had their own legends. Even related stories about their disciples, such as those about Rabbi Hayim Vital, the primary disciple of Rabbi Isaac Luria, often constitute a story cycle of their own.

These tale cycles often begin with legendary accounts of the lives of these masters, from their miraculous births to the legends surrounding their deaths, as well as sporadic reports of their spirits returning after death. This pattern of return from the beyond first takes form in the many legends about the reappearance of the Prophet Elijah in this world, often disguised as a wandering beggar.[8] In the majority of Jewish folktales, Elijah draws upon his miraculous powers to assist Jews in need. But his role changes when he studies with mystics such as Rabbi Shimon bar Yohai and the Ari. He does not conceal his identity from them. Rather, he reveals mysteries of heaven, serving as a kind of heavenly master, the model for all the living masters who follow.

The first of the talmudic sages whose spirit returns after death is Rabbi Shimon bar Yohai, who spent thirteen years hiding from the Romans in a cave, where he was reputed to have written the Zohar, the primary text of Jewish mysticism.[9] So powerful is Bar Yohai's soul that there are many accounts of him appearing in the world long after his death. In one such story, "The Dancing of the Ari," he appears at the Lag ba-Omer celebration of Rabbi Isaac Luria and dances with him. In another he returns in a dream, as in this early midrashic tale:

> One of the disciples of Rabbi Shimon bar Yohai forgot what he had learned and went weeping to the cemetery. After this Rashbi appeared to him in a dream and said: "When you throw three pebbles at me I will come to you." The disciple went to a dream interpreter, who told him to repeat each lesson three times and Rabbi Shimon would come to him, and he would no longer forget what he had studied. This turned out to be true. Every time he repeated the lesson three times, Rabbi Shimon came to him and his memory was restored.[10]

What this midrashic tale suggests is that the spirit of Rabbi Shimon bar Yohai returned in the form of an *ibur*, literally an impregnation, a positive kind of possession in which the spirit of a great sage who has died is bound to one of the living in order to increase the man's wisdom and faith.[11] This is in contrast to possession by a *dybbuk*, where the evil spirit of one who has died takes possession of one of the living.[12]

The presence of an *ibur* was regarded as a great blessing by Jewish mystics, especially those of Safed in the sixteenth century, while the same mystics strove greatly to exorcise *dybbuks* from those who were possessed by them. However, accounts of *dybbuks*, such as "The Widow of Safed," were widespread in this period, while tales of possession by *iburs* are rare and are found only among mystical tales.[13]

A fascinating oral variant, which is a clear retelling of this midrashic tale, has been collected in modern Israel. In "A Kiss from the Master," the spirit of Shimon bar Yohai comes in a dream to a man uneducated in the Torah. The spirit kisses him, and afterward the man discovers that he has become a master of the Torah, possessed with the spirit of Bar Yohai. It is characteristic of these tales that the possession by the *ibur* is not permanent, but is triggered by something, such as the study of a particular text, or, as in the case of "The *Tefillin* of the Or Hayim," the wearing of *tefillin*.

One of the primary characteristics of Jewish literature is that the earlier texts serve as models for the later ones, as can be seen in these two stories about Rabbi Shimon bar Yohai, separated in time by well over a thousand years. Certainly, in the case of the later mystical tales, it is almost always possible to find a prototype in the early rabbinic texts. In general, these tales are a natural outgrowth of the Aggadah, the legendary material of the Talmud, just as the mystical commentary in the Zohar, the central text of the Kabbalah, often seems to be built on earlier midrashic commentary. The difference is that the rabbinic commentary is primarily legal or legendary, while that found in the Zohar is chiefly mystical. So too are the tales found in the Zohar of a mystical nature. Here, for example, Shimon bar Yohai and his disciples see signs that reveal God's intentions, speak with an angel in the form of a rock, meet saints from the Other World, ascend to the celestial Academy, and read the book that Adam was once given by an angel.[14]

The links between the classic rabbinic tales and those of kabbalistic, Hasidic, or folk origin also reveal how the later rabbis sought their personal models in the lives of the earlier sages. The primary models were the talmudic sages Rabbi Akiba, Rabbi Ishmael the High Priest, Rabbi Yohanan ben Zakkai, and Rabbi Shimon bar Yohai. Of these, the most extensive legendary tradition is that surrounding Bar Yohai. It is this legendary model, especially as found in the Zohar, that transformed Bar Yohai into the foremost archetype of Jewish mystics.

Among those who modeled themselves after Shimon bar Yohai was Rabbi Isaac Luria of Safed, known as "the Ari," and the Baal Shem Tov, the founder of Hasidim, known as "the Besht." The Ari once took his disciples to the place where Shimon bar Yohai used to meet with his disciples. He had each of them sit in the place of one of the disciples, and he himself sat in the place of Shimon bar Yohai, making the parallel between them explicit, and even hinting that he was the reincarnation of Bar Yohai in that generation.[15]

Later, this model of the master was taken up by the Hasidim, beginning with the Baal Shem Tov. Other key mystical masters among the Hasidim include Reb Pinhas of Koretz, Reb Elimelech of Lizensk, and Reb Nachman of Bratslav, as well as several others. The role of the rebbe, the Hasidic master, in these tales is of primary importance, for the rebbe was believed to possess divine knowledge and to be in communication with the world above. Certainly a major purpose of these tales was to create a legendary tradition about these rabbis, to demonstrate the level of their spiritual attainment and the extent of their mystical powers. For this reason, the tales in this collection have been arranged to focus on the cycles linked to these key figures.

It is no accident that the Ari would hint that he was the reincarnation of Shimon bar Yohai, for *gilgul*, the transmigration of souls, was one of the most influential mystical doctrines in sixteenth-century Safed. Drawing on this doctrine, it was common to assert that one rabbi was a reincarnation of another or that one rabbi had sparks of the souls of several great figures. The concept of sparks of souls derives from the tradition that 600,000 souls gathered at Mount Sinai. Later, when there were more Jews than this, whole souls were not available to everyone, and instead one person could have the sparks of several souls. Rabbi Hayim Vital, the primary disciple of the Ari, asserted several times that his soul was the soul of Rabbi Akiba, while Reb Nachman of Bratslav stated that his soul contained sparks of the souls of Moses, the Ari, and the Baal Shem Tov. And Rav Kook was reported to have said: "I am the soul of Reb Nachman," as if he were the reincarnation of Reb Nachman or that the spirit of Reb Nachman had taken possession of him in the form of an *ibur*. Thus the sense of spiritual continuity with specific sages of the past pervades the accounts of the great Jewish mystical masters.

Concerning the soul of Reb Nachman, there is a remarkable tradition among Bratslaver Hasidim about his wandering spirit. On his deathbed, Reb Nachman indicated to his Hasidim that they would not need to appoint a successor, for he would always be their rebbe. His

Hasidim followed this directive, and even to this day they function without a living master. That is why they are known by their opponents as the "Dead Hasidim." There are many accounts of how Reb Nachman's spirit returned to assist them in time of need. In the most famous of these, "Reb Nachman's Chair," it became necessary to carve the rabbi's chair into pieces in order to smuggle it past the Nazis. Each of the Bratslaver Hasidim was given one piece of the chair, and all vowed to meet in Jerusalem. And despite the grave dangers they faced in making that journey, every one of them bearing a piece of that chair arrived safely in the Holy Land. This miracle is attributed to the spirit of Reb Nachman. As for the chair, it has been reconstructed and can be found in the Bratslaver synagogue in Jerusalem.

Among the tales the Hasidim told, there are many in which a Hasidic rebbe takes on the characteristics of one of the legendary sages, especially those of the talmudic era. Since the Hasidim were well schooled in the Talmud, they would recognize at once the link between the ancient tale and that of their master. In this way the Hasidic rebbe was elevated, in the eyes of his Hasidim, to the level of the ancient sages. Eventually this focus on the master led to the doctrine of the *tzaddik*, where the master played an almost messianic role for his followers, and each group of Hasidim believed that their rebbe was the *tzaddik ha-dor*, the potential Messiah of that generation.[16] And some of these rebbes, including Reb Nachman, strongly hinted to their disciples that their role was a messianic one.[17]

Each of the masters takes a different path, something that the Ari recognized when he turned away some of those who sought to be his disciples. In one instance the Ari comforted a distraught rabbi he had turned away by telling him that in this lifetime it was his destiny to study the literal meaning of the sacred texts, while the Ari's destiny was to study the mystical meaning. But in a future incarnation, they were destined to study together.[18]

So too does each of the mystical masters demonstrate his mastery in a different way. The Ari knows the history of every soul, and he knows on Yom Kippur whose name has been inscribed in the Book of Life and who is destined to die. The Baal Shem Tov can go into a trance and guide his soul to heaven in order to open a heavenly gate that is preventing the prayers of the Jews from ascending on high. When Reb Pinhas of Koretz opens a page of the Zohar, he is transformed into the Angel of the Zohar. Rabbi Naftali Katz has the power to project his image to distant places and to control events there, as does Reb Issachar Dov of Belz, who appears in a vision to Franz

Kafka's friend Jiri Langer in Prague while Issachar Dov is actually in Belz.[19] The spirit of Shimon bar Yohai returns from the dead to assist those who study the Zohar, while the spirit of Reb Nachman of Bratslav guides and protects his Hasidim to this day.

Perhaps the most astonishing of the powers demonstrated in these tales is the ability to cause a person to experience an illusion out of time, where many years seem to pass in the space of a minute. These can be described as Jewish tales of illusion, for those who experience these spells are astounded to discover that they have been living in a world of illusion. But in every case they learn an important lesson that transforms their lives. These tales are remarkably parallel to many Indian myths, such as those concerning Vishnu, which also portray an illusory world, that of *Maya*.[20]

One of the earliest examples of these illusion tales is "The Magic Flock," of midrashic origin. Here the patriarch Jacob meets another herdsman crossing the river Yakkok, and they agree to help each other forge the river with their flocks. But no matter how many flocks Jacob carries across, the number of those still to be carried across keeps multiplying, until Jacob realizes that it is an illusion and that the other herdsman is some kind of sorcerer, and he wrestles with him until dawn. The other turns out to be the guardian angel of Esau, who has come to weaken Jacob before meeting Esau the next day, and the story itself is a midrashic commentary on the identity of the mysterious figure Jacob wrestled with in the biblical account (Gen. 32:23–33).

In later Jewish folklore, King Solomon experiences the powers of illusion firsthand as a beggar king.[21] This tradition is carried on by rabbis such as the medieval sorcerer Rabbi Adam,[22] as well as Reb Pinhas of Koretz and Reb Elimelech of Lizensk in stories such as "The Underground Forest" and "The Young Magician." In "The Underground Forest," for example, Reb Pinhas causes a student descending into a *mikveh* to enter another world, where he has a series of adventures lasting for many years, only to discover that it was all an illusion. But as a result, he learns that he is destined to wed the daughter of Reb Pinhas.

"The Tale of the Kugel" is another fine example of the illusion tale. Here Rabbi Menachem Mendel I of Lubavitch demonstrates great powers of illusion, showing a man a vision of the path his life will take if he divorces his wife for not having borne a child.

In addition to drawing on these mystical powers as they are needed, these masters transmit the mysteries of the Torah to their disciples. In their hands the Torah is revealed to be a secret code about the mythic truths of the universe. When this truth is deciphered, the role of the

Jews in the fabric of creation is revealed, and it turns out to be crucial in repairing the cosmic rents that took place at the time of creation, as well as in bringing together God and His Bride, the *Shekhinah*, who have been torn apart. According to the myth of the Exile of the *Shekhinah*, at the time of the the destruction of the Temple, God's Bride went into exile with her children, Israel. Somehow God and His Bride had to be brought together. The Ari provided many special prayers for this purpose, known as *yihudim*. By prefacing every *mitzvah* or commandment with these prayers, it became possible to assist in repairing the world.

From these examples it is apparent that the Jewish mystical tale emerged out of a highly charged spiritual environment, filled with mystical expectations. In this context, accounts of the miraculous became inevitable, as well as legendary embellishments. So too was this aspect enhanced by the mode of transmission. Virtually all of these tales were first circulated orally, primarily among the followers of these masters, and they were written down only after the rabbi's death. And eventually they too became a kind of sacred text.

Among the mystical themes most often found in the tales of these rabbis are those concerning the Divine Presence, the mysteries of creation and of the Chariot, as well as mysteries of the Torah, of the Word, and of prayer. There also are tales of the power of prayer and repentance, the mystery of the Sabbath, communication with the world above, and heavenly journeys. Many of these tales recount visits to Paradise or the Garden of Eden or journeys to the Holy Land through enchanted caves. There are many accounts of wandering souls and reincarnation, of experiences beyond time and space. Other tales offer examples of kabbalistic magic, miracles about masters and hidden saints, encounters with angels and demons, and many legends about the Messiah and the World to Come.

It is common to find accounts of out-of-body experiences in these tales, as well as events that take place out of time. In the former are many accounts of the ascent of the soul, a kind of astral projection in which the soul is guided toward Paradise. Another kind of soul travel is found in the tales of those rabbis who could cast their image to distant places and affect events there. There is also a form of enchanted journey, known as *Kfitsat ha-Derech*, the "Leaping of the Way," in which masters such as the Baal Shem Tov travel from one place to another by mystical means. In these stories the hooves of the horses no longer touch the ground, for the carriage is flying to its destination, much as did the *Merkavah*, the Divine Chariot in the vision of Ezekiel.

There are two primary branches of Kabbalah. One is known as "Practical Kabbalah." It makes use of the powers inherent in Kabbalah through manipulation of letters and numbers and by drawing on the powers of holy names. These are usually one of the many names of God, of which the Tetragrammaton (YHVH) is the holiest and most powerful of all. Or the names are the those of angels, each of which brings with it its own unique powers of mythical proportions. There are the archangels, Gabriel, Michael, Uriel, and Raphael, who serve as messengers of God. In addition, there are hundreds of other angels, including Raziel, the angel of secrets and mysteries; Rahab, the angel of the sea; Sandalphon, who weaves a garland of flowers out of the prayers of Israel for God to wear on the Throne of Glory; and Metatron, who was once Enoch, chief among the angels and the heavenly scribe. These are only the best known of the angels. There are many others, whose names themselves are secrets. Often these holy names are combined into keys that can unlock the gates of heaven. The purpose of drawing on these powers is usually to protect the Jewish community or the lives of individuals. Otherwise, the use of these powers is forbidden.

The other branch is that of "Speculative Kabbalah," sometimes referred to as "Contemplative" or "Theosophical Kabbalah." It is more inwardly directed, where mystical longing finds its focus in prayer and in mystical contemplation of the text of the Torah, as well as in the interaction of the Ten *Sefirot*. So intense is this contemplation that it not only includes the words of the Torah, but even regards the letters and numbers as gates of mystery, and prayers as virtual ladders of ascent, as in "The Ladder of Prayers," where the Baal Shem Tov ascends the ladder of the prayers of his Hasidim all the way to the palace of the Messiah. Some of the meditative exercises practiced, such as trying to combine the names of God in prayers of unification, produce mystical effects, such as visions of the Divine Throne and the *Shekhinah*. These visions should be regarded as a Jewish kind of *unio mystica*, the unitive mystical experience, even though there does not appear to be a loss of awareness of the self. For such visions and mystical illuminations were regarded as the ultimate goal of kabbalistic contemplation.

Likewise, these stories might be regarded as a legendary portrayal of the mystical experience in its Jewish representation, demonstrating the concept of *devekut*, of cleaving to God. Certainly, many rabbis are portrayed in these tales in a state of possession that resembles mystical ecstasy. However, while reports of mystical union in which the self dissolves into the Divine are found in the writings of Abulafia and others, few such accounts are found in these mystical tales. Most of the rabbis in these tales, no matter how profound the experience or to what heights they may ascend, retain a strong sense of self-identity even at moments of ecstasy. Those who lose themselves, as was said to have happened to Ben Azzai, one of the rabbis in the legend of the four who entered Paradise, often lose their lives.

Further, one of the goals of mystical endeavors was to obtain knowledge of the divine mysteries. Such knowledge required continued awareness of the self in order to be able to recall every detail of the experience. For it is important to remember that the primary focus of the Kabbalah is on a comprehensive understanding of the mystical meaning of the Torah. Thus mystical knowledge was as highly regarded as transcendental experience.

These two branches of Kabbalah, the Practical and the Speculative, are portrayed in different kinds of Jewish mystical tales. But both branches have a substantial number of tales linked to them, and a proper definition of the Jewish mystical tale must include tales drawn from both. Among the kinds of tales that demonstrate Practical Kabbalah are those drawing on kabbalistic magic, such as "Rabbi Shimon's Escape," where a rabbi uses the power of the Name to make a drawing of a ship become real, and in this way escapes execution for himself and his companions.

The themes of the tales of Speculative Kabbalah, on the other hand, concern the mysteries of the Torah and the power of the word, such as several tales about the theme of flying letters, including "The Book of Flying Letters," where a disciple of Shimon bar Yohai has a vision of his master's soul ascending, followed by the flying letters that make up the book of his wisdom, which was also departing from this world. Likewise, in "The Flying Letters," the letters of a Torah scroll in one town take flight because of the evil inhabitants and fly to another town, where they land on an empty scroll a scribe is about to write.

Jewish tradition holds that the sky opens at midnight on Shavuoth and the glory of heaven is revealed. This kind of revelation is at the core of these stories. In each one there comes a time when the Divine realm is suddenly glimpsed, and there is a moment of revelation. At this moment, the rabbis often appear possessed or surrounded by a Divine presence. In "The Circle of Fire," a disciple of the Baal Shem Tov sees him lying on the floor, surrounded by a fiery circle. Such a sacred fire surrounds both Rabbi Eizek of Kallo and the hidden saint who comes to visit him in "The Prayer Leader." These examples highlight the difficulty of portraying mystical experience in these tales. It is generally reported by an outsider, who witnesses the effects, or an account is given afterward by the one who has undergone the experience. Both of these perspectives are found in "Unlocking the Gates of Heaven." First, the Baal Shem Tov is seen in a catatonic state, with bulging eyes. Then, when the vision has ended, he reports what took place during his heavenly journey.

Once these stories were recorded, a transformation took place, and they themselves become a kind of mystical text, with several levels of meaning. Not only do they have strong mystical and legendary dimensions, but metaphorical ones as well. From this perspective, the heavenly journey can be seen as an archetypal symbol linking this world with that of the divine. Or an encounter with an evil angel can represent an inner struggle between the forces of good and evil. Such multiple levels of meaning were not lost on the rabbis, who created a system of four levels of interpretation known by the acronym *PaRDeS*, in which all levels of meaning were regarded as equally valid. This system of interpretation recognizes the literal, symbolic, allegorical, and mystical meanings of any sacred text, especially the Torah.[23]

There also is a strong mythical dimension underlying these mystical accounts. Four kabbalistic myths, in particular, are most influential in these tales: myths of creation, of the Divine Chariot, of the Bride of God, and of the Messiah. The first two of these myths constitute the roots of Kabbalah in the Bible, emerging as a kind of mythic commentary on creation and the vision of Ezekiel. Virtually all kabbalistic texts and tales grow out of at least one of these root myths, although other biblical episodes of a mystical nature, such as the giving of the Torah at Mount Sinai, are also the focus of kabbalistic commentary. The kabbalistic term for the study of creation is *Ma'aseh Bereshith*, the Work of Creation, while the term for the study of the Divine Chariot is *Ma'aseh Merkavah*, the Work of the Chariot. In this context "Work" can be understood as "Mysteries."

The first of these primary kabbalistic myths, that of creation, actually consists of three separate but related myths. In addition to the account of creation found in Genesis, in which God created the world in six days and rested on the seventh, there are two additional kabbalistic cosmologies. One is that of the Ten *Sefirot*, often illustrated in a diagram of the kabbalistic Tree of Life, which proclaims creation in ten primary stages of emanation. There are specific kinds of interactions between these *Sefirot*, which are known as the "Thirty-two Paths." These paths represent the infinite possibilities of the interaction of the Divine, as revealed through the symbols of language. Each of the *Sefirot* is a symbol of an aspect of God, as well a stage in the emanation of creation. The *Sefirot* function in kabbalistic texts as archetypes of the interaction of God and existence. Attached to each of the *Sefirot* are rich and varied meanings, some of which are mystical, some mythical. In the kabbalistic mythology associated with the *Sefirot*, Samael, the fallen angel, comes to represent the masculine principle of evil, while Lilith, the demoness, is transformed to represent the feminine. Countering Lilith is the positive feminine principle, identified with the *Shekhinah*, the Sabbath Queen and Bride of God. One important facet of the *Sefirot* is that they could be influenced by special prayers of unification, known as *yehudim*. This made potentially great powers available to those mystics who understood the secret of making these unifications effective. They held the power, for example, of bringing God and his Bride closer together, as well as the potential to unleash the End of Days, the messianic era.

It is hard to reconcile the creation myth in Genesis with the emanations of the *Sefirot*, and in fact they are separate myths of creation. Yet both myths are drawn upon by the third primary Jewish myth of creation, that of the Ari. This is the most cosmological of the Jewish creation myths. The central teachings of the Ari concern the mysteries of creation: how God had to contract himself in order to make space for the creation of the world, in a process known as *tzimtzum*, and how God then sent forth vessels of primordial light that somehow split apart, scattering the sparks of holy light all over the world, but especially in the Holy Land. These scattered sparks must be sought out and raised up so that the broken vessels can be restored and the world returned to its primordial condition. And this repair of the world, known as *tikkun*, can be accomplished by fulfilling the *mitzvot*, the divine commandments.

This myth of the Ari was the last major new myth to take root in Jewish tradition. But while it is essentially an original myth drawn from Gnostic themes, it is also a remarkable commentary on *Ma'aseh Bereshith*, has discernible links to the system of the *Sefirot*, and also links two other primary Jewish myths, those of the creation and of the Messiah. For the return to the primordial condition of the unshattered vessels is equivalent to the initiation of the messianic era. Thus the broken vessels initiated the cosmic Fall, and the messianic era will restore the world to its prelapsarian condition. This combined megamyth serves as a framework for all of Jewish history.

The links between the myth of the Ari and the system of *Sefirot* become apparent upon closer observation. Like the *Sefirot*, the Ari's myth describes a process of emanation in which the vessels of light progress from one realm of existence to another. The *Sefirot*, however, represent an ongoing process of transformation, while the Shattering of the Vessels took place at the early stages in creation and was a cosmic catastrophe, similiar in impact to the exile from Eden or the destruction of the Temple in Jerusalem. Yet because the first stage of the Ari's myth is inextricably linked to the second, that of Gathering the Sparks, it too can be regarded as an ongoing process. Thus, one way of viewing the myth of the Ari is as a reworking of the doctrine of the *Sefirot,* and some kabbalistic schools regard the Ari's teachings as a direct and detailed explication of the *Sefirot.*

The deepest mystery of all among the students of the Ari concerns the true reason for the Shattering of the Vessels.[24] The most important consequences of it, however, are apparent: it shifts the responsibility for the fallen state of existence from man to God, and it sets the stage for the second phase of the myth, that of Gathering the Sparks. Here the scattered sparks are gathered together in the belief that when enough have been raised up, the broken vessels will be restored and the world returned to its primordial condition. This myth also gives a positive explanation to the problem of Jewish exile, especially after the expulsion of the Jews from Spain in 1492. It suggests that there was a Divine purpose behind the exile, and that the Jews are the chosen people in the sense that they were created to search for and raise up the scattered sparks. Yet at the same time, since more sparks fell on the Holy Land than anywhere else, that is the best of all places to go to gather the holy sparks.

This myth, in its apparent simplicity, conveyed kabbalistic principles in a way that could be readily understood. As a result, it was taken up by the Jewish community at large, breaking the lock on the mystical tradition that had been the domain of a select group of rabbis since ancient times. This myth spoke to the people, turning the curse of exile into a blessing. It gave meaning to their wandering in the Diaspora, for the scattered sparks had to be found and raised up wherever they were hidden. And it held out hope for a messianic era that could be brought closer by acts of human piety.

This myth can also be recognized as the source behind many tales concerning the principle of *tikkun olam,* or repair of the world. Here the role of the rabbi is often that of a healer. In "Repairing Souls," Rabbi Hayim ben Attar goes into the mountains to repair the souls gathered there. In "Redemption of the Lost Souls," the famous kabbalist Shalom Sharabi seeks out lost souls among the "Sons of the Desert," as the Bedouins were known, and redeems them. Nor is this repair limited to the events of this world. After all, the Shattering of the Vessels was a cosmic catastrophe, and the heavens themselves require repair. This is the secret work of the hidden saints, such as

Shimon Pilam in "The *Tzaddik* of the Forest" or Hayim the Vine-keeper in "The Prayer Leader."

The second primary myth is that of the Divine Chariot, based on the vision of Ezekiel. As with creation, Ezekiel's vision gave birth to more than one myth. There is the myth of the Divine Chariot, which represents the mystery of the Divinity. Just as Ezekiel's vision is perplexing, so is the study of this mystery, known as *Ma'aseh Merkavah*, the Work of the Chariot, an almost impenetrable enigma. The *Merkavah* represents both God's Throne of Glory and the Divine Chariot, which are mystically regarded as one. Visions of this chariot are extremely rare in these mystical tales, but the mere act of contemplating this mystery often triggers mystical experiences, as in "The Mystery of the Chariot."

The second myth to emerge from Ezekiel's vision is the myth of ascent. This myth represents the longing to come into the Divine presence, which is the ultimate goal of mystical ascent. This longing, then, consists of a yearning for personal experience of the Divine, to come into the presence of the King, to behold Him personally, rather than to remain outside the palace and hear rumors of the King. It is not necessarily a longing for mystical union in the traditional sense, where the mystic's identity dissolves into that of the Divine. Somehow the rabbis retain a sense of themselves in these visions, no matter how exalted. This, then, should be seen as a unique characteristic of Jewish mysticism. This myth of ascent finds expression both in the tale of the four sages who entered Paradise and in the many accounts of heavenly journeys found in the Hekhaloth texts. In these texts the individual comes into the presence of God and experiences complete awe, in ways that are often overpowering. And, as these texts make clear, there is an inherent danger in these Divine visions, as well as great rewards.

The third of these kabbalistic myths is the Exile of the *Shekhinah*, God's Bride. In its earliest use in the Talmud and Midrash, the term *Shekhinah* referred to God's presence in the world. Later kabbalistic myth turned the *Shekhinah* into a separate mythic being, who separated from her spouse, God, when the Temple in Jerusalem that served as her earthly home was destroyed, and went into exile with her children, Israel. Furthermore, it is believed that the *Shekhinah* will remain in exile until the days of the Messiah, when the Temple will be rebuilt. This belief links the myth of the *Shekhinah* to the myth of the Messiah.

One of the earliest personifications of the *Shekhinah* is as Mother Zion, as found in this midrashic text:

When Jeremiah saw the smoke of the Temple in Jerusalem rising up, he broke down. And when he saw the stones that once were the walls of the Temple, he said: "What road have the exiles taken? I will go and perish with them."

So Jeremiah accompanied them down the road covered with blood until they reached the river Euphrates. Then he thought to himself: "If I go on to Babylon, who will comfort those left in Jerusalem?" Therefore he took his leave of the exiles, and when they saw he was leaving, they wept, as it is written, *by the waters of Babylon, there we sat down, yea, we wept* (Ps. 137:1).

As he was returning to Jerusalem, Jeremiah lifted his eyes and saw a woman seated at the top of a mountain, dressed in black, crying in distress, in great need of comfort. So too was Jeremiah in tears, wondering who would comfort him. He approached the woman, saying, "If you are a woman, speak, but if you are a spirit, depart at once!" She said: "Do you not recognize me? I am she who has borne seven sons, whose father went into exile in a distant city by the sea. Then a messenger brought the news that my husband, the father of my children, had been slain. And on the heels of that messenger came another with the news that my house had fallen in and slain my seven sons."

Jeremiah said: "Do you deserve any more comfort than Mother Zion, who has been made into a pasture for the beasts?"

And she replied: "I am Mother Zion, the mother of seven, as it is written, *She that has borne seven anguishes*" (Jer. 15:9).[25]

This personification of Mother Zion eventually evolved into that of the *Shekhinah*, one of whose roles is that of the mother of Israel. The *Shekhinah* is typically portrayed as a bride in white or as a grieving woman in black, mourning over the destruction of her home, the Temple, and the scattering of her children. In "A Vision at the Wailing Wall" both personifications are found, while the image of the bride is found in "A Vision of the Bride" and "The Sabbath Guests." The *Shekhinah* is also identified as the Sabbath Queen, a beloved figure whose presence makes the Sabbath holy. It is the Sabbath Queen that the Ari and his disciples, dressed in white, went out to meet at sunset in the hills of Safed in the ritual known as *Kabbalat Shabbat*. The Sabbath Queen is welcomed with the famous hymn *Lecha Dodi* every Friday evening at the beginning of the Sabbath.

The arrival of the Sabbath Queen is closely linked to the belief that every person receives an extra soul on the Sabbath. The talmudic source for this belief is in Betza 16a: "Rabbi Shimon ben Lakish said: 'On the eve of the Sabbath the Holy One, blessed be He, gives man an enlarged soul and at the close of the Sabbath He withdraws it from him.'" This *neshamah yeterah* or extra soul is closely identified with the *Shekhinah*, and especially with the personification of the *Shekhinah* as the Sabbath Bride or Queen. This tradition can be considered an *ibur* visitation in the broadest sense of the concept. Because they are loath to lose their extra soul, many Hasidim put off the *Havdalah* ceremony that marks the end of the Sabbath as long as possible, sometimes until long past midnight. See "Three Stars" for an example of this custom and the controversy it caused.

The fourth and last of the primary kabbalistic myths to influence these mystical tales is the myth of the Messiah. Here, too, the myth is found in two distinct formulations, which are ultimately linked. One of these concerns a Messiah who is the son of Joseph, and the second a Messiah who is the son of David. Messiah ben Joseph, as he is known, will be a human, the *tzaddik* of his generation, who will prepare the way for Messiah ben David, who is sometimes identified as a human being and sometimes as a celestial Messiah, who lives in a heavenly palace.[26]

The longing for the Messiah has been palpable throughout Jewish history. In addition to several false messiahs, such as Shabbatai Zevi, many attempts to hasten the coming of the Messiah are recorded in these tales. See, for example, "The Chains of the Messiah," about the monumental failure of Rabbi Joseph della Reina, who sought to force the coming of the Messiah by capturing Asmodeus and Lilith, the king and queen of demons. But one fatal error at the last minute caused him to lose everything. So too are there many tales about moments in time that would have been perfect opportunities to bring the Messiah but were somehow lost. In "The Journey to Jerusalem" the Ari announces his plan to set out for Jerusalem at once with his disciples. Some of them agree to go unquestioningly, but others hesitate, and this causes them to lose the opportunity to bring the Messiah. In "The Sabbath Guests,'" Rabbi Eizek of Kallo seeks a blessing from two visiting Hasidim for a mysterious couple who have come to his Sabbath table. The Hasidim, scandalized by the rabbi's warmth toward the woman, refuse. Only afterward do they learn that their guests were the Messiah and the Sabbath Queen, and if the Hasidim had given their blessing, the wedding would have initiated the messianic era. Accounts of these lost opportunities to bring the Messiah make up one characteristic type of these Jewish mystical tales.

Even in present-day Israel, messianic longings are widespread in the most religious circles. A few years ago there was a report that three rabbis in Jerusalem had dreamed on the same night that the Messiah was coming. This sent a wave of messianic expectation through the community. At the same time, there are many explanations about why the Messiah has not yet come, as in this legend recently collected in Israel by the IFA:

> For many generations the Messiah has sat captive, chained with golden chains before the Throne of Glory. Elijah has tried to release him many times, but he has never succeeded. So Elijah descends to earth and explains that in order to break the chains of the Messiah, he needs a magic saw whose teeth are the deeds of Israel. Every deed adds a tooth to this saw, but every sin takes one away. When there are twice as many good deeds as there are sins, then the saw can be used. That is why it is said that the Messiah will not come until we bring him.[27]

In addition to these four primary myths, there are many other mythic concerns reflected in these tales, especially those involving journeys to heaven or hell. Many details about these mythic realms emerge in these tales. From these a remarkably detailed knowledge of the Divine realm can be gained, as well as how to invoke its powers through the use of holy names, prayers of unification,[28] astral projection, sympathetic magic, and other mystical techniques. With these powers it becomes possible to enter into the sacred dimension where angels are often encountered and where visions of the Divine Presence, in the form of the mythic figure of the *Shekhinah*, are regarded as the ultimate revelation, as in "A Vision of the Bride."

At the same time, the use of these mystical powers was reserved for exceptional situations, such as countering an evil decree against the Jewish community. These tales recount how certain rabbis are able to affect events far away by soul travel and projection of their images to distant places, where they accomplish miraculous feats. In "A Bowl of Soup," Rabbi Elimelech of Lizensk spills a bowl of soup at the Sabbath table, and later it is learned that at the same moment, as the Emperor was about to sign a decree against the Jews, the bottle of ink spilled on it, and he took this as a sign that the decree must not be signed.[29] Likewise, Rabbi Naftali Katz draws upon his mystical powers in "Rabbi Naftali's Trance," not only to locate a missing husband in *Gehenna*, the Jewish hell, where he is being punished, but to set up a meeting, in the presence of witnesses and avenging angels, between the husband and the wife he abandoned in order to obtain the divorce.

So too are there many accounts of rabbis who use their powers to raise up the souls of the dead, who often call upon them for their help. Reb Nachman of Bratslav asked to be buried in the cemetery in the city of Uman so that he could raise up the souls of those buried there

who had lost their lives in a pogrom.[30] So too, in "The Field of Souls,"
does a rabbi who prays in a field on Yom Kippur unknowingly free the
many souls stranded there, while in "The Boy Who Blew the Shofar,"
a boy is called upon by the souls of the dead to set them free.

From this it can be seen that these tales are set in a world where the
boundary between the living and the dead, between earth and heaven
and hell, between spirit and body, is a fluid one, and the world is seen
as a place populated with all kinds of spirits, including angels, demons, and spirits of the dead. The rabbis in these tales are masters of
this spiritual realm. They have a remarkably complete knowledge of
its workings, and possess holy names that serve as spells in calling
upon angels and other spirits to do their bidding. Their goals are both
spiritual and practical, their most pressing desire, of course, to hasten
the coming of the Messiah.

But the mystical quests found in these tales are not limited to attempts to hasten the messianic era. Indeed, the primary quest is that
for mystical knowledge, knowledge of God and the perfection of the
world, which is linked to the coming of the Messiah. This starts by
seeking the mystical meaning of the Torah and other sacred texts,
where the letters of the words are as significant as their meaning, and
where words that have the same numerical total are believed to be
mystically linked.[31]

Thus the word is seen in these tales as a gateway to the realm of
celestial mysteries. This is a natural extension of the primary rabbinic
belief that the Torah, dictated by God to Moses at Mount Sinai, is the
source of all truths, mysteries, and hidden meanings. The Zohar, the
primary kabbalistic text, describes a celestial Torah written in black
fire on white. In "The Flaming Letters,'" Reb Shnuer Zalman creates
a set of Hebrew letters that prove to be identical to the celestial model,
lifting yet another veil of the celestial mystery. Even the blank portions of the page on which the words are written are regarded as being
meaningful, suggesting a figure/ground reversal of the text, which is
seen to reveal a world of mysteries.

With the mystical experience in Judaism so remarkably focused on
the page, it is not surprising that there are many tales involving the
power of the word, or of potent combinations of words such as incan-
tations. Above all, there is the power of prayer. And the essence of this
power derives from the intensity of the prayer, known as the *kavanah*.
So too are there mystical techniques known as *yihudim* or unifications
that seek celestial unity by creating an interaction among the *Sefirot*,
with the ultimate goal of bringing God and His Bride closer together.
These *yihudim* combine letters from different names of God in a very

complex mental exercise that was believed to produce profound effects in this world and the world above.[32] In addition, the *yihudim* were used to exorcise evil spirits. There are also holy names that are used to call forth angelic figures such as the Prince of the Torah or to open the gates of heaven. With the powers made available through these mystical methods, it became possible to enter into the sacred realm, where angels are often encountered and visions take place in Paradise.

From the multitude of accounts of heavenly journeys found in the pseudepigraphical texts and rabbinic lore, as well as in many a Hasidic tale, a vivid portrait of heaven emerges, with a celestial Jerusalem that is the mirror image of Jerusalem on earth, except that the Temple on high still exists, while that in this world has been destroyed. And there are a multitude of secret places, treasuries, heavenly academies, and, of course, palaces of heaven, including the palace of the Messiah, known as the "Bird's Nest," after the golden dove of the Messiah that makes its nest in a tree that grows there. It is a complex, labyrinthine vision of the celestial world, which is ruled by its own laws and exists on its own terms. There is a place for every purpose in creation, such as the *Guf*, the Treasury of Souls, from which souls are drawn,[33] or the House of Treasures, where God keeps all the things He created before the creation of the world, including the Torah, the rainbow of Noah, and the ram that was sacrificed at Mount Moriah. All in all there are seven heavens, the highest of which is known as *Arabot*, and in each successive heaven the merits of the righteous who are found there increase. So too do the great sages have their own academies in heaven, where the souls of the righteous and angels gather together to hear their teachings of the Torah.

Human beings are by nature explorers, motivated by curiosity, and in many ways heaven has traditionally been considered the final frontier. Thus, from the perspective of the knowledge gathered from these heavenly journeys, the rabbis can be seen as celestial explorers. Whatever realm they entered, whether in this world or in the spiritual realm, they explored in great detail. Part of this interest, of course, comes from the belief that heaven is the location of the *Olam Haba*, the World to Come, where the righteous will receive their rewards. And for those generations largely deprived of material rewards, and more often than not subject to persecution, the dream of a realm in which they would be justly rewarded served as a great solace.

The first figure to be credited with journeying into heaven and exploring it was Enoch. Very little is said about Enoch in the Torah. His name appears in a genealogy linking Adam and Noah, and all that distinguishes him is the way his death is reported. For while it is said about everyone else that "he died," about Enoch it is said that *And Enoch walked with God, and he was not; for God took him* (Gen. 5:34). Even the slightest variation in biblical phrasing was taken to have profound significance; extensive conclusions were drawn from the unusual statement about his death.

In three major postbiblical texts found in the Apocrypha and the Pseudepigrapha, Enoch came to be described as one of the few righteous men in the evil generation preceding the Flood. He was taken up into Paradise in a chariot at God's command and taught the secrets of the universe. Then he came back to earth to instruct men, and finally he returned to heaven, where he was transformed into the fiery angel Metatron, who became the attendant of the Throne of Glory, the prince of the treasuries of heaven, and the ruler and judge of all the hosts of angels, executor of the Divine decrees on earth and the heavenly scribe.

One of the primary purposes of the ascent of Enoch was to provide a detailed description of the rewards and punishments awaiting the righteous, as well as to map the landscape of these distant and mysterious realms. And such a map of heaven and hell does emerge from the extensive literature about Enoch.

Not only is the heavenly Paradise explored in great detail in Jewish mystical texts and tales; so too is the earthly Paradise, the Garden of Eden. In one legend, "The Gates of Eden," Alexander the Great, a popular figure in Jewish lore, comes to the Garden of Eden and receives an eye that outweighs all his gold—until it is covered with dust. In another, "A Crown of Shoes," the Baal Shem Tov is transported in an instant to the Garden of Eden, where he finds angels gathering shoes that flew off the feet of those dancing on Simhat Torah. They flew off with such joy that they flew all the way to the Garden of Eden. There the Baal Shem Tov learns that an angel makes a crown out of these shoes for God to wear on the Throne of Glory, just as He wears a crown woven from the prayers of Israel. In another tale, "The Tree of Life," the Baal Shem Tov uses his great powers to transport not only himself, but also his Hasidim, to the Garden of Eden. He tries to lead them to the Tree of Life, but one by one they become fascinated with some lesser mystery, and by the time the Baal Shem Tov reaches the Tree of Life, he is alone.

There also are a multitude of encounters with angels in these tales. Foremost among these is the angel Gabriel, who serves as the primary celestial guide. In "The *Tzohar*" Gabriel assists Joseph in the pit, where his brothers had cast him, and in "Rabbi Ishmael's Ascent" the angel meets Rabbi Ishmael as he ascends on high and reveals secrets that he has heard from behind the *Pargod*, the curtain that separates God from the angels. In "Gabriel's Palace," Gabriel visits the imprisoned Rabbi Meir of Rottenberg in a dream and brings him the celestial Torah to read from on the Sabbath.

But not all angels are good, as one student learns in "The Evil Angel." So too does he learn how to distinguish the good ones from the evil ones: both have God's Name inscribed on their foreheads, but the letters of the name of the good angel are inscribed in white fire, while those of the evil angel burn in black.

In addition, there are beings that are neither spirit nor angel, but a combination of both. These spirits, known as *maggidim*, come into being as a result of intense study of the sacred texts, and they speak through the mouths of great sages, such as Rabbi Joseph Caro, the author of the *Shulhan Aruch*, the Code of Jewish Law. That such a respected scholar of the Law as Joseph Caro could at the same time be a mystic possessed by the spirit of the Mishnah may appear to be a great paradox. Yet in one book, *Maggid Mesharim*, he kept a diary of the knowledge he had received from this spirit, who came to him and spoke through his mouth—often in the presence of others, as recounted in "The Angel of the Mishnah."[34]

From a psychological perspective, the accounts of both the *ibur* and the *maggid* can be seen as a kind of automatic speaking from the unconscious. It has also been suggested that parts of the Zohar, the central text of Kabbalah, were written automatically by the author, Moshe de Leon. Also, many forms of kabbalistic meditation, such as the *yihudim*, the prayers of unification, seem intended to invoke unconscious powers. This underscores one important aspect of kabbalistic study— it seems to call forth unconscious forces, which reveal themselves through symbolic language. In a very real sense, the letters of the alphabet and the Ten *Sefirot* serve as gates of spiritual forces, and function in ways that are quite similiar to both the Platonic archetypes and C. G. Jung's concept of the archetypes of the collective unconscious.[35] Indeed, this parallel is even more striking in terms of the key feminine figure of the *Shekhinah*, the Bride of God, and Jung's concept of the *anima*, the symbolic feminine aspect of every man. Jungian thought requires the seeking out and uniting with the *anima* in order to attain psychic wholeness, which Jung calls "Individuation." In the arts this figure is identified as the muse, and the artist can flourish only when he is in the presence of the muse, just as nothing is considered to be sacred that does not take place in the Divine Presence, which has been traditionally identified with the *Shekhinah*. Thus, from a Jungian perspective, one of the effects of kabbalistic study was the discovery by the kabbalists of the feminine within themselves. From this point of view, their attempts to unify God and His exiled Bride through prayers of unification can also be seen as an attempt to unite with their own *anima*. These mystical tales, as well, can be seen as products of this unconscious process, with a strong symbolic component and many levels of meaning. The tales of Rabbi Nachman of Bratslav, in particular, lend themselves to this kind of interpretation, where, for example, the search for the princess in his famous story "The Lost Princess" can be seen to represent a quest not only for the Bride of God, but also for the exiled *anima*.[36]

One further important parallel between the kabbalistic view of existence and Jungian theory concerns the understanding of evil. In the Kabbalah the world of evil is known as the *Sitre Ahre*, the Other Side. This grows out of the talmudic view that "for everything God created, He also created its counterpart."[37] All in all, the kabbalistic world is a polar one precisely in the Jungian model, where the forces of the unconscious are understood to be arranged in a polar configuration.

Just as heaven is thoroughly mapped out in the Enoch and Hekhaloth texts, so too is the realm of evil fully explored. This world is portrayed in very different ways. There is *Gehenna*, the Jewish hell, where the souls of those who sinned are punished, in ways that are as explicit as those recounted by Dante in *The Inferno*. There is also the *Sitre Ahre*, filled with evil forces and swarms of spirits, some of them poor souls who are being punished by endless wandering. It functions as a distorted mirror of existence ruled by the forces of evil. And only the rabbis who have mastered the mysteries of Kabbalah have it within their power to assist these lost souls and bring their wandering to an end, as in "The Blind Angel," where Rabbi Mordecai of Chernobyl uses the gift of a precious menorah to guide the soul of the Hasid into heaven.

The existence of demons and the portrayal of evil in kabbalistic literature draw on several sources, among them popular demonological traditions, as well as the influence of magical texts such as *Sefer ha-Razim* and the widespread use of magical amulets, which inevitably included magical spells. In the Zohar and other kabbalistic texts, these traditions are transformed into more abstract forces of good and evil.

Then there are other spirits who travel through the cycles of rebirth, known as *gilgul*, and are reincarnated in a variety of forms, such as a stone, a flower, or a tree, as well as in both animal and human form. Often the same soul will be forced to undergo all these transformations, as in "The Voice in the Tree." More than anything else, these souls long to be freed from the chain of reincarnation to ascend on high, as happens in "The Sabbath Fish."

This focus on *gilgul*, the transmigration of souls, gave the Jewish mystics a completely different perspective, in which the history of a person's soul was the primary factor in shaping his life. It is said about the Ari that he could look at a man's forehead and read his soul's history in the Hebrew letters invisibly inscribed there. He could listen to the dialogue of two birds and recognize one of them as the reincarnation of Balaam. He could recognize that a black dog that continued to haunt him was the reincarnation of Joseph della Reina, who fell into evil ways after he failed to hasten the coming of the Messiah.[38] And he could even recognize a soul trapped in one stone in the wall of an ancient synagogue, as he does in "A Stone in the Wall." This kind of knowledge of the history of souls was rare even among the mystical masters, but in "A Wandering Soul" one of the Belz Hasidim knows that he has been reborn three times: once as a sheep in Jacob's flock; once as a follower of Korah, who rebelled against Moses and was punished, along with his followers, when the earth swallowed them up; and once as himself. The concept of *gilgul* in many ways resembles that of *samsera*, the cycle of death and rebirth in Hindu thought, including the law of *karma* that is involved in the *samsera* process. Yet it has also been formed by the Jewish mystical context out of which it emerged.

As for the fate of the souls of the living, this is said to depend on the state of their soul-candles, as described in "The Cottage of Candles." A person lives only as long as his soul-candle continues to burn. And it is forbidden to try to steal oil from one candle for another, as the doomed man in this story finds out. Indeed, these stories teach reverence for every kind of living being. Even trees have souls, as Reb Nachman of Bratslav discovers in "The Souls of Trees."

Above all, such tales reveal the longing to communicate with the world above and the belief that such communication is possible, at least for the greatest figures. And based on the evidence of the tales, these communications took many forms, including heavenly voices, angelic messengers, omens, visits of the patriarchs and matriarchs, heavenly books, prophecy, and divine messages such as letters falling from heaven, as well as divination by the holy spirit, known as *Ruach ha-Kodesh*. Another popular method of divination was *Sheilat Sefer*, divining from a book. In reply to an important question, a holy book is opened at random and a passage blindly selected, which serves as the reply. See "The Souls of Trees" and "Divining from the Zohar" for examples of this kind of divination. And, above all, such communication with the world above took place in the form of visions or dreams. These visions might involve heavenly ascents, as in "Reb Ishmael's Ascent," or the *Shekhinah*, as in "A Vision at the Wailing Wall" and "A Vision of the Bride." In some stories, such as "The Vision of the High Priest" and "The Enchanted Island," there is even a vision of God.

Let us return to the four sages who entered Paradise. It can now be seen that this brief, enigmatic talmudic legend has multiple levels of meaning, where ascent may be understood as a visionary experience, on the one hand, and as a metaphor for mystical contemplation on the other.[39] Therefore it is important not to overlook the metaphorical dimensions of this account.

In the original talmudic legend, the four sages enter *Pardes*. This means, literally, that they entered an orchard. But because of the dire consequences of their actions, it is clear that the passage is not intended to be understood solely on the literal level. Of course, the orchard also suggests a garden, which suggests the Garden of Eden, which is sometimes referred to as the "earthly Paradise." From this interpretation it is not far to the notion that they actually entered Paradise, referring to the celestial Paradise. This reading is confirmed by one version of this legend that concludes that "Only Rabbi Akiba ascended in peace and descended in peace" rather than "entered in peace and departed in peace."[40]

What, then, does the story mean? Probably that these four, among the greatest sages of all time, engaged in some kind of mystical contemplation. Observe how well this legend manages to work on two levels at the same time—the essential factor in forming an allegory. On the literal level the sages have entered an orchard. This is demonstrated when Elisha ben Abuyah cuts the shoots. On the allegorical level, there is no doubt that this talmudic legend is using *Pardes* to refer to Paradise, because some of the companion legends describe the sages in the heavenly realm.[41] But since "Paradise" itself is a metaphor for mystical contemplation, *Pardes* refers to the enticing but dangerous realms of mystical speculation and contemplation symbolized by heavenly ascent.[42]

The dangers of mystical contemplation are also recounted in a talmudic account of a child of exceptional understanding who read the Book of Ezekiel at his teacher's home. He comprehended the true meaning of the word *hashmal* in the passage *And I looked, and, behold, a stormy wind came out of the north, a great cloud, with a fire flashing up, so that a brightness was round about it; and out of the midst thereof as the color of electrum (hashmal), out of the midst of the fire* (Ezekiel 1:4). At that instant a fire went forth and consumed him, like the flame that goes forth from the mouth of a furnace.[43] That is why it is written in the Mishnah:

> The Mysteries of Creation should not be expounded before two persons, nor the Mysteries of the Chariot before one, unless he is a sage and has an independent understanding. For whoever ponders on four things, it would have been better for him not to have been born: What is above, what is below, what is before time, and what will come after.[44]

The four sages likewise entered into this dangerous realm of mystical contemplation, and only Rabbi Akiba emerged intact. What was it that they were contemplating? It was almost certainly either *Ma'aseh Bereshith*, the mysteries of creation, or *Ma'aseh Merkavah*, the mysteries of the Chariot. Since the journey of the sages is understood as an ascent into Paradise, it seems likely that they were contemplating *Ma'asseh Merkavah*, which is concerned with ascent.

The brief account of the four who entered Paradise is clearly a barebones summary of a much longer legend. A few remaining fragments of this legend are found in the same tractate of the Talmud and shed a little more light on the fate of two of the three lost sages.[45] We learn that Elisha ben Abuyah "cut the shoots," meaning that he cut his ties to his religion, after seeing the angel Metatron sitting on a heavenly throne and concluding that "There must be, God forbid, two powers in heaven."[46] The legend goes on to tell us that God sent Elijah to punish Metatron with sixty lashes of a flaming whip for giving Elisha ben Abuyah this false impression. After this Elisha becomes known as *Aher*, the Other, because of his subsequent apostasy.

There is also a brief legend concerning the fate of Ben Zoma, who looked and lost his mind. He is said to have encountered another rabbi who was walking with his students. This rabbi greeted Ben Zoma, who replied: "Between the upper waters and the lower waters there are but three finger-breadths." Hearing this the rabbi said to his students: "Ben Zoma is gone," meaning that he had lost his mind.[47] Here Ben Zoma's statement about the upper and lower waters seems to be linked to something he had seen during his heavenly ascent. Referring to the creation of the firmament, where God *divided the waters which were under the firmament from the waters which were above it* (Gen. 1:7), Ben Zoma seems to be expressing amazement that the upper waters and the lower waters—symbolizing heaven and earth—are so close.[48]

As for Ben Azzai, his fate is the most uncertain. In one midrash Rabbi Akiba tells Ben Azzai: "I heard that you sit down and study, and flames surround you. I said, 'Ben Azzai has descended to the Chambers of the Chariot.'"[49] Here Ben Azzai is portrayed as a great mystic, which reinforces the tradition that he died by the kiss of the *Shekhinah*, meaning that his soul was taken directly into heaven. This tradition contradicts that which assumes that Ben Azzai died from the shock of mystical revelations. According to this view, Ben Azzai was drawn to the mysteries of heaven like a moth to a flame, and in this way he lost his life.

Together these legends constitute the primary account in the Talmud of the legend of the four sages. Over the ages they were recognized as referring to an esoteric, mystical tradition within Judaism that was at the same time both alluring and dangerous. This tradition later became identified as Kabbalah, and these talmudic legends about the four sages play a central role in the creation of a mystical mythology.

On the one hand, the legend of the four sages was generally interpreted to mean that mystical contemplation, which was regarded as synonymous with study of either the creation or the vision of Ezekiel, was dangerous. As a result, barriers were established limiting the study of these subjects, as noted in the previous quotation from the Mishnah. In addition, it was required that those who studied be rabbis who were at least forty years old, married, and learned in the Talmud. (It goes without saying that women were forbidden to consider these subjects.) It was believed that when a man had reached this age and had a family, he was sufficiently grounded to be trusted with these dangerous subjects. Later, the prohibition against the study of *Ma'aseh Bereshith* and *Ma'aseh Merkavah* was extended to include all kabbalistic texts, which are in any case based upon one of these two primary biblical sources.

These strictures deriving from the disaster that befell three of four of the greatest sages were not, however, the only reaction to this famous episode. For there was also the opposite reaction: their ascent into Paradise was regarded by some as a model for subsequent heavenly journeys. These sages regarded mystical contemplation, as symbolized by the heavenly journey, as the ultimate mystical objective. They are the authors of what are known as the "Hekhaloth texts," which describe in great detail journeys into Paradise. "Hekhaloth" means "palaces," and this refers to the palaces of heaven. So is this field of mystical contemplation known as *Merkavah* Mysticism, because of its focus on ascent, as symbolized by the *Merkavah*, the heavenly chariot in the vision of Ezekiel. Several of these important texts have been discovered in recent years, and they are the subject of intensive scholarly study at this time. What has not yet been determined is whether those who wrote these Hekhaloth texts regarded them as actual guides to bodily ascent or to the ascent of the soul. While Hekhaloth texts seem to describe bodily ascent, later accounts of heavenly journeys describe instead the ascent of the soul. But even in some of the earlier texts, such as "Rabbi Ishmael's Ascent," which is drawn from the legend of the Ten Martyrs, it is clear that Rabbi Ishmael's body remains on earth while his soul ascends on high.[50]

Sometimes these mystical ascents were said to take place in meditative states, after long fasting and prayer, and sometimes in dreams, as the soul was believed to leave the body every night and wander in the celestial realms, returning to the body shortly before waking. In any case, the Hekhaloth texts themselves are quite explicit about the nature of each of the palaces of heaven, plus the names of the angels that stand outside their gates and what holy names must be pronounced in order to get past them. Indeed, they read as a precise map of heaven, drawing on the explorations of Enoch, and recounting journeys of other sages, including Rabbi Akiba and Rabbi Ishmael, into the heavenly realms. Yet even today the true meaning and purpose of the Hekhaloth texts—like the legend of the four sages—is elusive and open to interpretation.

While mystical ascent is one method of bringing the living into contact with the heavenly realm, dreams are the most common medium by which spirits communicate with the living and by which the souls of the living are able to wander from world to world. And, of course, this tradition of dreams goes all the way back to the Bible, to the prophetic dreams associated with Joseph. It is one more example of how the patterns established in the earliest texts, especially the Torah, are repeated in new variations in later phases of Jewish literature. No matter what their source, sacred or secular, these tales place great emphasis on the dream as a doorway to the spiritual realm, which may take the form of one of the realms of Paradise, the Garden of Eden, the Holy Land, or even an enchanted cave. In one tale, "The Handwriting of the Messiah," Rabbi Hayim Vital dreams that his master, the Ari, returns from the dead and brings him a message from the Messiah. In another, "The Sword of the Messiah," a rabbi ascends in a dream to the palace of the Messiah. And in "The Cave of Mattathias," a Hasid trapped in a snowstorm lights the Hanukah oil he has with him and dreams of meeting the father of the Maccabees in a cave in the Holy Land.

The distinction between sacred and secular tales in postbiblical Jewish literature is difficult to make because of the close interaction between the rabbinic circles linked to the sacred literatures and the common folk. In general, the rabbinic sources offer legends and tales as exempla, for their allegorical meaning and moral intent, without placing undo emphasis on the narrative. Beginning in the sixteenth century in Constantinople, however, collections of Jewish folklore were published that were not considered to be sacred texts, and the stories in these collections place their primary emphasis on narrative embellishment, while the link to the sacred text is at least once removed.

It is true that many of the mystical folktales have their origin in one of the sacred sources, often the Talmud, whose lore is the primary source and model for all subsequent Jewish literature. But the themes that are emphasized draw from the folk elements in these rabbinic models—the magical powers of the Name; encounters with angels, spirits, and demons; and similiar folk motifs.

To some extent, the mystical folktale—for there is such a tale type—mirrors the folk understanding of the complex kabbalistic mythology. Only certain aspects of these esoteric rabbinic theories became a part of the folk tradition. These include the great kabbalistic emphasis on the potency of the letters of the Hebrew alphabet. Thus tales focusing on letters, numbers, and holy names, especially on the Tetragrammaton, God's most sacred Name, are often found. However, the folk influence is not limited to these tale types, for some of the mystical themes are closely associated with themes of great folk popularity, such as visits to the Garden of Eden, encounters with one of the Thirty-Six Hidden Saints, or accounts of angels, demons, and wandering spirits. Certainly the fact that the mystical tale can also be found in medieval Jewish folklore, as well as in all of the sacred sources, confirms it as a primary type of Jewish tale.

Thus it becomes apparent that the tales collected here, covering a period of two thousand years and ranging from Eastern Europe to the Middle East, belong to the same genre of mystical tales. They are linked by the mystical themes they have in common, as well as by the later masters who found their models in the earlier ones. "Kabbalah" means tradition, and the manner of transmission of these esoteric mysteries is a chain linking one mystical master to the next, whether or not they lived at the same time. As Reb Nachman of Bratslav said:

> Two men who live in different places, or even in different generations, may still converse. For one may raise a question, and the other who is far away in time or space may make a comment or ask a question that answers it. So they converse, but no one knows it save the Lord, who hears and records and brings together all the words of men, as it is written: *They who serve the Lord speak to one another, and the Lord hears them and records their words in His book* (Mal. 3:16).[51]

Thus the Ari considers himself to be a disciple of Rabbi Shimon bar Yohai, who lived more than a thousand years earlier. So too does the Baal Shem Tov regard the Ari as his model, while Reb Nachman of Bratslav found his model in his great-grandfather, the Baal Shem Tov. As a child, Reb Nachman spent many hours lying on the grave of the Baal Shem Tov, communing with him. So too is the chain of generations demonstrated in midrashic legends such as "The *Tzohar*," which links the generations from Adam to Seth to Enoch to Methuselah to Lamech to Noah to Abraham and the other patriarchs, and so on, down through the generations. The glowing jewel of the *Tzohar* itself, containing the primordial light, symbolizes the Jewish mystical tradition. Just as the *Tzohar* is handed down in each generation, so do the generations perpetuate this chain of tradition by transmitting the ancient and arcane secrets of the Kabbalah.[52]

Above all, these tales served as examples of how a mystical life could be lived. It was necessary to enter a world of signs and symbols, where everything that took place had meaning, a world of mythic proportions in which the forces of good and evil were engaged in a continual struggle. It was a world in which the spirits of the dead were no longer invisible, nor the angels. And a heavy responsibility hung on the master and his disciples to repair the world in order to make it possible for God and His Bride to be brought back together, for the broken vessels to be restored, and for the Messiah to be freed from the chains that have held Him back for so long. These tales illustrate this sacred, mythical world and preserve the legends of the greatest Jewish mystics.

Notes

1. For examples of Sufi and Zen tales, see *Tales of the Dervishes*, edited by Idries Shah, and *Zen Flesh, Zen Bones*, edited by Paul Reps. For accounts of Christian mystical experience see *The Lives of the Saints* by Alban Butler. See the Bibliography for additional information about English-language books referred to in these notes.

2. This legend is found in two versions in the Talmud. B. Hag. 14b uses the phrasing "Rabbi Akiba entered and departed in peace," and B. Hag. 15b and Tosefta Hag. 23 have "Rabbi Akiba ascended in peace and descended in peace."

3. In addition to these primary biblical roots of Kabbalah, other biblical episodes play an important role in the evolution of a Jewish mystical consciousness, including the visions of Isaiah and Daniel and the Giving of the Torah.

4. The term "kabbalistic" has both a broad and a narrow definition. The definition offered on p. 4 is the broad one. The narrow definition refers specifically to the period between the appearance of the Zohar in the thirteenth century and the failure of the messianic movement of Shabbatai Zevi in the seventeenth century.

5. In fact, de Leon gave several accounts of how it was found: in a cave in Palestine, and later sent to Spain by Nachmanides; or by an Arab boy digging for treasure; or that it was discovered among the plunder of a library. All later evidence, including testimony by de Leon's wife after his death, indicates that it was indeed a work of pseudepigrapha, of de Leon's creation, or that it was the creation of the circle of mystics to which Moshe de Leon belonged. For more on the theory of group creation of the Zohar, see *Studies in the Zohar* by Yehuda Liebes, chapter 2, "How the Zohar Was Written," pp. 85–138.

6. See *Shabbatai Zevi: The Mystical Messiah* by Gershom Scholem.

7. Two novels have been written about the Maid of Ludomir. One is *Ha-Betulah mi-Ludomir* by Yohanan Twersky (Tel Aviv: 1949), and the other is *They Called Her Rebbe* by Gershon Winkler. The other woman recognized as a rabbi is Asenath bat Samuel Barazani of Kurdistan. See "Asenath's Dove," p. 148.

8. See, for example, "The Three Tasks of Elijah" in *Miriam's Tambourine: Jewish Folktales from Around the World*, edited by Howard Schwartz, p. 56. See also *Tales of Elijah the Prophet*, by Peninnah Schram.

9. See "The Cave of Shimon bar Yohai," p. 69, and the accompanying note.

10. Kohelet Rabbah 10:10. Because of the ambiguity of the text, it is not completely clear if it is Rabbi Shimon bar Yohai himself (or his spirit) who comes to the disciple, or simply that the disciple remembers the lesson. But since Bar Yohai clearly states in the dream that he will come to the disciple, it is reasonable to assume that this is what takes place. This interpretation is confirmed by the oral variant "A Kiss from the Master," p. 79.

11. The concept of the *ibur* is suggested in the Zohar II:100b: "The Supernal Holy King does not permit anything to perish, not even the breath of the mouth, which emerges into the world as a new creation." Possession by an *ibur* should be distinguished from *gilgul*, the transmigration of souls. In the latter, the soul of a person who has died is reincarnated in the body of a person born later. In the case of an *ibur*, the soul of a sage who has died fuses with the soul of one who is living, and this kind of metempsychosis is usually temporary rather than permanent.

12. For more on the subject of possession by *dybbuks* see *Lilith's Cave: Jewish Tales of the Supernatural*, edited by Howard Schwartz, pp. 11–13.

13. See *Sippure ha-Dybbuk*, edited by Gedalya Nigal (Jerusalem: 1983), for a comprehensive collection of accounts of possession by *dybbuks*.

14. The stories referred to are, respectively, "The Cave of Shimon bar Yohai" (where the sign is the bird escaping from the hunter's net), "The Decree," "A Saint from the Other World," "The Celestial Academy," and "The Book of Adam."

15. *Shivhei ha-Ari*, p. 26, and *Shivhei ha-Rabbi Hayim Vital*, p. 28a.

16. The traditional belief is that there is one *tzaddik*, or righteous one, who is the greatest in that generation, and if the conditions are right, he could serve as the Messiah. See the discussion about the myth of the Messiah beginning on p. 20. See also *The Zaddik* by Samuel H. Dresner.

17. See Arthur Green's biography of Rabbi Nachman, *Tormented Master*.

18. *Shivhei ha-Ari*, p. 37b.

19. See "A Vision," p. 264.

20. Heinreich Zimmer, *Myths and Symbols in Indian Art and Civilization*, pp. 32–33.

21. See "The Beggar King" in EV, pp. 59ff.

22. For examples of Rabbi Adam's use of illusion, see "The Enchanted Journey" and "The King's Dream" in *Elijah's Violin and Other Jewish Fairy Tales*, edited by Howard Schwartz, pp. 181ff. and 197ff., respectively.

23. The method of interpretation known by the acronym *PaRDeS* was most likely invented, or at least codified, by Moshe de Leon, author of the Zohar, according to the widely accepted findings of Gershom Scholem. Moshe de Leon was also the author of a volume, since lost, entitled *Sefer Pardes*. Scholem speculates that this volume was a theoretical treatise of *Pardes* as a method of explication, a concept that in any case dates from the same period, the thirteenth century.

PaRDeS is an acronym for four levels of understanding: *peshat*, *remez*, *drash*, and *sod*. *Peshat* is the literal level. *Remez* is the first hint of another level of meaning; in literary terms it is the use of metaphor. *Drash* stands for midrash when the interpretation takes the form of a legend, or in literary terms, of allegory, which itself is simply an extended metaphor. *Sod* is the level of mystery, of Kabbalah. Here literary meaning remains inseparable from mystical meaning; both provide entry into the realm of the transcendent. The existence of the level of *sod* is also a reminder that metaphor is a kind of veil, and that ultimate truth transcends it and must remain imageless and unknown, like the remotest aspect of God, known in Kabbalah as *Ein Sof*. The choice of the word *Pardes* as the acronym for this system derives from its use in the talmudic legend about the four sages who entered *Pardes*. See the discussion of this legend beginning on p. 28.

24. This matter is regarded as highly esoteric because it seems to imply a flaw in God's essential being. Since God is responsible for all of creation, it follows that any flaw in creation, such as the Shattering of the Vessels, must be God's responsibility.

25. From *Pesikta Rabbati* 26:7. This legend grows out of the *drash* of Jeremiah's lamentation over the destruction of the Temple in Jerusalem and the Babylonian exile. Mother Zion is the personification of Zion, who is grieving and in need of comfort. At the same time, Mother Zion is an early incarnation of the *Shekhinah*, whose home was the Temple in Jerusalem.

26. Some traditions view both Messiah ben Joseph and Messiah ben David as human figures. The separate traditions of an earthly and a heavenly Messiah are sometimes resolved by identifying the heavenly Messiah as the celestial soul of the earthly Messiah, whose fusion with his earthly soul will transform the human Messiah and unleash his destiny. This is the position taken by Jacob Immanuel Schochet and other Lubavitch Hasidim. For more on the complex traditions linked to the Messiah, see *The Messiah Texts*, edited by Raphael Patai.

27. IFA no. 6928, collected in Israel by Uri Resler from his uncle.

28. For additional information about these prayers of unification see *The Hebrew Goddess* by Raphael Patai, third edition, chapter 8.

29. It is sometimes difficult to distinguish between the kind of astral projection practiced in these tales and sympathetic magic. The former requires some form of soul travel, while the latter draws upon the powers of magic to make an action that is performed in one place have effect in another. "A Bowl of Soup" is an example of a tale in which it is particularly difficult to make this distinction.

30. *Hayey Moharan* no. 88 by Reb Nathan of Nemirov (Jerusalem: 1982). While traveling to Uman from Bratslav, Rabbi Nachman told a story to his scribe, Reb Nathan of Nemirov, about the Baal Shem Tov going to a city where souls had been waiting for three hundred years to ascend on high (*Hayey Moharan* no. 87). This tale about his great-grandfather, the Baal Shem Tov, probably explains Reb Nachman's

desire to be buried in Uman, where over twenty thousand Jews were killed by Cossacks on June 19, 1768. Reb Nachman explicitly referred to this on the day before he died, saying: "'Do you remember the story I told you?' 'Which one?' Reb Nathan asked. 'The story of the Baal Shem Tov which I told you on the way to Uman.' 'Yes,' said Reb Nathan. Reb Nachman said: 'For a long time now they have had their eyes on me, to get me here. There are not just thousands of souls here, but hundreds upon hundreds upon hundreds of thousands'" (*Hayey Moharan* no. 88).

Rabbi Nachman is said to have seen a dead soul for the first time when he was a child. He prayed to see such a soul, and one did indeed seek him out, terrifying him. Later he was said to have seen many such souls of the dead, and at the end of his life he became "The Master of the Field," sought out by thousands of souls for the *tikkun* or repair he could do for their souls (*Hayey Moharan* no. 7). The phrase "Master of the Field" comes from one of Reb Nachman's teachings (*Hayey Moharan* no. 48) in which he spoke of a field where souls grow, and how they require a master of the field to repair them.

31. There are a variety of kabbalistic techniques in which the letters of the words of the Torah are manipulated. The most popular technique is *gematria*, where the numerical total of a word is believed to link it to any other words with that same total, making it possible to insert the alternate word or words in the same context as a means of revealing secrets concealed in the Torah. The use of *gematria* was especially popular in trying to determine when the coming of the Messiah was to take place. See *The Spice of Torah—Gematria* by Gutman G. Locks, which lists all the words of the Torah according to their numerical value.

32. An example of combining the letters from different names of God is found in Hayim Vital's diary of his visions, *Sefer Hezyonot* V:32. Here Vital describes prostrating himself on the grave of the talmudic sage Abbaye and attempting a unification in which he combined the letters of the Tetragrammaton with those of the name *Adonai*. In this case the attempt failed, as his thoughts became confused and he was unable to combine the letters.

33. There are several rabbinic depictions of the abode of the souls of the unborn. Hagigah 12b describes it as the seventh heaven, while B. Yebamot 62a and Sanhedrin 98a speak of the *Guf*, where the souls of future generations are stored, noting that the Messiah will not come until the Guf is emptied: "The Messiah will not come until all the souls in the heavenly chamber of souls (*Guf*) have entered bodies and have been born into this world." The film *The Seventh Sign* is based on the premise that the *Guf* is empty, and that the first child without a soul is about to be born. Other sources identity the *Guf* with the *Pargod*, the curtain that separates God from the angels, on which all souls are portrayed. Still others speak of a Quarry of Souls.

34. See *Joseph Karo: Lawyer and Mystic* by R. J. Zwi Werblowsky. Here the point is made that there are significant links between kabbalah and *halachah*, the body of Jewish law. Indeed, most of the great kabbalists, including Joseph Caro and the Ari, were also masters of the *halachah*.

35. A number of rabbinic legends strongly suggest the concept of the archetype. One common legend lists a number of things that God created before the creation of the world: "Seven things were created before the world was created. They are: The Torah, Gehenna, the Garden of Eden, the Throne of Glory, the Temple, Repentance, and the Name of the Messiah" (*Pirke de Rabbi Eliezer* no. 3). In Numbers Rabbah 15:10, God shows a heavenly model of a candlestick to Moses so that he will

know how to fulfill the injunction *"And thou shalt make a candlestick of pure gold"* (Ex. 25:31).

36. See "The Lost Princess" in *Elijah's Violin and Other Jewish Fairy Tales,* edited by Howard Schwartz, p. 210.

37. B. Hag. 15a. The passage goes on to say: "He created mountains and hills. He created seas and rivers. . . . He created the righteous and the wicked. He created the Garden of Eden and Gehenna."

38. For the legend of Joseph della Reina, see "The Chains of the Messiah," p. 106. This is the classic tale of attempting to force the coming of the Messiah.

39. Such multiple interpretations of the same passage are common under the system of interpretation known by the acronym *PaRDeS.* See note 23 for a further discussion of this method.

40. There is a scholarly controversy over the meaning of the term *"Pardes"* in its original context, concerning whether or not it had already acquired a mystical meaning. Gershom Scholem held that it did have such a meaning, while Ephraim Urbach and David Halperin concluded that in the original legend it had only a literal meaning of "garden/orchard/park," as it does in most other places in rabbinic literature. But it took on a metaphorical/mystical meaning of "Paradise" when it was inserted into its literary context in the Talmud. For further discussion of this issue, see David Halperin's *The Merkavah in Rabbinic Literature,* pp. 86ff. See note 2 for the sources of these variant readings.

41. B. Hag. 15a.

42. Thus *Pardes* may be understood as a metaphor inside a metaphor. The orchard represents Paradise, which in turn represents mystical contemplation. This becomes clearer when cast in terms of the system of interpretation known as *PaRDeS,* where the orchard represents the literal interpretation, Paradise the allegorical one, and the mystical meaning takes the form of mystical contemplation. See note 23 for a further discussion of the system of *PaRDeS.*

43. B. Hag. 13a.

44. Mishnah Hag. 2:1.

45. B. Hag. 15a.

46. B. Hag. 15a.

47. B. Hag 15a.

48. The upper waters and lower waters are personified in the midrash as male and female, respectively. Midrash Konen 25 describes the male and female waters as locked in a passionate embrace, and that God had to tear them apart in order to separate them. Ben Zoma was especially interested in the division of the upper and lower waters. In Bereshith Rabbah 4:6 he disputed the verse *And God made the firmament* (Gen. 1:7), saying: "He made—how remarkable! Surely it came into existence at God's word, as it is written, *By the word of the Lord were the heavens made, and all the host of them by the breath of his mouth"* (Ps. 33:6).

49. Rabbi Azriel of Gerona's *Commentary on Talmudic Aggadot,* p. 40. Note that by an enigmatic kabbalistic reversal, "descending to the *Merkavah"* means the opposite, to ascend on high. This statement about Ben Azzai appears in several variations, including Leviticus Rabbah 16:4: "Ben Azzai was sitting and expounding Torah, and a flame was burning around him. They said to him: 'Are you perhaps engaged in the study of the *Merkavah?'* He replied: 'No, I am but finding in the Torah parallels to the Prophets, and in the Prophets parallels to the Aggadah. And the words of the Torah

are joyful even as they were on the day they were being given at Sinai, and they were originally given in fire, as it is said, *And the mountain burned with fire*'" (Deut. 4:11). For a further discussion of these passages about Ben Azzai, see *Kabbalah: New Perspectives* by Moshe Idel, p. 318, note 99.

50. There are several versions of "The Legend of the Ten Martyrs." The earliest of these is found in *Hekhaloth Rabbati*, one of the most important of the Hekhaloth texts of *Merkavah* mysticism. The best-known version is that found in *Midrash Eleh Ezkerah*. See the note to "Rabbi Ishmael's Ascent," p. 52. For a further discussion of the background of this legend, see *Rabbinic Fantasies*, edited by David Stern and Mark Jay Mirsky, pp. 143–46.

51. *Shivhei ha-Ran*, edited by Rabbi Nathan of Nemirov (Ostrog: 1816).

52. The midrashim about the *Tzohar* resolve two important problems in the biblical text. The first concerns the identity of the light of the first day, in contrast to that of the fourth. What was this light? The midrash answers that it was the primordial light. The identity of the term *"Tzohar"* in the passage about the building of the ark is also resolved, with the gem of the *Tzohar* said to contain the primordial light. See "The *Tzohar*," p. 59 and the accompanying note.

I

RABBINIC TALES

THE GOLDEN DOVE

Rabbah bar bar Hanna was once traveling in a caravan with several other sages. After riding for many hours, they came to an oasis and stopped to eat and rest. Later, after they had resumed their journey, Rabbah suddenly realized that he had forgotten to say the blessing after meals. He did not think it was permitted to say those prayers at a distance from where he had eaten, so he decided to return to the previous site.

Now Rabbah was a master of the Law, but so were the other sages in the caravan. They might not agree with him, and by the time the matter was decided, they would be even farther away than they were. Instead Rabbah told his companions he was returning to the oasis to recover a golden dove he had left behind. They all agreed that such a great treasure could not be abandoned, and they wished him luck in finding it.

So Rabbah turned back on his own until he reached that place. There he uttered the blessing, and just as he finished, he looked down and saw something glittering in the sand. Rabbah dug it out and saw that it was a golden dove. As he held it, the heat of his hands warmed its wings, and the dove began to throb as if it were alive. This so surprised Rabbah that he opened his hands and the dove took flight, ascending all the way to Paradise. There it built its nest in the branches of the tree outside the palace of the Messiah, where its song fills the heavens. That is why the palace of the Messiah is known as the "Bird's Nest."

And every year, on Rosh Hashanah, the Messiah sends forth the dove to see if the world is ready to hear his footsteps, just as Noah did to see if the waters had receded. And if the time is right, the returning dove will perch on the gates of the palace to signal that it is time for them to be opened. But if the world is not yet ready, the dove returns to its nest and is silent for three days. For the time of the coming of the Messiah has been delayed once more.

□ Babylon: c. Fifth Century

2

AN APPOINTMENT WITH DEATH

One morning, as King Solomon awoke, he heard a chirping outside his window. He sat up in bed and listened carefully, for he knew the language of the birds, and he overheard them say that the Angel of Death had been sent to take the lives of two of his closest advisers. King Solomon was startled by this unexpected news, and he summoned the two doomed men. And when they stood before him, he revealed what he had learned of their fate.

The two were terrified, and they begged King Solomon to help them. Solomon told them that their only hope was to find their way to the city of Luz. For it was well known that the Angel of Death was forbidden to enter there. Therefore the inhabitants of Luz were immortal—as long as they remained within the walls of the charmed city. Very few knew the secret of how to reach that city, but King Solomon was one of those few.

So it was that King Solomon revealed the secret to the two frightened men, and they departed at once. They whipped their camels across the hot desert all day, and at nightfall they finally saw the walls of that fabled city. Immortality was almost within reach, and they rode as fast as they could to the city gates.

But when they arrived they saw, to their horror, the Angel of Death waiting for them. "How did you know to look for us here?" they asked. The angel replied: "This is where I was told to meet you."

□ Babylon: c. Fifth Century

⁂ 3 ⁂

Isaac's Ascent

When the knife touched Isaac's throat, his soul flew from him. While his body lay on the stone altar, his soul ascended on high, rising up through the palaces of heaven. And the angels on high brought Isaac's soul to the celestial academy of Shem and Eber. There he remained for three years, studying the Torah, for in this way Isaac was rewarded for all he had suffered when he was about to be slain.

So too were all the treasuries of heaven opened to Isaac: the celestial Temple, which has existed there since the time of the creation, the Chambers of the Chariot, and all of the palaces of heaven; and all the treasuries of ice and snow, as well as the treasury of prayers and the treasury of souls. There Isaac saw how he had descended from the seed of Adam. So too was he permitted to see the future generations that would arise from the seed of Abraham. Even the End of Days was revealed, for no mystery of heaven was deemed too secret for the pure soul of Isaac.

During all this time Abraham remained frozen in place, the knife in his upraised hand. But to him it seemed but a single breath. Then the angel spoke: "Lay not thy hand upon the lad," and at that instant Isaac's soul returned to his body. And when Isaac found that his soul had been restored to him, he exclaimed: *"Blessed is He who quickens the dead!"* And when Abraham unbound him, Isaac arose, seeing the world as if for the first time, as if he had been reborn.

□ Palestine: c. Eighth Century

✠ 4 ✠

THE MAGIC FLOCK

When Jacob arrived at the River Jabbok, he sent his servants across first, then his wives and children. He himself wished to remain alone there, to rest after his escape from Laban, and to prepare himself for his encounter with Esau the next day.

Soon after everyone else had crossed the river, a shepherd arrived there with his flocks. He proposed to Jacob that they help each other in crossing their flocks, and Jacob agreed. They started with Jacob's flock, and in a twinkling the shepherd succeeded in transferring all of them to the other side. Then they turned to the shepherd's flock, and Jacob assisted him by carrying the animals, two by two, across the river. Jacob worked without pausing, but after he had forded the river with a great many animals, he saw that the flocks of the shepherd had not grown smaller but seemed to have increased.

Still, Jacob continued to bear the flocks across the river hour after hour. But as the day began to grow dark, he saw that the flocks of the shepherd still reached to the horizon, with no end in sight. Then Jacob understood that this was no ordinary shepherd, but some kind of magician, and that all the flocks he had carried were only an illusion. In his fury Jacob accused the shepherd of enchantment and deceit. Then the shepherd touched his finger to the earth, and a great fire burst forth. But this display of his power did not frighten Jacob, and the two began to struggle, and they continued to wrestle all night.

During their struggle the magician wounded Jacob in his thigh, but Jacob still continued to fight. And as dawn approached the magician sought to depart, but Jacob refused to let him go. In this way Jacob received his adversary's blessing, and his name was changed from Jacob to Israel.

Some say that shepherd was Samael, the guardian angel of Esau, who came to Jacob to weaken him before his encounter with Esau.

Others say it was the angel Michael, who had been sent by God to show Jacob that he, like the angels, was made of fire, and that he had nothing to fear from Esau. And, in truth, after this struggle Jacob was a changed man, who put down his weapons and his pride and bowed seven times to his brother, *and Esau ran to meet him and embraced him* (Gen. 33:4), and at last they came together in peace.

□ Ancient Israel: Fifth Century

5

THE ASCENT OF MOSES

With the children of Israel assembled at the foot of Mount Sinai, Moses ascended the mountain, and when he reached the top he saw that a cloud was floating there. As he came closer the cloud opened, and Moses stepped inside. There he found himself in the presence of a great light, like that he had witnessed at the burning bush, and as the cloud started to ascend, Moses knew that he was being borne up by God's blessing.

As the cloud rose up toward heaven, Moses lost track of time, so filled was he with awe. Then all at once he reached the gates of the firmament and the cloud opened, so that Moses could step out. The angel Kemuel, who guards that gate, rebuked him for seeking to enter heaven. But when Moses replied "I have come to receive the Torah," the gate opened of its own accord. And when the angel saw this, he knew that it was God's wish that Moses should enter there, and he made way for him to pass.

After that Moses reached the river Rigyon, a river of fire whose waves can consume angels as well as men. There he was met by angels of destruction, who sought to burn him with their fiery breath. And Moses cried out: "Master of the Universe, I fear they will consume me with their fire!" And at that moment a great fiery wave rose up from the river and washed over the angels of destruction, and they were all consumed. But not a spark of that fire touched Moses, who learned, in this way, that all things exist by the mercy of the Holy One, and that every life is in His hands.

Now when the angels saw Moses there, they cried out to the Holy One: "Master of the Universe, what is this man doing here?" And the Holy One, blessed be He, replied: "He has come to receive the Torah." And the angels said: "You created the Torah before You created the world. How can such a precious treasure pass into the hands of a mere man?" And the Holy One replied: "It was created for that very purpose."

Then the Holy One reached down and pulled Moses up to Paradise. There Moses saw the Holy One seated on His Throne of Glory, and behind Him was an angel so large that Moses shook with terror. And when the Holy One saw this, He stepped down from His Throne of Glory to comfort him. After that Moses found his strength again, and he grew calm in that high place.

When he had recovered, Moses asked to know the identity of that angel, and the Holy One replied: "That is the angel Sandalphon, who weaves garlands out of the prayers of Israel." Just then Sandalphon completed one of those garlands, and it rose up of its own accord and came to rest on the head of the Holy One, blessed be He, as He sat on His Throne of Glory. And at that moment all the hosts on high shook with awe, and the wheels of the throne revolved, and the creatures of the Chariot, who had been silent, began to roar like lions, all of them crying out *Holy, holy, holy is the Lord of hosts* (Isa. 6:3). That is when Moses saw that God was weaving something. He asked Him what it was, and the Holy One replied: "These are the crowns of the letters of the Torah. I have been weaving them since the time of creation, so that a time will come when Rabbi Akiba ben Joseph will interpret every crown and letter of the Torah." And Moses said: "I would like to see him." And God said: "Turn around." And when Moses did, he found himself seated in the back of the classroom of Rabbi Akiba, a thousand years in the future, and he listened to Rabbi Akiba explain one of the laws of the Torah, but try as he might, Moses could not understand, for he had not yet received the Torah. Then one of the students asked Rabbi Akiba where he had learned this, and Rabbi Akiba said: "From Moses, at Mount Sinai." And when he heard this, Moses understood that the words of the Torah would take root and flourish in the days to come.

At that moment Moses heard someone call his name, and when he looked up he found himself back in Paradise, standing before the Holy One, blessed be He, who said: "The time has come for you to receive the Torah. Take hold of my Throne of Glory." This Moses did, and all at once the Holy One opened the seven firmaments and showed Moses the Sanctuary on high. Then He opened the portals of the seven firmaments and appeared over Israel, in all His fullness and splendor. And when the Children of Israel heard the words *"I am the Lord thy God* (Ex. 20:2), they fell down in fear and their souls departed. Then the Holy One caused the dew of the Resurrection, which will revive the souls of the righteous at the End of Days, to fall upon them. And every one of them was revived.

After that the Holy One sent one hundred twenty myriad angels to earth. There were two angels for each of the Children of Israel, one to put its hand over each of their hearts, so that they would not stop beating, and the other to raise up their heads, so they could gaze at the Holy One, blessed be He, in that moment of glory. And so they did.

Then, while the portals were still open, the Holy One transmitted the Torah to Moses, while every word echoed among the people gathered below. For forty days and nights the Holy One spoke the words of the Torah to Moses during the day, and at night He explained it to him. And that which he wrote down during the day is the Written Law, and that which he learned at night is the Oral Law, which reveals the seventy meanings of every word of the Torah like the many facets of a perfect jewel.

At the end of forty days and nights the cloud returned, and Moses descended to Mount Sinai. And there he proclaimed the sovereignty of the Lord over all of Israel and declared that *The Lord will reign forever, thy God, O Zion, unto all generations. Hallelujah* (Ps. 146:10).

□ Palestine: Ninth Century

6

THE CHRONICLE OF SERAH BAT ASHER

Only a handful of the Children of Israel were brought into heaven alive. Moses was one, his sister Miriam another, and there were also Enoch and Elijah. Not only was Serah bat Asher one of those so blessed, but she also lived longer than anyone else, even longer than

Methuselah, for she lived from the time of Jacob until the ninth century, when she was taken into heaven.

Serah was the daughter of Asher, one of the sons of Jacob. She was among the sixty-nine who ascended with Jacob to Egypt, and she was among those who crossed the Red Sea and were counted by Moses in the census of the wilderness. Joseph sent his brothers to bring the House of Jacob to Egypt because of the famine in the land. They had to find a way to break the news to Jacob that Joseph was still alive. So they decided to have Serah, who was seven years old, play the harp for Jacob and sing the words "Joseph is alive." This Serah gladly did, and when Jacob suddenly understood what she was saying, he cried out, "Is it true?" And when Serah assured him that it was, Jacob, in his joy, gave her a great blessing, which caused Serah to live for so long. Later she served as a midwife, but when the Israelites were enslaved in Egypt, she too was enslaved and forced to bend over a mill.

When Serah was among the multitude at the Red Sea, she had a vision in which she saw things that none of the others saw. In the vision she saw the multitude of angels who had gathered to watch the Children of Israel cross the Red Sea. So too did she see the Divine Presence, who descended among them when Miriam played the tambourine and sang the Song of the Sea. And in that vision Serah even saw the Holy One commanding the waters of the Red Sea to part. For other than Moses, Serah was the only one alive in that generation who could look upon the Holy One and live.

It was also Serah who showed Moses where the coffin of Joseph could be found. Before his death, Joseph vowed that when the time came for the Children of Israel to return to the Holy Land, they should bring his bones with them. And when that day arrived, Moses searched everywhere for Joseph's coffin, but no one knew where it was. Finally he encountered Serah, who said: "My Lord Moses, why are you so tired?" Moses replied: "For three days and nights I have been searching for Joseph's coffin, and I cannot find it." She said to him: "Come and I will show you where it is." Moses was amazed. He asked: "Who are you?" She said: "I am Serah bat Asher, and I was present when the coffin of Joseph was sunk into the Nile." She led him to the river and said: "In this place the Egyptian magicians and astrologers made a coffin for Joseph and cast it into the water. Then they returned to Pharaoh and said: 'Your wish will be fulfilled. These people will stay here, because they won't be able to leave unless they find the bones of Joseph.'"

Then Moses leaned over the bank of the Nile and called out: "Joseph, Joseph, we are leaving. If you want to come with us, come now.

If not, then we have done our best." At that moment Joseph's coffin suddenly rose up from the depths, and when Moses lifted it out of the water, it was as light as a feather for him, so relieved was the spirit of Joseph that his bones were at last being taken to the Holy Land.

When the time came to be freed from slavery, it was Serah who identified Moses as the Redeemer. For there was a secret sign that God had communicated to Jacob, who passed it on to Joseph, who revealed it to his brothers, and in this way Serah came to learn of it from her father, Asher. The sign of the true redeemer is that he would say, "I will surely visit you." And thus when Moses said these words, Serah identified him as the Redeemer at once.

After that there were two arks that accompanied the Children of Israel in the wilderness: the coffin of Joseph and the Ark of the Tabernacle, the one representing the past and the other, the Torah, defining the future that lay before them.

There are many reports of Serah in the succeeding centuries. It was she who showed King David the location of the Foundation Stone, so that he knew where to build the Temple in Jerusalem. So too was it she who assisted Jeremiah in hiding the temple vessels after the Temple was destroyed.

Rabban Yohanan ben Zakkai once asked his students to describe the appearance of the walls of the Red Sea when the waters parted for the Children of Israel to cross. When none could do so, Rabban Yohanan described them as resembling a wall of sprouting bushes. Then, all at once, they heard a voice say: "No, it was not like that at all!" And when they looked up, they saw the face of a very old woman peering in the window of the House of Study. "Who are you?" demanded Rabban Yohanan. "I am Serah bat Asher," came the reply, "and I know exactly what the walls resembled, for I crossed the Red Sea." "And what did they look like?" asked Rabban Yohanan. She replied: "They resembled shining mirrors, mirrors in which every man, woman, and child was reflected, so that it seemed like an even greater multitude crossed there, not only those of the present, but also those of the past and future as well." And when Serah had finished speaking, none dared contradict her, for her knowledge was firsthand.

All of her days Serah bat Asher wandered wherever Jews could be found. In the ninth century she lived in Persia, in the city of Isfahan. One day, while she was alone inside the synagogue, a fiery chariot descended from heaven and surrounded the synagogue with flames. Then the chariot ascended and the flames disappeared. There were many witnesses of this event. Afterward they rushed to the synagogue and saw with amazement that there was no damage to the synagogue at all. But when they went inside, Serah was gone. For she had ascended into Paradise alive, and was spared the taste of death. And that synagogue, which became known as the synagogue of Serah bat Asher, is still standing to this day.

□ Persia: c. Twelfth Century

ඝඝඝඝඝඝ   7   ඝඝඝඝඝඝ

MYSTERIES OF THE CHARIOT

Rabban Yohanan ben Zakkai and his student, Rabbi Eleazar ben Arakh, once rode through a field on their donkeys. And Rabbi Eleazar said: "Please, rabbi, teach me something about the Mysteries of the Chariot."

"Surely you know that such mysteries may not be revealed to a single student unless he is able to comprehend them on his own," said Rabban Yohanan. "Therefore you may begin the discussion, and I will decide whether to speak of such secrets."

At that moment Rabbi Eleazar dismounted from his donkey, wrapped himself in his prayer shawl, and sat down beneath an olive tree. "Why did you dismount?" asked Rabban Yohanan, surprised. Rabbi Eleazar replied: "When we discuss *Ma'aseh Merkavah*, the Mysteries of the Chariot, the *Shekhinah* descends to listen, accompanied by the Angel of the Torah and many other angels. Should I, then, be seated upon a donkey?"

Rabbi Eleazar then began to discourse upon these very mysteries, and as he spoke, a circle of fire descended from heaven to surround that field and a song of praise rose up from the trees. And in the center of that circle an angel appeared, who stood before them and said: "Indeed, these are the very same Mysteries of the Chariot that are spoken of behind the Curtain." Then the angel disappeared, and they heard nothing more than the wind.

At that moment, Rabban Yohanan turned to his student and kissed him on the forehead. "How blessed is God to have a son like Abraham, and how blessed is Abraham to have a son such as you, Rabbi Eleazar."

Rabbi Yehoshua learned of this incident from Rabbi Yossi ha-Kohen while they were also traveling along a road. They too agreed to stop and discuss the Mysteries of the Chariot. All at once the skies became covered with clouds, and a splendid rainbow appeared. And the rabbis saw that clusters of angels had gathered around to listen, like guests at a wedding who rejoice with the bride and groom.

Later, Rabbi Yossi told Rabban Yohanan ben Zakkai what had happened. And Rabban Yohanan replied: "Fortunate are we to have been so blessed. And now I know why I dreamed last night that you and I were sitting together on Mount Sinai when we heard a heavenly voice telling us to rise, for magnificent palaces and golden beds awaited us in Paradise, where we were to join the souls that sit before the Divine Presence."

□ Babylon and Ancient Israel: c. Fifth Century

8

THE FOUR WHO ENTERED PARADISE

Four sages entered Paradise—Ben Azzai, Ben Zoma, Aher, and Rabbi Akiba. Ben Azzai looked and died. Ben Zoma looked and lost his mind. Aher cut himself off from his fathers and became an apostate. Only Rabbi Akiba entered and departed in peace.

It is said about Ben Azzai that when he sat down to study, flames surrounded him, and the words of the Torah burned like fire in his sight, and they were as joyful to him as they were on the day they were given at Mount Sinai. In this way he descended to the Chambers of the Chariot and passed through the palaces of heaven and saw with his own eyes the celestial glory, and his soul could not tear itself away, for he felt he had returned to his true home at last. And that is how he took leave of this world.

About Aher it is said that when he ascended on high, he reached the realm of the angel Metatron, whom he saw seated on a throne. In great confusion he cried out "There are—God forbid—two powers in heaven!" and from that moment he lost his faith. Then God commanded that Metatron be lashed sixty times with a fiery whip for not rising up before Aher and showing him that he was wrong.

In those days Rabbi Joshua ben Haninah saw Ben Zoma, and Ben Zoma was so lost in thought that he did not stand up before his master. Rabbi Joshua asked "Whence and whither, Ben Zoma?" And Ben Zoma replied: "I was gazing at the mysteries of creation, and between the upper waters and the lower waters there are only three finger-breadths." Hearing this, Rabbi Joshua said to his disciples: "Ben Zoma is gone." Nor did Ben Zoma live long after that.

Four sages entered Paradise. But only Rabbi Akiba ascended on high, passed through the palaces of heaven, and descended in peace.

□ Babylon: c. Fifth Century

9

RABBI ISHMAEL'S ASCENT

One of the Roman emperors called in ten of the finest sages and demanded to study the Torah with them. They began at the beginning of Genesis, and all went well until they reached the passage in Exodus that reads *He who kidnaps a man—whether he has sold him or is still holding him—shall be put to death* (Ex. 21:16). When he read this, the Emperor remembered how Joseph's brothers had sold him into slavery. Yet they had not been punished by death, as the law required.

The Emperor asked the sages if this ruling applied to Joseph's brothers, and they agreed that it did. Then he demanded that the law be fulfilled and the executions carried out. The sages tried to explain that Joseph's brothers had died long ago. The Emperor told them that he knew this—the brothers could no longer be punished. But in that case, the punishment must be carried out on those who represented Joseph's brothers in that age. And he pointed to each of the ten sages and told them that surely none represented the leaders of the tribes of Israel more than they did.

Then the Emperor signed a decree commanding that the ten sages be put to death, among them Rabbi Akiba, Rabbi Ishmael, Rabbi Haninah ben Teradion, and seven other of the greatest sages who ever lived.

All of the sages were placed in a cell together, so that none might escape before the execution was carried out. There in that cell they turned to Rabbi Ishmael and begged him to use the power of the Name to overturn the Emperor's decree, for they knew that he alone could do it. Rabbi Ishmael told them that he could indeed overturn the decree, but first they must find out if it was solely that of the Emperor, or if in condemning them the Emperor was carrying out a decree of the Holy One, blessed be He.

Then Rabbi Ishmael put on his *tallis* and *tefillin* and chanted a long prayer. And as he prayed, his soul ascended from this world to Paradise, until he reached Gabriel's palace, in the sixth heaven. Gabriel greeted him and asked to know why he had come there, and Rabbi Ishmael told him of the Emperor's decree, and that he had ascended to learn if it was a Divine decree or not.

Then Gabriel swore that he had heard the decree pronounced from behind the *Pargod*, the heavenly curtain. But he told Rabbi Ishmael not to mourn, for the ten sages would shortly be reunited in Paradise. Meanwhile their martyrdom would free the world from the evil that had entered it when Joseph's brothers sold him into slavery. And when that terrible sin had been lifted from the world, one of the chains that held back the Messiah would be broken, and the days of the Messiah would be that much closer. Rabbi Ishmael was greatly comforted to learn this and accepted his fate at once. Then he and the angel Gabriel took their leave of each other, and Rabbi Ishmael returned to this world.

When he opened his eyes, Rabbi Ishmael saw that all of the other sages had gathered around him, waiting for his soul to return from on high. He told them at once all he had learned from the lips of the angel Gabriel. And when the other sages learned that they had been chosen to lift the sin of Joseph's brothers from the world, and to break one of the chains of the Messiah, they embraced their destiny. And one by one they went bravely to their deaths.

□   Palestine: Eighth Century

10

THE WATERS OF THE ABYSS

Every night King David's soul ascended on high and wandered through the Temple in the Celestial Paradise. There he learned that he and his son Solomon were destined to build a Temple on earth that would be the mirror image of the one in heaven. So too did David learn that the Temple was destined to be built above an ancient stone, which God had set into the earth at the time of creation.

But where was this Foundation Stone to be found? King David commanded that shafts be dug to a depth of fifteen hundred cubits. And lo, they struck a stone in one of those shafts. As soon as he learned of it, King David went there with Ahitophel, his counselor, and with other members of the court. They descended into the pit, and there, at the bottom, they saw the immense stone, shining like the darkest emerald.

All those who saw it were amazed, and they knew that it must indeed be that fabled stone, which served as the world's foundation. Yet all at once King David was possessed by a great curiosity to see what lay beneath it. King David ordered the stone to be raised, but a voice came forth from the stone, saying: "Be warned that I must not be lifted. For I serve to hold back the waters of the Abyss."

King David and the others stood in awe of that voice, but still King David's curiosity was not sated. He decided to ignore the warning, and once more he ordered the stone to be raised. None of his advisers dared say anything, for they feared his wrath. After a great effort, a corner of the Foundation Stone was lifted up, and King David bent down and peered into the Abyss beneath it. There he heard something like the sound of rushing waters, and all at once he realized that by lifting the stone he had set free the waters of the Deep. Once again the world was in danger of being deluged, as in the time of Noah.

King David trembled with fear, and he asked the others what they might do to cause the waters to fall back, but no one spoke. Then King David said: "Perhaps if I wrote the Name of God on a potsherd and cast it into the depths, we might still be saved. But does anyone know if this is permitted?" Still the others said nothing, and King David grew angry and said: "If any one of you knows this and still refuses to answer, then your soul will bear the curse of the end of existence!" Then Ahitophel spoke: "Surely the Name can be used to bring peace to the whole world." So David picked up a potsherd and scratched the four-letter Name of God into the stone and cast it into the bottomless pit, and they replaced the stone. All at once the roar of the waters grew fainter, and David knew that they had been saved by the power of the Name.

In the days to come King David repented many times for his sin, and he gave thanks to God for sparing the world from another flood. And his son Solomon had the Holy of Holies of the Temple built exactly above the Foundation Stone, for both the stone and the Temple bore the seal of God's blessing.

□ Babylon: c. Fifth Century.

11

THE VISION OF THE HIGH PRIEST

Once, when Rabbi Ishmael ben Elisha, the High Priest, went into the Holy of Holies of the Temple, he looked up and saw Akatriel Yah, the Lord of Hosts, seated on a high and exalted throne. And the Lord spoke to him and said: "Ishmael, My son, bless me." And Rabbi Ishmael raised his hands in a blessing and said: "May it be Your will that Your mercy overcomes Your justice, and may Your children be blessed with Your compassion." And when Rabbi Ishmael raised his eyes, the Lord inclined His head toward him.

□ Babylon: c. Fifth Century

12

THE KEYS OF THE TEMPLE

The Temple in Jerusalem had been set on fire, and the moment of destruction had arrived. The High Priest went up to the roof, the keys of the Temple in his hand. There he called out: "Master of the Universe! The time has come to return these keys to You." Then he threw the keys high into the air, and at that instant a hand reached down from above and caught them and brought them back into heaven.

▢   Babylon: c. Fifth Century

13

THE SPIRIT OF IDOLATRY

When the Israelites returned from the Babylonian exile, they found the Temple in Jerusalem destroyed and they *cried with a loud voice unto the Lord their God* (Neh. 9:4). They said: "Woe, woe, it is the evil spirit of idolatry that has destroyed the Sanctuary, burnt the Temple, killed all the righteous, and driven Israel into exile. And behold, he is still dancing among us." And they prayed to the Lord: "You, who brought this evil spirit into being so that we could receive a reward through resisting him—we want neither him nor the reward!" Thereupon a tablet fell from heaven among them, with the word "truth" inscribed on it.

After this miracle had taken place, the people fasted for three days and nights, and at the end of that time the spirit of idolatry was delivered into their hands, and he came forth out of the Holy of Holies like a fiery lion. But they approached him fearlessly and plucked out one of his hairs, whereupon the lion raised his voice and roared so loudly that it could be heard for four hundred parasangs. And when the people heard this, they said among themselves: "Let us hope that heaven does not have mercy upon him." Then they cast the lion into a huge leaden pot and closed its only opening with lead, because lead absorbs sound.

They imprisoned the evil spirit for three days; then they discovered that there was not a fresh egg in all of the land. From this they realized that if they killed him, the whole world would also be destroyed. So they let him go.

□ Babylon: c. Fifth Century

14

THE ANGEL OF CONCEPTION

Among the angels there is one who serves as the midwife of souls. This is Lailah, the angel of conception. When the time has come for conception, Lailah seeks out a certain soul hidden in the Garden of Eden and commands it to enter the seed. The soul is always reluctant, for it still remembers the pain of being born, and it prefers to remain pure. But Lailah compels the soul to obey, and that is how new life comes into being.

While the infant grows in the womb, Lailah watches over it, reading the unborn child the history of its soul. All the while a light shines upon the head of the child, by which it sees from one end of the world to the other. And Lailah shows the child the rewards of the Garden of Eden, as well as the punishments of Gehenna. But when the time has come to be born, the angel extinguishes the light and brings forth the child into the world, and as it is brought forth, it cries. Then Lailah lightly strikes the newborn above the lip, causing it to forget all it has learned. And that is the origin of this mark, which everyone bears.

Indeed, Lailah is a guardian angel who watches over us all of our days. And when the time has come to take leave of this world, it is Lailah who leads us to the World to Come.

□ Babylon: c. Ninth Century

15

THE GOLDEN TABLE

Rabbi Haninah and his wife were very poor. All that Rabbi Haninah ate to sustain himself from one Sabbath to the next was a measure of carobs. Every Friday his wife would light the oven and throw twigs into it to produce smoke, so as not to be put to shame. She had a nosy neighbor who said: "I know that they have nothing to eat. What then is the meaning of all this smoke?" One day she came over, walked to the oven, and opened it, saying, "The smoke is so thick that I am afraid your bread might be burning." The wife of Rabbi Haninah was humiliated, but when they looked into the oven, they found it was filled with loaves of bread, and the odor of the baking bread filled the room. Then the neighbor was greatly surprised and said: "Hurry and bring your shovel before your bread gets charred."

One day Rabbi Haninah's wife said to him: "How long shall we go on suffering so much?" He asked her what he should do, and she told him to pray that something be given to them. He did so, and the next morning they found the leg of a golden table in their house. Rabbi Haninah's wife was delighted, but Rabbi Haninah found the miracle unsettling. And that night he dreamed that he feasted with the righteous in Paradise, but while all of them sat at golden tables with three legs, his table had but two. When he awoke Rabbi Haninah told his wife this dream, and he said: "Are you content to use now part of the blessings that are reserved for us in the world to come?" She

said: "Pray that the golden leg be taken away." This he did, and all at
once the leg vanished from before their eyes.

□ Babylon: c. Fifth Century

16

THE *TZOHAR*

When the world was first created, God filled the world with a sacred
light, known as the "primordial light." It came into being when God
said, *"Let there be light"* (Gen. 1:3). It was not the light of the sun, for
that did not come into being until the fourth day, when God created
the sun and the moon and the stars. It was a miraculous light by which
it was possible for Adam to see from one end of the world to the other.
And what was the source of that light? Some say that God wrapped
Himself in a *tallis* of light, while others say that it was cast from the
robe of the *Shekhinah*.

When Adam and Eve ate the forbidden fruit, the first thing they lost
was that precious light. Without it, the world seemed dark to them, for
the sun shone like a candle in comparison. But God preserved one
small part of that precious light inside a glowing stone, and the angel
Raziel delivered this stone to Adam after they had been expelled from
the Garden of Eden as a token of the world they had left behind. This
jewel, known as the *Tzohar*, sometimes glowed and sometimes hid its
light.

Before his death, Adam gave the *Tzohar* to his son Seth. By peering
into that jewel, Seth became a great prophet. In this way it was passed
down until it reached Enoch. Enoch peered deeply into the jewel and
saw that the flame burning in it formed itself into Hebrew letters, and
by reading those letters he was able to read the Celestial Torah, which
was imprinted in the flame of that glowing jewel. Enoch grew in his
wisdom until he was taken into Paradise in a chariot and transformed
into the angel Metatron, the heavenly scribe and prince of the treasuries of heaven.

Before departing from this world, Enoch gave the *Tzohar* to his son, Methuselah. Methuselah slept in its glowing light, and that is why he lived longer than anyone else. And Methuselah passed on the jewel to his son Lamech, who gave it to his son Noah, who brought it with him on the ark. Indeed, the Lord instructed Noah to do so when he said *"Put the* Tzohar *in the ark"* (Gen. 6:16). Noah hung it on the deck, and for forty days and nights it illuminated the ark.

When the ark landed on Mount Ararat, the first thing Noah did was to plant grapes, and when they grew ripe, he made wine and became drunk, and at that moment the *Tzohar* fell from where it hung in the ark, rolled into the water, and sank to the bottom of the sea. There it was carried by the currents until it came to rest in an underwater cave.

Years later, after the waters had subsided, the child Abraham was born in that cave. His mother had gone there to give birth to escape King Nimrod's decree that all newborn boys be put to death. For Nimrod had seen a sign that a child born at that time would overthrow him. After giving birth, Abraham's mother began to fear that the presence of the infant would bring the rest of the family into danger. And with a broken heart she abandoned the infant in the cave and returned home alone. Then the angel Gabriel descended to the cave and fed the infant with his thumb, through which milk and honey flowed, and because he was fed in that miraculous way, the boy began to grow at the rate of a year every day. And on the third day, while exploring the cave, he found a stone glowing in one of the crevices of the cave. Then the angel, who knew how precious it was, put it on a chain and hung it around Abraham's neck.

Thirteen days later Abraham's mother returned to the cave, for she could not put the fate of her infant out of her mind. She expected to find that the child was no longer living, but instead she found a grown boy, who said that he was her child. She refused to believe it at first, but when he showed her the glowing stone and the sacred light it cast, she came to believe that a miracle had taken place.

Abraham wore that glowing jewel all the days of his life, and it was said that whoever was ill and looked into that stone was soon healed. So too did he use it as an astrolabe to study the stars. Before his death, Abraham gave the *Tzohar* to his son Isaac, and Isaac gave it to Jacob at the time he gave him the stolen blessing. For Isaac had intended to give the glowing stone to Esau, but Rebecca, who was a seer, knew well that it was destined to belong to Jacob.

Jacob was wearing the *Tzohar* when he dreamed of the ladder reaching to heaven, with angels ascending and descending on it. And he, in turn, gave the stone to his beloved son, Joseph, when he gave him the coat of many colors. Now when he gave it to him, the stone was dark, and Jacob did not reveal its power, for he wanted Joseph to discover this for himself. And because Joseph's brothers did not know how precious the stone was, they did not take it from Joseph when they stripped him of the coat of many colors and cast him into the dark pit.

Now that pit was an old well, now dry, with snakes and scorpions living at the bottom. And Joseph, who heard them slithering and creeping in the dry leaves, shivered in the darkness at the bottom of the pit. All at once a light began to glow, and Joseph saw that it was coming from the stone he was wearing around his neck. Just then Joseph looked up and saw that a glowing figure stood before him. And he was amazed to find that he was no longer in a pit, but in a palace! That incandescent palace surrounded him in all its glory. Joseph felt as if he were in a trance, and he said: "Who are you, and what is this place?" And the glowing figure replied: "I am the angel Gabriel, and this is my palace. For as long as you are left in the pit, you will remain in this palace." Then Gabriel reached out and took Joseph's glowing amulet in one hand, and with his other hand he drew forth a cloth woven out of the amulet's light. And he wrapped Joseph in that garment so that he was no longer naked. Then the angel pointed to a window, and when Joseph looked out of it, he saw the history of future generations revealed.

For three days and nights Joseph remained in Gabriel's palace, drinking in the glory of the Torah and the future history of the Children of Israel. At the end of the third day the amulet suddenly grew dark, and Joseph found himself once more at the bottom of the well and heard Medianite traders calling out to him from the top of it. When they checked to see if the well contained water, they discovered Joseph there. They lowered a bucket for Joseph and pulled him up to the top. So it was that the Medianites sold Joseph into slavery and to the destiny that fate held for him, which was to become the Prince of Egypt.

Joseph placed the glowing stone of the *Tzohar* inside his silver cup, and discovered that by peering into it he could read the future and interpret dreams. That is how he interpreted the dreams of the butler and baker, and later the dreams of Pharaoh that prophesied the seven years of famine. It was that same cup that Joseph hid in the saddlebags of Benjamin, about which his servant said, *Is this not the cup from which our master drinketh, and with which he divineth?* (Gen 44:5).

That cup, with the precious jewel in it, was placed inside Joseph's coffin at the time of his death, and it remained there until Moses recovered Joseph's coffin with the help of Serah bat Asher. Soon after that Moses was told in a dream to take out the glowing stone and hang it in the Tabernacle. This he did, and that is the origin of the *Ner Tamid*, the Eternal Light. And that is why, even to this day, an eternal light burns above every Ark.

□   Babylon and Ancient Israel: c. Fifth Century

17

THE GATES OF EDEN

During his journeys, Alexander the Great once stopped by a stream. He had some salted fish with him, and when he washed it in the waters it gave off a wonderful fragrance. Alexander then drank some of that water and felt remarkably refreshed. He said: "This stream must come from the Garden of Eden. Let us see if we can find its source." So Alexander followed the stream until he reached the Gates of Eden. The gates were guarded by an angel with a flaming sword. The others in his company hid from the sight of the angel, but Alexander stood before the angel and said: "Open the gates for me!" The angel replied: *"This is the gate of the Lord, the righteous shall enter into it"* (Ps. 118:20). When Alexander saw that he would not be admitted, he said: "I am a king who is highly regarded. Give me something!" Then the angel gave him an eye. Alexander went and weighed it against all his gold and silver, but the eye outweighed them all. He asked the angel how this was possible, and the angel said: "The eye of a human being is never satisfied." Alexander asked: "How can you prove that this is true?" the angel answered: "Take some dust and cover the eye and you will see for yourself." Alexander did this, and all at once the eye was restored to its true weight.

□   Babylon: c. Fifth Century

18

THE LAW IS NOT IN HEAVEN

Rabbi Eliezer ben Hyrcanos was among the sages who were debating a point of the Law. All of the sages, except Rabbi Eliezer, ruled one way, but Rabbi Eliezer continued to insist that they were wrong. He used every possible argument to support it, but the others did not agree. Then he said: "Let this carob tree prove that the Law is as I state it is." The carob tree then uprooted itself and moved a distance of one hundred ells. But the other sages said: "The carob tree proves nothing."

Then Rabbi Eliezer said: "Let the waters of the spring prove that I am right." Then the waters began to flow backward. But again the sages insisted that this proved nothing.

Then Rabbi Eliezer spoke again and said: "Let the walls of the House of Study prove I am right." And the walls were about to collapse when Rabbi Yehoshua said to them: "If scholars are discussing a point of the Law, why should you interfere?" Thus they did not fall, in deference to Rabbi Yehoshua, but neither did they straighten out, out of respect for Rabbi Eliezer, and they are inclined to this day.

Rabbi Eliezer then said: "If the Law is as I say, let heaven prove it." Thereupon a *bat kol*, a heavenly voice, came forth and said: "Why do you quarrel with Rabbi Eliezer, whose opinion should prevail everywhere?"

Then Rabbi Yehoshua stood up and said: *"The Law is not in heaven"* (Deut. 30:12). "What does this mean?" asked Rabbi Yermiyahu. "It means that since the Torah was given to us on Mount Sinai, we no longer require a heavenly voice to reach a decision, since it is written in the Torah: *Follow after the majority* (Ex. 23:2).

Later Rabbi Nathan encountered Elijah and asked him how the ruling was accepted on high. And Elijah said: "At this the Holy One, blessed be He, smiled and said: 'My children have overruled me!'"

□ Babylon: c. Fifth Century

19

THE VOICE IN THE ATTIC

Before his death, Rabbi Eliezer ben Shimon had a vivid dream in which a vital matter waited to be decided, and he understood that it was a question for the dead. In the dream, he and three other rabbis journeyed to a burial cave after a ceremony that lasted long into the night. There Rabbi Eliezer descended to the secret entrance and entered, with no reluctance. Little by little he exhumed the body of one of the ancient priests, which was perfectly preserved. Then, with his torch extinguished, he bent low in a position of prayer, bringing his ear next to the mouth. It was dawn when he emerged from the cave, greeted by those who had been waiting. The decision was final.

When Rabbi Eliezer awoke he was powerfully moved by this dream, which seemed to portend matters of grave importance. But he did not know what it meant. Therefore he decided to go to the other three rabbis who had made the journey with him in the dream. He found all three rabbis studying together and told them the dream.

The first rabbi to speak said: "It is hard to avoid concluding that this dream reveals that you may soon be called to the Other World to join the ancient ones."

The second rabbi nodded in agreement at this interpretation but added: "Even so, the dream portends more than this. It also portends a miracle: that your body, Rabbi Eliezer, will not decay like every other, but will remain perfectly preserved."

The third rabbi concurred: "All that the others have said seems true to me. But the dream also tells us that the voice of the forefathers will speak through you after your death."

Even so did all of these things come true. Rabbi Eliezer told his wife about the dream and about the interpretation of the three rabbis, and after his death his wife hid his body in the loft. And the miracle came to pass as the rabbis had foretold: those who addressed a vital matter to him in that house heard a clear voice come forth from the attic, announcing the reply. And while his body lay there, no beasts or thieves dared approach that place.

The voice in the attic continued to speak all during the lifetime of Rabbi Eliezer's wife, but upon her death the voice became silent. And before the time of the Kaddish had passed, all three rabbis who long ago had interpreted Rabbi Eliezer's dream, now dreamed on the same night that he came to them and asked that they intern his body, for the time had come. Then the three rabbis went together to the loft to carry out his request, and there they found his body perfectly preserved, looking as it did on the day he had died more than ten years before.

□ Babylon: c. Fifth Century

20

FORCING THE END

Elijah used to frequent Rabbi Judah ha-Nasi's academy. One day he failed to come. When they asked him why he delayed, he replied: "I had to wait until I awoke Abraham, and he washed his hands and prayed; likewise for Isaac and Jacob."

They asked: "But why not wake them together?"

Elijah replied: "I feared that they might pray together and bring the Messiah before his time."

"And is their like to be found in the world?" they asked.

Elijah said: "There are Rabbi Hiyya and his sons."

Thereupon Rabbi Judah decreed a fast, and Rabbi Hiyya and his sons were called upon to read. As Rabbi Hiyya said *"He causeth the wind to blow,"* a wind began to blow; when he said *"He causeth the rain to descend,"* a heavy rain began to fall.

When he was about to say *"He quickeneth the dead,"* the world trembled, and in Heaven it was asked, "Who has revealed this secret?" "Elijah," they replied. Elijah was then brought forth and ordered to stop them. So Elijah went forth, disguised as a fiery bear, and chased them from that place.

□   Babylon: c. Fifth Century

II

KABBALISTIC TALES

The Circle of Shimon Bar Yohai

21

THE CAVE OF SHIMON BAR YOHAI

Near the village of Peki'in in the Galilee there is a cave known as the cave of Shimon bar Yohai. That is the cave in which Shimon bar Yohai and his son, Eleazar, hid from the Romans after they passed a decree calling for his execution. Shimon bar Yohai and his son remained in that cave for thirteen years, devoting themselves to the study of the Torah.

Many miracles took place while they lived in that cave. During the first night they spent there, a well of living water formed inside the cave and a large carob tree grew outside it, filled with ripe carobs, that completely hid the entrance. When Shimon bar Yohai and his son discovered the spring and the tree that had appeared overnight, they drank from the water and tasted the fruit. The water was pure and delicious and the fruit was ripe, and they knew that their faith had been rewarded and that the Holy One, blessed be He, was guarding them. And they gave thanks.

After that, Rabbi Shimon and his son cast off their clothes and spent each day buried in the sand, studying the Torah. Only when it was time to pray did they put on their white garments, and in this way they preserved them through the long years of their exile.

Then a day came when Elijah the Prophet arrived at the cave to study with them. Elijah revealed great mysteries to them that had never been known outside of heaven. And in the days that followed Elijah often returned, and Shimon bar Yohai wrote down those mysteries on parchment that Elijah brought them, which came from the ram that Abraham had sacrificed on Mount Moriah in place of Isaac. Now that was an enchanted parchment, for it expanded to receive his words as Shimon bar Yohai wrote. And every letter he inscribed there burned in black fire on white. And the name of the book that he wrote down there, filled with the celestial mysteries, was the Zohar.

One day, as they watched from inside the cave, Rabbi Eleazar saw a bird repeatedly escape from a hunter, and he recognized this as a sign that they were free to leave the cave, for the Emperor had died and the decree had been annulled. But before they left, they hid the book of the Zohar in that cave, for they knew that the world was not yet ready for its secrets to be revealed.

There the book of the Zohar remained for many generations, until an Ishmaelite who happened to find it in the cave sold it to peddlers. Some of its pages came into the possession of a rabbi who recognized their value at once. He went to all the peddlers in that area and found that they had used the pages of the book to wrap their spices. In this way he was able to collect all of the missing pages, and that is how the Zohar was saved and came to be handed down.

▫ Babylon: c. Fifth Century

❦❦❦❦❦❦ 22 ❦❦❦❦❦❦

THE DECREE

Once Rabbi Shimon bar Yohai went outdoors during the day and found that the world had grown dark. He wondered greatly at this and set out with his son, Rabbi Eleazar, to find out why this had happened. While they were walking, they came upon a great rock that had never been there before, and they were very surprised to see it. Suddenly thirty tongues of fire shot forth from the rock and a voice emerged, and Rabbi Shimon realized that an angel had appeared to them in the shape of that rock.

Rabbi Shimon said to the angel, "Why have you taken this form?" The angel replied, "In each generation there must be thirty righteous ones. But these thirty flames show that these righteous ones are missing from this generation. Therefore I have been commanded to bring about the destruction of the world." Then Rabbi Shimon commanded the angel, "Return to the Holy One on high and remind Him that I am still in this world." So the angel took flight and the rock vanished from before their eyes. And when the angel stood before the Holy One, blessed be He, he reported what Rabbi Shimon had said and asked what he should do. And the Holy One replied, "Carry out your command. Destroy the world!"

But when the angel returned to carry out the Divine decree, Rabbi Shimon stood before him and said, "Return at once to on high, or else I will condemn you to sink into the Abyss! Go and report my message to the Holy One: 'If there are not thirty righteous ones in the world, then accept twenty. And if there are not twenty, then accept ten. And if there are not ten, then accept two—my son, Eleazar, and myself. And if there are not two, then there is surely one. I know I am that one!'"

Just as Rabbi Shimon finished speaking, a voice came forth from heaven, which said, "Praised be Shimon bar Yohai, for he has been able to change the evil decree sent forth from heaven!"

□ Spain: Thirteenth Century

23

THE CURTAIN OF FIRE

One day, as Rabbi Hiyya came to visit Rabbi Shimon bar Yohai, he saw a fiery curtain inside the house, with a celestial being on one side of the curtain and Rabbi Shimon bar Yohai on the other. And they were studying Torah in that way.

Rabbi Hiyya was so electrified by this sight that he could not even knock on the door. All at once the door opened, and Rabbi Hiyya looked inside. As he did, he glimpsed the glory of the Divine Presence. And he lowered his eyes and stood frozen in place.

When Shimon bar Yohai saw that Rabbi Hiyya had been struck dumb, he said to his son, Rabbi Eleazar: "Go to Rabbi Hiyya and pass your hand over his mouth." Eleazar did this, and at last Rabbi Hiyya recovered his senses.

□ Spain: Thirteenth Century

༄༅ 24 ༄༅

A Saint from the Other World

Rabbi Eleazar, son of Rabbi Shimon bar Yohai, and Rabbi Abba were journeying together, accompanied by a porter who carried their baggage. When they had first set out, the porter said, "The journey before us is a long one. Therefore let us not waste it, but let us discuss matters of the Torah." These words, coming from a porter, greatly moved Rabbi Eleazar, and he embraced that man and said, "Your place is not behind us, but before." But the porter insisted on remaining behind them and said, "Let us openly speak of the mysteries of the universe." Now these words greatly surprised the rabbis, for few are capable of speaking of these mysteries. And they said to him, "Tell us who you are and where you come from." He replied, "I am Rav Hamnuna Sava. I live in a tower suspended in the heavens. In it lives the Holy One, blessed be He, the Lord of Hosts. My father makes his home in the sea. He is of great size and ancient of days. He swallows the fish of the sea and then gives them new life. His power is so great that he can travel from one end of the sea to the other in a single instant. He took me out of the sea and hid me in the tower on high. Then he returned and hid himself in the sea."

The two rabbis were amazed to hear all that the man told them, and they bowed their heads and prostrated themselves before him. But when they lifted their heads, they found that he had vanished from their sight. Then they were sad because he had not remained with them longer. And Rabbi Abba said, "It is true, as we have been told: Whenever two travel together and speak of the Torah, they are joined by a saint from the other world."

□ Spain: Thirteenth Century

THE GOLDEN SCEPTER

Rabbi Eleazar and Rabbi Abba were once traveling from Tiberias to Sipphoris. On the way, Rabbi Yoezzer ben Yaakov joined them. They began to discuss the shape of the soul after death. Rabbi Eleazar said: "The soul and the body consist of the same elements—earth, wind, fire, and water. But the soul is composed of spiritual elements emanating from the Throne of Glory."

Then Rabbi Yoezzer said: "There is a tale I can tell you concerning this: I was once walking at the edge of the desert, and I lost my way. In the distance I saw an ancient tree. As I drew near, I saw that it hid the entrance of a cave, from which drifted the scent of balsam. I entered the mouth of the cave and found it was well lit, although I never saw even a single torch.

"I came to a crossroads in the cave and went in the direction of the fragrant scent. At the end of a long passage, I found a man with a golden scepter who guarded the way to the rest of the cave. He stood up and asked me who I was. My knees began to tremble, and I replied that I belonged to the holy circle of Rabbi Shimon bar Yohai. Then he welcomed me and gave me a small book. He told me to take it back with me, to share with those in Rabbi Shimon's circle, who would understand the mysteries it contained. I opened the book and just as I read the first words, I felt a blow. Turning around, I saw that the man had struck me with the golden scepter. All at once, I grew drowsy and lay down to sleep.

"In my dream, I found myself carried under the wing of the *Shekhinah*, flying through the heavens at night. From a great height I looked down on the world below, my breath drawn through countless stars. We approached a glowing star, which turned out to be the House of the World. That is where souls are created for their descent into this world. In that house I saw how the souls are clothed in the spiritual elements of water, wind, and fire. But they are not clothed in the element of earth until the soul and body are bound to each other. At that moment everything disappeared, and I found myself back in the cave. The man with the scepter was not to be seen, but the book that he had given me was still there, and I picked it up and made my way out of the cave."

Rabbi Eleazar asked him: "Surely you have been blessed. But where is the book that you received?"

Rabbi Yoezzer took the book out of his pack and gave it to Rabbi Eleazar. And as soon as Rabbi Eleazar opened the book, he was suddenly surrounded by fire. And the letters he read there also burned, in black fire on white. And before he had finished one page of that book, mysteries beyond imagining were revealed to him. But when he finished that page, the book flew out of his hands and disappeared. And Rabbi Eleazar wept, saying, "Blessed be the way and the hour in which this happened!" For two in that generation had been found worthy of having those mysteries revealed to them.

□   Spain: Thirteenth Century

$$\text{⧉⧉⧉⧉⧉⧉⧉⧉} \quad 26 \quad \text{⧉⧉⧉⧉⧉⧉⧉⧉}$$

THE BOOK OF ADAM

Rabbi Yosse and another disciple of Rabbi Shimon bar Yohai arrived at a distant place, and Rabbi Yosse said, "My father once brought me here when I was a boy, and he told me that when I was forty years old, I would find a supreme treasure in this place. He said he knew this because he had seen a sign—two birds had flown over my head. But I am already forty years old, and yet I have not found the treasure."

Rabbi Yosse had little hope, but he searched between the rocks, and lo and behold, he found a hidden book. Amazed, he opened it and found that it contained the seventy-two-letter Name of God. This secret Name had long ago been confided to Adam when the angel Raziel had brought him that book. And it was known that whoever knew that secret holy name would have the portals on high opened to him.

Rabbi Yosse and his friend were greatly excited by the discovery of the book and sat down to study it together. Mystery after mystery was revealed, but all at once a flame, borne by a powerful wind, tore the book out of their hands and carried it off, and although they hunted for it, it was gone. Then Rabbi Yosse said sadly, "We must not be considered worthy of possessing that book. Perhaps we have even sinned by taking it from its hiding place."

When they returned, they told the Master, Rabbi Shimon bar Yohai, all that had taken place. He told them that had they pronounced the secret Name of God, they would have been empowered to bring the Messiah. But since the Holy One did not deem that the time was right for the Messiah to come, He deprived them of that secret. And it was true. Not only had they lost the book, but even the mysteries they had read there had been erased from their memory.

□ Spain: Thirteenth Century

27

RABBI GADIEL THE CHILD

Two disciples from the circle of Shimon bar Yohai went to another city. There they were invited into a man's home. But his child refused to join them. The child said that the rabbis had not yet said the prayer of the *Shema* that day. The rabbis were astonished to hear this, for in fact they had hurried so to reach the city by nightfall that they had not said the prayer. They looked at each other, wondering what kind of child this was.

The rabbis said the prayer and then the child joined them. Each time he spoke, mysteries from on high were revealed. The rabbis began to feel that they were in the presence of an angel. They asked the child how it was possible that he was acquainted with such mysteries, and he told them that his soul was the soul of Rabbi Gadiel, who had been martyred in an earlier life at the age of seven. Even then he had been recognized as a great scholar and one of great purity. His soul had been received at once in heaven, where he was made head of his own yeshivah. Still, even though the greatest sages in Paradise sat at his feet, he had longed to know what it meant to live a full life. And when the Holy One, blessed be He, recognized his great longing, Rabbi Gadiel had been reborn into that family, but he had brought all of his knowledge with him.

After that, the rabbis addressed the child as "Rabbi Gadiel" and showed him the great honor he deserved as one of the greatest sages. So too did they study at his feet. And when they returned to Rabbi Shimon bar Yohai, they told him the marvelous tale of Rabbi Gadiel the child.

□   Spain: Thirteenth Century

28

THE CELESTIAL ACADEMY

Soon after the death of Rabbi Shimon bar Yohai, Rabbi Hiyya went to visit his grave. Rabbi Hiyya prostrated himself and said: "Dust, be not proud, for Rabbi Shimon, the pillar of the world, will never waste away in you." Rabbi Hiyya wept, and when he left there he was still weeping.

That is when Rabbi Hiyya began to fast so that he might be permitted to see Rabbi Shimon's place in Paradise. After fasting for forty days, he dreamed that an angel came and told him that he could not see Rabbi Shimon. Then Rabbi Hiyya continued to fast and weep for another forty days. And on the eightieth day, Rabbi Hiyya dreamed that he saw Rabbi Shimon in Paradise. He was teaching while thousands listened, sages and angels alike. Then, in the dream, Rabbi Shimon said: "Let Rabbi Hiyya enter here, to see what awaits him in the World to Come."

That is when Rabbi Hiyya awoke, and when he opened his eyes, he saw a winged angel standing beside the bed, and he understood that it had been sent to bring him to Paradise. Then Rabbi Hiyya mounted the angel, and they ascended at once to the Celestial Academy. There Rabbi Hiyya saw Rabbi Shimon standing exactly as he had seen him in his dream, discussing the same point of the Law.

All at once there was a heavenly voice saying, "Make way for King Messiah, who is coming to Rabbi Shimon's academy." And all of the righteous stood and made a path for the Messiah. Just then the Messiah saw Rabbi Hiyya and said: "Who brought this mortal here?" Rabbi Shimon replied: "This is Rabbi Hiyya, who is the light of the lamp of the Torah." And the Messiah said: "Then let him be gathered here." "No," said Rabbi Shimon, "Let him be given more time." When the Messiah heard the words of Rabbi Shimon, he nodded in assent, and at that moment the winged angel brought Rabbi Hiyya back to this world. And an instant later he found himself alone in his room, and he could not stop shaking.

□ Spain: Thirteenth Century

29

THE BOOK OF FLYING LETTERS

Not long after the death of Shimon bar Yohai, Rabbi Judah fell asleep beneath a tree, and in a dream he saw Rabbi Shimon ascending on high, bearing a scroll of the Torah in his arms. Behind him flew a flock in formation. Then Rabbi Judah looked closer and saw that it was not a flock of birds but a flock of flying letters that followed Rabbi Shimon. At first, Rabbi Judah was mystified. Then he suddenly understood that what he was seeing was a book of flying letters that Rabbi Shimon was taking up with him. And in the dream, Rabbi Judah watched them ascend until they disappeared.

When Rabbi Judah awoke and remembered this dream, he knew that when Rabbi Shimon had died, the world had lost the precious store of his wisdom. For now that book of celestial mysteries had returned to its place on high.

▫ Spain: Thirteenth Century

❧❧❧❧❧❧❧❧ 30 ❧❧❧❧❧❧❧❧

CANDLES IN THE SYNAGOGUE

All of Israel observed the holiday of Lag ba-Omer by lighting fires in honor of the great rabbi Shimon bar Yohai. And in the village of Peki'in, near the cave where Shimon bar Yohai spent thirteen years writing the text of the Zohar, Lag ba-Omer was respected above all other holy days.

Now one Lag ba-Omer the *shammash* in the synagogue of Peki'in went to the treasury of the synagogue and took out every candle, and placed them all around the synagogue and lit them, so that the whole synagogue was illuminated with their light.

As it happened, the new treasurer of the synagogue was a stingy man. And when he saw all those candles burning, all he could think about was how much they cost. And he demanded that the *shammash* blow out half the candles. This the *shammash* sought to do, but no matter how hard he tried, not a single candle went out.

The treasurer thought that the *shammash* was just pretending to blow them out, so he decided to do it himself. But the first time he tried, he fell to the ground in terror and fainted.

Later, when the man found that he was still alive, he gave thanks to God and begged the *shammash* for his forgiveness. And he said: "When I bent over to blow out the candles, I looked into the flames and I saw two eyes staring at me, and then I saw a face. Somehow I knew it was Shimon bar Yohai, and when I saw his angry countenance, I was filled with terror, lest the wrath of his anger descend. And now I know that I was wrong to tell you to blow the candles out."

After that the treasurer saw to it that the synagogue was filled with candles every Lag ba-Omer, and he left a bequest so that this would always be done, as it is to this day in the village of Peki'in.

□ Palestine: Nineteenth Century

<∘⟩⟨∘⟩⟨∘⟩⟨∘⟩⟨∘⟩ **31** ⟨∘⟩⟨∘⟩⟨∘⟩⟨∘⟩⟨∘⟩

A Kiss from the Master

During the days when the cave of Rabbi Shimon bar Yohai was still open, the wise men of Safed would enter it on Lag ba-Omer. Once, a rich man who was visiting in Safed on the eve of Lag ba-Omer was invited by his host to visit Rabbi Shimon's grave in Meron. When they arrived, he saw that the sages were sitting around the grave of Rabbi Shimon bar Yohai rejoicing. They invited the rich man to join them, and they gave him an honorable place among them.

Then, one at a time, they read passages from the Zohar, as was their custom. But when the guest received the book, he could not read the Aramaic in which it was written, and he was deeply ashamed.

After they had finished reading, all but the rich man returned to their tents. But he remained in the cave, weeping bitterly for his lack of knowledge of the Torah, until at last he fell asleep. And no sooner did he sleep than he dreamed that Rabbi Shimon bar Yohai appeared to him and comforted him, and before he departed he kissed him on the mouth. And that is when the rich man woke up.

From the moment he opened his eyes, the rich man felt as if a new spirit were within him. He picked up the book of the Zohar and opened it to the first page. There he found, much to his amazement, that he could now read the Hebrew letters. Not only that, but the true meaning of every letter rose up in his vision, for the spirit of Rabbi Shimon had joined his soul. In this way his eyes were opened to the hidden meanings of the Torah, and its mysteries were revealed to him.

Later the others returned to the cave, and they began to discuss one difficult passage in the Zohar, which none of them could comprehend.

Then the rich man spoke and explained that passage to them as if it were elementary, and their eyes were opened to its true meaning. Even more, they were amazed at his wisdom, for they knew he could not even read the language, and yet what he said could only come from a master of the Torah.

Then the sages demanded that the rich man explain how this transformation had taken place. So the rich man revealed his dream about Shimon bar Yohai. And when the sages heard this dream, they understood that a miracle had occurred, and that the rich man had been possessed by an *ibur*, the spirit of a great sage who joins his soul to the soul of another, and in this way gives it strength and guidance. So too did they know that this sage could be none other than Shimon bar Yohai, since that was the cave in which he wrote that very book of the Zohar during the thirteen years that he was in hiding from the Romans.

After that, the rich man found that all he had to do to call forth the soul of Rabbi Shimon was to open the book of the Zohar. Then he would be able to understand the mysteries of the Zohar as if they were the *aleph bet*. And in the days that followed, the sages invited him to remain in Safed and to bring his family to join him. This he did, and before long they made him the head of the kabbalists of Safed, for they knew that he spoke with the wisdom of Shimon bar Yohai.

□   Israel: Oral Tradition

The Circle of the Ari

32

THE PILLAR OF CLOUD

As Rabbi Moshe Cordovero lay on his deathbed, his disciples begged him to reveal his successor. But the "Ramak," as the rabbi was known, refused to do so. Instead he told them to watch for a sign: whoever saw a pillar of cloud at his funeral would be the one they should follow. Soon after Rabbi Cordovero died, and all of Safed was filled with mourning.

As the funeral procession reached the graveyard, a young disciple named Rabbi Isaac Luria approached Rabbi Joseph Caro and said: "Ever since we left the synagogue, there has been a pillar of cloud going before us." He pointed to it, but it was invisible to all the others. And when he entered it, he vanished from their sight. For a long moment everyone stood in disbelief. Then Rabbi Isaac stepped out of the cloud, which only he could see, and his face was glowing like the face of Moses as he descended Mount Sinai. And indeed it was the same cloud that had enveloped Moses at the top of Sinai and carried him into heaven, so that he could receive the Torah from the finger of God.

Then they all understood that this was the sign the Ramak had given them, and that Rabbi Isaac was fated to be their teacher. So it was that after the funeral, many of the disciples of the Ramak came to Rabbi Isaac and asked to study with him. At first "the Ari," as he came to be known, was reluctant, for until then he had concealed his holy ways. But at last he agreed, and for the two years that he remained in this world, he was their master of Torah, and his teachings still echo to this day.

◻ Palestine: Sixteenth Century

෴෴෴෴෴ 33 ෴෴෴෴෴

THE ANGEL OF FORGETFULNESS

While Rabbi Isaac Luria was still living in Egypt, the prophet Elijah came to visit him. Elijah revealed that Isaac's days were numbered, and that the time had come for him to journey to the Holy Land, to the city of Safed. There he must seek out Rabbi Hayim Vital and make him his disciple. For it was to teach him that he had come into the world.

The Ari made ready to leave for the Holy Land the next day. On the night he arrived in Safed, he had a dream in which he saw a flock of birds flying backward and followed them. As they traveled, they merged into one another, until at last there was only one bird left. That bird flew directly to the tree that stood beside the Ari and addressed him: "Do you know why the flock flew backward?" "No," said the Ari, "but I want very much to know." "Every bird is the spark of a soul," the bird replied. "And who, then, are you, who contains every spark?" asked the Ari. "I am the soul of Shimon bar Yohai, and among those who bear the sparks of my soul are you, Isaac. For in this generation, half of my soul belongs to you and the other half to another, whom you must seek out." "And who is it who bears the other half of your soul?" asked the Ari. "Hasn't Elijah already told you that?" asked the soul of Shimon bar Yohai, and at that instant the bird took flight, and the Ari awoke. He realized at once that the bird must have meant Hayim Vital, of whom Elijah had spoken. And the Ari realized how important it was to find him.

The next day the Ari made inquiries and learned that Hayim Vital lived in the city of Damascus, where he was the head of a kabbalistic school. However, the Ari did not go to Damascus. Instead, his soul left his body every night and approached the soul of Hayim Vital to draw it closer. At first Hayim Vital resisted this approach, although he was well aware of it. For he was already recognized as a master, and he did not want to become a disciple. Thus he refused to travel to Safed.

Therefore the Ari called upon the Angel of Forgetfulness and commanded the angel to deprive Hayim Vital of his memory. This the angel did when Hayim Vital was engaged in an explanation of a difficult passage of the Zohar. Hayim Vital found that his understanding of that passage had vanished, and he could remember nothing of his interpretation. So he left that passage and turned to another and the same thing happened, once, twice, and three times. He understood this as a sign that he must approach the Ari, and soon after that he left Damascus and traveled to Safed.

Even before Hayim Vital arrived, the Ari told his students that a great rabbi from Damascus would soon arrive and that they must treat him with respect, for his soul was very holy.

When Hayim Vital arrived in Safed and came to the yeshivah of the Ari, everyone treated him with honor and respect. He took a seat near the Ari, and the Ari turned to him and said: "Why did it take you so long to come here?" And Hayim Vital confessed that he had resisted the pull of the Ari's soul, but now something terrible had happened, for he had lost his memory and he was in need of the Ari's help.

And the Ari said: "Fear not for your memory, or for me, for your memory will soon be restored, and I have already forgiven you. Then the Ari picked up an empty pitcher and led Hayim Vital to the shore of the Kinneret. There they found a boat, and when they got in, the Ari said: "When I tell you to fill the pitcher with water, do so at once."

Then the Ari rowed in the direction of the tomb of Rabbi Meir Baal ha-Ness, until they reached the place in the Kinneret that is the final resting place of Miriam's well, which had followed the Israelites so faithfully in their forty years of wandering. And when they reached the sacred waters of the well, the Ari told Hayim Vital to fill the pitcher. Then the Ari told him to drink of that water, and the moment he did, his memory was restored to him.

And that is how Hayim Vital and the Ari came to be together. Nor were they ever separated again until the day of the Ari's death.

□   Israel: Oral Tradition

꧁꧂ 34 ꧁꧂

The Dancing of the Ari

Every Lag ba-Omer the Ari led his students to the grave of Rabbi Shimon bar Yohai in Meron. And there they danced at the resting place of the holy rabbi.

Now one Lag ba-Omer, an old man danced with them. He could be seen swaying at the outer edge of the circle, as if he were being carried on waves of song. He had a beautiful white beard and was dressed all in white, with a white prayer shawl covering his head. His eyes were closed, and his whole body radiated mystical glory.

All at once, the Ari took his hand and started dancing with him. A great light shone between them, a sacred radiance, like the light of many candles, tinged with blue and gold. All the students watched spellbound as the Ari and the old man danced.

Their dancing lasted for hours. It was well after midnight when they stopped, and the old man took his leave. Then the disciples of the

Ari crowded around him to learn the identity of the old man. And he told them that it was none other than Shimon bar Yohai himself who had joined in the celebration.

□   Israel: Oral Tradition

35

THE BLESSING OF THE *KOHANIM*

One Yom Kippur in Safed the Ari joined all of the *kohanim* for the Blessing of the *kohanim*. Standing together, facing the congregation, they covered their faces with their prayer shawls, bent their fingers into the sign of the *kohanim*, and held them out in blessing. And everyone knew that while their faces were covered, no one was permitted to look up. It was strictly forbidden.

Even so, all during the blessing, Rabbi Hayim Vital was overcome with the desire to look up at the Ari. He wrestled with himself, but finally he could resist no longer. And when he looked up, he saw that the *Shekhinah*, the Bride of God, had descended and stood before them. And Hayim Vital could not tear his eyes away, even though he knew that it was forbidden to see such a thing. When at last he managed to look down, the world began to grow dim. At first Hayim Vital was terrified that he had gone blind. Then, little by little, the world came back, although it was much dimmer than before. And Hayim Vital knew that he had been punished for his sin.

Afterward he went to the Ari in grief and confessed. The Ari told Hayim Vital that his sin had been very great, and so must be the punishment. He had seen something forbidden to him; that is why his eyes had begun to grow dim. And Hayim Vital begged the Ari to save him from going blind. And after a long silence, the Ari said:

"If you will fast from one Sabbath to the next, and at the time of *Kabbalat Shabbat* go out to greet the Sabbath Queen, filled with repentance, then perhaps you will be forgiven."

Hayim Vital began his fast at the end of the next Sabbath, and he neither ate nor drank anything all week. And every night, without exception, he had nightmares in which he suffered the punishments of Gehenna. Those nightmares lasted until dawn, and Hayim Vital never got a moment's rest. At last the week came to an end. Then Hayim Vital prepared himself for the Sabbath, bathing in the *mikveh* and putting on a white robe.

Not long before the beginning of the Sabbath, he left his home and walked out into the fields around Safed, on his way to greet the Sabbath Queen. Because of his fast, he felt very light, as if he were floating. The world around him was still dim, and he could not tell if he were standing on the earth or floating over the field like a leaf. Nor could he tell which way was up or down. Sometimes he felt as if he were rising on high, and sometimes he felt as if he were plunging into the depths. And all the time he floated, he knew that his life hung in the balance.

Then all at once the dim world around him began to part, as if it were a curtain, and he saw that he was standing on the earth, and out of the mist he saw the face of a woman standing before him. Hayim Vital tried to focus on that face, but it seemed as if that one face contained a multitude of others. And among those faces were many that he recognized: the faces of his grandmothers, of his sisters, and even that of his mother, who had died that very year. His mother opened her arms and reached out to him, and Hayim Vital felt himself cradled in her loving embrace. And at that moment all the terror that he had carried with him since the time of his sin vanished, and he understood that he had been forgiven.

And when Hayim Vital looked again, he saw the face of the *Shekhinah* exactly as he had seen her standing before the *kohanim*. But this time he had been permitted to see her.

After that, Hayim Vital found that his sight had not only been restored, but that it was much finer than it had ever been. For now he could make out the aura that surrounded everyone, which had been hidden from him until then. So too did he perceive the presence of the Bride descending every Sabbath when he went out to greet the Sabbath Queen.

□   Palestine: Sixteenth Century

36

THE JOURNEY TO JERUSALEM

One day the Ari turned to his disciples and declared that they must set out for Jerusalem at once. The disciples were taken aback, but half of them had such perfect faith in the Ari that they stood up, ready to depart. But the others grew afraid. After all, they had not told their families, nor had they made any preparations for the journey. They begged the Ari to give them enough time to do these things before they departed. And the Ari looked at them, brokenhearted, and said: "I heard a heavenly voice proclaim that if we journey to Jerusalem at once, without the slightest hesitation, the footsteps of the Messiah will soon be heard. But as soon as you raised your objections, I heard the voice say that the chance to bring the Messiah had been lost."

□   Palestine: Sixteenth Century.

37

THE PRECIOUS PRAYER

One Yom Kippur, while the Ari was praying in the synagogue, an angel came to him and whispered in his ear about a man whose prayers had reached the highest heavens. The angel told him the name of this man and the city where he lived, which was Tiberias. And when

Yom Kippur was over, the Ari went there to seek him out. For he wanted to learn the secret of his prayers.

When the Ari reached that city, he first looked for the man in the House of Study. But he was not to be found among any of the men there. Then he sought him in the market. And there he was told that the only man by that name in Tiberias was a poor farmer who lived in the mountains.

So the Ari climbed into the mountains to find that man. When he reached his house, he was surprised to see that it was just a hut. The poor farmer greeted him and invited him to come in. And when they were together at last, the Ari did not waste any time. He asked the man to tell him the secret of his prayers. The man was very surprised by this and said: "But rabbi, I am afraid that I cannot pray. For I cannot read. All I know are the letters of the alphabet from *aleph to yod*."

The Ari was astonished to hear this, for had not the angel said that the prayers of this man were precious to God? Then the Ari said: "What did you do on Yom Kippur?" The man replied: "I went to the synagogue, of course. And when I saw how intently everyone around me was praying, my heart broke. And I began to recite all that I know of the alphabet. And I said in my heart: 'Dear God, take these letters and form them into prayers for me, that will rise up like the scent of honeysuckle. For that is the most beautiful scent that I know. And that is what I said with all my strength, over and over.'"

When the Ari heard this, he understood at once that God had sent him to learn this secret: while man sees what is before his eyes, God looks into the heart. And that is why the prayers of the simple farmer were so precious.

□   Eastern Europe: Sixteenth Century

38

A VISION AT THE WAILING WALL

On the day of Yom Kippur the decision is made on high as to whether or not each person's name will be sealed in the Book of Life. Rabbi Isaac Luria of Safed, known as "the Ari," was able to divine the future, and he always knew from Yom Kippur who among his disciples would live or die. This knowledge he rarely disclosed, but once, when he learned that there was a way to avert the decree, he made an exception. Summoning Rabbi Abraham Beruchim, he said: "Know that a heavenly voice has gone forth to announce that this will be your last year among us—unless you do what is necessary to abolish the decree."

"What must I do?" asked Rabbi Abraham.

"Know, then," said the Ari, "that your only hope is to go to the Wailing Wall in Jerusalem and there pray with all your heart before God. And if you are deemed worthy, you will have a vision of the *Shekhinah*, the Divine Presence. That will mean that the decree has been averted and your name will be inscribed in the Book of Life after all."

Rabbi Abraham thanked the Ari with all his heart and left to prepare for the journey. First, he shut himself in his house for three days and nights, wearing sackcloth and ashes, and fasted the whole time. Then, although he could have gone by wagon or by donkey, he chose to walk to Jerusalem. And by the time Rabbi Abraham reached Jerusalem, he felt as if he were floating, as if his soul had ascended from his body. And when he reached the Wailing Wall, the last remnant of Solomon's Temple, Rabbi Abraham had a vision standing before the Wall. Out of the Wall came an old woman, dressed in black, deep in mourning. And Rabbi Abraham suddenly realized how deep was the grief of the *Shekhinah* over the destruction of the Temple and the scattering of her children, Israel, all over the world. And he became possessed of a grief as deep as the ocean, far greater than he had ever known. It was the grief of a mother who has lost a child; the grief of Hannah after losing her seven sons; the grief of the Bride over the suffering of her children, scattered to every corner of the earth.

At that moment Rabbi Abraham fell to the ground in a faint, and he had a vision. In the vision he saw the *Shekhinah* once more, but this time he saw her dressed in her robe woven out of light, more magnificent than the setting sun, and her joyful countenance was revealed. Waves of light arose from her face, an aura that seemed to reach out and surround him, as if he were cradled in the arms of the Sabbath Queen. "Do not grieve so, my son Abraham," she said. "Know that I shall restore my sons to their borders and my daughters to their homeland. Nor will my inheritance go to waste. And for you, my son, there shall be a great many blessings."

Just then Rabbi Abraham's soul returned to him from its journey on

high. He awoke refreshed, as if he had shed years of grief, and he was
filled with sparks of hope.

When Rabbi Abraham returned to Safed he was a new man, and
when the Ari saw him, he said at once: "I can see that you have been
found worthy of seeing the *Shekhinah*, and you can rest assured that
you will live for another twenty-two years. Know that each year will
be the blessing of another letter of the alphabet, for the light of the
Divine Presence shines forth through every letter. And you, who have
stood face to face with the *Shekhinah*, will recognize that light in every
letter of every word."

So it was that Rabbi Abraham did live for another twenty-two
years, years filled with abundance. And all who saw him recognized
the aura that shone from his face, for the light of the Divine Presence
always reflected from his eyes.

□   Palestine: Sixteenth Century

&&&&& 39 &&&&&

READING THE LIPS OF THE ARI

One day Rabbi Abraham Halevi, one of the disciples of the Ari,
went to see his master and found him asleep, with his lips moving.
Rabbi Abraham was very curious to know what the Ari was saying,
and he leaned over him to hear the words. There Rabbi Abraham
heard the Ari speaking of mysteries far beyond his comprehension.
And as the Ari spoke, Rabbi Abraham saw for the first time that angels
filled the room, and that they, too, were listening intently to the words
that arose from the Ari's lips. Then Rabbi Abraham perceived a
Divine Presence in the room, as if the *Shekhinah* had descended as well.

At that instant the Ari opened his eyes, and all the angels disappeared, along with the Holy Presence. That is when the Ari saw
Rabbi Abraham standing over him, and he asked him what he was
doing there. Rabbi Abraham confessed that he had seen the lips of the

Ari moving and had come closer to hear the words the master was speaking.

"And did you hear what was spoken?" asked the Ari.

"Yes," said Rabbi Abraham. "The words reached my ears, but their meaning eluded me. Yet as I listened I had a wonderful vision, in which I saw this room filled with angels, and it felt as if it were the Sabbath."

"In that case," said the Ari, "you understood."

□ Palestine: Sixteenth Century

#################### 40 ####################

THE SPEAKING FLAME

One Sabbath evening Rabbi Yosef Ashkenazi sat with the Ari, studying the Mishnah by the light of one candle. All at once the flame began to sputter. As they watched, it almost went out; then it flickered back to life. Finally, the sputtering stopped, and the candle burned with a single flame.

The Ari said nothing about it at that time, but after *Havdalah*, when the Sabbath was over, the Ari accompanied Rabbi Yosef to his home, and as they walked the Ari asked him about his family. Rabbi Yosef replied that with God's blessings they were fine. Then the Ari asked him about his younger brother. Rabbi Yosef replied: "He is a wonderful lad. But he prefers to be in the field, serving as a shepherd, than in the House of Study."

That is when the Ari told him that his brother was in grave danger. For when the flame of the candle sputtered, it had spoken, and the Ari understood what it said: the brother's life was in peril, and only Rabbi Yosef could save him.

"What must I do?" asked Rabbi Yosef.

"The voice of the flame did not reveal this," said the Ari, "but it said that the secret would be found in the Mishnah. Then I knew that it must lie in the last passage we were reading, when the flame began to flicker."

"I remember it!" cried Rabbi Yosef. And he quoted it from memory: "If a man finds a pair of *tefillin* left in an open field, he should bring them inside."

"Yes," said the Ari. "And now let us ask what it might mean in terms of your brother."

"Now I understand!" cried Rabbi Yosef. "My brother has a very special pair of *tefillin*, which were given to him on the day of his *brit* by an old man. My father often told my brother 'Keep the *tefillin* with you at all times.' And on his deathbed, those were the last words my father spoke. Perhaps my brother has lost the *tefillin*."

"Surely the passage from the Mishnah has the clue. He must have left them in the field."

"Yes! Yes!" said Rabbi Yosef. "That must be it. Somehow he must have forgotten to bring the *tefillin* in when he returned before the Sabbath, and once the Sabbath began, he could not go out to get them."

The Ari said: "Surely the spirit of prophecy has taken hold of you. Now, let us search for those *tefillin*."

"But how can we find them in the dark?" asked Rabbi Yosef.

The Ari replied: "Perhaps the Sabbath candle can tell us." The Ari relit the candle that had first revealed the mysterious danger, and he peered into the flame. It flickered in the night wind and began to sputter. Then all at once, the flame went out.

"What did it say?" Yosef pleaded.

The Ari replied: "Who gave your brother those *tefillin*?"

"It was an old man who was present at the *brit*. We had never seen him before. Nor did we ever see him again."

"Know," said the Ari, "that he was Elijah. And those are no ordinary *tefillin*. For Elijah saw at your brother's birth that he would die while still an infant unless he was given special protection. Therefore Elijah brought him the *tefillin* of one of the hidden saints who had just died. Before he left your brother's *brit*, Elijah revealed the truth about those *tefillin* to your father. That is why your father urged your brother never to part from those *tefillin*. For the spirit of that hidden saint has protected him from that day until now. But if your brother has forgotten them, he is vulnerable, for the forces of the Other Side will recognize that he is unprotected. Therefore let us search together for these *tefillin*."

So it was that Rabbi Yosef led the Ari to the field where his younger brother served as the shepherd. When they reached the vast field, however, they saw that there was little light from the moon to aid in their search.

"How will we ever find the *tefillin* here?" Rabbi Yosef asked.

And the Ari replied: "Surely the candle that has led us this far will help." And he lit the candle again. This time, however, he did not stare into the flame, but carried the candle as they walked across the field. And they quickly saw that when they went in one direction the flame grew stronger, but when they turned in another it grew dim. So they let the candle lead them until they came to a tree in the center of that field. And by the light of that candle they saw someone standing beneath its branches, deep in prayer, who was wearing *tefillin*.

Now that was a strange figure whose eyes seemed to glow in the darkness, and he struck terror into Rabbi Yosef's heart. But the Ari was not frightened, for he knew at once that this must be the hidden saint to whom the *tefillin* had once belonged, for he was wearing the *tefillin* at night, which is not the practice of the living. And he went up to the praying figure and said: "*Shalom Aleichem.*"

"*Aleichem Shalom,*" the ghostly figure replied.

"We have come to lead you back to the boy, for without you he is in great danger."

"Yes," said the other. "I have been waiting for you."

So it was that the figure wearing the *tefillin* followed the Ari and Rabbi Yosef until they came to Rabbi Yosef's house. Rabbi Yosef led them to the window, where they could see his brother sleeping, tossing from side to side. The window was open, and the figure took off the *tefillin* and placed them on the window sill. Then he disappeared.

"Now your brother will be safe," said the Ari. "But in the morning, tell him all that has happened, so that he will understand how close he came to losing his life. And after that, I am sure he will never let himself be parted from those *tefillin* again."

This Rabbi Yosef promised to do, and he thanked the Ari with all his heart. In the morning, he told his brother of the miracle of the speaking candle and the hidden saint. And when his brother saw those precious *tefillin* and heard the tale that Rabbi Yosef told, he vowed never to be parted from them again. And he remained true to that vow all the days of his life.

□ Palestine: Sixteenth Century

41

GREETING THE SABBATH QUEEN

Every Sabbath eve, at sunset, the Ari led his students to greet the Sabbath Queen as she descended upon the rolling hills outside of Safed. Many were those who saw them leaving Safed, every one dressed in white, and later saw them returning, singing Sabbath songs.

Now in the city of Safed one of the leading rabbis was Rabbi Moshe Alshich. When he heard of the marvelous teachings of the Ari, he wanted to study with him. But the Ari never consented to let him be his student. One day, in great frustration, Rabbi Moshe demanded to know why the Ari always turned him away.

The Ari replied: "Know that in this lifetime it is your duty to seek out the literal meaning of the sacred texts, and it is my duty to seek out their mystical meaning. Yet I also see that in a previous life you were a great kabbalist, and in the next life, as well, you will be again. Surely you have already studied with me in an earlier life, and perhaps we are destined to study together again. But not now. If you do not believe me, do as I say: You know that every Sabbath eve we go out to greet the Sabbath Queen, and you know there is only one road that leads out of Safed. Go to that road before the Sabbath and watch for us. If you see us passing by, you may join us. But if you do not, then you will understand that this is a matter of fate."

Rabbi Moshe Alshich stood in awe at the Ari's words, but his longing to study with him was still strong. So he accepted the Ari's offer at once and agreed to meet them the following Sabbath. And on that day, long before the sun began to set, Rabbi Moshe stood at the entrance of the road that led from Safed, waiting for the Ari and his disciples to come forth. He watched for hours, but he saw nothing.

Meanwhile, the Ari led his followers out of Safed to greet the Sabbath Queen. When he saw Rabbi Moshe waiting for them, the Ari turned to the others and made a sign to be silent. So it was that they passed right before Rabbi Moshe, but he saw nothing. All that he noticed was some dust in the wind.

Soon after that the Ari and his students arrived at the hills outside of Safed, and they began to sing the songs greeting the Sabbath Queen. And the melodies of those songs were carried upward on the wings of prayer and formed a beautiful garland of prayers that the Sabbath Queen carried with her as she descended from on high. And a wonderful aura surrounded the face of every student, for the glory of the Sabbath Bride was reflected in their eyes.

Meanwhile Rabbi Moshe continued to stand on the road even after it had grown dark. He too prayed to welcome the Sabbath, but the truth is that he could not understand why he had not seen the Ari. All at once he heard the sound of singing voices, and in the dark he recognized the melodies of the Ari, so unlike any other. And when Rabbi Moshe saw them returning, he accepted his fate. And when the Ari greeted him with the Sabbath blessing, Rabbi Moshe returned the blessing and said: "Now I know that I am not destined to be your student in this lifetime. But surely I will be in the next." And the Ari confirmed with a nod that it was true.

□ Palestine: Sixteenth Century

⧉⧉⧉⧉⧉ 42 ⧉⧉⧉⧉⧉

GATHERING SPARKS

One Rosh Hodesh the Ari led his disciples outside at night and told them to follow him. He led them without a torch, so that only the stars lighted their way. Yet it seemed to them that there was another light that guided them, an aura that emanated from the Ari.

At last they reached their destination, the tomb of Rabbi Shimon bar Yohai. There the Ari began to pray with great intensity, and all the others joined him, swaying back and forth, until it seemed as if they were being rocked in a cradle of stars.

At last they completed the prayers, and there was silence. This lasted long into the night, and for all of them it was as if they had discovered the world on the first day of creation.

Then, at midnight, the Ari began to speak. And every word seemed to them like one of the words with which the world was created. For there he revealed the mystery of the Shattering of the Vessels and the Gathering of the Sparks. How, long before the sun cast a shadow, before the Word was spoken that brought the heavens and the earth into being, a flame emerged from an unseen point. And how sparks of light sprang forth from the center of that flame, concealed in shells that set sail everywhere, above and below, like a fleet of ships, each carrying its cargo of light.

How the frail vessels broke open, split asunder, and all the sparks were scattered, like sand, like seeds, like stars.

That is when they learned why they had been created—to search for the sparks, no matter where they were hidden, and as each one was revealed, to raise it up and redeem it. For when all the scattered sparks had been gathered, the vessels would be restored, and the footsteps of of the Messiah would be heard at last.

Just as the Ari finished speaking, a comet streaked across the sky. And when they saw this, all of them were filled with wonder, for they understood that they were not the only ones who had heard the words of the Ari that night. The words had also been heard in heaven.

□ Palestine: Sixteenth Century

43

DELIVERING A MESSAGE

One of the disciples of the Ari was Rabbi Israel Sarug, who also made his home in Safed, in the north of the Holy Land. He was a master of every kind of Kabbalah, and it was whispered among the disciples of the Ari that his powers were very great indeed.

Once the Ari learned through his mystical vision that Rabbi Shlomo
Luria of Poland had been told by travelers that the Ari was revealing
the mysteries of the Torah. Now Rabbi Shlomo Luria, who was
known as "the Maharshal," felt that these mysteries must be kept
secret, and he was about to ban the teachings of the Ari. When the
Ari learned this, he called upon Israel Sarug and told him to travel
from Safed to Poland at once, by using holy names. He must go
directly to the home of the Maharshal and tell him, face to face,
of the true teachings of the Ari. And the Ari gave him a verse, which
he said he was to reveal to the Maharshal at once, so that he would
know he was telling the truth when he said he had come directly from
Safed.

Rabbi Israel understood that a great task had been placed on his
shoulders, but he readily accepted it. He did not ask the Ari any
questions, for he knew that he only had to pronounce one of the
Divine names, and he would reach his destination. And that is what he
did, and a moment later he found himself standing before the door of
the Maharshal.

Now all that day the Maharshal had been in a state of confusion, for
the night before he had dreamed that he had opened the Bible at
random and read the verse *I will send unto him wanderers* (Jer. 48:12).
When he awoke, he wondered greatly about the verse and why he had
received it. And all day he sought to comprehend the meaning of this
dream.

Just then Israel Sarug knocked on the door, and when the Maharshal answered it, he saw a young man wearing a white robe, as if he
were dressed for a warm climate, while snow was piled high everywhere. At first the Maharshal thought that the young man must have
lost his mind, but then he remembered the verse in his dream, and he
invited him in from the cold at once. Then he asked him who he was
and where he had come from, and Israel Sarug identified himself and
said that he had been sent there by the Ari.

"And how long ago did you leave on this journey?" asked the Maharshal.

"This morning," Israel Sarug replied.

"That is impossible!" said the Maharshal.

And Israel Sarug said: "The Ari told me that if you did not believe
me, to mention a specific verse to you."

"What verse is that?" the Maharshal shouted. "Tell me at once!"

Then Israel Sarug repeated the verse that the Ari had revealed to
him, and it was exactly the same verse that the Maharshal had

read in his dream! Then the Maharshal understood that the powers of the Ari must be very great indeed, and from that moment on, he dropped his opposition to the Ari and became one of his most fervent followers.

□   Palestine: Sixteenth Century

⧉⧉⧉⧉⧉⧉   44   ⧉⧉⧉⧉⧉⧉

A STONE IN THE WALL

Once, when the Ari and his disciples were passing the great academy of Rabbi Yohanan in Tiberias, the Ari showed them a stone in the wall. "In this stone there is a soul crying out for us to pray on its behalf. It has suffered through the wheel of transmigration, and now it has finally purified itself in this holy wall, which has stood since the days of Rabbi Yohanan. All that it needs is a prayer to set it free. And this is the secret meaning of *The stone shall cry out in the wall* (Hab. 2:11)."

Then, without hesitation, all of them began to pray. And they prayed with joy, knowing that their prayers would serve the great *mitzvah* of setting a soul free. And just as they finished praying, they heard a flutter of wings, although there was no bird to be seen anywhere.

□   Palestine: Sixteenth Century

❧❧❧ 45 ❧❧❧

THE WIDOW OF SAFED

A widow living in Safed, whom everyone considered pious, suddenly began to speak with the voice of a man, until it became apparent that a wandering spirit, a *dybbuk*, had taken possession of her body. The woman was greatly tormented by this spirit, and she sought help among the disciples of Rabbi Isaac Luria, known as the Ari. Rabbi Joseph Arsin was the first to visit her, and when the voice addressed him by name, he was amazed. Then the *dybbuk* revealed that he had once been a pupil of Rabbi Arsin's when they had both lived in Egypt, and he gave his name. Rabbi Arsin recalled that he had once had such a pupil and realized that the former pupil's soul was now addressing him.

Rabbi Arsin demanded to know why the soul of this man had taken possession of the pious widow. The *dybbuk* readily confessed that he had committed a grievous sin. He had caused a married woman to break her marriage vow and had fathered a child with her. And because of this sin, he had been enslaved after his death by three evil angels, who had dragged him by a heavy chain and had punished him endlessly. He had taken possession of the widow's body in order to escape this terrible punishment.

Then Rabbi Arsin asked the *dybbuk* to describe the circumstances of his death, and the spirit said: "I lost my life when the ship on which I was sailing sank. Nor was I able to confess my sins before dying, because it happened so quickly. When the news of the wreck reached the closest town, my body was recovered along with the others who had drowned, and I was buried in a Jewish cemetery. But as soon as the mourners left, an evil angel opened the grave with a fiery rod and led me to the gates of Gehenna. But the sinners of Gehenna refused to allow me to enter, so great did they consider my sin, and instead I was condemned to wander, pursued by three avenging angels.

"Twice before I tried to escape from this endless punishment. Once I took possession of a rabbi, but he invoked a flock of impure spirits, and in order to escape them I had to abandon his body. Later I became so desperate that I took possession of the body of a dog, which became so crazed that it ran until it dropped dead. Then I fled to Safed and entered the body of this woman."

Rabbi Arsin then tried to command the *dybbuk* to depart from the widow's body but the *dybbuk* refused, and at last the rabbi realized that he did not have the power to expel him. Therefore he went to the Ari and asked him to exorcise this unfortunate spirit. The Ari asked his disciple, Rabbi Hayim Vital, to do this in his name and gave him a formula, consisting of holy names, that would force the *dybbuk* to depart.

Now when Rabbi Hayim Vital entered the house of the poor widow, the *dybbuk* forced her to turn her back to him. And when Hayim Vital asked the *dybbuk* to explain this, the spirit told him that he could not bear the holy countenance of his face. Then Hayim Vital asked the *dybbuk* to tell him how long it had been cursed to wander, and the spirit replied that its wandering would last until the child he had fathered had died. Finally, Hayim Vital asked to know how the *dybbuk* was able to enter the body of the widow. The *dybbuk* explained that the woman had made it possible because she had little faith, since she did not believe that the waters of the Red Sea had truly parted.

Hayim Vital asked the woman if this was true, and she insisted that she did believe in the miracle. He made her repeat her belief three times, and on the third time Hayim Vital uttered the formula that the Ari had taught him. After that he commanded the *dybbuk* to depart from the woman by the little toe of her left foot. At that moment the *dybbuk* did depart with a terrible cry, and the woman was freed from the agony of that possession. The next day, when the Ari ordered that the *mezuzzah* on her door be checked, it was found to be empty, and that is why it did not protect against that evil spirit.

□ Palestine: Sixteenth Century

46

THE BODY OF MOSES

Rabbi Hayim Vital once dreamed that it was the custom of Israel to bring the body of Moses to the synagogue once a year on Shavuot to commemorate the giving of the Torah at Mount Sinai. Now the day of the festival had arrived, and the body of Moses was brought to the synagogue in Safed. It took many men to carry the body into the synagogue, for it was at least ten ells long. Then the body, wrapped in a white robe, was placed on a very long table that had been prepared in advance. But as soon as the body of Moses was stretched out on the long table, it became transformed into a scroll of the Torah that was opened to its full length, from the first words to the last. And in the dream they began to read the words of the Torah, starting with the creation, and they continued until they reached the last words, *in the sight of all Israel* (Deut. 34:12).

All this time the rabbi of Safed sat at the head of the table, and Hayim Vital sat at the foot. And in the dream it occurred to Hayim Vital that while the rabbi of Safed sat closest to the account of creation, he was closest to that of the death of Moses. And when the scroll of the Torah had been completely read, the rabbi said, "The time has come to bring the garments to clothe the body of Moses." And at that moment the scroll of the Torah became the body of Moses once again, and they clothed it and set a girdle around it. That is when Hayim Vital awoke, and for hours afterward it seemed to him as if the soul of Moses was present in that very room.

□   Palestine: Sixteenth Century

47

A VISIT TO THE CITY OF THE DEAD

At midnight the voice of the wind woke Rabbi Hayim Vital, and he was certain that it was calling to him. He got up, put on his white garment, and let the voice of the wind lead him to a crossroads. There he saw his father, who was no longer among the living, coming down one road, and two departed sages, Rabbi Moshe Cordovero and Rabbi Moshe Sagis, coming down the other.

Rabbi Hayim Vital looked around in confusion. He realized that he was no longer in Safed, but that somehow he had entered the Kingdom of the Dead. And he wondered if in this way he had passed from one life to another without noticing.

When the others reached him, Hayim Vital embraced them and asked where he was. They told him that he had entered the City of the Dead, where all the souls of the dead are found. The road in that city is round, so that all who set out on it eventually meet all the others following its path.

So Hayim Vital accompanied them along the road of that city. As darkness fell, all those they passed were weeping. He asked them why, and they told him that the Messiah had been delayed for so long that they could not bear it. For they had continued to wait for the Messiah even after they had entered the World to Come.

Just then Hayim Vital saw an old man dressed like a dervish—a hermit with hair so long that it reached down to his legs. He was traveling alone, and as the old man came closer, Hayim Vital heard him singing about the coming days of the Messiah. His voice was haunting and his songs were of sublime beauty. But when Hayim Vital asked the others about him, they were unable to hear his voice, nor did they know his name. But when the old man and Hayim Vital passed each other, the sun began to shine, even though it was many hours until dawn.

Hayim Vital turned around to watch the old man as he departed, but he had already disappeared. And when he turned back, the others also were gone, and he was alone at the crossroads of that city, where he had first arrived. And that is when he woke up.

□   Palestine: Sixteenth Century

∞∞∞∞∞∞∞∞∞∞∞∞ 48 ∞∞∞∞∞∞∞∞∞∞∞

THE ANGEL IN THE MIRROR

For the first year after the Ari died, Rabbi Hayim Vital never dreamed of his master. In time he began to fear that the Ari was angry with him or thought him to be an unworthy disciple. Hayim Vital confided these fears to Rabbi Yehoshua Albuv. Rabbi Yehoshua told him that he knew a holy name that could invoke the angel Tsadkiel, and that this angel could reveal to him the reason for the Ari's absence. But this angel could be seen only in a mirror.

Rabbi Yehoshua taught the secret name to Hayim Vital. For the next week he fasted and immersed himself in the *mikveh*. Then, on the fifth of *Av*, the *yahrzeit* of the death of the Ari, Hayim Vital stood before a mirror and pronounced the holy name. All at once there was a blinding light in the mirror, and Hayim Vital shut his eyes. And when he opened them, he was barely able to make out a presence in the mirror. And as his eyes adjusted to that great light, he recognized that it was indeed an angel.

The angel spoke first and said: "I have come at your command. What is it you wish to know?" And Hayim Vital replied: "Tell me first who you are and what is your heavenly role." And the angel said: "My name is Tsadkiel, and I am the angel who dresses each soul that enters Paradise in a garment of great purity, woven by the Bride of God. So too was I the rabbi of Abraham. I taught him the ways of wisdom. And now I am ready to reveal my wisdom to you."

Then Hayim Vital asked the angel for help in contacting the Ari in the World to Come, for since his death the Ari had been silent. And

Hayim Vital also asked if he had somehow sinned and was therefore unworthy of the Ari's presence in his dreams.

In reply Tsadkiel said: "Know the holy Ari has prepared a place for you in Paradise, at his side, along with Rabbi Akiba and Rabbi Yohanan ben Zakkai. For you are a true *tzaddik* in the eyes of God. Yet there is one sin that holds the Ari back from visiting you in the world of dreams."

And Hayim Vital asked: "What sin is this?"

The angel replied: "In your life, you are perfect. But you have not done enough to see that others truly repent, to make the coming of the Messiah possible. Until you accept the burden of being a *tzaddik* and bring others to repentance, the Ari will hold back from visiting you. But if you accomplish this, he will guide you in your dreams as he did when he was in this world."

Then Hayim Vital swore that he would do everything to make others aware of the power of repentance to hasten the End of Days. And when the angel had witnessed this vow, he vanished from the mirror and was gone. So night and day Hayim Vital devoted himself to fulfilling his vow, and before the year was out the Ari began to visit him in his dreams, and once more became his guide.

□ Palestine: Sixteenth Century

49

THE HANDWRITING OF THE MESSIAH

On the third *yahrzeit* of the death of the Ari, Rabbi Hayim Vital dreamed that he was home alone, reading the Zohar, when someone knocked at the door. When he opened it, he saw the Ari. But even in the dream he remembered that the Ari was no longer among the living, and he understood that if the Ari had come to him from so far away, he must have something very important to tell him.

The Ari said: "It was always your desire to see the handwriting of the Messiah. See, I have brought you a letter in his own hand, a message from the Messiah. Open it!"

Hayim Vital asked the Ari to swear three times that the letter was truly written by the Messiah. And this the Ari swore. So Hayim Vital unsealed the letter, and there he saw words written in black fire on white, and the shape of those letters was like those of a Torah scroll. And from those flaming letters he learned that the footsteps of the Messiah would soon be heard in the Land of Israel and that everything must be made ready. When Hayim Vital finished reading, he looked up and saw that the Ari had disappeared. He turned back to the letter, but this time it was written in white fire on black. There, in the the letters of white fire, the mysteries of the Messiah were revealed. And Hayim Vital trembled in awe as he read those momentous words.

At the moment that Hayim Vital read the last word written in white fire, he woke up. And the first thing he saw when he opened his eyes was a dove, fluttering outside his window, with something in its beak that looked like a letter. Then the dove took flight and he followed it until it disappeared.

□ Palestine: Sixteenth Century

Other Kabbalistic Tales

ᏪᎿᏪᎿᏪᎿᏪᎿᏪᎿᏪᎿᏪ 50 ᎿᏪᎿᏪᎿᏪᎿᏪᎿᏪᎿᏪ

THE PALACE OF VANITIES

Two rabbis were once traveling on horseback on the eve of the Sabbath when they met a man on crutches. He greeted them and said: "I have heard that you are the great sages in our generation. Tell me, where are you going?" The rabbis replied that they were going to a distant village. To which the lame man replied: "If you wish, I can go ahead of you and prepare a place for you for the Sabbath."

Now this mystified the rabbis. And they said: "How can you go ahead of us when we are on horseback and you are not?" And the man replied: "Even though you are on horseback and I am lame, I can set a place for you for the Sabbath—if you wish."

The rabbis stared at him, amazed. They had expected to spend the Sabbath in a field by themselves. One of the rabbis said: "Yes, of course, we would love to spend the Sabbath with you." At that instant the lame man began to move as fast as a falling star. Yet, somehow the rabbis remained close behind him. That is when they realized that the hooves of the horses were not touching the ground. And suddenly they found themselves at the entrance of a cave.

The astonished rabbis found their host waiting for them, and he motioned for them to enter. They followed him inside, but the cave they entered turned into a great palace, while the man had divested himself of his lame body and clad himself in another. Now his face shone like the sun, and he was seated upon a great throne. And in the presence of such glory the rabbis lowered their eyes, and they were afraid. But when the ruler saw how they trembled, he said: "Fear not, for your merits have made it possible for you to join me for the Sabbath."

Then the ruler led the rabbis through that palace, which was linked to six others, one more magnificent than the next. But the seventh palace was the most beautiful by far.

Now the rabbis saw that above the entrance to every palace it was written: "Vanity of vanities." They wondered greatly about this, and they asked about it. The ruler replied: "I have built this edifice out of this verse. For it is a heritage from my father, and from my father's father. By using it I can fly around the world seven times. But now it is time to welcome the Sabbath."

So it was that the two rabbis spent the Sabbath in that seventh palace, filed with the glory of the Sabbath Queen. And at the very moment the Sabbath ended, they found themselves transported to the distant village to which they had been traveling.

□   Spain: Thirteenth Century

51

THE CHAINS OF THE MESSIAH

There once was a man named Joseph della Reina who lived in the city of Hebron in the Holy Land. His longing for the Messiah was so great that he spent his life in mystical study and prayer, seeking to learn how the coming of the Messiah might be hastened. It was in those days that the holy book of the Zohar was discovered, and Joseph della Reina saw this as a sign. Surely the gate of the Messiah's palace was open, and the time had come for the Messiah to pass through that gate, so that his footsteps could be heard in the world.

Thus della Reina sought out ten other scholars who, like himself, devoted themselves to mystical meditation. Together they fasted and mortified themselves, so that they might purify their souls, Joseph della Reina more so than any of the others. They studied the Kabbalah day and night, immersing themselves in its mysteries. And they scattered ashes on their heads, crying and mourning over the destruction of the Temple.

At last Joseph della Reina so purified his soul that the Prophet Elijah descended from on high and taught him mysteries that had never been revealed outside of heaven. In this way he learned that the soul of the Messiah was being held captive by the forces of evil, and not until those forces had been defeated could the chains of the Messiah be broken. Most of all, Joseph della Reina wished to know how to set free the captive soul of the Messiah. But Elijah was reluctant to tell him any more, for it was forbidden to reveal this mystery. Then Joseph della Reina said to Elijah: "If you yourself cannot reveal this secret, can you give me the name of an angel I might invoke?" And at last Elijah relented and revealed the holy names that invoke the angel Metatron, who once had been Enoch before being transported to heaven in a chariot and transformed into the fiery angel Metatron, the Prince of the Presence.

Then Joseph della Reina and his followers began to fast from the end of one Sabbath to the beginning of the next. And, as Rabbi Shimon bar Yohai had done, they ate only carobs and drank only water. Now it is said that at midnight on the eve of Shavuoth the heavens split open, and any prayer said at that time reaches to the highest heavens.

So Joseph della Reina and his followers waited until that moment, and then he pronounced the holy names that Elijah had given him to invoke the angel Metatron. Thunder rang out all around them and lightning split the sky, and the heavens parted and a great light shone from on high that so blinded them that they fell on their faces in fear. And the voice of Metatron rang out so loudly that the earth shook beneath their feet. "What is it you want?" the voice demanded. At first Joseph della Reina was speechless, but he finally found the strength to supplicate himself before the Prince of the Presence and he said: "Surely the time has come for the Messiah to be set free from his chains. Tell us how this can be done, and we will set out to accomplish this quest, no matter how difficult."

"The victory that you seek over evil would bring you into the gravest danger. Now is the time to turn back," said Metatron. But Joseph della Reina refused to give up and begged the angel to assist them. And at last Metatron revealed this fateful secret: that the rulers of the forces of evil, Asmodeus, the King of Demons, and Lilith, his Queen, could be found in the form of black dogs living on Mount Seir. And if they could be captured and put in chains and led away from that mountain, which was their home and the source of their strength, they could be defeated. Then the chains holding back the Messiah would break, and the time of his coming would be at hand. But, Metatron warned him, those demons were very powerful, and the only way to weaken them was to deny them every kind of sustenance. They must be given nothing, neither food nor water, until they were led away from the mountain, or all would be in vain. So too did Metatron reveal the holy names that would transport della Reina and his followers to the Mount Seir and permit them to capture the demons who reigned there.

When Joseph della Reina heard this, his soul exulted, for now the quest that he had sought for so long lay open before him. And he thanked Metatron from the depths of his soul and vowed that he would do everything in his power to fulfill that quest. But before departing, Metatron warned him not to take on such a great responsibility unless he was certain he would not fail, for if he did, the time of the coming of the Messiah would be delayed much longer. And at that moment the heavens closed and the vision came to an end, but Joseph della Reina and his followers felt that they had been reborn, for now the path of their destiny had opened before them.

Once again they fasted and prayed and prepared themselves for the day of reckoning. So too did they prepare many links of chain with which to restrain the demons. At last Joseph della Reina, surrounded by his ten disciples, pronounced the holy names in the proper combination, and an instant later they found themselves at the foot of Mount Seir. There they heard an unearthly howling, and certain that this must be a sign, they set out in that direction.

At last they caught sight of two great black dogs howling at the moon. That howling was so terrible that it filled them with dread, but still they crept closer until they were right behind them. And just as they threw the chains around the dogs, Joseph della Reina pronounced the holy names that made them his prisoners. As soon as he did, Asmodeus and Lilith were restored to their true forms and tried to break free. But when the demons realized they could not, they no longer struggled but began to beg for something to eat or drink. Their pleas were piteous indeed, but Joseph della Reina spurned them, and he and his followers led them in chains down the mountain.

Now when they had almost descended the mountain, Asmodeus and Lilith became so weak that they had to be dragged, and their pleas for sustenance grew more urgent. But when they saw that della Reina would show them no mercy, they begged instead for a single whiff of incense to revive them. Then della Reina took pity on them, for he did not see any danger in that, and he lit the incense and let them each take a whiff of it. But at that instant Asmodeus shot up many times his size and the chains that held him shattered, as did Lilith's. Asmodeus was filled with rage, and he picked up the ten followers of Joseph della Reina and cast them a great distance, so that all of them lost their lives. And when he found Joseph della Reina cowering behind a rock, he picked him up and and cast him a distance of hundreds of miles, where he landed with a great crash.

The next thing Joseph della Reina knew, he found himself transformed into a large, black dog, wandering through the streets of a city. And the soul of Joseph della Reina, which was trapped in the body of that black dog, recognized that city at once as Safed. Now Joseph della Reina was horrified to discover himself in the body of that dog, and he suffered the pangs of hell. Now, too, all hope he had once held for the coming of the Messiah was shattered, and his singular longing was simply for his own soul to be set free.

So it was that the black dog that bore the soul of Joseph della Reina hid near the windows of the yeshivahs of Safed and listened to the teachings of the sages and learned, in this way, that there was a righteous man living in the city of Safed at that time who was known as the Ari, and that he alone possessed the mystical powers to set della Reina's soul free.

Soon the Ari found that a black dog followed him everywhere. There was nothing he could do to get rid of it. At last the Ari's disciples asked him about the dog that pursued him like a shadow, and the Ari replied: "That dog was once the holy sage Joseph della Reina, who sought to shake the heavens so that the footsteps of the Messiah might be heard. Instead he failed in his task and brought the wrath of heaven upon himself, and now he has been reborn as this black dog. He wants me to set him free, but that is not his fate. This is just the first of a thousand rebirths he will have to suffer through before his soul can be freed of the taint of his sin." And when the black dog, who had listened carefully to every word, learned of his fate, he lost his mind and ran howling into the wilderness and was never seen again.

□ Palestine: Fifteenth Century

꧁꧂꧁꧂꧁꧂꧁꧂꧁꧂꧁꧂ 52 ꧁꧂꧁꧂꧁꧂꧁꧂꧁꧂꧁꧂

THE *TZADDIK* OF THE FOREST

In the days of the Ari there was a student named Shimon Pilam in the city of Safed who was said to know the Torah, the Talmud, and the Zohar by heart. And in the same city there lived a man who was educated and wealthy, who had a large orchard and many fields, as well as two ancient forests. Now this wealthy man had one daughter, who was of marriageable age. He had great difficulty in finding a worthy groom for her. No one was a fine enough scholar. Then it happened that he heard of Shimon Pilam, and with the help of a marriage broker, he was determined that such a scholar would be his son-in-law. And the betrothal was made.

So it was that Shimon Pilam met both his bride and his father-in-law for the first time on the day he was wed. And the love between Shimon Pilam and his bride was a deep one, which had been ordained in heaven. But it was also hidden. After the morning prayers, Shimon Pilam rode a horse into one of the forests, and he was not seen again until the sun was about to set and it was time for the afternoon prayers.

What he did in that forest was a mystery, but he could not be accused of shirking his studies, for he carried the sacred books in his memory, and that way he could study them at any time. And the rich man saw that Shimon Pilam was honorable and treated his daughter well. So he never questioned his ways and went back to his life of luxury.

Now the rich man had hired two Jews to serve as the guards of the two ancient forests he owned. Each had a hut at the entrance of one of the forests, and there they watched for those who sought to cut down the trees. Once in a while they would leave their huts and walk through the forests. And it happened that one of the guards saw a horse tied to a tree. When he went closer, he saw his employer's son-in-law lowering himself into the dark, insect-infested waters. What kind of *mikveh* was this?

The man spent a long time in those waters. And when he emerged, he dressed, untied the horse, and rode out of the forest. Then the guard came out of hiding and saw, to his amazement, that those waters had turned completely pure. He bent down and drank from them, and the waters were clear and sweet. And he realized that he had witnessed a miracle of one of the hidden saints.

So it was that the guard secretly observed Shimon Pilam as he made his way through the forest, and he saw many other kinds of miracles take place. Whatever barren tree he sat beneath soon had blossoms appear on it, and whatever path he walked on had flowers spring up overnight. All of nature welcomed his presence as if he were an angel. And he secretly went on his way, healing whatever needed to be healed with a power that seemed to emanate from his very being. And indeed he was searching for the scattered sparks in that holy forest, so that he could gather them and in this way repair the world.

Now that guard was childless, and when he told his wife about the miracles he had witnessed in the forest, she begged him to go to the *tzaddik* and ask for his blessing in having a child of their own. And one day, when he could not hold himself back any longer, he approached the *tzaddik* and said: "I know that you are a great *tzaddik*, who hides his ways from the world. There is only one thing that I would ask of you, and if you help me, I promise I will never reveal your secret. All I ask is that you pray for my wife and me to have a son." The *tzaddik* saw that his secret had been discovered, and he promised the man that within a year he and his wife would be hugging a baby boy. And so it was that the guard's wife gave birth at the end of the year to a healthy son.

Now the guard kept his word and never revealed the secret of the *tzaddik*. Then one day his companion guard, who watched over the other forest, came to visit him. This guard's life had been tragic, for each of his sons had died before reaching the eighth day. And he said: "I see that God has blessed you and you have had a son. May there be many more. Tell me, was there anything you did that brought you such a blessing? Perhaps you can help me so that I can be blessed as well."

Now the guard had no intention of betraying his vow, but at the same time he wanted to help the other guard. So he said: "I will help you on one condition—that you not ask any questions but do whatever I tell you to do." The other guard quickly agreed to these terms, and the first one said: "What we have to do is to switch places, so that you will guard my forest, and I will guard yours. Then everything will be all right."

So it was that the guards switched places. And after a while the second guard observed the ways of the hidden *tzaddik*, who brought miracles to pass wherever he went. When he saw these miracles, the guard understood why the other had advised him to switch places. And at last he approached the *tzaddik* of the forest and told him of the disaster that had haunted the birth of every son. And he asked for his blessing, so that his future sons would live.

The *tzaddik* was silent for a long time, and at last he said: "Do you remember that when you were young you went with some friends to swim in the river and to wash in its waters? There was a large tree near the shore of that river, and at the bottom of the trunk, near the roots, there was engraved the image of a hand. And you had the urge to laugh and be merry. So you took a ring and placed it on the finger of the hand and said the wedding vows."

The guard grew pale when he heard this, for he himself had forgotten about that incident. He lowered his eyes and admitted that it was true. And the *tzaddik* said: "At that moment an evil spirit that lived in that place was wed to you. And since you married someone else, this evil spirit comes and kills your sons because you betrayed her and didn't fulfill the wedding vow."

The guard was staggered by these words. And he said: "I remember that day as if it were yesterday. Afterward I was ashamed of what I had done, and I put it out of my mind until now. Please, tell me, what must I do in order to free myself of that evil spirit?"

The *tzaddik* said: "I will write the bill of divorcement for you, and you must take it there, to the same place, and put the get at the place where the hand is engraved. And you will say: 'Shimon Pilam orders you to divorce me.'"

And the guard went there, and he found the place where the hand was engraved, and he did as the *tzaddik* told him to do, and at last he was freed of that spirit. And the sons that were born to him after that all lived and studied the Torah and led happy and full lives.

□ Palestine: Sixteenth Century

⁂ ⁂ ⁂ 53 ⁂ ⁂ ⁂

THE ANGEL OF THE MISHNAH

Rabbi Joseph Caro was deeply devoted to studying the Mishnah. One day when he opened the Mishnah, an angelic spirit known as a *maggid* came to him and whispered secrets of the Torah. That was the angel of the Mishnah, who brought him secrets from on high.

So too did the spirit appear when Joseph Caro recited the Mishnah to himself. For the words of the Mishnah invoked the presence of the *maggid*, and once it had appeared it revealed great mysteries to him, and Joseph Caro recorded these revelations in his book, *Maggid Mesharim*.

Once Solomon Alkabetz, author of the hymn *Lecha Dodi*, stayed up all night with Joseph Caro and several others on Shavuoth, and they never stopped studying the Torah for even a moment. They sang every word with a beautiful melody, from the creation to Moses to the Song of Songs and the Book of Ruth. And then they began to read the Mishnah, and as soon as they did, the voice of the *maggid* began to speak out of the mouth of Joseph Caro. All of them heard it, but they could not understand what it was saying, for so profound were those words that they fell on them like rain, and when they tried to comprehend them, the words simply vanished from their memory.

Then all of those present were filled with awe and fell on their faces. And at that instant they found that they could understand everything the spirit said: "I am the Mishnah, and I have come to converse with you. Had there been ten of you, you would have ascended even higher. But look down now and see where you are."

At that instant, all of them looked down and saw that they had ascended on high above the city of Safed, and the city seemed to be no larger than a glowing spark. And all of them, except for Joseph Caro, were afraid to find themselves at that height. Then the angel said: "Remember Rabbi Akiba, who ascended and descended in peace." And no sooner did the angel say this than they were filled with the spirit of Rabbi Akiba, and they were no longer afraid.

When the angel of the Mishnah saw this, he said: "Know that I can remain here only as long as you study the Mishnah. For I am the *maggid* of the Mishnah that has come into being because of Rabbi Joseph Caro's love of the Mishnah." Then they all turned their eyes to the words of the Mishnah, and they continued singing the words out loud. And as they sang each word, they suddenly understood it as they had never done before, and the words of the Mishnah shone before them like a pillar of fire in the wilderness.

Just before dawn the angel of the Mishnah informed them that he must go, and once more told them to look down. And when they did, they saw that they were lying on the floor in Joseph Caro's house, and that Joseph Caro was now speaking to them in his own voice. And there was no trace of the *maggid*'s presence. But the mysteries of the Mishnah that had been revealed to them were inscribed in their memory, as if they were black fire burning on white. Nor was that the last time the angel revealed itself in their presence. Over the years this took place many times, and in this way they learned great mysteries of the Mishnah.

□ Palestine: Sixteenth Century

ᘓᘓᘓᘓᘓᘓᘓ 54 ᘓᘓᘓᘓᘓᘓᘓ

A New Lease on Life

Every man is allotted a certain number of years in his life. This is true even for the holy sages. It is said that King David was only given a few hours to live, but when Adam was permitted to read in the book of the future, he considered David's soul so worthy that he gave him seventy years of his own life. That is why King David lived until seventy and Adam lived for nine hundred and thirty years, rather than the one thousand years he had originally been given.

Now Rabbi Joseph Caro, the author of the *Shulhan Aruch*, had an angel, which he called his *maggid*, that came to him and revealed the secrets of heaven. So it was that Rabbi Caro learned that he had been allotted eighty years of life. One day when the angel came to teach Rabbi Joseph the Torah, he found him deep in sorrow. The angel asked why he was so dejected, and Rabbi Joseph replied that his days in this world were coming to an end, yet he was full of the desire and the power to create. So the *maggid* revealed to him that in the faraway land of Poland there was one shepherd, and only one, who could give him more years of life. So too did the *maggid* reveal that his name was Moshe Pastech and that he lived in the city of Lublin.

Soon after this, Rabbi Joseph called in two of his best students and sent them on a mission to Poland to find this shepherd, and to ask him in the rabbi's name to have mercy on him and add a few more years to his life. The students did as the rabbi ordered, and when they finally reached Lublin, they learned that a man by the name of Moshe Pastech lived in an isolated place on a small mountain there. He worked as a shepherd in a nearby village. Everyone was surprised that they had come such a long way to see an illiterate shepherd, but the messengers knew in their hearts that the shepherd must be a hidden *tzaddik*, whose influence was great in the upper worlds.

The two came to the shepherd and brought the rabbi's blessings. At first he paid them no heed, but when they sought mercy for the man who had collected and arranged all the commandments of Israel, he said: "I contribute seven years of my life to Rabbi Joseph Caro." And at that moment, in Safed, the seventh and last child of Rabbi Joseph Caro was born, and from this sign he knew that he had been blessed with seven more years of life.

□   Israel: Oral Tradition

55

REDEMPTION OF THE LOST SOULS

In the seventh century, seven hundred Jews of Yemen found refuge with the "Sons of the Desert," as the Bedouins were known. Some of their descendants were said to be found near Jerico, and Rabbi Shalom Sharabi of Jerusalem often sought them out to redeem their holy sparks.

One night, during the Days of Awe between Rosh Hashanah and Yom Kippur, Rabbi Sharabi was reading in the Beth El Synagogue by the light of a candle. No one else was there except for Meshullam, the *shammash*, and Rabbi Sharabi asked not to be disturbed for any reason.

The *shammash* went to sleep, but he was awakened during the night by some kind of disturbance in the synagogue. He ran to the terrace and looked down through the dome, and there he saw a very strange sight. The synagogue was filled with the Sons of the Desert, who, with their shirts removed, were chastising themselves in the presence of the rabbi, who repeated the words "He whom God loveth is chastised, even as a loving father to his son."

Frightened by this strange sight but remembering the rabbi's warning, the *shammash* returned to bed and finally fell into a restless, fearful sleep. But suddenly he was awakened by the sound of music. He returned to the terrace and saw that the synagogue was now filled with light. The Sons of the Desert, dressed in white, each one wrapped in a *tallis*, circled the Ark, holding scrolls of the Torah in their embrace. A holy light streaming from the open doors of the Ark surrounded them and was reflected in their faces. They walked like Bridegrooms of the Law on Simhat Torah, but in silence, enveloped in that holy light. As for Rabbi Sharabi, who stood in their midst, the *shammash* thought that Moses must have looked like that when he descended Mount Sinai with the Tablets of the Law in his hands.

As the *shammash* stood there, it seemed that the synagogue began to rise up in the air, ascending on high until it become a part of the dome of heaven. There a heavenly host surrounded it, floating in that river of light, chanting prayers of joy. At that moment the *shammash* ran off to wake his wife, but when they returned all that they saw was Rabbi Sharabi sitting in the dimly lit synagogue, reading by the light of one candle.

□ Palestine: Oral Tradition

❧❧❧❧❧❧ 56 ❧❧❧❧❧❧

REPAIRING SOULS

Rabbi Hayim ben Attar, known as the "Or Hayim," would often leave his house after Shabbat was over and spend the whole week in the mountains of Jerusalem. He would take seven challas with him and a pitcher of milk, and he would return home only on the eve of Shabbat. Then he would start chanting the Song of Songs with great fervor.

While he was saying the Song of Songs, there was a sound of flying wings all around. Everyone who was present there heard it. And when he was asked about it, the Or Hayim said: "Those are the souls I repaired during the week, while I was in the mountains."

It was said that even when his wife threw out the crumbs of the challas, the sound of wings could be heard, for those souls came to share the crumbs of the *tzaddik*.

□ Morocco: Oral Tradition

THE *TEFILLIN* OF THE OR HAYIM

When the time came for the Or Hayim to take leave of this world, he called his wife closer. She saw how weak he was and bent nearer, and he said: "After my death a wealthy man will come from Kushta and offer you three hundred gold pieces for my *tefillin*. Don't refuse his request. But be sure to tell him to be careful with the *tefillin* and never let himself become distracted for the slightest time while wearing them." The wife of the Or Hayim vowed to do as he had asked, and then he closed his eyes and breathed his last.

All of Israel was saddened by his death. Many mourned for him for thirty days. And after the thirty days had ended, a wealthy man from Kushta came to the rabbi's wife and asked to purchase the rabbi's *tefillin*, exactly as he had foreseen. She informed the man of the rabbi's request that he take care not to be distracted while wearing the *tefillin*. And he, in turn, vowed to receive the *tefillin* on those terms. In this way did the rabbi's wife fulfill her vow to her husband, and the gold she received saved her from a life of poverty for the rest of her days.

The morning after returning home, the wealthy man put on the *tefillin* for the first time. As he did, he felt a transformation. It was almost like the feeling he had on the Sabbath, when each person receives an extra soul. It was the very soul of the Or Hayim accompanying his own. That day the man prayed with a fervor he had never known, nor even imagined that he could attain. But with the soul of the rabbi like a wind soaring beneath his own, his prayers ascended on high. After praying he took the *tefillin* off in the prescribed manner, and when he did, he felt the extra soul depart, exactly as happens at the end of the Sabbath. And he was filled with wonder at the miracle of those *tefillin*.

From that day on, the wealthy man guarded the *tefillin* as his most prized possession. Each time he put them on, he took care that his concentration was complete. And each time he finished binding the *tefillin*, the spirit of the Or Hayim returned to him, and his prayers soared to the palaces on high. During this time his thoughts were much clearer, his soul much calmer, and he saw as never before the harmony of creation and the presence of God in the world.

But once, while the man was wrapped in his *tallis* and *tefillin*, a servant distracted him with a matter concerning his store. And when the man returned to his prayers, he found that the holy spirit that had been with him was gone. Nor in all the times he put on the *tefillin* after that did the soul of the Or Hayim return.

At last, in desperation, the man took the *tefillin* to a *sofer*. And when the *sofer* opened the houses of the *tefillin* and took out the parchments, he was amazed to find that they were blank, with not a single letter written on them. For the instant the man had turned away, every letter had taken flight, along with the soul of the Or Hayim.

□   Palestine: Nineteenth Century

III

MYSTICAL FOLKTALES

GABRIEL'S PALACE

In the city of Worms there is an ancient Torah inscribed on parchment of deerskin. It is said that this scroll was written by Rabbi Meir of Rothenburg, known as the "Maharam," while he was imprisoned. No possession of the Jews who live there is more precious, for its origin was miraculous. Rabbi Meir had been libeled and cast into jail, and a huge ransom of twenty thousand gold coins had been placed on his head. Nevertheless, the Jews of that generation decided to raise the sum. They sent a delegation to Rabbi Meir, but he rejected their offer, saying: "I regret to deprive you of the *mitzvah* of redeeming a captive. Still, I prefer to remain in prison rather than to encourage this kind of extortion. All I ask is that you bring me the tools of a scribe so that I may write down my thoughts about the Torah. For, as you know, I have been forbidden to have any books." With no other choice, the delegation respected his wishes and saw to it that he received a scribe's quill, ink, and pieces of parchment.

So Rabbi Meir remained imprisoned, much to the disappointment of those who had expected to receive the ransom. And even though he had been deprived of every book, he had long since memorized not only the Torah, but both Talmuds and many other holy texts as well, so he lacked for nothing. Indeed, all that he truly needed was a scroll of the Torah to read on the Sabbath, since it is written that the Torah must be studied on that day from a text.

One Friday night Rabbi Meir fell asleep, and while he slept his soul took wing and ascended on high. When he opened his eyes, he was blinded by a bright light. But when his eyes grew accustomed to the light, he found himself in a palace chamber, and there was a glowing figure standing before him, an angel. Just then the angel spoke and said: "Welcome, Rabbi Meir. I am the angel Gabriel, and you have ascended to my palace. The heavenly hosts are aware of how distressed you are, because you lack a scroll of the Torah. You have been brought here to receive one. This is one of the thirteen scrolls that

121

Moses himself wrote before his death. One scroll was given to each of the twelve tribes, and the thirteenth was brought to the heavenly academy. This is that Torah. Now it is to remain with you. All that we ask is that you read loud enough that it can be heard here. For the sages on high will be listening to every word, since it is their Torah that you will be reading." And with awe and wonder Rabbi Meir received that celestial Torah from the arms of the angel Gabriel, and then he awoke.

When Rabbi Meir opened his eyes, it was the first crack of dawn. He looked around, still in a daze, and it was then that he saw the scroll of the Torah lying upon the table—and he knew that the dream had been true. Rabbi Meir washed and dressed, staring with amazement at the Torah that had been brought to him from on high. For a long time he did not dare to touch it, lest it all be a dream.

Then he began to recite the Sabbath prayers, and when the time came to read the weekly portion, the scroll of the Torah rolled open to the right place. And as Rabbi Meir began to read, the room filled with a holy light, and he felt the presence of all of the *tzaddikim* on high. He read slowly and clearly, taking his time with every word. And he read loud enough that not even a single one would be lost. And when he finished reading, the scroll of the Torah rolled closed on its own, and the light vanished from the room.

So it was that Rabbi Meir lived in the presence of that sacred scroll, reading the Sabbath portion from it every week and studying it night and day. And during that time he discovered many truths that could only be discerned by one who read in that celestial scroll.

One day it occurred to Rabbi Meir to copy that scroll of the Torah for the generations to come, for all of the other scrolls that Moses had written had been lost over the ages. So it was that every day he sat at the table transcribing every word from the sacred parchment, counting out each letter as if it were a golden coin. He worked on it for twelve months, and at last he completed transcribing it without a single error. And when he reread what he had written, he discovered that heaven had assisted him in creating a perfect replica of the celestial Torah.

When Rabbi Meir awoke the next morning, he discovered that the scroll of Moses was gone, and he knew that Gabriel must have descended during the night to take it back. And Rabbi Meir knew that this meant that heaven had found the Torah he had written to be perfect and that it would now serve as a model for future generations.

Now Rabbi Meir remained imprisoned for six more years. During that time, he fashioned a wooden ark to hold the scroll of the Torah and covered it with pitch to make it waterproof. When he felt the end of his life drawing near, he sealed the ark with the scroll inside it, lowered it from his window into the Rhine River, and consigned it to its fate.

In the days that followed, the ark floated down the river until at last it approached the city of Worms. Some Gentile fishermen tried to catch it in their nets, but it always eluded them. Soon word spread about this elusive box. It became the talk of the city, and many tried their luck at capturing it, but no one succeeded.

Among the Jews of the city there was an intense debate about the box. Some said that it had a demon inside, while others insisted that it was being guided by the Holy Spirit, which is why it eluded all the Gentiles who had tried to ensnare it. At last the Jews decided to see if they had any better luck. They rented a boat and set out near the last place where the box had been sighted. And sure enough, a current soon carried the box in their direction, and they were quickly able to pull it into the boat.

When they returned to shore, however, the owner of the boat, who was not Jewish, claimed the box as his own, since it was caught with his boat. The Jews were forced to give it up, but when the Gentiles tried to lift it, they could not. Even when a dozen men tried to pick it up, they could not budge it an inch. At this they became frightened and ran away. But the Jews had no difficulty in lifting and carrying it into the synagogue. There they opened the box with trepidation. Inside they found the scroll of the Torah, inscribed on deerskin. And along with it was a message, also on parchment, from Rabbi Meir, giving it as a gift to the community of Worms.

When the Jews of the city learned of this miracle, they celebrated and gave thanks to God. And that Torah has remained there for many generations, guarding them from danger and serving as a great blessing in their lives.

As for Rabbi Meir, he died in jail soon after he lowered the ark into the river, and his soul ascended directly to Gabriel's Palace. There he makes his home in the World to Come, serving every Sabbath as the reader of the celestial Torah kept in the Ark on high.

▫ Germany: Oral Tradition

❧❧❧❧❧❧ 59 ❧❧❧❧❧❧

The Cottage of Candles

There once was a Jew who went out into the world to seek justice. He looked in the streets and the markets of cities but could not find it. He traveled to villages and he explored distant fields and farms, but still justice eluded him. At last he came to an immense forest and he entered it, for he was certain that justice must exist somewhere. He wandered there for many years and he saw many things—the hovels of the poorest peasants, the hideaways of thieves, and the huts of witches in the darkest part of the forest. And he stopped in each of these, despite the danger, and sought clues. But no one was able to help him in his quest.

One day, just as dusk was falling, he arrived at a small clay hut that looked as if it were about to collapse. Now there was something strange about this hut, for many flickering flames could be seen through the window. The man who sought justice wondered greatly about this and knocked on the door. There was no answer. He pushed the door open and entered.

Before him was a small room crowded with many shelves. And on the shelves were a multitude of oil candles. Together their flames seem to beat like wings, and the flickering light made him feel as if he were standing in the center of a quivering flame. He held up his hand, and it seemed to be surrounded with an aura, and all the candles were like a constellation of stars.

Stepping closer, he saw that some of the flames burned with a very pure fire, while others were dull and still others were sputtering, about to go out. So too did he now notice that some of the wicks were in golden vessels, while others were in silver or marble ones, and many burned in simple vessels of clay or tin. The plain vessels had thin wicks, which burned quickly, while those made of gold or silver had wicks that lasted much longer.

While he stood there, marveling at that forest of candles, an old man in a white robe came out of one of the corners and said: "*Shalom Aleichem*, my son, what are you looking for?"

"*Aleichem Shalom*," the man answered. "I have traveled everywhere searching for justice, but never have I seen anything like all these candles. Why are they burning?"

The old man spoke softly: "Know that these are soul-candles. Each candle is the soul of one of the living. As long as it burns, the person remains alive. But when the flame burns out, he departs from this life."

Then the man who sought justice turned to the the old man and asked: "Can I see the candle of my soul?"

The old man led him into a corner and showed him a line of tins on a low shelf. He pointed out a small, rusty one that had very little oil left. The wick was smoking and had tilted to one side. "This is your soul," said the old man.

A great fear fell upon the man and he started to shiver. Could it be that the end of his life was so near and he did not know it?

Then the man noticed that next to his tin there was another, filled with oil. Its wick was straight, burning with a clear, pure light.

"And this one, who does it belong to?" asked the man, trembling. "That is a secret," answered the old man. "I only reveal each man's candle to himself alone."

Soon after that the old man vanished from sight, and the room seemed empty except for the candles burning on every shelf.

While the man stood there, he saw a candle on another shelf sputter and go out. For a moment there was a wisp of smoke rising in the air, and then it was gone. One soul had just left the world.

The man's eyes returned to his own tin. He saw that only a few drops of oil remained, and he knew that the flame would soon burn out. At that instant he saw the candle of his neighbor, burning brightly, the tin full of oil.

Suddenly an evil thought entered his mind. He looked around and saw that the old man had disappeared. He looked closely in the corner from which he had come, and then in the other corners, but there was no sign of him there. At that moment he reached out and took hold of the full tin and raised it above his own. But suddenly a strong hand gripped his arm, and the old man stood beside him.

"Is this the kind of justice you are seeking?" he asked. His grip was like iron, and the pain caused the man to close his eyes.

And when the fingers released him, he opened his eyes and saw that everything had disappeared: the old man, the cottage, the shelves, and all the candles. And the man stood alone in the forest and heard the trees whispering his fate.

□   Afghanistan: Oral Tradition

60

RABBI SHIMON'S ESCAPE

Among the prisoners of the Inquisition on the island of Majorca was Rabbi Shimon ben Tsemah Duran. Many of his fellow Jews were also confined in that prison, where they were often tortured because they were unwilling to abandon their faith. At last they were condemned to death, for the inquisitors saw that they would never turn their backs on the Torah.

As they awaited the day of execution, which was to take place in thirty days, Rabbi Shimon drew a ship on the wall of the jail. Now Rabbi Shimon had never been known as an artist, and the others marveled at his skill. For he drew every detail as if he had sailed for many years, while, as far as they knew, he had never set foot in a ship.

For three weeks, as the days until the date of the execution passed, his cellmates watched him at work on the drawing. Once they asked him why he was so exacting, and he answered: "I intend to escape on this ship. Who among you would like to accompany me?" And all of them announced their readiness at once, for they knew that Rabbi Shimon was a master of miracles.

Before the drawing of the ship was completed, Rabbi Shimon added himself and all of the others, so that they could be seen standing on the deck, looking out to sea. Every prisoner recognized himself at once, for the resemblance was uncanny.

Then, on the very day of their execution, when they heard the keys of the soldiers turning in the lock, Rabbi Shimon told them it was time to go. And he turned to the ship and pronounced the Holy Name. At that instant all of them found themselves on the deck of a great ship in the middle of the ocean, sailing by itself to the beaches of North Africa. And, indeed, they were.

□ The Balkans: Oral Tradition

61

THE BOY WHO BLEW THE SHOFAR

Long ago in the city of Kiev there lived a young boy named Eliyahu. He was a fine student in the yeshivah, and he had great faith in God.

One night Eliyahu had a strange dream. In the dream he was walking at night on the path that led to the synagogue. And when he arrived, he entered and found that it was empty. But he saw that a shofar and a large prayer shawl had been left on the *Bimah* where the rabbi led the prayers. Just then a man entered, and, strange as it may seem, he was wearing a shroud, the garment worn by the dead. And stranger still, Eliyahu was not afraid. And as the man came closer to Eliyahu, the boy saw at once that he had a troubled appearance. The man said: "I am one of forty-eight souls from the world of the dead who have been forced to wander between heaven and earth. Our souls have been trapped, unable to ascend, since the time of our deaths at the hands of the Cossacks. The forces of evil have held us back. But we cannot bear waiting any longer to be set free. Please, Eliyahu, you must help us."

"But how can I help?" the boy asked in the dream.

"You must take the prayer shawl and the shofar from the synagogue and go to the cemetery outside of town, where we are gathered. And you must sound the shofar, but this must be done before the close of Rosh Hashanah. Then the gates of heaven will open, and our wandering will be ended."

Eliyahu was even more shocked than before. "But I am only twelve years old. I don't even wear a prayer shawl," he answered, "and I don't know how to blow the shofar."

The man looked straight into the boy's eyes. "Eliyahu, if the gates of heaven do not open for us before the close of Rosh Hashanah, we will have to wander for another year," he said. "Only you can set us free." Then the shrouded man departed, just as the boy awoke.

When he realized that he had been dreaming, Eliyahu sighed with relief. But all day long he was haunted by the man's words: "Only you can set us free."

Now Eliyahu could not imagine stealing a shofar and prayer shawl from the synagogue. Nor could he imagine blowing the shofar in a cemetery, for such a thing is never done. So, even though the man's words came to him again and again, Eliyahu did not do as the man had asked, and so a whole day passed by.

The next night Eliyahu dreamed again that he followed the path at night to the synagogue. This time there was a figure wrapped in a shawl, standing and facing the Ark. As he entered, the figure turned around, and Eliyahu saw that it was a woman. He could hardly believe his eyes—a woman standing at the Holy Ark, and a shrouded woman at that! Yet when this eerie figure approached him, the boy did not take fright, but instead felt sad for her, for he saw the look of suffering in her eyes. Then the woman spoke: "Eliyahu, only two days remain before Rosh Hashanah. I am speaking for forty-eight souls, whose fate is in your hands. You must take up the prayer shawl and the shofar and blow great blasts on it to open heaven's gates for us. Hurry to the cemetery, Eliyahu. Only you can set us free." Then the shrouded woman departed, and no sooner had she passed through the doorway than Eliyahu awoke.

This time the boy was paralyzed with fear. "I am losing my mind. Who will forgive me for stealing from the synagogue? And who will believe my reason for doing so?" With these thoughts tormenting him, another day passed, and Eliyahu did not do as the woman had asked. And yet he wanted to free those poor souls from their wandering. And the words of the woman returned to him again and again: "Only you can set us free."

Eliyahu was tired. He could not think clearly. But as it grew dark, he fell into a deep sleep. And he dreamed again that he entered the synagogue, and everywhere he looked he saw worshipers, men and women, all wearing shrouds, all chanting prayers. He recognized the shrouded man who had approached him in the first dream and the shrouded woman who had spoken to him in the second. He quickly counted and saw that there were twenty-four men on one side of the aisle and twenty-four women on the other, separated by a curtain. What a strange congregation they were! Yet he did not feel terror at the sight of them, for he saw that they were all suffering.

And then Eliyahu noticed that there was no one leading the congregation. He turned to the nearest man and said: "How is it that you are praying without a prayer leader?"

"It is because we are waiting for him to put on the prayer shawl and take up the shofar," said the man.

"And when do you expect him to come?" asked the boy.

"He has already arrived," said the man.

"Where is he?" the boy asked, for he was curious to know who the leader was.

"Eliyahu, it is you we have been waiting for," said the man. Eliyahu looked around and saw that every eye in the congregation was fixed on him. Then the man said: "Only a short time remains. Hurry, Eliyahu. Only you can set us free."

Just then Eliyahu woke up. He was covered with a cold sweat. He leaped from bed as if some great invisible force were pushing him and ran in the darkness to the synagogue. And when he reached it, he noticed that the door was open, and his heart almost stopped beating. He stepped inside and saw, to his great relief, that the synagogue was empty. His eyes were drawn to the prayer shawl and the shofar lying there. And he recognized the large prayer shawl as that of the rabbi himself. For a moment he stopped. Did he dare put on the rabbi's prayer shawl? Yet time was passing. Soon it would be too late. Quickly he picked up the prayer shawl and wrapped it around himself like a long robe. And, strange to say, the moment the prayer shawl was on his shoulders, he felt greatly strengthened. Then he picked up the shofar and ran from the synagogue.

In a short time, he reached the cemetery and entered the place where spirits and demons are said to roam. But now he gave no thought to fears of ghosts and demons. His only fear was that he would not be on time. "Lord in heaven, let me not be late," he said aloud. And as he stood amid those tombstones, in the presence of all those departed souls, he had the same feeling that he had had in the dream: that all eyes were fixed on him.

Then, hesitating no longer, Eliyahu lifted the shofar and blew on it: The first long, unbroken note rang clearly through the night air. Then, one after the other, the broken notes came forth, sounding like sobbing and wailing. And as he blew those notes, Eliyahu thought he heard sobbing and wailing all around him. He repeated the long, unbroken blast and held it for what seemed to be forever. And the instant he finished blowing that long note, the sound of rushing winds encircled him for several seconds, as if they were hugging and embracing him, and he heard a distant creaking sound as if, somewhere far away, a great gate had opened.

Then suddenly the winds grew calm, and for a few moments Eliyahu stood in the cemetery, wrapped in the large prayer shawl, holding the shofar in his hand. He felt a sense of calm and peace and stillness. But all at once, he remembered that the men would be in the synagogue to pray, and he had to return the shofar and the prayer shawl. So, in a panic, he ran back as fast as his legs would carry him.

When he arrived, Eliyahu saw that there was only one person there, one man who was praying. And he was without a prayer shawl.

The man turned around as Eliyahu entered, and the boy saw that he was none other than the rabbi himself. The boy was overcome with terror. Would the rabbi ever forgive him?

But the rabbi smiled broadly as he approached the boy and put his arms around Eliyahu, who was still wearing his prayer shawl. And when the boy looked up in confusion, the rabbi said: "You were chosen, Eliyahu, because your faith is so strong. And, because you opened the gates of heaven for them, those souls have been freed from their wanderings, and at last have reached their final destination. They were right, you know, Eliyahu. Only you could have set them free."

□   Israel: Oral Tradition

※☆※☆※☆※☆※☆ 62 ※☆※☆※☆※☆※☆

THE ENCHANTED INN

There once was a wealthy man who was very generous, but his wife was very stingy. From the front door her husband would welcome every guest, while she turned away every beggar from the back. Only once did she ever give any kind of charity. Then some sisters came to her house, crying out that their mother was about to give birth, and they were so poor that they didn't have a sheet. That day the wife of the wealthy man pulled the white satin cloth off the dining room table and handed it to the girls without saying a word. They thanked her profusely and hurried off.

This man and his wife were the parents of three sons. Then tragedy struck the family, and within a short time both the father and the mother died. Only the family servant, an old woman whose name was Miriam, was left to care for the children.

Now it had always been the dream of the merchant to ascend to the Land of Israel with his family, so the old woman decided to take the boys there, where they could be assured of receiving the finest training in the Torah. So she sold everything that was left and traveled with the boys to Jerusalem. There she purchased a fine home for the boys and continued to serve them.

Miriam wanted to choose the best possible teacher for the brothers, and she searched for one with great care. Then she had a dream in which an old man came to her and told her to seek out a certain Rabbi Nachshon. On waking the old woman remembered this dream clearly, and she set out at once to find this rabbi, for she had great faith in dreams. When she did, she told him her dream, and he said: "Send me the oldest one."

The next day Miriam brought the boy to the rabbi, who welcomed him and said: "Go and fast for today and come to me in the afternoon and I will teach you Torah."

When the boy came back the next day at the appointed time, the rabbi showed him a goat that was tied to a tree outside his house and said: "Untie the goat and follow it wherever it leads you. But remember this: If you are hungry, you may not eat, but if you are thirsty, you can drink."

The boy did as he was told. And as soon as he untied the goat, he had to hurry to keep up with it. The goat led him on a long chase, and at last they came to an inn, one he had never seen before. No sooner did the boy reach the inn than the goat leaped in through an open window. The boy followed the goat inside and found that the inn was empty. Still, the scent of fresh food reached him, and he saw a delicious meal waiting on the table. He didn't wonder where it came from, but he was so hungry from fasting and the chase that he sat down and ate the entire meal without once remembering that this had been forbidden. While he was eating, the goat leaped back outside. When at last he finished, the boy discovered that the goat was gone. In shame the boy returned to the rabbi empty-handed. He confessed that he had lost the goat and had failed to keep his fast.

The rabbi showed the boy the goat, which was tied to the same tree. Then the rabbi said: "As you can see, the goat came back on its own. Now go home and send me your brother. You don't deserve to study Torah because you ate during the day of fasting."

The same thing happened with the second brother. Rabbi Nachshon gave him the same instructions, and he too followed the goat to the inn and could not restrain himself from breaking the fast. And when he returned, the rabbi also sent him away and asked to see the youngest son.

When the third brother came to him, Rabbi Nachshon asked him also to fast and sent him to follow the goat, which led him by a long route to the same inn. There he saw all the food set at the table, but he didn't touch it. Instead, he went into a different room. That room was full of burning candles. He saw among them one candle that was about to go out, so he added oil to it and fixed the wick so that it would keep burning.

Then he came to a third room from which seven stairs descended. And he saw a woman sitting at the bottom of the stairs before an open pit. From where he stood he could not see her face. While he was watching, two men came and threw the woman into a pit filled with snakes and scorpions. Then they pulled her out of the pit and cleansed her with a white tablecloth. After that they threw her into the pit again. They kept repeating this over and over.

The boy became very frightened and left that room and went into a different one. There he saw an old man coming toward him, who offered him a cup of fresh water. And the boy remembered that he was permitted to drink if he was thirsty, and his thirst was very great. And when he drank of those miraculous waters, his heart opened to the Way of the Torah, and it was as if a hidden palace had been revealed. That is when he noticed that the glass was still as full as it was when the old man had given it to him. And he understood that it would never run dry. And as his eyes opened wider, he became filled with the wisdom of the Torah. That is when he saw the door to another room. He was drawn to that door, and when he opened it he saw an old man wrapped in a white *tallis*, which covered him so that the boy could not see his face. He was teaching Torah to students, and while the boy stood there and listened, the rabbi and his students discussed a fine point of the Law, which the rabbi interpreted one way and the students another. And the boy was amazed to find that he understood what they were saying, and he couldn't help but get involved in it as if he were a true scholar. And in the end he not only joined the rabbi in his opinion, but convinced the others that the rabbi was right.

At that instant everything disappeared. The inn was suddenly gone, as well as the goat, and the boy found himself standing alone in a field. He was filled with dread. For a while he stood there, lost in confusion; then he caught sight of a path and decided to see where it would lead him. And before long he found his way back to the city.

When the boy entered the city, he went to the rabbi and told him what had happened. And the rabbi said: "You must know that the room of the food and drink was this world. And every candle that burned in the next room was a living soul. And the candle you preserved is your own, and now your life has been greatly lengthened. Know also that the room with seven stairs was Gehenna. As for the woman that you saw, she is your mother, who was stingy all her days and only gave a gift to the poor once. That was a white tablecloth she gave to a woman about to give birth. And with that tablecloth they cleanse her from the pit. Thus is she punished until her soul shall be pure enough to ascend the seven stairs and leave Gehenna behind. And the old man you met, who let you drink, that was Elijah, and that water was the water of the Torah. That is why the glass always remained full—for the wisdom of the Torah is inexhaustible. And last, but not least, there was the rabbi and the students. Know that the rabbi was your father, who gave charity all his days. And when he died, he came to the World of Truth and received his reward. And he sits in the yeshivah on high, teaching the Torah, blessed be he."

And the rabbi blessed him to continue in the ways of his father, striving equally in Torah and in good deeds. And before he gave him a final blessing, he told him to fast for seven days, for on each day of the fast he could raise his mother up another of the seven stairs and thus save her from the judgment of Gehenna. And this, indeed, is what the young man did.

□   Eastern Europe: Nineteenth Century

63

LEAVES FROM THE GARDEN OF EDEN

The largest stable in the city of Ludomir was owed by Shepsel. From morning until nightfall mail coaches would arrive, exchanging their tired horses for fresh ones. Shepsel was helped in his work by the boy Hayim, an orphan who made his home with Shepsel and his family. Hayim's parents had died while he was very young, and he had roamed the streets before Shepsel had taken him in. Soon, however, they all regarded him as a member of the family. And he was especially close to Shepsel's daughter, Leah. They were like brother and sister.

Now Hayim was a hard worker in the stables, just like Shepsel. They worked side by side all day long. But one day Hayim took ill, and each day he seemed to grow weaker. Leah nursed him during his illness, and she was deeply grieved at his death, as was Shepsel and the rest of the family.

When the period of mourning had ended, however, Leah did not seem to recover from her grief. She had loved the boy deeply, and she could not bear the loss. Shepsel and his wife sat at her bedside every day, praying for her recovery. One day, while Shepsel was sitting at her bedside, he fell asleep and began to dream. In the dream, Hayim the stable boy appeared before him, his face glowing with joy.

"Where did you come from?" asked Shepsel, who remembered, even in the dream, that the boy was no longer in this world. "And why are you so joyful?"

"Let me tell you all that has happened to me. When I left this world, I was brought before the heavenly court. I explained that I only knew a few prayers, for that is all I had been taught. But I had served you, my master, as faithfully as I could. So too did I tend the horses with care. And I always tried to be honest.

"The court ruled that I had earned a place in the Garden of Eden, and that is where I make my home. And because I had tended horses in my earthly life, I have been put in charge of the heavenly horses that pull the golden coaches of the *tzaddikim.*"

Then the boy asked Shepsel about his family. And Shepsel broke into tears and told him how much his daughter had grieved over his death, and now she too was in grave danger. And the boy said: "Don't worry. There are leaves that grow in the Garden of Eden that heal any illness. Wait, and I will fetch you some." And a moment later, the boy brought Shepsel a handful of leaves and said: "Boil these in a pot of water and give them to Leah to drink." And as Shepsel accepted the leaves, he awoke. And scattered all over the bed were leaves that had blown in from the open window. And when he picked them up, he saw that those leaves did not grow anywhere in that land. So too did they bear a wonderful fragrance, like that in his dream.

Shepsel hurried to boil some of those leaves in water, and he gave it to his daughter to drink. As he did, he told her about his dream, and about the leaves that Hayim had given them from the Garden of Eden. And, to everyone's amazement, Leah began to recover at once. So swift was her recovery that by the third day she was out of bed and walking around.

Soon after that, Leah was betrothed and wed. And she named her first son Hayim, after the stable boy. And it is said that she loved her child as much as she had loved her adopted brother.

□ Eastern Europe: Nineteenth Century

64

THE TENTH MAN

For many years only a few Jews were permitted by the Moslem authorities to live in Hebron, where the Patriarchs Abraham, Isaac, and Jacob and their wives are buried. Once there were so few that on the eve of Yom Kippur, only nine Jews had gathered in the House of Prayer in the city of Hebron, and there was no one else they could call on to complete the minyan. The sun was setting, but they could not begin *Kol Nidre*.

Just then there was a knock on the door, and when the *gabbai* answered it, he found an old Jew standing there, a stranger with a long white beard, wearing a white robe, carrying a white *tallis*. The *gabbai* gladly invited him in and asked to know his name. The old man said it was Abraham. Then, since the tenth man had arrived, they began the prayers, and the old man joined in with them. As they listened to him chant his prayers, many of them felt certain that they had heard his voice before, although they did not know where.

The old man remained there with them, praying all night and the next day, until Yom Kippur had come to an end. Never before had they prayed for so long without stopping, but somehow not one of them felt tired, nor did hunger pangs trouble them. All were aware that the power of the Divine Presence filled the House of Prayer.

When the Day of Atonement had ended, the old man took his leave, but he left his *tallis* behind. The *gabbai* hurried after him to return it, but he was nowhere to be found.

That night the *gabbai* had a dream in which the old man returned to him and revealed that he was actually the Patriarch Abraham. So too did he reveal that he had left the *tallis* behind for him and that it was sacred. For if he wore it when he prayed, he would be permitted a vision of the Divine Presence. The *gabbai* told the others his dream, and they were filled with wonder to learn the true identity of the old man.

The *gabbai* put on the *tallis* of Abraham when he prayed that day. And during the silent prayer, when he closed his eyes for an instant, he saw a vision of the Divine Presence glowing in the dark. Afterward, whenever he closed his eyes, the vision would return, as if it were imprinted there.

As for the *tallis*, it is said that Abraham returned to the *gabbai* in a dream shortly before he died, and told him to request that he be buried in it. This was done, and no sooner did they cover his body with that prayer shawl than his soul found itself in Paradise, inside the synagogue of Abraham the Patriarch. There he was made *gabbai* in that heavenly House of Prayer, where he serves the Patriarch Abraham to this day, still wrapped in that sacred *tallis*.

□ Persia: Nineteenth Century

65

THE RAM WHOSE HORNS REACHED TO HEAVEN

The ram that Abraham found caught in the thicket at Mount Moriah was one of the seven things created before the creation of the world, along with the Torah, the rainbow of Noah, and other precious things. The ram waited in Paradise for many centuries until that fateful day on Mount Moriah. All this time the ram knew it had been created, but it was not afraid. Instead, it looked forward to fulfilling its destiny.

Then the day came when the angel brought the ram from Paradise to serve as the sacrifice in place of Isaac at Mount Moriah. There, its horns caught in the thicket, it waited for Abraham to set it free.

Nothing of the ram that was sacrificed there was wasted. The skin of the ram became Elijah's mantle, the gut was used in David's harp, one horn was sounded by Moses at Mount Sinai, and the other will be blown by Elijah at the End of Days. And the sacrifice itself was accepted; the fire of the Lord descended to consume the burnt offering.

Yet there was one part of the ram that was not used—its soul. The soul of the ram returned to Paradise, to the Messiah's palace, where it remained for centuries. And all that time it longed to do something more in the world of men. At last the soul of the ram addressed the Holy One, blessed be He: "Master of the Universe, I know that I was created to be sacrificed at Mount Moriah. My taste of the world was brief, and would have been bitter had I not known that I was fulfilling my fate. Nothing of my body was wasted, but my soul longs to return to the world, for surely I have more to give."

The Holy One listened to the words of the ram, and a moment later the Angel of the Torah, who had once brought it to Mount Moriah, led it back to earth, where it found itself in the only shape it had ever known, that of a ram. But because it was no ordinary ram, it was given horns so long that they reached all the way to heaven.

In this way it was possible for the ram to be in both worlds at the same time, with its feet on the earth and its horns cradling the sun, the moon, and the stars, sharing in the mysteries of the Torah whispered among the angels.

So the ram walked among men for many centuries, seeking to help those in need in any way that it could. If a husband and wife were childless and their prayers had not been answered, the ram would take their prayers and lift them all the way to Paradise. There it would place them in the hands of the angel Sandalphon, who would weave garlands of prayer out of them for the Holy One to wear on His Throne of Glory. And with the help of the ram, the man and woman were at last blessed with a child.

Or if a child was lost in the night, the ram would let it take hold of one of its horns and lead it home.

And sometimes the ram would whisper in a man's ear some secret about himself that it had overheard among the angels.

Now one night the ram was wandering through the streets of a Polish town when it saw a very sad man passing by. The ram asked him why he was so downcast, and the man replied: "I am a poor man, of few possessions. And now I have lost the finest thing I owed, a snuffbox made out of horn. I will never be able to afford another like it."

The ram wanted to help the man, so he said: "My horns are very long. Why don't you cut off a bit of one of them and make yourself another snuffbox?"

The man was very grateful for such a generous offer, and the ram lowered its horns so that the man could cut off what he needed. And from that horn the man made a beautiful snuffbox and filled it with tobacco. And the very next day he discovered that the tobacco left in the snuffbox had acquired the most wonderful fragrance, for the horn from which the box was made had come from the sacred ram.

Now the man shared a bit of that tobacco with everyone in his *minyan*, and all of them wanted to know where they could get such a precious snuffbox. So the man told them about the ram, and each and every one of them sought it out. And the ram always lowered its horns and let them cut off a little bit, enough for each to make a snuffbox of his own.

In time the wonder of these snuffboxes became known in many cities, and many were those who sought out the sacred ram. Nor did the ram ever refuse anyone who asked for some of its horn, for, after all, it was the ram of sacrifice. At last its horns became so short that they barely reached the clouds, and before long they barely reached the top of the trees, and finally, they could not be seen at all.

Now those who seek out the ram can no longer find it. It looks like every other ram, and without its horns there is no way of knowing. Nor can we be sure if it is still wandering among us, or if it has gone off alone into the wilderness, until its horns grow back. And how long will that take? It could be a very long time. For some say that until the horns of the ram again reach all the way to heaven, the footsteps of the Messiah will not be heard.

□ Eastern Europe: Nineteenth Century

66

THE CAVE OF KING DAVID

One night the Turkish Sultan disguised himself and walked about his city. When he entered the Jewish quarter, he heard singing, and when he went closer, he saw that the people were dancing in a great circle. He asked about the song and was told that the words were "David, King of Israel, is alive and still exists."

When the Sultan heard this, it confirmed all his suspicions about the Jews. The Jews were not loyal to him, but to their own king.

The next day the Sultan called in the kabbalist Rabbi Rafael Recanti, who was the leader of the Jewish community, and made these accusations. The rabbi insisted that King David had died long ago, but the Sultan would hear none of it. He demanded that the rabbi bring him a gift that could come only from King David, and if he did not, he would destroy all the Jews of that land.

Rabbi Recanti was very frightened. And he knew that he must turn to heaven for guidance, for only a miracle could make it possible for him to fulfill the king's command. So he fasted for several days and immersed himself in the *mikveh*, and at last he heard a heavenly voice announce that he must go to the city of Luz in the Holy Land. There he would find King David, who, in truth, was still alive. So too did the heavenly voice reveal the holy name that would make it possible for him to go there.

Now the way to the city of Luz is one of the most closely guarded secrets. The histories of the city, reaching back for centuries, are filled with every detail of learning and life. Yet these same histories, though complete, do not record a single death, nor a single flood or fire, for all who live inside its walls are immortal, and even the Angel of Death can do them no harm.

Now that heaven had opened a path for him, Rabbi Recanti rushed down it, as did the Children of Israel when the waters of the Red Sea parted. He pronounced the holy name that had been revealed to him, and in a single breath he found himself inside the walls of that city. There he saw an old, old man, far older than any he had ever seen before. He asked the old man if King David could be found there. And the old man said: "No. King David lives in a cave out in the desert, near a spring. Once a year a flock of birds fly in that direction, and today is the day they will arrive here. Follow the birds to the spring, and immerse yourself in the waters before you enter the cave."

Rabbi Recanti thanked the old man and left the city. Just as he stepped beyond its gates, he heard a flapping of wings and saw a flock of birds that filled the sky. Once more he pronounced the holy name that had brought him to that place, and he found himself flying as fast as that flock to the spring the old man had spoken of, with the cave nearby.

Rabbi Recanti immersed himself in that spring and then entered the cave. There he saw King David reclining on a couch. Above him hung his sword and the crown of the kingdom. King David welcomed him, for he too had heard the heavenly voice announcing the rabbi's visit, and he knew of the danger facing the Turkish Jews.

King David brought forth two pitchers of water and gave them to Rabbi Recanti. He told him to wash his hands in the waters of the first pitcher. And the instant the waters touched the rabbi's hands, his skin grew white as snow, as happens with leprosy. The rabbi was very frightened, but King David told him not to worry, just to pour the water of the other pitcher over his hands. And as soon as he did this, Rabbi Recanti's skin was restored to its healthy state. Then King David said: "Now that you know the power of the waters in these pitchers, take them to the Sultan. He will understand that this gift could come from no one but me. For the waters of the first pitcher are from Gehenna, and those of the second are from the Garden of Eden."

When Rabbi Recanti took his leave of King David, he pronounced the holy name for the third and final time. And in an instant he found himself back in the land of Turkey, before the palace of the Sultan. There he was granted an audience, and he gave the Sultan the two pitchers that he had received from King David.

The Sultan wanted to know what was so precious about the water in those pitchers. Rabbi Recanti suggested that the Sultan pour the water from the first over his hands. When the Sultan did, his skin turned leprous and the Sultan was horrified. He knew that if anyone found out, his reign would be over, for the disease would be seen as a sign that he was no longer fit to rule. The Sultan pleaded with Rabbi Recanti to cure him, and the rabbi assured him that he would if he promised not to harm the Jews of Turkey in any way. The Sultan quickly vowed to do so, and the rabbi told him to wash his hands in the water of the second pitcher. And as soon as the Sultan did, he recovered. Then the Sultan knew that none could have sent him those enchanted waters but King David himself, and never again did he threaten the Jews of his kingdom.

□ Eastern Europe: Nineteenth Century

◊ 67 ◊

THE SHINING ROBE

It is said that Rabbi Eleazar and Rabbi Joshua journeyed together to Jerusalem one year in order to pray at the Temple on Yom Kippur. As they reached the courtyard of the Temple, they each had a vision in which they saw a great light, and an angel revealed itself to them in all its glory. The angel had in its hand a shining robe, which gave off a light as bright and pure as the angel's. The two rabbis wondered greatly for whom that celestial garment was intended, knowing it must be for one of the righteous.

The two rabbis blessed the angel, who returned their blessing and revealed to them that they had been inscribed for another year in the Book of Life. The two rabbis felt joy and relief at this news, but they were very curious to know for whom the shining robe was intended. This they asked the angel, who told them he was taking it to Joseph the Gardener, who lived in Ashkelon. The angel pointed out that the robe was not quite perfect, for it was missing its collar. And the angel revealed that the celestial robes of the two rabbis would be even finer than that one.

At the end of Yom Kippur, when they had recovered their strength, the two rabbis undertook to journey to Ashkelon, for they wanted to meet this Joseph. When they reached the city they were made welcome by every sage, each of whom asked them to share his hospitality. But they refused every one, saying that they would only stay with Joseph the Gardener. This surprised the rabbis of Ashkelon, who knew nothing of this Joseph. It was one of the servants of the rabbis who knew where he could be found, and he took Rabbi Eleazar and Rabbi Joshua to see him, for he lived outside the city.

When they arrived they found Joseph bent over in his garden, picking herbs. They greeted him, and he returned their greetings and asked how he could be of help. The rabbis asked if he would permit them to stay with him that night, and Joseph said he would be greatly honored, but he was a very poor man who could offer them nothing more than two loaves of bread. The rabbis assured him that would be sufficient, and so they remained as his guests.

That night the two rabbis engaged Joseph in conversation. They asked about his life, and he told them that his father had been wealthy, but that he had lost his inheritance in a short time and had been driven out of town when the people learned he had nothing left. Then he said, "I came to the city of Ashkelon and found this plot of land outside the city, where I have planted my small garden. And this garden sustains me. For out of what I receive from its fruits, I retain half for myself and give the rest to charity."

When the rabbis heard this, they recognized that Joseph the Gardener was indeed one of the righteous, worthy of that shining robe. Then they told him of that celestial garment. And when Joseph learned that such a blessing awaited him, his soul was filled with such joy that it leaped from his body in the very presence of the two sages, and at that very moment the angel appeared, bearing the shining robe. But this time the robe was complete, and even the collar could be seen. For Joseph the Gardener was one of the blessed ones, along with Moses, who died by the kiss of the *Shekhinah*. And at the moment of his death, the soul of Joseph put on that shining robe and was equal in his glory to the angel, who led him directly to Paradise. And Rabbi

Eleazar and Rabbi Joshua knew they had been in the presence of one of the hidden saints, who had now taken leave of the world.

□ Tunisia: c. Eleventh Century

❦❧❦❧❦❧❦❧❦❧ 68 ❧❦❧❦❧❦❧❦❧❦

THE EVIL ANGEL

The head of a yeshivah had a daughter who was modest and virtuous, and he sought to find a suitable match for her. Now among the students at his yeshivah was a young scholar who was filled with the fear of heaven. He devoted himself to the study of Torah day and night; he even awoke at midnight to continue his studies. The head of the yeshivah realized that this young man, who came from a fine family, would make an ideal son-in-law.

He proposed the match to the young man's family, and they were delighted to approve it, as was the young man himself, who had the highest respect for the *rosh yeshivah*. A fine wedding was held, and after the wedding the head of the yeshivah made it possible for the groom to devote himself completely to the Torah. So it was that in time the young man became a master of the Torah and achieved a high level of holiness.

One night, while the young man was alone in the House of Study, a light suddenly filled the room, and when he looked up he saw an angelic presence. The angel explained that it had descended from on high to teach him the Torah of the angels. And before it departed at dawn, the angel revealed secrets of the Torah that the young man had never even imagined.

Now the young man knew that an angel sometimes descends to this world to serve as a *maggid*, an angelic teacher. This had happened with Joseph Caro and a handful of other great sages, and the young man was thrilled that such an angel should seek him out. At the same time, he was very modest and dared not reveal such a thing to anyone, not even to his wife or his father-in-law.

After that the angel returned to the young student only late at night, when he was alone in the House of Study. There the angel continued to reveal mysteries that are only known on high.

Then one night the student asked the angel a question, and the angel refused to reply. What the young man wanted to know, the angel said, could force the coming of the Messiah. Now that is what the student longed for more than anything else, and night after night he begged the *maggid* to share this powerful secret, but the angel continued to refuse.

The young man tried every way he could think of to extract this secret from the angel, but without success. At last the angel agreed to reveal it if he would first obey a single request. The young man was ready to do anything, until he learned that the angel wanted him to commit a sin.

The young man was thrown into great confusion. He struggled with himself and told the angel that he would have to think the matter over. In the following days he continued to resist the sin, but at the same time his longing to know the secret grew even greater. At last he confided his confusion to his wife, who could barely believe what her husband told her and was appalled by the sin that the angel had called on him to commit.

She, in turn, went to her father and asked for his help. He was shocked at what she told him and saw that his son-in-law was in great danger. He went to see the young man at once and told him that he knew his secret. Then the *rosh yeshivah* explained that there are two kinds of angels, those from the Side of Holiness and those from the *Sitre Ahre*, the Other Side. How could they be distinguished? By the appearance of the Name of God on their foreheads. For God's Name is written on the forehead of every kind of angel, but in the case of the angels from the side of holiness, the Name burns like a white flame, while on the angels from the Other Side it is inscribed in a black flame. He asked the young man which kind of angel it was, but the young man was not certain, for he had not dared to look at the angel's face.

Then the head of the yeshivah told his son-in-law that the next time the angel came to him, he must find out the truth at once. And if it was an evil angel who had approached him—and surely it must be, for what other angel would call upon him to commit a sin?—he was in grave danger. He gave the young man a small round mirror and told him to be sure to keep it with him at all times. And should he discover that it was indeed an evil angel, he must hold up the mirror before the angel at once.

Now the next time the angel came to visit, the young man looked carefully at its forehead, and he saw that the Name of God did glow darkly there, confirming that he had been led astray by an evil angel. The angel realized at once that the young man had perceived its true identity, and it was prepared to slay him, but the young man pulled out the mirror and held it before the angel's face. And when the angel saw its image reflected in that mirror, it was forced to confront its own evil nature, and in that instant it ceased to exist.

So it was that the young yeshivah student was saved from the evil angel, and he lived a long life filled with a love of Torah that he never lost. And never again did the forces of evil seek to seduce him with forbidden knowledge.

□   Eastern Europe: Nineteenth Century

69

THE YOUNG MAN WITHOUT A SOUL

There once was a young man possessed of great powers whose name was Aaron. He had been born with the knowledge of these powers, but he kept them secret from everyone. Now his father, Samuel, had a mill, and one day, when Aaron was left in charge of the mill, a lion came and devoured their trusty mule. This made Aaron so angry that he pronounced a holy name, causing the lion to become his slave, as meek as a lamb. He harnessed the lion in the place of the mule, to turn the grinding stones. But when Aaron's father returned and saw the harnessed lion, he exclaimed: "What have you done? You have humiliated the lion and broken his will! God made him to be a king, walking erect, and you have forced him to become a slave. For this you must go into exile and wander for three years before you return."

So it was that Aaron left his native land and wandered until he came

to the port of Joppa, where he boarded a ship and set sail for the city of
Gaeta. Here Aaron disembarked on a Friday afternoon and wandered
through the city until he reached the synagogue. He joined the *minyan*
there, and afterward a Sephardic Jew befriended him and invited him
to his home. But when the meal was served, Aaron saw that the man
did not eat, even though it was the Sabbath. He asked him why he
abstained on God's day of delight, and the man said: "Forgive me for
grieving on the Sabbath, but I cannot help myself, for I have heard
nothing from my son in more than a year, and I do not know if he is
dead or alive."

Aaron then said to him: "Let us observe the Sabbath properly, and
then we shall go together through the streets and lanes in which he
lived and see what we can learn." This greatly surprised the man, and
after the Sabbath they set out together. They visited friends of his son
and learned that the boy had last been seen entering a house nearby
and was never seen again. Aaron and the boy's father went to the
house and were met by a woman whom Aaron, with his powers,
recognized at once as a sorceress. The woman claimed to know nothing about the young man, and they were ready to leave when one of
the woman's mules, tied up behind the house, began to cry out. And
Aaron, who had always understood the language of the animals, realized that the mule was the very boy for whom they were searching.
The witch had cast a spell on him.

"Let us hurry to the back of the house," Aaron said to the woman,
"for perhaps someone is trying to steal your mule." And there they
found a dozen mules tied up. And when the one who was braying saw
the father, it began to kick and pull at its tether. Aaron asked the
woman if she might sell the mule, for he liked its spirit. The woman
replied that the price would be very high, and Aaron agreed at once to
pay it. He handed her a leather pouch and said: "Open it and take as
much as you like." The sorceress was overcome with greed and
reached in and filled her fist with gold coins, but when she tried to pull
her hand out, she could not. The more she tried, the tighter the pouch
seemed to grow around her hand, like the jaws of a beast. Finally, she
began to panic and screamed for him to pull it off. Then he looked in
her eyes and said: "If you ever want to pull your hand free of the Jaws
of Death—for that is what has you in its grip—free the boy whom you
have turned into a mule. The witch glowered at him, but by then half
her arm was inside the pouch, so she pronounced a spell. And suddenly the boy stood among them, while the mule was nowhere to be
seen.

Father and son embraced, but the witch still shrieked from pain as the jaws inched up her arm. And when Aaron saw this, he said: "What other evil deeds have you done? Set free all these mules or the jaws will swallow your whole body!" This time the witch did not hesitate but pronounced a series of spells, and suddenly there were a dozen young men and women weeping among them, giving thanks. But nevertheless the witch was suddenly pulled inside the pouch. Her evil was too great for her to escape. She vanished, leaving nothing behind but the echo of her last long shriek. For she had been devoured by the Jaws of Death.

Now when these events became known, the people of the town all recognized Aaron as a great master and begged him to live among them. He agreed to remain there, and he was given great honor by everyone. Not long afterward, on the Sabbath, an esteemed young man arose to read the prayers. He chanted with a pleasing voice, but Aaron noticed that when he reached the Name of God in the prayers, he did not pronounce it. And Aaron realized at once that the boy must not be one of the living, but was one of the living dead. For the dead are not allowed to pronounce God's Name.

Then Aaron stood up and called out: "Stop. For the dead are not permitted to pray before God." Of course, everyone was astonished by this, but they were even more surprised when the young man broke into sobs and confessed that it was true—that he was not alive. Then Aaron spoke to him gently and asked him to explain how this strange thing had come to pass. And the boy told them his tale. He had been invited on a journey by a family friend, whose name was Ahimaaz. Ahimaaz had vowed to the boy's parents that he would bring him back safely. Then the two companions had journeyed to Jerusalem. They had traveled together throughout the length and breadth of the Holy Land, and on the night before their departure when they went to say goodbye to the Elders, one of the old men wept. When Ahimaaz asked why, the man revealed that God had decreed that the boy was shortly to die before he could return to his home. When Ahimaaz heard this, he rent his clothes and hair: "How can I return to this boy's house if he is not with me? Have I not made a vow before God that I would do so?"

Seeing his grief, this Elder wrote out the Name of God on a slip of parchment, made an incision in the boy's right arm, and inserted the Name there. Not long afterward, as the companions were walking up the plank to board a ship for home, the boy slipped off and fell into the water. When they pulled him out, the living spirit had departed from his body, yet he still remained alive. He told no one of this, not even Ahimaaz, who accompanied him back to the home of his parents. And never did Ahimaaz learn how soon the prophecy of the Elder had been fulfilled.

Then Aaron told the boy it was time to take out the parchment that had kept him alive without a soul. This the boy was more than willing to let them do, for nothing was more terrible than to be without a soul. And when the parchment was removed, he slumped down dead. Aaron saw to it that the young man received an honorable burial and that his father was informed of his death. Then Aaron set out to return to his own father, for three years had passed, and it was time for him to go home. When he came back, he told his father of all that had happened to him on his journey. And when his father learned how he had saved one young man from a witch and redeemed another from the curse of living without a soul, he rejoiced in the wisdom of his son.

□   Italy: Eleventh Century

❦❦❦❦❦ 70 ❦❦❦❦❦

ASENATH'S DOVE

Rabbi Samuel Barzani of Kurdistan had a daughter, Asenath, whose knowledge of the Torah and even of the Kabbalah was said to be as great as his own. She was renowned for performing wonders, and she had a pet dove as white as the dove of Noah. She did not keep this dove in a cage, but let it make its nest on a branch outside the door. Once this dove was shot by a hunter, and when some children told him it was Asenath's dove, he took the lifeless dove to her at once and begged for her forgiveness. Asenath carried the dove inside the house and closed the door. A few moments later the man, standing outside, heard the fluttering of a bird within. A moment later Asenath opened the door, and the dove flew out of the house into its nest.

After that it was whispered among the people that the spirit of her father, Rabbi Samuel, rested upon her, and that Asenath knew the secret of the Name. Her blessing was often sought out by women wanting to conceive. So too was she sought out by those who were sick. And it was said that her touch had a healing power, especially in the case of children.

Now Asenath was not only wise, but also beautiful. Once, when she was spreading laundry on the roof, a Gentile saw her and lusted after her. At midnight he started to climb upon the roof, filled with evil thoughts. At that moment the dove cried out, and when Asenath heard it she looked up and and saw the man outside her window. At that instant she pronounced a holy name, and he found himself hanging from the beams of the roof, frozen in place.

In the morning people gathered to see the strange sight, but none of them could remove him from that place. So it was that he hung there for days, until the governor came to see for himself. The man begged the governor to have her set him free, and the governor asked Asenath to do so, but she refused, saying: "Did he only intend to steal from my house, I would have done nothing. But he intended to do an evil deed to me." Then the governor swore that if she set him free, he would be properly punished. So Asenath freed him, and soon after that he was hung from a tree.

□   Kurdistan: Seventeenth Century

࿔࿔࿔࿔࿔   71   ࿔࿔࿔࿔࿔

THE TALE OF THE KIDDUSH CUP

Rabbi Hayim Pinto, the kabbalist, was a master of miracles who liked to invite the poor to his seder. One year, on the eve of Passover, Rabbi Hayim sent his students to every corner of the city to look for poor people, and they found a Jew who seemed very downcast sitting under a tree. They invited him to the rabbi's seder. But he refused to come, saying: "For you it is the holiday of Pesach, but for me it is a time of mourning."

The students went back to Rabbi Hayim Pinto and asked for advice, but all the rabbi would say was, "If you can't convince him to come here, whisper this word in his ear"—and he whispered it to each of his students. They ventured forth and again asked the Jew to come with them. But still he refused, so they whispered the word that the rabbi had told them. And when the man heard it his eyes opened wide, and he agreed to accompany them at once.

When that Jew arrived at the rabbi's house, he asked: "How is it, Rabbi, that you knew the name of the ship that brought about my misfortune?" And Rabbi Pinto replied: "Join our seder and you will understand how it became known to me."

When they were all seated, Rabbi Pinto introduced the guest and asked him to tell the others his story. This he did: "I was born in the city of Marrakesh, and I traveled to Spain and worked until I had become quite wealthy. I wanted to return to my native town, and with all that I had saved I bought precious jewels. So too did I carry the jewels of a widow, to bring to her daughter as a wedding gift. I carried everything in a wooden case. But the case was lost at sea when a storm sank the ship in which I was traveling. Somehow I managed to grab hold of a plank and reached the shores of this city. I know that I am fortunate to be alive. But after all these years, I have nothing. So too do I grieve because I cannot fulfill my mission for the widow."

Rabbi Hayim Pinto said: "Be happy and watch." And the rabbi took the holy kiddush cup and pronounced a holy name that invoked Rahab, the Prince of the Sea, and he called upon Rahab for help in finding what had been lost. All at once the kiddush cup began to grow larger and larger, and the wine in it was transformed into the waves of the sea. One after another the waves rose and fell, and eventually they cast up a small wooden case that floated on the surface. The guest, who could hardly contain himself, cried out: "Master, that is my case!" And Rabbi Pinto said: "Take it out." So the man reached into the enormous cup and took out the wooden case and set it on the table. At that instant the cup returned to its original shape, and the waters in it became wine once more. Then everyone watched in awe as the man opened the case and saw that nothing was missing. So it was that he celebrated the seder with them in great joy. And soon afterward he returned to his native town. There he delivered the jewels to the widow's daughter and joined in the celebration of her wedding.

□   Syria: Oral Tradition

72

THE MIRACLE IN THE SUKKAH

Three Hasidim came to the house of the Samaritan sage Abraham Tsedaka to dine in his sukkah, which was inside the house, according to the Samaritan tradition, rather than outside it. The house was filled with multicolored fruit—oranges, dates, olives, and pomegranates—for the festival.

After they had dined, one of the Hasidim said: "Why do the Samaritans built their sukkahs indoors rather than outdoors?" Abraham replied: "Throughout the ages we have been persecuted because of our beliefs, and in order to protect ourselves and our families we were forced to build our sukkahs indoors. Over time this has become our tradition, and that is why we continue to do it this way."

"Yes," said the Hasid, "but is it not true that the Divine Presence is less present in an indoor sukkah than in an outdoor one?" "No," said Abraham, "about this you are wrong. Let me show you. I will sing a song about Sukkot, and after that I will recite the *Shema*. And when I finish, the fruit in this room will begin to dance. But first, please close the windows, so that you don't say afterward that the dancing was caused by the wind."

This they did, and then Abraham sang the song and recited the prayer. And just as he finished, all of the fruit in the room began to leap and dance, much to the amazement of the Hasidim. And it continued to do so until Abraham told it to stop.

□ Israel: Oral Tradition

RABBI NAFTALI'S TRANCE

Among the followers of Rabbi Naftali Katz in the city of Posen was a rich man who was determined to find a righteous groom for his daughter. He asked Rabbi Naftali to select one of his finest students for her, and this the rabbi did. The rich man gave the student a large dowry and a new wardrobe, and the wedding soon took place.

Then it happened that a short time after the wedding the groom abandoned his bride and disappeared. For thirteen years no one heard anything from him. All this time the rich man's daughter could not remarry, for they had not been properly divorced.

As time passed, the rich man and his daughter became increasingly bitter, and they went to Rabbi Naftali every day, begging him to find the whereabouts of the missing groom. But Rabbi Naftali always put them off. Not until the rich man broke down crying, did the rabbi tell him that he would do something to save his daughter.

After that Rabbi Naftali brought three of his finest students into his study, and he said: "Know that I need your assistance. I am going to search for the groom who has vanished, to try to find where he is in this world. While I am sitting in my chair, sleep will appear to come over me. Then you should watch me carefully. If something about my appearance should change, you should awaken me at once. That way my spirit will be restored to me."

So Rabbi Naftali closed his eyes and went into a trance. After half an hour the students noticed that he had grown very pale. They became worried and awakened him, as he had told them to do. When he had recovered, he said to them: "I did not find him, so I will have to search for him elsewhere. Keep watch as before, and be sure not to give up until you have awakened me, even if it takes great effort."

Then Rabbi Naftali went back into the trance, and this time it lasted an hour before he became pale and his head slumped on his chest. The students rushed to awaken him, but at first he did not respond. They kept trying, as he had told them to do, and in the end they succeeded in bringing him out of the trance. Afterward he told them that he had found the groom at last.

Then Rabbi Naftali called in the rich man and his daughter and said: "You will find the missing groom in an inn outside the city of Vienna. Travel there at once with a scribe and two witnesses. In the inn you will see three soldiers sitting together. The groom will be the one in the middle. When you find him, demand that he give your daughter a bill of divorce. But do not think it will be easy to get him to agree."

The rich man and his daughter hired a carriage at once and set out to Vienna with the scribe and witnesses. Outside the city they found the inn the rabbi had named and went inside. And there, sitting in one corner, they saw three soldiers. They soon recognized the one sitting in the middle as the missing groom, although he had changed very much since they had last seen him. And they noticed as well that each of the soldiers sitting next to him had a terrible countenance. When the daughter saw the one who had abandoned her, she screamed and fainted. Then the rich man demanded, in the strongest terms, that the vile groom sign the bill of divorce at once. But the groom refused, and he could not be swayed. So the rich man told the two soldiers the whole story of how he had abandoned his wife, and they agreed with him that the groom must give his wife the divorce. But the groom continued to refuse their request. At last one of the soldiers stood up, drew his sword, and cut off the young man's head. All of them gasped at the sight. Then the soldier said: "Now you won't need a divorce, because, as you see, he is dead."

When the rich man recovered from the shock, he asked the soldiers if he might take the body of the groom with him to Posen to prove that the groom was dead. But they refused, telling him that the witnesses would testify to all they had seen. The witnesses confirmed this, and the rich man and his daughter returned to Posen at once. They went directly to the home of Rabbi Naftali Katz and told him everything. And Rabbi Naftali said: "I want you to know that the man you saw was not in this world anymore. Not long after he left you, he encountered thieves who threatened to kill him unless he agreed to join them. This he did, and in time he himself murdered several people. One day he fought with his fellow thieves, and they killed him. Since then his soul has been punished in the bottom pit of Gehenna. I was able to raise him from the dead to meet you in that inn, accompanied by two avenging angels."

Then Rabbi Naftali released the daughter so that she could re-marry, and she soon found another to wed. And all this was accomplished through the powers of Rabbi Naftali Katz.

□ Eastern Europe: Nineteenth Century

74

INTERPRETING THE ZOHAR

It was the custom of the Jews of Haleb in Syria to read the book of the Zohar from beginning to end during the winter nights. One of the Jews came upon a passage that was very difficult for him to compre-hend. He read it over many times, but still he could not understand it. He became very upset and cried and fasted. Then one night he had a dream in which he was told: "Rabbi Rabbah bar bar Hannah sits at midnight in the House of Study in Haleb. Go there and he will explain that difficult passage to you."

When he awoke, the Jew was very happy to have received this dream, and the next day he went to the House of Study a little before midnight. It was empty except for one person studying in a corner by the light of a candle. He approached the man and saw that it was Rabbi Mordecai Abbadi. So he asked the rabbi to explain the difficult passage in the Zohar to him. The rabbi was very surprised, and he asked the man how he knew that he would be there at that time. And the man said: "I was told in a dream to come here, and that Rabbah bar bar Hannah would explain this passage to me. And since I came here and found you, I have no doubt that you are the reincarnation of Rabbah bar bar Hannah."

Rabbi Mordecai told the man: "I am willing to explain this passage to you on one condition—that you keep this incident secret and not tell anyone about it as long as I live." The man promised, so Rabbi Mor-decai Abbadi revealed the meaning of the difficult passage, which contained great mysteries. Afterward the man returned home, and he kept this matter secret for many years. Only after the death of Rabbi Mordecai did he tell this story to others.

□ Syria: Oral Tradition

&⟡&⟡&⟡&⟡&⟡ 75 ⟡&⟡&⟡&⟡&⟡&

THE SECRETS OF KABBALAH

There was a scholar in one of the congregations of Israel in Holland who became famous for being a master of the Zohar. Many students came to him from faraway places to study the Kabbalah. And if it happened that the rabbi did not know the answer to one of their questions, he would pronounce a certain holy name and a spirit would descend from heaven and reveal the meaning of the mystery. And the students marveled at the rabbi's knowledge of the powers that could be called forth.

One day the rabbi became tired while studying and fell asleep on his open book. Around him sat four of his best students, and they continued to delve into the secrets of Kabbalah. Before long they reached a passage they could not decipher, which mattered greatly to them. They didn't want to wake the holy rabbi, so they decided to pronounce the holy name themselves. One of them dared to say it, and the spirit descended from on high and replied to all of their questions.

Then it was time to pronounce the holy name that made it possible to send the spirit back. But none of them remembered what it was. And the spirit told them that if they did not pronounce the name at once, their lives were as good as lost. The appalling danger they had brought on themselves now became clear to the students, and in their desperation they woke the rabbi and quickly revealed their dilemma. The instant he understood, the rabbi pronounced the name that sent the angel back to the place from whence it came, and the lives of the students were spared.

At first they breathed a great sigh of relief, but then they saw that the rabbi was deeply angry with them for having used the holy name without his permission. In his anger the rabbi cursed the students to wander in exile for all the days of their lives, and the words of the rabbi singed them as if the mark of Cain had been burned into their foreheads. And they knew that they would never escape that curse.

Of the four, one of them died in his sleep not long after this and became a wandering soul, circling the lost worlds. One of them ran away and boarded a ship that sailed endlessly around the seas. It was said that he never set foot on land again. The third turned his back on his faith and followed a false messiah who led him further and further away from the truth. And the fourth became a wandering rabbi, restlessly traveling through the countryside of Holland, seeking out Jews who lived in isolated villages and towns.

The name of this wandering rabbi was Rabbi Moshe Pinto, and he was often called upon by the Jews of the towns he passed through to remain as their rabbi. They gave him a good bed and fed him, but he never stayed in one place for very long. For he knew that it had been decreed for him to wander, and wander he did until the day he died.

□   Holland: Nineteenth Century

76

THE FLYING LETTERS

This story is told about two Polish towns separated by many miles. The inhabitants of one town were very wealthy, but they also were very sinful. They had a beautiful synagogue with a well-crafted wooden Ark. And in that Ark was an ancient scroll of the Torah. No one knew just how old it was. Now the sins of these inhabitants were hidden from the eyes of men, but God looked into their hearts. And the letters of the Torah shuddered at being so close to sin.

The inhabitants of the other town were very poor. They had a small synagogue, but the Ark was empty, for they were too poor to buy the parchment or pay for the services of the scribe who writes the Torah. Yet little by little they saved up, and at last they sent for a scribe, who connected the portions of the parchment into a scroll and planned to start writing the next day.

That midnight, the letters of the Torah in the evil town took flight, forming a flock of letters that flew in the moonlight from the evil town to the righteous one. Before long the scribe, who slept in a room connected to the synagogue, was awakened by a bright glow. He stared in amazement as the flock of flying letters streamed in the window and flew to the empty scroll, each letter taking its place among the letters of the Torah.

The scribe knew at once that he was witnessing a great miracle, and when every letter was in place, he looked at that Torah and saw that it was complete, from the creation to the death of Moses. Then he hurried out into the night to tell the others. Soon a crowd had assembled inside the synagogue, where they all saw the miraculous Torah, which became known as "the Torah of the Flying Letters." The members of the congregation never failed to touch that Torah with their *tallises* when the Torah was carried around the synagogue, for it was said to have great healing powers. And the inhabitants of that town never forgot the miracle of that Torah, and they treasured it as their most precious possession.

□ Eastern Europe: Oral Tradition

㋡㋡㋡㋡㋡ **77** ㋡㋡㋡㋡㋡

THE CURSE

Among the Karaites of Poland there was a doctor whose name was Ezra. This doctor had cured the Polish King Kazimir of a terrible disease, and in return the king had given him a portion of land adjoining the palace, with a mansion on it in which the king himself had lived when he was a prince. This fortunate doctor had one child, a daughter, whose name was Esther, and like Esther the queen she was blessed with charm and beauty. Of course, her father adored her and was very proud of her in every respect.

Even before Esther was old enough to be married, handsome and wealthy men sought to make her their bride. But she always found flaws in every one. Her father tolerated this at first, but as the years passed and she did not marry, he began to worry, for until she was wed his happiness would not be complete. But Esther passed all the days of her youth rejecting those who sought her hand, and when those days had passed, no suitors appeared. Thus it happened that she never married and never gave birth.

Her father could not understand why his daughter had proven to be so impossible to please. And as he grew old, he began to resent that no Karaite offspring would come from his line at a time when his people were very few. Thus it happened that on his deathbed the old doctor's love for his daughter suddenly turned to hatred, and the last words he spoke were a curse on her. He told her that because she didn't want life, death would avoid her, and she would be deprived of a place not only in this world, but in the next.

No sooner had he spoken these words than the old doctor took leave of his soul. And at that very moment a great fire rose up from the deep, from Sheol, and engulfed the mansion until nothing remained of it but ashes. And these same flames enchanted Esther and imprisoned her as if with iron chains, so that she remained bound in that place of ashes, neither dead nor alive, her beautiful hair turned to serpents, her heart turned to stone. And all that hints of her presence there is an occasional sigh carried in the wind, and when it is heard by those who live nearby, they recall her sad tale among themselves.

□   Eastern Europe: Nineteenth Century

࿇࿇࿇࿇࿇࿇࿇࿇ 78 ࿇࿇࿇࿇࿇࿇࿇࿇

The Miracle of the Ring

In one of the cities of Persia lived a wealthy man who had an only son. When this man was on his deathbed he called his son to him, gave him a ring, and said: "Take this ring and don't show it to anyone. When I die, bury me yourself, and don't bring anyone along with you. And place this ring in my hand."

When the man died, the son did as his father had asked, although he did not know the reason for the strange request. But he greatly loved and respected his father, and he did not hesitate to fulfill his last request.

Meanwhile, in another city, there was a beautiful girl who was of the age to marry, but she was unable to find a groom whom she wished to wed. Then one night, in a dream, an old man came to her and told her that he knew of the right groom for her, who was his son. The girl remembered this dream very clearly when she woke up, and she told it to her father, but he dismissed the dream.

The next night again the old man appeared and repeated the things he had said the night before. But in the morning, when the girl told her family about the second dream, no one paid any attention to it.

Then, on the third night, the old man again came to the girl in a dream and said: "Leave your house and travel to my city." And he told her the name of the city. Then he said: "And so that you will know that what I have told you is true, here is my ring. Show it to my son when you find him, and he will know that all you say is true." At this point the girl awoke, and to her astonishment she found that very same ring the old man had given her in the dream still in her hand.

Then the girl hurried to her family and told them of the dream and showed them the ring. And at last they did believe her, for the miracle of the ring convinced them. Then her father gave her a dowry of silver and golden vessels and many diamonds, and sent her with a trusted servant to the city the old man had mentioned in the dream.

When the girl reached the city, she disguised herself as a man and bid farewell to the trusted servant. Then she sold one of the diamonds she had received from her father, and she rented a store. When customers came into the shop, she showed them the silver and golden vessels her father had given her, and she always showed the ring that she had received in the dream. But no one ever recognized it.

After three months the girl began to grow worried that she had not yet met the destined young man. So, still disguised as a man, she went to an agent and said that she wanted to sell the shop and the things in it, and she asked if he knew of a buyer. He told her of a wealthy young man who might be interested and set an appointment. The next day the young man came into the shop, and the moment the girl saw him she knew that he must be the one. But this time she did not show the ring, and she only discussed the details of the sale. When these had been completed, the young man invited her to have dinner at his home, assuming that she was a young man of his own age. And the disguised girl readily agreed to come.

On the day of the dinner, the girl arrived at the young man's house, still dressed as a man. The young man's mother served them a fine dinner, and they spent most of the time discussing matters relating to the shop. After dinner the girl said: "Although you are clearly a wealthy man, I have something that cannot be bought for all the money in the world." The young man was very curious to know what this was, and he begged her to show it to him. And that is when she took out the ring.

Now when the young man saw the ring of his father, he almost fainted. His mother was also amazed, for she recognized the ring of her husband. They asked the disguised girl where she had gotten it, and she told them of the three dreams. The young man could not understand at all, since he believed he was speaking to a man. Then the young woman let down her hair, and when the young man saw how beautiful she was, he was very, very happy, for the ring proved that what she had said was true.

So it was that the young man married the girl according to the laws of Moses and Israel, and they lived together in happiness and joy. And all of this came to pass because the soul of the young man's father had brought them together.

□   Persia: Oral Tradition

༄༅༆༄༅༆༄༅༆༄༅༆ 79 ༄༅༆༄༅༆༄༅༆༄༅༆

THE ANGEL'S DAUGHTER

There once was a young man who decided that he would only marry the daughter of an angel. His widowed mother and friends tried to talk him out of this, but they could not. He would not consider any other match. And every day he prayed that he might be blessed with such a wife.

One night Elijah the Prophet came to him in a dream in the form of an old man and told him that God had heard his prayer and that he would be able to marry an angel's daughter, but only on the condition that he would never question anything she did. The next day, early in the morning, there was a knock at the door, and a beautiful and pleasant girl entered the house, and indeed she was the daughter of an angel.

The boy and his mother quickly accepted the lovely girl, and the boy soon married her. For the first year of their marriage they were very happy, and at the end of that year the girl gave birth to her first child, a son. But on the eighth day, after the circumcision, the angel's daughter carried the child into the forest and came home alone. The young man and his mother were very distressed at this, but since the young man had been warned by Elijah not to question her acts, they remained silent.

A year later the angel's daughter gave birth to her second child, also a son, and on the eighth day she repeated the strange act. So it was as well with their third son, born in the third year. Each time the young man could barely restrain himself, but he remembered how blessed he was to have such a wife, and he remembered the warning of Elijah, and therefore he said nothing. So too did his mother follow her son's wishes and remain silent. In time the old woman died, and at her funeral the angel's daughter walked at the head of the procession holding a thick stick in one hand and one shoe in the other. No one understood what this meant, and everyone thought she was crazy.

When they returned home after the funeral, the son was in a fury. He shouted at his wife, demanding to know the reason for her behavior. He told her that he had accepted the strange disappearance of their sons because no one else had known of them, but now she had brought shame on him in front of everyone. His wife warned him that he was not to question her acts and would regret it, but he insisted that she tell him the meaning of all that she had done.

Then the angel's daughter explained to him that their sons had not been destined for life in this world, but for life in heaven as angels. Even now they were serving as guardian angels who protected them in all that they did. As for her actions at the funeral, his mother had once chased a beggar away with the same stick, and she had once refused to help an orphan who begged for a pair of shoes. She had carried these objects at the funeral to remind those in heaven that these were her only evil actions, and that she had also performed many good deeds. And as a result, his mother's soul had been accepted into the World to Come.

When the young man heard these explanations, he understood that his wife had only done these things for the best, and he regretted his anger. But then it was too late: the angel's daughter vanished before his eyes, and he never saw her again all the days of his life.

□ Buhara: Oral Tradition

80

THE BRIDEGROOM AND THE ANGEL OF DEATH

There once was a righteous man named Reuben who had but one son, whom he had begotten after his eightieth year. During Reuben's long life he had committed a sin but once. On that occasion he came into the synagogue and found another man sitting in his place. He rebuked him, and the man immediately went away and sat by the door weeping bitterly. When his tears reached the Throne of Glory, God took pity on his plight. Therefore, he sent the Angel of Death to take Reuben's son, who was about to be wed.

When the Angel of Death came into his house, Reuben recognized him at once and said: "Why have you come here? Has the time come for me to accompany you?" "No," replied the angel, "God has sent me to take your son's life." "Why? He has not yet even stood beneath the marriage canopy and known his hour of joy." "Because you rebuked the poor man who sat in your place," the angel replied. And Reuben understood that his sin had counted greatly against him, and that the punishment was much worse than if his own life were sought.

Reuben pleaded with the angel to give his son thirty days in which he might marry and taste a little joy before his life was snatched away. And because of Reuben's merits, the angel agreed to wait that long before he returned to take his son's soul.

Now God was very angry with the Angel of Death for postponing the death of Reuben's son, and He rebuked the angel for disobeying. So the angel decided to revenge himself when the time came to take Reuben's son by taking him with the same fourfold anger that the Lord had shown against the angel. When twenty-nine days had passed, and one day remained before the wedding was to take place, the Prophet Elijah came to Reuben's door. The young man, who opened the door, trembled when he saw him and asked to know why he had come. Then Elijah said: "Know, my son, that tomorrow the Angel of Death will come to take your soul." The young man grieved greatly to learn this, since that was also to be the day of his wedding.

Then the young man pleaded with Elijah and asked if there was anything he could do to save himself. Elijah said: "When you are standing beneath the marriage canopy, you will notice a poor man dressed in dirty and torn clothes. Give honor to him, for that is how the Angel of Death will disguise himself, and perhaps he will have mercy upon you."

The next day, as the bridegroom stood with his bride beneath the wedding canopy, he saw the poor man that Elijah had described sitting beside the door. He went over to him and said: "Master, I wish to do you honor. Come, sit in the distinguished place before the Ark." To which the old man replied: "May He to whom honor is due have compassion upon you." He then went and sat by the canopy, with the young man before him. And the father of the young man, who knew that the Angel of Death was due to come that day, recognized him and prostrated himself before him and sobbed and pleaded for the life of his child, entreating the angel to take his life instead.

Then the Angel of Death clothed himself with his garments of cruelty, anger, wrath, and severity, unsheathed his sword, and put his foot upon the old man's neck, in order to slay him. At this the father's limbs trembled and shook, and he stood up and fled from the angel, saying: "Go ahead, take him for whom you have been sent, for I cannot bear thee." Now when the bridegroom's old mother saw this, she fell down and entreated the angel to spare her son and to take her life instead. And while she was sobbing and weeping, the Angel of Death again donned his garments of cruelty, so that he appeared like a warrior going forth to battle. He unsheathed his sword and placed his foot upon her neck to slay her, but she fled from him in terror and said: "Spare me. Take him for whom you have been sent. For I cannot bear to look upon you."

Now the bride, standing beneath the canopy, had witnessed all that had happened. She prostated herself before the Angel of Death and said: "I entreat you to spare the life of my bridegroom and to take my life instead. And again the angel clothed himself in his terrible garments, so that all who saw him shrank away in terror. He drew his sword and placed his foot upon her neck. Yet she did not run away, as had the others, but said: "Finish the bidding of the King of Kings, who has sent you." And when the angel saw that she was not afraid to die for her groom, a tear of mercy fell upon her from his eye.

Then God, who had witnessed all that had taken place, said: "If this cruel one has mercy upon them, shall I, who am called the God of

Mercy, not have compassion?" And God thereupon granted seventy more years to them both.

□   Yemen: Fourteenth Century

⌘⌘⌘⌘⌘⌘ 81 ⌘⌘⌘⌘⌘⌘

THE CAVE TO THE HOLY LAND

There once was a poor Hasid and his wife who lived in a small hut in the forest outside the city of Shebreshin. This Hasid was very poor, for all that he and his wife possessed were two skinny goats. With the milk of the goats the Hasid and his wife made butter and cheese, but the goats gave so little milk that they could hardly make a living.

Now every Sabbath the Hasid came to town to pray in the House of Prayer, and he always prayed that he might someday live in the land of milk and honey. For his fondest desire was to travel to the Holy Land, even though he was far too poor to go there.

One day the Hasid's wife went to milk the goats, but they were not there. Then she remembered that she had forgotten to tie them up, and she hurried to get her husband and together they searched for the goats in the forest. But even though they searched all day long, there was no sign of the goats, and when it began to grow dark they returned home with heavy hearts. For how would they make a living without their goats?

But later that evening the goats returned home by themselves, and they gave a lot of milk, much more than they usually did. So too was that milk far sweeter than it had ever been. And the Hasid's wife understood that the goats must have found a new place to graze, so she did not tie them up the next day either. And once more the goats were gone all day, but in the evening they returned on their own. So too was the milk they gave as sweet as it had been the day before.

Now when the Hasid sold that milk in the city, the people soon saw that it was not like any other. It cured anyone who was sick, and before long there were no more sick people in the city of Shebreshin.

After this the Hasid decided to follow the goats to see where they went. So he followed them into the forest, to a place where there were two overlapping trees, and there they disappeared. The Hasid hurried to that place and found that it concealed the entrance to a cave. He entered that cave and saw the goats before him, walking toward a dot of light that could be seen in the distance. And the Hasid followed after them.

Now it did not take the Hasid very long to discover that it was an enchanted cave, for on the way, black demons with red tongues of fire jumped out to frighten him, and he heard the sound of money falling from behind him and naked women beckoned him as he passed. But the Hasid kept walking forward. He didn't look to the left or right, for he had faith in God. And the powers of Satan that tried to obstruct his way were overcome one by one.

That is how the Hasid arrived at the other end of the cave. When he stepped outside it, he saw blue skies and a boy playing the flute, while his two goats grazed nearby. The boy approached the Hasid and said in Hebrew, "Are you new to our land?" The Hasid became afraid and his legs began to tremble, because he understood that he must be standing in the land of Israel. And the boy continued to speak and said, "I am also new in the area of Safed. Until now I walked with my goats in the mountains of Judah and Jerusalem."

And the Hasid fell to the ground and kissed the earth and gave thanks to God. Then he wrote a long letter to the Jews of his town and to all of the Jews in the Diaspora. He called upon them to join him in the Holy Land by means of that enchanted cave. He warned them about the obstacles of the cave and assured them that these were only illusions. Then he wrapped the letter in a fig leaf and tied it to the neck of one of the goats.

In the evening the goats came back home, but when the Hasid's wife saw that he was not with them, she became frightened. She was so worried about her husband that she did not notice the fig leaf on the neck of the goat. She waited one day, two days, three days, but still her husband did not come back. She was certain that robbers had slain him in the forest. Then she decided to move to the city of Shebreshin, for she could not bear to be alone. And since she was moving there, why did she need the goats? So she sold them to a butcher, and only after the goats had been butchered did they notice the fig leaf and find the letter inside it. They called the rabbi of the city at once, as well as the man's wife, and and when the rabbi read the letter out loud, they all started crying, for the goats could not be brought back from the dead, and they were the only ones who had known the way to the enchanted cave. And because the letter had been found too late, they could not go to the Holy Land.

The rabbi kept that letter for many years in the synagogue of Shebreshin until it was lost in the great fire. And they still speak of it to this day.

□   Poland: Oral Tradition

82

THE CAVE OF TEMPTATIONS

There was a Jewish farmer who had three sons. This farmer had a lease on a noble's land, where his sons often served as shepherds. Now one day everyone noticed that the milk of one of the goats was exceptionally delicious. So the oldest brother decided to see where the goat was grazing, and in this way he learned that the goat disappeared each day and only returned just as the sun was about to set, when it was time for all of the animals to return.

The oldest son was very curious about where the goat went. One day he followed it and saw it enter a cave. Although he thought he had explored every inch of that land, he had never seen that cave before. The next day he followed the goat back to the same cave, and this time he carried a torch. When he entered, he could still hear the bells of the goat echoing through the cave. On the first turn he came into a small cavern and saw something gleaming in the half light. He came closer and saw a pile of golden coins. He could barely believe his luck. He bent down and scooped up a handful of coins, but the moment he touched them, the gold coins disappeared, along with the cave itself, and the oldest son found himself back in a field, and there was no sign of the cave anywhere.

The oldest son returned home, confused about all that had taken place. When he told his brothers about it, the second brother offered to follow the goat. So the next day the second brother took a torch with him, and when he saw the goat run into the entrance of a cave, he followed it. He too saw the gold piled in the small cavern and leaned close to look at it. Yes, it was quite amazing, but the young man was no fool. He remembered what had happened to his brother. And he decided to continue following the goat, whose bells still echoed.

So it was that the young man turned the passage and found another small cavern. And in the light of the torch, he saw something that amazed him. There was someone sleeping in the cave. He came closer and saw that it was a beautiful woman curled up on the floor. When he came closer, the woman's eyes opened and she sat up, and he saw that she was naked. Her eyes, filled with desire, looked into his own. And without saying a single word, he came close to embrace her. And the instant he touched her, the woman vanished, as well as the cave. And the second brother found himself in a field. Nor was there any cave to be seen anywhere.

This brother, too, returned in confusion and told the others all that had happened to him. And when he heard these strange occurrences, the youngest brother decided that he too would follow the goat to see if he could learn any more about that mysterious cave.

So it was that the goat led the youngest brother to the cave, and he quickly followed it. He too encountered the gold coins and the beautiful woman. But he barely paused to look at the coins, lest they tempt him to touch them. Nor did he return the lascivious gaze of the naked woman. Instead, he hurried after the sound of the goat's bells, lest they grow faint.

In this way he was led through the third turning of the cave and found himself in another cavern. There he saw, much to his amazement, that a pulpit had been set up, and there was a man standing before it who was reading a book by the light of a torch. "Who are you, and what are you doing here?" he asked the man. "I come here to study where nothing can disturb me. Indeed, this is the first time that another has come here while I was studying. But perhaps you have come just in time, for I have been wrestling with a problem in the Talmud."

Now the youngest son was the brightest boy in his yeshivah, and many were the hours he had spent weighing one matter or another. So he gladly offered to discuss the point of the Law. But soon he saw that the issue the scholar had raised was a thorny one, indeed, one that might take months, or even years, to resolve. Just then he heard, very faintly, the sound of the goat's bells. For a moment he wrestled with himself; then he politely said goodbye to the scholar and hurried off after the goat.

At last the youngest son reached the other end of the cave. And as soon as he stepped out of the cave, he found himself in a beautiful

orchard. Trees with an abundance of fruit were to be seen everywhere, and wandering streams filled with fish. He knew at once that
he had reached the land of his dreams, a land of milk and honey. And
he understood that the goat had grazed on those sweet grasses, and
that is why its milk was so delicious.

Now that young man wanted to return through the cave, to bring
his family with him. But when he looked for the cave, he could not
find it, for it had disappeared. So he took the goat with him and made a
new life for himself. And he is still living there to this day.

□   Poland: Oral Tradition

83 THE HOLLOW OF THE SLING

There once was a yeshivah student who was betrothed to a young
woman in a nearby town. On the day of the wedding, as he sat alone in
the house, he looked out the window and saw a beautiful woman
passing by. She raised her eyes to his and then walked on. But that one
glance filled him with passion, and he made a wish that his own bride,
whom he had never met, would be as beautiful.

Later that day, as the bride and groom stood beneath the *huppah*, the
bridegroom looked up and saw the same woman who had passed by
his window. She was standing close to the canopy, so that he glimpsed
her several times during the ceremony. And she gazed shamelessly at
the bridegroom, who fell under her spell. And even as he was wed to
another, in truth he bound his soul to her.

That night, in the bridal chamber, the bridegroom found the other
woman waiting for him instead of the one he had wed. Greatly confused, he said to her: "How is it that you are here instead of my bride?"
And she replied: "It was I that you wed. Is that not true?" And all at
once the bridegroom became afraid, for he remembered how he had
bound himself to her. And he said: "Who are you? Where did you
come from?" She answered: "My name is Naamah. My mother's name
is Lilith."

"No!" he cried. And the student backed away from the demoness, for that is who she was. "Have you forgotten your craving for me?" she answered. And she dropped her gown. And when the student saw her, his desire returned tenfold, and he gave himself up to that daughter of demons.

Afterward, however, the student was filled with fear and remorse. What had he done? Then, as he looked around, he saw that the mirror on the wall was covered, as was done at the time of Shiva, when someone had died, but never for a bride and groom!

Quaking with fear, he asked: "Where are we?" And she replied: "This is the Palace of Illusion, although it has many other names. You may know it as 'the Hollow of the Sling.'" And the student jumped back in terror. For that was the very pit of hell. And he saw that his soul was imperiled, and without considering the consequences, he ran away from there as fast as he could.

All at once, he found himself back in the same town where his wedding had taken place. He went from house to house searching for his bride, for he was certain that if he could only find her, he could break his bond with Lilith's daughter. But no one in that town had ever heard of her, even though she had lived there all her life. And when he had searched everywhere, he left that city and traveled from one city to the next, always hoping to find her.

For three hundred years he wandered without finding any trace of his bride. By then he had lost all track of time and wandered at random from place to place. It was then that he came to a house that seemed strangely familiar, and he knocked, as he had done so many times before. A voice told him to come inside, and when he did he found himself back in the bridal chamber, with the demoness still reclining on the bed. That is when he realized, to his horror, that he had never escaped her at all. And at the instant he understood, the demoness disappeared, the room vanished as well, and the bridegroom found himself still standing beneath the bridal canopy, and the ceremony was still taking place.

And when the bridegroom realized where he was, he looked out to the place where the demoness had stood, and there he saw instead the face of the Serpent. And this time, after the wedding vows, as he crushed the glass beneath his foot, he imagined it was the head of that Serpent that was being crushed. And that night he clung to his true bride with all of his being, and at last he escaped the Hollow of the Sling.

□   Eastern Europe: Nineteenth Century

84

How Rabbi Judah the Pious Became a Great Scholar

Rabbi Samuel the Pious of Regensburg had two sons, Abraham and Judah. From the first, Abraham was a fine student of the Torah, but Judah refused to study at all, preferring to shoot his bow and arrow.

No one could understand why Samuel the Pious permitted him to be so wayward when all of his ancestors had been great scholars. At last Rabbi Samuel's own pupils asked how this could happen, but he assured them that Judah, too, was destined to become a great scholar.

One day, when Judah was eighteen, Rabbi Samuel told him that it was time for him to begin the study of the Torah. Judah did not dispute this at all, and the next day he stood beside his brother, Abraham, in the House of Study. Then Rabbi Samuel turned to Abraham and said: "You have been a fine scholar all your life, but Judah will soon prove to be a greater one. For he will know what takes place in heaven as well as on earth. Nothing will be hidden from him."

Then Rabbi Samuel pronounced the holy Name of God, and the entire House of Study was suddenly filled with a great light. This light so overpowered Judah that he covered his face and fell to the ground. And when he rose up his eyes had been opened, and he saw all that was holy for the first time.

After that, Judah remembered every word that he studied and asked more questions than anyone else. He turned out to be one of the greatest scholars of all time, the famous Rabbi Judah the Pious, whose deeds are recounted in many a tale.

□ Eastern Europe: Sixteenth Century

85

THE WORDS IN THE SAND

There once was a pious man named Rabbi Amnon, who lived in the city of Mayence. Rabbi Amnon had only one son, Rabbi Eliezer, and in his will, Rabbi Amnon said it was forbidden for his son to cross the river Danube, for it was his wish that he remain in his native city.

Now Rabbi Eliezer was anxious to study with Rabbi Judah the Pious of Regensburg, to whom he was related. So he crossed the Danube, despite his father's wishes.

Rabbi Judah the Pious recognized at once that Rabbi Eliezer had disobeyed his father's will. Still Rabbi Judah greeted him, out of respect for his father's memory, and let him remain as a student. Now Rabbi Eliezer was very eager to learn all that he could of the hidden mysteries. But for many months Rabbi Judah put him off, and Rabbi Eliezer learned nothing.

When the eve of Passover came, Rabbi Eliezer was very sad, for he wished that he were home to lead the seder. Rabbi Judah recognized this and offered to let him return home that day. Rabbi Eliezer could not understand how that was possible, for it was a journey of several days. But Rabbi Judah told him to join him in baking matzohs, and when they were ready, it would be time for him to go home.

So they baked matzohs together. And when they were ready, Rabbi Judah said: "I know that you came here to study the mysteries, and that you are disappointed not to have learned anything. But you disobeyed the express wish of your father, and that is reason enough not to teach you. Still, because your father was a pious man to whom I was related, I will teach you something."

Then Rabbi Judah took his staff and wrote holy names in the sand. He told Rabbi Eliezer to read those words, and when he did, Rabbi Eliezer found that he knew as much as Rabbi Judah himself. But a moment later Rabbi Judah covered the words with sand, and at that instant Rabbi Eliezer forgot everything. Rabbi Judah the Pious did this three times, and three times Rabbi Eliezer was filled with great knowledge, and three times he grieved when it was gone. The fourth time Rabbi Judah wrote the words in the sand, he told Rabbi Eliezer to eat the words of sand. And when Rabbi Eliezer swallowed the sand on which those words were written, the knowledge remained with him, and he never forgot it again.

Then Rabbi Judah pronounced the priestly blessing, followed by a pair of holy names. And a moment later, Rabbi Eliezer found himself at the door of his home in Mayence.

That evening, when Rabbi Eliezer met the other worshippers in the synagogue, they asked where he had spent the night, for it is not proper to travel on the eve of a festival. Rabbi Eliezer told them that at noon he had been in Regensburg, and as proof he showed them a matzoh that was still warm, which he had baked with Rabbi Judah. So too did he deliver a letter that Rabbi Judah had sent to the community. And Rabbi Eliezer led the seder in his home that night, and his family rejoiced at his miraculous homecoming.

□   Eastern Europe: Sixteenth Century

86

THE COUNT WHO WANTED TO STUDY KABBALAH

In the days of Rabbi Judah Loew of Prague, known as "the Maharal," there lived a wealthy Count who devoted himself to the study of astrology and alchemy and to finding the Philosopher's Stone. This Count knew that the Maharal was well versed in the secrets of the Kabbalah, so he invited him to his castle.

There the Count told the Maharal that he wanted to be initiated into the study of the Kabbalah, but the Maharal refused his request. He told the Count of the great difficulties involved, even for one who was Jewish. How much more so for one who was not? But the Count demanded that the Maharal serve as his teacher, and he threatened to go to the Emperor and bring great harm upon the Jews if he did not. When the Maharal saw that he had no other choice, he agreed to begin their studies at once.

The Count led the Maharal to a room he had prepared for his mystical studies. It was dark and empty, except for a single lamp, and filled with a sense of foreboding. For a long time the Maharal was silent, but at last he said: "Before we begin, I must ask you if you are free of all guilt. For any guilt that you bring with you could lead you into danger."

"I am," said the Count.

"In the case," said the Maharal, "look behind you!"

And when the Count looked around, he saw a woman standing there with an infant in her arms. The Count began to tremble with fear.

"Do you know who they are?" the Maharal asked.

"It is my sister and her child. But how can they be here? They are both dead!" cried the Count.

"They are here because you killed them!" said the Maharal. "For that child was your child, and you killed them to keep your sin a secret."

Then the Count fainted. And when he came to his senses, he told the Maharal that he would abandon his quest to study the Kabbalah. But he warned the Maharal never to reveal his secret, lest he seek revenge against the Jews. The Maharal promised to kept the secret and went on his way. But every night after that, the Count saw his sister and their infant in his dreams, and he woke up screaming. Nor did he go back to his mystical studies, but for the rest of the his days he was a broken man.

□   Eastern Europe: Nineteenth Century

87

The Dream Question of the Maharal

To protect the Jews of Prague from the Blood Libel and the pogroms that followed every Passover, Rabbi Judah Loew created a man of clay known as the "golem" and brought him to life with the power of the Name. After that the golem guarded the Jews of Prague against every danger, not only from without, but also from within.

One Yom Kippur a terrible incident occurred. One of the worshippers, who had been called to lift the scroll of the Torah after the portion had been read, lost his grip and dropped it. Everyone was horrified, for they knew that this was an evil sign on the very Day of Judgment, when a person's fate for the coming year is sealed in the Book of Life.

The Maharal, more than anyone else, wondered about this incident and prayed for an answer. And that night, in a dream, he overheard an angel say a string of words. When he awoke he remembered this cryptic message and wrote it down, but it made no sense. Then the Maharal decided to write each letter of those words on a separate slip of paper. Then he called in the golem and asked him to arrange those fifteen letters as he saw fit. Without any hesitation, the golem arranged them, but no word was formed. The Maharal was puzzled at first, but all at once he recognized that those were the initial letters of a biblical verse that is read on Yom Kippur: *Moreover you shall not lie with your neighbor's wife and defile yourself with her* (Lev. 28:20).

Then the Maharal met with the man who had dropped the scroll and demanded that he confess to having sinned with someone's wife, for that is why the scroll had fallen on Yom Kippur. The man, who knew of the Maharal's powers of perception, saw that there was no escape, and he confessed his guilt. And he and the woman who had sinned with him were punished according to the Law.

□   Eastern Europe: Nineteenth Century

⚛⚛⚛⚛⚛⚛ 88 ⚛⚛⚛⚛⚛⚛

THE RUIN

Just outside Prague, near the road leading to the city, stood an old ruin. It had been abandoned for such a long time that no one alive remembered what it had once been used for. But everyone knew that it was a place of danger. It was said that demons frolicked there at night, and what sounded like a band of musicians was often heard playing there. So too were hundreds of black dogs seen roaming the building after dark. And because of these tales, most inhabitants were careful to avoid that side of the road after dark.

It happened that a Jew from Prague was returning home at night and was not careful. He walked close to the ruin and a black dog dashed up, barking and circling him. At last the dog ran off, but by then the merchant was a broken man. When he reached home, he told his family what had happened in a very meek voice and then lay down to sleep.

During the night the household was frightened to hear the sound of barking coming from his room, and when they checked they found him barking in his sleep. They hurried to wake him up and dry him off, for he was covered with perspiration. He told them that in his dream he was riding a black dog, together with many others like him, in a single file. And as all the other riders were barking like dogs, so too was he forced to bark. For he was warned that if he did not, the dogs would eat him alive. So he was barking with all his might.

His family tried to dismiss the importance of the dream and urged him not to worry about it. They advised him not to dwell on it during the day and then he would sleep peacefully by night.

On the second night he was again heard to bark, and this continued night after night until the merchant became terribly weak. He grew thin and could no longer provide for his family. When they saw that their trouble was great indeed, the man and his wife went to the home of the Maharal. They pleaded for help and told him all that had taken place.

First, the Maharal ordered that the fringes of the man's *tallis* be checked to see that they were in order. And one fringe was found to be invalid. Then he ordered that the man's *tefillin* be examined, and the head *tefillin* were also found to be flawed. The Maharal said that because of these circumstances the man was unguarded, and he was unable to protect himself. Therefore, he had fallen into mire and dung.

So it was the Maharal ordered the man to have his *tallis* and *tefillin* repaired at once, and he also ordered him to immerse himself in the *mikveh*. Then he summoned his scribe and ordered him to write an amulet on parchment to protect him, which included the passage *But against any of the children of Israel shall not a dog move his tongue* (Ex. 11:7).

And the Maharal enjoined him to wear this amulet day and night, and for the next seven days not to sleep at home, but in the House of Study.

The man did all of these things, and the first night he dreamed that he was still riding in the line of dogs, but he did not bark; neither did they try to harm him for not barking. The second night he dreamed that he rode his dog away from the line of the others and they did not follow after him. The third night he dreamed that he dismounted the dog, but it did not try to attack him. The fourth night he dreamed that he returned to the ruin, but no dog ran out of it to frighten him. The fifth night he dreamed that he lit a torch and approached the ruin, and no demon dared to get in his way. The sixth night he dreamed that he set fire to the straw near the roof of the ruin, and it burned to the ground. And that night, at midnight, it did happen that the ruin caught fire and burned until it was ashes.

And the seventh night the man's sleep was sweet and his strength restored, and he was as healthy and strong as ever.

□   Eastern Europe: Nineteenth Century

⊱⊰⊱⊰⊱⊰⊱⊰⊱⊰ 89 ⊱⊰⊱⊰⊱⊰⊱⊰⊱⊰

THE VOICE IN THE TREE

A Jew once died and was brought to rest. Among the mourners was an old rabbi. It was a hot day, and as the grave was being dug, the old rabbi sat down under a nearby tree. All at once the branches and leaves began to tremble. The rabbi could not understand how this was possible, for there was no wind that day. Nor was there any kind of earthquake. What made the tree shudder?

Just then a voice spoke from within the tree: "Dear rabbi, surely you remember me. I was once your neighbor." And the voice gave the name of a man who had died many years before. "Please, rabbi, listen to what I have to tell you, for I need your help that I may be spared suffering in the other world." And the rabbi said: "Speak, for I remember you, and I will do all that I can."

Then the voice went on to say: "After death a man's soul suffers four transformations. First, it crosses the sea. And if the soul falls there, it enters the body of a fish. And if that fish is caught, and someone cooks and eats that fish after saying the proper blessing, that soul is spared its suffering and ascends to the Garden of Eden.

"Then there are the souls that cross the ocean and pass above the trees. If the soul falls and enters a fruit-bearing tree, and if those fruits are later picked and blessings pronounced on them, that soul also enters the Garden of Eden, its sufferings at an end.

"So too are there souls that pass over the crops, such as wheat. If the soul enters the wheat and bread is made of it, and the blessings are said over it, that soul is also saved. But if the soul enters crops that are eaten by animals, it remains in sorrow.

"For if an animal eats the crops containing this soul, it enters the animal. It suffers there until the animal is slaughtered and blessings are made over the food. And that is the soul's last chance of being saved from its suffering. For if it is not saved, it will continue to suffer until the End of Days.

"Know, dear rabbi, that my soul passed over the ocean, over the trees, and entered the crops. It has been revealed to me that I am about to enter a sheep that I can identity for you. I beg you to be good enough to come on a certain day next week, purchase that sheep, and slaughter it. And when a meal has been made and the blessings said, you will have saved my soul. But if you do not, my soul will be condemned until the footsteps of the Messiah are heard in the world."

So the rabbi did as the soul requested and purchased that sheep. He had it slaughtered and invited all of the students of the yeshivah to the meal. That night the neighbor came to the rabbi in a dream and said: "Your compassion saved me from great suffering. I now make my home in the Garden of Eden. Know that you will find your reward by digging beneath the fireplace of my old house, which now stands in ruins."

The next day the rabbi went to the ruins of that house and dug there, and he found a treasure in gold and silver. After that the rabbi inquired about the man's family and found out that his granddaughter was still alive. He married his son to her and gave them a lavish wedding. The couple lived a good life and a happy one, and the rabbi's son became famous as a Torah scholar. And the day came when the wife of the rabbi's son gave birth to a son of their own, and they named him after her father, whose soul had brought them together.

□ Israel: Oral Tradition

ᘓᘺᕽᘓᘺᕽᘓᘺᕽᘓᘺᕽᘓᘺᕽ 90 ᕽᘓᘺᕽᘓᘺᕽᘓᘺᕽᘓᘺᕽᘓᘺᕽ

A Vision in the Cemetery

When Rabbi Moshe Sofer became the Rabbi of Mattesdorf, he was given an apartment on the third floor, while the cantor, Rabbi Nathan, lived on the second floor, above the House of Prayer. The house, which was owned by the congregation, was directly across from the cemetery.

One night, at midnight, the rabbi looked out the window and saw someone in the cemetery, wrapped in shrouds and walking between the gravestones. Looking closer, Rabbi Sofer recognized Rabbi Nathan, but he could not believe his eyes. He was certain that Rabbi Nathan had gone to sleep, and he hurried downstairs to check on him. And, indeed, Rabbi Nathan was asleep in his bed.

Then Rabbi Sofer knew that it must have been a vision, and he began to worry about the well-being of the cantor. The next night he saw the same vision again at midnight, and in the morning he directed his students to say the Psalms along with him for the sake of Rabbi Nathan. And when Rabbi Nathan heard the melody of the Psalms rising up to his room, he hurried to the House of Prayer and took his place in front of the Ark. Everyone noticed how beautifully he sang that day, and it brought tears to every eye, for Rabbi Nathan did not know for whom the Psalms were intended.

That same day Rabbi Nathan became very ill. Close to midnight, Rabbi Moshe again saw the vision of Rabbi Nathan wearing shrouds and walking between the gravestones. Because this was the third time he had seen this vision, and because the shape of Rabbi Nathan was the most vivid this time, there was no doubt in Rabbi Moshe's heart about the fate of Rabbi Nathan. And within a week Rabbi Nathan took leave of this world, leaving an orphan son. But because of the vision, Rabbi Sofer brought up the boy and saw that a fine match was made for him. And on the day of the wedding, Rabbi Nathan came to Rabbi Sofer in a dream and thanked him for all he had done.

□ Eastern Europe: Nineteenth Century

91

THE SPIRIT OF HAGIGAH

There once was a pious man who devoted his life to only one book—the tractate Hagigah of the Talmud. He read it over and over until he knew it by heart. And he meditated on the many mysteries contained therein, any one of which, he believed, was itself worthy of a lifetime of study. So it was that with every breath this man recalled the sacred passages of Hagigah and meditated on them night and day. Even in his dreams he pursued these mysteries, his soul ascending on high.

And one night his soul ascended all the way to the Palace of Hagigah in the highest heavens. When his soul entered there, his quest was complete, and at that moment this pious man took leave of this world.

But because he lived alone, no one knew what had happened to him. So a figure of a woman, dressed in white, came and stood by him and raised her voice in mourning, and her cries alerted others that he had died.

When they came there, they saw that she was not of this world, and they were stricken with awe and fear. She said: "All of his life this man studied nothing but the book of Hagigah. Now his soul has taken its place on high and he deserves your mourning. Therefore bury him with honor and respect his grave, and you too will be blessed in the world to come."

Then all the women gathered and sat with her, and they mourned over him, and the men were busy with the arrangements of his burial. She remained among them until after the funeral. And before she left, they asked her who she was, and she told them her name was Hagigah, and then she disappeared. For she was the spirit of that very book. And that is how they learned that the good deeds a person performs in this world plead for them in the world to come.

□   Italy: Sixteenth Century

IV

HASIDIC TALES

The Circle of the Baal Shem Tov

92

THE BOOK IN THE CAVE

There once was a holy man whose name was Rabbi Adam. He lived alone in a small hut in the forest, where he studied the Torah day and night. In this way he had gained knowledge of many mysteries and thus attained great powers. But he used these powers only to serve the ways of righteousness, for his soul was very pure.

In those days there was also an evil sorcerer in league with Samael, who discovered, through his knowledge of the stars, the existence of the Book of Mysteries and even the location of it. This fabled book contained all of the celestial mysteries, and by reading it, it was possible to penetrate great secrets of knowledge. But because of the spell that the angel Hadarniel had cast, it was impossible for the sorcerer to enter the cave where the book was hidden in order to bring it out. For only one of the pure souls who had fled from the Garden before the sin of Adam and Eve could remove the book from that place. And in every generation there was only one such soul to be found. So it was that the evil sorcerer searched in the stars and discovered that the pure soul in that generation was Rabbi Adam. And the sorcerer thought of a way to trick Rabbi Adam into turning over the sacred book to him. For once the sorcerer had it in his possession, he could become ruler of the world, since the book would give him almost infinite power.

The sorcerer thought long and hard about how he could make Rabbi Adam perform this deed for him. At last he decided to cast a spell, causing an illness to fall upon him, a contagious disease. And this was the first step in his plan.

Now Rabbi Adam was very surprised when he became ill, for he had never been sick a day in his life, and he decided he had better see a doctor. So he walked into town and went to visit the finest doctor there, as the evil sorcerer had known he would. Meanwhile the sorcerer, who could make himself resemble anyone else through his magical powers, kidnapped the doctor and took his place. And when Rabbi Adam came to him, the sorcerer warned him that the disease was quite contagious, and that he must go to a very remote place so as not to endanger others. Naturally Rabbi Adam did not want to bring harm to anyone else, so he obeyed the order. And the sorcerer saw to it that this distant place was near the cave where the Book of Mysteries had been hidden.

Rabbi Adam vowed to remain in that desolate place until he had been cured of his illness. Yet despite all the remedies he tried and all the prayers he offered up, he remained as sick as ever. Then one day a wanderer came to the hut where Rabbi Adam lived. Rabbi Adam covered his face and told the man to depart because of his illness, but the man, who was the evil sorcerer in another disguise, said he knew of a cure for it.

Now Rabbi Adam was very encouraged to learn that there might be a cure, for while he remained in that isolated place he could not assist his fellow Jews. So he listened to what the wanderer had to say. Thus he learned that the man wanted him to enter a nearby cave to retrieve a certain manuscript, preserved in a golden casket, and in exchange, the wanderer would cure him of his disease. Rabbi Adam vowed to do as the man had asked. And the evil sorcerer passed his hand over Rabbi Adam's body, and he was healed. Now Rabbi Adam wondered greatly at the powers of this man, but at the same time he was very grateful that the disease had been cured. Then the wanderer led him to the cave in which the book was hidden. But before Rabbi Adam entered it, the wanderer said: "Remember, you have vowed to give this book to me, and a holy man such as yourself would never break a vow. Also, you must not open the book at all, nor read from it, for it does not belong to you, but to me."

So Rabbi Adam crawled into the entrance of the cave to search for the book. At last he found it, concealed in a crevice, and when he held it in his hands he sensed at once that it was sacred. Then he began to wonder about the wanderer who had the power to cure him with a wave of his hand but had not been able to enter the cave to retrieve the book. And he began to suspect that the man who had brought him to that cave might serve the powers of evil rather than the powers of good.

So Rabbi Adam decided to examine that book, and when he opened it a sacred light rose up, and Rabbi Adam read in black fire on white that it was the fabled Book of Mysteries. And there it was stated that the book should never be in the possession of anyone but the one who had found it in that cave. Furthermore, any vow that had been made to give the book to another had been made in error, extracted by deceit, and was therefore null and void. And there too, Rabbi Adam found, were certain holy names for protection against such an adversary, who would surely be a powerful sorcerer, if not the Evil One himself.

While still in that cave, Rabbi Adam turned the pages of the Book of Mysteries and read its history. In this way he learned that it had first been revealed to Adam while he was still in the Garden of Eden, to let him know the forms and features of his descendants and all that was destined to take place among the generations of men. It was the angel Raziel who had been sent to read to Adam from the book, inscribed in the angel's own hand from the words spoken by the Holy One, blessed be He. But when Adam heard the first words issue from the mouth of the angel, he fell down in fear. Therefore God permitted the angel to leave the book with him to read on his own. In this way Adam came to know the future and was made wise in all things.

For that book contained all the celestial mysteries, many of which were hidden even from the angels. Whenever Adam opened it, angels gathered around him to read in it as well. Thereupon the angel Hadarniel was secretly sent to him and said: "Adam, Adam, reveal not the glory of your master, for to you alone and not the angels is the privilege given to know these mysteries."

After that Adam kept the book by him secretly, and studied it diligently until he discovered mysteries that had been hidden on the other side of the *Pargod*, the heavenly curtain that separates God from the angels. Still, the jealousy of the angels grew, and at last it became so great that they stole the book from Adam and cast it into the sea. Adam searched for it in vain and then fasted for many days until a celestial voice announced: "Fear not, Adam, I will bring the book back to you." Then the Holy One, blessed be He, called upon Rahab, the Angel of the Sea, and ordered him to recover the book from the depths and give it to Adam, and so he did.

When Adam transgressed and was expelled from the Garden of Eden, the book flew away from him. He then begged God for its return, and beat his breast, and entered the river Gihon up to his neck, until his body became wrinkled and his face haggard. God thereupon made a sign to Raziel to return the book to Adam, so that its wisdom might not be lost among men. And this is the book of the generations of Adam.

As Rabbi Adam continued to read, he learned that after the death of Adam the book had disappeared, but later the cave in which it was hidden was revealed to Enoch in a dream. It was from this book that Enoch drew his vast knowledge of the mysteries of creation, and before he was taken up into heaven and transformed into the angel Metatron, Enoch entrusted the book to Methuselah, who read the book and transmitted it to Noah, who made use of its instructions in building the ark. Noah took the book with him into the ark, preserved in a golden casket, and in this way it was successively revealed to Abraham, Isaac, Jacob, and Joseph, who consulted it to discover the true meanings of dreams. The book was buried with Joseph, but it was recovered when his coffin was raised by Moses from the Nile and carried beside the Tabernacle throughout the wandering in the wilderness.

Thus the book came into the possession of King Solomon, who made good use of its wisdom and sought its assistance in constructing the Temple. However, the book again disappeared after the destruction of the Temple in Jerusalem, and it was presumed to have been lost forever. So believed all of mankind. But Samael, the Evil One, knew the Lord had commanded the angel Hadarniel to conceal the book in the cave, allowing only the pure souls born among men to take it from that place.

After they had read it and made its knowledge their own, they returned the book to that cave. In this way it had come into the possession of great sages, such as Simeon bar Yohai and Rabbi Isaac Luria, known as the Ari, who revealed some of its infinite truths in their teachings. For in every generation some long hidden truth is finally permitted to be revealed.

And how did these sages discover the secret of where the book was hidden? Some, such as Enoch, learned of it in a dream, while to others, such as Abraham, an angel revealed its hiding place.

Rabbi Adam also read the list of those who were destined to open that book, and there he found his own name, along with those who would illuminate the world in future generations, including the name of his successor.

After he had read in the Book of Mysteries, Rabbi Adam understood that it had been his destiny to acquire the book in that cave. And he was quite certain that the wanderer who had brought him there had known this but had concealed it from him in the hope that he might take possession of the book. And Rabbi Adam thanked God that he had decided to examine the book and had not brought it out unopened, as he had been told to do.

No sooner did Rabbi Adam emerge from the cave with the book than the man approached with his hand outstretched and said: "Why did it take you so long? Was it so hard to find? Here, give it to me!" But Rabbi Adam refused to part with the book, and nothing the man said convinced him to change his mind. He explained that his vow to give up the book had been forced upon him, due to his illness, and therefore had no effect. And when the evil sorcerer saw that Rabbi Adam had recognized how precious the book was, and how sacred, he grew furious and shouted: "If you refuse to give me the book, I shall swallow you alive!" And he immediately stretched himself until he reached the sky. But Rabbi Adam quickly pronounced the holy names he had read in the book, and the evil sorcerer was restored to his actual shape. The man ran away terrified and later found that all of his evil knowledge had been erased. He never pronounced another spell.

So it was that Rabbi Adam returned to his home completely healed. There he continued to study the Book of Mysteries all of the days of his life. And with the knowledge he obtained from it he was able to perform extraordinary deeds. Before his death, Rabbi Adam summoned his only son and instructed him to transmit the holy writings to Israel ben Eliezer in the city of Okup, later to become known as the Baal Shem Tov, whose name he had read in the book following his own.

□   Eastern Europe: Nineteenth Century

93

THE PRINCE OF FIRE

Rabbi Adam was the *tzaddik* of his generation. And when the time came for him to prepare for his departure from this world, he called upon his son and gave him an important mission. He revealed where he had hidden secret writings, and he directed that those writings be taken, after his death, to Israel ben Eliezer in the city of Okup. So too did he warn his son that those writings were intended only for this Israel, and that he should not, for any reason, try to read them himself. And all this Rabbi Adam's son promised to do.

Not long afterward Rabbi Adam died. And after the period of mourning, his son set out for the city of Okup. When he arrived there, he began to search for Israel ben Eliezer. But there was no one by that name in the city, except for an orphan who lived in the House of Study. Everyone was certain that this boy could not be the one he was looking for. They said he slept all day or wandered off into the forest.

But since there was no one else by that name, Rabbi Adam's son sought out this Israel and secretly observed him for any signs of holiness. He saw that he did indeed sleep most of the day, and there was nothing about him that seemed out of the ordinary. But once, when Rabbi Adam's son came back at night to observe him, he saw that the boy woke up at midnight and studied with great fervor.

Then he knew that he had found the right one. So the next day he left one page of the secret writings near the bench on which Israel slept. And then he hid himself.

When Israel awoke at midnight, he noticed the page and picked it up. And when he read the first words, a light seemed to rise up from the page, until Rabbi Adam's son saw that it was reflected from Israel's face, for a holy aura surrounded him, dispelling all doubts about his worthiness. Rabbi Adam's son stepped out from where he was hidden and revealed himself. And he told Israel how he had been sent by his father to give him the secret writings.

Israel was still under the spell cast by the mysteries he had read on that page. He was deeply grateful to receive those sacred writings, but he begged Rabbi Adam's son to keep his secret, for he was not ready to reveal himself. This Rabbi Adam's son agreed to do, but at the same time he begged the boy to share the secret writings with him. He suggested that they study together, and although Israel ben Eliezer had grave doubts about this, he did not feel that he could turn down the one who had brought him such a great blessing. In the days that followed, Rabbi Adam's son devoted himself to those mysteries, while Israel, who was far more advanced, served as his tutor. From reading there, they gained knowledge of the highest forces, including the angels. And a day came when Rabbi Adam's son revealed his greatest wish to Israel, which was to invoke the Prince of Torah to join them in their mystical study. This Israel strongly resisted, because he knew that great dangers faced them in such an undertaking. But Rabbi Adam's son insisted that he would do it himself, and rather than permit him to face those dangers alone, Israel agreed to join him.

So they fasted from Sabbath to Sabbath after immersing themselves in the *mikveh*. Then Rabbi Adam's son pronounced the holy name that was intended to invoke the Prince of the Torah. But Israel realized at once that he had made an error, and instead he had invoked the Prince of Fire. Terrified, he told Rabbi Adam's son that their only hope was to remain awake all night, or else the Prince of Fire would descend and cause great damage. They prayed fervently through the night without stopping, but just before dawn Rabbi Adam's son was overcome with exhaustion. He closed his eyes—and never opened them again, for he had lost his life.

Israel grieved over Rabbi Adam's son, but he was not afraid to continue to study those writings, for he knew that it was his destiny to do so. And finally a time came when Israel ben Eliezer revealed himself, and before long he became known as the Baal Shem Tov, whose purity and powers had not been seen in the world since the days of the Ari.

□ Eastern Europe: Eighteenth Century

94

THE ANGEL'S SWORD

In the years before he revealed himself as the Baal Shem Tov, Israel ben Eliezer spent his time in study and meditation. Once some robbers observed him deep in contemplation. He was walking near a ravine between two mountains, and he was getting closer and closer to the edge. "He will probably fall and break his neck," said one of the robbers. At that moment, as Israel stepped over the edge, the two mountains suddenly moved together, closing the ravine, and he continued walking as if nothing had happened. The robbers, all of whom witnessed this miracle, then realized that he was a holy man, and they decided to reveal their secret cave to him.

In those days, robbers often searched for caves in which they could hide. That is how they found an enchanted cave that led directly to the Land of Israel, even though the Holy Land was actually a six-month journey from there by ship. Such caves were created so that the bones of the righteous would roll through them to Jerusalem at the End of

Days, when the age of the Messiah had begun. But, of course, they were secret, their locations known to very few in any generation. Now these robbers had stumbled on such a sacred cave.

When the robbers went to see the Baal Shem Tov, they noticed that he was not afraid of them, even though everyone else who saw them ran away. They indicated to him that they had come in peace, and they told him of the existence of the cave. He was greatly intrigued, for he wished more than anything else to travel to the Land of Israel.

The Baal Shem Tov thanked the robbers and asked them to lead him into the cave. With one of the robbers carrying a torch, they all descended into the dark passages. Now anyone else would have feared for his life in the company of such robbers, but the Baal Shem thought of nothing except the miracle of the cave that might help him reach the Holy Land. Nor did he have anything to fear, for the robbers were in awe of him.

Before they had gone very far, though, they saw the reflection of something like flames in one of the passages, and the robbers became afraid. They refused to go on, so the Baal Shem took the torch and continued on his own. When he entered that passage he saw how bright the light was, although he could not see its source. He also saw that the light had a holy aura about it, and he knew that he was indeed in a sacred place. And the Baal Shem greatly wondered about the source of that light.

At last he reached a turn in that passage, and there he was almost blinded by a flaming circle of light that forced him to avert his eyes. Slowly, however, he raised his eyes and saw that the light came from a flaming sword spinning there. The sight of this sword sent a chill down his spine, for he recognized at once that it must be *the fiery ever-turning sword* (Gen. 3:24) that the angel of the Lord was said to spin outside the gates of Eden, to guard the way to the Tree of Life.

And in that moment the Baal Shem Tov realized that his quest to the Holy Land had been forbidden by heaven and that he could go no further in that enchanted cave. At first his heart sank, but then he realized that it had been a great blessing merely to discover the existence of that cave and to witness the flaming sword itself. That meant that a time would come as well when the sword would stop spinning and the cave would serve its intended purpose of leading directly to the Holy Land. Then the footsteps of the Messiah would be heard throughout the world.

After that the Baal Shem Tov no longer attempted to travel to the

Land of Israel but fulfilled his destiny in his own land. For it had been decreed in heaven that if the Baal Shem Tov had set foot on the Holy Land, it would have brought on the End of Days. And that is why he was forbidden to complete his quest.

□ Eastern Europe: Eighteenth Century

95

THE LADDER OF PRAYERS

Once, while the Baal Shem Tov was praying with his Hasidim, the soul of the Baal Shem ascended all the way to Paradise, to the palace of the Messiah. There he saw the golden dove that makes its nest there and heard its song.

Now when the Hasidim had completed their prayers, they saw that the Baal Shem was still praying. At first they waited for him, but eventually they began to grow impatient, and one by one they departed.

Afterward the Baal Shem came to them and said: "Know that while I was praying I ascended the ladder of your prayers into Paradise. There I reached the palace of the Messiah, known as the Bird's Nest. There too I heard the song of the golden dove, which is indescribable. I knew that if I could only capture that dove and bring it back, the Messiah would be sure to follow, for he cannot bear to be without its song.

"I was within arm's reach of the golden dove. But just as I reached for it, the ladder of prayers suddenly collapsed."

□ Eastern Europe: Eighteenth Century

❧❧❧❧❧❧ 96 ❧❧❧❧❧❧

THE TREE OF LIFE

It was the practice of the Baal Shem Tov to go out into the forest alone. What he did there was a mystery that greatly intrigued his Hasidim. So one morning, when the Baal Shem asked three of his Hasidim if they would like to accompany him into the forest, all of them readily agreed to go. These three were Reb Sendril, Reb Yehiel Mikhal, and the Baal Shem's brother-in-law, Reb Gershon.

Everyone climbed onto the wagon, and this time the Baal Shem himself served as the driver. And although he never cracked the whip, the horses responded to his presence by racing forward, and it seemed to the Hasidim that the hooves of the horses and the wheels of the wagon flew over the ground.

Soon they arrived at the entrance of a pristine forest in a place that none of the Hasidim recognized. Without saying a word the Baal Shem dismounted, unhitched the horses from the wagon, and motioned for the others to follow. Now they wondered why he did not tie the horses to a tree, and Reb Sendril asked the Baal Shem if he wanted him to do this, and the Baal Shem replied: "It is not necessary to tie up the horses in this place, but if you are worried about them wandering off, Sendril, you could stay here with them until we return." But Reb Sendril had no intention of being left behind, and he quickly joined the others walking into the forest.

Never had the Hasidim seen a forest like this. The trees were so ancient that some of them were as wide as a house and so high that they seemed to reach into the heavens. Now when Reb Yehiel tried to peer into the top branches of an especially tall and magnificent tree, he glimpsed a nest high in its branches and saw, at the same time, a golden bird of such great beauty flying into the nest that he remained rooted in that place, trying to get another glimpse of it. Meanwhile the others continued into the forest, leaving their companion behind.

A little further on they came to a beautiful pond, and when the Hasidim saw the Baal Shem lean over and peer into the pond, they followed his lead. But that was no ordinary pond, and what they saw was not an image of themselves, but an angelic presence that seemed to peer back at them from beneath the waters. Now the Hasidim greatly wondered about this and raised their eyes to ask the Baal Shem Tov, but when they did, they saw that he had already left the pond behind, and Reb Sendril hurried off to catch up with him. But Reb Gershon remained staring at that angel, for he understood that it was his own guardian angel that he was seeing, and he could not tear himself away from the remarkable sight.

Further in the forest they came to trees that seemed to be shimmering as if they were on fire, yet they were not consumed by the flame. Reb Sendril wanted to stop to explore this strange sight, but the Baal Shem barely paused to glance at the trees and continued on his way. But Sendril, remembering well the vision of Moses and the Burning Bush, remained behind, trying to discern the mystery of that fire, and he did not notice that the Baal Shem had left him behind.

In this way hours or days passed, and the three Hasidim were lost in the mysteries of that forest. Then, all at once, they found themselves back at the House of Study, where they had started their journey. They could not understand how they had gotten there, and when they looked to the Baal Shem for an explanation, he said: "When Moses left Egypt he knew that some of the Children of Israel would never reach the Promised Land. And, indeed, some of them crossed the Red Sea but were no longer present at the giving of the Torah, and some who were present both when the sea was crossed and the Torah was received did not reach the Promised Land. So it is that I brought you with me into Paradise. And the further we went, the fewer were those who followed. And when I came to the Tree of Life, I found that all of you had lagged behind."

□   Eastern Europe: Eighteenth Century

97

A CROWN OF SHOES

One Simhat Torah, the Hasidim of the Baal Shem Tov were celebrating with great fervor. That year, however, the Baal Shem seemed very solemn. This worried the Hasidim, who knew that it is commanded to be joyous on the day commemorating the Giving of the Torah. So they watched him closely even as they danced wildly. Suddenly a shoe from the foot of Rabbi Dov Baer flew into the air. At that instant a beatific smile appeared on the face of the Baal Shem Tov. Soon after that he joined the Hasidim in dancing with a fervor they had never seen before.

Afterward one of the Hasidim asked the Baal Shem why he had smiled after having been so solemn. The Baal Shem replied: "While you were dancing, I was transported from here into the Garden of Eden. As I looked around, I saw that there were scattered fringes of prayer shawls and straps of worn *tefillin*. But I also saw such things as heels and soles and shoelaces, and sometimes even whole shoes. And all of these objects were glowing like so many sparks, even the shoes.

"Now I was not surprised to see the sacred objects, but I wondered what the shoes were doing there. Just then a shoe flew into the Garden of Eden, and I recognized it at once as yours, Dov Baer. And I realized that your *kavanah* was so complete that your shoe had flown all the way there. And then I understood why there were shoes in the Garden of Eden. And that is why I smiled.

"Before I left the Garden and returned here, I saw two angels who had come to sweep and clean in the Garden. I asked the angels what they were going to do with the shoes, and one of them replied: 'Know that we tend the Garden of Eden and keep it, so we are gathering the shoes that have flown here from the feet of Jews dancing with the Torah in their arms. For just as the angel Sandalphon weaves crowns of prayer out of the prayers of Israel for the Holy One, blessed be He, to wear on His Throne of Glory, so does the angel Gabriel make crowns out of the shoes falling from the feet of those who dance on Simhat Torah.'"

And all who heard the Baal Shem were filled with awe. Nor was Dov Baer's shoe ever found—for it had indeed flown into the Garden of Eden.

□ Eastern Europe: Eighteenth Century

98

THE FLAMING TREE

In the coldest time of the winter the Baal Shem Tov was traveling through the forest with several of his disciples, including Rabbi Baruch of Kameka. The Baal Shem announced that they would pray the afternoon prayer in a certain place, quite a distance ahead. The disciples could not imagine how they could endure the cold until they reached that faraway place. They began to whisper about this, and the Baal Shem overheard them. At last he had the wagon stopped and he dismounted, followed by his curious Hasidim. He approached a tree that was covered with ice and snow, and he touched it with his finger. And the instant he did, the tree burst into flames and burned with a fire that did not consume. The Hasidim were completely astonished to see such a miracle and joined the Baal Shem Tov in fervent prayer, warmed by the fire of that burning tree.

After they departed, Rabbi Baruch started to turn back to see the flaming tree. But the Baal Shem warned him to remember Lot's wife, who was turned into a pillar of salt, and not to look back.

□ Eastern Europe: Eighteenth Century

⟨⟩⟨⟩⟨⟩⟨⟩⟨⟩ 99 ⟨⟩⟨⟩⟨⟩⟨⟩⟨⟩

A VISITOR FROM THE OTHER WORLD

Rabbi Wolf Kitzes had a beloved student who was dying. When the student was so near death that it was time for his confession, Wolf Kitzes hurried to his home. When he got there, he was surprised to see the Baal Shem Tov leaving. Wolf Kitzes was a fierce opponent of the Baal Shem Tov, and he could not imagine that his dying student had turned to him.

When Wolf Kitzes reached his student's bed, he demanded to know why the Baal Shem Tov had been there. The student, who was so near death that he could barely speak, was deeply hurt by his rabbi's anger and was filled with remorse. "What did you ask of him?" Wolf demanded to know. And the student weakly replied: "For help in the World to Come." And Wolf Kitzes said: "Then let us make a vow with each other. Come back to me after your death and let me know if he helped you or not. And then the truth will be known. And if it is true that the Baal Shem Tov helps you, then I will drop my opposition and go to him." The student nodded in agreement, and both of them took this vow. And soon afterward the student took leave of this world.

In the days that followed, Wolf Kitzes grieved over the loss of his student, yet he also wondered if the young man would fulfill his dying vow. But when the thirty days of mourning were over and there was no sign of the student, Wolf decided that he had not found a way to come back.

That night, however, just after Wolf Kitzes blew out the lamp, he heard footsteps, and he was amazed to see his student standing there. He looked exactly the same, but there was an aura that surrounded his body, and his face glowed as brightly as any lamp.

"I have come back to fulfill my vow." said the student. "They would not let me remain in Paradise until I had done so, for every vow must be fulfilled."

"And did you see the Baal Shem Tov there?" Wolf asked.

"Yes," said the student, "it was he who led me inside the gates of *Gan Eden*."

"And is he that highly regarded in Paradise?" Wolf asked.

"More than you could imagine. I myself heard him reveal mysteries to the Fathers, mysteries, they said, that until then had been hidden behind the *Pargod*."

"And can you reveal these mysteries to me?" asked Wolf Kitzes.

"I cannot reveal every word," said the student, "but this much I am permitted to say." And the student repeated one part of the Baal Shem's heavenly *drash*, word for word. Wolf Kitzes listened very closely, as if in a trance.

When the student had finished, he said: "Now I can return to my place in the Yeshivah on High. Goodbye, my rabbi." And the student walked out of the room and was gone.

In the days that followed, Wolf Kitzes struggled with himself, for he felt that he must go to the Baal Shem Tov. But he was such a well-known opponent that he was ashamed to be seen there. Finally, after a week in which he got very little sleep, Wolf Kitzes went to the House of Study, where he knew the Baal Shem would be addressing his Hasidim. When he entered, he found that the room was crowded with Hasidim, who hung on the Baal Shem's every word. He hid behind a post, where he hoped none would recognize him. But as soon as he began to listen to the words of the Baal Shem, he almost fainted. For they were the exact words that his student had repeated to him!

At that moment the Baal Shem said: "Not long ago I spoke these same words in Paradise, and there is someone here who can confirm that this is true. Is that not right, Wolf Kitzes?"

Hearing his name, Wolf Kitzes grew dizzy and had to grab hold of the post so that he wouldn't faint. For a long moment he was silent, but at last he managed to say: "Every word is true."

In the days that followed, Wolf Kitzes became one of the most devoted of the Baal Shem's Hasidim and remained with him for many years. And his name and that of the Baal Shem Tov are linked to this day.

□   Eastern Europe: Eighteenth Century

100

THE MASTER KEY

Once the Baal Shem Tov dreamed that he was walking outside his hut, and he saw a tree, shaped like a shofar, twisting in and out of the earth, as if a giant ram's horn had taken root. The sight of that great shofar took the Baal Shem's breath away. And in the dream the Baal Shem gathered all of his Hasidim together by that tree and told them to see who among them could sound it. So, one by one, they approached the mouth of that mighty shofar, but none of them could bring forth a single sound. At last Reb Wolf Kitzes approached it, and this time a deep and long-sustained blast came forth, like a voice from deep in the earth. He blew only that one note, but it rose up into heaven.

When the Baal Shem awoke, he was still being borne by that long note, and he sighed because there was no such shofar in this world, only in the world of dreams.

The next day the Baal Shem called upon Wolf Kitzes and told him that he wanted to teach him the secret meanings of the blasts of the shofar so that he could serve as the *baal tekiah* for the High Holy Days. Of course, Wolf Kitzes relished this chance to delve into the mysteries with the Besht. So it was that he learned, over many months, that every blast of the shofar is a branch of the Tree of Life, and that there are great powers residing in the shofar. So mighty is its blessing that a note blown with the right meaning and intensity could rise on a single breath all the way to the Throne of Glory.

Now Wolf Kitzes listened carefully to the words of the Baal Shem, and wrote down the secret meaning of each and every sound, so that he could remember it precisely as he blew on the shofar.

Then it happened that on the day of Rosh Hashanah, when he was about to blow on the shofar before the Ark for the first time, the notes with all the secret meanings vanished. He frantically searched for them everywhere, but to no avail.

Then, weeping bitter tears, he blew on the shofar with his broken heart, without concentrating on the secret meanings. And the sound of the shofar rose up in long and short blasts and carried all of their prayers with it into the highest heavens. And everyone who heard him blow the shofar that day knew that for one moment heaven and earth had been brought together in the same place.

Afterward, the Baal Shem said to Wolf Kitzes: "In the palace of the king there are many chambers, and every one has a lock of its own. But the master key is a broken heart. When a man truly breaks his heart before the Holy One, blessed be He, he can pass through each and every gate."

□   Eastern Europe: Nineteenth Century

101

THE ENCHANTED ISLAND

One of the earliest disciples of the Baal Shem Tov was Rabbi Wolf Kitzes, who was famous for his ability to blow the shofar. So resonant were the sounds he drew forth that the Baal Shem called upon him to blow the shofar during the Days of Awe, so that its voice would ascend on high all the way to the Throne of Glory.

Now it was the dream of Wolf Kitzes to travel to the Holy Land, and at last he was about to set out on his journey. Just before he left, he went to see the Baal Shem, who embraced him and said: "God willing, you will blow the shofar in Jerusalem this year. But remember this: when anyone asks you a question, take care to consider the reply."

So Wolf Kitzes set out for the Holy Land, and when he reached the Black Sea he took a ship to Istanbul. Now for the first few weeks things went well, but one day the ship was struck by lightning during a terrible storm, and it split apart. All the passengers lost their lives except for Wolf Kitzes, who somehow managed to grab a long plank that floated nearby. He clung to that plank for three days and nights, until at last the current carried him to an island.

There the exhausted man crawled onto the shore and collapsed. Later, when he regained a little strength, he got up to explore the island, for he was famished from the three days he had spent at sea. Now the island seemed to be deserted, and he didn't find any fruit or anything else he might eat, although he did find a freshwater brook that satisfied his thirst. Following it to its source, he discovered a spring, and there beside it was a magnificent mansion, a palace far greater than that of any king.

Wolf made his way to the door of that mansion and used the last of his strength to knock on the door. To his surprise, the door opened by itself, although no one appeared to be there. At first he stood in the doorway and called out, but no one replied, so he decided to see if anyone lived there. He walked through the halls, opening every door. Every room was magnificent, but still no one was to be seen. At last he opened the door to a large dining room, and there he saw the longest table he had ever seen in his life. It was so long that he could not see the other end, which seemed to be enclosed in some kind of fog. At another time he might have wondered at this, but at that moment all he noticed was that there was one place setting at the table, although there was no food to be seen.

When he came closer to the table, Wolf saw that two precious objects had been placed there. One was the largest and most beautiful shofar he had ever seen, and the other was a golden horn whose value he could not begin to guess. He stood before the two precious objects and wondered which he should examine first. Just then a single grape rolled out of the golden horn, and this decided the matter for him. He picked up the horn, and as he did, an immense amount of the finest food fell out of it, rolling across the table.

Wolf was overwhelmed at this unexpected abundance and quickly sat down so that he might partake of that delicious food. He pronounced the blessings before eating, and just as he was about to take his first mouthful, he heard a deep voice that seemed to come from the far side of the table: "So, how are my children faring?" Now all that Wolf could think of was that delicious food, and he quickly replied: "So, how should they be faring?" and he took the first bite. Then the voice replied: "So be it." At that instant the fog lifted. Wolf was able to see to the other end of the table, but no one was there. That is when he noticed that the shofar was missing, although the golden horn still remained. He decided to look for the shofar once he had finished eating, and he turned back to his plate. But each time he lifted his head, it seemed that the table had grown smaller. When he had eaten his fill, he looked down and saw that the table was no bigger than a plank. At that moment a deep exhaustion came over him, his head sank down, and he fell asleep.

All at once Wolf was awakened by cold water washing over him, and when he opened his eyes, he found himself back in the sea, still clinging to the plank. And he could not decide if his visit to that mysterious mansion had been a dream or if it had really taken place. But when he realized he was no longer famished, he knew that some kind of miracle had occurred.

Not long afterward, a fishing boat found him floating in the sea and brought him back to shore. Then he knew that he must not attempt to continue his journey to the Holy Land but must return to the Baal Shem Tov, to tell him all that had taken place.

When Wolf reached the small hut of the Baal Shem Tov, the Baal Shem greeted him sadly and said: "What a shame, Wolf, that you did not pick up that shofar and blow on it, as you and only you can do so well. For if you did, the footsteps of the Messiah would have been heard throughout the world. For that is the shofar made from the horn of the ram that Abraham offered on Mount Moriah in place of Isaac. It is said that Elijah will blow that shofar at the End of Days. And it was within your grasp to do so, so that all our waiting would come to an end.

"Or at least if you had held on to that golden horn, hunger would have been banished from the world. For that is the Horn of Plenty, and if you had brought it back, no one would ever know hunger again.

"Or if you had replied otherwise to the question that was asked of you and told the Holy One, blessed be He, about our suffering in this world, surely everything would be different.

"But at least you were wise enough to say the blessings before you ate. For if you had not, you would have been lost at sea, as were all of the others who set out in that unfortunate ship."

□   Eastern Europe: Eighteenth Century

102

THE CIRCLE OF FIRE

One day, while Rabbi Jacob of Annopol and Rabbi Elijah were visiting Rabbi Dov Baer, the *Maggid* of Mezhirich, the *Maggid* grew faint. Rabbi Jacob asked him what was wrong, but there was no reply. Then Rabbi Jacob asked the others in the household if the *Maggid* had left the house that night. They reported that he had, and that he had been faint ever since he had returned. Rabbi Jacob then asked the *Maggid* where he had been.

The *Maggid* replied: "At midnight the *gabbai* of the Besht came to the door and said that the Besht had sent for me. Of course, I went at once. When I arrived I found the Besht seated, wearing a wolf's fur that had been turned inside out. A holy aura shone from his face. He asked me if I had studied Kabbalah, and I replied that I had.

"Now there was a book lying open on the table, and the Besht instructed me to read aloud from it. Each of the short paragraphs began: 'Rabbi Ishmael said: "Metatron, the Prince of the Presence, told me."' I read a page to him, and then the Besht asked to continue. And as he began to read, he trembled. He completed another page, then beckoned for me to come closer, and when I did he said in a low voice: 'What is it that can only be taught in a whisper?' And when I replied '*Ma'aseh Merkavah*,' the Mysteries of the Chariot, he nodded yes.

"At that moment the Besht lay down on the floor and curled up in a circle, and all at once he was surrounded by a fiery circle and I could no longer see him. I heard many voices and musical instruments playing, and I saw the circle of fire burn as if it were a single flame, white and pure, which seemed to resemble a living figure, some kind of spiritual being. Indeed, at that moment I was certain I was seeing the very Prince of the Presence. I grew afraid and lowered my eyes for a long time. And when I raised my eyes, the fire was no longer present, but the face of the Besht was still radiant."

In the years that followed, the *Maggid* of Mezhirich rarely spoke of this incident. But whenever anyone asked to know where he had learned his Torah, he would reply that he had received his soul's Torah from the Besht amid lightning and thunder and the sound of musical instruments.

□ Eastern Europe: Nineteenth Century

ᦉᦉᦉᦉᦉᦉ 103 ᦉᦉᦉᦉᦉᦉ

THE TALE OF THE FROG

Once the Baal Shem Tov went out for a walk, and he was so lost in his meditations that he paid no heed to where he was going. Instead, he let his legs lead him for three days and nights, until at last he arrived at the bend of a river.

Somehow the Baal Shem knew that this was the place he had been sent to, so he made camp there. During the night, he heard the sound of a frog croaking. But to the Baal Shem it sounded like sobbing. And the longer he listened, the more it began to resemble prayer, the sobbed prayer of a broken heart. Then the Baal Shem knew that he had been sent there because of the mystery of that strange sound.

As soon as the sun rose, the Baal Shem awoke and went to the river and washed and prayed. Then he began searching for the frog, and at last he caught sight of it, perched on a stone near the water. It was the largest frog he had ever seen, one that looked very old. The Baal Shem stared at the frog for a long time, and at last he said: "I know you are no ordinary frog. Tell me, then, who are you?" And just as the Baal Shem had expected, the frog replied: "I was once a scholar who sinned. And I was sent back to this world as a frog. For five hundred years I have prayed for this torture to end."

The Baal Shem asked: "What was your sin?" And the frog replied: "My sin was to conceal an ancient scroll I discovered that contained a holy text that had been lost for many centuries. For as long as I kept it for myself and refused to reveal it, the mysteries in it were condemned to the waters of oblivion. And that is why I have been sentenced to live by these waters, so that I can never forget my sin."

The Baal Shem replied: "Indeed, your sin was very great. Yet there must be some way for your soul to be set free."

"Yes," said the frog, "I heard from behind the Curtain that if I led a scholar to the lost book, then my punishment would come to an end."

"Where is the book?" asked the Baal Shem Tov.

"Follow me," said the frog. And he hopped from the stone to the riverbank and led the Baal Shem to an ancient tree not far from that place. And he stood next to the tree and directed the Baal Shem to dig there. And when he did, the Baal Shem Tov found a buried urn, and inside it was an ancient scroll concerning many mysteries, including the very ones that the Baal Shem had been meditating upon when his legs had brought him to that place. And as the Baal Shem unrolled that scroll for the first time, the soul of the scholar took leave of the frog's body and was free at last to ascend on high.

□   Eastern Europe: Nineteenth Century

104

THE FIELD OF SOULS

It was the custom of Rabbi Nathan to pray in the House of Study of the Baal Shem Tov on Yom Kippur, and so he did, year after year. He let nothing stop him.

One year, as he traveled in his wagon to the Besht's house, a wheel broke. So Rabbi Nathan left the wagon and went to the nearest village to buy another wheel. While he was gone, a thief stole his horse. When Rabbi Nathan discovered this, his heart sank, not for the loss of the horse, but because his timely arrival at the Besht's house now was in doubt.

Still, Rabbi Nathan was determined to go on. He picked up his possessions and continued on foot. He prayed to arrive there in time, even if it required a miracle, but none took place. The sun started to set while he was crossing a field, and he realized that he could go no further, but must spend Yom Kippur in that place.

In the center of that field there was a pond that had been formed by the rain. He went there and washed his hands, took out his white coat, wrapped himself in his *tallis*, and began to pray Kol Nidre. He wondered what he had done to deserve finding himself there on that holy day. And he remained standing all night and all the next day, pouring out his heart before the Holy One, blessed be He.

That evening, soon after three stars appeared in the sky, he heard something traveling in the distance, and all at once he found a carriage standing next to him. The driver asked him to be seated and loaded his possessions. And when he was seated in the carriage, it flew across the fields to the house of the Baal Shem Tov. And as soon as Rabbi Nathan descended from the carriage, it disappeared from sight.

Rabbi Nathan told the Besht all that had happened to him and wept because he had remained apart from the Congregation of Israel on that holy day. And the Besht comforted him and said: "You did not arrive at that field by accident. You were sent there by God. In that field are souls that have been lost for more than five hundred years. You, with your prayers and your broken heart, repaired their sins, and now they rest peacefully."

□ Eastern Europe: Nineteenth Century

105

UNLOCKING THE GATES OF HEAVEN

On the eve of one Yom Kippur, the Baal Shem Tov perceived that a serious charge had been brought against the Jews in heaven. So grave was the accusation that even the Torah, the most precious possession of the Jews, was in danger of being lost. Grief-stricken, the Baal Shem went to the synagogue and preached harsh words of warning, but even these, he knew, would not be enough.

Recognizing the extent of the Baal Shem's fear and desperation, everyone prayed with great intensity and beat his breast and wept tears of remorse. But toward evening, perceiving that the threat had grown even worse, and that the greatest sages of the past had been brought to testify before the heavenly court, the Baal Shem urged all the prayer leaders to hurry so that he would be able to pray the Neilah prayer while it was still daylight.

Before Neilah began, the Baal Shem wept and looked so agonized that the entire congregation was terrified. Then, while he was praying the silent blessings, he slumped forward and hung his head between his legs. And when the cantor began to chant the voiced eighteen benedictions, the Baal Shem did not join him when he reached the words "Open the gates of heaven." Instead the Baal Shem began to make terrible gestures, as if he were possessed, and everyone feared for his very life. But no one dared to approach him in that state, for they knew the great miracles of which he was capable.

This continued for what felt like an eternity, when suddenly the Baal Shem stirred and stood up. He prayed in a great hurry and completed the prayers, and afterward all the people surrounded him, begging to know the outcome of the charges in heaven.

The Baal Shem said: "Yesterday and today I found that I was unable to pray, so disconcerted was I at the grave danger facing us. Only during the silent benedictions did I find that I could pray again, and then I ascended from one of the palaces of heaven to another with little difficulty, along with our prayers, threading my way into Paradise. For I knew that I had to appeal directly to the Holy One, blessed be He, for mercy.

"In the final palace I found all the prayers of the past fifty years that had not been able to ascend into heaven, and I realized that because of the failure of all those prayers to ascend, grave danger had come to pass. And I was determined to shepherd them through the final gate. But when I came to that gate, I saw that an angel had placed a lock on it so huge that it was larger than this entire city. Nor could I even find the place for the key, much less the key itself. But with the aid of all the prayers, I searched every inch of that vast lock, and at last the place for the key was found, but the key was still missing. And I knew that the time to open the lock was short, for once the sun had set, the judgment would be inscribed forever.

"At that moment great grief possessed me, so great that had I not overcome it, I would have plunged from that great height and my life would surely have been lost. And while I teetered on the brink between life and death, I looked up and saw that my teacher, Ahijah the Prophet, had joined me. And he said 'Come with me to the palace of the Messiah. For only the Messiah has the key to unlock this terrible lock.' With a sudden surge of hope I followed him to the palace of the Messiah, and when the Messiah saw me from afar, he called out to me and beckoned me to him. And he embraced me, and in his embrace I recovered all my hope and shed all my fear. And he said: 'I do not know whether you will open the gate, but if you do, redemption will surely come to Israel.' Then he gave me a key that consisted of two holy letters of the alphabet.

"I thanked the Messiah with all my heart for myself and for every one of us, and I hurried back, used the key, and the gate flew open at my touch. Then the myriad prayers that had been held back so long rushed forward, carrying me with them, and we entered into the highest heaven. And at that moment, the moment of judgment, the accuser suddenly became silent and I did not need to argue, for the presence of the prayers spoke for itself, and the decree was canceled."

□ Eastern Europe: Eighteenth Century

106

THE HEALING SPRING

Once the Baal Shem Tov and his Hasidim traveled far away from any city. There they walked in the fields and forests, and the Baal Shem revealed mysteries such as had not been passed down since Sinai. When it was evening, they found that there was no water to wash with before the evening prayers.

Now there were a great many souls circling there, waiting for the Baal Shem to pray, so that they could be freed to ascend on high. The Baal Shem was aware of their presence and revealed it to the others, and as soon as he did, they saw those souls circling everywhere around them.

So too did the Baal Shem Tov see that the hour was right. It was a time for ascending, for repairing the soul. And the Baal Shem motioned for his Hasidim to form a circle around him. When they did, the Baal Shem Tov took his staff and struck a rock, and pure water came forth. In great joy they drank of that water and washed their faces and their hands in it. Then they began to pray with great intensity.

While they were praying, the water continued to flow, until it formed a spring. And that spring continued to pour forth in that place long after the Baal Shem Tov and his Hasidim had departed. So too were all the lost souls set free, ascending on high in a single bound.

When the miraculous origins of the spring became known, many Jews sought it out. Among them was one who had leprosy. He poured that water on his face three times, and he was healed. That is how the healing powers of that holy spring were discovered.

But those waters not only healed the body, they healed the soul. Every bitter soul who drank there was healed. Indeed, everything that came into contact with those waters flourished, barren trees started to bring forth fruit, and the flocks that drank from those waters grew bountiful.

Many years later, a landslide covered the holy spring. Many Jews came there to search for it, but none could find the right place. And they went away greatly disappointed. They were like the pilgrims who came a great distance to give their sacrifices at the Temple and found it destroyed. And those whose souls were thirsty for those living waters cried out in their bitterness.

Then one night an old Jew, who had been a child when the landslide covered the spring, had a dream in which the Baal Shem Tov came to him and revealed its true location. He told the old man to get up and dig there. And when the old man awoke, he took a shovel and went to that place. And the third time he put the shovel into the earth, water rose up from where it had been hidden. And the old man fell on his face and gave thanks. And the news quickly spread that the waters of the holy spring had returned, and there was rejoicing everywhere.

□   Eastern Europe: Nineteenth Century

❦ 107 ❦

LIGHTING A FIRE

The Baal Shem Tov always knew if his prayers had ascended on high, as most of them did. But once in a while, a prayer would somehow be lost and never reach the angel Sandalphon, who weaves the prayers of Israel into garlands of prayer for the Holy One to wear while He sits on His Throne of Glory. Now the Baal Shem Tov perceived that not only his prayers, but all the prayers of Israel, had somehow been refused and that a time of great danger had come upon them.

Late that night, the Baal Shem came to Dov Baer and asked him to accompany him into the forest. There was a full moon that night, and the Baal Shem hurried along a path to a place that only he knew about. In that secret place, as Dov Baer watched, the Baal Shem lit a fire merely by touching the branches, so that they resembled a burning bush. Nor were the branches consumed in the flames. The Baal Shem said nothing about this, and Dov Baer dared not ask. Then, seated by the fire, the Baal Shem closed his eyes in deep meditation. For a long time there was only the sound of the wind in the trees. Then the Baal Shem opened his eyes, stood up, and began to pray with great intensity. Dov Baer heard the words of that prayer for the first and only time that day. Yet they remained imprinted in his memory all the days of his life.

At last the Baal Shem stopped praying, and there was a great smile on his face. He said: "The prayers of Israel will no longer be turned back."

Years later, when Dov Baer was known as the "*Maggid* of Mezhirich," another grave danger faced Israel, concerning the Blood Libel. The *Maggid* knew what he must do. He went to his Hasid, Reb Moshe Leib of Sassov, and led him into the forest to the secret place of the Baal Shem Tov. But he did not light a fire, for he knew that a soul such as that of the Baal Shem Tov burned only once in a hundred generations. He told the story to Reb Moshe Leib, and he said: "Per-haps we can no longer light the fire, but let us meditate and pray, for I still remember the prayer of the Besht." And he repeated the words of the prayer out loud for the first time since he had heard them many years before, and not a single word was missing. Reb Moshe Leib listened with complete concentration, but he was not able to recall any of the words. And when they returned to the city, they learned that the danger had passed.

A generation later, Reb Moshe Leib of Sassov was himself called upon to fulfill a great task concerning the redemption of a great many captives. But because there was no one to accompany him, he went into the forest alone. He knew that he could not light the fire, nor did he know the prayer, but at least he knew the place. And that proved to be enough.

But when the time came in the next generation for Reb Israel of Rizhin to perform the task, he said to his Hasidim: "We cannot light the fire, we cannot speak the words of the prayer, we do not even know the place. But we can tell the story of what happened." And he did. And that was enough.

□ Eastern Europe: Nineteenth Century

The Circle of Rabbi Pinhas of Koretz

108

OPENING A VERSE

One day, in the brief study period between the afternoon and the evening prayers, Reb Pinhas of Koretz was discussing a passage from the Zohar with his Hasidim. He noted that each *drash* from the Zohar began with the words *Rabbi Shimon patah*, "Rabbi Shimon opened with the verse . . ." Reb Pinhas said: "This is generally understood to mean that Rabbi Shimon bar Yohai opened his lecture. But it does not. It means that he literally *opened* the verse of the Torah."

"But Rebbe, what can this mean?" asked one of the Hasidim.

"Let me assure you that the meaning will become clear to you. Let us study today's verse, that of Korah."

The Hasidim began to read the verse out loud together, as was their custom, and when they reached the words *And the earth opened her mouth, and swallowed them up* (Num. 16:32), the ground beneath them broke open, and they tumbled into the earth. That fall seemed to take an eternity, as if they were falling from one side of the world to the other.

After what seemed like years of falling in that dark place, the initial terror wore off, and they tried to take stock of where they were and what had happened. And since they were all falling together, they found that they could discuss it among themselves. One of them called out: "We are being punished for doubting the words of Reb Pinhas." "Yes," shouted another, "surely we are falling to Gehenna, about to burn in hell!" And a third one cried out: "Now I understand what Reb Pinhas meant about 'opening the verse!'" And as soon as he said this, all of them understood.

At that moment the ground beneath their feet became firm again, and they found themselves seated in the House of Study, and Reb Pinhas said: "Where have you been? It's time for the evening prayers." And the Hasidim understood that they had been falling for only a few minutes, although it had seemed like an eternity to them. And they looked toward Reb Pinhas in confusion, and he said: "Your merits saved you from falling into Gehenna, as did the followers of Korah. Instead, you knew the falling of a wandering soul, who falls from one world to the next. The falling ended as soon as you understood the secret of how to open a verse."

□ Eastern Europe: Nineteenth Century

109

The Angel of the Zohar

Every sacred book has its own angel. Just as there is the "Prince of the Torah," as the Angel of the Torah is known, so too is there an angel for every sacred book. Reb Pinhas of Koretz had such a great love for the Zohar that his guardian angel was said to be the Angel of the Zohar. He communed with this angel as had Rabbi Joseph Caro with the angel he called his *Maggid*. It was said that the Angel of the Zohar remained in the presence of Reb Pinhas whenever he opened the pages of the Zohar, and that a glowing light, like that of the angel, could often be seen from outside the door of his study.

One of the Hasidim of Reb Pinhas was possessed by a great longing to see the angel for himself. So one day he hid himself in the rebbe's cabinet and peeked through a crack. Not long afterward, Reb Pinhas entered the study, closed the door, took down a volume of the Zohar, and brought it to his study stand. From within the cabinet, the Hasid had a clear view of Reb Pinhas as he opened the Zohar and began to read. All at once a bright light began to glow from Reb Pinhas's face. It was so intense that the Hasid was temporarily blinded, as if he had peered into the sun. When he regained his sight, one glance confirmed what he could barely believe—light filled the room, and Reb Pinhas was the source of the light. In his hiding place the Hasid trembled in awe, for he had learned the truth: when Reb Pinhas opened the pages of the Zohar, he was transformed into the Angel of the Zohar himself.

□ Eastern Europe: Nineteenth Century

110

THE ANGEL OF FRIENDSHIP

Among the Hasidim of Reb Pinhas of Koretz were Ze'ev Wolf of Zhitomir and Aaron Samuel ben Naftali Hertz Hacohen, who had been study partners for many years and were the closest of friends. For more than a year, both Hasidim had been separated from Reb Pinhas and from each other. Aaron Samuel had traveled to the Holy Land, to the Holy City of Jerusalem, and had just returned to Koretz that day. Ze'ev Wolf, as it happened, returned on that same day from more than a year spent in the Yeshivah of the *Maggid* of Mezhirich, where Reb Pinhas had sent him to study.

As each Hasid entered the House of Study, they greeted their rebbe with the traditional blessing recited when seeing a great scholar of Torah: "Blessed art thou, Oh Lord Our God, King of the Universe, Who has given of His wisdom to those who fear Him." But when the two friends laid eyes on each other after such a long time, they each instinctively cried out the traditional blessing recited when seeing a friend again after more than a year has passed: "Blessed art thou Oh Lord our God, King of the Universe, who raises the dead."

The rebbe and his students all rejoiced at this fortunate and coincidental reunion. Then one of the younger students asked the rebbe: "Why is it, Reb Pinhas, that when we see a friend whom we have not seen for a whole year, we are commanded to bless God for reviving the dead? Surely this is a strange commandment, since none of us has died. Whom has God raised from the dead?"

Reb Pinhas replied: "We learn in the Zohar that everyone has a light burning for them in the world above, and everyone's light is unique. When two friends meet, their lights above are united, and out of that union of two lights an angel is born. That angel has the strength to survive for only one year, unless its life is renewed when the friends meet again. But if they are separated for more than a year, the angel begins to languish and eventually wastes away. That is why we bless the dead upon meeting a friend we have not seen for more than a year, to revive the angel."

Just as the rebbe finished speaking they heard a sound like the rustling of wings, and a sudden wind swirled around the room, brushing against them. Then they knew that the angel had been reborn.

□   Eastern Europe: Nineteenth Century

111

THE UNDERGROUND FOREST

On the eve of the third anniversary of his father's death, the student Reuven dreamed that his father came to him and told him to go to the town of Koretz. When Reuven awoke, he marveled at this dream, and at how real his father had seemed to him. And he wondered about the strange message: to go to a place where he didn't know anyone. To whom and for what purpose? And how could he leave the yeshivah? Surely they would forbid him to go on the basis of a dream.

All day Reuven strongly felt his father's presence, and the next night the dream was repeated, except that this time his father told him to go to the town of Koretz for Rosh Hodesh, the Feast of the New Moon. Now Reuven realized that a decision must be made—whether to act on the dream or not.

The dilemma resolved itself the third night, when the dream recurred, except that this time Reuven's father told him to go to Koretz for Rosh Hodosh and seek out Reb Pinhas.

After this third dream, Reuven decided that he must go, no matter what. His father had compelled him. He understood that. And he wrote a letter to the head of the yeshivah explaining that he had left on business, to claim an inheritance in Koretz. This, he reasoned, would be more acceptable to him than his father's command in a dream.

Reuven took a carriage to Koretz. In the carriage were two Hasidim of that town. As Reuven listened, they spoke about Reb Pinhas. "It is said," said one Hasid, "that Reb Pinhas can read the thoughts of men." "That is true," said the other, "for I myself have heard of a man who came to Reb Pinhas when he was full of doubts that God could read his thoughts. When he knocked on the door, Reb Pinhas opened it and said: 'Young man, I myself know what you are thinking. And if I know, should not God know?'" And Reuven wondered what kind of man he had been sent to, who could read the thoughts of men.

Reuven arrived only a few hours before the eve of Rosh Hodesh. Reb Pinhas greeted him and told him that he would be welcome to use the *mikveh* before the Feast of the New Moon that night. The young man thanked the rabbi and took his leave. He asked one of the servants where the *mikveh* could be found, and he was directed to a hut behind the rabbi's house.

The young man walked to the little hut and stepped inside. He saw a stairway, but from the top of the stairs he could not see the water below. Instead, he heard a deep warbling sound, like the call of an exotic bird. How strange, he thought to himself, that this calling seems to come from within the *mikveh*.

Curious to see for himself, the student descended the stairs. Much to his amazement, the stairway was very long, much longer than that of any other *mikveh* he had ever seen. And he soon found that he could see neither the top of the stairs nor the bottom from where he stood. He feared that something strange was taking place, as if he were descending from one world into another. Surely, he thought, no stairway could be this long!

Each step of the way, the noise from below grew louder. Soon he could make out a cacophony of forest sounds—birds whistling, wolves howling, the wind shaking the trees. He wanted to turn back, but he controlled himself and continued on. Surely, he thought, I am almost there.

At last the student reached the bottom of the abyss, but he found no sign of a *mikveh*. Instead, he found himself standing on the floor of a dense forest. Had he entered the wrong hut? The young man decided to turn back. But when he turned around, the stairs were gone. There was no sign of them at all. How would he ever return to the world above?

With no other choice, the student peered around him and saw that it was growing dark. He knew it was unsafe to stay where he was, so he looked for a tree in which to spend the night. He found one in a nearby clearing and pulled himself up into the branches. He was comfortable, but he knew he must not fall asleep or he might tumble to the ground.

When it was completely dark, a band of robbers came into that clearing and made a campfire not far from the very tree into which the student had climbed. He was well hidden in the branches, but he was terrified that the robbers would find him and strip him of everything, perhaps even his life. And it was true that they were a vicious band, for they bragged about their exploits, how many men they had killed, and who among them was the most ruthless. They bragged half the night, until they fell into a drunken sleep. And all the while the poor student trembled in the tree, holding his breath for as long as possible and then breathing very quietly. When they were asleep at last, the student was exhausted. He would have loved to sleep himself, but he knew that his life depended on remaining awake.

So it was that the student in the tree saw a serpent slither toward the branch on which the robbers' wineskin had been hung, still open. The snake slid inside the wineskin and stayed there a long time, filling itself with the wine, until it was so engorged that it spit up the wine, mixed with its own poison. Then the snake crawled out and disappeared into the forest.

When the robbers awoke in the morning, the student watched them take swigs of the wine. Then, one after another, they began to choke from the poison, and soon they all lay dead on the ground.

Now the student carefully lowered himself from the tree and made sure that every one of the robbers was dead. Then he looked for something to eat. In one of the robbers' bags he found a loaf of bread, but mostly the bags were crammed with stolen riches, with gold and silver and jewels of every kind. Reuven emptied bag after bag onto the ground and was amazed at all they had carried away. But when he shook out the last bag, he could feel that it had a false bottom. He took a knife and cut it open, and all at once a shining object came tumbling out—a round, glowing jewel. He held it up and turned it around, but try as he might, Reuven could not see the source of the light inside it. Surely, he thought, that was a priceless treasure. And he recognized that such a precious object could only be owned by a king.

Now this student cared little for material goods. His concerns were those of the spirit. He would not have minded leaving all the gold and silver behind, but he could not abandon that glowing jewel, so he put it into his own bag. Then he buried the robbers and said a prayer over their souls, for surely they had found terrible punishments for their evil deeds in the World to Come. And then he went on his way, going in the direction the robbers had come from, in the hope that he would find a city or town of some kind. And he gave thanks to God for letting him survive that dangerous night.

Little by little, the faint path he followed become well worn, and that, in turn, led him to a road wide enough for the king's horse and carriage. Soon he reached the gates of that underground city.

There the student saw that the people of the city were dressed for mourning, and he asked a young man passing by what had happened. "Two tragedies have struck our kingdom at the same time. First, our king died without leaving any heir except for his daughter, the princess. And second, the king's enchanted jewel was stolen by thieves. Now this glowing jewel has always revealed who will succeed the king. But now no one knows where it is. Even so, the princess has declared that she will marry whoever brings that glowing jewel to her, for the jewel has always succeeded in reaching the one who was destined to be king. For that jewel is guided by the hand of fate."

Now the student shivered when he heard this, for he was carrying the glowing jewel in his pack. He took his leave of the young man and set off for the palace. And when he reached it, he asked for an audience with the princess, saying that he had news of the glowing jewel.

When the guards heard this, they took him to the princess at once, and he was overwhelmed by her great beauty and by the wisdom and radiance of her eyes. "Tell me," she said, "what you know about the jewel." The student was speechless, but he pulled the jewel out of his pack and gave it to her. The princess looked at him with amazement and said, "Then it is you who is destined to be my husband, and you who are destined to rule. But how did you come into possession of the jewel?"

So the young man told her of his night in the forest and all that he had witnessed. He offered to lead guards to that very place, to confirm his account and to recover the other items the robbers had stolen along with the glowing jewel. This was done, and the guards confirmed everything he had said. So it was that the wedding soon took place, and the young man, who had been a poor student, now found himself a great king in that underground country.

Now the young man ruled using the principles of the rabbis, as he had learned in his studies of the Talmud, and the kingdom flourished. So too did the young man fall in love with the princess, now his queen. Together they had three children, two boys and a girl, and he loved all of them as much as life itself.

Then one day it happened that there was a sudden downpour that grew into a great torrent. A great wave washed through the palace and

carried the king out an open window and away from his family forever. For a long time the current carried him further and further
downstream, and suddenly it thrust him into a great whirlpool. As he
was pulled down, the young man was certain that his life had come to
an end. Still, he fought against the whirlpool and tried to rise to the
surface as best he could. All at once the young man found himself
above the water, and he saw that he was standing in a *mikveh*. That is
when he recalled having descended the stairs in search of the *mikveh*
just before coming come to the underground forest. Now he looked up
and saw a short stairway nearby, with no more than ten steps. He
climbed out, greatly confused, and stumbled back to the home of Reb
Pinhas. The moment the rabbi opened the door, the student burst into
tears and asked the rabbi how long he had been gone. "Why, no more
than an hour," Reb Pinhas said. Then the student told the rabbi of all
the years that he had lived through since he had gone into the *mikveh*,
and he poured out his heart and begged the rabbi to explain how such
things had happened to him. For it seemed to him that the world had
been turned upside down.

Reb Pinhas said, "Let me first introduce you to my daughter, and
then I will explain." He called forth his daughter, and when the
student saw her, he almost fainted. For she was the very princess he
had wed in the underground city! The rabbi saw that the young man
was overwhelmed, and he quickly said: "Listen carefully to what I tell
you. I learned from a heavenly voice that it was you who were destined to marry my daughter. And when you arrived here, I recognized
you at once. That is why I sent you to the *mikveh*, for in this way you
traveled the path of your own destiny, and now you can understand
that you are indeed destined for my daughter."

So it was that the young man married the daughter of Reb Pinhas,
and they loved each other as if they had already been married in
another life. And they had three children, two boys and a girl, who
were identical to the children he had had when he was king. And
Reuven loved all of them with all his heart and thanked God for
restoring his family to him. And at the same time he held them dear to
him at all times, for he remembered well how quickly they had been
lost.

□   Eastern Europe: Nineteenth Century

112

REB PINHAS AND THE ANGEL OF DEATH

At the end of his life Reb Pinhas of Koretz was visited by the Angel of Death. But the angel did not appear in his most fearsome form, with a hundred eyes; instead he disguised himself as a visiting Hasid, revealing his true identity only in the *kvittel*, his petition to the rabbi.

When Reb Pinhas read that petition and saw the holy name that served as its seal, he knew that the Angel of Death had really come calling. Indeed, Reb Pinhas, in the fullness of days, had been expecting him. But now he realized that just as the angel had contacted him through that petition, so could Reb Pinhas reply in the same way. He sat down at his desk and took out his finest pen, dipped it in ink, and wrote the following reply on the same page:

"I welcome the presence of the eminent angel, who has been honored to attend to all of the Fathers, guiding them from this world to the next. Know that I am prepared to accompany you wherever it is that you want to take me. But if I were given the choice of going to Gehenna or to the Garden of Eden, I would choose to enter Gehenna. There I would suffer the pangs of Gehenna with all the other Jews who live there. Nor would I budge from that place until every other Jew had been released."

When the Angel of Death, disguised as a Hasid, received this reply, he was thrown into a dilemma. For he had been commanded not to deny any wish of Reb Pinhas, who was so highly regarded in heaven. Now Reb Pinhas had asked to go to Gehenna—how could he take such an eminent sage there? At the same time, how could he refuse Reb Pinhas's request? The angel dared not make such a momentous decision, so he folded the note, put it in his pocket, and took his leave of that house. He returned to Paradise to find out what he was supposed to do.

He stood outside the *Pargod*, the heavenly curtain, and asked for advice. Then he put his ear to the curtain and listened for the whispered reply. And when he heard it, the Angel of Death descended to earth and returned to the house of Reb Pinhas.

Once again the angel, disguised as a Hasid, presented a petition. When Reb Pinhas opened it, he saw that in addition to the words that were written there, there was one word on the last line that seemed to be inscribed in black flames. This time the petition informed Reb Pinhas that heaven had presented him with that holy name, to use as he wished. But he should know that there were two ways to pronounce that name, and if he should pronounce it one way, he would find himself in Paradise, where he must remain. But if he pronounced the name the other way, he would be taken to Gehenna, as he had wished. And he could remain there as long as he wanted. The name itself was so secret that its true pronunciation was known by only one angel, Metatron. Not even the Angel of Death could have told Reb Pinhas how to pronounce it, even if he had wanted to.

When he read this, Reb Pinhas realized that heaven had put his fate back in his own hands, if he could only discover how to use that secret name. For he had recognized at once that the word could be pronounced two ways, but he could not decide which one would take him to Gehenna and which one to Paradise. He thought of Rabban Yohanan ben Zakkai, near the time of his death, who wept because he knew that there were two paths, one leading to Gehenna and one to Paradise, and he did not know which one he would be taking. Now Reb Pinhas, however, was seeking to take the path leading to Gehenna; indeed, he was determined to go there.

Thus Reb Pinhas, knowing that there was not much time, studied that word from every perspective. He sought some clue in Gematria and used other mystical methods to find a clue. But in the end the two ways seemed completely balanced. What was Reb Pinhas to do? Just then there was a knock at the door of his room, and Reb Pinhas knew that the Angel of Death was waiting for his decision. At that instant Reb Pinhas simply pronounced the word the way he had first read it.

All at once Reb Pinhas found himself in Paradise, in the company of the great sages who had gone before him. They welcomed him, even though they knew that he had not intended to join them until he had liberated all the souls in Gehenna. And they told him that in his honor, the Holy One, blessed be He, had agreed to set free all those being punished in Gehenna until that day. But in the future, those who deserve to be punished in Gehenna would still be sent there. And

Reb Pinhas knew that he had accomplished as much as he could, and he gave thanks to God for all of His blessings. Then he joined the other sages in Paradise in the study of Torah that he loved more than anything else.

□   Eastern Europe: Nineteenth Century

The Circle of Rabbi Elimelech of Lizensk

⁙⁙⁙⁙⁙ 113 ⁙⁙⁙⁙⁙

THE WOMAN IN THE FOREST

When Rabbi Elimelech of Lizensk was a young man, he spent all day in the House of Study, and at night he walked home through the forest, always taking the same path. One night, as he was walking home, he saw a light in the distance he did not recognize. Curious to know what it was, he left the path and walked closer to the light. Before long he saw that it was coming from a cottage, one that he had never before seen in the forest. And through the window he saw a woman with long hair who was wearing a very thin nightgown.

Reb Elimelech knew that he did not belong there, and he started to leave. At that very moment the door to the cottage opened, and a voice called out: "Reb Elimelech. Wait!" Reb Elimelech turned and saw that the woman was standing in the doorway. And she said: "Please, come in."

So Reb Elimelech went inside. And after she closed the door, she said: "Reb Elimelech, I have seen you pass through the forest many times, and I have often hoped you would stop by. Just now I have come from the spring, and I am clean. Surely you know that the sin would be slight, but the pleasure would be abundant." And she dropped her gown.

Reb Elimelech stared at her with disbelief and struggled with himself, as did Jacob with the angel. And at last he wrenched out the word "No!"

At that instant the woman vanished, and the cottage disappeared, and Reb Elimelech found himself standing alone in the forest. And there were glowworms at his feet.

□   Eastern Europe: Nineteenth Century

&&&&&&&&&&&&& 114 &&&&&&&&&&&&

A Bowl of Soup

One Friday afternoon, not long before the Sabbath, it became known that the King was planning to sign an evil decree against the Jews. There was dismay everywhere, but Rabbi Elimelech of Lizensk insisted on celebrating the Sabbath as always, for, he said, "You must never turn away from the Sabbath Queen."

After saying the Sabbath blessings, they sat down to the meal. Among the guests was the Rabbi Menachem Mendel, who was to become the Rabbi of Riminov. A bowl of soup was set before Rabbi Elimelech. The others waited for him to begin eating, but he did not. He waited, saying nothing, a distant look on his face. All at once he knocked over the bowl of soup, spilling it all over the table. Seeing this, Rabbi Mendel pushed his chair back in terror and said: "Rabbi, what are you doing? Surely you realize the danger!" And Rabbi Elimelech said: "Don't be afraid. The danger has already passed."

Later it was learned that at the very time the King was to sign the evil decree, he accidentally knocked over the inkwell. Ink spilled all over the parchment. And when he saw this, the King tore up the decree and ordered that none like it ever be drawn up again.

□   Eastern Europe: Nineteenth Century

115

THE WINE OF PARADISE

One Shavuoth as Reb Elimelech and his Hasidim sat around the table of the feast, he said: "Surely we have everything we need here. We lack for nothing."

"Only the wine of Paradise," one young Hasid said in jest.

Reb Elimelech frowned. "It is not too late even for that. Take the pole and attach two buckets to it. Go directly to the graveyard and through the gates. Take three steps inside it. Once you are there, put down the buckets, turn your back, and wait until you can see the full moon. Then pick up the buckets and bring them back here. But remember: Don't talk to anyone for any reason. No matter who it is. And don't spill a single drop."

The young Hasid did as he was told. When he stepped out of the house, he saw that it was very dark outside. The moon was completely hidden behind the clouds. It was very windy that night, and the leaves on the trees were trembling, as was the young man. Still, he carried the empty buckets to the cemetery, opened the iron gate, and went in. He took three steps inside, put down the buckets, and turned his back. He looked up at the sky, searching for the moon, but not a glimmer of it could be seen. Meanwhile, the howling of the wind had grown louder, but he could not tell if it was really the wind he was hearing, or if it was ghostly cries in the night.

It seemed to the young man that he stood there, frozen in place, for hours. At last he heard the sound of something being poured, and a moment later the full moon suddenly emerged from the clouds. Then the young man picked up the pole and felt that the buckets were full. So too did he hear the splash of wine in the buckets. He quickly left the graveyard and made his way carefully to Reb Elimelech's house, for he knew that the rabbi would not forgive him if he spilled even a single drop.

Now the wind seemed to blow against him, and every step he took was difficult. Then he heard a voice emerge out of the wind, begging for a drop of that wine. All at once there was a great chorus of voices begging him, because even a single drop would take them to Paradise. Then he knew that he was surrounded by the souls of the dead, who had followed him from the graveyard. They made every step he took a nightmare, and their pleas were terrible to hear.

Still, the young Hasid did his best to ignore them and to remember his mission. And all at once he found himself on the threshold of Reb Elimelech's house. He cried out with great relief: "So I've escaped you after all!" At that instant the pole cracked, and the buckets fell down and spilled every drop of that precious wine. Suddenly it was deathly silent. Then the door opened and Reb Elimelech said: "Come in, fool, and sit down at the table."

□   Eastern Europe: Nineteenth Century

ଷଅଓଵେଓଵେଓଵେଓଵେ 116 ଵେଓଵେଓଵେଓଵେଓଵେଓ

THE YOUNG MAGICIAN

There was a young man in the city of Lizensk who was known to have delved into the secrets of kabbalistic magic. On learning this, Reb Elimelech invited this young man to come to his home for the Sabbath. While he was seated at the table, the young man suddenly became very hot. When the heat became unbearable, he asked Reb Elimelech's permission to take off his long black coat. Reb Elimelech readily agreed to his request. But even when the coat was off, the young man felt as if he were suffocating.

When Reb Elimelech saw his discomfort, he suggested that the young man step outside for a few moments to cool off. The young man accepted this suggestion and excused himself from the table. A cool breeze greeted him as he stepped outside the door. The young man relished the wind and took a deep breath. Just then he saw something glowing in the distance between the trees. Curious about it, he followed that light, which always seemed to glow before him. At first he was certain it was quite close, and yet it always seemed to remain the same distance ahead of him.

The young man completely forgot about the Sabbath dinner at Reb Elimelech's house, and he became obsessed with following that light. Soon he reached the outermost boundary of the distance he was permitted to walk on the Sabbath. But still he did not pause, even for an instant. He continued to chase that light through the forest. Now it seemed to move faster, and he had to push the branches aside in order to keep his eye on it.

Before long the young man reached the banks of a river that ran through that forest. From where he stood, he saw the light glowing on the other side. But there was no way to get there, for only a rope had been strung across the river.

When he saw this, the young man hesitated for a moment, but the glowing light on the other side beckoned him on. He stepped into that river and took hold of the rope and used all his strength to pull himself across the river. But, strangely enough, the glowing light was as far off as ever.

At last, when it seemed that he had been crossing that river for hours, the young man grew afraid. He looked behind him, to see which shore was the closer, for he was ready to turn back. But they seemed equally distant. The young man feared that he was being punished for breaking the Sabbath, and he began to tremble. It became harder and harder to pull himself along the rope. Just when he felt that he was about to lose his grip, he reached the other side.

Using the last of his strength, the young man climbed out of the water. But no sooner did he step on the other bank than the river disappeared, as well as the forest, and he found himself standing before Reb Elimelech's house, staring at the candlelight within. He did not understand how he had gotten there, and he felt himself grow faint.

Just then Reb Elimelech opened the door and greeted the young man. He said: "In the time you have been out here, we have sung three Sabbath songs. Tell me, are you ready to return to the table?"

□ Eastern Europe: Nineteenth Century

117

REB SHMELKE'S WHIP

Two men, one poor, the other wealthy and influential, came before
Reb Shmelke as litigants. As Reb Shmelke listened carefully, each
presented his side of the case. Then he rendered his judgment in favor
of the poor man. The rich man became livid and declared that he
would not abide by the verdict. Reb Shmelke remained calm and said:
"You will obey. When a rabbi renders his decision, it must be
obeyed."

At this the rich man became furious and said: "I abhor you and all
your rabbis!" Then Reb Shmelke stood up, looked the man in the
eyes, and said: "If you do not obey my order this instant, I'll take out
my whip." Hearing this, the rich man began to heap abuse on the
rabbi, who reached over to his desk and pulled a drawer open. At that
instant the Primal Serpent sprang forth and wrapped itself around the
rich man's neck. He fell to his knees, filled with terror, and begged for
forgiveness. Reb Shmelke said: "Warn your children, and let them
warn their children, to follow the way of the rebbe or fear his whip."
And then he removed the snake.

□   Eastern Europe: Oral Tradition

118

THREE STARS

The holy Reb Shmelke lived next door to a *mitnagdid*, a fierce opponent of the Hasidim, who understood the letter of the Law in the most rigid way. Therefore he performed *Havdalah*, the ceremony ending the Sabbath, as soon as three stars appeared in the sky. Reb Shmelke, on the other hand, continued to observe the Sabbath far into the night. And this bothered his neighbor to no end.

This neighbor took it on himself to save Reb Shmelke from this transgression. So as soon as three stars appeared, he would open his window and shout: "Three stars! Time for *Havdalah!*" These shouts would disturb Reb Shmelke's reveries. Nonetheless, Reb Shmelke restrained himself and never said anything about it to his neighbor. Instead, he continued to savor the Sabbath for many hours after his neighbor had reminded him that the Sabbath was over.

Seeing that he had failed to convince Reb Shmelke to change his ways, the neighbor decided on a more drastic approach. As soon as the three stars appeared, he went outside, picked up some pebbles, and threw them through Reb Shemlke's window. One of those pebbles struck Reb Shmelke, tearing him from the arms of the Sabbath Queen. And Reb Shmelke not only felt the pain of his own loss, but knew as well that his neighbor had made a terrible mistake. And before many months had passed, the neighbor became sick and died.

Some months after that, when Reb Shmelke was sitting at the Sabbath table, about the time the three stars first appeared, he suddenly smiled mysteriously. And he mumbled the words "From below they look above, from above, below." None of his Hasidim understood what he meant, but Reb Shmelke refused to tell them until the end of the Sabbath. Then he said: "The soul of our neighbor was sent to Gehenna for his sins, where he is punished all week long but spared on the Sabbath. But as soon as three stars appear, the angels drag him back to Gehenna. And all the way there he shouts, 'But Reb Shmelke is still celebrating the Sabbath!'"

□   Eastern Europe: Nineteenth Century

119

THE SHADOW ON THE WALL

One morning, as Reb Zushya of Hanipol awoke, he saw the silhouette of his brother, Reb Elimelech, on the wall of his room. Reb Zushya rubbed his eyes, certain that it was a momentary illusion, but when he looked again, the shadow had moved, and now it resembled Elimelech more than ever. Zushya sat up and peered at it, and this time the shadow seemed to be beckoning to him. There was no doubt about it—it resembled Elimelech in every way.

Zushya caught his breath. Surely Elimelech had drawn upon his great powers to summon him. Zushya knew he must go. He leaped from bed, dressed in a rush, and shook his driver, who was still sound asleep. But when the driver awoke and saw the look in Zushya's eyes, he asked no questions, dressed as quickly as he could, and hurried outside to get the wagon ready.

So it was that Zushya left the town of Hanipol and went to the city of Lizensk, directly to the home of Elimelech. There he saw Elimelech pacing back and forth outside the house. When Elimelech saw the wagon, he rushed over to greet Zushya. They embraced, and together they went into Elimelech's house.

Elimelech was the first to speak: "What took you so long?" he asked with a smile.

Zushya replied: "Then it is true that you have summoned me."

"Of course," said Elimelech, "and a good thing too, for if you were not here, you would be in jail!"

"What do you mean?" asked Zushya, who could barely believe what he heard.

"This morning, when I awoke," said Elimelech, "I saw a shadow on the wall of my room—your shadow. And there were bars surrounding that shadow, and I understood that you were in great danger of being arrested and jailed—perhaps for a very long time. So I sent my shadow to you, to tell you to come here, where you would be safe."

Zushya was staggered to learn this, and he was in awe of the powers of Elimelech. "I will do whatever you tell me to do," he said.

"You will simply stay here for one week. By that time the one who accused you will have lost his credibility, and you will no longer be in danger."

"But how do you know this?" asked Zushya.

"Look at the clock," said Elimelech.

Zushya did. It was exactly seven o'clock.

"Now, look behind you," said Elimelech. Again Zushya did as he was asked. This time he saw his own shadow cast on the wall.

Elimelech said: "That is the same wall I saw your shadow on this morning. But now there are no bars before you. From the clock I know that we must wait seven days. When that time has come, surely you will no longer be in danger."

And so it proved to be true. Reb Zushya had been denounced by an enemy of Israel, who knew how much his loss would dishearten the Jews of Hanipol. Because of this false charge, guards were sent to arrest Zushya, but he was nowhere to be found. Then, before the week was out, the accuser was discovered to be a liar and a thief and was himself imprisoned, and all charges against Reb Zushya were dropped.

□ Eastern Europe: Nineteenth Century

 120

THE GARDEN OF THE TORAH

Reb Shmelke tried to stay awake all the time to study Torah. He held a candle in one hand, so that if he fell asleep the flame would wake him when the candle burned down. Reb Elimelech once visited Reb Shmelke and noticed this, and he told him that it was imperative that he rest. He said: "You can serve God in many ways, even in your sleep."

Reb Shmelke took these words to heart and agreed to lie down on a couch in his study. He fell into a very deep sleep, and he had a dream in which he was traveling through a cave with Reb Elimelech, and Elimelech was holding a torch in his hand that illumined the cave from one end to the other. They traveled through this cave for years, but as they never stopped discussing the Torah, the time flew by for them, so the years seemed like hours and the hours like minutes.

At last they came to the other end of the cave and stepped out into a beautiful garden, with olives and dates so large that they shone like precious gems. Together with Reb Elimelech, Reb Shmelke explored every corner of that garden, and Reb Shmelke never wanted to leave it, for everywhere he went he saw the Name of God before him. In this way he recognized that they had reached the Garden of the Torah, which is also known as *Gan Eden*, the Garden of Eden.

Meanwhile, Reb Shmelke remained asleep. Everyone knew he was exhausted, so no one worried when he slept for a full day without waking. But by the end of the second day they were concerned, and by the end of the third day they were quite anxious. But no matter what they tried, they could not awaken him.

At the end of the seventh day they were desperate, and they begged Reb Elimelech to try to wake him, for they knew that no one else could succeed. Now all this time Reb Elimelech had not seemed the least bit worried about Reb Shmelke, but since they had asked for his help, he led them into Shmelke's study and placed his hand over the *mezzuzah*.

At that moment, in his dream, Reb Shmelke and Reb Elimelech had found their way to the gate at the entrance of that garden. And there, on the doorpost, Reb Shmelke had seen a *mezzuzah*. He looked at that *mezzuzah*, which seemed very familiar, and realized it looked exactly like the one on the door of his study. At that instant the Name of God, which had been before him all the time he had been in that garden, disappeared, and Reb Shmelke gasped and opened his eyes. That is when he found himself lying on the couch in his study, with a dozen bystanders watching him.

At first Shmelke was grieved to have been awakened out of that perfect dream and forced to leave that immortal garden. But when he learned how Elimelech had placed his hand over the *mezzuzah*, he understood that he had been permitted to remain in that Paradise, the Garden of the Torah, as long as possible, and now he had to return to the world of men. For when Reb Elimelech had placed his hand over the *mezzuzah*, he had covered the Name of God, and that is why it had vanished for Reb Shmelke. But now that he was awake he continued to see the Name of God before him, and this lasted all the days of his life. Reb Shmelke smiled at Reb Elimelech and said: "If only you had been with me!" And Reb Elimelech replied: "But of course I was!"

The next day, when Reb Shmelke preached to the congregation about the crossing of the Red Sea, it was said that the lapping of the waves could be felt, and the sound of the waters filled their ears. For that long sleep had restored him to his full powers, which rarely have been seen in this world.

□ Eastern Europe: Nineteenth Century

The Circle of Rabbi Nachman of Bratslav

121

A VISION OF LIGHT

Even when Reb Nachman of Bratslav was a little boy, he had a great longing to welcome the Sabbath with sanctity. One Friday afternoon when he was six, he went to the bathhouse and purified himself in the *mikveh*. Then he returned home and put on his Sabbath clothes and went alone into the House of Study.

There he anxiously awaited the extra soul that comes with the Sabbath. He was certain that at any moment he would be filled with its presence. But as time passed, nothing happened. Meanwhile, people came into the House of Study and began reciting the Song of Songs, as is customary prior to the Sabbath. The boy hid under a desk, where no one noticed him. And as the men recited the prayers, he wept quietly with his eyes tightly closed. He cried for several hours, long after the Sabbath candles had been lit. And when at last he opened his eyes, the light of the candles' flames beat against them.

Everything was very bright, and in that moment he was filled with the *Ruach ha-Kodesh*, the Holy Spirit.

Afterward a great calm came over him, for he felt the second soul strongly within him, and everywhere he looked he saw the Divine Presence.

□   Eastern Europe: Nineteenth Century

122

THE SCRIBE

The teachings and tales of Reb Nachman of Bratslav have come down to us only because one of his disciples also became his scribe. Reb Nathan of Nemirov recorded everything his *tzaddik* said, including his tales. Sometimes Reb Nachman would tell these tales on the eve of the Sabbath, and then his Hasidim would retell the stories among themselves, until the Sabbath ended and it was permitted to write again. Then Reb Nathan would write the stories down, word for word, as close to the original as he could recall.

It is said that Reb Nathan became a disciple of Reb Nachman's after having met him in a dream. In the dream, Reb Nathan dreamed of a ladder that rose up from earth into heaven. Reb Nathan began to ascend that ladder in order to reach the heavenly realm. But after climbing only a few rungs, he fell backward to the ground. Many times Reb Nathan attempted to ascend the ladder, and each time he climbed closer to heaven, but each time he fell backward before he reached the top. Then, at last, Reb Nathan succeeded in climbing close to the top rung. Suddenly the figure of a man whose face was radiant appeared at the top. And this man said to Reb Nathan: "If you never allow yourself to give up hope, Nathan, you will surely reach the top." And then he woke up.

A year later, while on business in Bratslav, Reb Nathan decided to spend the Sabbath at the house of Reb Nachman in order to hear his discourse on the Torah. As Reb Nathan entered the house, he found that the Hasidim had already begun to pray. Slowly Reb Nathan made his way through the maze of Hasidim and found a place just behind the rebbe. When Reb Nachman began to distribute the wine of the Kiddush and turned in the direction of Reb Nathan, their eyes met, and Reb Nachman said, "Welcome. We have already known each other a long time." Then Reb Nathan remembered the dream of the year before and recalled the radiant face of the man who had spoken to him out of the heavens. And they were one and the same. And in this way began the lifelong bond in which Reb Nathan came to serve as Reb Nachman's scribe.

□   Eastern Europe: Nineteenth Century

፡ቯፇ፡ቯፇ፡ቯፇ፡ቯፇ፡ቯፇ፡ 123 ፡ቯፇ፡ቯፇ፡ቯፇ፡ቯፇ፡ቯፇ፡

The Sabbath Fish

Reb Nathan of Nemirov, Reb Nachman's scribe, once had a dream in which he was told that a man would offer him a fish in the morning. He was to buy that fish and to take it at once to Reb Nachman. When he awoke, Reb Nathan recalled this dream and wondered about it. Just then there was a knock at the door. A poor Jew stood there with a wagonload of fish. Reb Nathan saw that he was holding a single fish, a white one. He raised his hands, silently offering the fish to Reb Nathan. And Nathan, with the dream still vivid in his memory, gave him a substantial amount of money and thanked him for the fish with all his heart.

Then Reb Nathan hurried to Reb Nachman. As soon as he came in, Reb Nachman said: "Where is the fish?" Reb Nathan quickly handed the white fish to the rebbe. Then Reb Nachman said: "Your father came to me in a dream last night and told me that his soul had been placed inside this fish. If that fish were to be cooked for the Sabbath, the soul would be free to take its resting place in the World to Come. So too did his soul come to you unseen and whisper in your ear while you were asleep. That is how you knew not to turn away the fish seller."

"But who was the fish seller?" Reb Nathan asked.

"Elijah, of course," Reb Nachman said.

So it was that the fish was served for dinner on that Sabbath, and the soul of Reb Nathan's father was set free to ascend on high.

□   Eastern Europe: Nineteenth Century

༄༅࿐࿇࿐࿇࿐࿇࿐ 124 ࿐࿇࿐࿇࿐࿇࿐࿇༄

THE SWORD OF THE MESSIAH

Among Reb Nachman's best-known disciples was Reb Shmuel Isaac. Like Reb Nachman, he had great prophetic powers. Not only could he see into the future, but he also had visions in which he ascended into Paradise. Several of these visions were recorded in a small notebook that was lost after his death. Only one of Reb Shmuel's visions was preserved.

In this vision Reb Shmuel found himself walking at night through a snow-covered forest. There he saw a light glowing far off, as distant as a star, and with nothing else to guide him, he followed it. He made his way through that dark forest, ignoring the icy wind and the howling of wolves. He kept his eyes fixed on the distant light, certain that it held his salvation.

At last, deep in the forest, Reb Shmuel came to a clearing in the shape of a circle. That clearing was filled with light, and when Reb Shmuel came closer, he saw that a ladder of light rose up there. Reb Shmuel looked at it in amazement, certain that it was none other than that seen by Jacob in his dream. But while Jacob had seen angels ascending and descending that ladder, Reb Shmuel saw none.

He stood at the base of it and peered up into the sky. He saw how the ladder ascended as far as he could see, into the very heavens. And at the top of the ladder he saw the light that had guided him to this place, the heavenly star that drew him ever closer. And he knew that he would have to ascend that ladder, wherever it would take him.

When Reb Shmuel stepped on the first rung, he found that it somehow held him, though it consisted only of light. Indeed, the ladder felt very secure, as if it were anchored in the most solid of foundations. Then Reb Shmuel lost his fear and climbed from rung to rung, determined to reach that distant light.

Reb Shmuel climbed until he finally reached the top of the ladder. There he saw that the source of that light was a magnificent palace. Outside that palace grew a tree with branches that seemed to reach into every corner of heaven, and in the branches he saw a golden nest, with a golden dove in it. The song of that dove filled the air, and it was so beautiful that he felt like weeping. Then Reb Shmuel realized that he had ascended to the very palace of the Messiah, and that the bird he saw was none other than the golden dove of the Messiah, whose heavenly song is immortal.

When Reb Shmuel realized that it was the light of the Messiah's palace that had guided him there, he was overwhelmed. And he was drawn to that incredible palace like a moth to a flame. He came to its door and saw that it consisted of black flames burning on white, and he drew in his breath and walked through that door, knowing full well that it might be impossible to turn back. Inside he found a chamber of awesome beauty, and while he marveled at its uniqueness, he suddenly saw that a gateway had opened leading to another chamber, and from there to yet another, and so from room to room and from story to story. Thus he found that every entrance led to the next, and everything was connected to everything else with the profoundest wisdom and beauty.

Reb Shmuel moved from room to room in that fiery palace until he came to a door with a flame that burned much brighter than any other. And somehow he knew that he had come to the end of his quest, that behind that door he would find the Messiah, who had guided him to that place.

Gathering all his courage, Reb Shmuel stepped through that fiery door into the inner chamber. There he was blinded by a brilliant light that filled every corner of the room. Shielding his eyes, Reb Shmuel could make out an old man with a white beard seated on a throne before him. He was holding a sword, and Reb Shmuel saw that his face was the source of the light that filled the room. Then he knew with certainty that the old man must be the Messiah, who has waited all these years for his time to come.

"Do you see this sword?" the Messiah asked. Reb Shmuel nodded that he did, for he was speechless. "With this sword I shall conquer the world!"

Bewildered, Reb Shmuel could not comprehend what the old man meant. Then the Messiah said: "Go to your rebbe. He will explain everything to you."

At that moment Reb Shmuel's vision ended, and he found himself standing before the House of Study in Bratslav. In great confusion he entered, knowing that his only hope was to ask Reb Nachman to explain his vision. As he stepped inside, he saw that Reb Nachman was teaching a lesson. And the first words Reb Shmuel heard Reb Nachman say were: "And the sword of the Messiah is prayer!"

□   Eastern Europe: Nineteenth Century

125

THE SOULS OF TREES

Reb Nachman was once traveling with his Hasidim by carriage, and as it grew dark they came to an inn, where they spent the night. During the night Reb Nachman began to cry out loudly in his sleep, waking up everyone in the inn, all of whom came running to see what had happened.

When he awoke, the first thing Reb Nachman did was to take out a book he had brought with him. Then he closed his eyes and opened the book and pointed to a passage. And there it was written "Cutting down a tree before its time is like killing a soul."

Then Reb Nachman asked the innkeeper if the walls of that inn had been built out of saplings cut down before their time. The innkeeper admitted that this was true, but how did the rabbi know?

And Reb Nachman said: "All night I dreamed I was surrounded by the bodies of those who had been murdered. I was very frightened. Now I know that it was the souls of the trees that cried out to me."

□   Eastern Europe: Nineteenth Century

126

DIVINING FROM THE ZOHAR

While Reb Nachman of Bratslav was in the Holy Land, he became famous even among the Ishmaelites, because they knew that he was a great miracle maker. And for a long time after his return to Bratslav, the Ishmaelites approached his Hasidim in Jerusalem and asked for their influence in obtaining the rabbi's assistance.

When Reb Nachman learned of their pleas, he was always willing to help, for in time of trouble he did not distinguish between Jew and non-Jew.

Now it happened that three years after Reb Nachman returned from the Holy Land, the son of the Kadi suddenly disappeared, and his family could not be comforted.

One day, when the Kadi learned that one of the Hasidim was traveling to Bratslav, he asked the traveler to tell the story of his son's disappearance to Reb Nachman and to ask him to decipher the mystery.

When the Hasid reached Bratslav and reported this to Reb Nachman, the rabbi opened the book of the Zohar to the *parasha* of *Mishpatim*. As if in a clear mirror, he saw everything there, and he said to the Hasid: "When you go back to Jerusalem, tell the Kadi that there are two Ishmaelites in the city of Jerusalem who kidnap boys to sell them into slavery. And if the Kadi goes to the city of Rhodes, he will find his son there."

And that is exactly what happened. The Kadi traveled to Rhodes and there he found his son, who had been sold as a slave. The tale of the boy's release involved great dangers, but at last he was set free.

▫ Eastern Europe: Oral Tradition

127

THE ANGEL OF LOSSES

Late one evening, when Reb Nachman and his Hasidim were gathered together, a strong wind blew in the open window and extinguished all the candles. Some of the Hasidim rose to relight them, but Reb Nachman stopped them, telling them to remain in the dark. So they did. For a long time there was silence. Then one of the Hasidim said: "Tell me, rebbe, is the blowing out of the candles a good omen or bad?"

"Surely it is a sign that another presence is among us, an angel who watches over us even in the dark. This is Yodea, the Angel of Losses. Even now he is watching our lives unfold, recording every detail before it fades. This angel has servants, and his servants have servants. Some of these servants are angels, and some are not. Each of the angels carries a shovel, and they spend all their time digging, searching for losses. For a great deal is lost in our lives.

"So too is every *tzaddik* a servant of the Angel Yodea. That is because even a *tzaddik* who searches after lost things is himself sometimes lost. And as you know, it is necessary to search in the dark, in the realm of the unknown. And with what do you search in the darkness? With the light of the soul. For the soul is a light planted in the *tzaddik* to seek after whatever has been lost.

"What kind of light is it? Not a torch, but a small candle. Yet even so, with it you can search inside deep wells, where darkness is unbroken, peering into every corner and crevice. So for once let us be guided by that light, small though it may be."

That is when the Hasidim all saw the flame that was burning before Reb Nachman's face. And even though they were in complete darkness, still they saw his face as if it were glowing in the dark. And indeed it was, for every one of them to see.

□   Eastern Europe: Nineteenth Century

≋≋≋≋≋≋≋≋≋≋ 128 ≋≋≋≋≋≋≋≋≋≋

The Book that was Burned

Between Purim and Pesach, when Reb Nachman was in Lemberg, he went into a special room every day and cried. At last he called Reb Shimon and said: "I have a terrible dilemma. In my house in Bratslav there is a book in which I invested my soul. And because that book contains truths taken from on high, it has already caused me a great tragedy. For its very existence caused my son, Shlomo Ephraim, to lose his life. And now a *bat kol*, a heavenly voice, has told me that if that book is not burned, my own life will be lost."

When Shimon heard this, a shiver passed through his body, but he remained silent, for he realized that such a momentous decision could be made only by Reb Nachman. As far as Shimon was concerned, the life of his rebbe was the most precious thing in the world. But he was worried that Reb Nachman might think that the truths revealed in that book were more precious than life itself.

Then Reb Nachman said, "All of the secrets contained in that book were revealed to me in dreams, for in dreams the soul is free to ascend into the highest heavens. And I had to overcome great obstacles when I awoke in order to recall all that I learned there, for the angels did everything in their power to make me forget. I paid a great price for my loyalty to this book, and its continued existence will now cost me my life." Reb Nachman began to weep, and Shimon saw that his heart was broken. Then Shimon decided to speak up and he said, "It is far better, in my opinion, to burn the book so that the rebbe will remain alive."

Reb Nachman replied, "The mysteries of this book must not be hinted at, but it is the other truths—the ones I am still permitted to reveal—and not my own life, that must be weighed in the balance." Reb Nachman was silent for a long time, and Shimon dared not interrupt.

Suddenly Reb Nachman took a key from his pocket, handed it to Shimon, and said, "If the book must be burned, here is the key to the bookcase in which it is kept. A second copy is hidden in the trunk beneath my bed. Go quickly, before I change my mind. Run, don't walk. Take a carriage and go to Bratslav and see to it that both copies of the book are burned. And do not burn only one copy and keep the other, for that would be the same as not burning either one." When Shimon took the key, he saw that the rebbe's hand was shaking. And he hurried off to complete the terrible task. For next to taking a life, what is more terrible than burning a book?

Shimon immediately hired a carriage to go to Bratslav. And when the carriage finally arrived, he hurried into the rebbe's house, set a fire in the stove, and burned the two books. And their truths were returned to smoke and rose into the heavens, whence they had come.

About this book Reb Nathen, Reb Nachman's scribe, adds the following: "When I was writing down the book for Reb Nachman that was burned according to his order, the rebbe said to me, 'If only you knew what it is you write.' And I said to him, 'Surely I do not know.' And he said, 'You don't know how much you don't know.'"

□ Eastern Europe: Nineteenth Century

❧ 129 ❧

A LETTER FROM THE BEYOND

When Reb Yisrael Dov Odesser was a young man, he mistakenly ate on the 17th of Tammuz, a fast day, and he became very depressed. He was so downcast that he even contemplated suicide. But before taking such a terrible step, he decided to open a book at random to see if he could find a reason to live. He closed his eyes and took down a book from the shelf. When he looked at it, he found it was one of Reb Nachman's. He opened the book, and tucked among the pages he found a letter from Reb Nachman to himself—a letter that spoke to him directly and transformed his life. In the letter Reb Nachman told him to live and to affirm life, for that was his true destiny, and that he—Reb Nachman—would always be with him. This letter transformed Reb Yisrael's life, and he always maintained that Reb Nachman had sent it to him from heaven.

□ Israel: Oral Tradition

130

REB NACHMAN'S CHAIR

Before he died, Reb Nachman of Bratslav said to his Hasidim: "After my death it will not be necessary to appoint a successor, for I will always be your rabbi." Nor did anyone ever take his place. And Reb Nachman's spirit did indeed guard and guide his followers. Many tales are told of how Reb Nachman's spirit came to their assistance. One of these tales concerns Reb Nachman's chair.

Shortly before Rosh Hashanah in 1808, the *shohet* of Teplik brought Reb Nachman a beautiful chair that he had made for him. He had worked on carving the chair for many months with all the love in his soul. From the first everyone realized it was a very special chair, as beautiful and intricate as any throne. And the Bratslav Hasidim regarded it as the throne of their rebbe.

That night Reb Nachman dreamed that someone brought him a throne, surrounded by fire. Everyone, men, women, and children, came to see it. Engraved on that throne were all the world's creatures, along with their mates. And as the people turned to go, bonds were formed between them and marriages were arranged at once, for each had been able to find his mate. And in the dream Reb Nachman sat down on the chair, and all at once he found himself flying through the heavens, and before him he saw Jerusalem, glowing like a jewel in the distance. It was indescribably beautiful, and as he approached it, he woke up.

Reb Nachman shared this dream with his Hasidim, and it became part of the lore of the chair. Reb Nachman used that chair all the days of his life. And when he died, his Hasidim kept the empty chair next to the Ark, for they never forgot the last words of their rebbe: that he would always be with them. The chair remained with the Bratslavers until the Second World War. Then, after the Nazis invaded, the Hasidim realized they must escape as soon as possible. But what were they to do with the chair? They decided to cut it into small pieces and to give one piece to every Hasid. Then they made a vow to meet in Jerusalem and to reassemble the chair there. And they took leave of each other and set out, each in his own way, to reach the Holy Land.

Now that was a very dangerous time, and few were those who escaped unharmed. But every Bratslaver who carried a piece of that chair arrived safely in Jerusalem and there it was reassembled. And as much care was taken in restoring that chair as in repairing a shattered vessel. And when it was finished, the chair looked exactly as it did when Reb Nachman first received it. And it is standing to this day, in the Bratslaver synagogue in Jerusalem, next to the Ark.

□   Israel: Oral Tradition

⚙⚙⚙⚙⚙⚙ 131 ⚙⚙⚙⚙⚙⚙

Reb Nachman's Tomb

Now in Jerusalem there was a wonderful violinist among the Bratslavers whose name was Reb Moshe Shilge. This Moshe was a *baal teshuvah*, one who has returned to the fold. Before he had come back to the ways of his fathers, he had played the violin to earn his living, but now he dedicated his music to the Holy One, blessed be He, for when he played the violin he felt he was singing in praise of all that is sacred.

This Reb Moshe joined a group of Bratslavers on a pilgrimage to Reb Nachman's tomb in Uman, in Russia. For every Bratslaver Hasid seeks to go there at least once in his lifetime. That is because on his deathbed Reb Nachman made a promise. He said that anyone who went to his tomb, gave charity to the poor, and recited with intensity the ten psalms he told them to say, in the proper order, would be saved from Gehenna if, God forbid, the Hasid should arrive there.

In that old cemetery in Uman there was a mass grave for tens of thousands of martyrs who were killed there in the terrible pogrom of 1768. Reb Nachman had asked to be buried there so that he could redeem the souls of the dead, much as the Baal Shem Tov had once done in another town.

Now the journey to Reb Nachman's tomb was fraught with danger. For the Russian government threw many obstacles in the way of those who sought to reach the rebbe's grave. And many of the Hasidim were stopped and had to turn back or were arrested and charged with being spies. In fact, shortly before Reb Moshe planned to go to Uman, another Hasid had been arrested while making the attempt. A considerable ransom was demanded and everyone contributed something to free the Hasid, no matter how poor they were. Although this incident might have discouraged others, it did not discourage Reb Moshe.

Now before he departed, Reb Moshe asked his wife for permission to set out on such a journey. And his wife concurred because she was certain that a messenger intent on performing a mitzvah would not be harmed. For Reb Moshe's wife shared his devotion to the study of the Torah and his love for Reb Nachman, whose spirit pervaded their lives.

So Reb Moshe took his beloved violin and set out. The way brought him into contact with other Bratslavers, who were traveling from all over the world to complete this essential quest. The Bratslavers met in Europe, and from there they traveled together. There were twenty-two of them in all. They arrived on the eve of Rosh Hashanah in Kiev, about a hundred miles from Uman. Reb Moshe felt that his heart was about to explode from his longing to reach the rebbe's tomb. He felt as if he were being pulled there by a powerful magnet. Then he noticed that a special light shone from the others' faces, clear and bright. And Moshe was certain it was the presence of Reb Nachman's soul that had created this intense longing in them.

So it was that all of the Hasidim were deeply disappointed when they were unable to reach the Rebbe's tomb by Rosh Hashanah. They remained in Kiev, and there they spent the days of the holiday and the Sabbath.

After the Sabbath they left Kiev before dawn and set out for Uman. On the way they stopped at a freshwater pond, and all immersed themselves in its waters. After this they prayed together under the sky. And as their words rose in unison, so did their souls bind themselves into one, imprinting that moment in their memories for all the days of their lives. Then they continued the journey to Uman.

And when they arrived at Uman, they entered the cemetery and raced about, trying to find the rebbe's tomb. A Gentile woman showed them the way.

When at last they reached the rebbe's tomb, they lay down at the foot of it, and Reb Moshe cried with relief for having been blessed to reach that place. Then he put on his *tallis* and *tefillin* and said the ten psalms Reb Nachman had chosen with great emotion, and there he understood them as never before.

Now Reb Moshe was named after his father, who had passed away two months before he was born. So there at the tomb Reb Moshe said the orphan's Kaddish with tears running down his face. After this he took his violin and played the melodies of his rebbe. And as he played he felt a great calm come over him, and he knew a closeness to God he had never experienced before in his life. He played quietly, simply, without flourishes, but with great longing and desire. And there, surrounded by the other tombs and by great trees, the melodies of Reb Nachman rose in the air, pulling all of them up one rung after another, ascending the stairway of the soul.

□   Israel: Oral Tradition

⚜ 132 ⚜

The Soul of Reb Nachman

It was well known among the followers of Rav Kook that a great change had come over him when he came to the Holy Land. So great was the transformation that even his handwriting changed, as if he had become a different person. And, indeed, Rav Kook was once heard to say: "I am the soul of Reb Nachman."

For years after his death, Rav Kook's followers debated the meaning of these words among themselves. Some of them said that the soul had come to him as an *ibur*, a spirit that possessed him and combined with his own. This was none other than the very soul of Reb Nachman of Bratslav, whose soul fused with Rav Kook the moment he set foot on the Holy Land. And that is why a change came over him, for two souls had fused into one.

But others insisted that by those words Rav Kook had meant precisely that his soul and the soul of Reb Nachman were one and the same, and that the soul of Reb Nachman had been reincarnated in his body. The reason a change came over him when he reached the Holy Land was that Rabbi Nachman greatly loved the Holy Land, and his soul celebrated when Rav Kook arrived there.

Nor has this debate among the followers of Rav Kook been settled even to this day.

☐ Israel: Oral Tradition

Other Hasidic Masters

░░░░░░░░░░ 133 ░░░░░░░░░░

A VISION OF THE BRIDE

Soon after his thirty-sixth birthday, Reb Levi Yitzhak of Berditchev traveled to the city of Kallo, arriving after dark on the twentieth day of counting the *Omer*. The carriage brought him to the house where he was to stay, and the driver departed. But when Levi Yitzhak knocked on the door, no one answered it, for no one would open the door that late at night. All Levi Yitzhak wanted to do was to pray the evening prayer and count the *Omer*, but now he had nowhere to spend the night.

Levi Yitzhak had no idea what to do, and he became dejected. He fell through a bottomless pit that he had never known to exist, and just when he thought he would continue to fall forever, a Jew passed on the street and asked if he could be of any help. Levi Yitzhak was greatly relieved to see him and told him of his plight. And the man offered to let him stay in his house.

Levi Yitzhak followed the Jew to his home and went inside. The man had Levi Yitzhak wait in the living room, and while he was gone Levi Yitzhak noticed an unusually large collection of holy books. He took down a prayer book, but when he opened it, he saw to his horror that the Name of God had been blotted out every time it appeared. And Levi Yitzhak rushed away from that house, which he knew must be the pit of hell, for that is how far he had fallen.

As Levi Yitzhak wandered through the streets of the empty city, he wondered if it were the city of the dead, and if he had died and been cut off from men, so that now he was prey to demons. And as he walked, he cried bitter tears.

After he had been walking for a long time, he saw a spark of light in the distance. He said to himself: "Perhaps that is a House of Study over there." And, indeed, it was. Levi Yitzhak went inside, but no one was there. So he prayed alone until midnight, and still he could not escape from a boundless grief. All that consoled him was the certainty that the sorrow of the Bride's exile must surely be much greater, for she too was in the darkness, waiting for someone to let her in.

Again he cried bitterly until he fell asleep from exhaustion. And in a dream he saw a vision of a bride whose veil radiated a light brighter than the sun. And in the vision he heard a heavenly voice say: "Be strong, my son Levi Yitzhak, be strong. A hard time is upon you. But fear not, for I am with you." And when the vision ended, Levi Yitzhak felt the presence of the Bride everywhere, in the stars, in the wind, in the night. And his grief gave way to great joy, for now the Bride had torn away the veil.

▫   Eastern Europe: Nineteenth Century

134 THE FLAMING LETTERS

The *Maggid* of Mezhirich once asked his student, Reb Shneur Zalman, to create a new style of letters for the Torah, the *tefillin*, and the *Mezzuzot*. He asked that it be very intricate and special, with each letter's shape made according to its kabbalistic meaning.

Reb Shneur Zalman took this assignment very seriously, and before beginning it, he fasted from Sabbath to Sabbath and then immersed himself in the *mikveh*. As soon as he began to work, he felt the presence of the *Shekhinah* in the room. And while he was drawing the letters, it was as if they drew themselves. And all that time Reb Shneur Zalman felt exactly like a vessel, ready to receive the holy spirit filling him with its abundance.

When he finished the last letter, Reb Shneur Zalman found that he had created a shape for the letters according to their mystical meanings. And everyone who looked at those letters agreed that each and every one resembled a flame, burning first in the shape of one letter and then another.

As soon as the letters were finished, Reb Shneur Zalman took them to the *Maggid* of Mezhirich. When the *Maggid* saw those letters, he was filled with joy. And he said: "You have done well. But now I must ask that you go at once to Reb Moshe Sopher, for he will surely want to use them to write a Torah. For that would be a flaming Torah, with every letter a flame of its own."

So Reb Shneur Zalman took his leave of the *Maggid* and set out for the city of Annopol, where Reb Moshe Sopher lived. Now that was also the town of Reb Zusya, and Reb Moshe Sopher was a follower of Reb Zusya, and he was often called upon to serve as a holy scribe.

Reb Shneur Zalman arrived in the city at night, and when he reached Reb Moshe's house, it was already quite late. And when he knocked on the door, no one came to open it. Finally, after a long wait,

Reb Moshe came to the door. He apologized and said that he had been about to write the Holy Name, and he could not stop. Shneur Zalman well understood the importance of *kavanah* when a *sopher* wrote a sacred text, and he begged Reb Moshe to continue until he was finished.

So Reb Moshe went back to work on the text for the *tefillin*, and Reb Shneur Zalman waited until he had finished writing the parchment. But when Shneur Zalman looked at the parchment for the first time, he saw, to his complete amazement, that the flaming letters were identical to those that he himself had just created. He could not believe his eyes. He asked Reb Moshe: "Where did you find these letters?" And Reb Moshe answered: "Several days ago Reb Zusya came to me and asked me to write the letters for the text of the *tefillin* according to the shapes of the letters revealed to him by heaven in a dream."

□   Eastern Europe: Nineteenth Century

135

THE SABA KADISHA IN THE UPPER WORLD

When the Saba Kadisha of Shpola was a young man, he was a Hasid of Reb Pinhas of Koretz. One night he dreamed that he had already taken leave of this world and come to his place in the Garden of Eden. Never had he felt so completely at home. Then he was summoned by an angel to the upper world, to stand before the heavenly Sandhedrin. So he left Eden and ascended to the Sanhedrin on high. And when he stood before them, they told him that he had to go back to the world to save the people of Israel. But in the dream the Saba Kadisha did not want to go. He said he had been reborn enough times; now he wanted to remain in the Garden of Eden. Just as he said this, he heard the gates of Eden close, and he understood that he had been barred from there. But still he refused to descend to the world below. Instead he decided it was better to remain in the upper world, even if he was condemned to be a wandering soul.

That, indeed was his punishment by the Sanhedrin, and in this way many years passed, three generations in all. And all that time he knew nothing except for the circles of a wheel that never stopped spinning.

Then one day he saw a Jew who appeared in the upper world wearing a long coat with a belt of rope, and on his back he carried a shovel. And when the Saba Kadisha saw him, a great fear fell upon him, so intense was that man's gaze and so bright the aura he cast. And that Jew shouted at him in a great voice, saying: "What are you doing here? Go down at once to the world and save the people of Israel!" This so terrified the Saba Kadisha that he quickly agreed to go, and at that instant the Jew in the old coat disappeared, and an angel came and brought him to the world of men.

On the way to this world, the Saba Kadisha asked the angel who that Jew was and why he was carrying a shovel. The angel did not reveal his name but told him that he was the pillar on which the House of Israel was leaning, and with the shovel he set free souls that had been all but forgotten, as his own had been. And that is when the Saba Kadisha awoke from his dream, but the memory of it haunted him for days.

Some time later the Saba Kadisha accompanied his master, Reb Pinhas of Koretz, to the house of the Baal Shem Tov, whom the Saba Kadisha had never met. Just as they reached the entrance of his house, the Saba Kadisha saw the glowing shape of the Baal Shem Tov through the window and recognized him at once as the Jew carrying the shovel on his back, who had met him in the upper world. And he became dizzy and fainted.

And when the Saba Kadisha opened his eyes, he found himself seated inside the house, in the presence of the Baal Shem Tov. And the Baal Shem said: "Why did it take you so long to come here?"

□   Eastern Europe: Nineteenth Century

136

THE WANDERING WELL

One year, on the eve of Yom Kippur, just as the congregation was gathering in the synagogue before sunset, Rabbi Eizik of Kallo whispered to Rabbi Yaakov Fish that he wanted him to harness his horse. Rabbi Yaakov could not believe his ears, but he knew better than to question the ways of his rebbe. So he went to fetch the horse and wagon. And Rabbi Eizik, still wearing his white robe and prayer shawl, climbed into the wagon and directed them toward the outskirts of town.

They drove until Rabbi Eizik told Rabbi Yaakov to stop. Then Rabbi Eizik stepped down and went into the fields. Rabbi Yaakov followed him, greatly wondering why they had come there. Soon Rabbi Eizik led him to a small pool. Now Rabbi Yaakov was truly mystified, for he knew that area very well, and he had never seen a pool there. And he watched, almost in a trance, as Rabbi Eizik disrobed and stepped into the waters. There he dipped himself several times and then emerged from the waters and quickly dressed.

Then they returned to the wagon and drove back to the synagogue, and when they arrived, Rabbi Yaakov was amazed to find that the *Kol Nidre* prayers had not yet begun. Indeed, it seemed as if time had stood still. Then, just as they entered the synagogue, the prayers began, and Rabbi Yaakov knew that his questions would have to wait.

All that Yom Kippur, Rabbi Yaakov was wrapped in the mystery of Rabbi Eizik's strange deed, and he prayed with a greater intensity than ever, so that he would be worthy of understanding it. At last, when Yom Kippur had ended and the fast was broken, Rabbi Yaakov went back to that same place and searched for the pool, but it was not to be found anywhere. He returned to Rabbi Eizek and said: "Please, rebbe, tell me why you went to that pool and what pool it was, for it has already disappeared."

Rabbi Eizik said: "As you know, Miriam's well followed the Israelites during their forty years of wandering, and it is still traveling
from place to place, wherever Jews are to be found. And when I heard
a heavenly voice say that it was passing near here, I knew that I had to
go at once. And if you had any sense, you would have dipped yourself
in it too!"

□ Hungary: Nineteenth Century

⊱⧉⊰⧉⊰⧉⊰⧉⊰⧉⊰ 137 ⊱⧉⊰⧉⊰⧉⊰⧉⊰⧉⊰

THE SABBATH GUESTS

Two traveling Hasidim arrived in the city of Kallo on the eve of the
Sabbath and sought out the hospitality of the Rabbi of Kallo, about
whom they had heard so much. Already tales were being told of his
miracles throughout Hungary, and the visiting Hasidim greatly antici-
pated spending the Sabbath in his company.

Soon everyone had gathered together to celebrate the Sabbath, and
all looked toward the *tzaddik* of Kallo for the signal to welcome the
Sabbath Queen. But the *tzaddik* did not stir. Not a single muscle
moved. Every eye remained upon him, yet he seemed detached, in
deep concentration.

The visiting Hasidim were startled at such behavior, for no one ever
delayed the beginning of the Sabbath for even an instant. Could it be
that the rabbi had lost track of time?

All at once there was a knocking at the door, and when it was
opened a couple came in. The young man was dressed in a white robe,
as was worn in the Holy Land. The young woman, who was also
wearing a white robe, was hauntingly beautiful, with very dark eyes,
her head covered with a white scarf. The *tzaddik* rose, at the same time
signaling for the Sabbath to begin. The Hasidim began singing *Lecha
Dodi*, the song that welcomes the Sabbath Queen, as the Rabbi of
Kallo went to meet his guests. He treated them with every kindness,
paying as much attention to the woman as to the man. This was too

much for the visiting Hasidim, but they were guests, and there was nothing they could do.

All during the Sabbath meal the Rabbi of Kallo paid attention only to the young couple, completely ignoring the other visitors. As far as they were concerned, this only made matters worse.

After the meal the Rabbi of Kallo rose and said: "This couple has come here to be wed this day. And I have agreed to wed them." Now these words were a deep shock to the visiting Hasidim, for weddings are forbidden on the Sabbath. And they began reciting psalms to themselves to protect themselves from the desecration of the Sabbath. At that moment the Rabbi of Kallo turned to the two Hasidim and addressed them. He said: "Of course, the consent of everyone present is necessary if the wedding is to be performed. Please tell us if we may have your consent?" And there was almost a pleading tone in his voice.

Now it is one thing to witness such a desecration and quite another to perform one. But the two Hasidim did not dare turn down the *tzaddik* to his face. Instead they each dropped their eyes and continued reciting psalms, and a great fear was in their hearts.

At last, when they raised their eyes, they saw that the couple was gone. The Rabbi of Kallo was slumped in his chair. For a long time there was silence. At last the rabbi said: "Do you know who they were?" Each of the visiting Hasidim shook his head to say no. And the rabbi said: "He was the Messiah. She was the Sabbath Queen. For so many years of exile they have sought each other, and now they were together at last, and they wanted to be wed. And, as everyone knows, on the day of their wedding our exile will come to an end. But that is possible only if everyone gives his full assent. Unfortunately, you did not, and the wedding could not take place."

▫   Hungary: Nineteenth Century

138

FROM THE BEYOND

In the city of Karaster in Hungary there was a *melamed* whose name was Rabbi Mordecai. He taught the best students, and everyone in town respected him. He was learned in the ways of the Hasidim and was known as a master of the Kabbalah.

Once the *melamed* was invited to a *bris* in a nearby village. After the ceremony the father served a fine meal, as was the custom. And during the meal, when everyone was enjoying himself, Rabbi Mordecai the *melamed* said: "Ladies and gentlemen, if you want to see Joav ben Tsrouya, King David's general, I will call him forth." And the guests replied: "Who doesn't want to see such a thing? Let the rabbi bring forth one of the greatest figures of Israel."

At once Rabbi Mordecai stood up. He lifted his eyes, then lowered them, then looked toward each of the four corners of the room. While he did this, he whispered holy names. The guests watched in awe as the foundation of the house began to shake and then broke apart, and from the earth emerged the head of a man, wearing a copper helmet. And the head rose up until the shoulders emerged, and soon they saw that the man had a sword on his thigh and a dagger in his hand. Never had they seen a soldier so imposing. Before he emerged fully from the earth, his head reached the ceiling and then broke through it. When the guests saw this, they screamed in terror. So the *melamed* raised his hand and ordered the figure to go back to his place. But the gigantic soldier ignored him and continued to rise, destroying everything in his way. Again the *melamed* urged him to return to his resting place, and Joav answered, "Why did you bother me? Tell me, what do you want of me? Do you think I will return so easily? No, now that I am here, I won't go back to my place until I destroy the whole city!" And these words struck terror in everyone.

Now at that moment a simple man, Hayim the Vinekeeper, heard the cries of terror. He entered the house and saw the enormous man coming out of the earth, armed for combat. Without hesitation, he approached the giant figure and said: "Go back to the place where you came from!"

All at once the unearthly soldier started to sink into the earth. Soon the last of his helmet disappeared, and the roof and the floor were restored to the way they had been before the *melamed* had disturbed the dead. Everyone thanked Hayim the Vinekeeper for saving them and hurried away, glaring at the *melamed*. After this the *melamed* went back home and packed his bags and was never seen again. And Hayim went back to his vineyard.

▢ Hungary: Nineteenth Century

৪৫৩৫৫৫৩৫৫৫৩৫৫৫৩৫৫৫   139   ৵৫৫৫৫৩৫৫৫৩৫৫৫৩৫৫৫৩

THE PRAYER LEADER

One year the Holy Rabbi of Kallo became sick after Rosh Hashanah. He told his congregation that he would not be able to stand in front of the Ark on Yom Kippur, and that they should find another prayer leader. They tried to change his mind, but when they saw they could not, they began to search for someone worthy to take his place. But they were not able to find anyone. And when the Days of Awe were almost at an end, the heads of the congregation returned to the rabbi and begged him again to be the Master of Prayer, as he had been for so long, or to tell them whom to approach. So he sent them to the village of Saag to ask Hayim, the keeper of the vineyard, to be the prayer leader. And what if Hayim turned them down? In that case they were to give him a sealed letter that the rabbi had written, but they were to give it to him only if he refused to accompany them.

So the leaders of the congregation went to Saag and found Hayim the Vinekeeper. They were very surprised that their rabbi had se-

lected such a simple man. Still they asked him to come with them to
Kallo to be the Master of Prayer on Yom Kippur. "How is it possible
that I am the one chosen for this honor?" Hayim asked. "The truth is
that I have never stood before the Ark, except for the day my father
died." When the leaders saw that he was reluctant to go, they gave him
the sealed letter from the Holy Rabbi of Kallo. And when he read it,
he packed a few things at once and went with them.

When they arrived in Kallo, Reb Yaakov Fish, a Hasid of the Rabbi
of Kallo, was very curious to see how the holy rebbe would welcome
the vinekeeper and to hear what they would talk about. So he went
to the house of the rabbi and hid behind the curtain in the room where
the rabbi would meet with his guest. For several hours he waited for
the new Master of Prayer. When Hayim arrived at last, the Rabbi of
Kallo received him with happiness and told him to sit down, and they
both began to sing. All of a sudden the whole room was filled with
song and light, and fire came out and danced around them, and they
sat inside it, singing. When the hidden Hasid saw this, he grew very
frightened and was afraid for his life. And he rushed out from behind
the curtain and ran out of the house.

What took place that year at Yom Kippur is impossible to describe.
Whoever heard Hayim the Vinekeeper praying on that holy day
learned for the first time what prayer is. Angels and seraphim gathered
to hear his prayers before God, and everyone sensed the Divine Presence that pervaded the sanctuary.

But after Yom Kippur, despite the pleading of the congregation,
Hayim went back to the village to work as vinekeeper. And that is
what he did until the end of his days.

□   Hungary: Nineteenth Century

140

The Pact

In every generation there are three sages who together possess the power to force the coming of the Messiah. In the time of the ancient sages, it was Rabbi Hiyya and his sons. In the time of the Ari, it was the Ari and two of his disciples, Hayim Vital and Israel Sarug. And in the time of the Hasidim, it was three masters: the Seer of Lublin, Reb Menachem Mendel of Riminov, and Reb Baruch of Medzibozh.

Over the generations these three sages existed, but rarely did they live near each other, nor did they know that this great power could be theirs if they joined together. But the Seer of Lublin uncovered this secret and revealed it to the other two sages. All of them were filled with a terrible longing for the Messiah. So they made a pact to force the Messiah to come on Simhat Torah of that year.

Now it happened that just before Rosh Hashanah, Baruch of Medzibozh took sick and died. Twenty-two days later, on Simhat Torah, the news of Rabbi Baruch's death had reached the Riminov rabbi, but not the Seer of Lublin. The Riminov rabbi recognized at once that he must not proceed with the plan to force the End of Days. But the Seer of Lublin knew nothing about it, so on Simhat Torah he danced with the Torah in his arms, and then he went to the second floor of the synagogue and prayed alone there for several hours.

Just as he reached the conclusion of his prayers, the Seer of Lublin suddenly felt a great force from behind push him out of the open window. He would have met a certain death, but just before he struck the ground, he felt as if a net had caught him. Looking up, he saw Baruch of Medzibozh standing there, and found that he had landed on his *tallis*, which Rabbi Baruch had spread out below. Then the Seer understood that Rabbi Baruch must have died, and that he had come back from the Other World to save him. And he understood as well that the time had not come for the footsteps of the Messiah to be heard in this world.

Not long afterward the Seer of Lublin also took sick, and he died on the Ninth of Av of that year, the day the Temple in Jerusalem was destroyed.

□ Eastern Europe: Nineteenth Century

༄ 141 ༄

THE CLOCK OF THE SEER OF LUBLIN

After the Seer of Lublin died, his son, Rabbi Joseph of Torchin, received as his inheritance his father's belt, his silken Sabbath garments, and the clock that had hung in his father's study.

When the days of mourning were over, Rabbi Joseph left Lublin and returned to Torchin. Along the way it began to rain very hard, making it impossible to go on. Rabbi Joseph found lodging in a nearby village in the home of a Jew. It turned out that he was stranded there for several days, and before he left, the owner and his wife asked to be paid for his lodging. Rabbi Joseph told them that he was penniless but that he was carrying some holy objects. He opened the sack and showed them his inheritance, and he told them to take whatever they wanted. On the advice of his wife, the owner took the clock as payment for the debt.

Some years later Reb Issachar Ber of Radoshitz, a disciple of the Seer of Lublin, was passing that village and stayed in that same house. The owner of the house heard the rabbi pacing around his room all night. In the morning he asked him why he could not sleep. But instead of answering his question, Reb Issachar said: "Please tell me, where did you get the clock in that room?" And the owner told him how he had received it as payment for lodging from a man who had no money.

Then Reb Issachar said: "When I heard the chimes of that clock, I knew at once it was the clock of the Seer of Lublin. While other clocks tell a man that he is one hour closer to death, the clock of the Seer of Lublin always rings out in jubilation that there is one less hour until the coming of the Messiah. That is why I couldn't sleep, for I danced with joy at every note."

After that Reb Issachar purchased the clock for a fair price and hung it in his study. And as the years passed, he became known as a miracle worker, for he followed the instruction of that clock, joyously awaiting the footsteps of the Messiah.

□ Eastern Europe: Nineteenth Century

❧ 142 ❧

THE SOUL OF THE ARI

One winter morning Reb Zevi Hirsch of Zhidachov rose very early, when it was still dark outside. Although no candles in the house had been lit, a light pervaded the rooms as if it were day. Curious to know the source of this light, Reb Zevi searched until he found that it was coming from a little cupboard. There he found a precious stone as large as an egg that glowed with a bright light from within. Reb Zevi realized that the value of that stone could not be calculated, and he hid it away.

Then he fasted from the end of one Sabbath until the beginning of the next so that heaven might inform him of what it was. And in a dream he was told that this stone had been a gift to him from heaven. If he chose to keep it, he and all of his descendants would be very wealthy. But if he chose not to keep it, then the soul of the holy Ari would become fused with his own.

Now Reb Zevi did not desire wealth, and the choice was not difficult for him to make. He asked in a dream question how he should return the precious stone, and he was told to fling it up toward heaven. This he did, and fiery sparks flew from it from until nothing more could be seen.

Later one of Reb Zevi's students, who slept in the room next to his, heard a voice speaking to his master during the night. He knew that no one else was with Reb Zevi, so he rose and washed his hands and stood beside the wall and listened. The voice that spoke was interpreting a passage of the Zohar, casting great light on its mysteries. And the student was filled with wonder, but he dared not ask the rabbi about it.

During the next Sabbath, Reb Zevi began to expound on a passage from the Zohar, and the student recognized the teachings of the mysterious voice he had heard. And when Reb Zevi finished, he said: "This is what I learned from the very mouth of the Ari." Then the student knew whose voice he had heard that night.

□ Eastern Europe: Nineteenth Century

143

THE BLIND ANGEL

Among the Hasidim of Reb Mordecai of Chernobyl was Rabbi Eliakim, a merchant of great wealth and a collector of rare and precious religious objects. So wealthy was Reb Eliakim that he even owned his own scroll of the Torah, which was prominently displayed in an Ark that had been built into one wall of his living room.

Once Reb Mordecai came to pay him a visit, and Reb Eliakim was beside himself with joy, proudly showing off his precious objects to his rabbi. And each time Reb Mordecai seemed pleased by a particular object, Reb Eliakim had it wrapped and placed in a crate for the rabbi to take back with him.

Before long the crate was almost filled with silver goblets, embroidered matzah and challah covers, and other precious treasures of Reb Eliakim, and at last the rabbi rose to take his leave, thanking Reb Eliakim for his generosity. At that moment the rabbi's eye fell on a beautiful antique silver menorah, which was one of Reb Eliakim's most prized possessions. For a long time the rabbi stared at that menorah, and Reb Eliakim and everyone else clearly saw that he desired it, yet Reb Eliakim could not bring himself to offer it, for it was a priceless heirloom.

Finally it was the Rabbi of Chernobyl who broke the silence, asking, as a special favor, for the silver menorah. Everyone watched Reb Eliakim closely, for they knew how much he prized that menorah, and they saw that he was struggling with himself. At last Reb Eliakim ordered his servant to wrap the menorah, place it with the other gifts, and carry the crate to the rabbi's carriage.

When they returned home, the rabbi had the crate opened, and displayed all of the gifts he had received from Reb Eliakim except for the silver menorah, which was kept in storage. His Hasidim did not understand why he had asked for it or why he did not display it, but they dared not question the rabbi.

Time passed, and Reb Eliakim took his leave of this world, and eventually the episode of the silver menorah was forgotten. Ten years later, on the eve of Hanukah, Reb Mordecai had the menorah brought out of storage and prepared for lighting. As the flames burned brightly, reflected in the polished silver of the menorah, Reb Mordecai told his Hasidim a tale.

"This menorah once belonged to Reb Yosef David, who was a rich man for most of his life but then fell upon hard times. Reb Eliakim desired this menorah for many years and often tried to purchase it, but no matter how much he offered, Reb Yosef David refused to sell it, for this menorah had been in his family for many generations. However, when his situation grew desperate, Reb Yosef David went to Reb Eliakim for a loan. Reb Eliakim agreed to give him a generous loan, with the silver menorah to serve as security. But when the loan was due, Reb Yosef David could not repay it, and thus he had to relinquish the menorah to Reb Eliakim.

"Now, as we know from Reb Pinhas of Koretz, every good deed creates an angel. But if a deed is imperfect, it produces an imperfect angel. In giving Reb Yosef David a loan, Reb Eliakim did a good deed, and therefore an angel came into being. However, because his intentions were not completely pure, Reb Eliakim's angel was blind.

"After his death, Reb Eliakim was brought before the heavenly court. His good deeds and bad deeds were weighed, and they balanced exactly. All at once the blind angel took its place on the right side of the scale, and it tipped in Reb Eliakim's favor. Seeing this, the heavenly court ruled that Reb Eliakim might be permitted to enter Paradise, but since his margin was so narrow, he would have to be led there by the blind angel.

"Ever since, Reb Eliakim and the blind angel have wandered, and his soul has found no rest. For the blind angel could not find the way to Paradise. And without some special merit, he would have remained a wandering soul for many years to come. But tonight the light of this menorah reached all the way to the upper world, restoring the angel's sight. Now, at last, the angel has been able to lead the soul of Reb Eliakim to his resting place in Paradise.

"Now you know why, long ago, I asked Reb Eliakim for his menorah. For it was the merit of this gift that he needed in order to repair the eyesight of the angel. I never used it until now, as I was waiting for the right moment. Last night, I saw Reb Eliakim, led by the blind angel, in a dream. From this I knew that they were close, and tonight, as the flames ascended, that they were passing over. And now Reb Eliakim is basking in the sacred light of Paradise."

□ Eastern Europe: Nineteenth Century

144

THE CAVE OF MATTATHIAS

In a village near the city of Riminov there was a Hasid whose custom it was to bring newly made oil to Reb Menachem Mendel of Riminov, and the rabbi would light the first candle of Hanukah in his presence.

One year the winter was hard, the land covered with snow, and everyone was locked in his home. But when the eve of Hanukah arrived, the Hasid was still planning to deliver the oil. His family pleaded with him not to go, but he was determined, and in the end he set out across the deep snow.

That morning he entered the forest that separated his village from Riminov, and the moment he did, it began to snow. The snow fell so fast that it covered every landmark, and when at last it stopped, the Hasid found that he was lost. The whole world was covered with snow.

Now the Hasid began to regret not listening to his family. Surely the rabbi would have forgiven his absence. Meanwhile, it had become so cold that he began to fear he might freeze. He realized that if he were to die there in the forest, he might not even be taken to a Jewish grave. That is when he remembered the oil he was carrying. In order to save his life, he would have to use it. There was no other choice.

As fast as his numb fingers could move, he tore some of the lining out of his coat and fashioned it into a wick, and he put that wick into the snow. Then he poured oil on it and prayed with great intensity. Finally, he lit the first candle of Hanukah, and the flame seemed to light up the whole forest. And all the wolves moving through the forest saw that light and ran back to their hiding places.

After this the exhausted Hasid lay down on the snow and fell asleep. He dreamed he was walking in a warm land, and before him he saw a great mountain, and next to that mountain stood a palm tree. At the foot of the mountain was the opening of a cave. In the dream, the Hasid entered the cave and found a candle burning there. He picked up that candle, and it lit the way for him until he came to a large cavern, where an old man with a very long beard was seated. There was a sword on his thigh, and his hands were busy making wicks. All of that cavern was piled high with bales of wicks. The old man looked up when the Hasid entered and said: "Blessed be you in the Name of God."

The Hasid returned the old man's blessing and asked him who he was. He answered: "I am Mattathias, father of the Maccabees. During my lifetime I lit a big torch. I hoped that all of Israel would join me, but only a few obeyed my call. Now heaven has sent me to watch for the little candles in the houses of Israel to come together to form a very big flame. And that flame will announce the Redemption and the End of Days.

"Meanwhile, I prepare the wicks for the day when everyone will contribute his candle to this great flame. And now, there is something that you must do for me. When you reach the Rabbi of Riminov, tell him that the wicks are ready, and he should do whatever he can to light the flame that we have awaited so long."

Amazed at all he had heard, the Hasid promised to give the message to the rabbi. As he turned to leave the cave, he awoke and found himself standing in front of the rabbi's house. Just then the rabbi himself opened the door, and his face was glowing. He said: "The power of lighting the Hanukah candles is very great. Whoever dedicates his soul to this deed brings the time of Redemption that much closer."

□   Eastern Europe: Oral Tradition

145

A NEW SOUL

Hannah Rochel, the Maid of Ludomir, had a very lonely childhood.
She lost her mother when she was very young, and she rarely saw her
wealthy father. So she spent hours praying at the grave of her mother
or learning the Torah. She insisted on studying the Midrash, and the
time came when she was as knowledgeable as any young man.

One day, when Hannah Rochel went to the grave of her mother, she
fell asleep. And when she awoke, she discovered she was alone in the
graveyard. It was midnight, and it seemed as if spirits were swarming
everywhere. She was terrified. She started running and fell into an
open grave.

That is where they found her, barely alive. For a long time her soul
fluttered between this world and the next. At last her soul ascended on
high, and she found herself in a heavenly court. There she was told
that she was to receive a new soul. And this, indeed, is what happened.

When Hannah Rochel opened her eyes, the first thing she said to
her father was, "I have just returned from the Heavenly Court, and I
have received a new soul." After that, Hannah Rochel wrapped herself
in a *tallis* and put on *tefillin*. At her father's funeral she recited Kaddish
for him. And she spent her days in the study of the Torah, delving
into the mystical texts.

In time her wisdom was recognized, and she was regarded as a rabbi
among some of the Hasidim. A synagogue was built in her honor, with
her room attached to the House of Study. Rabbis and scholars assembled there, and the "Maid of Ludomir," as she was now known,
discoursed from behind a curtain, and all were held spellbound by
what she said.

A time came when the Maid of Ludomir decided to ascend to the
Holy Land. There in Jerusalem she met an old kabbalist, who was a

descendant of the great Yemenite kabbalist Rabbi Shalom Shabazi. The old kabbalist recognized the great knowledge of the Maid and how great was her longing for the Messiah. He, too, as he neared the end of his life, had grown impatient for the coming of the Messiah. They decided to meet on a certain day at twilight to pronounce the prayers that would make the footsteps of the Messiah heard in this world. The place where they met was one of the hidden caves leading directly to the Holy Land, through which the bones of the righteous will roll to reach the Mount of Olives in Jerusalem, where the resurrection of the dead will take place.

The Maid of Ludomir came to the cave on that day, but the old kabbalist was late, for an old man came to his house just as he was about to leave, and delayed him past twilight. And that old man was Elijah, who had been sent by heaven to stop the two from offering their prayers at the same time and forcing the End of Days. When the old kabbalist did not arrive, the Maid of Ludomir went ahead without him, so great was her longing. She prayed the prayers of unification and pronounced the secret name of the Prince of the Torah. And at that instant her soul took flight and returned to its place on high. Nor could the old kabbalist ever find the entrance to that cave again when he searched for her, and no one knows where her bones are to be found.

□ Eastern Europe: Nineteenth Century

❧ 146 ❧

A VISION

In the city of Prague lived Jiri Langer, who left his family when he was eighteen and traveled to Belz, where he became a disciple of Reb Issachar Dov the First, the *tzaddik* of Belz. There he learned how to tie the knots of his *tallis* and how to welcome the Sabbath Queen. He became one of the Belz Hasidim, who treasured every crumb discarded by the rebbe and entrusted him to be their guide.

For more than a year he made his home in Belz. But a time came when he grew lonely for the life he had left behind and returned to Prague.

One night, when he could not sleep, he lay in his bed facing east. He had just put down the sacred text he had been reading. The window was open, and Belz beckoned. All at once the small room filled with a silver light, as if the moon had slipped inside. Although every light was out, there was a bright presence on the other side of the open door. It was the *tzaddik* of Belz who stood there, while at the same time he sat in his room in Belz, looking right at him. On his face was a sublime smile full of wisdom.

The vision lasted long enough to make a deep impression, and suddenly the apparition ended. The room was dark again, although the presence of the rebbe was still very strong.

A few days later, Jiri Langer returned to his Hasidim.

□ Prague: Twentieth Century

147

THE TALE OF THE ETROG

One year the Reb of Kamionka came to the city of Belz for Sukkot in order to be with his master, Reb Sholem of Belz. As he walked into the House of Prayer, he heard Reb Sholem's voice praying the Hallel prayer. He looked up, expecting to see the rebbe at the *bimah*, but he was not there. The Rabbi of Kamionka looked around the synagogue in confusion, for he could still hear the rebbe's voice ringing out, as clear as ever.

The visiting rabbi looked around again slowly, ever so slowly. Surely Reb Sholem was there somewhere. And at last he saw him where few would think of looking. For somehow Reb Sholem had entered entirely into an etrog, an etrog so perfect that it could only have been a gift of heaven. Barely able to believe that such a miracle was taking place, Reb Sholem stared at that etrog, so doubly blessed.

As he peered at it, the etrog began to glow. It became transparent in his vision, and he saw that the source of its light was within, and that it was the light of Reb Sholem, who filled the shell of the etrog.

The Rabbi of Kamionka closed his eyes for an instant and still saw the glowing etrog as clearly as when his eyes were open. He marveled at this, and when he opened his eyes again, he saw Reb Sholem standing before the Ark, with the light of the etrog glowing from his face and the fruit itself cradled in his hand.

□   Eastern Europe: Twentieth Century

ꙮ 148 ꙮ

A WANDERING SOUL

Every soul has its own history, although this is hidden from almost everyone at the moment of birth. For the holy Yismach Moyshe of Ihel, however, the history of his soul was no secret. He knew that this was the third time his soul had entered this world, and he knew what he had been before.

The first time, he had been a sheep tended by Jacob when he worked for Laban. Many saw with their own eyes the strange scars he still carried on his body from birth, scars left from the blows of Jacob, who was a very strict shepherd.

The second time his soul descended, he was among those who followed Moses out of Egypt, and he was blessed to be among those who stood at Sinai. But he was also cursed to be a follower of Korah, who rebelled against Moses, for somehow he had found the words of Korah convincing. And like all who followed Korah, he had been swallowed up by the earth and punished in Gehenna. After that his soul had been sentenced to wander for many generations, traveling from one world to another, never resting.

Until, at last, he had been reborn.

And how was it that he remembered so clearly that which everyone else has forgotten? When asked about this, Yismach Moyshe replied: "After all those years of punishment, the last thing I wanted was to forget. So before I was born I begged the angel Lailah, who accompanied me from one world to the next, to let me remember the history of my soul. The angel conveyed my wish to the Holy One, blessed be He. And because of the merits of that angel, who pleaded my case, none of the history was erased."

□ Eastern Europe: Twentieth Century

149

TRYING TO PRAY

Reb Dovid Din was sought out in Jerusalem by a man who was suffering a crisis of belief. Whatever Reb Dovid said to him, he disputed. Reb Dovid quickly recognized that it was the man's intention to provoke him, so he restrained himself and refused to be drawn into an argument. He listened and listened to the man, who ranted and raved for hours. At last he said to him: "Why are you so angry with God?"

This question stunned the man, as he had said nothing at all about God. He grew very quiet and looked at Dovid Din and said: "All my life I have been so afraid to express my anger to God that I have always directed my anger at people who are connected with God. But until this moment I did not understand this."

Then Reb Dovid stood up and told the man to follow him. He led him to the Wailing Wall, away from the place where people pray to the site of the ruins of the Temple. When they reached that place, Reb Dovid told him that it was time to express all the anger he felt toward God. Then, for more than an hour, the man struck the wall of the *Kotel* with his hands and screamed his heart out. After that he began to cry and could not stop crying, and little by little his cries became sobs that turned into prayers. And that is how Reb Dovid Din taught him how to pray.

□ United States: Oral Tradition

150

THE TALE OF THE KUGEL

A Hasid who was a wealthy merchant once came to Reb Menachem Mendel of Lubavitch, the *Zemach Tzaddik*, for permission to divorce his wife. The Hasid was worried, for he knew the rabbi regarded marriage as one of the pillars of existence and rarely gave his blessing for divorce. Nor would the man do anything without his rebbe's permission, for the rebbe was the pillar of his life. So he was quite tense when he came to the rebbe's house and requested an audience.

The Hasid arrived just before breakfast. Indeed, the first thing that struck him as he walked inside was the delicious smell of the food. He had left before dawn in order to reach the rebbe's house, for he hoped to return to his work before the end of the day. The rebbe's wife seated him in the living room, but she did not invite the man to join them for breakfast.

From where he sat, the man saw the rebbe enter his study to put on his *tefillin* and heard him chanting prayers. Even though the rabbi twice passed by the door of the living room, he did not look up and he did not seem to notice the Hasid sitting there.

The morning passed. The rabbi did not emerge from his study. Nor did any others come to the house. The man wondered why no other petitioners came that day and why the rebbe did not call him into his study.

Before long it was time for lunch. The man, who had not eaten since the night before, was tormented by the tantalizing scents of the cooking food. But still he was left to sit alone. Again the rebbe passed the doorway twice but did not give any indication that he had seen him.

By evening the man was exhausted with hunger and waiting, but still there was no sign of the rabbi. Now the delicate smells of dinner reached him, tormenting him, in particular the smell of kugel, which he loved. If only they would take notice of him and invite him to join them for dinner! But they did not.

By the time the dinner ended, the man was deeply worried about the meaning of the rabbi's actions. So he was greatly relieved when the rabbi's wife came to him shortly thereafter and led him to the rabbi's study.

When the man walked into the study, he was struck again with the smell of kugel, even more potent than it had been in the living room. At the same moment he saw the rabbi with a plate of kugel before him. Reb Menachem Mendel looked up at him, his eyes gleaming, and asked him why he had come. Then the Hasid poured out his heart about his wife, who had failed to give him a child in almost ten years, so that there would be no one to say the Kaddish, the prayer for the dead, for him. And since it is permitted to divorce a childless woman after that time, he had come to seek the rebbe's permission.

The rebbe stood up, taking the plate of kugel in his hand, and offered it to the Hasid. "Here," he said, "first, eat some kugel; then we will talk." At that moment the man remembered he was famished, and he gladly took the plate of kugel, picked up a piece, and took a bite of it. It was the most delicious food he had ever tasted. And yet, strange to say, he had taken no more than a single bite when his hunger was gone.

At that moment the rabbi spoke: "Go now and know that I have approved your request. There shall be a *get*, a bill of divorce, on your tenth anniversary. Be there with your wife on that day, and bring your wedding contract."

Amazed at how the rebbe had agreed without any objections, the man left, and he was back there on his tenth anniversary to divorce his wife. Not long afterward he remarried, and before a year was out he was the father of a beautiful girl. Indeed, every year after that he became the father of another daughter, until he had six girls but no boy who could say his Kaddish. And in despair he went back to the rebbe.

This time he was given an audience as soon as he entered the door. Back in the rebbe's chamber, the smell of kugel again struck him, and soon the rebbe was standing, offering him to taste some. Remembering the good luck it had brought him last time in obtaining the rebbe's approval, the man took a single bite, and at that very moment the rebbe again gave him permission to divorce his wife.

By the time he had left his wife and six daughters, he was a much poorer man in silver and in spirit. But at least he was free to seek out his Kaddish. And in less than a year he was married again. This time his wish came true, and his wife's first child was a son. The man knew that he had been right all along to persevere for his son, even at the price he had paid, and he lavished love and gifts on him. And by the time the boy was three years old, he was recognized as a prodigy, and all who saw him predicted that he would be a great scholar in Torah.

It happened that the Hasid had to travel by ship on business. He could not bear the thought of leaving his son behind, so he hired a tutor and brought the boy with him on the voyage. Then one day there was a storm at sea, and the boat started to sink. It all happened so fast that the man was not able to save his son. He watched in horror as a great wave carried the boy off, and that was the last he ever saw of him. So great was his grief that he almost welcomed death so that he could be with his son again. But just then the mast of the ship floated by, and the man's instinct to save himself took over. He grabbed it just as a giant wave picked up the mast and bore it across the water for many hours, until he found himself washed up on a distant shore. Eventually the heartbroken father made his way back to his home town, but he could hardly bear to break the terrible news to his wife. So he went to see the rebbe first.

This time the rebbe himself opened the door, and he recognized the man's grief at once. He gently led him into his study and gave him a seat. Then the rebbe brought over a plate of food. "Would you like some kugel?" the rabbi asked. And the man, remembering all the misery that his divorces had brought on, whispered "No" and began to weep. And he wept with all his heart. When at last he looked up, he heard the rebbe say, "No, you may not have a *get*."

This greatly confused the man, and he said: "What do you mean, rebbe? I have not come to you for a *get*. Far from it. I have had enough of divorces. After two divorces I finally got the son of my dreams, and I lost him, due to my own foolishness in taking him with me on a dangerous voyage. If only it had been me, and not him, who had died!"

"Let me assure you," said the rebbe, "that you have not been divorced even once. It is only now that you have requested your first divorce. Nor do you have any children."

"What do you mean?" the man shouted. "My first divorce was many years ago. Oh, if only I had not been divorced, my life would not have been ruined."

"Here," said the rebbe, picking up a copy of a newspaper and showing it to the man. And he saw that it was the same day that he had come asking for his first divorce. And then he realized that only a short time had passed, while for him it had seemed like half a lifetime. And he realized that a strange miracle had taken place, for he had seen the futility of divorcing his wife, whose only flaw was a failure to give him a son. The man was awed by what had happened to him, and he took leave of the rebbe.

So too did he remain married, and before the twelfth year of marriage had passed, he was the father of a fine son, much to his amazement. And he loved that son with all his heart, and from the day the boy was old enough to understand, he made him take a vow that he would never set foot in a ship. So too did the boy keep this vow, and his life flourished. And when the merchant died, his son said Kaddish for him and always kept his memory alive.

□ Eastern Europe: Oral Tradition

 V

SOURCES AND
COMMENTARY

SOURCES AND COMMENTARY

The tales collected here are drawn from the legendary dimension of the Jewish mystical tradition, growing out of a ritualistic, mythic system rich in religious and literary conventions. It was widely understood that these mystical tales were intended to have multiple meanings, following the system of interpretation known by the acronym *PaRDeS*, which postulates four levels of interpretation: the literal, the symbolic, the allegorical, and the mystical. The following notes offer relevant commentaries on these mystical tales, drawing on these sources, conventions, and levels of interpretation. These tales function in two primary ways: as legendary accounts of the lives of the primary mystical masters and their disciples, and as mystical texts in themselves. In portraying the lives, albeit legendary, of these *tzaddikim*, as well as their teachings, they suggest models for the life of a mystic, based primarily on the legendary model of Rabbi Shimon bar Yohai, as portrayed in the Zohar. The mystical tradition can take many different forms, from ecstatic visions of heaven to attempts to hasten the coming of the Messiah. These tales draw on either Practical or Speculative Kabbalah, and sometimes both. There is no one primary type of tale, but rather many characteristic types. The editor has sought to include a representative number of the major types of these tales, selected from the principal phases of postbiblical rabbinic literature and Jewish folklore.

The major sources for Part I, Rabbinic Tales, are the Talmud, the Midrash, and other rabbinic sources.

Part II, Kabbalistic Tales, is drawn chiefly from two periods—the thirteenth century in Spain and the sixteenth century in the city of Safed in the Holy Land. The primary source of the thirteenth-century material is the Zohar, and there are many collections of tales about Rabbi Isaac Luria, known as the Ari, and the other mystics of sixteenth-century Safed. The first of these was *Shivhei ha-Ari*, which is said to have been based on the letters of Shlomo Shmulil about the miracles of the Ari, sent from the Holy Land to Eastern Europe. This same collection served, to a considerable extent, as the model for *Shivhei ha-Besht*, the first collection of tales about the Baal Shem Tov, which was published in Poland in 1814. Other important sources for Part II are the writings of Rabbi Hayim Vital, the primary disciple of the Ari, especially *Shivhei Rabbi Hayim Vital* and his diary of visions and other experiences, *Sefer ha-Hezyonot*. It is interesting to note that folktales about the circle of Safed mystics are still told orally in present-day Israel, some of which are included here. So too have many Hasidic tales of Eastern European origin been collected there. Many of these are variants of the earlier written tales, although there are also many tales that are not to be found in written sources. These oral tales were collected by the Israel Folktale Archives (IFA), founded by Professor Dov Noy of Hebrew University and presently under the direction of Professor Aliza Shenhar of Haifa University. The curator is Edna Hechal.

The primary sources for Part III, Mystical Folktales, are medieval collections of Jewish folklore published between the sixteenth and nineteenth centuries. There also are tales collected orally by the IFA. The tales have been drawn both from Eastern European collections such as *Kav ha-Yashar* and Middle Eastern ones such as *Sefer ha-Ma'aysiot* (Baghdad). Samaritan and Karaite tales also have been included. One of the finest modern collections of medieval lore and Hasidic tales drawn upon is Mordecai Ben Yehezkel's *Sefer ha-Ma'aysiot* (Tel Aviv: 1937).

The stories in Part IV, Hasidic Tales, are selected from the collections about the various Hasidic rebbes, beginning with the tales about the Baal Shem Tov in *Shivhei ha-Besht*, first published in 1805. Other important collections are *Midrash Pinhas*, tales about Reb Pinhas of Koretz; *Ohel Elimelech*, tales about Rabbi Elimelech of Lizensk; and tales from the extensive writings of Reb Nathan of Nemirov, the scribe of Rabbi Nachman of Bratslav, such as *Hayey Moharan*, as well as many early anthologies of Hasidic tales such as *Sipurei Ya'akov* and *Sipurei Hasidim*.

All of the sources cited here are in Hebrew except where noted. A few sources are from other languages, primarily Yiddish. The Babylonian and Jerusalem Talmuds are primarily in Aramaic, as is the Zohar, the central text of Jewish mysticism. The Babylonian Talmud is abbreviated as "B.," followed by the appropriate tractate. The Jerusalem Talmud is abbreviated as "Y.," followed by the tractate. The Jerusalem (or Palestinian) Talmud was codified around 425 C.E., and the Babylonian Talmud was codified around 500 C.E.

The editor's previous collections of Jewish folklore are abbreviated as follows: *EV* for *Elijah's Violin and Other Jewish Fairy Tales; MT* for *Miriam's Tambourine: Jewish Folktales from Around the World;* and *LC* for *Lilith's Cave: Jewish Tales of the Supernatural. Gates to the New City: A Treasury of Modern Jewish Tales* is abbreviated as *GNC*. Refer to the Appendix for additional information on the mystical themes in these tales. For further information about English-language books cited, see the Bibliography. Information on foreign-language books is included in these notes. See the Glossary for definitions of Hebrew- and Yiddish-language terms used throughout.

I RABBINIC TALES

1. *The Golden Dove* (Babylon and Ancient Israel)
From Berakoth 53b. The origin of the legend of the golden dove probably derives from Psalms 68:14: *The wings of the dove are covered with silver, and her pinions with the shimmer of gold.* The identification of the golden bird with the Messiah is found in Zohar 2:8a–9a: "Then the Holy One, blessed be He, beckons that bird, and it enters its nest, and comes to the Messiah, and it calls what it calls, and stirs up what it stirs up, until the Bird's Nest and the Messiah are called three times from inside the Holy Throne, and all ascend." Additional material about the Bird's Nest is found in Zohar 3:196b and in *Seder Gan Eden* in *Beit ha-Midrash* 3:132–33.

Among the talmudic sages, Rabbah bar bar Hannah was the great wanderer. He traveled by ship and by caravan and told many tall tales of the sea and desert, which have been subjected to many allegorical interpretations. Many of these tales resemble the voyages of Sindbad in *The Arabian Nights*, which they predate in writing by at least two centuries, as the Talmud was codified in the fifth century, whereas the first manuscripts of *The Arabian Nights* are dated from the seventh century. The tale of the golden dove is, however, more of a mystical tale than a tall tale. Rabbah deceives his fellow sages in the caravan so that he can hurry back to the previous resting place to recite *Birkat ha-Mazon*, the blessing after meals, which he had forgotten to say. In order not to engage them in a debate about the appropriateness of his actions, he tells them he has left a golden dove behind. Then, as soon as he completes his prayers, he sees a golden dove in the sand. Above all, this miracle reveals how much God appreciates Rabbah's tenacity in obeying the Law as he understands it. Of course, this issue of understanding is at the core of the tale, in the form of a *Halachic* debate over whether or not *Birkat ha-Mazon* must be said in the same place in which one has eaten. Rabbah interprets the Law in the strictest fashion and therefore returns to the previous site, even though he risks being left behind by the caravan. He is rewarded for his determination to fulfill the letter of the Law by a miracle. As for the golden dove, it is a celestial image of the earthly dove. Just as there is a heavenly Jerusalem as well as an earthly one, so too is the symbol of Noah's dove transformed into a messenger for the Messiah as well as a singer of celestial songs. An additional talmudic legend about the golden dove is found in B. Yoma 44b concerning King Solomon's miraculous throne: "The throne of King Solomon was made entirely of gold. Golden lions and golden bears stood on each step leading to the throne, and facing the lions were golden eagles. Over the throne was a kind of canopy, and in the midst of it was a golden chain, and from the chain hung a golden dove, in its beak a golden crown in which was a precious stone that illuminated the world. When King Solomon took his place on the throne, the golden dove came to life and opened the Ark and took out the scroll of the Torah, and placed it before him, its wondrous stone illuminating the letters of the Law." Another interesting variant of the theme of the miraculous dove is found in B. Shab. 49b, where a man whose name is Elisha is caught wearing a pair of *Tefillin*, which was at that time forbidden by the government. Elisha takes off the *Tefillin* and puts them in his hand. When asked what he is holding, he replies "The wings of a dove." He opens his hands and that is what they find, for the *Tefillin* have been transformed into wings. This is an appropriate metaphor for *Tefillin*, which transmit the prayers of the righteous to heaven on wings of prayer. After that he became known as "Elisha of the Wings." Note that in both tales the dove is associated in some way with prayer. For a companion tale, see "The Ladder of Prayers," p. 191, and the accompanying note.

2. *An Appointment with Death* (Babylon)
From B. Sukka 53a. A variant is found in Y. Kil. 9:32c.
This famous legend is found in many cultures, and its theme of a city of immortals has been the focus of many works of fiction, including John O'Hara's *Appointment in Samara* and James Hilton's *Lost Horizon*. This version from the Talmud appears to be the earliest form of the legend and is derived from the reference in Genesis 28:19 to Luz as the original name of the place where Jacob had his dream of the heavenly ladder. In order to explain why this was such a holy place, one of the "gates of heaven," the Talmud (B. Sota 46b) identifies it as a city of immortals, where the only way that the old people could die was to leave the city, since the Angel of Death was not permitted to enter. The location of the city of Luz was regarded as a well-kept secret, since it would otherwise be deluged by those seeking immortality, but such secret knowledge was easily accessible to King Solomon. The primary moral of this tale is that it is impossible to escape that which has been fated. It is one of several tales concerning King Solomon in which he tries to outfox fate and fails. See "The Princess

in the Tower" in *EV*, p. 47, for the most famous of these. See also "The City of Luz" in *EV*, p. 279, which recounts many of the traditions associated with this city of immortals. In the present tale the Angel of Death has the final word, but in a related talmudic tale (B. Ket. 77b) the angel is unable to conquer Rabbi Joshua ben Levi, who steals his sword and leaps into the Garden of Eden, refusing to give it back. In this manner Rabbi Joshua ben Levi is able to enter Paradise alive, and only after divine intercession does the Angel of Death recover his sword.

3. *Isaac's Ascent* (Palestine)

From *Genesis Rabbah* 56. Also Targum Jonathan, Genesis 22:19. Also *Pirke de Rabbi Eliezer*, chapter 31. Also *Hadar Zekenim* 10b in *Beit ha-Midrash*, edited by A. Jellinek (Jerusalem: 1967, V:157). Also Commentary on *Sefer Yetsirah*, p. 125.

Although it is clearly stated in Genesis 22:12 that the angel of the Lord commanded Abraham not to raise his hand against Isaac, this late midrash, which probably echoes Christian influence, asserts that Abraham did in fact slay Isaac and that Isaac's soul ascended to Paradise, where he studied in the academy of Shem and Eber. The basis of this midrash is the conclusion of the *Akedah* episode of the binding of Isaac, where it is Abraham alone who returns to his servants, and no mention is made of Isaac (Gen. 22:19). The themes of dying and resurrection here echo the Christian belief in the death and resurrection of Jesus. The parallel of the three days after the death of Jesus, when the resurrection takes place, and the three years in this midrash about Isaac underscores the similarity. It is interesting to note that the traditional Christian interpretation of the Binding of Isaac views it as an allegory for the sacrifice by God of His only son. See Melito of Sardis, *Peri Pascha* (On Passover). This legend about the ascent of Isaac is linked to the Resurrection of the Dead by adding that when Isaac arose, "he knew that in this way the dead would come back to life in the future, whereupon he began to recite, 'Blessed art Thou, O Lord, who quickens the dead.'" (*Pirke de Rabbi Eliezer* 31). For further discussion of the legends of the *Akedah*, the binding of Isaac, see *The Last Trial* by Shalom Spiegel. The academy of Shem and Eber is often referred to in the Midrash. Abraham is said to have told Sarah that he was taking Isaac to study there at the time he set off for Mount Moriah (*Sefer ha-Yashar* 43a–44b, Venice: 1613). While this academy may once have been on earth, in most rabbinic legends it is identified as the Yeshivah on high. Therefore Isaac's ascent to Paradise to study in this academy verifies Abraham's statement to Sarah, affirming his honesty. The origin of this legend is the identification of *the tents of Shem* in Genesis 9:27 with a *Beit Midrash* or House of Study, which evolved in midrashic literature into an academy led by Shem and his great-grandson Eber. Later legends identify the academy as a heavenly one where the greatest sages study. There also is a strong identification of prophecy with Shem, who was said to have had the gift of prophecy. Note that in the Midrash this "academy" existed long before the giving of the Torah at Mount Sinai, underscoring the rabbinic belief of the preexistence of the Torah.

4. *The Magic Flock* (Ancient Israel)

From Genesis Rabbah 77:2 and *Midrash Tanhuma* Vayishlach 1.

This legend is closely related to the account of Jacob's wrestling with the angel in Genesis 32:25–33. The identity of the sorcerer thus depends on the identity given to the angel or whoever it was with whom Jacob wrestled. Most accounts identify this figure as the angel Michael or as the guardian angel of Esau, who, disguised as a shepherd, first got Jacob to agree that they would assist each other in carrying their flocks across the river Yabbok, and then created the illusion of so many flocks that he succeeded in exhausting Jacob before they wrestled and before Jacob's encounter with Esau the next day. This story is of particular importance, as it is an early example of an illusion tale, a particular type of tale that has a distinct and prominent place in Jewish lore. Several other examples of these illusion tales are collected here, including "The Enchanted Inn," p. 130, "The Underground Forest," p. 214, "The Cave of Temptations," p. 166, "The Young Magician," p. 224 and "The Tale of the Kugel," p. 268. This particular theme was probably drawn into Jewish lore from oriental sources, where it also is very popular. For additional examples of these illusion tales, see the cluster of tales about Rabbi Adam in *EV*, including "The Enchanted Journey," p. 181, and "The King's Dream," p. 197. See also "The Beggar King" in *EV*, pp. 59ff., an early illusion tale about King Solomon that finds its origin in the Talmud, in B. Gittin 68b, but adds the theme of illusion in later midrashic and folk variants.

5. *The Ascent of Moses* (Palestine)

From *Pesikta Rabbati* 20:4. Also drawn from B. Shab. 88b–89a, B. Men. 29b, and *Ma'ayan ha-Hohmah* in *Beit ha-Midrash*, edited by A. Jellinek (Jerusalem: 1967, Vol. 1, pp. 60–61).

It was widely assumed in rabbinic literature that Moses did not only climb to the top of Mount Sinai to receive the Torah, but that he also ascended into Paradise. Inevitably, Moses encountered the angels, who had never been enthusiastic about the creation of man in the first place and were loath to see the Torah transmitted to him. The angels attempt to obstruct Moses and cast him out of heaven, but God always intercedes to protect him. There are several versions of this legend of heavenly ascent; that in *Pesikta Rabbati* is the most extensive. Among the prophets, Moses is the only one said to have seen God. In these legends of Moses he stands before the Throne of Glory and sees God weaving the crowns of the letters of the Torah; most amazingly, there is an account of God stepping down from his Throne of Glory to assure Moses, who has been frightened by the awesome sight of the angel Sandalphon. Subsequent prophets hear the voice of God, but visions of God are extremely rare. In another midrash, Moses finds God studying the portion of the Torah concerning the Red Heifer (Number 19:2). God quotes Rabbi Eliezer's commentary on it and Moses asks for Rabbi Eliezer to descend from his seed (Num. Rab. 19:7). See, for example, "The Vision of the High Priest," p. 55, which recounts the High Priest's vision of Akatriel Yah in the Holy of Holies. In many ways the account of the ascent of Moses in *Pesikta Rabbati* closely resembles a Hekhaloth text, and these texts, such as *Hekhaloth Rabbati*, probably served as its model. See "The Pillar of Cloud," p. 80 for a tale that draws on the imagery of the enchanted cloud.

6. *The Chronicle of Serah bat Asher* (Persia)

The legend of Serah informing Jacob that Joseph is alive is from *Sefer Yashar* (Venice: 1613, 109b–110a). The legend that Serah was enslaved in Egypt is found in *Pesikta Rabbati* 17:5. The legend of Serah revealing that Moses is the Redeemer is from Exodus Rabbah 5:13. The legend about Serah revealing the location of the coffin of Joseph is found in *Mekilta de-Rabbi Ishmael*, Beshallah 24a–24b, and in B. Sota 13a–b, based on Exodus 14:19: *And Moses took the bones of Joseph with him*. The account of Serah and the walls of the Red Sea is found in *Pesikta de-Rab Kahana* 11:13. That Serah enters heaven alive is found in *Sefer Yashar* 110a and *The Alphabet of Ben Sira* 28a.

This is a classic example of a chain midrash. There are only three references to Serah bat Asher in the Bible. In Genesis 46:17 she is identified as one of the sixty-nine who go into Egypt with Jacob. Some say that Serah should be counted as two because of her long life, bringing the number to seventy. See Gen. Rab. 94:9. In Numbers 26:46 she is listed in the census that Moses takes in the wilderness. She is also mentioned in I Chronicles 7:30 as a sister of the sons of Asher. In each case virtually no information is given about her, although she is said to have been a slave in Egypt. The fact that the name "Serah bat Asher" appeared in both lists led the rabbis to conclude that it referred to the same person. In order to explain why she lived so long, the midrash explains that Jacob blessed her for letting him know that Joseph was still alive. In one version, the blessing is given as a sign of happiness. In another, Jacob is infuriated when he thinks that Serah is taunting him about Joseph, the greatest loss of his life, and he curses her with the words "You should live so long!" In this case, the curse turns into a blessing. Subsequent legends make use of her longevity, as in the midrash in which she informs Moses of the location of Joseph's coffin. Thus the legend of Serah becomes a kind of Jewish version of the Wandering Jew legend, blessed rather than cursed, as was the Wandering Jew, to virtual immortality. According to one version of the legend, she lost her life in a fire in a synagogue in Isfahan in the ninth century, while in another she was one of the nine who were taken into heaven alive. A legend in the Zohar builds on this latter version, describing four heavenly palaces that are presided over by four women: Batya, the daughter of Pharaoh, Serah bat Asher, Yocheved, and Deborah. Serah's palace is said to contain thousands of women who tended the old and infirm in their lifetimes, just as Serah cared for her grandfather, Jacob, and revived him by telling him that Joseph was alive. There Serah often visits with Joseph and also teaches Torah to the women in her palace.

7. *Mysteries of the Chariot* (Babylon and Ancient Israel)
From Y. Hag. 77a and B. Hag. 14.

There are two primary categories of early kabbalistic contemplation: those linked to *Ma'aseh Bereshith* or The Work of Creation, and those linked to *Ma'aseh Merkavah*, or The Work of the Chariot. The former focuses on the mystical meaning of the creation as described in Genesis and the latter on the vision of Ezekiel. Here the discussion of Ezekiel's vision and its mystical implications invokes yet another vision, shared by two rabbis, of angels dancing in a field. In many ways this talmudic tale defines the essential kabbalistic experience, presenting it in a positive and powerful fashion and making it clear that Jewish mysticism is not merely a text-oriented study, but involves actual mystical experiences. Rabban Yohanan ben Zakkai was one of the great talmudic sages, but here the sage accompanying him is the one who invokes the mystical vision. This tale serves as a primary model for many tales found in the Zohar, where two or more rabbis discover that the lowly Jew traveling with them is actually a hidden saint, who reveals great kabbalistic mysteries to them or invokes a mystical vision. See, among the tales linked to the circle of Shimon bar Yohai, "A Saint from the Other World," p. 72, "The Golden Scepter," p. 73, and "The Book of Adam," p. 74. See also David Halperin, *The Merkavah in Rabbinic Literature* and *The Faces of the Chariot*.

8. *The Four Who Entered Paradise* (Babylon)
The primary account is found in B. Hag. 14b. An alternate version is found in

Tosefta Hag. 23. The legend about Ben Azzai is found in Leviticus Rabbah 16:4 and Song of Songs Rabbah I:10. The legend about Ben Zoma is from B. Hag. 15a and Y. Hag. 77a–b. The legend about Aher and Metatron is from B. Hag. 15a.

This brief, ambiguous legend about the four sages who entered *Pardes* is one of the central mystical tales in the Jewish tradition. It became the focus of opposing traditions—one that saw it as the model for mystical contemplation and heavenly ascent, as found in the Hekhaloth texts, and another that saw in its conclusion, in which three of the four greatest talmudic sages are somehow harmed, a warning that such contemplation and/or ascent was extremely dangerous and that access to the study of such material should be limited to those who were well grounded. But the tale of the four who entered Paradise (for this is how it was commonly understood) impressed others in an entirely different way. For this legend also became an entry into the mysteries of *Pardes* by an esoteric Jewish sect that sought, by engaging in mystical contemplation, to discover the means to enter *Pardes*, which in their meta-phorical system represented the heavenly Paradise. This is a form of contemplation of *Ma'aseh Merkavah*, or the Mysteries of the Chariot, and such mystical ascent is para-doxically identified as a descent, as in the account of Ben Azzai. The texts pro-duced by this sect are called "Hekhaloth texts," since they describe travels through the palaces (*hekhaloth*) of heaven. These texts were written either to record the experiences of the travelers or to prepare a guidebook for mystical ascent. To a large extent, the very ambiguity of the legend of the four sages is the reason for its primacy. Many have wondered what it was that Ben Azzai saw that caused him to lose his life, what Ben Zoma saw that caused him to lose his mind, and what Elisha ben Abuyah (Aher) saw that caused him to "cut the shoots," that is, become an apostate. There are clues in the Talmud concerning the fates of Ben Zoma and Aher, while the clues about Ben Azzai are found in Leviticus Rabbah and Song of Songs Rabbah, as noted. Ben Azzai's mysterious death has been linked to the mystical tradition of those who give up their souls without reservation during a mystical experience. This is equivalent to dying by the Kiss of the *Shekhinah*, as Moses did. As is the case with the alchemists, who either sought to turn lead into gold or the leaden *soul* into the golden *soul*, it is impossible to ascertain whether the authors of the Hekhaloth texts believed in and sought actual heavenly journeys, or whether it was implicit that the heavenly journey itself was a metaphor for the mystical ascent, in which the heavenly palaces signify degrees of spiritual elevation. In any case, Gershom Scholem speculates that this sect actively engaged in techniques to bring about mystical experiences, including the use of yo-galike positions and the singing of rhythmical hymns in unison for long periods of time. Standard Jewish practices of purification were also used, including the *mikveh* (ritual bath), fasting, and extensive prayer. Emphasis was also placed on the power of the word—on prayers, on amulets containing invocations, and, above all, on the secret pronunciation of the ineffable Name of God, the Tetragrammaton. For further dis-cussion of the legend of the four who entered Paradise, see the Introduction, pp. 28–31.

9. *Rabbi Ishmael's Ascent* (Palestine)

From The Legend of the Ten Martyrs. The earliest version of this legend is found in *Hekhaloth Rabbati*. The best-known version is that found in *Midrash Eleh Ezkerah* in A. Jellinek, *Beit ha-Midrash* (Jerusalem: 1967, Vol. 2, pp. 64–72). A critical synoptic edition, *Die Geschichte von den Zehn Martyern*, was published by Gottfried Reeg (Tubingen: 1985). A version of this legend is the liturgical poem *Eleh Ezkerah*, included in the prayer book for Yom Kippur, and another poem, *Arzei ha-Levanon Adirei ha-Tovah*, is recited on the Ninth of Av.

While most texts describing heavenly journeys make the ascent the focus of the tale, "Rabbi Ishmael's Ascent" is a portion of a longer midrashic narrative known as "The Legend of the Ten Martyrs." Here ten of the most famous Jewish martyrs, including Rabbi Akiba and Rabbi Ishmael, are linked as victims of the same evil decree, even though historically they did not all live at the same time. Rabbi Ishmael then undertakes an ascent into Paradise to discover if this is actually a heavenly decree or not. If not, he has it within his power to overthrow the Emperor's decree by drawing on the power of God's Name. So far the tale reads like a fairy tale. If it had followed this pattern, Rabbi Ishmael would have learned that it was not a heavenly decree, and on his return he would have defeated the Emperor, saving himself and his fellow sages. But this account has fused the Hekhaloth-type tale of ascent with the accounts of the deaths of these great sages culled from rabbinic sources, primarily from the Talmud. Thus Rabbi Ishmael learns that heaven has approved the decree against the sages to erase the sin of Joseph's brothers in selling Joseph. Note that this explanation gives the deaths of the sages cosmic meaning, in righting what was perceived as an epic wrong in the Torah, where Joseph's brothers are never punished for selling him into slavery. For it is clearly stated in the Torah that the punishment for such a sin is death: *He who kidnaps a man—whether he has held him or is still holding him—shall be put to death* (Gen. 21:16). In "The Legend of the Ten Martyrs" it is the Emperor, who has commanded the sages to teach him the Bible, who raises the question of whether or not Joseph's brothers were punished. But this was clearly a question on the minds of the rabbis, who scrutinized the events prior to the giving of the Torah for evidence that the laws were fulfilled, and this was not always the case, as for example, where Abraham appears to serve the angelic wanderers both meat and milk in Genesis 18:7–8. Also, the rabbis sought precedents for evil behavior in the biblical text. They wanted to know how Cain died, which is not reported. In fact, there are four different versions of how Cain died that are found in the aggadic texts. It is therefore possible to see the imprint of four basic kinds of Jewish narratives combined into one here: (1) the tale of ascent; (2) the linking tale, which links key figures from various generations into a chain midrash; (3) the tale that responds to a specific point of the Law, in this case the punishment required for the sin of Joseph's brothers; and (4) the martyrological tale. In addition, this tale can be seen to have major theological ramifications. It shifts the blame for the Roman oppression to God, much in the same way that the myth of the Ari shifts the blame for the Fall from Adam and Eve to God. This is a natural consequence of monotheism: if there is only one God, then everything that takes place must have been brought into being by that God, including evil acts. One strange notion found in this important tale is that it would be possible, much less expected by God, that anyone other than Joseph's brothers be punished for their sin. Yet this is what the tale implies. This is an essentially kabbalistic premise. The sin of Joseph's brothers has cosmic implications; it created a taint in existence, much in the way that the person of Cain is transformed into a principle of evil in the Kabbalah. Therefore the deaths of the ten martyrs has a meaning that transcends their earthly loss: a major taint has been removed from the world. From this perspective the deaths represent a monumental sacrifice, which has the effect of serving as a cosmic act of *tikkun*, of repair and restoration. (Note that this sacrifice has Christian overtones.) The accounts of the deaths of the rabbis, drawn from diverse time periods and sources, are very moving. For example, Rabbi Haninah ben Teradion was burned along with the

Torah: "They took him, wrapped him in the scroll of the Torah, placed bundles of branches around him and set him on fire. . . . His disciples called out, 'Rabbi, what do you see?' He answered: 'The parchments are being burnt but the letters are soaring on high'" (Avodah Zarah 18a). The other rabbis who were martyred in addition to Rabbi Ishmael, Rabbi Akiba, and Rabbi Haninah ben Teradion, include Rabbi Simeon ben Gamaliel, Rabbi Yuda ben Baba, Rabbi Yuda ben Dema, Rabbi Hutzapit, Rabbi Hanina ben Hakhinai, Rabbi Yeshivav the scribe, and Rabbi Eleazar ben Shammua. *Midrash Eleh Ezkerah* includes an interesting legend about Rabbi Ishmael that identifies the angel Gabriel as his true father. For so pious was Rabbi Ishmael's mother that the Holy One, blessed be He, told Gabriel to appear to her in the shape of her husband, Rabbi Yose. So it was that Gabriel took Rabbi Yose's form and met her at the bathhouse and held her hand as they walked to her home. And that night Rabbi Ishmael was conceived, who, everyone agreed, was as beautiful as an angel. This legend makes the meeting of Rabbi Ishmael and Gabriel in Paradise much more meaningful.

10. *The Waters of the Abyss* (Babylon)

From B. Sukkah 53a–b and Y. Sanh. 29b. Additional legends about the *Even Shetiyah* (Foundation Stone) are found in in the Mishnah, Yoma 5:2, in B. Yoma 54a–b, and in Zohar II:222a–222b.

One of the primary themes of this tale is a stern warning against tampering with the primary forces of creation. Here the tampering takes the form of lifting the Foundation Stone that covers the Abyss. Even though King David is more than sufficiently warned not to proceed by a voice coming from the stone, he insists on lifting the Foundation Stone purely to satisfy his curiosity and almost provokes a flood that will inundate the world. Then he reverses the process by dropping a potsherd with God's Name inscribed on it into the Abyss. The water recedes and the danger passes. Note that King David is not certain if such a use of God's Name is permitted and virtually forces the others to approve his action. This clearly indicates that he recognizes the grave step he is taking in making use of God's Name. A talmudic variant of this tale gives the origin of the Foundation Stone and its history. According to this legend, God restrained the waters of the deep, known as *Tehom*, from rising up, and enforced this by placing a stone above it, on which God engraved His Name. God removed this stone only once: to bring on the flood in Noah's day (Y. Sanh. 29a). This is one of several instances of the use of the Tetragrammaton in the Talmud. Another concerns King Solomon's magic ring, with God's Name inscribed on it, which is used to capture Asmodeus, the King of Demons (B. Gittin 68b). Rabbi Nachman of Bratslav wrote about the Foundation Stone in *Sihot ha-Ran* 60 (Ostrog: 1816), interpreting it in mythic and allegorical terms as follows:

The world has a foundation stone. This stone serves as the starting point of all that was created and serves as a true foundation. Now there are channels which emanate from this stone, reaching every land. King Solomon, in his wisdom, understood the nature of these channels, and was therefore able to plant every kind of tree. But there are many types of fruit which do not grow in our land, and this is because people do not understand this secret. For if the location of these subterranean channels was known, every fruit could be grown here as well, for each channel has the power to bring forth a particular species. And even if some channels do not pass directly beneath our land, the fact is that all of these channels are intertwined, and each flows into the other. Therefore it would still be possible, if the nature of these channels were truly understood, to plant any tree, no matter what kind it was. Furthermore, if the location of these channels were known, it would be possible to dig anywhere and locate a well, which would sustain these species of trees, and thus the trees would flourish. But this knowledge seems to have been lost from the world. Once it was revealed, but for many generations now it has been concealed. And while it is often said that the world is gaining knowledge, in truth the earlier generations made the primary discoveries, and this took the greatest wisdom. And if the secrets of the earlier generations were recovered, the world would flourish where today it merely languishes in its ignorance.

Rabbi Nachman also discusses this mystical interpretation of the Foundation Stone in *Lekutei Moharan* (Ostrog: 1808, 61:6). For further discussion of the legend of the *Even Shetiyah* see *Aggadot ve-Toledotehen* by J. Heinnemann and "On Sealing the Abysses" by Daniel Sperber in *Journal for Semitic Studies*, 11 (1966), 168ff. For a similiar theme about cosmic catastrophe, see "The Prince of Coucy" in *MT*, p. 173, where a rabbi lifts the curtain covering the Cave of the Four Winds and comes close to unleashing winds that would demolish the world.

11. *The Vision of the High Priest* (Babylon)
From B. Ber. 7a.
This tale is a talmudic retelling of a biblical incident, exemplifying the pattern of retellings that continues through postbiblical Jewish literature. Here the biblical account of Moses speaking with God inside the tent of meeting is reworked into a tale of the high priest having a vision of God in the Holy of Holies. In the biblical version, Moses does not see God but speaks to him: *And when Moses went into the tent of meeting that He might speak with him, then he heard the Voice speaking unto him from above the ark-cover that was upon the ark of the testimony, from between the two cherubim; and He spoke unto him* (Num. 7:89). The talmudic tale grows out of traditions linked to the Temple in Jerusalem. No one was permitted to enter the Holy of Holies in the Temple except for the High Priest, and then only on Yom Kippur. This talmudic legend recounts how Rabbi Ishmael, the High Priest, had a vision of God inside the Holy of Holies. The name he attributes to God, Akatriel Yah, is a very strange one, leaving open the possibility that this was also an angelic figure. However, the traditional readings of this tale have always identified Akatriel Yah as one of the many names of God. Most remarkable is God's request to Rabbi Ishmael—that Ishmael bless Him, rather than the reverse. This makes it one of the primary examples of the rabbinic tradition by which God's need for man is as great as man's need for God. Rabbi Ishmael does bless God, and in return the Lord nods his approval. At the root of this legend is the belief, of primitive origin, that there is a kind of interdependence between man and God. This is represented in the legend of the angel Sandalphon, who is said to weave the prayers of Israel into crowns of prayers for the Holy One to wear on His Throne of Glory (B. Hag. 13b). Here, however, the tradition has been modified to the extent that God wears the crowns of prayer not because He needs to in order to be complete, but out of a great love that He holds for the prayers of Israel.

12. *The Keys of the Temple* (Babylon)
From *Pesikta Rabbati* 26:6. Other versions of offering the keys to heaven are found

in the J. Shekalim 50a and B. Ta'anit 29a. In some versions, not only the High Priest leaps into the flames, but the other priests and Levites as well. A variant is found in 2 Baruch 6:8–9. Here the High Priest offers the temple vessels to the earth, which opens, swallowing them up.

The destruction of the Temple in Jerusalem brought an era of Jewish life to an end. All of the rituals connected to the Temple could no longer be performed. Therefore this talmudic legend recounts how the High Priest returns the keys to the Temple to God, and in a strongly anthropomorphic image, a giant hand reaches down from heaven to retrieve them. The theological implications of this legend are considerable. It presumes both that heaven was well aware of the destruction of the Temple and that it was no accident, but rather God's intention. Of course, it is also a tragic event. From this perspective, the act of the High Priest in returning the keys to heaven is one of great despair. Nevertheless, even at this tragic moment in Jewish history, the link between God and His people, Israel, remains intact in the act of God's accepting the keys to the Temple. The motif of returning a precious gift to heaven is also found in "The Golden Table," p. 58, and "The Soul of the Ari," p. 258.

13. *The Spirit of Idolatry* (Babylon)
From B. Yoma 69b.

The spirit that is captured in this talmudic tale is the incarnation of the *Yetzer ha-Ra*, the Evil Inclination. (There is also a Good Inclination, the *Yetzer ha-Tov*.) Rabbinic literature shows considerable ambiguity on this subject. While always urging that this impulse be resisted, the rabbis also recognized its essential role in the world, as this tale makes clear. Here the spirit of idolatry is overcome and captured. It is only then, however, that the people discover its role in the divine scheme—for without the Evil Inclination, sexual desire in all creatures ceased, causing all procreation to stop. Had this continued, all animal life would have died out. In this way, the rabbis acknowledge a necessary and perhaps even positive role of the Evil Inclination. Note the strongly mythical aspects of this tale, in which the Evil Inclination is personified as a fiery lion. It has strong echoes of the rabbinic legends about the golden calf, which was said to have come to life and charged around, out of control (*Midrash Shir* 13a–b and *Pirke de Rabbi Eliezer* 45). This tale also has distinct echoes of far Eastern mythologies, such as those portraying fiery dragons. The roaring of the fiery lion in this tale is reminiscent of that in the well-known talmudic tale, "The Lion of Ilai" (B. Hullin 59b):

> Caesar called in Rabbi Yehoshua ben Hananiah to question him about the ways of the Jews. He said to him: "Your God is likened to a lion, as it is written in your Holy Scriptures: *The lion hath roared, who will not fear?* (Amos 3:8) What is so great about this? A hunter can kill a lion." Rabbi Yehoshua replied: "You would not want to see this lion." But Caesar insisted, saying: "Indeed, I want to see him. If I do not, the lives of the Jews will be in grave danger!" Then Rabbi Yehoshua saw that he had no choice, so he prayed that the lion might come from its place in the forest Ilai. And before long his prayer was answered, and the lion emerged from the forest and set out for the city of Rome. And when the lion was at a distance of four hundred parasangs, it roared once, the ground shook, and all the bridges of Rome collapsed. When it was at a distance of three hundred parasangs it roared a second time, the molars and front teeth of the people fell out, and Caesar himself fell off his throne. Then

Caesar said to Rabbi Yehoshua: "Enough! I beg you, pray that the lion be
returned to its place." This Rabbi Yehoshua did, and the lion turned around
and returned to the forest from which it had come.

The literal meaning of the Hebrew term for "forest Ilai" is "Supernal House."
Using the term to echo both meanings, this tale suggests the terrifying power and
glory of the Lord, who is compared to the lion of the forest Ilai. For a further
description of the "Supernal House," or "House of the World," see the note to "The
Golden Scepter," p. 291.

14. The Angel of Conception (Babylon)

From *Midrash Tanhuma Pekude* 3, first published in Constantinople in 1522. The
exact date and country of origin are uncertain. An alternate edition was edited by
Solomon Buber (Vilna: 1885). Also found in Zohar Hadash 68:3.

This legend is sometimes identified as "The Formation of the Child." One version
of it is found in *Sefer ha-Zikhronot*, edited by Jerahmeel ben Solomon, and another in
Be'er ha-Hasidut, edited by Eliezer Steinmann (Tel Aviv, vol. 1, p. 216). The divine
origin of the soul is here revealed to have been drawn from on high and sent to this
world reluctantly. Such a legend affirms the rabbinic belief in the essential purity of
the human soul, which is subjected to the power of the *Yetzer Hara*, the Evil Inclination. The portion of the legend concerning the touch of the angel's finger to the child's
lip is very popular and serves as the framework to a satiric midrashic novel, *The Book of
Paradise*, by Itzik Manger. Note that the angel Lailah has distinctly feminine characteristics. Although angels are generally regarded as androgynous, most bear male
names and have male characteristics. Here the angel Lailah seems to have the female
characteristic of being responsible for the fetus, for assisting at birth, and for guiding
the soul from this world to the next.

15. The Golden Table (Babylon)

From B. Ta'anit 24b–25a.

Rabbi Haninah ben Dosa was a beloved talmudic sage. His honesty was legendary,
as was his poverty. In this tale, his wife's subterfuge of burning sticks in the oven so
that the neighbors will think she is baking bread for the Sabbath is challenged by a
nosy neighbor who wants to humiliate her. To prevent this from happening, a miracle
takes place, and the oven is filled with beautiful *challas*. This is both heaven's reward
and a divine way of preventing her humiliation (B. Ta'an. 25a). It was an article of
faith among the rabbis that although the material rewards of the righteous in this
world might be few, a great reward awaited them in the World to Come. Knowledge
of the rewards of the righteous is gained from the heavenly ascents of Enoch and Rabbi
Ishmael and the four who entered Paradise, among others. In "The Golden Table,"
the poverty of Rabbi Haninah and his wife becomes so extreme that Rabbi Haninah's
wife begs him to request some of his reward in the World to Come while he is still
alive. When he accedes to her wish, he receives a golden leg from heaven, but later
dreams that his golden table in Paradise is short one leg. The Talmud adds that the
latter miracle of returning the golden leg to heaven was even greater than that of first
receiving it, for there is a tradition that a miracle may be given only once and is then
never taken away. For another tale about Rabbi Haninah's honesty, see B. Ta'anit
25a. Another tale concerning heavenly rewards is "The Shining Robe," p. 141. See

"Challahs in the Ark," another famous tale about *challahs*, from *Shivhei ha-Ari*. A version of this tale can be found in *GNC*, p. 240.

16. *The Tzohar* (Babylon and Ancient Israel)

The legend of the primordial light is found in B. Hag. 12a, where it is said that in that light "one could see from one end of the world to another." Here it is said that at the time of the Fall, God hid the primordial light for the righteous in the World to Come. Another version of this legend states that the light was hidden in the Garden of Eden (Lev. Rab. 11:7). Still another version holds that this light was hidden in the Torah. In *Shivhei ha-Besht* the Baal Shem Tov adds to this tradition that "One who sees this light in the Torah is capable of viewing the entire world from end to end." In Genesis Rabbah 3:3 the primordial light is linked to the verse in Psalms *Who coverest Thyself with light as with a garment* (Ps. 104:2). See also Genesis Rabbah 3:6, where this light is said to be stored up for the righteous in the messianic era. The source of the legend of the primordial light is B. Hag. 12a. The complete legend of the primordial light is found in Zohar 1:31b. The image of God wrapping Himself in a *tallis* of light is found in Gen. Rabbah 24:2 and *Midrash Tanhuma*, ed. Buber, Ber. 28. See also *Pesikta de Reb Kahana* 21:5. For more on the primordial light see *The Lamp of God: A Jewish Book of Light* by Freema Gottlieb, pp. 142–52. The legend of the glowing gem that Noah hung in the ark is found in Genesis Rabbah 31:11: "During the whole twelve months that Noah was in the ark he did not require the light of the sun by day or the light of the moon by night, but he had a polished gem which he hung up: when it was dim he knew that it was day, and when it shone he knew that it was night." There is another version of the theme of the angel Gabriel coming to earth to save the infant Abraham in the cave where he has been abandoned. Here Israelite mothers said to fear for the lives of their infants gave birth in the secrecy of the orchards, seen by no one. And angels came down from heaven to help them (Ex. Rab. 1:16). This midrash is linked to the verse *I raised you up under the apple tree; there thy mother brought you forth* (Song of Songs 8:5). The story of the precious stone of Abraham is found in B. Baba Batra 16b. This account offers an alternate fate for the precious stone, saying, "When Abraham passed away from the world, the Holy One, blessed be He, hung it on the wheel of the sun." The legend about Joseph in the pit is found in *Midrash Asseret Harugei Malchut* in *Otsar HaMidrashim*, p. 444. The story of Joseph's cup being carried off by his brothers is found in Gen. 44:5. The *Ner Tamid* or Eternal Light is first mentioned in Exodus 27:20: *And thou shalt command the children of Israel that they bring unto thee pure olive oil beaten for the light, to cause a lamp to burn continually.* This lamp was later placed above the Ark.

This tale is a classic example of a chain midrash—a series of midrashim that are linked to each other by a common object or character. The object here is the glowing stone known as the *Tzohar*. The term *"Tzohar"* appears in the Bible only once, at the time that God instructs Noah on how to build the ark. God tells him *A Tzohar shalt thou make to the ark* (6:16). *Tzohar* has been variously translated as "light," "opening," "window," "dome," and in other ways, implying that it should admit light into the ark. This interpretation derives from the assumption that *Tzohar* is linked to the Hebrew word *Zohar*, meaning "splendor" or "illumination." In the Aggadah, however, *Tzohar* is taken to refer to the sacred jewel given to Adam and thereafter passed down through the generations to Seth, Enoch, Methuselah, Lamech, Noah, the Patriarchs, Joseph, and Moses. This legend evolves out of an attempt to resolve two problems in the biblical text: the nature of the light of the first day of creation, before the creation of the sun and moon and stars, and the meaning of *Tzohar* in the passage about building the ark. The Midrash explains that the light of the first day was a sacred light, which, according to some accounts, was cast from God's garment of light, and, according to others, was reflected from the robe of the *Shekhinah*. The midrash emphasizes the difference between this light and the ordinary light of the sun, so that it was possible for Adam to see to the ends of the earth. The fact that no such light still exists is explained by adding it to the list of the things that were lost at the time of the Fall and the expulsion from Eden. However, God decided to retain a bit of the sacred light and encased it in the glowing jewel of the *Tzohar*. The vehicle of the chain midrash makes it possible for it to be transmitted from Adam to Noah, and then from Noah to Abraham and the following patriarchs. The imprinting of the Torah inside the *Tzohar* follows from the midrashim that explain that the Torah was one of the things that God created before the creation: "Seven things were created before the world was created. They are: The Torah, Gehenna, the Garden of Eden, the Throne of Glory, the Temple, Repentance, and the Name of the Messiah" (*Pirke de Rabbi Eliezer* 3, Constantinople: 1514). Further evidence of the preexistence of the Torah is found in Genesis Rabbah 1:1: "God consulted the Torah and created the world." According to the Zohar, Rabbi Shimon bar Yohai also had possession of the *Tzohar*: "Our companion, Bar Yohai, has a jewel, a precious stone, and I have looked upon the light emitted by it, and it is like the light of the sun, illuminating the whole world. This light extends from the heavens to the earth, and will continue to illumine the world until the Ancient of Days comes, and sits upon his throne" (Zohar I:11a–b). The *Tzohar* also is found in various Jewish folktales. See, for example, "The Man Who Escaped Misfortune" in *MT*, p. 331. It is possible that J. R. R. Tolkien made use of some of the legends about the *Tzohar* in *The Silmarillion*, in which the central motif concerns jewels containing the last of a primordial light.

17. *The Gates of Eden* (Babylon)
From B. Tamid 32b.
There are many legends about Alexander the Great in Jewish lore. This legend from the Talmud teaches Alexander the lesson that the lust of the human eye is limitless but is easily quenched by dust, that is, by death. Alexander learns this at the gates of the Garden of Eden, which is the one place that Alexander cannot conquer in the world, just as he cannot conquer death. Thus the moral of the tale is that there are built-in limits to human desire, a moral that is appropriately directed at Alexander, a folk symbol of one who sought to go beyond all human limits. For other Jewish tales about the exploits of Alexander, see "Alexander Descends into the Sea" in *MT*, p. 118, and "The Waters of Eternal Life," in the same book, p. 122.

18. *The Law Is Not in Heaven* (Babylon)
From B. Baba Mezia 59b. The subject of the disagreement between Rabbi Eliezer and the others was the purity of a certain type of oven, known as the oven of 'Aknai.
This rather startling legend vividly demonstrates the rabbinic belief that once the Torah had been given on Mount Sinai it became the possession of the Jews, and the responsibility for interpreting it fell to the rabbis. So extreme is this tale that it suggests that the rabbis were not willing to let any authority—even that of God—overrule them. And as the coda to the tale reveals, God seems to accept their determination to decide the Law as they see fit. Rabbi Eliezer ben Hyrcanos, one of the great talmudic sages, disagrees with his fellow sages, and insists on his interpretation

to the extent that he provokes miracles—the moving of the carob tree, the reversal of the waters of the spring, and the imminent collapse of the walls of the House of Study. Finally, he calls upon heaven to confirm the correctness of his interpretation—and heaven replies in his favor. None of this, however, deters the other rabbis from their interpretation. Instead, Rabbi Yehoshua virtually tells heaven to keep out of this matter, since, as he says, *The Law is not in Heaven* (Deut. 30:12). And, indeed, the full context of this passage does in fact seem to shift the burden of responsibility for the interpretation of the Law from God to man: *From this commandment which I command thee this day, it is not too hard for thee, neither is it far off. It is not in heaven, that thou shouldest say: "Who shall go up for us to heaven, and bring it unto us, and make us to hear it, that we may do it." Neither is it beyond the sea, that thou shouldest say: "Who shall go over the sea for us, and bring it unto us, and make us to hear it, that we may do it." But the word is very nigh unto thee, in thy mouth, and in thy heart, that thou mayest do it* (Deut. 30:11–14). On the other hand, the biblical passage that serves as the basis of Rabbi Yehoshua's assertion that the rabbis, and not God, must decide the Law, *Follow after the majority*, from Exodus 23:2, has had its meaning reversed from its original context: *Thou shalt not follow a multitude to do evil.* This is a radical example of the rabbinic reinterpretation of the text. Indeed, it is a willful misinterpretation, and it demonstrates the extent of the rabbinic determination to assume all responsibility for the interpretation of the Law.

19. *The Voice in the Attic* (Babylon)
From B. Baba Mezia 83b-85a.
Because of his great piety, Rabbi Eliezer is singled out to reply to important queries after his death, while his body is preserved. Speaking from the beyond, the rabbi functions as a kind of oracle. In this tale can be found the rabbinic belief of a metaphysical link to the patriarchs, prophets, and sages of the past. Indeed, one of the primary characteristics of midrashic literature is the assumption that all generations exist simultaneously. See "Past and Present in Midrashic Literature" by Marc Bregman in *Hebrew Annual Review* 2(1978), 45–59. In this sense, the voice in the attic is still speaking. The primary folk motif of this tale, of the voice of one who has died continuing to speak, is rare in Jewish lore. The closest motif is that of the *dybbuk*, the spirit of one who has died, who takes possession of someone living, and must be expelled. This *ruach* or spirit speaks through the living person, although often in a voice of its own. Such forms of possession are, of course, recognized as cursed, and each such tale ends with the exorcism of the *dybbuk*. See "The Widow of Safed," p. 98. An even closer parallel to the present tale is the concept of the *ibur*, the spirit of a dead sage who fuses his soul with that of a living one to give him comfort or instruction. But in the case of both the *dybbuk* and the *ibur*, the voice of the one who has died is speaking through one who is living, unlike the voice of Rabbi Eliezer, which continues to speak from the attic.

20. *Forcing the End* (Babylon)
From B. Baba Metzia 85b.
This is an exceptionally important talmudic legend concerning the attempt to hasten the coming of the Messiah. Here Elijah inadvertently reveals one of the key secrets of heaven—that Rabbi Hiyya and his sons have the righteousness and purity of the Patriarchs, and therefore have the power to force the coming of the Messiah. This they attempt to do by reading prayers that cause the actions they describe to take

place. This causes consternation in heaven, for they are on the verge of forcing the coming of the messianic age, and Elijah is sent to earth as a fiery bear, chasing everyone out of the synagogue before the Messiah is forced to come. Later Elijah is punished with sixty fiery lashes for revealing this heavenly secret—much as Elijah whips the angel Metatron sixty times for not standing up in the presence of Elisha ben Abuyah when he ascended into Paradise, thus giving him the false impression that there is more than one power in heaven (B. Hag. 15a). This hastening of the messianic era is known as "Forcing the End," and this legend serves as the model for many subsequent tales about the attempt to hasten the coming of the Messiah. There is great ambivalence in the rabbinic literature about these attempts, since such an effort is sinful. But this one sin was tolerated and even encouraged by many rabbis whose longing for the coming of the Messiah grew so great that they were willing to do anything so that the footsteps of the Messiah could be heard in the world. One classic example is the tale of Joseph della Reina. See "The Chains of the Messiah," p. 106. There also are many Hasidic tales on this theme of trying to force the coming of the Messiah. See, for example, "The Pact," p. 256.

II Kabbalistic Tales

The Circle of Shimon bar Yohai

21. *The Cave of Shimon bar Yohai* (Babylon)
From B. Shabbat 33b. This legend is also found in *Beit ha-Midrash*, edited by A. Jellinek, IV:22; *Pesikta de-Rab Kahana*, edited by Solomon Buber, 88b; and *Koheleth Rabbah* 10:8. The legend is amplified in *Zohar Hadash, Ki tavo* 59c–60a. The legend about the finding of the Zohar is from the introduction to *Or Hahama* I, edited by A. Azulai, published in 1816.

Although this legend originated in a talmudic source, it became the basis for the kabbalistic legends about the talmudic sage Shimon bar Yohai. According to this legend, Bar Yohai spent thirteen years in a cave, hiding from the Romans, who had condemned him. Moshe de Leon, who lived in Spain in the thirteenth century, attributed the text of the Zohar, which he claimed to have discovered, to Shimon bar Yohai, who was said to have written it during the years spent in hiding. However, modern scholars, especially Gershom Scholem, have demonstrated that the Zohar was actually the creation of Moses de Leon. The Zohar is a mystical commentary on the Torah, but it also contains many legends about Shimon bar Yohai and his disciples. The portrayal of Shimon bar Yohai in the Zohar became the model of the master for later sages, especially the Ari. And the Ari became the archetype of the master for later rabbis, such as Shalom Shabazi and the Baal Shem Tov. So an imagined portrayal of a master by Moshe de Leon led to a real life emulation of the model.

22. *The Decree* (Spain)
From *Zohar Hadash, Va-yera*, 26b.
In this legend from the Zohar, Shimon bar Yohai singlehandedly causes heaven to reverse a decree to destroy the world. This tale strongly recalls Abraham's negotiations with God over the fate of Sodom (Gen. 18:20–33). It also echoes a famous talmudic tale about Shimon bar Yohai, but with an opposite moral. In it, Bar Yohai and his son Eleazar emerge from the cave after twelve years and are so distraught at what they find that whatever Bar Yohai gazes upon withers, and he and his son are

ordered by God to return to the cave for another year (B. Shab. 33b). But as the central figure of the Zohar, the latter legend finds Bar Yohai saving the world from destruction rather than threatening it, as in the talmudic tale.

23. *The Curtain of Fire* (Spain)
From the Zohar II, 14a–15a, *Midrash ha-Ne'elam.*

This is one of a cycle of tales about Rabbi Shimon bar Yohai that is found in the Zohar. For more about Shimon bar Yohai, see the note to "The Cave of Shimon bar Yohai," p. 290. In all of these tales Bar Yohai is portrayed as a consummate mystical master, guiding his disciples to experience the divine mysteries. Mystical union is the most essential aspect of any mystical tradition. Yet it is rarely portrayed as openly as it is here, where Rabbi Hiyya sees the Divine Presence inside Shimon bar Yohai's house. He perceives that Shimon bar Yohai is studying the Torah with an angel, with a curtain of fire separating them. Note that what Rabbi Hiyya sees is not presented as a vision, but it affects him as a visionary experience. Indeed, he is so caught up in the moment of mystical union that Rabbi Shimon sends another disciple to cover his mouth, which brings him back to this world. One of the fascinating mysteries of this tale is why Bar Yohai chooses to have Rabbi Hiyya's mouth covered, and not his eyes, which had witnessed the vision. One possible answer is that he does not want to cut off the vision, but rather to prevent Rabbi Hiyya's soul from leaving his body during the instant of mystical union. Another is that since Rabbi Hiyya has been struck dumb, the gesture of the hand restores his speech. The curtain of fire that separates Bar Yohai from the divine force suggests both the *Pargod*, the heavenly curtain that separates God from the rest of Paradise, and the curtain in the Holy of Holies in the Temple beyond which only the High Priest was permitted to go. The fact that a curtain remains separating Rabbi Hiyya and the heavenly being suggests that even in the grip of powerful mystical experiences, there was not a complete loss of self-identity for Jewish mystics, as is so often associated with mystical union. There is also the suggestion that just as God remains apart from the angels, so humans must remain separated from divine beings.

24. *A Saint from the Other World* (Spain)
Zohar I:5a–7b.

For the early Jewish mystics the prime concern was deciphering the mysteries of creation and of the *Merkavah*, the Divine Chariot seen in the vision of Ezekiel. These are the two subjects on which all other kabbalistic speculation is based. The kabbalistic mythology presumes the existence of heavenly discussions similiar to those practiced by the rabbis in this world. Here one of the righteous in Paradise comes down to earth to encourage the discussion of these esoteric mysteries, revealing secrets from on high. This divine figure is identified as Rav Hamnuna Sava, and his divine origin is apparent from his description of where he lives—in a tower suspended from the heavens—and from the mythic description of his father as some kind of sea being, resembling Leviathan. Such encounters are quite common in the kabbalistic literature. Naturally the saint, who plays a role similiar to that of Elijah, vanishes when identified, as does Elijah in similiar instances.

25. *The Golden Scepter* (Spain)
From the Zohar 2:13a–b.

This tale, like "The Curtain of Fire," portrays a moment of mystical union, although it is presented in a more allegorical manner here. The union comes at the instant Rabbi Yoezzer opens the book of mysteries he has received from a mysterious man in a cave. This man strikes him from behind with a golden scepter, and he then has a vision of the House of the World. This is a kabbalistic symbol for the place that is the center and core of the spiritual universe. In the following passage, also from the Zohar, the nature of this archetypal house is described further:

> This House forms the center of the universe. It has many doors and windows on every side and provides sacred and exalted abodes where the celestial birds build their nests, each according to its kind. In the House are stored many precious and undiscovered treasures. From the midst of it rises a large tree, with mighty branches bearing an abundance of fruit providing food for all. The tree rears itself to the clouds of heaven and is lost to view between three rocks, from which it again emerges, so that it is both above and below them. From this tree the House is watered. The tree in the midst of the House is visible in the day but hidden by night, whereas the House becomes manifest in the night and is hidden by day. As soon as darkness sets in and all the doors on all its sides are closed, innumerable spirits fly about, desiring to know what is in the House. They flit around and see many things until the darkness in which the House is enveloped is aroused and sends forth a flame, causing the doors to be opened. This flame descends to the world below and ascends into the heavens above and calls forth a herald, who makes proclamation. Then innumerable voices chant hymns, and songs of praise ascend. Soon the house is lit up on every side, brilliant and resplendent, and from thence flow rivers of balsam from which all the animals of the field are watered. These praises continue until daybreak, when the stars, the constellations and their hosts all commence to chant songs of praise and hymns. (Zohar I: 172a–b)

Who is it that triggers Rabbi Yoezzer's vision? It is possible to identify the man with the golden scepter with the highest angels, such as Metatron or the Archangels (Michael, Gabriel, Uriel, and Raphael), or else with the Messiah. Because of the way the mysterious figure is encountered, and because he is a hidden ruler, he most closely resembles the Messiah. One point is clearly made: the reason that Rabbi Yoezzer has been privileged to experience this revelation is that he is part of the circle of Shimon bar Yohai. The vision of the letters inscribed in black fire on white fire is a common image in the Zohar deriving from Song of Songs Rabbah 5:11: "Rabbi Shimon ben Lakish said: 'The scroll which God gave Moses was of white fire and its writing of black fire.'" A variant of this legend is found in Deuteronomy Rabbah 3:12.

26. *The Book of Adam* (Spain)
From Zohar I:117b-118a. The legend of the book that the angel Raziel gave to Adam is found in Zohar I:55a.

This tale echoes the legend about the book given to Adam by the angel Raziel in order to reveal the nature of the future generations to him. According to the legend, Adam fainted when he heard the angel read from the book, and so it was left with him, and in this way it came into the possession of Enoch, Noah, Abraham, Joseph, and Solomon, among others. According to most accounts it was destroyed along with the Temple, but others legends hint that it was among the Temple vessels preserved and hidden by Jeremiah. In "The Book of Adam" Rabbi Yosse finds a book of divine mysteries much like the Book of Raziel, but since he is not destined to read in it, a great wind tears it from his grasp after he has read one page. In any case its truths are too great for him to comprehend, as he realizes when he discovers that they have been erased from his mind. Note the reference to the age forty, which is the traditional age to begin the study of Kabbalah. The legend of the book of Raziel is retold in Hasidic lore in "The Book in the Cave," p. 183. The Hasidic legend follows essentially the same line of descent, but has the book survive the destruction of the Temple and reaches Rabbi Adam, whose son later passes the book on to the Baal Shem Tov in "The Prince of Fire," p. 187. The legend of the book of Raziel is an example of a chain midrash, one of the most popular types of rabbinic tales. The chain midrash is one kind of mega-myth, and the myth of the Ari, which links the myths of creation and the Messiah, is another. Both view history as a chain of related events focused on the covenant between God and Israel. In these tales one biblical figure is linked to another in a series of legends. Among the examples included here are the chain legends of "The Tzohar," p. 59, and that of the remarkable legendary figure Serah bat Asher, who lived longer than Methuselah, in "The Chronicle of Serah bat Asher," p. 47. The legend of the book of Raziel is generally regarded as talmudic or early posttalmudic. One version of this legend is found at the beginning of *Sefer ha-Razim*, edited by M. Margoliot (Jerusalem: 1966).

27. Rabbi Gadiel the Child (Spain)

From *Seder Gan Eden* in *Beit ha-Midrash*, edited by A. Jellinek (Jerusalem: 1967, Vol. III, pp. 136–37). Also found in *Otsar Midrashim* I:87. A variant is found in The Zohar III:186a–192a.

One interesting kabbalistic legend is that of a holy child. This legend is found in several versions. In all of them the child is a prodigy of the Torah. In the legend of Rabbi Gadiel the child was martyred, and because of its pure soul and immense knowledge, it was made head of a heavenly yeshivah. In other versions, the child is the reincarnation of a great sage. In another variant of this legend, found in The Zohar III:186a–192a, the holy child is identified as the son of the mythic figure Rav Hamnuna Sava (Zohar I:51–7a). See "A Saint from the Other World," p. 72, where a hidden saint is identified as Rav Hamnuna Sava. The present version draws on both of these variants. The legend of the holy child serves to illustrate the mystical concept of *gilgul*, demonstrating the cycles of rebirth. This belief has survived to this day in certain Orthodox circles, especially those of Sephardic origin. The motif of a holy child is still found among oral tales collected by the IFA. See, for example, "The Reincarnation of a *Tzaddik*" in *MT*, p. 217.

28. The Celestial Academy (Spain)

From the Zohar, I:4a–4b. The tradition of the Celestial Academy is found in B. Avodah Zarah 18.

Here Rabbi Hiyya fasts to achieve something that is not permitted to the living—to see Shimon bar Yohai's place in Paradise. After eighty days of fasting and weeping he has a dream in which he sees bar Yohai teaching thousands in Paradise, and when he awakes he finds an angel in his room, who bears him to Paradise. There the Messiah asks why a mortal has been brought there, and he commands that his soul remain in Paradise. But Shimon bar Yohai asks that Rabbi Hiyya be given more time among the living and the Messiah agrees to this. This tale confirms the taboo of a human entering into Paradise, which finds its model in the tale of the ascent of Moses into heaven to receive the Torah. The angels sought to cast him out of Paradise, for none of the living are permitted there (B. Shab. 88b). This tale also confirms the greatness of Shimon bar Yohai, who is presented as a great leader in Paradise who even has influence over the Messiah. Rabbinic lore portrays the great rabbis as leading their own yeshivahs in Paradise, and this legend thus depicts Shimon bar Yohai as being recognized as one of the greatest sages of all time.

29. *The Book of Flying Letters* (Spain)
From the Zohar I:216b–217a.

The earliest examples of the theme of flying letters are found in rabbinic lore concerning the Tablets of the Law that Moses threw down when he saw the golden calf (Ex. 33:1a). The tablets broke, but the letters ascended to heaven (*Avot de Rabbi Natan* 2:11). The other famous tale about flying letters concerns the execution of Haninah ben Teradion, who was wrapped in the scroll of the Torah. When asked what he saw as the flames burned, he replied: "The parchments are being burnt but the letters are soaring on high" (Avoda Zara 18a). "The Book of Flying Letters" emphasizes how much the world lost at the time of the death of Shimon bar Yohai. Here Rabbi Judah has a dream in which he sees Bar Yohai ascending on high, followed by a flock of flying letters. These are the letters of the book of his wisdom, which has been lost due to his death. See "The Flying Letters," p. 156 and the accompanying note. Rabbinic lore often attributes remarkable events to the deaths of the rabbis, as is indicated in this list from *Mor Uktsia*: "When Rabbi Yakov bar Acha died, the stars appeared in the day. When Rabbi Assi died, all the trees were uprooted. When Rabbi Hiyya died, stones of fire came down from heaven. When Rabbi Himnona died, hail stones fell from heaven. When Raba and Rabbi Yosef died, the shores of the river Pratt came closer together. And when Abaya and Raba died, the shores of the river Hideckel came closer. When Rabbi Narshiya died, thorns grew on all the trees, and all of these were to show a change that came upon the world."

30. *Candles in the Synagogue* (Palestine)
From *Anshe Shem*, edited by Solomon Buber (Jerusalem: 1967). Also found in *Tsfunot Ve Aggadot*, edited by M. J. Bin Gorion (Berditchevsky) (Tel Aviv: 1956).

Shimon bar Yohai has remained a great hero in Israel, especially in the Galilee, to this day. The holiday of Lag ba-Omer, which commemorates the end of the plague that killed many of Rabbi Akiba's students, is also linked to Shimon bar Yohai, who is said to have died on Lag ba-Omer, the 18th day of Iyar. On this holiday bonfires are lit throughout Israel, and many Jews journey to Meron, where Shimon bar Yohai is said to be buried. This tale takes place in the village of Peki'in, near the cave where Shimon bar Yohai and his son were said to have spent thirteen years and where, according to legend, Bar Yohai wrote the Zohar, the central text of Jewish mysticism. See "The Cave of Shimon bar Yohai," p. 89. The present tale emphasizes how Shimon bar Yohai's spirit is still present in that place. The *shammash* of the synagogue has lit many candles in honor of Rashbi, and when the stingy treasurer of the synagogue of Peki'in orders half of them blown out, this proves to be impossible. The treasurer then attempts to blow out the candles lit in honor of Rashbi and almost loses his life. At the same time he has a vision of Bar Yohai, which further underscores the master's presence in that place. This tale reaffirms the fierce characteristics of Shimon bar Yohai, which are exemplified in the talmudic account of how, on leaving the cave near

Peki'in, he gave the evil eye to those who provoked his disfavor, causing so much havoc that God returned him to the cave for another year (B. Shab. 33b).

31. *A Kiss from the Master* (Israel)
IFA 612, collected by S. Arnest.

This oral tale almost certainly finds its source in Ecclesiastes Rabbah 10:10. See the Introduction, p. 7, for a discussion of this midrash. Both tales recount how someone who had forgotten or lacked knowledge received it miraculously from the intercession of the spirit of Rabbi Shimon bar Yohai. Both incidents also occur in dreams, making the two clear variants, despite the fact that they are separated by about 1500 years. However, it is also understood in both cases that their new knowledge derives from the spirit of Bar Yohai that possesses them in the form of an *ibur*. The presence of an *ibur* was regarded as a great blessing by Jewish mystics, especially those of Safed in the sixteenth century, while the same mystics strove greatly to exorcise *dybbuks* from those who were possessed by them. From a psychological perspective, the *ibur* represents the "inner being" that emerges to guide a person through a difficult time of transition. The fact that the presence of the *ibur* must be triggered in some way indicates that the presence of this inner being only emerges when it is required by internal or external circumstances. For further discussion of this type of metempsychosis see the Introduction, p. 7. The oral variant therefore makes explicit what is implicit in the midrashic tale—that the presence of the spirit of Bar Yohai makes their knowledge possible. Therefore the midrashic account in Ecclesiastes Rabbah may be regarded as one of the earliest, if not the earliest, account of possession by an *ibur*. For another example of an *ibur* tale, see "The *Tefillin* of the Or Hayim," p. 117, and the accompanying note. The motif of an untutored man suddenly becoming filled with knowledge is sometimes found in other sources. According to *Shalsheltet ha-Kabbalah*, for example, Rabbi Menachem ben Benjamin Recanati was once an ignorant man who miraculously attained wisdom.

The Circle of the Ari

32. *The Pillar of Cloud* (Palestine)
From *Divrei Yosef* by Rabbi Yosef Sambari, edited by A. Berliner (Berlin: 1896) and *Divrei Shaul*.

This is a fine example of a succession tale. It recounts how Rabbi Isaac Luria, later known as the Ari, became the successor to Rabbi Moshe Cordovero. It emphasizes how, as a recent arrival in Safed, the Ari does not have the stature or following to take Cordovero's place, but he alone is able to perceive the pillar of cloud that Cordovero predicts on his deathbed will be the sign of the one who should be his successor. The pillar of cloud, of course, is the sign that led the Israelites through the wilderness after the Exodus from Egypt. Thus this one tale links the Ari to both Moshe Cordovero and Moses. It is common in such succession tales to establish the link between one master and his successor, especially when the successor is an unlikely one, as in this case. See "The Ascent of Moses," p. 45, for one of the midrashic models for this tale.

33. *The Angel of Forgetfulness* (Syria)
IFA 7198, collected by Amnon Shiloach from Abraham Massalton of Syria. A variant of this tale is found, in a much condensed version, in *Shivhei ha-Ari*, edited by Shlomo Meinsterl (Jerusalem: 1905). Other variants are found in *Sefer Peri Etz Hayim*

361 by Hayim Vital and in *Nagid Umezave* by Y. Zemah (1798). The original legend of Miriam's well is found in B. Ta'an 9a and B. Shab. 35a. The oral version of this tale collected by the IFA is by far the most extensive.

The primary disciple of Rabbi Isaac Luria, the Ari, was Hayim Vital. Indeed, because the Ari did not commit his teachings to writing, it is the writings of Hayim Vital in *Etz Hayim* and other books that have preserved the teachings of the Ari. (It is interesting to note that the writings of other disciples of the Ari are often at odds with the interpretations of Hayim Vital, and Vital's objectivity can easily be called into question because of his elevated view of himself and his destiny. Nevertheless, it is Vital's interpretation that has been traditionally accepted as the authentic version of the teachings of the Ari.) At the time the Ari arrived in Safed, Vital lived in Damascus and was himself known as a master of the Kabbalah. He was therefore reluctant to come to Safed to become a disciple. This tale recounts the powers used by the Ari to reach Hayim Vital and make him understand that it was his destiny to become the Ari's disciple. The Ari's powers include invoking the Angel of Forgetfulness, who causes Hayim Vital to forget his mystical knowledge. Vital finally recognizes this as a sign that he needs to approach the Ari. To restore his memory, the Ari takes Vital out in a boat on the Sea of Galilee, and draws water from Miriam's well for him to drink. This does restore Vital's memory and at the same time creates a permanent bond between the two sages. The legend of Miriam's well recounts that God gave the Israelites an enchanted well of pure water in honor of the virtues of Miriam, sister of Moses, and that this well followed them in the wilderness. For another tale drawing on this legend, see "The Wandering Well," p. 250. Note that the Ari uses the tomb of Rabbi Meir Baal ha-Ness as a guide to locating Miriam's well. This revered tomb, which has many miracles linked to it, is reputed to be that of a Rabbi Meir who vowed never to lie down until the Messiah came, and was buried upright. (In Jewish folklore Meir Baal ha-Ness is sometimes identified with the talmudic sage Rabbi Meir. But they were almost certainly two separate figures living at two different periods.) Thus the Ari draws on the miraculous power of both this tomb and Miriam's well to restore Hayim Vital's memory. This tale was collected from a Syrian Jewish immigrant, showing that the oral tradition about the Ari and Hayim Vital continued to exist there at least until recently, a heritage of the period when Hayim Vital and other Jewish mystics lived in Damascus.

34. *The Dancing of the Ari* (Palestine)
IFA 3590, collected by Yeshayahu Ashni from Yisrael Schneerson, the head of a Yeshivah of mystical studies in Safed. A variant is found in *Ma'asiyot Yerushalayim* p. 260.

On Lag ba-Omer campfires are lit all over Israel, but especially in the Galilee, in honor of Shimon bar Yohai. It was the custom of the Ari to go to the grave of Shimon bar Yohai in Meron to celebrate Lag ba-Omer. Here, while the Ari and his disciples dance and sing, they are joined by a mysterious old man, whom the Ari recognizes as Shimon bar Yohai. This tale links the greatness of the Ari and of Shimon bar Yohai, who are, in fact, the two primary sages associated with the Galilee. In this respect it is a kind of succession tale, showing that Shimon bar Yohai has selected the Ari to be his successor. For another succession tale involving the Ari, see "The Pillar of Cloud," p. 80. That tale confirms the Ari's position as the leader of the Safed community in his generation. This tale confirms the Ari's importance to be equal to that of Shimon bar Yohai, legendary author of the Zohar as well as the hero of its tales. This tale and others about the circle of the Ari collected by the IFA demonstrate that a substantial share of the Safed oral tradition still exists in present-day Israel. These oral versions are often far more embellished than the existing written versions. For another example of a modern oral variant of these Safed tales, see "The Angel of Forgetfulness," p. 81.

35. *The Blessing of the Kohanim* (Palestine)
From *Divrei Yosef* by Yosef Sambari, edited by A. Berliner (Berlin: 1896).

The priestly blessing is performed by the descendants of the priestly sect, known as the *Kohanim*. In this ritual, known as *Birkat Kohanim*, *the Kohanim* stand before the congregation, and no one is permitted to look at them. This blessing was originally part of the Temple service, and after the destruction of the Temple it became a remnant of the priestly ritual. Every *Kohen*, or descendant of the priestly sect, is required to take part in the blessing, unless disqualified for one of several reasons. The blessing is recited with the prayer shawls of the *Kohanim* drawn over their heads, their hands raised, and the thumb and first two forefingers of each hand separated from the other two. There is a strong injunction against the congregation looking up at the *Kohanim* during this blessing, which Hayim Vital breaks in this case, with serious consequences, for his sight begins to dim. He is able to redeem himself, however, by begging forgiveness of the *Shekhinah* during *Kabbalat Shabbat*. For more on the background of *Kabbalat Shabbat*, see the notes to "Forcing the End," p. 65, and "Greeting the Sabbath Queen," p. 93.

36. *The Journey to Jerusalem* (Palestine)
From *Shivhei ha-Ari* 9b–10a, edited by Shlomo Meinsterl (Jerusalem: 1905). An oral variant is IFA 16159, collected by Shimon Shababo from Orna Fadida of Israel.

Here the Ari overhears a *Bat Kol*, a heavenly voice, announce that if he and his disciples undertake a journey to Jerusalem at once, the coming of the messianic era will begin. But half of the disciples hesitate, and the opportunity is lost. This is one of many legends concerning the wish of the kabbalistic sages and later Hasidic masters to hasten the coming of the Messiah, which according to talmudic tradition is within the powers of the greatest sages. For more on this type of tale, see the notes to "Forcing the End," p. 65 and "The Sabbath Guests," p. 254. Behind this tale also lies the talmudic assertion that if all Jews observed two Sabbaths, the Messiah would come.

37. *The Precious Prayer* (Eastern Europe)
From *Shaare ha-Emunah*, edited by N. Dinner (Warsaw: 1903). A variant is found in *Emunat Tzaddikim* (Warsaw: 1924). An oral variant is IFA 516, collected by Yeshayahu Ashani from Zusya Kahane of Israel.

This is a variant of a famous tale, which has many versions. Here the Ari learns that as precious as his prayers are to God, there is another whose prayers are even more precious. This turns out to be an illiterate farmer who, because he cannot read the prayers, recites the alphabet over and over, with great spiritual intensity. He has asked God to transform the letters into prayers, and God has done so. This tale affirms that knowledge is not the most important element when it comes to prayer, but rather prayer that emerges from the heart. This concept became one of the key principles of the Hasidic movement, for beginning with the Baal Shem Tov the most important element of prayer was *kavanah*, the intensity and inner depth of the prayer. In some of the other versions of this tale, a boy who doesn't know how to read blows a whistle on Yom Kippur in the synagogue. He is condemned by the others, but the rabbi realizes that the prayer of the boy has reached heaven, unlike the prayers of everyone else. See "The Simpleton's Prayer: Transformations of a Motif in Hebrew Literature" by Marc Saperstein in *Judaism*, 29, 3 (1980), 295–304.

38. *A Vision at the Wailing Wall* (Palestine)

From *Shivhei ha-Ari*, edited by Shlomo Meinsterl (Jerusalem: 1905). Variants are also found in *Kav Hayashar*, by Tsvi Hirsh Kaidanover (Livorno: 1837, chap. 92), and in *Ma'assiyot Noraim ve-Niflaim* (Cracow: 1896). For an oval variant see IFA 2632.

There is a rich tradition of visions of the *Shekhinah*, the Bride of God, at the *Kotel*, the Western or Wailing Wall. That is because the Temple, of which the *Kotel* is the last remaining retaining wall, was believed to be the earthly home of the *Shekhinah*. According to kabbalistic myth, once the Temple was destroyed, the Bride of God chose to go into exile with her children, Israel, rather than return to Paradise. This has major mythic implications concerning the separation of God and His Bride. It also leads to accounts of visions of the *Shekhinah* mourning at the Wall. There are three basic forms in which the *Shekhinah* appears: as a mourning dove, as a bride in white, or as an old woman in mourning, dressed in black. Here Rabbi Abraham Beruchim has visions of the *Shekhinah* both in mourning and as a bride in white. This double vision emphasizes the dual aspect of the *Shekhinah*, who still fulfills the mythic role of God's Bride, that is, the feminine aspect of God, and at the same time reflects the mourning of Israel over the loss of the Holy Land and the subsequent wandering in exile that became their fate. As a result of his vision, Rabbi Abraham's life is extended for twenty-two years (the number of letters of the Hebrew alphabet). From a Jungian perspective, the *Shekhinah* can be recognized both as a mythic and archetypal feminine figure, very close to the purest vision of Jung's concept of the Anima. In "A Vision at the Wailing Wall" the Ari recognizes that if Rabbi Abraham continues on his present path, he is going to shortly meet his death. That is to say, his life has reached a dangerous transition, and in order to survive it, he must undertake an extraordinary task. Therefore the Ari sends him on a quest to find the *Shekhinah* in the logical place where she could be found, the Wailing Wall, the remnant of her former home. Rabbi Abraham encounters her there both as a grieving old woman and as a radiant bride, and afterward he is a new man, who through this visionary experience has rediscovered his lost Anima and reintegrated his feminine side. That is why he is able to live for another twenty-two years, representing a whole new cycle of his life. In discussing this tale, Moshe Idel suggests that Rabbi Abraham's crying is an example of using weeping as a mystical technique (see *Kabbalah: New Perspectives*, pp. 80–81). However, this would seem to nullify the authentic grieving that is recounted here, which comes at the emotional climax of the tale.

39. *Reading the Lips of the Ari* (Palestine)

From *Shivhei ha-Ari* 5b–6a, edited by Shlomo Meinsterl (Jerusalem: 1905).

The ascent of the soul can take place when a person is either awake or asleep. Most often, the ascent of the soul takes place during sleep, when the soul is free to depart from the body and ascend on high. This appears to be what is happening to the Ari in this tale, in which one of the Ari's disciples hears him speaking in his sleep and has a vision of angels filling the room, who are also listening to the Ari's words. Although the disciple, Rabbi Abraham Halevi, does not understand the meaning of what the Ari is saying, the fact that he sees the angels means that he is in some way sharing in the Ari's vision. The tale implies, then, that the soul of the Ari has ascended on high, and the words from his lips are describing his celestial experiences, or, alternately, that his soul is giving some kind of *D'var Torah* on high, which his lips are repeating. This is an example of a tale in which the disciples are willing to go to any lengths to learn from their master. In some variants of this tale, the disciple who listens is identified as Rabbi Aaron Brochim. For another example of this type of tale, see "The Prayer Leader," p. 254, where a disciple of the Rabbi of Kallo hides in his cabinet to see what takes place in a meeting between the rabbi and one of the hidden saints.

40. *The Speaking Flame* (Palestine)
From *Shivhei ha-Ari* edited by Shlomo Meinsterl (Jerusalem: 1905).
The Ari is consistently portrayed as having the ability to read every kind of sign. He understands the language of the birds, can perceive omens everywhere, and can even detect the history of a soul in a stone in a wall. (For the latter, see "A Stone in the Wall," p. 97.) Here the Ari is able to understand the words spoken by a sputtering flame. The Ari has noted that a candle has begun to flicker while he and his disciple, Rabbi Yosef Ashkenazi, are studying the Mishnah. The Ari has learned from the flame that Rabbi Ashkenazi's younger brother is in mortal danger, and he links this knowledge to the passage in the Mishnah they are studying at that time. This echoes the method of divination known as *Sheilat Sefer*, in which a holy text, usually the Bible, is opened at random and a passage pointed to blindly. This passage, then, serves as the reply to the question. In this case, however, the Ari is alerted to the danger by the flicking candle and links its warning to the passage in the Mishnah (Er. 10:1) concerning *tefillin*. That is sufficient for Rabbi Ashkenazi to understand that the problem relates to the miraculous *tefillin* that his brother received as a child from a mysterious figure who turns out to have been Elijah. The *tefillin* in this tale serve as a protective amulet. Other similiar tales describe the use of actual amulets. The theme here is also similiar to the folk theme of the Wonder Child, who is born with some kind of jewel containing his soul and must never be parted from it. For a Jewish variant of this tale see IFA 6405, collected by Ilana Zohar from her mother, Flora Cohen of Egypt. This tale also echoes other tales concerning miraculous *tefillin*, including "The Tefillin of the Or Hayim," p. 117.

41. *Greeting the Sabbath Queen* (Palestine)
From *Divrei Yosef* by Rabbi Yosef Sambari (Jerusalem: 1981, p. 226).
As the reputation of the Ari spread in Safed, many of the leading figures of the city sought to study with him. The Ari turned away a number of these people, much to their distress, in the knowledge that his particular path was not right for them. This is one such tale, where Rabbi Moshe Alshich, having been turned down repeatedly by the Ari, agrees to a test in which he will wait for the Ari and his disciples as they go out to meet the Sabbath Queen. The Ari explains that if he is destined to become a disciple, he will see them, and if not, he will not. As it happens, the Ari and his disciples pass right by him, but they remain invisible to him. He sees them only as they return, which convinces him that the Ari was correct in refusing to accept him. This tale reinforces two aspects of the Ari's mystical powers—his ability to know precisely who he should accept as a disciple, by reading the history of their souls, and his great mystical powers, which in this case caused the group going out to greet the

Sabbath Queen to remain invisible to Rabbi Alshich. The custom of greeting the Sabbath Queen just before the beginning of the Sabbath, known as *Kabbalat Shabbat*, has talmudic roots. The Talmud, Shabbat 19a, recounts that Rabbi Haninah used to put on his Sabbath clothes and stand at sunset and say: "Come, let us go forth to welcome the Sabbath Queen." And Rabbi Yannai used to don his festive robes at that time and exclaim: "Come, oh bride, come, oh bride." Maimonides also suggested that this be done, except that the Sabbath King, rather than the Queen, should be welcomed. Shlomo Alkabetz, a disciple of the Ari, wrote the song "Lecha Dodi," which became the central song of the followers of the Ari when they performed *Kabbalat Shabbat*. The Ari made *Kabbalat Shabbat* a regular part of his Sabbath observance, and the custom is observed to this day.

42. *Gathering Sparks* (Palestine)
From *Sefer ha-Hezyonot* by Rabbi Hayim Vital (Jerusalem: 1914).

There are many accounts of mysteries revealed by the Ari at the tombs of various famous rabbis, especially the tomb of Rabbi Shimon bar Yohai, the key figure of the Zohar. Here the Ari reveals the mystery of the Shattering of the Vessels and the Gathering of the Sparks. This was the last of the great myths to enter Judaism. For more on this myth, see the Introduction, p. 16. In many ways the myth of the Ari prefigures the Big Bang theory. In both accounts there is an explosion at the beginning of time, and in both, the universe as we know it comes into existence. And there are even earlier rabbinic descriptions of the creation of the world that strongly prefigure this theory, such as the following: "When the Holy One, blessed be He, created the world, it started to expand in all directions. It could have gone on expanding forever. However, at a certain point, God stopped the expansion by calling out 'Enough!'" (B. Hag. 12a). Note that the myth of the Ari can be seen as a reworking of the messianic myth. Indeed, the description of the restored world that will come about when all the sparks have been gathered and all the broken vessels restored is virtually identical to that envisioned in the messianic age. The widespread and powerful response to the Ari's myth influenced the messianic expectations that led to the debacle of the false messiah Shabbatai Zevi and left a deep imprint on Hasidism.

43. *Delivering a Message* (Palestine)
From *Shivhei ha-Ari*, edited by Shlomo Meinsterl (Jerusalem: 1905). Also found in *Eden Tzion* (Jerusalem: 1955).

This tale is primarily intended to demonstrate the remarkable powers of the Ari. Here the Ari convinces an opponent, Rabbi Shlomo Luria, known as "the Maharshal," that his teachings should not be banned. In the tale the Maharshal is said to object to the revealing of kabbalistic mysteries, following the old tradition that these must be kept secret. But after the Ari demonstrates his powers by sending Rabbi Israel Sarug as a messenger from Safed to Poland using holy names, and by sending a message that replies to a verse that the Maharshal had read in a dream, the Maharshal withdraws his opposition and becomes a dedicated follower of the Ari. This tale follows the pattern of other tales about opposition to the Ari, such as "The Angel of Forgetfulness," p. 81. The pattern in these tales is for the Ari to win over those who are ambivalent about or opposed to his teachings. A clear indication that this tale is purely legendary is the presence of Israel Sarug, an Egyptian kabbalist closely identified with the Lurianic Kabbalah, who, however, was not one of the Ari's disciples in

Safed. He apparently had access to some of the writings of the Ari's disciples and led a kabbalistic school in Italy based on the Ari's teachings. As a result, his name came to be so closely associated with that of the Ari that the two are brought together in this legendary tale.

44. *A Stone in the Wall* (Palestine)

From *Emeth HaMelech*, edited by Naphtali Hirsh ben Elhanan (Amsterdam: 1653, 153:2).

This tale is an important example of the belief by the Ari in *gilgul*, the transmigration of souls. The soul can be reincarnated in a wide variety of shapes, including, as in this tale, a stone. That in itself is remarkable enough. But the Ari's power of perception includes reading the history of every man's soul in his forehead and recognizing souls in whatever form their *gilgul* takes. Here, then, he recognizes the soul of the man who has been reincarnated as a stone in a wall—not any wall, but a wall of the synagogue of Rabbi Shimon bar Yohai. What this seems to imply is that by taking the form of the stone, the man is shown to have been a sinner. But because that stone is in a holy wall, it shows that repentance is still available for his soul.

45. *The Widow of Safed* (Palestine)

From *Shivhei ha-Ari*, edited by Shlomo Meinsterl (Jerusalem: 1905).

The legends concerning *dybbuks*, spirits of the dead who take possession of the living, multiply in the later medieval and Hasidic literature. There are scores of such accounts of possession in Jewish lore. "The Widow of Safed" records the history of one such case, revealing, in the process, the basic pattern to which all possessions are subjected. The *dybbuk* has been able to enter the house because the *mezzuzah* is defective and has been able to take possession of the woman because of her lack of faith in the miracle of the crossing of the Red Sea. The latter was the standard test of true faith among Jews. Note that the Ari sends Hayim Vital to perform the exorcism in this tale, imputing to him powers similiar to those of his master. Another early account of possession by a *dybbuk* is found in *Ma'aseh Buch* 152, also dating from the sixteenth century, suggesting that the superstitious conditions both in Eastern Europe and the Middle East were right for this belief. Earlier cases of possession did not involve spirits of the dead, but rather demonic possession, as recorded in Josephus (*Antiquities*, 8:2.5) and the Talmud (B. Me'ilah 17b). It is interesting to note that the majority of these accounts of possession include details of name and place that far exceed the usual anonymity of folklore. Gedalya Nigal has compiled a Hebrew anthology of *dybbuk* tales, *Sipurei ha-Dybbuk* (Jerusalem: 1983), and virtually every account includes the place and year where the possession and exorcism occurred and the names of the witnesses. The scenario of the tales almost always follows the same pattern: (1) Someone becomes possessed by a *dybbuk*. (2) A rabbi confronts the spirit and demands that it reveal its name and history. (3) The *dybbuk* tells its tale. (4) The *dybbuk* is then exorcised, and the one who was possessed recovers. This suggests that the pattern established in the earliest of these tales, such as this one, was repeated in succeeding generations to those who were psychologically imprinted to expect it. It is interesting to note that such possession in this century has been identified primarily as a psychological aberration. In *Legends of the Hasidim*, the editor, Jerome Mintz, reports a case of such possession in which the Satmar Rebbe supposedly advised someone said to be possessed by a *dybbuk* to see a good psychiatrist (see pp. 411–412).

46. *The Body of Moses* (Palestine)
From *Shivhei Rabbi Hayim Vital*, edited by Menashe ben Naftali Feigenbaum (Ashdod: 1988, p. 38).

This astonishing dream of Hayim Vital shows the close link in the Jewish mind between the the Torah of Moses and Moses himself. In the dream the body of Moses is brought to the synagogue on Shavuot, which celebrates the giving of the Torah to Moses at Mount Sinai. Once the body, which is of gigantic proportions (as Moses was a giant among prophets), is carried inside and put on a long table, it turns into the scroll of the Torah. Hayim Vital sits closest to the end of the Torah, where the account of the death of Moses is found. Vital assumes that because he is closest to this end, he is the closest to Moses. Once the Torah has been read from beginning to end, it turns back into the body of Moses. Hayim Vital had one of the richest religious imaginations in all of Jewish history, and in his dreams and visions the line between mythology and religion is completely erased, as here, where the Torah and the body of Moses are one and the same. This dream also reveals that for Hayim Vital, Moses was the archetype of the messianic prophet. In his writings he strongly hints that his master, the Ari, had a messianic role, and in his dreams, visions, and other writings he likewise attributes such a role to himself.

47. *A Visit to the City of the Dead* (Palestine)
From *Sefer ha-Hezyonot* by Rabbi Hayim Vital (Jerusalem: 1914, part 2, no. 9). Also included in *Shivhei Rabbi Hayim Vital*, edited by Menashe ben Naftali Fiegenbaum (Ashdod: 1988, p. 26).

In *Sefer ha-Hezyonot* Hayim Vital indicates that this dream took place on Simhat Torah in 1570. It is interesting to note that many of Vital's most important dreams take place on the major holidays. The key figure in the dream is the old man, with hair to his knees, who is singing about the coming of the Messiah. The dream hints that this man may be the Messiah himself or a forerunner of the Messiah. What is important is that Hayim Vital alone among the others (who are dead) can hear the singing, indicating that he is able to perceive what the others present cannot. This suggests that he is somehow more attuned to messianic signs than the others, who include Rabbi Moshe Cordovero, the leader of the Safed kabbalists before the arrival of the Ari, and Hayim Vital's original master.

48. *The Angel in the Mirror* (Palestine)
From *Sefer ha-Hezyonot* by Rabbi Hayim Vital (Jerusalem: 1914, part 1, no. 23). This dream took place in 1609. Essentially the same account is found in *Shivhei Rabbi Hayim Vital* (Ashdod: 1988, p. 66). In the latter that the figure who assists Rabbi Hayim Vital is identified as Rabbi Yehoshua Albuv, while in the former he is identified as Rabbi Yehoshua Bom. Rabbi Hayim Vital also seeks the help of Rabbi Yehoshua in invoking Elijah in another story in *Sefer Shivhei Rabbi Hayim Vital*, p. 91.

Hayim Vital was very interested in the mystical process of invoking angels. Here he invokes the angel Tsadkiel, who is mentioned many times in the Zohar and early kabbalistic texts, including *Sefer Yetsirah*. Tsadkiel is identified as a companion of the angel Gabriel. He is also identified as the good angel in the famous legend of the Sabbath angels as follows: When the Sabbath prayers have been said, two angels follow a man home from the synagogue, a good angel and an evil one. If the man's house is in order and everything is ready for the Sabbath, the good angel blesses him and his family, and the evil angel is required to say "Amen." But if the house is disorderly and the Sabbath preparations are incomplete, it is the evil angel who makes the blessing and the good angel who is required to say "Amen" (B. Shab. 119b). According to *Siddur Sha'ar Shamayim*, Tsadkiel is the name of the good angel, and the evil angel is Samael, the Evil One. In the present story, Hayim Vital invokes the angel, which he must view in a mirror, as is customary, as divine beings cannot be seen face to face. The angel confirms, on the one hand, that heaven regards him as a *tzaddik*, but urges him, on the other, to use his powers to cause others to repent, suggesting that Vital's failure to do so has caused the soul of the Ari, his master, to keep his distance after death. Note that this tale, like the following one, emphasizes the almost messianic role in which Hayim Vital viewed himself while acknowledging some failure on his part to inspire others to repent. See the following note for more information about *Sefer ha-Hezyonot*, the source of this tale.

49. *The Handwriting of the Messiah* (Palestine)
From *Sefer ha-Hezyonot* by Rabbi Hayim Vital (Jerusalem: 1914), part 2, no. 42. The date is the 26th of Heshvan 1609.

Sefer ha-Hezyonot is a very unusual record of the dreams and visions of Hayim Vital. The book consists of accounts of mystical experiences, such as that found in "The Angel in the Mirror," p. 102, or of messianic dreams like the present tale. Most of the entries in this book clearly demonstrate a messianic complex on the part of Vital, who viewed himself in the most elevated terms. Indeed, Vital's perception of himself as a potentially messianic figure clearly emerges in almost every entry. In addition, Vital records visions others have had about him. One woman once saw a pillar of fire above Vital's head while he was speaking, and Elijah was supporting him on the right. Another time a Moslem who served as a guard at a Moslem temple told Hayim Vital that one night, around midnight, he had seen him flying in the air (*Shivhei Rabbi Hayim Vital* 2–3). In "The Handwriting of the Messiah" Vital not only receives a letter in a dream from the Messiah, but the letter itself emphasizes the importance of his role in bringing the messianic era, as well as linking him directly to the Messiah. An interesting variation on the theme of receiving a letter of great importance is found in Rabbi Nachman of Bratslav's parable "The Letter" as follows:

Once there was a prince who was separated from his father, the king, in his youth, and lived in a land far from his homeland. There he greatly yearned to be reunited with his father, so far away. But because of the great distance that separated them, this was not possible at that time. So it was that many years passed without any messages between the prince and his father. Then one day, to the prince's great joy, he received a letter from the king. This letter had traveled to him over a great distance, and the messenger had overcome many obstacles to see that it reached the prince's hand. The prince read the letter as if in a dream, so vividly did it evoke his father's presence. And when he had finished reading it, his heart was filled with longing to see his father again. And he thought to himself: "If I could only see my father now. If I could only touch his hand!" And while he harbored these longings, a thought crossed his mind: "Do I not have my father's letter? And was this letter not written in his very own hand? And is not the handwriting not unlike the very hand that penned it?" And with this thought he held the letter close to him and said over and over to himself: "The handwriting of the king—the hand of the king."

This tale of Rabbi Nachman's is from *Sipurei Ma'aysiot Hadashim* (Warsaw: 1909). It is a *drash* on the passage *When I look upon the heavens, the work of Your fingers* (Ps. 8:3). The fortunate prince who recognizes the importance of the handwriting of his father, which greatly closes the distance between them, can be identified with the *tzaddik*, who recognizes the Creator through His creation, that is, this world. In a broader sense, the Torah is the letter that God has delivered to his sons, the Israelites, and it is imperative to recognize in it not only God's word, but his hand as well. See "A Letter from the Beyond," p. 240, for another account of a mystical letter.

Other Kabbalistic Tales

50. The Palace of Vanities (Spain)

From *Tikkune Zohar* in *Midrash Talpiyot*, edited by Eliyahu ha-Cohen (Czernowitz: 1860, Vol. III, p. 138).

This tale closely follows the pattern of several others found in the Zohar, such as "The Golden Scepter," p. 73, where a hidden saint or divine figure reveals himself to sages he is traveling with, usually disguised as a servant. This grows out of the tradition that no one was supposed to walk further than four cubits (twelve feet) without discussing some matter of the Torah. This fulfills the injunction of the *Shema*, the primary prayer, that *These words, which I command thee this day, shall be upon thy heart . . . and thou shalt talk of them when thou sittest in thy house, and when thou walkest by the way . . .* (Deut. 6:6–7). Thus while the rabbis in these tales are engaged in such a discussion, often of a mystical nature, the servant joins in and reveals himself to be a great sage. In this case the lame servant turns out to be some kind of divine figure, who transforms his appearance completely in the cave, revealing his divine nature and causing a profound vision to take place for the two rabbis who are his guests. After this he even reveals a secret book to them, to take back to Rabbi Shimon bar Yohai. The model for this tale is the talmudic legend found in "Mysteries of the Chariot," p. 50. There it is the disciple of the rabbi who proves himself to be a great sage of kabbalistic mysteries. But the parallels between the two tales are quite distinct, including the vision that concludes the tale.

51. The Chains of the Messiah (Palestine)

From *Iggeret Sod ha-Ge'ullah* by Abraham ben Eliezer ha-Levi (Jerusalem: 1519). A later version is found in *Sippur Rabbi Yosef della Reina* by Shlomo Navarro. Another variant, based on the Navarro version, is found in *Eder ha-Yekar* in the *Samuel Abba Horodezky Jubilee Volume*, edited by Zalman Rubashov (Shazar) (Tel Aviv: 1947).

After the talmudic legend of the four who entered Paradise, this is probably the best-known kabbalistic tale of all. It exists in a number of versions and has been reprinted many times. The two primary versions are those of Eliezer ha-Levi and Shlomo Navarro. Ha-Levi's earlier account presents Joseph della Reina as a sincere, if over-ambitious, prophet who is willing to take great risks to hasten the coming of the Messiah and suffers a terrible failure. Navarro's version transforms the character of della Reina, emphasizing his hubris and adding a coda in which, having failed in his messianic quest, he becomes a student of black magic, taught by none other than Lilith, the demoness he originally sought to capture. His later exploits, in the version of Navarro, include using his powers to bring Queen Dolphina of France to his bed and attempting to bring Helen of Troy back from the dead for himself. The present version of this tale is based primarily on the earlier version. For a version based primarily on that of Navarro, see "Helen of Troy" in *LC*, pp. 42–52, and the accompanying note. Just as "The Four Who Entered Paradise" served as a warning tale about the dangers of the Kabbalah, so did the story of Joseph della Reina, and he became an archetype of the holy man driven mad by immersion in kabbalistic mysteries. The story of Joseph della Reina being reborn as a black dog, so full of poetic justice because of its echo of the forms taken by Asmodeus and Lilith when he sought to capture them, is associated with the legend of the Ari. It demonstrates that as early as the sixteenth century, della Reina had become a despised figure even by those who themselves still sought to hasten the coming of the Messiah.

52. The Tzaddik of the Forest (Palestine)

From *Sihot Hayim* (Piotrkow: 1904). Also found in *Sefer ha-Ma'aysiot*, edited by Mordecai Ben Yehezkel (Tel Aviv: 1937).

This story is of particular interest because it concerns a virtually unknown hidden saint, Shimon Pilam, who lived in the time of the Ari. The theme of the hidden saint is first found in the Talmud and recurs in virtually every phase of postbiblical Jewish literature. While mysterious figures, some human, some divine, are often found in the tales linked with the circle of the Ari, there is no mention of Shimon Pilam, although he is described as living in the same area of Safed at the same time as the Ari. This is not surprising in that Shimon Pilam works completely in secret, performing *tikkun olam*, repair of the world. These secret workings are characteristic of hidden saints, who rarely come in contact with others. However, this tale may also indicate that there were other mystical circles active in Safed whose history is virtually unknown, and that this tale emerges out of one of these circles. It is also possible that this is a later legend that was intentionally set in the period of the Ari. In any case, this rather extensive legend describes the wonders performed in the forest by the hidden saint, and how the guards of the forest each managed to have children with his blessing. It is very interesting that the final episode of this tale is a distinct variant of "The Finger," found in *LC*, p. 51. There a young man about to be wed slips his ring over a finger sticking out of the ground and finds himself wed to a corpse, who comes back to life. Here one of the guards is reminded of a distant episode when, as a young man, he put his ring on the finger of a carving of a hand at the base of a tree, and discovers many years later that this caused him to be wed to a demoness, who has been slaying his infant sons. Shimon Pilam tells the man how to divorce her, and he does, and after this his newborn sons survive. The carving on the tree has distinct pagan overtones, recalling the tree worship linked to the Canaanite goddess Asherah. For more on this subject see *The Hebrew Goddess* by Raphael Patai.

53. The Angel of the Mishnah (Palestine)

From *Shivhei ha-Ari*, compiled by Shlomo Meinsterl (Jerusalem: 1905). Also *Maggid Mesharim* by Joseph Caro (Amsterdam: 1704).

Among the sages of Safed, there are several accounts of their speaking with the voice of an angelic spirit known as a *maggid*. These spirits come into existence when there is very deep study of a particular text. One possible explanation for the phenomenon of the *maggid* is the talmudic statement that "From every utterance that goes forth from the mouth of the Holy One, blessed be He, an angel is created" (B. Hag. 14a). Since man was created in the image of God, angels or spirits such as the *maggid* come into being from the words spoken by the sages in their study of sacred texts. They then appear whenever that text is read, sometimes only after it has been read several times, three being the usual number. These spirits served to teach divine mysteries to those they spoke through and to those who heard these voices speak. The most famous of these spirits is that of Rabbi Joseph Caro, the author of the *Shulhan Aruch*, the code of Jewish law. Caro's *maggid* was the angel of the Mishnah. Caro kept a diary of the teachings of the spirit, *Maggid Mesharim*. There also are several accounts of those who were present when the *maggid* spoke. This kind of positive possession resembles that found in the accounts of possession by an *ibur*. This is the spirit of a dead sage who fuses with that of a living person and strengthens his faith and wisdom. These accounts are associated with a particular book or a specific object, such as *tefillin*. See, for examples of *ibur* tales, "A Kiss from the Master," p. 79, and "The *Tefillin* of the Or Hayim, p. 117.

54. A New Lease on Life (Israel)
IFA 479, collected by Shimon Ernest from Nissim Alnakava of Safed.

Joseph Caro was one of the greatest and most imposing Jewish scholars of all time and a man of great energy. This tale recounts how he added seven years to his life, receiving seven years from the life of a hidden saint living in the city of Lublin. This tale echoes the talmudic account of how King David received seventy years from Adam, who lived until 930 (Pirke de Rabbi Eliezer 19). For another tale of obtaining extra years to live, see "A Vision at the Wailing Wall," p. 87.

55. Redemption of the Lost Souls (Palestine)
From *Toledot Hakhmei Yerushalayim* by Aryeh Leib Frumkin (Vilna: 1874). Other legends about Sharabi can be found in *Yerushalayim shel Ma'ala*, edited by Menachem Gerlitz (Jerusalem: 1982).

Just as the Ari is the great mystic of the sixteenth century, Rabbi Shalom Sharabi was the kabbalistic master of the seventeenth century. He was Yemenite in origin and originally served in Jerusalem as the servant to the master Rabbi Gedaliah Hayon, the head of a kabbalistic yeshivah. Sharabi is said to have hidden his kabbalistic knowledge, but Rabbi Hayon became aware of his wisdom and appointed Sharabi to be his successor. Sharabi closely modeled his teachings on those of the Ari, whose teachings he knew by heart, and he even believed himself to be the reincarnation of the Ari. In this tale the *gabbai*, who cares for the synagogue, wakes at night and sees Rabbi Sharabi and a great many Arabs, probably Bedouins, whose souls he redeems. It appear that these Bedouins are of Jewish descent. According to Itzhak Ben-Zvi in *The Exiled and the Redeemed*, p. 17, "We gather from the accounts of Arab chronicles that Judaism was widespread among Bedouin tribes in southern Arabia." The *gabbai*'s vision concludes with the synagogue ascending on high. But when the vision ends, Rabbi Sharabi is seen sitting alone in the synagogue, and the *gabbai*—as well as the reader of the tale—is left wondering if he saw an illusion or an event that actually took place, or, perhaps, that Rabbi Sharabi redeemed their souls, but on a spiritual plane that the *gabbai* witnessed as a vision.

56. Repairing Souls (Morocco)
IFA 477, collected by S. Arenst from a new immigrant from Morocco.

As taught by the myth of the Ari, the most important actions that Jews can take are those of *tikkun olam*, repairing the world. For rabbis such as the Or Hayim (Rabbi Hayim ben Attar) and Rabbi Nachman of Bratslav, one of the most important duties of repair concerned raising up the souls of the dead who have somehow become trapped in this world. This theme is also found in "The Field of Souls," p. 204, and "The Boy Who Blew the Shofar," p. 127. Here the Or Hayim does this holy work during the week by going off into the mountains alone, and he returns only for the Sabbath, when he is followed by flocks of the souls he has set free. The Or Hayim was the most famous Jewish sage of his time living in the Holy Land. The Hasidim believed that the Baal Shem Tov had been barred by heaven from going to the Holy Land because the combination of his merits and those of the Or Hayim, along with those of the Holy Land, would force the coming of the Messiah. This indicates that the Or Hayim was regarded by the Hasidim as the equal of the Baal Shem Tov. See the following tale, "The *Tefillin* of the Or Hayim," for another tale about Rabbi Hayim ben Attar.

57. *The* Tefillin *of the Or Hayim* (Palestine)
From *Sefer Sgulat Moshe*. Also found in *Toldot Rabbenu Hayim ben Attar*, edited by Reuven Margarliot (Lemberg: 1904). Also in *Otsar ha-Ma'aysiot*, edited by Reuven ben Yakov Nana (Jerusalem: 1961, Vol. II, pp. 87–88). Also in *Sefer ha-Ma'aysiot*, edited by Mordecai Ben Yehezkel (Tel Aviv: 1937, Vol. 2, pp. 330–32). Additional variants are found in *Pe'er Layesharim* (Jerusalem: 1881). There also are oral variants of this tale, including IFA 9669, collected by Ephraim Haddad from Shimon Swissa, and IFA 12353, told by Nissim Malka of Morocco.

By their nature, *tefillin* are purely sacred objects, and it is natural that they are the focus of many Jewish folktales. "The *Tefillin* of the Or Hayim" is the most famous of these tales. It demonstrates possession by an *ibur*, the spirit of a departed sage that fuses with the spirit of a living person to strengthen him spiritually. Most commonly, in the tales of an *ibur*, this spirit is present only when the *tefillin* are worn. This kind of possession by the spirit of a sage can be contrasted with possession by a *dybbuk*, the spirit of an evil person who takes over the body of a living person. For an example of this latter kind of tale, see "The Widow of Safed," p. 98. The Moroccan oral version of this tale adds the following legends about the Or Hayim's death: "Rabbi Hayim ben Attar left the world on the 15th of Tammuz 1743 in Jerusalem. And all the great scholars of Israel and abroad mourned his death. There is a tradition among the Sephardim that at the time the Or Hayim died, Rabbi Jacob Abulafia was completing his prayers. He leaned his head on the table for a long time, and when he stood up, he said in deep sorrow: 'Rabbi Hayim ben Attar has just left this world, for I myself accompanied his soul to the gate of *Gan Eden.*' Also, the Baal Shem knew by *Ruach ha-Kodesh*, the holy spirit, when Rabbi Hayim ben Attar died. It was at the beginning of the third meal of the Sabbath, right after he said the blessing, that he told the students with him that 'The western candle has blown out.' But they did not understand what he meant, and at the end of the Sabbath, when the students asked him about it, he said: 'Our rabbi, Rabbi Hayim ben Attar, blessed be he, is gone, and he is from the western countries, therefore he is called the "western candle."'" And when the students asked him how he knew this, he answered, 'There is *kavanah* in washing the hands to eat that can only be revealed to one in a generation. And that was our rabbi, blessed be he.'" This enigmatic reply suggests that the Baal Shem Tov learned of the death while washing his hands before eating on the Sabbath, for now that the Or Hayim had died, the secret of the washing of the hands had been revealed to him, as the successor to the Or Hayim in that generation. Another oral variant, IFA 1892, collected by S. Arenst, records that the Baal Shem felt the death of Hayim ben Attar from a distance, and he stopped singing the *niggun* he had been singing on the Sabbath.

III Mystical Folktales

58. *Gabriel's Palace* (Germany)

From *Sefer ha-Ma'aysiot*, edited by Mordecai ben Yehezkel (Tel Aviv: 1937). Ben Yehezkel attributes the story to oral tradition. The legend of a celestial Torah is found in B. Pesahim 54, where the Torah is described as one of seven things created before the creation of the world, based on the passage *The Lord made me as the beginning of his way* (Prov. 8:22). The legend of the thirteen Torahs derives from *Peirat Moshe* in A. Jellinek, *Beit ha-Midrash* 1: 122–23 (Jerusalem: 1938). Here it states that Moses wrote all thirteen Torahs the same day he had been told he would die, as a means of preventing the Angel of Death from taking him, since the Angel is forbidden to take a person while he is studying the Torah. (See the legend of King David and the Angel of Death in B. Shab. 30a.) The best of the Torahs that Moses wrote was brought by an angel into heaven. The requirement to read the Torah from a written text on the Sabbath is stated in Tanhuma Buber Vayyera 6. It is also hinted at in B. Megillah 32a. An unrelated folktale about Rabbi Meir's imprisonment is found in *Ma'aseh Missim* (Yiddish), compiled by Jeptha Yozpa ben Naftali (Amsterdam: 1696, story no. 14). Here Rabbi Meir's body remains inside his prison cell for another fourteen years after his death, after the guard sent to remove it dies as he puts the key in the lock. Finally a righteous Jew is able to enter the cell and remove the body, which has not decayed, and transport it to a Jewish grave.

This story is a legend linked with the extended imprisonment of Rabbi Meir ben Baruch of Rothenburg, the leader of German Jewry in the thirteenth century. He was a great legalist, the author of more than one thousand responsa, and the most respected German Jew of his time. Rabbi Meir was captured and imprisoned because of his resistance to the decree of the German Emperor Rudolf I that the possessions of Jews were the property of the empire and could be taxed as the Emperor willed. This decree unleashed a vast exodus of German Jews, a movement led by Rabbi Meir. The Emperor used his capture to try to force the Jews to agree to the view that they were "serfs of the treasury." Rabbi Meir continued to resist this view and remained imprisoned for the rest of his life. In characteristic legendary form, the harsh conditions of his confinement gave birth to this legend about his receiving a celestial Torah. In this variation of the legend of the celestial Torah, the heavenly Torah is said to have been one of those inscribed by Moses, who, according to this legend, wrote thirteen Torahs, one for each of the twelve tribes, and the thirteenth, which was taken up into Paradise and used by the angels. The angel Gabriel delivers this Torah to Rabbi Meir and lets it remain with him until he succeeds in making a perfect copy of it. The fate of this copy is a miracle tale in itself, as Rabbi Meir is said to have put it in a casket and lowered it into the Rhine, where it floated until it reached the Jews for whom it was intended as Rabbi Meir's final legacy.

59. *The Cottage of Candles* (Afghanistan)

IFA 7830, collected by Zevulon Qort from Ben Zion Asherov. A variant is found in *Ha-Na'al ha-Ktanah* (Tel Aviv: 1966), edited by Asher Barash. Another variant, about a cave in which there are bottles of oil, where a person lives until the oil is exhausted, is IFA 8335, collected by Moshe Rabi from Hannah Haddad, in *Avotanu Sipru* (Jerusalem: 1976).

"The Cottage of Candles" is an example of a divine test, such as the one God subjected Abraham to when He commanded him to sacrifice Isaac on Mount Moriah.

The man seeking justice arrives at the cottage, where each soul is allotted exactly what it deserves in the form of a soul-candle. This in itself is a kind of justice. The identity of the old man who tends to the candles and conducts the test remains a mystery, although his supernatural aspect is quite clear. As the keeper of the soul-candles, he functions as an Elijah-type figure who is hidden in the forest in the model of the *Lamed-Vav Tzaddikim*, the Thirty-Six Hidden Saints, who are said to be the pillars of the world. This test surely takes place at the behest of God, so it remains a divine one. One way of reading the tale is to see that in arriving at this cottage, the man is on the verge of completing his quest to find justice, but he is first tested to see if he himself is just. Instead of proving worthy, he attempts to lengthen his life by depriving another of the years of life allotted to him. But he is caught and made to face the consequences of his action. In this sense he finds justice, for justice is exactly meted out. It is interesting to note that the man's quest is in many ways parallel to that of the man from the country in Kafka's famous parable "Before the Law," found in his novel *The Trial*, who comes to the gates of the Law seeking justice. And in each tale the man fails to find the justice he was seeking. Kafka's friend and biographer, Max Brod, comments on this apparent parallel: "Kafka's deeply ironic legend 'Before the Law' is not the reminiscence or retelling of this ancient lore, as it would seem at first glance, but an original creation drawn deeply from his archaic soul. It is yet another proof of his profound roots in Judaism, whose potency and creative images rose to new activities in his unconscious.'" (*Johannes Reuchlin und sein Kampf*, Shuttgart: 1965, pp. 274–75). Moshe Idel identifies the quest in this tale as the remnant of a mystical one. See *Kabbalah: New Perspectives*, p. 271. For a further discussion of Kafka's parable, see *GNC*, p. 648. See "The Enchanted Inn," p. 130, for a variation on the motif of the soul-candle.

60. *Rabbi Shimon's Escape* (The Balkans)

Collected by Max Grunwald from an unknown teller from the Balkans. From *Sippurei-am, Romanssot, ve'Orehot-hayim shel Yehudei Sefarad* by Max Grunwald, tale no. 28. Edited by Dov Noy (Jerusalem: 1982). Folklore Research Center Studies VI.

This tale concerns Rabbi Shimon ben Tsemah Duran (1361–1444) who did indeed live on the island of Majorca. But he did not experience the Inquisition. He actually left Majorca for Algiers after the massacre of 1391, in which his family lost their wealth. A similar blurring of chronology can be found in the story "Delivering a Message," p. 95. Here the Ari sends Israel Sarug on a mission, even though Sarug never met the Ari during his lifetime. He did, however, extensively promulgate the Ari's teachings, unlike Hayim Vital, the Ari's primary disciple, who refused to reveal his writings based on the Ari's teachings for most of his lifetime. This tale illustrates the mystical tradition of the Tetragrammaton, the mystical Name of God. Jewish tradition holds that the true pronunciation of this Divine Name, combined with the proper spiritual intention, provides virtually unlimited powers, but this secret is known only by the leading *tzaddik* in every generation. Rabbi Judah Loew of Prague was said to have used the Power of the Name to bring the golem to life. Here Rabbi Shimon uses it for another, equally compelling purpose. A variant is found in the same book, tale no. 48, concerning Rabbi Ephraim ben Yisrael Ankawa of Tlemcen, Tunisia. Rabbi Ephraim was the author of *Sha'ar Kvod Adonai*, a well-known Torah commentary. In this version the story continues after the escape from prison until they reach North Africa, where Rabbi Ephraim leaves the ship and mounts a waiting lion, using a serpent as a whip (a mythic symbol of power), and how, in exchange for curing the Sultan's daughter, Rabbi Ephraim made it possible for the Jews, who had been expelled, to resettle in the city of Tlemcen. On the motif of using the serpent as a whip, see "Reb Shmelke's Whip," p. 226. For the motif of riding the lion, see the Algerian story of the lion of the Sabbath collected by Moshe Rabi from Avner Azolai, IFA 6432, published in *Avotano Sippru*, edited by A. Rabi (Jerusalem: 1975). Here a rabbi who refuses to ride in a caravan on the Sabbath is rewarded by having a lion guard him during the Sabbath. The lion lets him ride on it after the Sabbath has ended until he catches up with the caravan. Both variants are North African folktales, demonstrating a popular type of tale attributed to leading rabbis well known for their mastery of the Practical Kabbalah. This particular tale of the miracle of the ship is so popular that there are more than one hundred variants of it in the IFA. The theme of riding the lion is well known in world folklore, as is the motif of the drawing that becomes real. One version is a Taoist fable of ancient China, "The Dark Maiden of the Ninth Heaven," in *Folktales of China* edited by Wolfram Eberhard, p. 39. For a modern reworking of this legend of the drawing of a ship that comes to life, see "How Wang-Fo Was Saved" by Marguerite Yourcenar in *Oriental Tales*.

61. *The Boy Who Blew the Shofar* (Israel)
Collected by Howard Schwartz from Yehuda Yaari.

A common theme in Jewish lore is the dependence of the spirit world on the righteous of this world. Here forty-eight souls need the intervention of the boy Eliyahu in order to ascend on high. They approach him through dreams, the traditional portal between this world and the Other World, which is inhabited by various spirits, angels, and demons. The boy tries to deny the message of the dream, for blowing the shofar in the cemetery is generally forbidden, except in case of the plague or some similiar disaster or on extraordinary occasions. But when the dream is repeated and becomes insistent, he overcomes all his reluctance, puts on the rabbi's *tallis*, and blows the shofar in a cemetery. In turn, the wise rabbi recognizes the necessity of the boy's actions and that no one else was pure enough to accomplish the task. For other tales on freeing souls, see "Repairing Souls," p. 116, and "The Field of Souls," p. 204.

62. *The Enchanted Inn* (Eastern Europe)
From *Va-Ye'esof David* (Jerusalem: 1859). Also included in *Sefer ha-Maaysiot*, edited by Mordecai Ben Yehezkel (Tel Aviv: 1937, II: 173–75).

This tale combines two basic tale types: the illusion tale and the test tale. Here the youngest of three brothers is the only one to pass the rabbi's test in the enchanted inn. In the rooms of this inn he perceives the fates of his father and mother in the afterlife, his father honored as a great teacher and his mother punished for her sins. This implies that one room of the inn leads to Paradise and the other to Gehenna. The goat often appears in Jewish lore as a guide. A goat leads Abraham into the cave of Machpelah in the midrashic account, and a kid leads a boy to a cave that leads either to the Garden of Eden or to the Holy Land in the many versions of another famous Jewish folktale. See "The Cave to the Holy Land," p. 164, and "The Cave of Temptations," p. 166. Indeed, this tale of the enchanted inn is essentially a variant of these tales. One interesting aspect is the explanation of all the mystifying events by the rabbi at the end of this tale. Here everything has a very clear meaning, and the rabbi demonstrates great powers in understanding every element. Ultimately the enchanted inn is a blend of a haunted house and a place of illusion, a kind of juncture between this world and the Other Side. Note the motif of the soul-candle found in this tale, which is the reverse of that found in "The Cottage of Candles," p. 124. Here adding oil to a candle that was about to go out adds years to his own life, while the same act in "The Cottage of Candles" leads to condemnation and death. The difference is that there is no indication in "The Enchanted Inn" that the oil the young man used came from any other's candle, while this was specifically the case in "The Cottage of Candles." Between these two tales it is apparent that there was a popular folk belief in the soul-candle. See the note to "Lighting a Fire," p. 209, for another variation of the candle motif.

63. *Leaves from the Garden of Eden* (Eastern Europe)
From *Nifla'ot ha-Tzaddikim* (Piotrkow: 1911)
Coleridge asked, "If a man could pass through Paradise in a dream, and have a flower presented to him as a pledge that his soul had really been there, and if he found that flower in his hand when he awoke—Ay!—and what then?" (*Samuel Taylor Coleridge: Selected Poetry and Prose*, edited by Elisabeth Schneider, 2nd ed., 1971, p. 617). This tale answers that question, in that a man finds enchanted leaves on his bed when he awakes one morning after a dream in which the soul of his stable boy brings him leaves from the Garden of Eden to heal the man's sick daughter. Her mourning over the boy's death provoked her illness, and his miraculous assistance heals her and makes it possible for her to wed later. The theme of leaves from the Garden of Eden is also found in the story "Miriam's Tambourine," where the patriarch Abraham is said to collect these leaves from the Garden and give them to his wife, Sarah, who crushes the leaves and scatters their powder to the wind on the eve of the Sabbath, so that all who breathe in that powder will have a taste of Paradise and a Sabbath filled with joy. See *MT*, p. 1. Reference to such magical leaves is also found in talmudic legends about the messianic era. In one, Elijah leads Rabbi Abbahu into the Garden of Eden and has him collect leaves in his cloak. The cloak absorbs the fragrance of the leaves, and he later sells it for twelve thousand dinars (B. Baba Mezia 114a–b). According to the other legend, "When the third holy Temple will be built, a magical tree will grow in Jerusalem. Some say that the leaves of that tree will cause the dumb to speak. Others say that the leaves of that tree will cause barren women to bear children" (B. Sanh. 100a). It is possible to see this tale as a benevolent version of S. Ansky's famous play *The Dybbuk*. There a yeshivah student who kills himself takes possession of Leah, whom he loved in vain, as she was betrothed to someone else. In both cases, the illness of the woman can be seen as a form of grieving over the death of the beloved. But in the case of *The Dybbuk*, a formal rabbinic exorcism is required to expel the soul of the dead student, while here a miracle makes it possible for the girl to recover her health and peace of mind. Ansky based *The Dybbuk* on many tales that he heard as an ethnographer. A folktale that is probably one of the major sources for the play can be found in Gedalya Nigal's *Sippure Dybbuk* (Jerusalem: 1983), pp. 146–60.

64. *The Tenth Man* (Persia)
From *Sefer ha-Maaysiot*, edited by Shlomo Bechor Chutsin (Baghdad: 1892). This version was collected by Howard Schwartz from Rabbi Yosef Landa of St. Louis.
One of the primary folk traditions associated with the synagogue is that of the tenth man. Since a *minyan* of ten men is required for a service, the tenth one is said to receive a special blessing. In many places it was difficult to assemble a *minyan*, and the tenth

man was of course welcomed, because it was then possible to begin praying. Because this tenth man was so singled out, a subsequent tradition holds that the tenth man is often a special one, as in this tale, where it is Abraham. As the first Patriarch, Abraham is regarded as deeply concerned about the lives of pious Jews. Like Elijah, he returns to this world to assist those in need of his help, although there are far more tales about Elijah than about Abraham. And in the tales about Abraham he usually comes to a synagogue or *sukkah*, as in this tale. Since this tale is set in Hebron, near the cave of Machpelah, where Abraham is buried, the link to Abraham is even stronger. Note the importance of the number 10 in this tradition. In addition to representing the number required for a *minyan*, it is the number of the Ten Commandments, the Ten *sefirot*, and the number of generations from Adam to Noah (Gen. 5:1–32), as well as the number separating Shem, Noah's son, and Abraham (Gen. 11:10–26).

65. The Ram Whose Horns Reached to Heaven (Eastern Europe)

Two tales are combined here. The midrash about all parts of the ram that Abraham sacrificed on Mount Moriah is from *Pirke de Rabbi Eliezer* (Constantinople: 1514, chap. 31). The second tale is found in *'Esser Tsahtsahot* by Y. Y. Berger (Piotrkow: 1910) and *Be'er ha-Hasidut*, edited by Eliezer Steinmann (Tel Aviv, 1960, vol. 1, p. 307). This tale is attributed to Reb Menachem Mendel of Kotzk. After a mysterious incident one Sabbath, in which some speculate that he blew out the Sabbath candles, Reb Menachem Mendel went into retreat for twenty years. He is said to have recounted this tale to Reb Yitzhak of Vorki, one of the few who were admitted to visit him. One way of reading the tale is that the rebbe himself is a kind of unique sacred goat. But his Hasidim wear him down with their demands, as symbolized by the cutting away of the ram's horns. Another way of reading the tale is to see the ram as the ram of sacrifice, who willingly gives up the potent enchantment of his horns in order to assist others but in the process loses his powers—until, at least, the horns grow back.

66. The Cave of King David (Eastern Europe)

From *Sipurei Yakov*, story 2, edited by Yakov Sofer (Dobromil: 1864).

In Jewish folklore there are a few key figures who either return from the dead or are described as never having died. These include Abraham, Moses, Elijah, and David. The famous song that insists that "David, King of Israel, is alive and still exists" derives from an incident recorded in the Talmud (B. Rosh Hashanah 25a) where Rabbi Judah ha-Nasi sent Rabbi Hiyya to Ein Tov to sanctify the moon and to report that this had been done by quoting this phrase about King David. Later this phrase was included in the liturgy for the sanctification of the moon (*Kiddush Levanah*) and became the basis of a popular song. It is this song that the Turkish Sultan overhears in this tale. Probably inspired by this passage and song about King David, there are a number of tales in which King David appears to the living or is found to be living himself in a distant place, usually the city of Luz, where the inhabitants are immortal, or, as in this case, in a nearby cave. One well-known legend about King David concerns his tomb in Jerusalem. Thieves who broke into it were said to have been punished by King David. See IFA 966, recorded by Nehama Zion from Miriam Tschernobilski. An English translation can be found in *Folktales of Israel*, edited by Dov Noy, p. 7. Another legend in which King David is alive can be found in *Dos Buch fun Nisyoynes* (Yiddish), edited by Israel Osman (Los Angeles: 1926). See also "David's Harp" in *MT*, p. 163. The King David of Jewish folklore is not the flesh and blood king of the Bible, but based on the traditional belief that he is the author of the Psalms, King David is portrayed as an Orpheus-like archetypal poet. He has a harp strung with gut from the ram sacrificed at Mount Moriah, and at midnight a wind blows through the window and plays beautiful melodies on that harp, waking King David and inspiring him to write the Psalms (B. Ber. 3a and *Midrash Tehillim* 22:8). This tale's type is that of the impossible quest, as in the famous tale of "The Golden Feather," where a king demands that a lad who has found a golden feather now find the whole bird. A version of this tale is found in *EV*, p. 137. Another fine example of an impossible quest is "The Princess and the Slave," also in *EV*, p. 36, where an old Hebrew slave is sent on a quest to find Moses and have him answer a riddle. The biblical archetype of this kind of tale is found in the Book of Daniel, when Nebuchadnezzar demands that his soothsayers not only tell him the meaning of his dream, but the dream itself (Dan. 2:5–6). Ultimately it is Daniel, with the help of God, who provides the dream and its interpretation. Note Rabbi Rafael Recanti's use of the Holy Name to journey in an enchanted way to the city of Luz. This tale is one of several accounts of journeys to that mythical city of immortals. See "An Appointment with Death," p. 42, and the accompanying note. See also "The City of Luz" in *EV*, p. 279.

67. *The Shining Robe* (Tunisia)

From *Hibbur Yafeh me-ha-Yeshuah*, compiled by Rabbi Nissim ben Jacob, edited by H. Z. Hirschberg (Jerusalem: 1953).

Rabbi Nissim lived in Kairouan, Tunisia, in the eleventh century. An early version of this book was published in Constantinople in 1519. The best-known edition was published in Ferrara, Italy, in 1557. The original language was Judeo-Arabic, which H. Z. Hirschberg translated into modern Hebrew. The shining robe the angel carries symbolizes the reward of the righteous man, while the lack of a collar on it symbolizes a few minor flaws. This tale was likely inspired by the talmudic parable "The Royal Garments," from B. Shab.152b, as follows:

Once a king of flesh and blood distributed royal garments among his servants. He told them that a time would come when he would take the garments back, and that they should be well cared for while they were in the servants' possession. The clever servants among them folded up the garments, placed them in a box, and wore them only on important occasions, while the foolish ones wore them even while they worked. Eventually the king asked for his garments back. The clever servants returned them to him cleaned and carefully folded, while the foolish servants returned them tattered and dirty. The king was as delighted with the clever servants as he was distraught with the foolish ones. Concerning the clever ones he said: "Let their clothes be put in the treasure house and they themselves should return to their homes in peace." And concerning the foolish servants he said: "Let their clothes be given to the seamstress and the launderer, and they themselves should be detained in the jail house until their clothes have been restored to their original state."

This talmudic parable is based on the passage *The spirit returneth unto God who gave it* (Ecc. 12:7). The garment that the king, representing God, gives to each servant is the sacred soul a human is entrusted with during his lifetime. The condition of the garment when it is recalled reflects how the soul has been treated during this lifetime. The Talmud comments additionally about this parable: "Thus the Holy One, blessed be He, says concerning the bodies of the righteous: *Let them enter in peace, let them rest on their couches* (Isa 67:2); and concerning their souls He says: *Let thy soul be bound in the bundle of life with the Lord thy God* (1 Sam. 25:29). About the bodies of the wicked He says: *There is no peace, saith the Lord, concerning the wicked* (Isa. 48:22); and about their souls He says: *Let the souls of thy enemies be slung out as from the hollow of a sling* (1 Sam. 25:29)." The jail to which the foolish servants are sent is Gehenna, where "soiled" souls are sent for eleven months. See Rabbi Nachman of Bratslav's tale "The Synagogue in Jerusalem," *LC*, pp. 253–54 (Oxford edition). For more on the meaning of *the hollow of the sling* see "The Hollow of the Sling," p. 168.

68. *The Evil Angel* (Eastern Europe)

From *Sipurei Tzaddikim* (Cracow: 1886). This tale is attributed to Reb Dov Hayalas, the Rabbi of Ladizin, a disciple of Reb Nachman of Bratslav, who is said to have recounted it to Reb Nachman.

Rabbi Nachman of Bratslav placed so much importance on tales that his Hasidim preserved not only Rabbi Nachman's own tales, but also some of those that were told to him by others. Among these tales is this one of the evil angel. This is a strongly kabbalistic tale in that it projects a heavenly realm divided between the side of good, where good angels are found, and the *Sitre Abre*, the side of evil. Associating the Tetragrammaton, the four-letter Name of God, with angels is an unusual motif. However, in *Pesikta de Rav Kahana* 12:22, every angel is said to wear a plaque with the word *El* on it, referring to God's name. The theme of evil angels is related to the account in Genesis 6 of the Sons of God and the daughters of men, where the Sons of God are identified as angels. The most common references to evil angels concern the angels of destruction, who haunt the souls of those who are evil after their deaths. In *Ma'aysiot Noraim ve-Niflaim* (Cracow: 1896), the gaon Rabbi Yehezkel of Prague describes evil angels who punished a woman for not having raised her son to be a rabbi. Here the evil forces are directly identified as the *Kleippot*, the kabbalistic shells to which evil clings.

69. *The Young Man Without a Soul* (Italy)

From *Megillat Ahimaaz* by Ahimaaz ben Paltiel, published in *Medieval Jewish Chronicles*, edited by A. Neubauer (Oxford: 1895), Vol. II, pp. 111-32.

The structure of *Megillat Ahimaaz* (*The Chronicle of Ahimaaz*) is a series of separate episodes involving the same character. As one who is born with the knowledge of holy names, Aaron has great powers at his command. He sets out on his travels after his father accuses him of misusing these powers in transforming a lion into a servile animal. This represents the traditional view that kabbalistic powers much be used with great caution. See "The Secrets of Kabbalah," p. 155, for another example of the consequences of misusing these powers. Along the way, Aavon has opportunities to demonstrate his powers and to grow in his understanding of how they must be used with great care. As such, this chronicle constitutes one of the warning tales about the dangers of the Kabbalah, in the tradition of the legend of the four who entered Paradise in B. Hagigah 14b. See "The Four Who Entered Paradise," p. 51, and the accompanying note. Here Aaron recognizes a young man without a soul and assists him in removing the parchment with God's Name, which has given him the appearance of life. As long as he is compelled to remain alive by virtue of the power of the Name, the young man remains one of the living dead, a tortured state of existence. Therefore Aaron does a great deed when he sets him free. The folk belief that the dead

were not permitted to pronounce God's Name gives the dead man away in the synagogue, when Rabbi Aaron notices that he avoids saying it. This episode recalls the
later tales of Rabbi Judah Loew of Prague, who brought the golem to life with the use
of God's Name, as portrayed in Yudel Rosenberg's *Nifla'ot Maharal*. See "The
Golem" in *MT*, p. 265. This theme is found in both talmudic and midrashic legends
and became increasingly popular in the Middle Ages, not only in the tales of the
golem, but in many others where a rabbi, such as Judah the Pious, was compelled to
bring a dead man to life in order to testify about the identity of his murderer. See "The
Dead Man's Accusation" in *LC*, p. 103. See also "The Sorcerer and the Virgin" in *LC*,
p. 87, and "The Homunculus of Maimonides" in the same collection, p. 29, for other
examples of the dead being brought to life. The expression "the jaws of death" is
personified in this tale, a terrible but vivid image of being swallowed up by death.
This is one of many ways in which death is personified. The most common image of
death, of course, is the Angel of Death. For a typical portrayal of this angel, see "The
Bridegroom and the Angel of Death," p. 162.

70. *Asenath's Dove* (Kurdistan)
From *Kehillot Yehude Kurdistan*, edited by Abraham Ben-Jacob (Jerusalem: 1961).
   This tale concerns a famous heroine of Kurdish lore known as "Rabbi Asenath bat
Samuel Barzani," in recognition of her knowledge of the Torah. She was a poet, a
kabbalist, and the head of a yeshivah in the seventeenth century who eventually
became recognized as the chief teacher of the Torah in Kurdistan. Her father was
Rabbi Samuel Barzani of Kurdistan, who appears as a great kabbalistic sorcerer in
Kurdish lore. It was reputed that both Rabbi Samuel and his daughter knew of the
secret pronunciation of the Name of God, the Tetragrammaton. Using the power of
the Name is the focus of many Kurdish legends and tales. Here it is implied that Rabbi
Asenath used her mystical powers to bring the dove to life, as well as to suspend her
attacker from the beams of the roof. From this tale it appears that she was a Baal
Shem, a Master of the Name, as well as a healer, who was especially sought out by
women. When she drew on her knowledge of holy names, she often pronounced the
names of angels. It should be noted that there are very few women in Jewish lore who
are honored as rabbis or the equal of rabbis. There are prophetic traditions linked with
Sarah, Rebecca, and Miriam, as well as Deborah. In the Talmud, the woman most
respected for her knowledge was Bruria, the wife of Rabbi Meir. In the Hasidic period
there was Hannah Rochel, the Maid of Ludomir, who had a following of male Hasidim. For a tale about her see "A New Soul," p. 263. Rabbi Asenath should be seen as a
figure in this tradition.

71. *The Tale of the Kiddush Cup* (Syria)
IFA 6628, collected by Moshe Rabi from Avraham Etia, *Avotanu Sipru*, story no.
47, edited by Moshe Rabi (Jerusalem: 1976).
   Here Rabbi Hayim Pinto shows himself to be a great kabbalistic conjurer, demonstrating powers similiar to those of the late medieval Jewish sorcerer Rabbi Adam or
the great Hasidic master Rabbi Elimelech of Lizensk. See, for example, "A Bowl of
Soup" p. 222, where another miracle takes place at the table. See also "The Magic
Mirror of Rabbi Adam" in *EV*, p. 187. In the present tale about Rabbi Pinto, he
invokes Rahab, the Prince of the Sea, to recover the sunken case of jewels lost by his
seder guest. The holy names that are used are usually the names of angels. In essence,
these holy names serve as keys, either to the gates of the palaces of heaven or to the

powers of the angels associated with them. Rahab is the angel of the sea, a kind of
Jewish Neptune. The theme of calling upon Rehab to recover something in the sea is
found in the Jerusalem Talmud in Sanhedrin 7:25. See "Rabbi Joshua and the Witch"
in *MT*, p. 35. Here Rabbi Joshua calls upon Rahab to send him an evil amulet sunk in
the sea. And as Rabbi Joshua stands at the shore, the waves wash up a box containing
it. And when Rabbi Joshua destroys the amulet, the witch who cast a spell of barren-
ness is quickly exorcised.

72. *The Miracle in the Sukkah* (Israel)

Collected by Howard Schwartz from Benyamim Tsedaka of Holon. He heard this
story from his grandfather, Yefet Tsedaka, the son of Abraham Tsedaka, who was
present during the miracle of the dancing fruit.

The Samaritans are an ancient Jewish sect that does not accept the divinity of any
text after the Torah. They once numbered more than a million, but because of
oppression and forced conversion, fewer than 600 Samaritans remain today, virtually
all living in Israel. Because the Samaritans have remained true to their ancient customs, their beliefs deviate in various ways from Jewish tradition. Benyamim Tsedaka,
a well-known Samaritan scholar, is of the one hundred twenty-fifth generation of
Samaritans who have lived in the Holy Land. According to Tsedaka, most Samaritan
legends are presented as accounts of actual incidents and include the names of the
participants, the date, and the place. Accounts of miracles are rare in Samaritan lore.
In that respect, this tale is an exception. Note the important distinction between the
sukkahs of the Samaritans, which were built indoors, and those of the Jews, which are
required to be built outdoors. For more on the construction of the sukkah, see Leviticus 23:34ff., Numbers 29:12 ff., and Deuteronomy 16:13. See also Mishnah Sukkah
1–2.

73. *Rabbi Naftali's Trance* (Eastern Europe)

From *Sipurei Ya'akov* no. 7, edited by Rabbi Yakov Sofer (Dobromill: 1864). A
variant, which does not identify the rabbi, is found in *Sippurim Mishekvar*, no. 27. For
a discussion of this variant, see below.

In this tale, Rabbi Naftali Katz of Posen uses his great mystical powers to search the
world for the groom who has abandoned the daughter of a wealthy disciple. It involves
an extraordinary effort, which almost costs him his life, for it turns out that the groom
is no longer in this world. Not only does Rabbi Naftali locate him in the World to
Come, he sets up a meeting between the soul of the man and his abandoned wife in the
presence of angels. The soul of the man is forced to return to this world in the form of
a soldier, while the two soldiers guarding him are avenging angels. Rabbi Naftali thus
demonstrates vast knowledge of the workings of the World to Come. So too is his
prophecy of the events that will take place fully realized. There are many tales about
agunot, abandoned wives, in Jewish lore, for Jewish law holds that the woman may
not remarry until she has obtained a *get*, or bill of divorce. Alternatively, in the event
that the man has died, the testimony of two witnesses is generally required. This has
provided great problems for women whose husbands abandoned them or refused to
give them a *get*. Likewise, women whose husbands died in faraway places, who had no
way to prove they were widows, were not permitted to remarry. The only other
alternative was for these women to consult with and receive written consent to
remarry from one hundred rabbis or, as in this tale of Rabbi Naftali, have someone
resort to supernatural methods. The tales about Rabbi Naftali often refer to his use of

his *tsura* or "shape" to accomplish his magic. This term seems parallel to that of *tselem*, which seems to refer to astral projection or soul travel. See *On the Mystical Shape of the Godhead* by Gershom Scholem, chapter 6, "*Tselem:* The Concept of the Astral Body." Reb Elimelech of Lizensk seems to use a similiar method to send his shape by astral projection. See "The Shadow on the Wall," p. 228. The variant of this tale found in *Sippurim Mishekvar* is very interesting. Instead of Rabbi Naftali Katz, the wonder-working is done by a water carrier who is understood to be one of the hidden saints. The water carrier covers the eyes of the father with a handkerchief and takes him out into the desert, using kabbalistic magic. There the dead man appears first as a cloud of dust and then as part of an army marching through the desert. In this version, the dead husband does not resist admitting that he was the woman's husband, and thus makes it possible for the rabbi and the father to serve as two witnesses proving that the husband who abandoned her is dead.

74. *Interpreting the Zohar* (Syria)
IFA 7336, collected by Moshe Rabi from Avraham Patal in *Avotanu Sipru*, edited by Moshe Rabi (Jerusalem: 1976, Vol. 3, No.8).

This tale recounts how a Jew of Haleb, Syria, learns that the soul of the talmudic sage Rabbah bar bar Hannah has been reincarnated in his generation, in the person of Rabbi Mordecai Abbadi. This secret is revealed to him in a dream, which is brought on by his intense desire to understand a difficult passage of the Zohar. The choice of Rabbah bar bar Hannah as the sage who is reincarnated seems an unusual one at first. For although Rabbah is associated with many miraculous events (see "The Golden Dove," p. 41, and the accompanying note) and with many incidents best described as tall tales, he is not associated with the Zohar, which, tradition holds, was written by the talmudic sage Shimon bar Yohai. However, Rabbah's tales have traditionally been interpreted as mystical allegories by rabbis such as the Vilna Gaon and Rabbi Nachman of Bratslav, and it is this association that may explain his presence in this tale. Here it appears that Rabbi Mordecai Abbadi knows the origin of his soul and is surprised that his secret has been revealed. That is why he insists that the Jew who has learned it in his dream keep it a secret as long as he lives. This story reflects the high esteem in which the Zohar has long been held, as well as the intense difficulties posed by its mystical text. It also reflects the belief in *gilgul*, or reincarnation, that was common in circles devoted to mystical studies. One of the primary motifs of the stories about the Ari concerns his ability to recognize the history of a man's soul and the assumption that many of the great sages had been reborn in their own generation. This story reflects these mystical assumptions.

75. *The Secrets of Kabbalah* (Holland)
From *Edot Messaprot*, edited by Abraham Shatal (Tel Aviv: 1969, pp. 113–15). This story originally was published in the Jewish weekly *Erev Shabbat*, January 23, 1925, p. 286. Part of this story is based on historical facts. Rabbi Moshe Pinto lived at the beginning of the nineteenth century and was active in the east of Holland. The main Jewish population of Holland was in the big cities in the west of the country, especially in Amsterdam, but there were some Jews who lived in the small towns and villages, and they were very isolated from the rest of the Jewish population. Usually the rabbis of the nearest towns took care of these Jews. Wandering rabbis existed in many countries, and did a lot to strengthen the belief of the Jews in the little towns and congregations. In Eastern Europe they were known as *maggidim*, who passed through

the villages and little towns. This is one of many stories that warn about the dangers of the Kabbalah. The archetype of such tales is "The Four Who Entered Paradise," p. 51. Refer to the note on this tale and the discussion in the Introduction, pp. 28–31. See also "From the Beyond," p. 253. In this century the famous drama *The Dybbuk*, by S. Ansky, is based on this same theme of the dangers inherent in Kabbalah. Here a young yeshivah student, who delves into kabbalistic mysteries on his own, loses his life. As for Rabbi Moshe Pinto, he experiences a great fall, followed by an attempt to come to terms with the rabbi's curse that has sentenced him to a life of wandering. It is clear that it was also a life of repentance, as he was much beloved as a wandering rabbi. Wandering as a punishment, of course, recalls the punishment of Cain to become a wanderer and an exile, as well as the Christian legend of the Wandering Jew. Above all, the tale warns that the gravest dangers await those who enter the realm of Kabbalah without the proper guide.

76. *The Flying Letters* (Eastern Europe)
Collected by Howard Schwartz from Yehuda Yaari.

The motif of flying letters is found in many variations in Jewish lore. It is first linked with the letters of the first tablets, which Moses smashed when he saw the golden calf. The legend explains that before the tablets struck the ground, the letters ascended on high. Here the letters of the Torah in one town fly to an empty scroll in another, suggesting that the holy letters of the Torah could not bear to be in the presence of evil. Thus it is also a warning tale to remind Jews that the Torah is a gift of God, and if it is no longer deserved, it will be lost. Here, as in the midrashic tale about the first tablets, the letters take flight in order to separate themselves from impurity. See "The Book of Flying Letters," p. 77, and the accompanying note for more on the theme of flying letters.

77. *The Curse* (Eastern Europe)
From *Me-Aggadot Ha-Karaim*, edited by Reuven Fahn (Vienna: no date).

This is a Karaite tale. The Karaites were a Jewish sect that rejected the Oral Law and broke away from rabbinic Judaism in the eighth century. Today only a handful of Karaites are still to be found, primarily in Eastern Europe. This background suggests why the father in this tale is so angered at his daughter's unwillingness to marry and have children—since there was no more pressing need for the Karaites than children. The theme of the bride (or her father) who cannot agree upon any groom is also found in "The Bridegroom" in *LC*, p. 123 (Oxford ed.). There the Angel of Death is the ultimate groom, while here the father's curse turns his daughter into a figure like Medusa, a creature with snakes for hair, neither dead nor alive.

78. *The Miracle of the Ring* (Persia)
From *Hodesh Hodesh Ve-sipuro: 1974–1975*, edited by Dov Noy (Haifa: 1975). IFA 10693, collected by Shlomit Sasson from Rachel Kalimi.

In this tale, the father's devotion to his son continues beyond the grave, as he manages to deliver a ring to the one he knows to be his son's destined bride in a dream. According to a talmudic dictum, forty days before a child is born, a voice goes forth that declares whom he or she will marry (B. Sota 2a). The soul of the departed father is thus able to use the knowledge gained in the World to Come to locate the destined one and see that the match takes place. Note the use of the dream to communicate with the bride-to-be and the unusual miracle of transmitting an object through a dream. For a parallel theme, see "Leaves from the Garden of Eden," p. ooo. One interesting detail of this story is the girl's decision to disguise herself as a man. This is forbidden by the Torah but is a common motif in Jewish folklore, demonstrating that the folktale, unlike the rabbinic tale, is less concerned with issues of the Law. For another example of a folktale in which a woman disguises herself as a man, see "The Disguised Princess" in *MT*, pp. 105ff.

79. *The Angel's Daughter* (Buhara)

From *Assarah Sipurei Am mi Buhara*, edited by Dov Noy. IFA 7705, collected by Jacob Pinhasi (Jerusalem: 1978).

A young man's determination to marry only the daughter of an angel is miraculously fulfilled, although he is made to vow not to question any of her actions. Yet these are so strange that in the end he breaks his vow and loses his celestial bride, only to discover that her actions had served him well. The motif of marrying an angelic husband or wife is not uncommon in general (it is especially popular in Chinese folktales), although it is rare in Jewish folklore. The primary precedent for it is in the midrash of the Sons of God and the daughters of men in *Yalkut Shimoni*, compiled by Shimon Ashkenazi (Frankfurt: 1687), which expands on Genesis 6:1–4. The figures of the Sons of God who descend and marry the daughters of men, that is, human women, are widely interpreted to be angels. The brief biblical account of this myth gave birth to many midrashic legends about two of the angels, Shemhazai and Azazel. See "The Princess Who Became the Morning Star" and "The Secrets of Azazel" in *MT*, pp. 79 and 85, respectively. There also are many examples of tales in which a human marries a demon—see, for example, "The Demon Princess" in *EV*, p. 107, and many examples of marriage with demons in *LC*—but marriage with angels is rarely found. One reason for this is that angels are almost always identified as male. Thus to find the daughter of an angel in this tale is quite unusual. Nor do we ever learn how an angel came to have a daughter, since angels do not procreate, as stated in *Avot de Rabbi Natan* 37. This tale about the angel's daughter is a variant of the tale type in which a person with extraordinary knowledge initiates acts that are confusing and mystifying to others, but that eventually are shown to have a good purpose. The earliest version of this tale is found in the Talmud, B. Gittin 68b, concerning the strange acts of Asmodeus. A similiar tale is found in *Hibbur Yafeh me-hay Yesuah* 2, where a rabbi follows Elijah, agreeing not to question whatever he does, but eventually becomes so disturbed at his strange actions that he is unable to restrain himself and insists on clarification, learning that all the actions served a worthy purpose. See also "The Reincarnation of a *Tzaddik*" in *MT*, p. 217, for another variant of this tale.

80. *The Bridegroom and the Angel of Death* (Yemenite)

From Bodleian Library, Codex Or. Gaster 82, published in *Sefer ha-Maaysiot* in *Exempla of the Rabbis*, edited by Moses Gaster. Also found in *Hibbur ha-Maaysiot ve-Midrashot ve ha-Aggadot* (Venice: 1551). An oral variant is IFA 10895 in *Hodesh Hodesh ve-Sipuro* 1976–1977, edited by Dov Noy, collected by Devora Wilk from Bela Baroz of Georgia (Jerusalem: 1979).

This striking tale refutes the common sentiment of those who wish they could take the place of a close relative who is dying. When the opportunity is given them, all back out, except for the bride. I. L. Peretz reworked this theme in the story "The Sacrifice," turning it into a horror tale when the Angel of Death does take up the offer of the bride, Sarah, rather than sparing the life of both bride and groom, as here. Tales about the Angel of Death are very common in all phases of Jewish lore, and belief in the angel was widespread. The motif of the angel revealing his true nature, which is more terrible than the father or mother can bear, is found earlier in the pseudepigraphal Greek text *The Testament of Abraham* 17, where Abraham begs the angel to reveal his true appearance: "Then Death made his appearance dark and more fierce than any sort of beast . . . and he showed Abraham seven fiery heads of dragons, fourteen faces of the most flaming fire . . . and a gloomy viper's face, and the face of a terrible precipice, and the fiercer face of an asp, and the face of a fearsome lion . . . and he also showed him the face of fiery sword . . . and another face of a wild sea raging and a river rushing and a fearsome three-headed dragon and a mingled cup of poisons" (quoted from *The Testament of Abraham*, translated by Michael E. Stone, Missoula: 1972). The great folklorist Haim Schwarzbaum completed a major study of the Angel of Death before his death, which is still unpublished.

81. *The Cave to the Holy Land* (Poland)
IFA 532. As remembered by Dov Noy.

This is a variant of one of the most famous oral tales in Jewish lore. The many variants of this tale all concern a goat or sometimes a cow that discovers a cave leading directly to the Holy Land. These enchanted caves were created so that the bones of the dead could roll through them to the Holy Land at the time of the End of Days. After returning from the cave, the animal starts to give unusually delicious milk, which, in the case of this tale, also serves as a healing potion. Then the shepherd who follows the animal finds that it travels through a cave that leads either to the Garden of Eden or to the Land of Israel. The majority of tales lead to a destination in the Land of Israel. For an exception to this rule, see "A Story with a Goat" in *GNC*, pp. 51–52, for a translation of a Yemenite variant of the present tale, also collected by the IFA. This is IFA 5842, from *Ha-Kamea ha-Kadosh*, collected by Rachel Seri, edited by Aliza Shenhar, no. 11. The linkage of Israel and the Garden of Eden seems natural enough, in that the Land of Israel was always portrayed as *a land flowing with milk and honey* (Ex. 3:8) in the Jewish lore of the Diaspora, when there seemed no better chance of returning there than to the Garden of Eden. This tale serves as a primary metaphor for the distance between those still living in the Old World and those who set out to live in the Holy Land, separating fathers and sons. S. Y. Agnon wrote a well-known version of this tale, known as "Fable of the Goat." See *GNC*, p. 459. The present tale is unusual in that it features two goats. Also, most versions of the tale concern a son who is separated from his family, not, as in the present case, a husband who is separated from his wife. Nevertheless, in bringing the rabbi of Shebreshin into the tale, the importance of the theme of separation of those in the Diaspora and those in the Holy Land is clearly indicated. Note that the shepherd in this tale is identified as a Hasid, suggesting that the tale is of Hasidic origin, and therefore that the Rabbi of Shebreshin served as this Hasid's rebbe.

82. *The Cave of Temptations* (Poland)
Collected by Howard Schwartz from Dov Noy.

This story is one of several interesting variants of the previous tale, "The Cave to the Holy Land." Like that tale, this one is an allegory about the desire to travel and live in the Holy Land. The existence, in legend, of a cave leading directly to the Holy Land demonstrates the great longing for the ancestral land. What distinguishes this version are the obstacles placed within the cave, temptations that distract the travelers as they set out for the Holy Land. Instead of the cave simply being a miraculous route, the forces of temptation use the power of illusion to create barriers in the cave. Only a person able to recognize those illusions can reach the far end. All the others become distracted along the way. The addition of the obstacles changes the tale in several interesting ways. It fulfills the requirement for obstacles found in fairy tales, which usually involve three episodes, as happens here. The theme of illusion here is echoed in a number of these mystical tales. See the note to "Isaac's Ascent," p. 278. All of the variants of tales of messianic caves can be seen as a kind of fantasy for Jews who were living such a great distance from the Holy Land. Sometimes, however, reality makes its way into these fantasies, as happens in this variant, in which the obstacles in the cave correlate with actual obstacles that stood in the way of those who wished to live in the Holy Land. These obstacles involve various kinds of distractions, including demonic seduction, as in the accounts of Lilith, the lure of money, and even excessive study. For the tale seems to question the pattern of continuous study found in the yeshivahs of Eastern Europe, which is here seen as an obstacle to *aliyah*, ascending to the Holy Land. These obstacles make the quest to the Holy Land that much more difficult, and consequently make the tale a more accurate representation of the difficulties involved in undertaking such a journey. For a further example of demonic seduction, see the following tale.

83. *The Hollow of the Sling* (Eastern Europe)

From *Sihot Moharan* in *Hayey Moharan* by Rabbi Nathan of Nemirov (Lemberg: 1874).

There are many names for hell in Jewish literature, including Gehenna, Sheol, and the Shadow of Death. See *Hell in Jewish Literature* by Samuel J. Fox, pp. 12–13 for a list of many of these names. One of the names for hell is *Kaph Kela*, "the Hollow of the Sling," which derives from I Samuel 25:29—*the souls of thine enemies, they shall he slung out, as from the hollow of a sling.* The numerical value of *Kaph Kela* is 300, and Rabbi Nachman of Bratslav linked this number to the number of years that the groom was a *fugitive and a wanderer* (Gen. 4:12). Thus this tale grows out of *gematria*, where words with the same numerical total can be substituted for each other as a way of shedding light on the meaning of a text. Here Rabbi Nachman goes one step further and is inspired by the number itself to a story that is a midrashic type of commentary on the meaning of *Kaph Kela* and the kind of hell it represents. The original was lost and was recorded in fragmentary form by Rabbi Nathan, Rabbi Nachman's scribe. The present version is an attempt to reimagine the lost story of the groom, which Rabbi Nachman attributed to Rabbi Yakov Yosef of Ostrog. Of this story, Rabbi Nathan writes: "There is a whole story about the groom—how when he came out from the bridal chamber he wandered from house to house and from city to city."

84. *How Rabbi Judah the Pious Became a Great Scholar* (Eastern Europe)

From *Ma'aseh Buch* (Yiddish), no. 166, compiled by Jacob ben Abraham of Mezhirech (Basel: 1601).

Rabbi Judah the Pious and his father, Rabbi Samuel the Pious, are legendary figures of twelfth-century Germany and the founders of the movement known as Hasidism, not to be confused with the Hasidic movement founded by the Baal Shem Tov in the eighteenth century. Rabbi Judah the Pious is the reputed author of *Sefer Hasidim*, and he and his father are the subject of numerous legends, a cycle of which are found in the *Ma'aseh Buch*, the best-known collection of sixteenth-century Yiddish

folktales. This story and the following one, "The Words in the Sand," are drawn from
that cycle. This story recounts how Judah the Pious experienced a mystical experience
after having avoided studying for many years. In essence, this experience changes him
from being an Esau-like figure, enamored of shooting his bow and arrow, into a Jacob-
like figure, who quickly becomes a master scholar. Much of this transformation is the
direct result of the mystical experience recounted in this tale, which not only awakens
his sense of spirituality and makes him receptive to knowledge, but almost seems to
give him a new soul, one that is already familiar with the teachings and mysteries of
Judaism. For another tale with this motif, see "A New Soul," p. 263. Accounts of such
direct and overpowering mystical experiences are rare in Jewish literature, and this
one closely resembles the classic descriptions of *unio mystica*, the unitive mystical
experience.

85. The Words in the Sand (Eastern Europe)
From *Ma'aseh Buch* (Yiddish), no. 173, compiled by Jacob ben Abraham of
Mezhirech (Basel: 1601).

One of the most popular types of Jewish folktales concerns a vow taken by a son at
the time of his father's death. The sons who remain true to the vow are eventually
rewarded, while those who do not meet a bitter end. For an example of the former
type of tale, see "The Princess with Golden Hair" in *EV*, pp. 169ff., and for an
example of the latter, see "The Demon Princess" in *EV*, pp. 107ff. "The Words in the
Sand" closely resembles this type of tale, except that the young man in the story does
not take a vow; rather, his father commands in his will that the son never cross the
river Danube. (The vow in these tales often concerns avoiding travel by water because
of the inherent dangers. It is this vow that the son breaks in "The Demon Princess.")
The son, however, desires to study with Judah the Pious, and crosses the river despite
his father's command. This puts Judah the Pious, a distant relative of the father, in a
difficult position. Out of respect for the father he takes in the son as a student, but
because the son has not honored the will, he refuses to teach him any mysteries. When
the time comes for the son to return home for Passover, Judah the Pious discusses
these matters for the first time and then performs the magic in which he writes a
phrase in the sand, which, when the son reads it, gives him knowledge as great as that
of Judah the Pious himself. Then, three times, Judah the Pious erases the sand, and
the son loses all the knowledge. This is his punishment for disobeying his father.
Finally, Judah the Pious lets him eat the words along with the sand, and as a result, he
gains the knowledge as his own at last. This method, because of its disagreeable
nature, also has an element of punishment, but the end result is that the boy gains the
knowledge he sought when he came to Judah the Pious in the first place. See the novel
Judah the Pious by Francine Prose, which is based on this cycle of legends.

86. The Count Who Wanted to Study Kabbalah (Eastern Europe)
From *Nifla'ot Maharal*, edited by Yudel Rosenberg (Piotrkow: 1909).

Rabbi Judah Loew of Prague, known as the "Maharal," is the most famous of the
medieval Jewish sorcerers, with powers approaching those of King Solomon. These
powers include knowledge of a person's hidden secrets, as demonstrated in this tale,
where the Maharal invokes the spirits of the murdered sister and child of the Count,
who had sought to study the Kabbalah with him. While the study of the Kabbalah is
an esoteric one in Jewish circles, it is completely forbidden to teach it to non-Jews.
Confronted with the Count's demand, the Maharal causes him to face his great sin

and in this way to withdraw his demand. Note that the Count is engaged in various esoteric studies, such as alchemy and astrology, and that he equates these with the study of the Kabbalah. Eventually there did emerge a form of Kabbalah that was studied outside of Jewish circles, which is generally referred to as "Christian Kabbalah." Here the use of kabbalistic numbers and letters is associated with those of the Tarot, and the result is a study that branches out on a path of its own, which Jewish scholars have inevitably regarded as a distortion and falsification of true kabbalistic studies.

87. *The Dream Question of the Maharal* (Eastern Europe)
From *Nifla'ot Maharal*, edited by Yudel Rosenberg (Piotrkow: 1909).
Rabbi Judah Loew, known as the "Maharal," is best known as the creator of the golem, a man made out of clay and brought to life with kabbalistic magic and the power of God's Name. The Maharal created the golem to protect the Jews of Prague from the Blood Libel, in which Jews were accused of ritual murder at the time of Passover in order to use the blood of Christians in the making of matzahs. This, of course, was a false accusation. The primary tales in the golem cycle involve the Blood Libel in some fashion, but there are also stories in which the golem assists Rabbi Loew in other ways, as in this tale. Here the golem arranges the letters from the dream message that the Maharal has received into one that he can interpret. He does not do this out of knowledge, but rather out of divine inspiration. When the mystery of the dream message has been deciphered, the Maharal learns the reason that the man dropped the Torah on Yom Kippur, the Day of Judgment. In kabbalistic literature there are different ways of solving problems with dreams. The most common method was the asking of a dream question before going to sleep, in the hope that heaven would send a dream that would serve as a reply. And such dreams were often received. See *Visions of the Night: A Study of Jewish Dream Interpretation* by Joel Covitz. *Nifla'ot Maharal* is the primary source of the legends of the golem. The editor, Yudel Rosenberg, claimed that the manuscript was written by a relative of the Maharal, but most recent scholars, including Eli Yassif, are convinced that it was written by Rosenberg himself, which changes its date of origin from the sixteenth to the nineteenth century. In that case, the earliest golem legends are those found in the first volume of *Sippurim*, a collection of the legends of Prague, edited by Wolf Pasceles and published in Prague in 1853. See "The Golem" in *MT*, pp. 265ff, for the primary legend of this man of clay.

88. *The Ruin* (Eastern Europe)
From *Nifla'ot Maharal*, edited by Yudel Rosenberg (Piotrkow: 1909).
Some of the tales in *Nifla'ot Maharal*, the primary collection of tales about Rabbi Judah Loew, do not concern the golem but demonstrate his wisdom and powers, as does this one. This is primarily about a strange kind of possession that occurs when a man walks too close to a haunted ruin. From a psychological perspective, the barking dog that started to attack the man when he walked near the ruin so traumatized him that he had terrible dreams of being turned into the rider on such a dog and being forced to bark like a dog himself. But the tale views this from a mystical rather than a psychological perspective, where the man has been the victim of demonic possession. The rabbi's solution frees him from the possession. In this sense, the ritual exorcisms and related methods of freeing those possessed by the forces of evil functioned in much the same way as modern psychoanalysis. Note the role of the black dogs in this

tale, which echoes that found in other tales, such as "The Chains of the Messiah," p. 106. In this and other variants, an evil person is reborn as a black dog as a punishment for his sins.

89. *The Voice in the Tree* (Israel)
From *Tova Be'ad Tova* by Rafael Babay, edited by Batya Maoz. Collected by Edna Babay from Rafael Babay. IFA 10200 (Jerusalem: 1980).

Jewish mystical lore outlines a complex fate of reincarnation for the soul of man after death. This tale summarizes these successive fates, known as *gilgul*, in an essentially didactic manner. The ultimate goal of the soul, from this perspective, is to be freed from the cycle of reincarnation, much as the goal in Hinduism is to achieve *nirvana* and be freed from any further rebirths. Here the principles of *gilgul* are explained so that the rabbi who learns of them can assist in freeing the soul from this cycle. In order for this to happen, the rabbi must slaughter the animal into which the soul has entered and make it holy by putting it to the holy purpose of being eaten. This action then releases the soul to ascend to heaven. The fate of the soul as outlined here involves great suffering. And an even worse punishment awaits those souls whose sins were so great that avenging angels chase them from one place to the next. When such a wandering spirit takes possession of a living person, it is known as a *dybbuk*. See, for example, "The Widow of Safed," p. 98, and the accompanying note.

90. *A Vision in the Cemetery* (Eastern Europe)
From *Anshe Mofet*. Also found in *Otsar ha-Ma'aysiot*, edited by Naftali Greenboim (B'nai Brak: 1988).

In this story Rabbi Moshe Sofer has a vision of his colleague, Rabbi Nathan, walking in the cemetery at midnight, wearing a shroud. The vision recurs three times, which is the essential number for prophetic visions or dreams, clearly indicating that they will come true. And, indeed, Rabbi Nathan takes sick at that time and soon passes away. Note also that the vision takes place at midnight, which is the enchanted moment in Jewish lore, as well as in many other cultures. The meaning of the vision is clear because of where the vision takes place—in the cemetery—and because Rabbi Nathan is dressed in a shroud. This story thus draws on many common folk elements, yet it also has strong Jewish overtones, taking place in a synagogue, concerning a rabbi and a cantor, and involving Jewish customs such as the reciting of the Psalms for those who are ill.

91. *The Spirit of Hagigah* (Italy)
From *Menorat ha-Ma'or* by Yitzhak Abohav (Mantua: 1573). The earliest edition derives from Constantinople in 1514. A variant of this tale is found in *Maaseh Buch* (Yiddish), no. 247, compiled by Jacob ben Abraham of Mezhirech (Basel: 1601).

Jewish lore asserts that there is an angel or spirit for every sacred text. In this tale, a man who devotes himself to a single tractate of the Talmud, Hagigah, has the spirit of that book, a woman, mourn for him after his death. This tale confirms the notion that heaven delights in the study of the sacred texts, and in this case, because of the man's devotion to Hagigah, that spirit takes a particular interest in him and ensures that he is properly mourned after his death. The choice of Hagigah as the tractate that is the focus of his study indicates the importance of that text to the subject of Jewish mysticism. Many of the key mystical legends of the Talmud, including those concerning the four who entered Paradise, are found in Hagigah. Indeed, in *The Merkavah in*

Rabbinic Literature (chapter 3, pp. 64–105), David Halperin refers to the cluster of mystical tales in tractate Hagigah beginning with 14b as "the Mystical Collection." This suggests that the man who studied Hagigah was involved in some kind of mystical contemplation, and in this context the appearance of the spirit of Hagigah is an appropriate mystical response to his lifelong study of this mystical text. Note that *Hagigah* means "celebration," and that the term sounds like a woman's name, making the feminine personification more likely than a masculine one. This tale also echoes some of the personification of the *Shekhinah* as a woman in mourning at the *Kotel*, the Western Wall in Jerusalem. See "A Vision at the Wailing Wall," p. 87. Also echoed is the personification of Mother Zion such as that found in Ecclesiastes Rabbah. See the Introduction, p. 18. For other tales about angels or spirits brought into being by mystical contemplation of a text, see "The Angel of the Mishnah," p. 112, and "The Angel of the Zohar," p. 212.

IV Hasidic Tales

The Circle of the Baal Shem Tov

92. *The Book in the Cave* (Eastern Europe)
From *Shivhei ha-Besht* by Rabbi Dov Ben Samuel, edited by Samuel A. Horodezky (Berlin: 1922). A far more extensive variant, which is the basis of the present tale, is found in *Sipurei Nifla'ot*. The earliest source of this legend is found in *Shivhei ha-Besht*, the first collection of tales about the Baal Shem Tov. See *In Praise of the Baal Shem Tov*, edited by Dan Ben-Amos and Jerome R. Mintz, for a complete translation of *Shivhei ha-Besht*.

This is a crucial story in Hasidic lore, linking the Baal Shem Tov with the legendary master Rabbi Adam. The link between them is a legendary book, handed down since the time of Adam, that Rabbi Adam bequeaths to the Baal Shem Tov. The opening of the Yiddish edition of *Shivhei ha-Besht*, also published in 1815, says that "All the miraculous acts that the Besht performed came to him from the writings received from Rabbi Adam." This book not only reveals great mysteries, but also proves that Rabbi Adam and the Baal Shem Tov are part of a chain of sages that goes all the way back to Adam. In the process, this legend links the whole Hasidic movement to the rabbinic past. It takes its model directly from the midrashic account of the Book of Raziel. This legend has a somewhat obscure history but is believed to have derived from the talmudic-midrashic period. The complete legend is found in the Zohar I:55b. A book with the title *Sefer ha-Razim* was published in Amsterdam in 1701. It contains fragments of earlier works, magical spells, and some Hekhaloth texts. In the original legend, the book of Raziel is passed down from Adam until it reaches King Solomon and is ultimately one of the treasures of the Temple that are destroyed. The Hasidic legend follows essentially the same line of descent but has the book survive the destruction of the Temple by being among the treasures of the Temple hidden by the Prophet Jeremiah in a cave, where Rabbi Adam found them. Later, Rabbi Adam passes the book to the Baal Shem Tov in "The Prince of Fire," p. 187. The legend of the book of Raziel is an example of the chain midrash, one of the most popular types of rabbinic tales. The chain midrash creates a kind of mega-myth in which all of the generations are linked together. It views history as a chain of related events focused on the covenant between God and Israel. Among the examples included here are the chain legends of "The *Tzohar*," p. 59, and that of the remarkable legendary figure Serah bat Asher, who lived longer than Methuselah, in "The Chronicle of Serah bat Asher," p. 47. Other examples include the legend of the garments of Adam and Eve, which God gave them as they left the Garden of Eden, and the staff of Moses, which he used to defeat Pharaoh's army and part the waters of the Red Sea. There is an extensive legendary tradition linked to Rabbi Adam, who is the archetypal Jewish sorcerer in the model of King Solomon. For additional tales about Rabbi Adam, see "The Enchanted Journey," "The Magic Mirror of Rabbi Adam," and "The King's Dream" in *EV*, pp. 181–202. See also "The Magic Lamp of Rabbi Adam," "Rabbi Adam and the Star-gazing King," "The Enchanted Palace," and "The King Descended from Haman" in *MT*, pp. 230–254.

93. *The Prince of Fire* (Eastern Europe)
From *Shivhei ha-Besht* by Rabbi Dov Ben Samuel, edited by Samuel A. Horodezky (Berlin: 1922).

This story continues that of the previous tale, "The Book in the Cave." In that tale, Rabbi Adam succeeded in obtaining the Book of Mysteries, and in this tale his son delivers it to Israel ben Eliezer, who later becomes the Baal Shem Tov. This story has a distinct Faustian theme and is one of many warning stories about the dangers of the Kabbalah, beginning with "The Four Who Entered Paradise." At the same time, it strongly echoes a biblical incident in which the sons of Aaron, the High Priest, brought "strange fire" into the sanctuary and were in turn devoured by fire: *And Nadav and Avihu, the sons of Aaron, took each of them his censer, and put fire in it, and put incense on it, and offered strange fire before God, which He commanded them not. And a fire went out from God, and devoured them, and they died before God* (Lev. 10:1–2). In the present tale, Rabbi Adam's son is apparently distraught that his father did not consider him worthy to receive the book himself. He fulfills his obligation to bring it to Israel ben Eliezer but then asks the boy if he might study it with him. Israel realizes that this is not right, but he does not feel that he can reject the one who has just brought him such a great treasure. Rabbi Adam's son seeks to invoke the angel of the Torah, known as the "Prince of the Torah." Instead, he mispronounces the name and ends up invoking the angel of fire, known as the "Prince of Fire." In doing so, he loses his life, as did Ben Azzai in the tales of the four who entered Paradise. This tale completes the transfer of the Book of Mysteries to the Baal Shem Tov, takes the form of a warning tale about the dangers of the Kabbalah, and demonstrates that even as a boy the Baal Shem was a holy figure with great mystical knowledge. For another example of a kabbalistic warning tale, see "The Secrets of Kabbalah," p. 155.

94. *The Angel's Sword* (Eastern Europe)
From *Shivhei ha-Besht* by Rabbi Dov Ben Samuel, edited by Samuel A. Horodezky (Berlin: 1922).

Every attempt the Baal Shem Tov made to reach the Holy Land was obstructed; here, he is prevented from passing through the cave to the Land of Israel by the spinning sword of an angel. This is clearly intended to indicate the angel guarding the Garden of Eden in Genesis 4:24: *And He placed at the east of the Garden of Eden the cherubim, and the flaming sword which turned every way, to keep the way to the Tree of Life.* In another case the ship he took to the Holy Land sank. This is explained in a Hasidic legend that attributes his inability to reach *Eretz Yisrael* to God's intention. That is because the powerful holiness of the Land of Israel, plus the powers of the Or Hayim, the most famous rabbi of the Holy Land, would combine to force the Messiah to come before his time. Later Rabbi Nachman of Bratslav, the great-grandson of the Baal Shem Tov, himself took a difficult journey to the Holy Land and walked only a few feet onto the land before he announced he was ready to return. For in setting foot on the Holy Land, he had accomplished the *tikkun*, the repair, he had set out to do. Thus, for Rabbi Nachman, his success in reaching the Promised Land somehow completed the quest started by his great-grandfather, with whom Rabbi Nachman felt a very strong bond. "The Angel's Sword" is one of a series of tales about the Baal Shem Tov before he revealed himself, at the age of thirty-six. Some of these tales concern his childhood. The cave itself is part of the tradition of messianic caves that lead directly to the Holy Land, so that the skeletons of the dead may roll there for the Resurrection when the messianic era begins. For tales with this theme, see "The Cave to the Holy Land," p. 164, and "The Cave of Temptations," p. 166.

95. *The Ladder of Prayers* (Eastern Europe)
From *Midrash Ribesh Tov*, edited by Lipot Abraham (Kecskemet: 1927, p. 42).
The Zohar tells of a dove that makes its nest outside the palace of the Messiah in Paradise. That is why the palace of the Messiah is also known as the "Bird's Nest." See the note to "The Golden Dove," p. 276, for the background and variants of this myth. "The Ladder of Prayers" builds on the earlier legendary accounts of the golden dove, reporting an attempt by the Baal Shem Tov to ascend on the ladder of prayers of his Hasidim into Paradise to capture the dove. The Besht believes that if he can use his mystical powers to snatch the miraculous bird of the Messiah, he can cause the Messiah to follow it, since the Messiah cannot bear to be apart from its enchanting song. The Besht fails at the last moment because the ladder of prayers of his disciples, on which he has ascended, collapses. The failure of the Baal Shem's Hasidim to provide the spiritual support needed for this great endeavor, as symbolized by the collapse of their ladder of prayers, is offered as the reason for the failure to bring the Messiah in their generation. Thus the tale illustrates the interdependency of the *tzaddik* and his Hasidim. This attempt to capture the golden dove and its failure marks one of the basic types of mystical tales—those concerning an attempt to hasten the coming of the Messiah. Several such tales are found in the Talmud. See, in particular, "Forcing the End," p. 65. Subsequently such tales are found in virtually every generation, explaining that there is a potential Messiah who, had all gone well, would have served as Messiah ben Joseph, preparing the way for Messiah ben David. In this tale of the Baal Shem, however, he ascends directly to the palace of Messiah ben David, determined to initiate the End of Days. For other tales of this type, see "The Journey to Jerusalem," p. 86, and "A Messiah in Every Generation" by Jiri Langer in *GNC*, p. 597.

96. *The Tree of Life* (Eastern Europe)
From *Shivhei ha-Besht* by Rabbi Dov Ben Samuel, edited by Samuel A. Horodezky (Berlin: 1922). The legend of the Tree of Life is expanded in *Midrash Konen* in *Otsar Midrashim*, edited by J. D. Eisenstein (Jerusalem: 1969), p. 255.
The quest to reach Paradise is echoed in many tales about the Baal Shem Tov. Sometimes this takes the form of a heavenly ascent, as in "Unlocking the Gates of Heaven," p. 205. Alternatively, as in this tale, the Baal Shem takes his disciples on a mystical journey. This is known as *Kfitsat ha-Derech*, the "Leaping of the Way," meaning that the wagon in which they ride suddenly begins to move at a great speed,

functioning much like the Divine Chariot in the vision of Ezekiel. This time the Baal Shem Tov leads his disciples closer and closer to the Tree of Life, but he does not reveal this to them, and little by little the Hasidim become fascinated with something they find on the way there. By the time the Besht reaches the Tree of Life, no one is still with him. This theme is strongly echoed in "The Journey to Jerusalem," p. 86, where the Ari directs his disciples to follow him to Jerusalem at once, and their hesitation causes the coming of the Messiah to be delayed. Both tales emphasize the theme of closely following the directions of the master in his teachings so as not to be left behind and both serve as warning tales. The legend most strongly echoed here is that of the four sages who entered Paradise. In that sense, a strong parallel is drawn between the Baal Shem Tov and Rabbi Akiba, who entered Paradise and safely departed as well. So too is the Baal Shem Tov the only one to reach the goal of the quest, the Tree of Life. And this clearly is also intended to be a symbol of the Torah itself that he is leading them to, as the Torah and the Tree of Life are often linked by the passage *It is a tree of life to those who cling to it* (Pr. 3:18), where "it" refers to "wisdom," and has traditionally been understood to refer to the Torah. In this sense, the tale serves as an allegory about how the master leads his disciples to the real treasure of the Torah.

97. *A Crown of Shoes* (Eastern Europe)

From *Gan Ha-Hasidut*, edited by Eliezer Steinmann (Jerusalem: 1957).

The location of the Garden of Eden is identified in various ways in the rabbinic texts. It is usually somewhere in this world, though no one knows where. Furthermore, the way into the Garden is blocked by the angel with the flaming sword (see the note to "The Angel's Sword," p. 189). But in other texts the Garden of Eden is one part of Paradise. Here the the Baal Shem Tov reaches the Garden of Eden and finds the shoes of the Hasidim that have flown off their feet as they celebrated Simhat Torah. Just how they got there is never explained and is understood as a miracle. The point of the tale is to emphasize how happy God is to see Jews celebrate on Simhat Torah, commemorating the completion of the reading of the Torah. Also echoed here is the beautiful talmudic legend about the angel Sandalphon, who weaves garlands out of the prayers of Israel for the Holy One to wear on His Throne of Glory (B. Hag. 13b). Here the shoes are substituted for the prayers, as they are seen by God as equally precious.

98. *The Flaming Tree* (Eastern Europe)

From *Shivhei ha-Besht* by Rabbi Dov Ben Samuel, edited by Samuel A. Horodezky (Berlin: 1922).

There are many miracle tales associated with the Baal Shem Tov, founder of Hasidism. Many of these tales are closely modeled on biblical, midrashic, or kabbalistic sources. In this tale the Baal Shem touches a frozen tree with his finger, turning it into a flaming one that is, of course, reminiscent of the burning bush seen by Moses (Ex. 3:2). Like the bush, it seems to burn without being consumed, this being the reason, perhaps, that the Baal Shem warns his Hasidim not to look back, echoing the warning given to Lot and his family (Gen. 19:17). But Lot's wife did look back and was turned into a pillar of salt (Gen. 19:26). The warning is thus clear at once to the Hasidim, and none of them do look back. The powers that the Baal Shem Tov draws upon are reflected in his name, "Master of the Good Name." Those given this title (the Baal Shem was not the only one; others include Rabbi Adam Baal Shem and Rabbi

Yoel Baal Shem) were believed to possess miraculous powers greater than those of any sorcerer. The difference is that the Baal Shems drew all of their power from God, using the various Names of God and the angels, and especially God's ineffable Name, known as the Tetragrammaton. By correctly pronouncing the Name, combined with the proper spiritual intention, they were able to accomplish anything, as long as it was for the good.

99. *A Visitor from the Other World* (Eastern Europe)

From *Kol Sipurei ha-Besht*. Edited by Yisroel Yakov Klapholtz. (B'nai Brak: 1966).

This tale provides a folk chronicle of how Rabbi Wolf Kitzes changed from being an opponent of the Baal Shem Tov to being one of his most important disciples, later serving as the shofar blower for the Baal Shem Tov. This follows the pattern of tales about the reluctant disciples. See "The Angel of Forgetfulness," p. 81, for another example of this type of tale. "A Visitor from the Other World," and the two that follow are the primary tales about Wolf Kitzes, whose descendant, David Antin, is a contemporary American poet. While many of the Baal Shem Tov's disciples went on to become rebbes on their own, little is heard about Wolf Kitzes in the later tales. In this tale, it takes the death of Wolf Kitzes's student, and his return from Paradise, to convince him that the Baal Shem Tov is an authentic master. But once he is convinced, he goes without hesitation to the Besht. The primary mystical theme here concerns the visiting of the living by the souls of the dead, as a result of an agreement they made while both were living, that the first one to leave this world would report to the other about the World to Come. Here the student hears the Baal Shem Tov teaching in Paradise and returns to this world to report to Wolf Kitzes about how the Baal Shem Tov is honored in heaven, and also to tell him of his heavenly teaching. Thus this tale is clearly an attempt to win over some of the opponents of the Hasidim, who would naturally identify with Wolf Kitzes's initial skepticism about the Baal Shem Tov, which he completely reverses. For another tale on the theme of the dead reporting back to this world, see "The Tale of a Vow" in *LC*, p. 192.

100. *The Master Key* (Eastern Europe)

From *Or Yesharim* (Warsaw: 1884). The primary meaning of this tale is addressed in the following parable of the Baal Shem Tov found in *Keter Shem Tov:* "There is a lock, and every lock has a key that opens it. Some locks can be broken by thieves who can open them without keys—they break the lock." This *mashal* or parable is followed by this *nimshal*, the interpretation: "Every hidden thing has a key. The master key is the miracle that breaks all the locks. The broken heart is the key to all the secrets." Thus the possibility exists that this tale of Wolf Kitzes and the Baal Shem Tov was somehow created around this parable or that the parable was drawn in to serve as the conclusion to the tale. Both tale and parable emphasize the Besht's belief that the true power of prayer lies in its *kavanah* or spiritual intention. For other stories with a similar theme see "The Precious Prayer," p. 86, and "The Field of Souls," p. 204.

101. *The Enchanted Island* (Eastern Europe)

From *Sipurei Tzaddikim* (Cracow: 1886).

Wolf Kitzes was one of the major early disciples of the Baal Shem Tov. His role as the Baal Shem's shofar blower brought him legendary status in the tales of the Baal Shem, and there are a handful of important tales in which he plays a central role. Here he misses the chance to bring messianic redemption, as occurs in many other tales, such as "The Journey to Jerusalem," "The Sabbath Guests," and "The Ladder of Prayers." In other tales, however, such as "The Master Key," he rises to the occasion. In any case, he is one of the most fascinating and complex figures in the circle of the Baal Shem Tov. In another variant of this story, Wolf Kitzes encounters Abraham, and they have a similiar dialogue, with the same results. "The Enchanted Island" is also an example of an illusion tale, a major tale type among these mystical tales. There is a famous parable attributed to the Baal Shem Tov about "The Palace of Illusion," which focuses on the nature of illusion. This parable is found in *Keter Shem Tov* by Aaron of Apt (Zolkiev: 1784, p. 87), as well as in *Degel Machane Ephrayim*, compiled by Moses Hayim Ephraim of Sudikov (Jerusalem: 1963):

> A great and powerful king who had mastered the secrets of illusion built a palace of many chambers that actually did not exist. But to all who approached it, the mirage seemed real. So too did the king surround the palace with obstacles, so that the way to reach it was fraught with danger. A wide river encircled the palace grounds, whose waters ran deep and were too wild to be crossed by boat. And only those who found some way to form a bridge could reach the palace. And even those few who managed this feat found themselves lost in a maze of garden paths that branched off in every direction. (It was said that a man could spend his days lost in that labyrinth.) And of the handful who ever found their way through the forking paths, further obstacles remained: seven walls, each impenetrable and with its own locked gate. And at each gate a guard was stationed, who had been commanded not to permit anyone to pass who could not reply correctly to a riddle. And even those who were clever at riddles and succeeded in reaching the third or fourth gate were usually turned back before they reached the seventh gate, for each succeeding riddle was more difficult. And in the unlikely event of anyone actually reaching the palace itself, his long quest was not complete, for the palace contained a great many chambers, and only one of them was that of the king. So it was that in all the years since the king had brought the palace into being, only one prince among men was said to have succeeded in reaching the door of the chamber of the king. At last there was a wise and righteous man who meditated on this matter and thought to himself: "How is it possible that this merciful king, who has given all his subjects such great abundance, should hide himself and conceal his face? Perhaps all of these obstacles are only an illusion, created to test the perseverance of those who would approach him." And then, for the first time ever, the sage stepped directly into the river, without attempting to build a bridge across it. And at that instant the waters vanished, along with the labyrinth and the seven walls and seven gates, and the inner chamber of the king was revealed.

This parable is a commentary on a line of the Torah: *And I shall surely hide and conceal my face* (Deut. 31:18). The notion of illusion that stands behind it illustrates the concept of *ahizat enayim*, which can be translated as "mirage," "sleight of hand," or "illusion." But behind the mirage that is this world stands the Holy One, who is eternal. In this allegory the king represents God, who has set up the world as a diversion and test. Those who recognize its true nature are then permitted to discern the true nature of God's existence, which is a far greater reward. Note the resemblance of the Baal Shem Tov's parable of illusion to the portrait of heaven found in the

Hekhaloth and other texts. The parallel is quite striking, as the system of symbols is virtually the same. A modern echo of this parable is found in Franz Kafka's famous parable, "Before the Law," from *The Trial*.

102. *The Circle of Fire* (Eastern Europe)

From *Shivhei ha-Besht* by Rabbi Dov Ben Samuel, edited by Samuel A. Horodezky (Berlin: 1922).

The subject of *Ma'aseh Merkavah*, the Mysteries of the Chariot, was considered so esoteric that it is rarely spoken of as directly as it is in this tale. Here the Baal Shem Tov reads one of the Hekhaloth texts, such as *Hekhaloth Rabbati* or, most likely, *3 Enoch*. This is a remarkable tale in that it offers direct evidence that the Hasidim studied these early mystical texts describing heavenly journeys and used them in much the original manner—as powerful invocations to the spirits and part of a process of mystical ascent. This tale also links several ancient Jewish mystical traditions. All of these are linked to *Ma'aseh Merkavah*, the Mysteries of the Chariot, beginning with the vision of Ezekiel and including the three books of Enoch, *1 Enoch*, *2 Enoch*, *and 3 Enoch*. (For translations of the Enoch books, see *The Old Testament Pseudepigrapha*, edited by James H. Charlesworth, Vol. 1, pp. 5–315.) *3 Enoch* is one of the primary Hekhaloth texts. Thus the mystical component in Hasidism can be traced back to the earliest texts of Jewish mysticism, which focus on mystical ascent. In the present tale, Rabbi Dov Baer shares in the visionary experience of the Baal Shem Tov and has a vision of the Prince of the Presence. This is the angel Metatron, the heavenly scribe, who was once Enoch before he ascended to heaven and was transformed into an angel. Some legends suggest that Elijah, who likewise ascended in a chariot, was also transformed into an angel, because he lives forever and often returns to assist those Jews in need of help. This tale indicates the identification of the Hasidim, and especially the Baal Shem Tov, with the ancient Enoch and Hekhalot sects and the use of these texts for mystical purposes. This tale is also unusual in its direct portrayal of mystical experience. Had it been told from the perspective of the Baal Shem Tov rather than that of Rabbi Dov Baer, it might have resembled the account of the ascent in "Unlocking the Gates of Heaven," p. 205. For additional discussion of this theme of mystical ascent, see the note to that tale, p. 332.

103. *The Tale of the Frog* (Eastern Europe)

From *Shivhei ha-Besht* by Rabbi Dov Baer ben Samuel, edited by Samuel A. Horodezky (Berlin: 1922). Also included in *Oseh Pele*, edited by Joseph Farhi (Jerusalem: 1959, p. 197).

This is a famous example of a tale about *gilgul*, or reincarnation. The soul of the sinner is reincarnated inside a giant frog. When he meets the frog, the Baal Shem Tov recognizes that freeing its soul is his purpose in coming to that remote place. The theme of reincarnation is especially strong in the tales of the circle of the Ari in sixteenth-century Safed. The Ari was a master at recognizing the history of a person's soul in all its incarnations. In many respects the first and primary book of tales about the Baal Shem Tov, *Shivhei ha-Besht*, was modeled on the book of tales about the Ari, *Shivhei ha-Ari*. This parallel is clearly indicated in the titles of the books and in the kind of hagiography or legendary biography, that is created. Both books portray a mystical childhood, a period of introspection and hiding, and remarkable accounts of wonders worked by each master. There are also substantial parallels in the types and themes of the tales, including this one. See, for example, "A Stone in the Wall," p. 97.

104. *The Field of Souls* (Eastern Europe)

From *Shivhei ha-Besht* 219, by Rabbi Dov Baer ben Samuel, edited by Samuel A. Horodezky (Berlin: 1922). In the mystical lore of the Jews of Eastern Europe, the souls of the dead often call upon the living to assist them in some way. This grows out of the tradition concerning the Kaddish, the prayer for the dead. The souls of those who have died are said to need the saying of this prayer in order to raise themselves from the world of punishment that is the lot of everyone but the saints and ascend on high. This period of punishment does not last for more than twelve months for those who are punished in Gehenna. Kaddish is recited for only eleven months on the assumption that no one's parents were so evil that they required the full twelve months for purification. In "The Field of Souls" fate sees to it that Rabbi Nathan prays on Yom Kippur at a place where there is a great gathering of souls in need of assistance to ascend on high. Rabbi Nathan views all that happens to divert him from reaching the Baal Shem Tov as a disaster. But it is actually his destiny, for his praying with a broken heart in that place is exactly what the souls require in order to be set free. For a parallel theme, see "The Boy Who Blew the Shofar," p. 127. In "The Field of Souls" Rabbi Nathan reveals the attitude of being a follower, not a master. For in the tales where a master, such as the Baal Shem Tov, becomes lost, he knows it is for a purpose, as in "The Tale of the Frog," p. 203. See also "Repairing Souls," p. 116, about the Or Hayim going off into the mountains alone to repair souls.

105. *Unlocking the Gates of Heaven* (Eastern Europe)

From *Shivhei ha-Besht* by Rabbi Dov Baer ben Samuel, edited by Samuel A. Horodezky (Berlin: 1922).

Hasidic tales often find their models in the earlier tale types found in Jewish literature. Among these models are the Hekhaloth texts, which describe heavenly journeys. Indeed, the Hekhaloth texts not only serve as models for many Hasidic tales, including this one, but quotations from them are sometimes found in such tales. See "The Circle of Fire," p. 202, for an example. Here the soul of the Baal Shem Tov ascends to Paradise during the Yom Kippur service. The way that his mystical trance is described strongly suggests the meditative states of the Hekhaloth sects, as well as the methods for inducing mystical states described by Abraham Abulafia. See *The Mystical Experience in Abraham Abulafia* by Moshe Idel. In the present tale, the forces of evil have succeeded in blocking the prayers of Israel from ascending for the past fifty years. When the Baal Shem ascends to the gates of heaven, he discovers that the gates have been locked with a gigantic lock as big as a city. This too strongly echoes the Hekhaloth texts, such as *Hekhaloth Rabbati*, where it is necessary to get past guards at various palaces in Paradise and in each case the key is a holy name. So too here the Baal Shem receives a holy name from his teacher, the Prophet Ahijah the Shilonite, which serves as the key to the lock, making it possible for all the accumulated prayers to break through to Paradise and reverse the evil decree against the Jews. The Baal Shem's identification of Ahijah as his teacher is significant in that it suggests that he had to turn to a teacher from the past rather than from his own time. The choice of Ahijah probably derives from the tradition that Ahijah was a master of mystical lore. The Talmud (B. Baba Batra 121b) identifies Ahijah as the sixth of seven men whose lifetimes encompass all time: "Seven men spanned the life of the whole world. For

Methuselah saw Adam; Shem saw Methuselah; Jacob saw Shem; Amram saw Jacob; Ahijah the Shilonite saw Amram; Elijah saw Ahijah the Shilonite, and he is still alive." There is a famous letter attributed to the Baal Shem Tov that describes a heavenly ascent, which strongly echoes this story. This letter was said to have been written by the Baal Shem Tov to his brother-in-law, Rabbi Gershom of Kittov, when the latter was in Israel. The letter, first printed in Koretz in 1781 and later published in *Ben Porat Yosef* by Yakov Yosef of Polonnoye in 1815, includes the following account:

> On Rosh Hashanah of 1750 I pronounced a holy name and ascended on high. This time I saw visions such as I have never seen, and what I learned words cannot express. . . . As I ascended, I entered the hidden palaces of heaven, one after another. All the mysteries of heaven are concealed in those palaces, and all the treasuries of heaven as well. . . . And I rose from rung to rung until I reached the palace of the Messiah, where the Messiah teaches Torah with all the authors of the Midrash, the saints and the seven shepherds. My joy was so great that for a moment I thought my soul had taken leave of my body. . . . I asked the Messiah, "When will my Master come?" and he replied, "When your teachings are known in the world."

106. *The Healing Spring* (Eastern Europe)
From *Kav ha-Yashar* by Tsvi Hirsh Kaidanover (Frankfurt: 1903).
This tale is a Hasidic retelling of the story of Moses striking the rock in the wilderness and water pouring forth (Ex. 17:5–6). It is one of several miracle tales that link the Baal Shem Tov to Moses. See also "The Flaming Tree," p. 195, which ties the Baal Shem to the story of Moses and the Burning Bush. There really are two tales here. The first recounts the miracle of the creation of the well by the Baal Shem Tov; the second tells the history of the well after that. In the course of the tale, the well clearly comes to symbolize the essential Jewish spirit, beginning to flow by a miracle. For a long time it flows strongly; then the flow comes to an end, symbolizing the absence of faith. At last it is rediscovered, signifying a spiritual renewal. If read this way, this tale can also be seen as a kind of commentary on Hasidism as a renewal and continuation of the path of the Ari, who served as the model of the Baal Shem Tov. Judaism at the time of the Baal Shem Tov was still reacting against the debacle of the false messiah, Shabbatai Zevi. Because kabbalistic prophecies pointing to the advent of the Messiah had been proven wrong, and because Shabbatai Zevi and his apostle, Nathan of Gaza, had presented him in kabbalistic as well as messianic terms, there was a countermovement against the study of the Kabbalah. From an allegorical standpoint, the story seems to indicate that the drought of the well lasts for a few generations, as did the conservative forces in Judaism who discouraged mystical studies. This mystical dimension, on the other hand, was an essential element in the teachings of the Baal Shem Tov. This is a good example of the hagiographic miracle tales that grew up around the Baal Shem Tov.

107. *Lighting a Fire* (Eastern Europe)
From *Knesset Israel*, edited by Reuven Zak (Warsaw: 1866, 13a).
The source of this tale is a collection of tales about Rabbi Israel of Rizhin, which firmly places him in the line of the key Hasidic rabbis. In the original version of this

legend, the Baal Shem Tov has a wax candle made and affixes it to the tree to light. This is a strange custom with no direct Jewish precedents, and probably for this reason most of the extensive retellings of this tale, including the present one, have described the Baal Shem Tov as lighting a fire, without specifying what kind of fire it was. Of course, candle lighting is commonly done by Jews every Sabbath, and the lighting of a *yahrzeit* candle is used to commemorate the death of a relative. But affixing a candle to a tree seems to have pagan overtones. According to Professor Dov Noy, however, the lighting of candles was done for those who were sick, with the wick of the candle measured by the base of the tomb of a highly regarded sage or saint. This tale stresses the importance of the intention of the heart. Even though much of the ritual is lost, it is effective because the intention is true. This tale also emphasizes a common theme in Jewish lore: that the ancients knew a great deal more than the generations that followed. For an additional discussion of this tale, see *Kabbalah* by Moshe Idel, pp. 270–71 and p. 397, notes 92–94. Noting that in the original version the candle is lit to cure an only son, a pious young man who is very ill, Idel identifies the candle as a substitute for the soul of the son, according to the verse *The spirit of man is the candle of God* (Prov. 20:27). He also identifies the tree as symbolizing the Tree of Souls. By affixing the candle to the tree and lighting it, he is affirming the boy's link to the Tree of Souls and thus to life. Thus the Baal Shem Tov is seen as the preeminent master, and each subsequent generation is a little less able to follow in his footsteps. Nevertheless, the tale stresses that it is worthwhile to retain whatever survives of the original tradition, and this in itself will be found to suffice. Such tales on the theme of how the earlier generations were greater than the later ones are common in Jewish literature. See *Jewish Preaching*, edited by Marc Saperstein, p. 425. A Hasidic tale on a very similiar theme is that of Rabbi Levi Yitzhak of Berditchev's "The King Who Loved Music," from *Toldot Aharon*, compiled by Aaron of Zhitomir (Lemberg: 1864), as follows:

There once was a king who loved music. Therefore he asked the finest musicians in the land to come to the palace at sunrise each morning to play for him. This suited the king well, as he was an early riser, but some of the musicians were not. Recognizing this, the king saw to it that those who arrived on time were given an extra reward, and that those who arrived even earlier, before sunrise, received a double reward. Nevertheless, it was not the reward that motivated the musicians to play for the king, but their love and respect for him and their mutual delight in music. For the musicians greatly loved to perform together, and the king loved to hear their music. These musicians served the king for many years, but in time they grew old and died, and the sons of the musicians sought to take their places. But unlike their fathers, they did not want to play out of respect for the king or love of music, but were intent only on the reward. Nor were they masters of their instruments, for although their fathers had sought to train them to be musicians, they had failed to practice, and as a result they had never acquired the art of making beautiful music. Needless to say, the music they played was harsh and offensive to the king's ears. Still, out of respect for their fathers, he did not send them away or replace them. Instead the king remained patient in the hope that they would eventually improve. And so it was that some of them did recover the love of music that had sustained their fathers, and they arrived even earlier to practice in a quiet corner and remained after the others had departed so that they might hone their skills. The king recognized these efforts and was pleased. And at last the day came when these few musicians formed the core of a new orchestra that played flowing melodies. True, their music did not attain the perfect harmony of their fathers, but it still sufficed to bring joy to the king, and thus he received it with favor.

This tale of Rabbi Levi Yitzhak is an allegory about prayer, and of the importance of *kavanah*, or spiritual intensity, in praying. The king, representing God, derives great pleasure from the harmonies attained by the musicians, representing devout Jews who arrive shortly after sunrise each day to pray together. The generational gap between fathers and sons, which has grown even wider in our time, can be traced, according to Rabbi Levi Yitzhak, to the failure to retain the spiritual intensity of prayer. But this parable is more optimistic than "Lighting a Fire" in that it holds out the possibility that an effort on the part of the later generation will eventually raise them up almost to the level achieved by their fathers.

The Circle of Reb Pinhas of Koretz

108. *Opening a Verse* (Eastern Europe)
Based on *Midrash Pinhas* by Rabbi Pinhas of Koretz (Warsaw: 1876).
Many Jewish mystical tales focus on the power of the Word. In the Kabbalah a word not only has meaning, but the power of its meaning. That is why God's Name, the Tetragrammaton, has the ultimate power of God—if its secret pronunciation is known. Since even the world itself was brought into being by words, when *God said, "Let there be light." And there was light* (Gen. 1:3), the rabbis sought to analyze words in a wide variety of ways, not only for their literal meanings, but for their symbolic meanings as well. Thus the letters were scrutinized, along with the traditions concerning those letters, as well as the number of letters and the total reached by adding together the letters of a word. (In Hebrew each letter also has a numerical value.) Then the numerical total of one word was matched against others in what is known as *gematria*. Here Rabbi Pinhas of Koretz, an early Hasidic figure, who was a contemporary of the Baal Shem Tov, demonstrates the power of a word of the Torah to his Hasidim. In fact, he triggers a mystical vision for them, using his great powers as the primary Jewish conjurer after the Baal Shem Tov, on a par not only with the Baal Shem but also with Rabbi Judah Loew of Prague, who created the golem. Reb Pinhas also taught Rabbi Elimelech of Lizensk, the last of the great Hasidic wonder workers. This is another example of the illusion tale, in which a short time is perceived as a very long one, with minutes lasting for what seem to be years. See the note to "Isaac's Ascent," p. 278, for further discussion of the illusion tale. For background information on Reb Pinhas of Koretz, see *The Circle of the Baal Shem Tov: Studies in Hasidism* by Abraham J. Heschel, edited by H. Dresner, pp. 1–43.

109. *The Angel of the Zohar* (Eastern Europe)
Based on *Tosefta Midrash Pinhas*, edited by Betzalel Joseph of Galina (Lemberg: 1896).
Because of Reb Pinhas's deep love of the Zohar, the Angel of the Zohar became his guardian angel, much as the spirit of the tractate Hagigah became the guardian of the man who studied Hagigah. See "The Spirit of Hagigah," p. 179. This tale takes an additional turn by identifying Reb Pinhas himself as the Angel of the Zohar, suggest-

ing that he was the angel incarnate, whose great secret was discovered by the Hasid hidden in the rabbi's cabinet. The Ari also was regarded by his followers as a human angel. This is a good example of the kind of legendary transformation found in Hasidic lore, where the rebbe is so idealized that he even transcends the human and becomes an angel. From a thematic perspective, this tale takes the motif of the *maggid*, the angel or spirit of a book who speaks through the mouth of a human, as in the case of the *maggid* of Joseph Caro, and carries it a step further, where Reb Pinhas is transformed into this angel when he studies the Zohar. See "The Angel of the Mishnah," p. 112.

110. *The Angel of Friendship* (Eastern Europe)
Based on *Midrash Pinhas* by Rabbi Pinhas of Koretz (Warsaw: 1876).

This haunting legend of the Angel of Friendship is one of the best known in Hasidic lore. For Reb Pinhas the angel symbolizes the love and affection that grow up between two people. But the angel's continued existence depends on them, and on how often they renew their friendship. If they do not, the angel dies. This tale grows out of the talmudic tradition that "Every day ministering angels are created from the fiery stream, and utter song, and cease to be" (B. Hag. 14a). The theme of the transformation of the angels is a common one in kabbalistic and Hasidic lore. The key passage behind the belief in imperfect angels is Mishnah Avot 4:2: "The reward for a good deed is a good deed, and the reward for a transgression is a transgression." Rabbi Hayim Vital offers the kabbalistic reinterpretation of this passage in *Sha'arey Kedushah*, where he writes that "The diligent study of the Law and the performance of the divine commandments brings about the creation of a new angel." This serves as an explanation for the existence of the *maggidim*, the angelic figures who are said to visit sages and bring them heavenly mysteries. Joseph Caro, author of the *Shulchan Aruch*, was famous for being visited by such a *maggid*. See "The Angel of the Mishnah," p. 112 and the accompanying note. A discussion of the transformation from evil angels into good ones is also found in the teachings of Reb Pinhas of Koretz in *Midrash Pinhas*: "Every good deed turns into an angel. But if the deed is imperfect, so is the angel. Perhaps it will be mute. What a disgrace to be served in Paradise by such an angel. Or it might have an arm or leg missing. And these imperfections can only be repaired by the repentance of the one who brought the imperfect angel into being." This kind of transformation is known as *tikkun* or repair, and it is parallel to the mystical cosmology of the Ari, where every good deed is said to raise up a fallen spark. For more on the theme of imperfect angels see "The Blind Angel," p. 259, and the accompanying note. Another source that is echoed here is found in *Ma'aysiot Noraim ve-Niflaim* (Cracow: 1896), concerning the gaon Rabbi Yehezkel of Prague. He was said to have stated that "The angels that are found in the upper world were created by the deeds of the *Tzaddikim*." Note that Reb Pinhas has the angel that comes into being as a result of friendship, or, by implication, love, function as a symbolic child. This expands the circumstances for the creation of an angel to include angels created by human interaction.

111. *The Underground Forest* (Eastern Europe)
From *Maaysiot ve'shichot Tzaddikim* (Warsaw: 1881). Also found in *Sefer ha-Maaysiot*, edited by Mordecai Ben Yehezkel (Tel Aviv: 1937, Vol. IV, p. 228).

This tale presents a classic example of Reb Pinhas of Koretz in the role of Jewish conjurer. He sends the student into a world of illusion, requiring a great struggle, which appears to last for ages, then breaks the illusion and reveals that only a short time has passed. The model for the conjurer in these illusion tales is King Solomon in "The Beggar King" in *EV*, p. 59, about Solomon's efforts to recover his throne. Many such tales are found concerning the late medieval wonder worker Rabbi Adam. See "The Enchanted Journey" and "The King's Dream" in *EV*, pp. 181 and. 197, respectively, and "The Enchanted Palace" in *MT*, p. 245. Here the journey is also an interior one, one of living out his own inner myth. Likewise, Reb Pinhas uses his powers to reveal the inner world to his Hasidim, which is also the world of the Divine.

112. *Reb Pinhas and the Angel of Death* (Eastern Europe)

From *Tosefta Midrash Pinhas*, edited by Betzalel Joshua of Galina (Lemberg: 1896). One of the primary types of tales about the Angel of Death has the angel come to a worthy rabbi and delicately raise the issue of death. The most famous such tales are found in the Talmud, concerning the death of Moses and Rabbi Joshua ben Levi and the Angel of Death (B. Ket. 77a). Moses refuses to be taken from this world by the Angel of Death, and instead he receives the Kiss of the *Shekhinah*, which carries his soul directly into the Other World. This is part of a tradition of the six who entered Paradise alive by the Kiss of the *Shekhinah* (B. Baba Batra 17a). The others are Abraham, Isaac, Jacob, Aaron, and Miriam. As for Rabbi Joshua ben Levi, he tricks the Angel of Death into letting him hold the angel's sword and jumps into the Garden of Eden and refuses to return it (B. Ket. 77a). In these cases, as well as in "Reb Pinhas and the Angel of Death," the *Malach ha-Moves*, the Angel of Death, is polite. Here the Angel of Death approaches Reb Pinhas disguised as a Hasid, giving him a *kvittel* or petition. Reb Pinhas responds with a petition of his own, expressing his desire to go to Gehenna, the Jewish hell, rather than to Paradise. Reb Pinhas believes he can assist the souls of those being punished there. This theme of assisting the souls of the dead is found in other tales, such as "Repairing Souls," p. 116, and "The Field of Souls," p. 204. After returning to heaven for further instructions, the Angel of Death comes back and gives Reb Pinhas a holy name that can take him to one place or the other—depending on how it is pronounced. This tale echoes as well the famous talmudic account about Rabban Yohanan ben Zakkai, who, when near death, wept because he was not certain if the path he would be required to take would lead to heaven or hell. In contrast, Reb Pinhas ends up in heaven despite his best efforts to go to Gehenna (Gen. Rab. 28). The point is that Reb Pinhas was destined for Paradise, and even he could do nothing about it. The echoes of rabbinic models in Hasidic tales serve, above all, to insist that the Hasidic masters were of the same stature as the great sages of the past. For an example of how the Angel of Death treats everyone else, see "The Bridegroom and the Angel of Death," p. 162. See also "The Bridegroom" in *LC*, p. 123 (Oxford edition), where the Angel of Death comes as a suitor and carries off a maiden whose father made her wait too long for her intended one.

The Circle of Reb Elimelech of Lizensk

113. *The Woman in the Forest* (Eastern Europe)

From *Ohel Elimelech*, edited by A. S. B. Michelson (Parmishla: 1870). Variants are found in *Sefer Or Yesharim*, story no. 199, edited by Moshe Hayim Kleinmann of Brisk, (Warsaw: 1884), *Zikaron Tov* (Piotrkow: 1892), and *Ohole Shem* (Bilgorai: 1910).

This story is linked to both Rabbi Elimelech of Lizensk and his famous student, the Seer of Lublin, whose vision occurs when he goes to visit his teacher. Thus this

temptation by Lilith takes place in every generation, with the best figures singled out
for her approach. The woman in this tale, who represents lust incarnate, is not
identified. But everyone who heard it knew exactly who she was: Lilith or one of the
daughters of Lilith. So vivid was the presence of Lilith in their lives that she became
the projection of their sexual fantasies and fears. In this tale, which can be viewed as a
Hasidic sexual fantasy, the woman's long hair indicates that she is unmarried, while
her comment about having bathed in the spring informs him that she has purified
herself in a *mikveh*. Indeed, she is appealing to his knowledge of the Law when she
tells him that the sin will be slight and the pleasure abundant. That is because, while
forbidden, Jewish law does not consider an intimate encounter between a married man
and an unmarried woman as adultery. (We can assume that Rabbi Elimelech is married, since the age for marriage was quite young.) By contrast, the reverse—an affair
between a married woman and an unmarried man—is defined as adultery (Deut.
22:22). Here Reb Elimelech resists, but barely. The power of the *Yetzer ha-Ra*, the
Evil Inclination, affects everyone on this earth, even rebbes. There is also a compen-
sating force, the *Yetzer ha-Tov*, the Good Inclination. But, as might be expected,
much more is heard of the *Yetzer ha-Ra* in Jewish lore than there is of the *Yetzer ha-
Tov*. Talmudic parallels to this legend are found concerning many of the great sages,
including Rabbi Akiba who is said to have barely resisted a naked woman he saw in a
tree; the woman turned out to be Satan in disguise (B. Kid. 81a). A similar tale is told
about Rabbi Meir (B. Kid. 80a). See the note to "The Temptations of Rabbi Akiba" by
David Pinski in *GNU*, p. 672, for further discussion of these talmudic tales.

114. *A Bowl of Soup* (Eastern Europe)
From *Em la-Binah*, edited by Yekutiel Aryeh Kamelhar (Lemberg: 1909). Also
found in *Me'or V'Shemesh*.

This is the most famous tale about Rabbi Elimelech of Lizensk in his role of Jewish
wonder worker. The powers he demonstrates here are reminiscent of those described
in the tales about Rabbi Adam. See especially "The Magic Mirror of Rabbi Adam" in
EV, p. 187. In its core, this is a tale about sympathetic magic. By using his great
powers of concentration and drawing on his kabbalistic knowledge, Reb Pinhas is able
to cause the inkwell of the king to spill at the very instant Reb Pinhas knocks over his
own bowl of soup. In almost all such stories where these mystical powers are drawn
on, the rabbi is responding to a dire situation, often the danger of a pogrom. The
people lived in great fear of these evil decrees, and the fantasy of magically reversing
them is a common theme in many Jewish folktales.

115. *The Wine of Paradise* (Eastern Europe)
From *Devarim Arevim*, edited by Dov Ehrmann (Munkacs: 1863). A variant is
found in *Ohel Elimelech*, edited by A. S. B. Michelson (Parmishla: 1870).

This tale can be seen as parallel to "The Underground Forest," p. 214, in which
Reb Pinhas of Koretz also creates an illusion for a student. It is an even closer variant
of the following tale, "The Young Magician." In the present tale, it is Reb Elimelech
of Lizensk, the primary disciple of Reb Pinhas, who creates a test for a student,
ordering him to the cemetery to retrieve the wine of Paradise. Above all, the tale
demonstrates the consummate mystical skills of Reb Elimelech, who transports the
student from this world to the Other Side. And though the student, who appeared
unworthy to begin with, fails the test, he learns a lesson about the power of the world
of the spirits that he will never forget.

116. *The Young Magician* (Eastern Europe)
From *Ohel Elimelech*, edited by A. S. B. Michelson (Parmishla: 1870). A variant is found in *Devarim Arevim*, edited by Dov Ehrmann (Munkacs: 1863).

This tale is a close variant of the previous tale, "The Wine of Paradise." Here a young student has delved into the study of kabbalistic magic, and Reb Elimelech gives him an unexpected lesson. There are many variants of this tale in Jewish lore, in which a sorcerer or rabbinical wonder worker teaches a would-be student to have respect for the powers of magic. See "The Enchanted Well" in *MT*, p. 150. "The Young Magician" also underscores the great powers of Reb Elimelech and is another example of the illusion tale, which is so popular in Jewish lore. For a further discussion of illusion tales, see the note to "The Magic Flock," p. 278. For a Kurdish variant of this tale see "The Elusive Diamond in *LC*, p. 117 (Oxford edition).

117. *Reb Shmelke's Whip* (Eastern Europe)
From *The Dybbuk*, Act I (Yiddish) by S. Ansky (1926).

This tale about Reb Shmelke of Nikolsburg was originally collected by S. Ansky during one of his expeditions and was included in the first act of his world-famous play *The Dybbuk*. Reb Shmelke is not usually portrayed as being this fierce, but his loyalty to the poor rather than the rich is well known, and the rich man in this tale rejects the authority of the rabbi, as well as that of the Torah. The "whip" that Reb Shmelke uses is the Primal Serpent, known as the *Nahash ha-Kadmoni*, a kabbalistic concept that represents a kind of archetypal serpent, over which Reb Shmelke has sufficient control to call upon as he wishes. This concept evolves in kabbalistic thought from the speaking serpent of Genesis into a more archetypal being, much as Lilith came to represent a principle of evil in the kabbalistic cosmology. This suggests that the great Hasidic masters not only understood how to align their lives with the side of good, but also how to control the elements of evil. It is interesting to note that in *The Dybbuk* four Hasidim discuss this tale after telling it, creating a kind of commentary about it. One of them argues that it couldn't have been the Primal Serpent that Reb Shmelke called forth, since that serpent was Satan, the Evil One. Another replies that there were many witnesses to this event, and therefore it should not be questioned. The first wonders if there are any names that can call forth the Evil One, and a third replies that he can be called forth only with God's Name, the Tetragrammaton. This, then, is what Reb Shmelke must have done. An interesting parallel to the concept of the Primal Serpent is found in the Midrash as a way of explaining what appears to be a fragmentary text in Exodus about the *bridegroom of blood* (Ex. 4:24–26). Here God sends the angels Af and Hemah (wrath and anger personified) in the guise of serpents to swallow Moses from his head to the place of the circumcision, then to spit him out and swallow him again, from his feet to the same place. Zipporah, the wife of Moses, concludes that God is angry because they have not circumcised one of their sons and does it at once (B. Ned. 32a and Ex. Rab. 5:8). In some versions of this legend only one angel, Uriel, is said to be present, and in other versions the angel is not named.

118. *Three Stars* (Eastern Europe)
From *Sipure Beit Din shel Ma'alah*, edited by Yisroel Yakov Klapholtz (B'nai Brak: 1978). This story is attributed to Miriam of Mohilev, the sister of Reb Shmelke, who is said to have told it to Reb Abraham Yehoshua Heschel, the Apter Rebbe.

This story reflects the tensions between the Hasidim and their neighbors, known as the *Mitnagdim* or "opponents" of the Hasidim. The Hasidim were more flexible in their interpretations of the time for prayer, which was unacceptable to the *Mitnagdim*. Also, the Hasidim created new traditions of their own, which quickly became regarded as *Minhagim* or local traditions. In particular, some Hasidic rabbis sought to preserve the holy presence of the Sabbath as long as possible and were loath to let it go, a practice, known as *Tosefet Shabbat*, with roots as far back as the Talmud. For they firmly believed that on the Sabbath every person received a second soul, and this soul remained with him throughout the Sabbath. But when the Sabbath ended and the *Havdalah* ceremony was performed, the extra soul departed until the following Sabbath. Therefore some rabbis delayed saying *Havdalah* as long as possible, even until the middle of the night. (Indeed, there were instances of those who extended the Sabbath until Wednesday, when they began preparing for the coming Sabbath.) In some interpretations, this second soul is identified with the Sabbath Queen, the *Shekhinah*, who is welcomed every Sabbath. Technically speaking, the arrival of the end of the Sabbath is defined by the ability to recognize three stars, as stated in Mishnah Brachot 1:1. It is at this precise time that a *Mitnagdid* would say *Havdalah*, the ceremony that separates the Sabbath from the rest of the week. But many Hasidim ignored the stars and continued to study Torah for several more hours, unwilling to let go of the spirit of the Sabbath that they so loved. As this story clearly indicates, this interpretation of the Law was frowned upon by the the the *Mitnagdim*. According to rabbinic lore, those punished in Gehenna are set free during the Sabbath. A ghost raised in *Pesikta Rabbati* 23 explains the policies of punishment after death: "We are punished on every day of the week, but we are allowed to rest on the Sabbath up to the time when the order of prayers for the close of the Sabbath is finished." This story of Reb Shmelke, which has the structure of a joke, implies that this extension of the Sabbath beyond the three stars is recognized on high as well. Nevertheless, the *Mitnagdid* is forced to return to Gehenna promptly at the end of the Sabbath, according to the interpretation he espoused while living. See the story "Sabbath in Gehenna" by I. B. Singer in *GNC*, pp. 185ff.

119. *The Shadow on the Wall* (Eastern Europe)
From *Siftei Tzaddikim*, edited by Solomon Mutsafi (Jerusalem: 1980). Variants are found in *Ahavat Shalom*, edited by Menahem Mendel ben Joseph (Jerusalem: 1976), and *Imrey Noam*, edited by Aaron Chorin (Pragne: 1798).
The mysterious shadow is the focus of many supernatural tales. Here Reb Elimelech, the great Hasidic sorcerer, is able to separate himself from his shadow and send it wherever he wishes. He sends it to Reb Zushya, his brother, to warn him of impending danger. Other tales, such as "A Bowl of Soup," p. 222, demonstrate Reb Elimelech's ability to affect events at a distance from himself. In "A Bowl of Soup" he draws on sympathetic magic. Here he detaches his "shape," a kind of image of himself, and sends it on a mission. In *Imrey Noam* it is written that "There are great Tzaddikim who are able to separate their shape from the material world, and send it to another place." This is one of several tales that involve both Reb Elimelech and his brother, Zushya. The Hebrew term for shadow or silhouette, *tsel*, is very close to *tselem*, which is the kabbalistic term for astral body. *Tselem* can also be translated as "image," as in Gen 1:27: *And God created man in His own image*. Thus Reb Elimelech's magic can be seen as a kind of astral projection and the image that appears on the wall as a kind of silhouette. For another example of this kind of magic, see "Rabbi Naftali's Trance," p. 152, and the accompanying note.

120. *The Garden of the Torah* (Eastern Europe)

From *Sipurei Ya'akov* by Yakov Sofer (Huzyatin: 1904). Also *Ohel Yitzhak* (Piatrakov: 1888) and *Ohel Elimelech* edited by by A. S. B. Michelson (Parmishla: 1870).

This tale provides another example of Reb Elimelech's great powers. Recognizing that Reb Shmelke needs rest, he encourages him to sleep, and he consequently sleeps so long he alarms everyone around him except Elimelech, who not only knows what he is dreaming about—a visit to the Garden of Eden—but is also there with him at the same time. This story offers a clear example of how the world of dreams serves as a gateway to the mystical world, and how mystical figures such as Elimelech can control events not only in this world, but in the world of dreams as well. The story also suggests that the power of God was really what sustained Reb Shmelke in his dream/vision. For when Reb Elimelech puts his hand over the *mezuzzah*, which contains God's Name, Reb Shmelke immediately awakens.

The Circle of Reb Nachman of Bratslav

121. *A Vision of Light* (Eastern Europe)

From *Shivhei Moharan* by Rabbi Nathan of Nemirov, no. 231 (Jerusalem: 1982).

This childhood mystical experience was recounted by Rabbi Nachman and recorded by his scribe, Rabbi Nathan of Nemirov. By all accounts, Rabbi Nachman was an unusual child, deeply concerned from an early age with spiritual matters. He was said to have spent many hours lying on the grave of his great-grandfather, the Baal Shem Tov, communing with him. He also was said to have subjected himself to fasting from a very young age, as well as other forms of self-denial. In this tale the young child seeks, in a child-like fashion, to experience the Divine. He purifies himself in the *mikveh* and goes into the House of Study, seeking some kind of affirmation of God. When this does not come as expected, he is greatly disappointed and weeps for many hours. At last, when he opens his eyes, the lights of the candles provoke an experience that has distinctly mystical overtones and produces a great sense of peace in the child. In another account of a childhood experience, Rabbi Nachman described how he wanted to see the soul of one who had died. He focused on this for so long that at last he did have such a vision, but because the one he saw was a sinner, the sight so frightened him that he ran from the room terrified [*Hayey Moharan* 7, (Lemberg: 1874)]. Later he was said to have seen the souls of many people and to have assisted these souls in any way that he could. Together these accounts suggest a child very sensitive to spiritual concerns, who took his heritage as a descendant of the Baal Shem Tov very seriously and consequently opened himself to spiritual forces at a very early age.

122. *The Scribe* (Eastern Europe)

From the memory of Rabbi Gedaliah Fleer. Further accounts of the first meeting of Rabbi Nachman and Rabbi Nathan are found in *Shivhei Moharan* 11a, no. 43 and no. 333.

Reb Nachman of Bratslav was blessed with an extremely devoted *sopher*, or scribe, Reb Nathan of Nemirov. This tale recounts how Reb Nachman first revealed himself to Reb Nathan in a dream. The dream has a strong echo of the dream of Jacob in Genesis 28:10–22, except that here Reb Nathan climbs the heavenly ladder and glimpses the mysterious man at the top, who turns out to be Reb Nachman. This tale emphasizes the element of destiny in their partnership, as well as hinting at Reb Nachman's ability to single him out even before they had met. It also echoes the legendary account of how Wolf Kitzes became a close disciple of the Baal Shem Tov. See "A Visitor from the Other World," p. 196. Note that dreams were of great importance to Reb Nachman, and that the dreams he reported to his Hasidim, recorded by Reb Nathan, strongly resemble the famous tales he told to his Hasidim. See the selection of Rabbi Nachman's dreams in *Rabbinic Fantasies*, edited by David Stern and Mark Jay Mirsky, pp. 333–47.

123. *The Sabbath Fish* (Eastern Europe)
From *Sipurei Tzaddikim* (Cracow: 1886). This tale was recounted by Reb Nachman Tulchiner, a close disciple of Reb Nathan of Nemirov.

This is a tale of *gilgul*, the transmigration of souls. The process of *gilgul* entails many stages and reincarnations, but after a certain number of reincarnations the soul reaches a point where it can be set free from the cycle of reincarnation. In some respects, this spiral of reincarnation resembles the Hindu concepts of *karma* and *nirvana*. *Karma* posits that the way a person lives in this life determines whether he will be reborn at a higher or lower level of *karma*. The highest stage is *nirvana*, where the spiral of reincarnation comes to an end. Here Rabbi Nathan of Nemirov receives the task of freeing his own father's soul in the shape of a Sabbath fish. The belief here is that the soul can be set free if the fish is eaten at a meal at which a blessing has been said. The sanctified soul, its body used for a good purpose, is consequently set free. But if this opportunity is missed, the soul is condemned to a new cycle of reincarnation. The fish is delivered, Rabbi Nathan fulfills the ritual of eating the fish, and his father's soul is set free. Compare this motif of the eating of the fish in the famous tale "The Fishhead," about possession in the time of Rabbi Isaac Luria, from *Shivhei ha-Ari*. Here a *dybbuk* has attached itself to that fish, and eating the fishhead brings on a terrible case of possession, requiring exorcism. But in "The Sabbath Fish" the fish bears a good spirit, the soul of Rabbi Nathan's father. If there is any hint of possession here, it is more like the positive possession of the *ibur*. See the Introduction for background on the *ibur*, p. 7. See also the notes to "The *Tefillin* of the Or Hayim," p. 307, and "A Kiss from the Master," p. 295. Note also Rabbi Nachman's role in "The Sabbath Fish": he has complete knowledge of the events. There is even a hint that he somehow arranged it, much as Rabbi Naftali does in "Rabbi Naftali's Trance," p. 152. There Rabbi Naftali conspires with heaven to have the soul of a man who has died come to earth to give his widow a *get*, a bill of divorcement. See "The Voice in the Tree," p. 177, for another tale about the transformations involved in the stages of *gilgul*.

124. *The Sword of the Messiah* (Eastern Europe)
From *Sipurei Tzaddikim* (Cracow: 1886).

This tale closely resembles the Hekhaloth texts describing heavenly journeys, as well as the talmudic legend of the four sages who entered Paradise (B. Hag. 14b). Reb Shmuel Isaac was one of Reb Nachman's close disciples, from the same circle as Reb Nathan of Nemirov, Reb Nachman's scribe, and Reb Shimon, his first disciple. This tale describes a prophetic vision of Reb Shmuel Isaac, the only one that was preserved. Shmuel Isaac is said to have had many such visions, which he recorded in a notebook that was lost. In this vision, Reb Shmuel Isaac ascends Jacob's ladder to the Messiah's palace. He does not specify if it is his soul or his body that ascends, for he does not distinguish between them here. Instead, he experiences the vision firsthand. See the Introduction, p. 30, for more on the issue of bodily or soul ascent. Such visions of heavenly journeys are rare in Hasidic literature. The most famous of these is described in a letter attributed to the Baal Shem Tov sent to his brother-in-law, Reb Gershon. Here the Baal Shem's heavenly ascent closely resembles the accounts in the Hekhaloth texts. See the note to "Unlocking the Gates of Heaven," p. 205. In this tale it is explicitly the soul of the Baal Shem that ascends, as his body remains on earth, observed by others, in a state of mystical possession. For other tales about the palace of the Messiah, see "The Golden Dove," p. 41 and "The Ladder of Prayer," p. 191.

125. *The Souls of Trees* (Eastern Europe)
From *Sihot Moharan* in *Hayey Moharan* by Rabbi Nathan of Bratslav, no. 535 (Lemberg: 1874).

Here Rabbi Nachman is portrayed as being so sensitive to the existence of surrounding souls that while sleeping in an inn he has a nightmare about a massacre, which turns out to have been brought on by the crying out of the souls of young trees that were cut down to build that inn. Of great interest is how Reb Nachman discovers this meaning of his dream, which otherwise does not point to the suffering of trees. By opening a book at random and pointing to a passage, Rabbi Nachman uses a method of Jewish divination known as *sheilat sefer*. But instead of doing it from the Bible, which is the most common method, Rabbi Nachman opens a book he has brought with him and blindly points to this passage: "Cutting down a tree before its time is like killing a soul" (B. Sukkah 29a). It gives him the essential clue to link the dream with the trees. As a master of allegory, Rabbi Nachman has no difficult understanding the meaning of the oracle. With this method of divination, it is understood that the reply is from God and contains an answer of some kind. Note that Rabbi Nachman does the act of divination at once on waking, despite the presence of all those who have come because of his crying out, and without explanation. For in divination it is important that nothing is permitted to cloud the reply.

126. *Divining from the Zohar* (Eastern Europe)
IFA 487, collected by S. Arnest from Reb Zaidel Buch.

This is an oral tale that portrays Rabbi Nachman using a well-established Jewish method of divination by opening a holy book at random. In "The Souls of Trees" p. 236, Rabbi Nachman opened a book that quoted the Talmud, but in this case it was the Zohar, the central text of Kabbalah, that he used. See the previous note. Here the precise passage that he received is not mentioned, except to say that it was from the *parashah* of *Mishpatim*. Somehow, Rabbi Nachman learns from it of a kidnapping half a world away, as well as where the kidnapped son of the Kadi had been taken. This tale differs from "The Souls of Trees" in that the text of the Zohar does not merely gave him a hint of the knowledge. Rather, it seems to hint that Rabbi Nachman was using the Zohar as a visionary tool, and that he was somehow transported to see the events he later described, which proved to be true. Of course, such a tale portrays the rebbe as having great magical powers, powers that Rabbi Nachman rarely calls upon except in times of great need. One of the intriguing aspects of this tale is its portrayal of the harmonious relations between Rabbi Nachman and the Kadi.

127. *The Angel of Losses* (Eastern Europe)
From *Be'er Hasidut*, edited by Eliezer Steinmann (Tel Aviv: 1960, Vol. I, p. 189).

Reb Nachman's teachings, as recorded by his scribe, Reb Nathan of Nemirov, are fascinating in that they often follow unlikely routes and arrive at mysterious conclusions. This tale is an example of such a teaching. Much like Reb Pinhas of Koretz, Rabbi Nachman was highly aware of the surrounding spirits. For Reb Pinhas these were often angels. See, for example, "The Angel of Friendship," p. 213. Here too Rabbi Nachman recognizes an angel that is invisible to all the others. In this case it is an obscure angel that he finds, the Angel of Losses. The angel Yodea and his servants search for what has been lost. The kind of work that this angel does is clearly linked to the myth of the Ari. For the second phase of this myth concerns gathering the scattered sparks. These are not unlike the losses that Yodea collects, for the sparks too have been lost. "*Yodea*" means "to know." Thus the angel's name reflects its purpose, which is to recall that which has been lost. It is possible that Rabbi Nachman created this angel for the purpose of making the myth of the Ari his own by transforming it into the myth of the angel Yodea, for there does not appear to be any prior reference to such an angel. This tale clearly indicates that the myth of the Ari is at the core of Rabbi Nachman's own teachings and how he had made the myth his own.

128. *The Book That Was Burned* (Eastern Europe)
From *Hayey Moharan* 66-73 by Rabbi Nathan of Bratslav, edited by Rabbi Nachman Goldstein of Tcherin. (Lemberg: 1874.)

The book that was burned was subsequently referred to as *Sefer ha-Nisraf*, "the burned book." The work consisted of four parts and was written down by Rabbi Nathan in the winter of 1805–6. Rabbi Nathan, Rabbi Nachman's scribe, said he understood nothing of the book but was overwhelmed by its greatness. Rabbi Nachman said that no one could understand a word of the book except one who was a great *tzaddik*, proficient in the seven branches of wisdom and a Torah sage. When Rabbi Nachman was in Lemberg in 1807–8, he perceived that he would either have to die or burn the book. After consulting Rabbi Shimon, he gave orders for him to return to Bratslav and burn the book. Later, after Rabbi Nachman died, Rabbi Shimon also burned a trunk of Rabbi Nachman's manuscripts, at the rabbi's request. Rabbi Nathan says about this: "Before Rabbi Nachman departed from this world, he left instructions to burn all his writings which, secreted in a special box, no one had been permitted to read. Immediately after his soul left him and his clothes were being removed, Rabbi Shimon hastened to open the box, took out all the hidden manuscripts, carried them to the stove, built a fire, and consigned them to the flames. I followed after him, in order to sniff the sacred fumes of the awesome Torah whose enjoyment was denied to our generation" (*Yeme Maharnat*).

129. *A Letter from the Beyond* (Israel)
Collected by Howard Schwartz from Avraham Greenbaum.

There are a substantial number of tales in which the spirit of Rabbi Nachman is reported to have returned to this world in order to help his followers, in the tradition of tales about Elijah the Prophet. This tradition derives from Rabbi Nachman's statement, as he was dying, that his Hasidim would not need to appoint a successor, for he would always be their rebbe. (See the following note for a further discussion of this matter.) These tales primarily exist in the oral tradition and are widely told in Bratslaver circles. This account of the miraculous letter from Rabbi Nachman that saved Rabbi Yisrael Dov Odesser from suicide and led him to become a loyal

Bratslaver for the rest of his life is particularly well known. Other accounts of the letter assert that Rabbi Nachman directed Rabbi Odesser to try to have Rabbi Nachman's remains moved from Uman to the Holy Land. Acting at the request of Rabbi Odesser, Haim Herzog, the President of Israel, received permission from the local authorities to move Rabbi Nachman's burial place, but this move was opposed by other leading Bratslaver Rabbis and the plan was canceled. See *The Forward*, Jan. 15, 1993.

130. *Rabbi Nachman's Chair* (Israel)

Collected by Howard Schwartz from Yehuda Yaari. The dream is recorded in *Sippurim Hadashim* in *Hayey Moharan* by Rabbi Nathan of Bratslav, edited by Rabbi Nachman Goldstein of Tcherin (Lemberg: 1874).

The account of the chair is widely told in Bratslaver circles, and the reassembled chair can be found next to the Ark in the Bratslaver synagogue in Meah Sha'arim in Jerusalem. As to whether or not Rabbi Nachman actually stated that he would always remain among his Hasidim, this is a somewhat controversial matter. According to some accounts, Rabbi Nachman did not state this directly, but when it appeared that he had died, Rabbi Nathan, his scribe, cried out: "Rebbe! Rebbe! To whom have you left us?" Rabbi Nachman then lifted up his head with an expression that said, "I am not leaving you, God forbid" (*Yemey Moharnat* 44a). Other Bratslav accounts record the rabbi as having said a few days earlier that he would always remain among them. In any case, the Bratslavers firmly believe that it was Rabbi Nachman's intention to always remain their rabbi, and they have observed that wish to this day. Note that the motif of the chair being broken apart and then reassembled has strong echoes of the cosmological myth of the Ari about the Shattering of the Vessels and the Gathering of the Sparks. There is a parable of Rabbi Nachman's, "The Tale of the Millstone," from *Sipurei Ma'aysiot Hadashim* (Warsaw: 1909), which presents a dilemma to which the wise prince finds a creative solution, much like that of the Bratslavers with Rabbi Nachman's chair:

A king once sent his son abroad to be educated. The prince was gone for several years, and when he returned he was well versed in all branches of knowledge. On his return the king informed him that he wished to test his wisdom. He showed his son a great millstone, of immense size, and told him that he wished for him, and for him alone, to bring that millstone into the palace and bear it up to the palace attic. The prince was astonished at this request, for the millstone was so large that it would require a regiment of soldiers to lift it, and even they would have to struggle. How could he do such a task on his own? It seemed impossible. For several days the prince sat dejectedly on the millstone, trying to think of a way to move it. He consulted all of the branches of knowledge he was familiar with, but none seemed to offer any clue. Just when the boy was about to go to his father and confess his inability to perform the task, he saw a squirrel open a huge nut and break it into many pieces. Then the squirrel carried the pieces one by one into its nest. Suddenly inspired, the prince took a hammer and began to pound at the millstone until he had broken it into a multitude of little pieces. Then he carried the pieces, one by one, into the palace attic, and at last he was able to present himself to the king and declare that the task had been completed. Then the king knew that his son had indeed become wise and was worthy of becoming his heir.

131. *Rabbi Nachman's Tomb* (Israel)
Collected by Howard Schwartz from Rabbi Moshe Shilge.

Before his death, Rabbi Nachman told his Hasidim that if they went to his tomb and pronounced ten psalms in the order he specified, he would come to them and protect them. There are many accounts of the travels by Bratslaver Hasidim to the city of Uman in order to pray at Rabbi Nachman's tomb. During the Soviet regime, this was a very dangerous quest, that large numbers of Hasidim still undertook each year. Rabbi Moshe Shilge joined one of the groups going to Uman, and here reports firsthand their experiences in reaching the burial place of their rebbe. It is interesting to note that at the time of this journey, Rabbi Moshe Shilge had been a Bratslaver for only a few years, having become a *ba'al teshuvah*. He was a well-known jazz violinist before becoming a Bratslaver, and he continued to play the violin for the Bratslavers, as evidenced in this account. For another such report, see "A Bratslaver Hasid" by Joseph Opatshau in *GNC*, p. 605. Although this is a work of fiction, it is obviously based on an account of one such journey to Reb Nachman's tomb. See the note to "A Letter from the Beyond," p. 240, for the controversial proposal to move Rabbi Nachman's grave from Uman to Israel.

132. *The Soul of Reb Nachman* (Israel)
Collected by Howard Schwartz from Y. David Shulman.

This very interesting tale comes from contemporary circles of the followers of Rav Kook living in Israel. Rav Kook's statement that "I am the soul of Reb Nachman" is a mysterious one that can be understood in several ways, suggesting a direct connection between the souls of the two great rabbis. Above all, it demonstrates how greatly Rav Kook admired Reb Nachman and how strongly he identified with him. Such a strong connection sometimes takes the form of a kind of spiritual possession in Jewish mystical lore known as an *ibur*. Or it can take the even stronger form of *gilgul*, reincarnation. The discussion in this tale concerns which type of link joins the soul of Reb Nachman to that of Rav Kook, but the link itself is left unquestioned. The existence of this tale is a clear indication that the mystical traditions portrayed in the ancient and medieval tales still exist in some circles in present-day Israel and other places. Reb Nachman's love for the Holy Land was legendary. A long account of it is found in *Shivhei ha'Ran* (Ostrog: 1816). After a journey that lasted for many months and was filled with bizarre incidents, Rabbi Nachman and his companion, who was probably Reb Shimon, his first follower, arrived in the Holy Land. After taking only a few steps onto the land, Reb Nachman turned to Reb Shimon and told him that they could turn back, for merely stepping on the Holy Land had been enough to complete the *tikkun*, the repair or restoration. However, he remained for a while, traveling through the land. Standing behind this journey to the Holy Land was the desire of Rabbi Nachman's great-grandfather, the Baal Shem Tov, to reach the Holy Land, which was never fulfilled. Rabbi Nachman often indicated his strong attachment to the Besht and said that he had sparks of the soul of the Baal Shem Tov in his soul. Thus one interpretation of Rabbi Nachman's longing to make this journey and his elation upon his arrival is that he felt that he had not only filled his own quest, but that of the Besht as well. Likewise, by a single phrase, "I am the soul of Reb Nachman," Rav Kook linked himself to this tradition, which reached back not only to Reb Nachman, but to the Baal Shem Tov as well.

Other Hasidic Masters

133. *A Vision of the Bride* (Eastern Europe)

From *Sipurei Hasidim*, edited by Shlomo Yosef Zevin (Tel Aviv: 1964). A close variant of this vision, also presented as a personal experience, is found in *Megillat Setarim* by Rabbi Isaac Yehuda Yehiel Safrin (Jerusalem: 1944, p. 19). Another version is found in *Ma'aysiot Noraim ve-Niflaim* (Cracow: 1896). It is also included in *Otsar ha-Ma'aysiot*, edited by Naftali Greenboim (B'nai Brak: 1988). Moshe Idel proposes that this vision actually occurred to Rabbi Safrin rather than Levi Yitzhak of Berditchev, although it has been widely attributed to the latter. See *Kabbalah: New Perspectives*, p. 314, note 54.

One of the characteristics of the visions of the *Shekhinah* is that they occur at times of intense grieving. In "A Vision of the Wailing Wall," the vision occurs as Rabbi Abraham Beruchim's life hangs in the balance. Here Rabbi Levi Yitzhak of Berditchev finds himself locked out of the house he has come to visit in another city and unable to count the *Omer*. He wanders the streets dejectedly until he finds a House of Study, where his vision of the *Shekhinah* takes place. After the vision occurs, there is great joy and relief, as always occurs after such events. There are several variants of this tale, suggesting that it reflects a central mystical experience in the life of Rabbi Levi Yitzhak.

134. *The Flaming Letters* (Eastern Europe)

From *Sipurei Hasidim* edited by Shlomo Yosef Zevin (Tel Aviv: 1964). Also found in *Otsar ha-Ma'aysiot*, edited by Naftali Greenboim (B'nai Brak: 1988).

Not only words have meaning in Kabbalah; every letter has a host of rich associations. One of the holiest professions is that of the *sopher*, or scribe, who writes the scroll of the Torah and also provides other sacred texts, including the texts of the *mezzuzah* and the *tefillin*, and writes marriage contracts, known as *ketubot*. In this tale Rabbi Dov Baer, the *Maggid* of Mezhirich, gives Reb Shneur Zalman, the founder of the Habad movement in Hasidism, an assignment to create a new style of letters for the Torah. This mission has strong mystical overtones, which Reb Shneur Zalman recognizes at once. To the best of his ability, which is considerable, he bases the shape of the new letters on their mystical meaning. The *Maggid* agrees that Shneur Zalman has succeeded and sends him on another mission to show the new alphabet to Reb Moshe Sopher, a master scribe. Shneur Zalman discovers on his arrival that the *sopher* is writing a Torah using the letters that Shneur Zalman has just invented, an example of divine synchronicity that also confirms the accuracy of Shneur Zalman's understanding of the mystical meaning of the letters. This story is remarkable in the way it links three major figures—the *Maggid* of Mezhirich, Reb Shneur Zalman, and Reb Zusya of Hanipol, plus Reb Moshe Sopher. It seems to suggest that the *Maggid* foresaw this sequence of events or even was responsible for them in some way. Compare "Rabbi Naftali's Trance," p. 152, where Rabbi Naftali Katz also seems to exercise control over events on earth and in heaven.

135. *The Saba Kadisha in the Upper World* (Eastern Europe)

From *Tiferet ha-Maharal* (Lemberg: 1914).

Reb Aryeh Leib of Shpola was known as "the Saba Kadisha," or holy father, of Shpola and also as "the Shpola Zeide," the Shpola grandfather. Legend holds that the Baal Shem Tov predicted his birth to his father and blessed him when he was born. The Saba Kadisha was originally a student of Reb Pinhas of Koretz, who emerged with his own brand of Hasidism at virtually the same time as the Baal Shem Tov. See the section of tales here of "The Circle of Reb Pinhas of Koretz," pp. 210–221. This tale links Reb Pinhas with the Baal Shem Tov and links the Saba Kadisha to both of them. Here the Saba Kadisha ascends to heaven in a dream and refuses to return to earth until he is driven there by a Jew carrying a shovel, whom he later discovers is the Baal Shem Tov. This dual meeting, in heaven and on earth, as well as in a dream and while waking, becomes a characteristic motif in Hasidic tales. Compare "A Visitor from the Other World," p. 196, which chronicles how Reb Wolf Kitzes became a disciple of the Baal Shem Tov, as well as "The Scribe," p. 232, which describes how Reb Nathan of Nemirov, the *sopher*, or scribe, of Rabbi Nachman of Bratslav, first met the rebbe in a dream. The Saba Kadisha was Rabbi Nachman's implacable enemy and caused him great torment. The conflicts between rebbes are rarely recorded in these hagiographic tales, but Reb Nachman's struggle with the Saba Kadisha is recorded in *Hayey Moharan* 11 by Reb Nathan of Nemirov (Lemberg: 1874). It is attributed to one man who became furious with Rabbi Nachman and denounced him before the Shpola Zeide. After this the latter stirred up tremendous opposition against Reb Nachman. As with virtually all of the other rebbes represented here, there are many legends associated with the Saba Kadisha's remarkable knowledge and powers. See, for example, "The Demon of the Waters" in *LC*, p. 202 (Oxford edition).

136. *The Wandering Well* (Hungary)
From *Esser Zahzahot* by Yisrael ben Yitzhak Berger (Piotrkow: 1910, p. 69). The legend about Miriam's Well is found in B. Ta'an. 9a and B. Shab. 35a.

The legend of Miriam's well grows out of Numbers 21:16: *That is the well whereof the Lord said unto Moses: "Gather the people together, and I will give them water."* This verse is followed by a list of places where the Israelites traveled, and it is interpreted by the rabbis as recording the places where the well went with them. This miraculous well, which could go uphill and down, was given by God because of the virtues of Miriam, the sister of Moses. Most versions of this legend report that the well followed the people into the Holy Land and can be found somewhere in the Kinneret (the Sea of Galilee). This legend is the basis of "The Angel of Forgetfulness," p. 81, where the Ari takes Rabbi Hayim Vital out in a boat on the Kinneret and gives him water to drink from Miriam's well, which restores his lost memory. Another version of the legend holds that Miriam's well went to the Garden of Eden. For a tale based on this legend, see "Miriam's Tambourine" in *MT*, p. 1. "The Wandering Well" offers a third version of the fate of the well. Here it is assumed that the well is still wandering around the world, and the great Hungarian mystic Rabbi Eizek of Kallo is aware of its presence on the eve of Yom Kippur and leads Rabbi Yaakov Fish on a journey out of time to the well, in which he immerses himself. Such journeys out of time are often found in these tales. See, for example, "The Underground Forest," p. 214, "The Wine of Paradise," p. 223, and "The Young Magician, p. 224. The linkage of Yom Kippur and the arrival of the miraculous well is clearly intended. At the holiest time of the year, God's presence in the world is strongest, and the appearance of the well is one expression of that presence. By immersing himself in this well, Rabbi Eizek sheds all of his sins, which otherwise would have been counted against him on Yom Kippur, which begins the moment they return to the synagogue.

137. *The Sabbath Guests* (Hungary)
From *Tortenetek a "Kalloi Cadik"—rol* (Hungarian) by Albert Neumann (Nyiregyhaza, Hungary: 1935).

Two of the major Jewish myths are those of the Bride of God, known as the *Shekhinah*, and that of the coming of the Messiah. For the most part, the myths concerning these two key figures are separate, but they converge on the same conclusion, which is the End of Days. The myth of the exile of the *Shekhinah* explains how at the time of the destruction of the Temple in Jerusalem, which was the earthly home of the *Shekhinah*, the Bride of God separated herself from her spouse and went into exile with her children, Israel. Nor will this exile end until the Temple is rebuilt in Jerusalem. It is here that the myths of the *Shekhinah* and the Messiah converge. For one of the consequences of the coming of the Messiah will be the rebuilding of the Temple, which is understood to be a magical re-formation of the Temple exactly as it was. Therefore the coming of the Messiah is essential to end the exile of the *Shekhinah*, and the two myths are eternally bound together. Nevertheless, it is rare to find tales in which both are active figures in the same tale, as we find in this one from Hungary. In this tale of Rabbi Eizik of Kallo, the Messiah and the *Shekhinah* arrive unexpectedly at his house on the Sabbath as a couple who wish to wed. The Rabbi of Kallo recognizes who they are, and understands that their union would herald the End of Days, the rabbinic vision of the messianic era. But the visiting Hasidim do not, and because of their blindness, the opportunity is lost. In a sense this tale of Rabbi Eizik makes the convergence of the two myths of the *Shekhinah* and the Messiah complete, as symbolized by their desire for union. Such mythic fusion is common, and often results in the creation of a new myth. From a Jungian perspective, this tale seems to advocate the fusion of the male and female "inner beings," as represented by the *Shekhinah* and the Messiah. Such a union can be viewed as the full integration of the male and female archetypal figures, and a symbol of psychic wholeness. Unfortunately, the tale tells us, the marriage has not taken place because you, the visitor to the realm of the unconscious, have not given your approval for it. Thus the conclusion of the story can be interpreted as if it were a dream, reporting the present state of psychic balance. From this perspective the story reports a lost opportunity for psychic unity, while from the traditional perspective it is a tale of why the Messiah has not yet come. Such stories explain how there are opportunities in every generation for the Messiah to come, if something does not go wrong. And there are a great many such tales, for the longing for the Messiah was very great. Explaining why the Messiah hasn't come yet is one of the major themes of Jewish mystical tales because, after all, his appearance has been intensely awaited for many generations. These tales explain how there are opportunities in every generation for the Messiah to come, if something does not go wrong. One example of this kind of tale is "The Ladder of Prayers," p. 191. Another example is "The Journey to Jerusalem," p. 86. The best-known story that symbolically brings together the *Shekhinah* and the Messiah is Rabbi Nachman's "The Lost Princess" (see *EV*, p. 210 ff.). Like "The Sabbath Guests," "The Lost Princess" can be interpreted as bringing together two myths, that of the *Shekhinah* and that of the Messiah, and linking them together. Here a king's minister searches for the lost princess. This princess has been traditionally identified as the *Shekhinah*, and one way to read the tale is to see the minister as the Messiah, which means that the Messiah has to search for the exiled *Shekhinah*. This makes the convergence of the two myths complete.

138. *From the Beyond* (Hungary)
From *Mei Be'er Yeshashy* (Solvaki: 1888). Also found in *Sefer ha-Maaysiot*, edited by Mordecai Ben Yehezkel (Tel Aviv: 1937, Vol II, pp. 68–71).

The primary intention of this tale is to warn against improper use of mystical powers, placing it firmly in the category of kabbalistic warning tales. Here Rabbi Mordecai, the *melamed*, or teacher, offers to bring forth King David's general, Joav ben Tsrouya, from the dead. This he succeeds in doing, provoking consequences of grave danger to all concerned. And only Hayim the Vinekeeper, a hidden *tzaddik*, is able to bring them back from the brink by invoking his own powers. The model for calling forth a spirit from the dead is the biblical account of King Saul and the Witch of Endor, in which he has her call up Samuel from the dead (II Sam. 28). Like the ghost of Samuel, Joav is angry at being disturbed. And since he was a warrior, he responds in a warlike manner. For another tale about Hayim the Vinekeeper, see the following tale, "The Prayer Leader." See also "Summoning the Patriarchs" in *LC*, p. 135 ff. (Oxford edition) for another tale in which great figures from the past are invoked with kabbalistic powers.

139. *The Prayer Leader* (Hungary)
From *Mei Be'er Yeshashyu* (Solvaki: 1888).
In the previous tale, "From the Beyond," Hayim the Vinekeeper reveals his powers. In the present tale he is again portrayed as a hidden saint, no doubt one of the *Lamed Vav Tzaddikim*, the Thirty-six Just Men who are the pillar of existence. Here Hayim agrees to take the Rabbi of Kallo's place as prayer leader for the Yom Kippur services when the rabbi becomes ill. The key moment of the tale comes when the two *tzaddikim* meet. A holy fire surrounds them, which is witnessed by one of the rabbi's Hasidim, who has hidden himself in the rabbi's room. This tale intentionally links the life of the Rabbi of Kallo with the legend of the hidden saint, Hayim the Vinekeeper. It also confirms the great difficulty in finding a successor to the Rabbi of Kallo. This clearly indicates that this tale emerged from the Hasidim of the Rabbi of Kallo and is intended as a testament to his greatness.

140. *The Pact* (Eastern Europe)
Collected by Jerome Mintz from a Satmar Hasid. Based on the account found in *Legends of the Hasidim* by Jerome Mintz, p. 180.
This tale is a Hasidic variant of the talmudic tale "Forcing the End," p. 65. There it is learned that in their generation only Rabbi Hiyya and his sons had the power to hasten the coming of the Messiah. "The Pact" identifies three great Hasidic rabbis— the Seer of Lublin, Reb Menachem Mendel of Riminov, and Baruch of Medzibozh— as the ones in their generation with such great power. In "Forcing the End," Elijah the Prophet, disguised as a flaming bear, chases Rabbi Hiyya and his sons from the synagogue to prevent them from completing the prayers invoking the coming of the Messiah. In "The Pact" the three rabbis agree to use a mystical secret to force the coming of the Messiah on Simhat Torah, but the death of Baruch of Medzibozh ends their plan. When the Rabbi of Riminov learns of this, he does not attempt to bring the Messiah. But because the Seer of Lublin did not receive word of Baruch's death in time, he does make the attempt, which almost costs him his life when a supernatural force throws him out a window. This clearly demonstrates the anger in heaven at this attempt. However, the Seer's life is saved by the spirit of Baruch of Medzibozh, who sees to it that the Seer lands on his *tallis*. And the Seer of Lublin understands at that moment that Rabbi Baruch must have died, and that his spirit had come back from the World to Come to save him. Both tales, "Forcing the End" and "The Pact," demonstrate the dangers of attempting to hasten the coming of the Messiah, as well as the

strong impulse to do so among the rabbis. Also, both are tales that explain why the Messiah has not yet come.

141. *The Clock of the Seer of Lublin* (Eastern Europe)
From *Sippure Hasidim*, edited by Shlomo Yosef Zevin (Tel Aviv: 1957, Vol. 2, pp. 292–93).

This tale is both a meditation on clocks and time and an affirmation of the Seer of Lublin's belief in the coming of the Messiah. The Seer's disciple recognizes the unique ticking of the clock in the house he stays in as having once belonged to his master. And his discovery of this clock awakens in him great faith that the messianic era is coming closer. Thus, while most people view the clock as an object announcing that the time of their death is coming nearer, the Seer of Lublin and his disciple take a much more optimistic view, seeing the passage of time as bringing them closer to the messianic era. Thus the Seer's clock has taken on the Seer's optimism, and instead of announcing that a person is one hour nearer to death, it issues notes of jubilation because the coming of the Messiah is one hour closer.

142. *The Soul of the Ari* (Eastern Europe)
From *'Ateret Tif'eret* (Bilgorai: 1910). A variant can be found in *Sefer ha-Ma'aysiot*, edited by Mordecai ben Yehezkel (Tel Aviv: 1937), who attributes it to oral tradition. There are many other variants of this tale, including *Sihot Tzaddikim* (Warsaw: 1921) and *Esser Kedoshot* (Piatrakov: 1906).

This tale draws on many now familiar mystical motifs and presents them in a unique fashion. Reb Zevi Hirsch of Zhidachov finds a precious glowing stone in his cupboard, a gift from heaven. This clearly recalls the legend of the *Tzohar*, the glowing stone containing the primordial light, which God gave to Adam and Eve upon their expulsion from Eden. This initiates a long chain legend in which the glowing stone comes into the possession of every major figure from Noah to Abraham to Moses. See "The *Tzohar*," p. 59, and the accompanying note. In the present tale the rabbi fasts to find out why he has received the stone, although it is clearly a heavenly reward, not unlike the leg of a golden table received by Rabbi Haninah ben Dosa in "The Golden Table," p. 58. In this way Reb Zevi learns that he can either keep the glowing stone, and he and his descendants will become rich, or else he can give it up and instead the soul of the Ari will become fused with his own. This latter option closely resembles that of possession by an *ibur*, where the spirit of one who has departed fuses with the soul of a living sage. See "The *Tefillin* of the Or Hayim," p. 117, and the accompanying note. This leads to a student of Reb Zevi's overhearing a voice other than that of the rabbi discussing a passage of the Zohar. This voice is later identified as that of the Ari, and the student understands that the Ari was, in some way, teaching Reb Zevi. This kind of speech closely resembles that of the *maggidim*, the spirits who come to scholars and speak through them, as happens with Rabbi Joseph Caro in "The Angel of the Mishnah," p. 112. Thus the link between Reb Zevi and the soul of the Ari seems to be a combination of the *ibur* and the *maggid*. When Reb Zevi returns the glowing jewel by casting it into heaven, there is an echo of the famous talmudic legend of the High Priest returning the keys of the Temple and of Rabbi Haninah ben Dosa praying that the leg of the golden table be returned. Indeed, the variant in *Sefer ha-Ma'aysiot* is much closer to this talmudic tale than the version from *'Ateret Tif'eret*. See "The Keys of the Temple," p. 56, and "The Golden Table," p. 58.

143. *The Blind Angel* (Eastern Europe)

From *Admorei Chernobyl* edited by Yisrael Yakov Klapholtz (B'nai Brak: 1971).

This tale grows out of the period of Hasidic decadence, when the transmission of the Hasidic masters was determined on the basis of family rather than knowledge and leadership. At this time many rebbes became very affluent. Rabbi Mordecai of Chernobyl was a son of Rabbi Menachem Nahum of Chernobyl, the founder of the Twersky dynasty. This tale was clearly intended to justify Rabbi Mordecai's wealthy lifestyle, and to refute the appearance of avarice by demonstrating that the silver menorah was not really of material importance to the rabbi but had deeper spiritual meaning. Note that Rabbi Mordecai has been able to see into the future, learning that the rich man will need the merit of giving away his precious silver menorah in order to guide his blind angel into Paradise. Because Rabbi Mordecai lights the Menorah on Hanukah, it can be assumed to have been a *Hanukiah*, a modified menorah for use during Hanukah. For another tale of future vision, see "The Tale of the Kugel," p. 268. The notion of the imperfect angel is found in the tales and writings of Reb Pinhas of Koretz. See "The Angel of Friendship," p. 213, and the accompanying note. The mystical aspects of the menorah in this tale suggest the even more symbolic interpretation of the menorah found in Reb Nachman of Bratslav's tale of "The Menorah of Defects," from *Sipurei Ma'aysiot Hadashim* (Warsaw: 1909) as follows:

> Once a young man left his home and traveled for several years. After he returned, he proudly told his father that he had become a master in the craft of making menorahs. He asked his father to call together all the townsmen who practiced this craft, that he might demonstrate his unrivaled skill for them. That is what his father did, inviting them to his home. But when his son presented them with the menorah he had made, not everyone found it pleasing. Then his father begged each and every one to tell him the truth about what they thought of it. And at last each one admitted that he had found a defect in the menorah. When the father told his son that many of the craftsmen had noted a defect, the son asked what the defect was, and it emerged that each of them had noted something different. What one craftsman had praised, another had found defective. And the son said to his father: "By this have I shown my great skill. For I have revealed to each one his own defect, since each of these defects was actually in he who perceived it. It was these defects that I incorporated into my creation, for I made this menorah only from defects. Now I will begin its restoration."

The commandment to use a menorah is found in Numbers 8:1: *And the Lord spoke unto Moses, saying: 'Speak unto Aaron, and say unto him: When thou lightest the lamps, the seven lamps shall give light in front of the candlestick.'"* This parable of Rabbi Nachman's has been subjected to various interpretations. Since the menorah is a traditional symbol of the creation of the world in seven days, with the center light representing the Sabbath, the craftsman in the tale may be seen to represent God, and the defects those of the world, with all its imperfections. The craftsman may also be seen to represent the rebbe, who must reveal the defects of his Hasidim to them, so that they may begin the process of *tikkun* or restoration.

144. *The Cave of Mattathias* (Eastern Europe)

From *Hag La'am*, edited by Eliezer Marcus (Jerusalem: 1990). Told by Shimon Toder. The original legend about Hanukah is found in B. Shab 21b.

Mattathias was the father of the Maccabees. Here the Hasid who risks everything to meet his rebbe on the day they share together is blessed with a dream of Mattathias still alive, living in a cave, preparing candles for the messianic era, and predicting its imminent arrival. This story builds on the rabbinic legends in which certain key biblical figures are portrayed as still alive, especially Moses and Elijah. At the same time, the Hasid is portrayed as a holy messenger, sent to the rebbe to inform him of the words of Mattathias. But the rebbe, Rabbi Menachem Mendel of Riminov, is aware of all that takes place, and acknowledges this when he greets the Hasid at the door. This links the powers of the Rabbi of Riminov to those of the sons of Mattathias, which serves to glorify the Rebbe in the eyes of his followers. Such linking of the Hasidic masters with the great figures of the past is one of the most common themes of Hasidic tales. At the same time, this is a tale of messianic tremors, the kinds of rumors that would often shake Jewish communities. Indeed, the message from Mattathias is that the messianic era is almost upon them, hinting that the Rabbi of Riminov can have an important role to play in this event. But the real importance of this dream is the way it provides salvation to the Hasid trapped in the snow. By creating the conditions to save himself, using the oil for the Hanukah candles, he saves himself from freezing and is able to sleep, and thus to dream. The dream first transports him from a cold place to a warm one, and then brings him face to face with Mattathias, who has remained alive all this time, waiting for the Messiah and preparing wicks to light when the messianic age arrives. This dream meeting with Mattiathias is a fateful one for the Hasid, for when he awakes he finds himself at the rabbi's door. A miracle has once more taken place, as it did to Rabbi Abraham when he had a vision of the *Shekhinah* in "A Vision at the Wailing Wall," p. 87, and as it did to the rich man who was kissed by Shimon bar Yohai in a dream in "A Kiss from the Master," p. 79. Above all, this tale reveals just how intense was the longing of the Hasidim for the Messiah.

145. *A New Soul* (Eastern Europe)
From *Froyen-rebbeyim un berihmte perzhenlikhkeyten in poylen* (Yiddish) (Warsaw: 1937).
One of the strangest and most fascinating episodes of Hasidic history was the emergence of Hannah Rochel Werbermacher, the Maid of Ludomir, as a rebbe. This tale describes her transformative experience, in which she believed that she had received a new soul, and after that took on some of the rituals of men, including the wearing of a *tallis* and *tefillin*, and was eventually recognized as possessing great knowledge and wisdom, and began to function, to a certain extent, like a rebbe. This lasted until her marriage, arranged by Rabbi Menachem Mendel of Chernobyl, which brought this period of her life to an end. In her later life she moved to the Holy Land, where legend has it that she participated in an attempt to hasten the coming of the Messiah, as described in this tale. Jewish lore has many stories about wise daughters who secretly listen in on the teachings of the Torah. See, for example, "The Donkey Girl" in *MT*, p. 202. I. B. Singer's famous story "Yentl the Yeshivah Boy" is about such a young woman who disguises herself as a student and joins the yeshivah. See *The Collected Stories*, p. 149.

146. *A Vision* (Czechoslovakia)
From *Devet Bran* by Jiri Langer (Czech) (Prague: 1937).
Jiri Langer left his home in Prague when he was eighteen and joined the Belz

Hasidim for several years. Eventually he returned to Prague and remained there until he had this vision of Rabbi Issachar Dov of Belz beckoning him to return. Note that in the vision Rabbi Issachar Dov appears in two places at the same time. This is a clear indication that Rabbi Issachar is contacting him with the use of kabbalistic magic. He has, in a sense, sent his "shape," as described in some of the stories about Reb Elimelech of Lizensk. This technique is also associated with Rabbi Naftali Katz. See "Rabbi Naftali's Trance," p. 152 and the accompanying note. See also "The Shadow on the Wall," p. 228. The mystical technique used here is a form of astral projection, where the rabbi not only sends his shape somewhere else, sometimes a great distance, but also controls the movements of the shape in that place. In the Langer tale, the sending of the shape is a demonstration of the rebbe's power over the disciple, who cannot escape the rebbe even when he tries. This is a common theme in Hasidic lore. See, for example, two tales about Reb Elimelech, "The Wine of Paradise," p. 223, and "The Young Magician," p. 224.

147. *The Tale of the Etrog* (Eastern Europe)
From *Devet Bran* by Jiri Langer (Czech) (Prague: 1937).
This tale recounts a mystical transformation, in which Reb Sholem of Belz so focuses his concentration on the etrog during Sukkot that he completely enters into it. This indicates the total meditative concentration of the rabbi and his complete identification with the etrog as a sacred object. This mystery is witnessed by his student, the Rabbi of Kamionka. The latter's perception of this transformation comes in the form of a mystical vision in which the rabbi vanishes within the etrog, illuminating it. The etrog is one of the four species of plants held together and shaken on the festival of Sukkot, according to Leviticus 23:40. Great emphasis is put on having a beautiful fruit for the festival, often at great expense, since the fruit has to be imported. Those who have succeeded in obtaining such a beautiful etrog for Sukkot are likely to appreciate it, or, as in this tale, make it an object of contemplation.

148. *A Wandering Soul* (Eastern Europe)
From *Devet Bran* by Jiri Langer (Czech) (Prague: 1937).
Many are those who experience the cycle of *gilgul* or reincarnation. But Jewish lore holds that at birth an angel presses its finger above our lips (the universal sign for silence), causing us to forget all we knew about our previous lives and many other mysteries. For more on this legend, see "The Angel of Conception," p. 57. Here Rabbi Yismach Moyshe of Ihel knows the history of his soul. This in itself indicates the remarkable level of his mystical attainment. His inclusion of one of his former lives as a follower of Korah is remarkable in that it shows a rare identification with the followers of Korah, who rebelled against Moses and were punished when the earth opened and swallowed them (Num. 16:31–33). In the Talmud the wandering sage Rabbi bar bar Hannah comes to the place where they fell into the fires of Gehenna, Jewish hell, and hears their cries, acknowledging that Moses was right and they were wrong (B. Baba Batra 73b). Perhaps Rabbi Yismach Moyshe is acknowledging the suffering of his soul or recognizing the struggles he had gone through before he attained the level of righteousness he did as a sage. This implies a view in which reincarnation is a kind of punishment, a notion not too far from the Hindu concept of *karma*, in which the soul ascends or descends the spiral of existence.

149. *Trying to Pray* (United States)
Collected by Howard Schwartz from Rabbi Zalman Schachter-Shalomi.

Rabbi Dovid Din was a distinguished Bratslaver rabbi who had a substantial following of his own. Here he pries a man from the grip of his crisis of belief and at the same time teaches him how to pray, breaking his heart at the *Kotel*, the Western Wall in Jerusalem that symbolizes so many Jewish griefs, and is therefore known as the Wailing Wall. The notion that a broken heart is the key to prayer is one of the primary themes of Hasidic teachings. See "The Master Key," p. 198, and the accompanying note. There are many tales set at the Wailing Wall, among them tales of visions of the *Shekhinah*, such as "A Vision at the Wailing Wall," p. 87. Each of these tales emphasizes the reverence in which the *Kotel* is held.

150. *The Tale of the Kugel* (Eastern Europe)
Collected by Rabbi Zalman Schachter-Shalomi from Reb Avraham Paris. A variant can be found in *Legends of the Hasidim*, edited by Jerome R. Mintz pp. 391–392).

This is a fine example of the illusion tale. It has been possible to trace this genre of tale from rabbinic lore to medieval Jewish folklore, kabbalistic tales, and other Hasidic models. For more background on this kind of tale, see the note to "The Magic Flock," p. 44. This tale portrays Rabbi Menachem Mendel I of Lubavitch as having great powers of illusion, as well as the powers to show a man a vision of the future path he will take. Here the man sees what his life would be like if he were to divorce his wife for not having any children. He experiences the time as if it were real—as if he were actually living out his alternate life. But when he emerges from the vision, very little time has passed. This is another example of the rebbe as wonder worker, in the model of the Baal Shem Tov and Reb Elimelech of Lizensk. Rabbi Menachem Mendel was the author of *Zemach Tzaddik* (1870–74), a book of responsa, in honor of which he was known as the *"Zemach Tzaddik."* He was the grandson of Rabbi Shneur Zalman, founder of the Habad movement. For a tale about Shneur Zalman, see "The Flaming Letters," p. 247.

Appendix: Mystical Themes and Thematic Contents

The thematic range of the Jewish mystical tale comprises certain key themes of a religious and folk nature. The following list of mystical themes represents the range of these mystical tales. Twenty-two primary themes have been identified, with several subthemes in each category. Each of the stories in this volume has been categorized according to the dominant theme and subtheme of the tale. In a few cases, where two or more themes seem to be of equal importance, they have been listed. Because of space limitations, it was not possible to include examples of every subtheme in the tales collected here, although each of the major themes is represented. The thematic categories and subcategories are identified by number and letter in the list of tales that follows that of mystical themes.

I MYSTICAL THEMES

1. THE DIVINE PRESENCE
   A. The Nature of God
   B. The Ineffable Name
   C. The Contraction of God
   D. The Bride of God
   E. Mystical Marriages
   F. The Extra Soul
   G. Allegories of the Divine Presence

2. MYSTERIES OF CREATION
   A. The Power of the Name
   B. The Secrets of Creation
   C. The Origin of the Soul
   D. The Fate of the Soul
   E. The Primordial Light

F. The Shattering of the Vessels
    and the Gathering of the Sparks
G. Repairing the World

3. MYSTERIES OF THE CHARIOT
   A. God's Throne of Glory
   B. Ascent by Chariot
   C. *Merkavah* Visions
   D. Dangers of Mystical Contemplation

4. MYSTERIES OF THE TORAH
   A. The Primordial Torah
   B. The Giving of the Torah
   C. The Letters of the Torah
   D. Numerical Mysteries
   E. The Torah of the Void

5. THE POWER OF THE WORD
   A. Vows
   B. Blessings
   C. Curses
   D. Fated Events

6. THE POWER OF PRAYER
   A. The Prayers of Simple Folk
   B. Prayers Unable to Ascend
   C. Learning to Pray

7. MYSTERIES OF THE SABBATH
   A. The Extra Soul
   B. The Sabbath Queen
   C. Sabbath Blessings
   D. Havdalah

8. COMMUNICATING WITH THE
   WORLD ABOVE
   A. Heavenly Voices
   B. Angelic Messengers and Maggidim
   C. Visits of the Patriarchs and Matriarchs
   D. Heavenly Books
   E. Prophecy
   F. Messengers of God
   G. Divine Messages
   H. Divination and Signs
   I. Returning Miraculous Objects to Heaven
   J. Heavenly Decrees

9. DREAMS AND VISIONS
   A. Dreams
   B. Visions
   C. Dream Questions

10. HEAVENLY JOURNEYS
    A. The Ascent of the Soul
    B. Ascent in Dreams
    C. Ascent of the Living
    D. Ascent by Pronunciation of the Name
    E. Ascent in a Chariot

11. THE CELESTIAL PARADISE
    A. The Heavenly Jerusalem
    B. The Heavenly Court
    C. The Celestial Academy
    D. The Palaces of Heaven
    E. The World to Come
    F. A Partner in Paradise
    G. Those Who Entered Paradise Alive

12. THE GARDEN OF EDEN
    A. Visits to the Garden of Eden
    B. The Tree of Life
    C. Paradise Lost

13. THE HOLY LAND
    A. Temple Legends
    B. Jerusalem
    C. Holy Sites
    D. Travels to the Holy Land

14. WANDERING SOULS
    A. Lost Souls
    B. Death and Resurrection
    C. Reincarnation
    D. Possession by Evil Spirits
    E. Possession by Good Spirits
    F. Visitors from the Other World
    G. The Grateful Dead
    H. Souls Returning to This World
    I. The Souls of Other Beings
    J. Souls Unable to Ascend
    K. Change of Soul

15. BEYOND TIME AND SPACE
    A. Tales of Illusion
    B. Enchanted Journeys
    C. The Narrow Bridge of Existence

16. MIRACLES
    A. God's Miracles
    B. Miracles of the Sages

17. THE EVIL INCLINATION
    A. The Evil Impulse
    B. The Golden Calf
    C. The Forces of Evil
    D. Lilith and Her Kind
    E. Exorcism of Evil Spirits
    F. The Punishments of Sinners

18. KABBALISTIC MAGIC
    A. Magical Combinations of Letters and Numbers
    B. Bringing the Dead to Life
    C. Sympathetic Magic
    D. Soul Travel

19. MASTERS AND HIDDEN SAINTS
    A. The Lamed Vav *Tzaddikim*
    B. Hidden Saints
    C. The Power of the *Tzaddikim*

20. MYSTICAL UNION
    A. Visions of God
    B. Union at the Moment of Death
    C. Mystical Experiences
    D. Parables of Mystical Union

21. ENCOUNTERS WITH ANGELS AND DEMONS
    A. Angelic Visitors
    B. Angelic Guides
    C. Angelic Adversaries
    D. Angels Fulfilling the Will of God
    E. Invoking Angelic Powers
    F. Bringing Angels into Being
    G. The Angel of Death
    H. Transforming Demons into Angels

22. AWAITING THE MESSIAH
    A. The Bird's Nest
    B. Forcing the End
    C. False Messiahs
    D. Messianic Caves
    E. Preparing for the Messiah
    F. Why the Messiah Has Not Yet Come
    G. The World to Come

II THEMATIC CONTENTS

I RABBINIC TALES

1.	The Golden Dove	16-A, 22-A
2.	An Appointment with Death	5-D, 21-G
3.	Isaac's Ascent	10-A, 14-B
4.	The Magic Flock	21-C
5.	The Ascent of Moses	10-C
6.	The Chronicle of Serah bat Asher	26-A
7.	Mysteries of the Chariot	3-C
8.	The Four Who Entered Paradise	10-C, 3-D
9.	Rabbi Ishmael's Ascent	10-A
10.	The Waters of the Abyss	1-B
11.	The Vision of the High Priest	9-B
12.	The Keys of the Temple	8-I
13.	The Spirit of Idolatry	17-B
14.	The Angel of Conception	21-C
15.	The Golden Table	8-I
16.	The *Tzohar*	2-E
17.	The Gates of Eden	12-A
18.	The Law Is Not in Heaven	16-B
19.	The Voice in the Attic	16-B
20.	Forcing the End	22-B

II KABBALISTIC TALES

The Circle of Shimon bar Yohai

21.	The Cave of Shimon bar Yohai	8-D, 8-F, 16-A
22.	The Decree	8-J
23.	The Curtain of Fire	9-B
24.	A Saint from the Other World	8-F
25.	The Golden Scepter	8-F, 9-B
26.	The Book of Adam	8-D
27.	Rabbi Gadiel the Child	14-C
28.	The Celestial Academy	11-C
29.	The Book of Flying Letters	4-C
30.	Candles in the Synagogue	14-H
31.	A Kiss from the Master	14-E

The Circle of the Ari

32. The Pillar of Cloud   16-A
33. The Angel of Forgetfulness   21-D
34. The Dancing of the Ari   14-F
35. The Blessing of the Kohanim   1-D
36. The Journey to Jerusalem   22-F
37. The Precious Prayer   6-A
38. A Vision at the Wailing Wall   1-D, 9-B
39. Reading the Lips of the Ari   8-E
40. The Speaking Flame   8-H
41. Greeting the Sabbath Queen   7-B
42. Gathering Sparks   2-F
43. Delivering a Message   2-A, 15-B
44. A Stone in the Wall   14-C
45. The Widow of Safed   14-D
46. The Body of Moses   9-A
47. A Visit to the City of the Dead   9-A
48. The Angel in the Mirror   21-D
49. The Handwriting of the Messiah   8-G

Other Kabbalistic Tales

50. The Palace of Vanities   8-F
51. The Chains of the Messiah   22-B
52. The Tzaddik of the Forest   19-B
53. The Angel of the Mishnah   8-B
54. A New Lease on Life   15-B, 19-B
55. Redemption of the Lost Souls   14-A
56. Repairing Souls   2-H
57. The Tefillin of the Or Hayim   14-E

III MYSTICAL FOLKTALES

58. Gabriel's Palace   4-A
59. The Cottage of Candles   2-D
60. Rabbi Shimon's Escape   2-A
61. The Boy Who Blew the Shofar   14-J
62. The Enchanted Inn   15-A
63. Leaves from the Garden of Eden   9-A, 12-A
64. The Tenth Man   8-C
65. The Ram Whose Horns Reached to Heaven   14-H
66. The Cave of King David   8-C

67. The Shining Robe   19-B
68. The Evil Angel   21-C
69. The Young Man Without a Soul   2-A
70. Asenath's Dove   2-A
71. The Tale of the Kiddush Cup   16-B
72. The Miracle in the *Sukkah*   16-B
73. Rabbi Naftali's Trance   18-D, 21-D
74. Interpreting the Zohar   14-C
75. The Secrets of Kabbalah   3-D
76. The Flying Letters   4-C
77. The Curse   5-C
78. The Miracle of the Ring   9-A, 14-H
79. The Angel's Daughter   21-A
80. The Bridegroom and the Angel of Death   21-G
81. The Cave to the Holy Land   13-D, 22-D
82. The Cave of Temptations   13-D, 15-B
83. The Hollow of the Sling   17-D
84. How Rabbi Judah the Pious Became
       a Great Scholar   2-A
85. The Words in the Sand   5-B
86. The Dream Question of the Maharal   9-C
87. The Count Who Wanted to Study Kabbalah   3-D
88. The Ruin   14-D
89. The Voice in the Tree   14-C
90. A Vision in the Cemetery   9-B
91. The Spirit of Hagigah   8-B

IV HASIDIC TALES

The Circle of the Baal Shem Tov

92. The Book in the Cave   8-D
93. The Prince of Fire   21-D
94. The Angel's Sword   22-D
95. The Ladder of Prayers   10-A, 22-A
96. The Tree of Life   12-B
97. A Crown of Shoes   12-A
98. The Flaming Tree   16-B
99. A Visitor from the Other World   14-F
100. The Master Key   6-B
101. The Enchanted Island   15-A
102. The Circle of Fire   3-C
103. The Tale of the Frog   14-C
104. The Field of Souls   14-J

105. Unlocking the Gates of Heaven   6-B, 8-J
106. The Healing Spring   16-B
107. Lighting a Fire   16-B

The Circle of Reb Pinhas of Koritz

108. Opening a Verse   6-C, 15-C
109. The Angel of the Zohar   8-B
110. The Angel of Friendship   21-F
111. The Underground Forest   15-B
112. Reb Pinhas and the Angel of Death   21-G

The Circle of Reb Elimelech of Lizensk

113. The Woman in the Forest   15-A, 17-D
114. A Bowl of Soup   18-C
115. The Wine of Paradise   15-A
116. The Young Magician   15-A
117. Reb Shmelke's Whip   17-A
118. Three Stars   17-F
119. The Shadow on the Wall   18-D
120. The Garden of the Torah   18-D

The Circle of Reb Nachman of Bratslav

121. A Vision of Light   9-B
122. The Scribe   9-A
123. The Sabbath Fish   8-F, 14-C
124. The Sword of the Messiah   10-A
125. The Souls of Trees   14-I
126. Divining from the Zohar   8-H
127. The Angel of Losses   21-D
128. The Book That Was Burned   8-D
129. A Letter from the Beyond   8-G
130. Reb Nachman's Chair   16-B
131. Reb Nachman's Tomb   6-C
132. The Soul of Reb Nachman   14-C, 14-E

Other Hasidic Masters

133. A Vision of the Bride   1-D, 9-B

134. The Flaming Letters   9-A
135. The Saba Kadisha in the Upper World   10-A
136. The Wandering Well   16-A
137. The Sabbath Guests   7-B, 22-F
138. From the Beyond   2-A, 3-D
139. The Prayer Leader   19-B
140. The Pact   14-H
141. The Clock of the Seer of Lublin   16-B
142. The Soul of the Ari   2-E, 14-E
143. The Blind Angel   21-B
144. The Cave of Mattathias   8-C, 9-A, 22-E
145. A New Soul   11-B, 14-K
146. A Vision   9-B
147. The Tale of the Etrog   9-B
148. A Wandering Soul   14-C
149. Trying to Pray   6-C
150. The Tale of the Kugel   15-A

Glossary

All of the following terms are in Hebrew unless otherwise noted.

Adonai   the name of God that is used most often in prayer to substitute for the four-letter Name known as the Tetragrammaton.

Aggadah (pl. *aggadot*)   the body of Jewish legends; specifically, those found in the Talmud and Midrash.

Agunah (pl. *agunot*)   a woman who is forbidden to remarry, either because her husband has abandoned her without a divorce or because there is no proof of his death, even though he is believed dead.

Aher   lit. "the Other." The name given to the talmudic sage Elisha ben Abuyah after he became an apostate.

Akatriel Yah   one of the names of God.

Akedah   the binding of Isaac by Abraham on Mount Moriah.

Aleph   the first letter of the Hebrew alphabet.

Aliyah   Lit. "going up." The term refers to those called up to the Torah as well as those who emigrate to the Land of Israel.

Amidah   the prayers also known as *Shmoneh Esreh* or the Eighteen Benedictions, which are found in all daily, Sabbath, and holiday services. This prayer is recited while standing.

Arabot   the highest realm of heaven.

Ari   the acronym for Rabbi Isaac Luria, who lived in Safed in the sixteenth century and is credited with having created the myth of the Shattering of the Vessels and the Gathering of the Sparks.

Aron ha-Kodesh   lit. "the holy Ark." The Ark of the Covenant, in which the scroll of the Torah is kept.

Asmodeus   the king of demons, the nemesis of King Solomon, and a familiar figure in Jewish folklore.

Ba'al Teshuvah   lit. "master of return." One who returns to the observance of Jewish life and ritual.

Baruch ha-Shem   lit. "Bless the Name." A phrase of thanksgiving.

Bat Kol   a heavenly voice.

Beit Din   a rabbinic court convened to decide issues relating to the *Halachah* or law.

Beit Knesset   a house of prayer.

Beit Midrash   a house of study, traditionally found next to the *Beit Knesset*.

Bereshith   lit. "in the beginning." The first word of the Torah.

Besht (BeSHT)   an acronym for the Baal Shem Tov, the founder of Hasidism.

Bet   the second letter of the Hebrew alphabet and the first letter of the first word of the Torah, *Bereshith*.

Bimah   the podium from which prayers are offered.

Birkat ha-Mazon   the blessing after meals.

Birkat Kohanim   the priestly blessing.

Brit   lit. "covenant." The circumcision given to every male Jewish child on the eighth day after birth. The complete term is *brit milah*, or "covenant of the circumcision."

Challah   bread baked for the Sabbath and holidays, which is often braided.

Daven   Yiddish for "to pray." Refers especially to the intense prayers of the Hasidim, who, following the dictum of the Baal Shem Tov, attempt to daven with *kavanah*, or spiritual intensity.

Devekut   cleaving to God, often of a mystical nature.

Drash   an interpretation of a passage of the Bible. Also the third level of the system of biblical interpretation known as PaRDeS, which represents allegory.

D'var Torah   lit. "word of Torah." A concise lesson in Torah, interpreting a portion of the Bible or Talmud or another sacred text.

Dybbuk   the soul of one who has died that enters the body of one who is living and remains until exorcised.

Ein Sof   lit. "endless" or "infinite." The highest, unknowable aspect of the Divinity.

Emeth   truth.

Erev   lit. "evening." The eve on which Jewish celebrations begin.

Eruv   A boundary around a city in which an observant Jew is permitted to perform actions on the Sabbath that would otherwise be considered work.

Etrog   the citron, one of the four species of plants carried and symbolically shaken as part of the Sukkot celebration.

Eretz Yisrael   the Land of Israel.

Even Shetiyah   the Foundation Stone of the world.

Gabbai an honorary synagogue officer.

Galut the forced exile of the Jewish people from the Land of Israel; the Diaspora.

Gan Eden the Garden of Eden. The term is also used to refer to the heavenly Paradise.

Gehenna the place where the souls of the wicked are punished and purified; the equivalent of hell in Jewish legend.

Gematria a technique used by Jewish mystics to discern secret meanings in the Torah. In this system each Hebrew letter has a numerical value, and the commentator seeks out words or word combinations that have the same totals, which are then regarded as linked.

Get a bill of divorcement.

Gilgul the transmigration of souls. The kabbalistic equivalent of the belief in reincarnation.

Guf the treasury of souls in Paradise.

Hagigah a tractate in the Talmud that contains many episodes of a mystical nature.

Halachah the code of Jewish religious law, which also includes ethical, civil, and criminal matters.

Hanukah festival celebrated for eight days to commemorate the successful struggle of the Jews led by Judah Maccabee and the rededication of the Holy Temple in Jerusalem.

Hasid (pl. *Hasidim*) lit. "a pious one." A follower of Hasidism, a Jewish sect founded by the Baal Shem Tov. Hasidim are usually associated with a religious leader, known as a "rebbe," as disciples.

Hatavat Halom a ritual in which a dream is interpreted.

Havdalah lit. "to distinguish" or "to separate." The ceremony performed at the end of the Sabbath, denoting the separation of the Sabbath from the rest of the week that follows.

Hazzan a cantor.

Hekhaloth lit. "palaces." Refers to the visions of the Jewish mystics of the palaces of heaven. The texts describing these visions and the ascent into Paradise are known as "Hekhaloth texts."

Hevra Kadisha the society that fulfills all the ritual requirements for a Jewish funeral.

Huppah the bridal canopy.

Ibur the spirit of a dead sage that fuses with a living person and strengthens his faith and wisdom. A positive kind of possession, the opposite of possession by a *dybbuk*.

Iyar the second month of the Jewish religious calendar.

Kabbalah lit. "to receive." The term designating the texts of Jewish mysticism. A Kabbalist is one who devotes himself to the study of those texts.

Kabbalat Shabbat a kabbalistic ceremony that takes place just before the onset on the Sabbath to welcome the Sabbath Queen.

Kaddish an ancient prayer, written in Aramaic, sanctifying the name of God, which is recited by mourners as a prayer for the dead. A son is required to say it for his parents three times a day for eleven months following their deaths.

Kadosh lit. "holy."

Kapparot lit. "expiation." A ceremony performed on the day before Yom Kippur in which a person's sins are symbolically transferred to a fowl.

Karaites A Jewish sect that emerged in the eighth century and rejected the Oral Law. Their rabbinic opponents made intermarriage between Jews and Karaites forbidden, and the Karaites have remained a small sect every since, no longer regarded as Jewish.

Kavanah lit. "intention." The spirit or intensity that is brought to prayer and other rituals, without which prayer is an empty form.

Kedushah holiness.

Kehillah the Jewish community.

Ketubah a traditional Jewish marriage contract.

Kfitsat ha-Derech lit. "leaping of the way." A kind of enchanted travel, often associated with the tales of the Baal Shem Tov, in which his wagon traveled great distances in a short time, without the wheels ever touching the ground.

Kiddush the blessing over a cup of wine preceding the Sabbath eve or holiday eve meal.

Kinneret the Hebrew name for the Sea of Galilee.

Kippot (sing. *kippah*) skullcaps worn by religious Jews.

Kleippot lit. "shells." A kabbalistic concept referring to the empty shells that represent the concentrated forces of evil and obstruction.

Kohanim the priestly sect among Jews.

Kol Nidre The opening words of the evening service commencing Yom Kippur, the Day of Atonement.

Kotel lit. "wall." The retaining wall that is the only remaining section of the Temple in Jerusalem still standing. It is also known as the Western Wall and the Wailing Wall.

Kugel a traditional Jewish noodle pudding.

Kvittel a note written by a petitioner to a Hasidic rabbi explaining why an audience with the rabbi has been requested.

Lag ba-Omer festival that falls between Passover and Shavuot.

Lamed Vav Tzaddikim   the thirty-six Just men who, according to legend, exist in every generation. By their merit, the world is sustained.

Liliah   the Angel of Conception.

Lilith   Adam's first wife, according to Jewish legend, who went on to become the Queen of Demons.

Lulav   a palm branch. It is used in the Sukkoth festival.

Ma'ariv   the evening prayer.

Ma'aseh Bereshith   lit. "the work of creation." The mystical doctrine of the secrets of creation.

Ma'aseh Merkavah   lit. "the work of the chariot." The mystical doctrine associated with the vision of Ezekiel.

Maggid   a preacher who confined his talks to easily understood homiletics, such as the *Maggid* of Dubno. Also, a spirit invoked by the study of a sacred text.

Mahzor   a prayer book of Jewish festivals.

Maharal   acronym for Rabbi Judah Loew of Prague.

Malach ha-Moves   the Angel of Death.

Mashal   a parable.

Mashiah   the Messiah. According to Jewish tradition there will be two Messiahs: Messiah ben Joseph, who will prepare the way, and Messiah ben David, who will bring the End of Days.

Mashumid   an apostate.

Matzah   the traditional unleavened bread baked for Passover.

Mehitzah   a partition used in Orthodox synagogues separating men and women during public prayers.

Melamed   a teacher, usually of young children.

Menorah   a seven-branched candelabrum, described in the Bible, used on Temple days. There is a special menorah, known as a Hanukiah, for the use of the festival of Hanukah, which has nine branches—one to be lit on each night and one to be used for the lighting of others.

Merkavah   "chariot." The Divine Chariot in the vision of Ezekiel.

Metatron   the angel into which Enoch was transformed, who serves as the heavenly scribe and is the highest among all the angels.

Mezuzzah (pl. *mezuzzot*)   lit. "doorpost." A small case containing a piece of parchment upon which is written the prayer that begins *"Shema Yisrael."* This case is affixed to the right doorpost of a Jew's home in accordance with the biblical injunction.

Midrash   a method of exegesis of the biblical test. Also refers to post-talmudic Jewish legends as a whole.

Mikveh   the ritual bath in which women immerse themselves after menstruation has ended. It is also used occasionally by men for purposes of ritual purification.

Minhag (pl. *minhagim*)   a local custom.

Minhah   the afternoon prayer.

Minyan   the quorum of ten males over the age of thirteen that is required for any congregational service.

Mishnah   the earliest portion of the Talmud, consisting of six orders, each divided into tractates. The Mishnah is believed to contain the Oral Law transmitted from the time of the giving of the Torah at Mount Sinai.

Mishpatim   Exodus 21:1–24:18

Mitnagdid (pl.: *Mitnagdim*)   an opponent of the Hasidim.

Mitzvah (pl.: *mitzvot*)   a divine commandment. There are 613 *mitzvot* listed in the Torah. The term has also come to mean a good deed.

Modeh Ani   the prayer that is said immediately upon awakening. It thanks God for restoring the soul, which dwells on high during sleep, to the body.

Mohel   one who performs the ritual circumcision of the *brit*.

Motze Shabbat   the period at the end of the Sabbath. Traditionally among the Hasidim a time of reflection or celebration.

Nahash Hadmoni   the primal serpent, one manifestation of the Evil One, or Satan. Primarily a kabbalistic concept derived from the encounter of Eve and the Serpent in Genesis.

Neilah   lit. "closing." The last of the five prayers recited on Yom Kippur.

Ner Tamid   the eternal light prescribed in Exodus 27:20–21 and Leviticus 24:2 as an essential part of the Sanctuary and later of the Temple.

Nekevah   the feminine aspect of the soul.

Neshamah   a soul.

Neshamah Yeterah   the extra soul that is said to be received on the Sabbath.

Niggun   a traditional chant to a prayer, especially popular among Hasidim.

Omer   the counting of the fifty days between Passover and Shavuoth.

Parashah   the weekly portion of the Torah that is read aloud during Sabbath (and festival) services, so divided that the reading begins and ends on Simhat Torah, then begins anew.

Pardes, PaRDeS   lit. "orchard"; also a root term for "Paradise." Also an acronym of a system of textural exegesis based on four levels of interpretation: *peshat* (literal), *remez* (symbolic), *drash* (allegorical), and *sod* (mystical).

Pargod   lit. "curtain." In Jewish mysticism it refers to the curtain that is said to hang before the Throne of Glory in Paradise, which separates God from the angels.

Pesach the holiday of Passover.

Peshat a literal kind of textural exegesis. Also the first level of interpretation in the system known as *Pardes*.

Pilpul a fine point of the Law. Literally, "pepper," to indicate the intricacies of talmudic argument.

Rashbi an acronym for Rabbi Shimon bar Yohai.

Raziel the Angel of Secrets, who also serves as a heavenly messenger.

Reb an honorific term used among Jews to address a man who is a scholar. It is also used among Hasidim to address each other.

Rebbe the term used for Hasidic leaders and masters. It is a Yiddish form of "rabbi."

Remez lit. "a hint." The second level of interpretation in the system known by the acronym *Pardes*. It implies the perception that the meaning has moved from the literal to the symbolic.

Responsa the replies of the rabbis to questions that relate to Jewish law.

Rosh Hashanah the Jewish New Year, which takes place on the first day of Tishri. Tradition says that the world was created on Rosh Hashanah.

Rosh Hodesh festival of the new moon.

Rosh Yeshivah the head of a Yeshivah.

Ruach lit. "spirit" or "wind." One of the three primary aspects of the soul, representing the spirit.

Ruach ha-Kodesh the Holy Spirit.

Samael the Evil One.

Sandalphon the angel in Paradise who weaves the prayers of Israel into garlands of prayer for God to wear on the Throne of Glory.

Sefer lit. "book." A book, especially a holy book.

Sefer Ezekiel The book of Ezekiel in the Bible.

Sefer Pardes a lost book reputed to have been written by Moshe de Leon.

Sefer Raziel a legendary book said to have been given to Adam by the angel Raziel at God's command. It was believed to have been destroyed along with the Temple in Jerusalem. In the Middle Ages, a book consisting largely of spells reclaimed the title and was a common text in many Jewish homes.

Sefer Yetzirah an early (eighth century) kabbalistic treatise.

Sefirot kabbalistic concept of emanations, ten in all, through which the world came into being.

Shabbat the Sabbath.

Shahareis the morning prayer.

Shammash lit. "servant." The beadle of a synagogue.

Shavuot   the Feast of Weeks festival, which falls exactly seven weeks after Passover. It is also identified as the anniversary of the giving of the Torah on Mount Sinai.

Sheilat Sefer   a method of divination in which a sacred text is opened at random and a passage pointed to that is understood to be the reply to the question.

Shekhinah   lit. "to dwell." The Divine Presence, usually identified as a feminine aspect of the Divinity, which evolved into an independent mythic figure in the kabbalistic period. Also identified as the Bride of God and the Sabbath Queen.

Sheol   the underworld limbo of the dead.

Shema   the central prayer of Judaism: *Shema Yisrael, Adonai Elohanu, Adonai Ehad*—Hear O Israel, the Lord our God, the Lord is One. It is based on Deuteronomy 6:4–9.

Shiur   the time between the Minhah and Ma'ariv services, often utilized as a study session.

Shivhei ha-Besht   (*In Praise of the Baal Shem Tov*) the earliest book of the tales of the Baal Shem Tov.

Shofar   the ram's horn that is ritually blown on the High Holy Days.

Shohet   a ritual slaughter.

Shtetl   a small rural village inhabited almost exclusively by Jews.

Shulhan Aruch   the Code of Jewish law, compiled by Joseph Caro.

Siddur   a prayer book.

Simhat Torah   the last day of the festival of Sukkot, on which the cycle of reading from the Torah is concluded and begun again.

Sitre Ahre   the side of evil in kabbalistic terminology.

Sod   the fourth level of the four-level system of biblical interpretation known as *Pardes*. It refers to secret or mystical interpretations.

Sopher   A scribe. One who writes holy texts and also records, as they are spoken, the teachings and tales of Hasidic rebbes.

Sukkah   a booth in which Jews are commanded to live for seven days so as to remember the Israelites who resided in booths during their exodus from Egypt. Its roof must be covered with boughs, which are not attached and through which the stars are visible.

Sukkot   the festival commemorating the completion of the harvest.

Tallis   a prayer shawl.

Talmud   the second most sacred Jewish text after the Bible. The term "Talmud" is the comprehensive designation for the Mishnah and the Gemara as a single unit. There are Babylonian and Jerusalem Talmuds, which have different Gemaras commenting on the same Mishnah. The material in the Talmud consists of both Halachah and Aggadah, law and legend, as well as discussions on philosophy, medicine, agriculture, astronomy, and hygiene.

Tanach the Bible. An acronym made up of *Torah* (the Five Books of Moses), *Neviim* (Prophets), and *Ketuvim* (Writings).

Targum lit. "translation" in Aramaic. The translation of the Bible into Aramaic.

Tefillin Phylacteries worn by men over the age of thirteen during the daily morning prayers (except on the Sabbath).

Tekhelet a blue dye that Jews were enjoined to use to color a thread in the fringes of the *tallis* (Num. 15:37–38). By the talmudic period it was no longer known which creature supplied the dye to make it, and the rabbis decided to leave the thread white rather than to dye it incorrectly.

Teshuvah lit. "return." Repentance.

Tetragrammaton the four-letter ineffable Name of God: YHVH. The true pronunciation is believed to have been lost, and the knowledge of it is believed to confer great power.

Tikkun lit. "repair." Restoration and redemption.

Tikkun Olam repair or restoration of the world.

Tisha B'Av the ninth of Av, traditionally the day on which the First and Second Temples were destroyed. It is a day of mourning on which disasters have recurred among the Jewish people.

Torah the first five books of the Bible, which, according to Jewish tradition, were given by God to Moses on Mount Sinai. The most sacred books of the Bible.

Tosefet Shabbat delaying the close of the Sabbath as long as possible.

Tsitsis the fringes of the prayer shawl.

Tu B'shvat the 15th of the month of Shevat, when it is customary to plant tree saplings in Israel. It is the day the almond blossoms are said to first appear.

Tzaddik an unusually righteous and spiritually pure person. Hasidim believed their rebbes to be *tzaddikim*.

Tzaddik ha-Dor the leading *tzaddik* of his generation.

Tzedakah charity/righteousness.

Tzimtzum the kabbalistic concept of the contraction of God that took place at the time of the creation to make space for the world to exist.

Tzohar the illuminating stone of Jewish legend, which Noah is said to have hung in the ark as a source of light at night.

Urim Ve'Thummim the oracular breastplate worn by the High Priest in the Temple.

Viduy a confession addressed directly to God for the purpose of repentance.

Yahrzeit Yiddish term meaning the anniversary of the death of a close relative.

Yenne Velt (Yiddish) lit. "the Other World." The realm of angels, spirits, and demons.

Yeshivah school for talmudic and rabbinic studies.

Yetzer ha-Ra the Evil Inclination.

Yetzer ha-Tov the Good Inclination.

Yom Kippur the most solemn day of the Jewish religious year. The Day of Judgment, in which God is believed to inscribe a person's name in the Book of Life for the coming year, sealing a person's fate.

Zohar The Book of Splendor. The primary book of Kabbalah, the body of Jewish mystical texts.

BIBLIOGRAPHY

The following is a selected bibliography of books and articles in English and in
English translation relevant to the subject of Jewish mysticism. For references
from other languages, see the sources to the individual stories.

Abelson, Joshua. *The Immanence of God in Rabbinical Literature*. New York: 1969.
Abelson, Joshua. *Jewish Mysticism: An Introduction to the Kabbalah*. New York: 1981.
Abrahams, Israel. *Jewish Life in the Middle Ages*. New York: 1975.
Achtemeier, Paul J., general ed. *Harper's Bible Dictionary*. San Francisco: 1985.
Agnon, Shmuel Yosef, ed. *Days of Awe*. New York: 1948.
Alter, Robert, and Frank Kermode. *The Literary Guide to the Bible*. Cambridge, Mass.:
    1987.
Andrew Handler, trans. *Rabbi Eizik: Hasidic Stories About the Zaddik of Kallo*. Ruther-
    ford, N.J.: 1978.
Ansky, S. *The Dybbuk*. Los Angeles: 1974.
Applefeld, Aharon, ed. *From the World of Rabbi Nahman of Bratslav*. Jerusalem: 1973.
Ariel, David S. *The Mystic Quest: An Introduction to Jewish Mysticism*. Northvale,
    N.J.: 1988.
Aron, Milton. *Ideas and Ideals of the Hasidim*. New York: 1980.
Aryeh, Isaiah, and Joshua Dvorkes, eds. *The Baal Shem Tov on Pirkey Avoth*. Jerusa-
    lem: 1974.
Attar, Farid Al-Din. *Muslim Saints and Mystics*. London: 1990.
Ausubel, Nathan, ed. *A Treasury of Jewish Folklore*. New York: 1948.
Bader, Gershom. *The Encyclopedia of Talmudic Sages*. Northvale, N.J.: 1988.
Baer, Yitzhak. *A History of the Jews in Christian Spain*. Philadelphia: 1961. Two
    volumes.
Bakan, David. *Sigmund Freud and the Jewish Mystical Tradition*. New York: 1965.
Bamberger, Bernard J. *Fallen Angels*. Philadelphia: 1952.
Band, Arnold J., trans. *Nahman of Bratslav: The Tales*. New York: 1978.
Barash, Asher. *A Golden Treasury of Jewish Tales*. Tel Aviv: 1965.
Baron, Salo Wittmayer. *A Social and Religious History of the Jews*, second ed. New
    York: 1957. Seventeen volumes.
Bazak, Joseph. *Judaism and Psychical Phenomena*. New York: 1967.
Ben Zion, Raphael. *The Way of the Faithful: An Anthology of Jewish Mysticism*. Los
    Angeles: 1945.
Ben-Ami, Issachar, and Joseph Dan, eds. *Studies in Aggadah and Jewish Folklore*.
    Jerusalem: 1983.

Ben-Amos, Dan. "Talmudic Tall Tales." In *Folklore Today: A Festschrift for Richard M. Dorson*, ed. by L. Degh, H. Glassie, and F. J. Oinas, 25–44. Bloomington, Ind.: 1976.

Ben-Amos, Dan. "Jewish Folklore Studies." *Modern Judaism* 11:1 (1991), 19–66.

Ben-Amos, Dan, and Jerome Mintz, trans. *In Praise of the Baal Shem Tov: The Earliest Collection of Legends About the Founder of Hasidism (Shivhei ha-Besht)*. Bloomington, Ind.: 1970.

Ben-Sasson, H. H., ed. *A History of the Jewish People*. Cambridge, Mass.: 1976.

Ben-Zvi, Itzhak. *The Exiled and the Redeemed*. Philadelphia: 1957.

Bension, Ariel. *The Zohar in Moslem and Christian Spain*. New York: 1974.

Bergman, Simcha, trans. *Likutey Moharan by Rabbi Nachman of Breslov*. Jerusalem: 1986–1990. Three volumes to date.

Bettan, Israel. *Studies in Jewish Preaching*. New York: 1976.

Bialik, Hayim Nachman. *And It Came to Pass: Legends and Stories About King David and King Solomon*. New York: 1938.

Bin Gorion, Micha Joseph (Berditchevsky). *Mimekor Yisrael: Classical Jewish Folktales*. Abridged and Annotated Edition. Bloomington, Ind.: 1990.

Birnbaum, Salomo. *The Life and Sayings of the Baal Shem*. New York: 1933.

Bloch, Abraham P. *The Biblical and Historical Background of the Jewish Holy Days*. New York: 1978.

Bloch, Chayim. *The Golem: Legends of the Ghetto of Prague*. Vienna: 1925.

Bloch, Chayim. "Legends of the Ari" in *Menorah Journal*, 14 (1928), 371–84, 466–77.

Blumenthal, David R. *Understanding Jewish Mysticism*. New York: 1978–1982. Two volumes.

Bokser, Ben Zion. *From the World of the Cabbalah*. New York: 1954.

Bokser, Ben Zion, trans. *Abraham Isaac Kook: The Lights of Penitence, the Moral Principles, Lights of Holiness, Essays, Letters and Poems*. New York: 1978.

Bokser, Ben Zion. *The Jewish Mystical Tradition*. New York: 1981.

Bokser, Ben Zion. *The Talmud: Selected Writings*. New York: 1989.

Borgen, P. *Bread from Heaven*. Leiden: 1965.

Braude, William G., and Israel J. Kapstein, trans. *The Midrash on Psalms (Midrash Tehillim)*. New Haven, Conn.: 1959. Two volumes.

Braude, William G., and Israel J. Kapstein, trans. *Pesikta Rabbati: Discourses for Feasts, Fasts and Special Sabbaths*. New Haven, Conn.: 1968. Two volumes.

Braude, William G., and Israel J. Kapstein, trans. *Pesikta de-Rab Kahana: R. Kahana's Compilation of Discourses for Sabbaths and Festal Days*. Philadelphia: 1975.

Braude, William G., and Israel J. Kapstein, trans. *Tanna Debe Eliyahu: The Lore of the School of Elijah*. Philadelphia: 1981.

Bregman, Marc. "Past and Present in Midrashic Literature." *Hebrew Annual Review* 2 (1978), 45–59.

Bregman, Marc. "Joseph Heinneman's Studies on the Aggadah." *Immanuel* 9 (1979), 58–62.

Bregman, Marc. "The Darshan: Preacher and Teacher of Talmudic Times." *The Melton Journal* 4 (1982), 3, 19, 26.

Breslauer, S. Daniel. *Martin Buber on Myth: An Introduction*. New York and London: 1990.

Brinner, William M., trans. *An Elegant Composition Concerning Relief After Adversity, by Nissim ben Jacob ibn Shahin*. New Haven, Conn.: 1977.

Broch, Yitzhak I. *Shir Ha-Shirim: The Song of Songs with a Midrashic Commentary*. Jerusalem and New York: 1968.

Broznick, Norman M. "Some Aspects of German Mysticism as Reflected in the *Sefer Hasidim*." M.A. thesis, Columbia University, 1947.

Buber, Martin. *Tales of the Hasidim: Early Masters*. New York: 1947.

Buber, Martin. *Ten Rungs: Hasidic Sayings*. New York: 1947.

Buber, Martin. *Tales of the Hasidim: Later Masters*. New York: 1948.

Buber, Martin. *The Way of Man: According to the Teaching of Hasidism*. New York: 1950.

Buber, Martin. *The Tales of Rabbi Nachman*. New York: 1956.

Buber, Martin. *Hasidism and Modern Man*. New York: 1958.

Buber, Martin. *Tales of Angels, Spirits and Demons*. New York: 1958.

Buber, Martin. *The Origin and Meaning of Hasidism*. New York: 1960.

Buber, Martin. *The Legend of the Baal-Shem*. New York: 1969.

Butler, Alban. *Lives of the Saints*. New York: 1956.

Buxbaum, Yitzhak. *Jewish Spiritual Practices*. Northvale, N.J.: 1990.

Campbell, Joseph. *The Hero with a Thousand Faces*. Princeton: 1975.

Campbell, Joseph. *The Masks of God: Occidental Mythology*. New York: 1964.

Campbell, Joseph, ed. *Myths, Dreams, and Religion*. Dallas: 1988.

Charles, R. H., ed. *The Apocrypha and Pseudepigrapha of the Old Testament*. Oxford: 1913. Two volumes.

Charlesworth, James H., ed. *The Old Testament Pseudepigrapha*. New York: 1983–1985. Two volumes.

Chitrik, Yehuda. *From My Father's Shabbos Table: A Treasury of Chabad Chassidic Stories*. Jerusalem: 1991.

Cohen, A. *Everyman's Talmud*. New York: 1975.

Cohen, Arthur A., and Paul Mendes-Flohr, eds. *Contemporary Jewish Religious Thought*. New York: 1987.

Coleridge, Samuel Taylor. *Selected Poetry and Prose*. 2nd edition. Edited by Elisabeth Schneider. San Francisco: 1971.

Cordovero, Moses. *The Palm Tree of Deborah*. London: 1960.

Covitz, Joel. *Visions of the Night: A Study of Jewish Dream Interpretation*. Boston: 1990.

Daiches, Samuel. *Babylonian Oil Magic in the Talmud and in the Later Jewish Literature*. London: 1913.

Dale, Rodney, ed. *The Kabbalah Decoded*. London: 1978.

Dan, Joseph. "The Beginnings of Jewish Mysticism in Europe." In Roth, Cecil, gen. ed. *The Dark Ages: Jews in Christian Europe*, Vol. 11, New Brunswick, N.J.: 1966, 282–90.

Dan, Joseph. "The Desert in Jewish Mysticism: The Kingdom of Samael" *Ariel*, no. 40 (1976), 38–43.

Dan, Joseph, ed. *Readings in Hasidism*. New York: 1979.

Dan, Joseph. "Samael, Lilith and the Concept of Evil in Early Kabbalah." *AJS Review*, 5 (1980), 17–40.

Dan, Joseph, and Frank Talmage, eds. *Studies in Jewish Mysticism*. Cambridge, Mass.: 1982.

Dan, Joseph. *The Teachings of Hasidism*. New York: 1983.

Dan, Joseph. *Three Types of Ancient Jewish Mysticism*. Cincinnati: 1984.

Dan, Joseph, ed. *Binah: Studies in Jewish History*. New York: 1985. Two volumes.

Dan, Joseph. *Jewish Mysticism and Jewish Ethics*. Seattle and London: 1986.

Dan, Joseph, ed. *The Early Kabbalah*. New York: 1987.

Dan, Joseph. *Gershom Scholem and the Mystical Dimension of Jewish History*. New York: 1988.

Dan, Joseph. *The Revelation of the Secret of the World: The Beginning of Jewish Mysticism in Late Antiquity*. Providence, R.I.: 1992.

Dan, Joseph. "Scholem's View of Jewish Messianism." *Modern Judaism* 12 (1992), 47–128.

Dan, Joseph. "Prayer as Text and Prayers as Mystical Experience." In *Torah and Wisdom: Studies in Jewish Philosophy, Kabbalah and Halacha*. Ed. Ruth Link-Salinger. New York: 1993.

Danby, Herbert. *The Mishnah*. London: 1933.

Davidson, Gustav. *A Dictionary of Angels*. New York: 1967.

Davies, Thomas Witton. *Magic, Divination and Demonology Among the Hebrews and Their Neighbors*. New York: 1909.

De Lange, Nicholas. *Apocrypha: Jewish Literature of the Hellenistic Age*. New York: 1978.

De Manhar, Nurho, trans. *Zohar*. San Diego, Calif.: 1978.

Dobh Baer of Lubavitch. *On Ecstasy*. Chappaqua, N.Y.: 1963.

Dorfman, Yitzchak. *The Maggid of Mezritch*. Southfield, Mich.: 1989.

Dresner, Samuel H. *The Zaddik: The Doctrine of the Zaddik According to the Writings of Rabbi Yaakov Yosef of Polnoy*. New York: 1974.

Dresner, Samuel H. *Levi Yitzhak of Berditchev: Portrait of a Hasidic Master*. New York: 1974.

Eberhard, Wolfram. *Folktales of China*. Chicago: 1965.

Einhorn, David. *The Seventh Candle and Other Folk Tales of Eastern Europe*. New York: 1968.

Elbaz, Andre E. *Folktales of the Canadian Sephardim*. Toronto: Fitzhenry & Whitehead, 1982.

Eliach, Yaffa, ed. *Hasidic Tales of the Holocaust*. New York: 1982.

Elworthy, Frederick Thomas. *The Evil Eye*. London: 1895.

Epstein, I., ed. *The Babylonian Talmud*. London: 1935–52. Eighteen volumes.

Epstein, Perle. *Kabbalah: The Way of the Jewish Mystic*. New York: 1978.

Fine, Lawrence. *Safed Spirituality: Rules of Mystical Piety: The Beginning of Wisdom*. New York: 1984.

Finkelstein, Louis. *The Jews: Their History, Culture, and Religion*, third ed. New York: 1960. Two volumes.

Fishbane, Michael. *Biblical Interpretation in Ancient Israel*. Oxford: 1985.

Fishbane, Michael. *The Garments of the Torah: Essays in Biblical Hermeneutics*. Bloomington, Ind.: 1989.

Fleer, Gedaliah. *Rabbi Nachman's Fire: An Introduction to Breslover Chassidus*. New York: 1975.

Fleer, Gedaliah. *Rabbi Nachman's Foundation*. New York: 1976.

Fox, Samuel J. *Hell in Jewish Literature*. Northbrook, Ill.: 1972.

Franck, Adolphe. *The Kabbalah: The Religious Philosophy of the Hebrews*. New York: 1940.

Frazer, James G. *Folklore of the Old Testament*. London: 1918. Three volumes.

Freedman, H., and Maurice Simon, eds. *Midrash Rabbah*. London: 1939. Ten volumes.

Friedlander, Gerald, trans. *Pirke de Rabbi Eliezer.* New York: 1970.

Friedman, Irving, trans. *The Book of Creation.* New York: 1977.

Gaster, Moses, ed. *Studies and Texts in Folklore, Magic, Medieval Romance, Hebrew Apocrypha and Samaritan Archeology.* London: 1896. Three volumes.

Gaster, Moses, trans. *Ma'aseh Book of Jewish Tales and Legends.* Philadelphia: 1934. Two volumes.

Gaster, Moses. *The Exempla of the Rabbis.* New York: 1968.

Gaster. Moses. *The Chronicles of Jerahmeel.* New York: 1971.

Gaster, Theodor, H. *The Holy and the Profane: Evolution of Jewish Folkways.* New York: 1955.

Gaster, Theodor, H. *Myth, Legend and Custom in the Old Testament.* New York: 1969.

Gaster, Theodor H. *The Dead Sea Scriptures,* third ed. New York: 1976.

Gersh, Harry. *The Sacred Books of the Jews.* New York: 1972.

Ginsburg, Christian D. *The Kabbalah: Its Doctrines, Development, and Literature.* London: 1920.

Ginsburg, Elliot K., trans. *Sod Ha-Shabbat: The Mystery of the Sabbath.* Albany, N.Y.: 1989.

Ginsburg, Elliot K. *The Sabbath in the Classical Kabbalah.* Albany, N.Y.: 1989.

Ginzberg, Louis. *The Legends of the Jews.* Philadelphia: 1909–35. Seven volumes.

Ginzberg, Louis. *On Jewish Law and Lore.* Philadelphia: 1955.

Glatzer, Nahum N. *A Jewish Reader.* New York: 1961.

Glatzer, Nahum N. *The Judaic Tradition.* New York: 1969.

Goldin, Judah, ed. and trans. *The Living Talmud.* Chicago: 1957.

Goldin, Judah. *The Song at the Sea.* New Haven, Conn.: 1971.

Goldin, Judah, trans. *The Fathers According to Rabbi Nathan.* New York: 1974.

Goldin, Judah. *Studies in Midrash and Related Literature.* Philadelphia: 1988.

Goldsmith, Arnold L. *The Golem Remembered: 1909–1980.* Detroit: 1981.

Goldstein, David. *Jewish Folklore and Legend.* London: 1980.

Goldwurm, Hersh. *The Rishonim.* New York: 1982.

Goodenough, Erwin. *By Light, Light: The Mystic Gospel of Hellenistic Judaism.* London and New Haven, Conn.: 1935.

Goodenough, Erwin R. *Jewish Symbols in the Greco-Roman Period.* New York: 1953–68. Thirteen volumes.

Gore, Norman C., trans. *Tzeenah U-Reenah: A Jewish Commentary on the Book of Exodus.* New York: 1965.

Gottlieb, Freema. *The Lamp of God: A Jewish Book of Light.* Northvale, N.J.: 1989.

Gratus, Jack. *The False Messiahs.* London: 1975.

Graves, Robert, and Raphael Patai, eds. *Hebrew Myths: The Book of Genesis.* New York: 1966.

Green, Arthur. "The Role of Jewish Mysticism in a Contemporary Theology of Judaism." *Shefa Quarterly,* 1,4 (1978), 25–40.

Green, Arthur. *Tormented Master: A Life of Rabbi Nahman of Bratslav.* University, Ala.: 1979.

Green, Arthur, trans. *Menahem Nahum of Chernobyl: Upright Practices, The Light of the Eyes.* New York: 1982.

Green, Arthur, trans. "Bratslav Dreams" in *Fiction,* nos. 1 and 2 (1983), 185–202.

Green, Arthur, ed. *Jewish Spirituality.* New York: 1986. Two volumes.

Green, Arthur. *Seek My Face, Speak My Name: A Contemporary Jewish Theology.* Northvale, N.J.: 1992.

Greenbaum, Avraham, trans. *Rabbi Nachman's Tikkun: The Comprehensive Remedy* (*Tikkun Haklali*). Jerusalem: 1984.

Greenbaum, Avraham, trans. *Garden of the Souls: Rebbe Nachman on Suffering*. Jerusalem: 1990.

Greenbaum, Avraham. *Under the Table and How to Get Up: Jewish Pathways of Spiritual Growth*. Jerusalem: 1991.

Gries, Zeev. "Hasidism: The Present State of Research." *Numen* 34, 97–108, 176–213.

Gruenwald, Ithamar. *Apocalyptic and Merkavah Mysticism*. Leiden and Cologne: 1980.

Halperin, David J. *The Faces of the Chariot: Early Jewish Responses to Ezekiel's Vision*. Tübingen: 1988.

Halperin, David J. *The Merkabah in Rabbinic Literature*. New Haven, Conn.: 1980.

Hammer, Reuven, trans. *Sifre: A Tannaitic Commentary on the Book of Deuteronomy*. New Haven, Conn., and London: 1986.

Harris, Maurice H. *Hebraic Literature*. New York: 1941.

Harris, Monford. "Dreams in Sefer Hasidim." *Proceedings of the American Academy for Jewish Research*, 31 (1963), 51–80.

Hartman, Geoffrey H., and Sanford Budick. *Midrash and Literature*. New Haven, Conn., and London: 1986.

Heinnemann, Joseph, and Dov Noy, eds. *Studies in Aggada and Folk Literature*. Jerusalem: 1971.

Heinnemann, Joseph, and Shmuel Werses, eds. *Studies in Hebrew Narrative Art Throughout the Ages*. Jerusalem: 1978.

Heschel, Abraham Joshua. *The Circle of the Baal Shem Tov: Studies in Hasidism*. Chicago: 1985.

Heschel, Abraham Joshua. *The Earth Is the Lord's: The Inner Life of the Jew in East Europe*. New York: 1950.

Heschel, Abraham Joshua. *The Sabbath: Its Meaning for Modern Man*. New York: 1951.

Heschel, Abraham Joshua. *God in Search of Man: A Philosophy of Judaism*. New York: 1955.

Heschel, Abraham Joshua. "The Mystical Element in Judaism." In Finkelstein, Louis, ed. *The Jews: Their History, Culture, and Religion*, third ed. New York: 1960, pp. 932–53. Two volumes.

Higgins, Elford. *Hebrew Idolatry and Superstition: Its Place in Folklore*. London: 1893.

Hilton, James. *Lost Horizon*. New York: 1933.

Himmelfarb, Martha. *Tours of Hell: An Apocalyptic Form in Jewish and Christian Literature*. Philadelphia: 1983.

Hirschman, Jack, trans. *The Book of Noah*. Berkeley, Calif.: 1975.

Hoffman, Edward. *The Way of Splendor: Jewish Mysticism and Modern Psychology*. Northvale, N.J.: 1989.

Holden, Lynn. *Forms of Deformity*. Sheffield, England: 1991.

The Holy Scriptures According to the Masoretic Text. Philadelphia: 1955.

Horowitz, Carmi. *The Jewish Sermon in 14th Century Spain: The Derashot of R. Joshua ibn Shu'eib*. Cambridge, Mass.: 1989.

Hsia, R. Po-chia. *The Myth of Ritual Murder: Jews and Magic in Reformation Germany*. New Haven, Conn., and London: 1988.

Hundert, Gershon David, ed. *Essential Papers on Hasidism: Origins to Present*. New York and London: 1991.

Hurwitz, Siegmund. *Lilith—the First Eve: Historical and Psychological Aspects of the Dark Feminine*. Einsiedeln, Switzerland: 1992.

Idel, Moshe. *Golem: Jewish Magical and Mystical Traditions On the Artificial Anthropoid*. Albany, N.Y.: 1990.

Idel, Moshe *Kabbalah: New Perspectives*. New Haven, Conn., and London: 1988.

Idel, Moshe. *Language, Torah, and Hermeneutics in Abraham Abulafia*. Albany, N.Y.: 1989.

Idel, Moshe. *The Mystical Experience in Abraham Abulafia*. Albany, N.Y.: 1988.

Jacobs, Louis. *Seekers of Unity: The Life and Works of Aaron of Starosselje*. New York: 1966.

Jacobs, Louis. "The Doctrine of the 'Divine Sparks' in Jewish Sources." In Loewe, Raphael, ed. *Studies in Rationalism, Judaism and Universalism in Memory of Leon Roth*. New York: 1966, pp. 87–114.

Jacobs, Louis. *Jewish Ethics, Philosophy and Mysticism*. New York: 1969.

Jacobs, Louis. *Hasidic Prayer*. New York: 1973.

Jacobs, Louis, trans. *The Palm Tree of Deborah*. New York: 1974.

Jacobs, Louis. *Hasidic Thought*. New York:1976.

Jacobs, Louis. *Jewish Mystical Testimonies*. New York: 1977.

Jacobs, Louis. *Holy Living: Saints and Saintliness in Judaism*. Northvale, N.J.: 1990.

Jacobson, David C. *Modern Midrash: The Retelling of Traditional Jewish Narratives by Twentieth Century Hebrew Writers*. Albany, N.Y.: 1987.

Janowitz, Naomi. *The Poetics of Ascent: Theories of Language in a Rabbinic Text*. Albany, N.Y.: 1989.

Josephus. *Jewish Antiquities*. Trans. by J. Thackeray. London: 1950. Nine volumes.

Jung, C. G. *The Archetypes and the Collective Unconscious*, second ed. Princeton: 1968.

Jung, Leo. *Fallen Angels in Jewish, Christian and Mohammedan Literature*. Philadelphia: 1926.

Kafka, Franz. *The Complete Stories*. New York: 1971.

Kafka, Franz. *The Trial*. New York: 1953.

Kaplan, Aryeh, trans. *Rabbi Nachman's Wisdom*. New York: 1971.

Kaplan, Aryeh. *Meditation and the Bible*. York Beach, Me.: 1978.

Kaplan, Aryeh, trans. *The Bahir*. New York: 1979.

Kaplan, Aryeh, trans. *Gems of Rabbi Nachman*. Jerusalem: 1980.

Kaplan, Aryeh, trans. *Outpouring of the Soul: Rabbi Nachman's Path in Meditation*. Jerusalem: 1980.

Kaplan, Aryeh. *The Light Beyond: Adventures in Hasidic Thought*. New York: 1981.

Kaplan, Aryeh. *The Living Torah: The Five Books of Moses*. New York and Jerusalem: 1981.

Kaplan, Aryeh. *Meditation and Kabbalah*. York Beach, Me.: 1982.

Kaplan, Aryeh, trans. *Rabbi Nachman's Stories (Sippurey Ma'asioth): The Stories of Rabbi Nachman of Breslov*. Jerusalem: 1983.

Kaplan, Aryeh. *Chasidic Masters*. New York: 1984.

Kaplan, Aryeh. *Jewish Meditation: A Practical Guide*. New York: 1985.

Kaplan, Aryeh. *A Call to the Infinite*. New York: 1986.

Kaplan, Aryeh. *Innerspace*. Jerusalem: 1990.

Kaplan, Aryeh. *Sefer Yetzirah: The Book of Creation*. York Beach Me.: 1990.

Kasher, Menahem M. *The Western Wall*. New York: 1972.

Kasher, Menahem M., ed. *Encyclopedia of Biblical Interpretation*. New York: 1980. Nine volumes to date.

Katz, Steven T. *Jewish Ideas and Concepts*. New York: 1977.

Kaufman, William E. *Journeys: An Introductory Guide to Jewish Mysticism*. New York: 1980.

Kirsch, James. "The Zaddik in Nachman's Dream." *Journal of Psychology and Judaism*, 3 (1979), 227–34.

Kitov, Eliyahu. *The Book of Our Heritage*. Jerusalem: 1970. Three volumes.

Klapholtz, Yisroel Yaakov, ed. *Tales of the Baal Shem Tov*. Jerusalem: 1970–71. Five volumes.

Klapholtz, Yisroel Yaakov. *Stories of Elijah the Prophet*. B'nai Brak, Israel: 1973. Four volumes.

Klapholtz, Yisroel Yaakov, ed. *Tales of the Heavenly Court*. B'nai Brak, Israel: 1982. Two volumes.

Klar, B. *The Chronicles of Ahimaaz*. New York: 1945.

Klein, Aron, and Jenny Machlowitz Klein, trans. *Tales in Praise of the Ari (Shivhei ha-Ari) by Shlomo Meinsterl*. Philadelphia: 1970.

Klein, Isaac. *A Guide to Jewish Religious Practice*. New York: 1979.

Kluger, Rivkah Scharf. *Satan in the Old Testament*. Evanston, Ill: 1967.

Koenig, Ester, trans. *The Thirteen Stories of Rebbe Nachman of Breslev*. Jerusalem: 1978.

Koltuv, Barbara Black. *The Book of Lilith*. York Beach, Me.: 1986.

Kugel, James L. *In Potiphar's House: The Interpretive Life of Biblical Texts*. San Francisco: 1990.

Lachs, Samuel T. "The Alphabet of Ben Sira: A Study in Folk Literature," *Gratz College Annual of Jewish Studies* (1973), 9–28.

Lamm, Norman, trans. "The Letter of the Besht to R. Gershon of Kutov." *Tradition*, 14,4 (Fall 1974), 110–25.

Lane, Edward William, trans. *Arabian Night's Entertainments; or, the Thousand and One Nights*. New York: 1927.

Langer, Jiri. *Nine Gates to the Chassidic Mysteries*. New York: 1976.

Laurence, Richard. *The Book of Enoch the Prophet*. London: 1883.

Lauterback, Jacob Z., trans. *Mekilta de-Rabbi Ishmael*. Philadelphia: 1935. Three volumes.

Lauterbach, Jacob Z. *Studies in Jewish Law, Custom and Folklore*. New York: 1968. Three volumes.

Lehrman, S. M. *The World of the Midrash*. London and New York: 1961.

Levin, Meyer. *Classic Hassidic Tales*. New York: 1975.

Levner, J. B. *The Legends of Israel*. London: 1946.

Liebes, Yehuda. *Studies in the Zohar*. Albany: 1993.

Locks, Gutman G. *The Spice of Torah—Gematria*. New York: 1985.

Lorand, Sandor. "Dream Interpretation in the Talmud." *The International Journal of Psychoanalysis*, 38 (1957), 92–97.

Maccoby, Hyam. *The Sacred Executioner: Human Sacrifice and the Legacy of Guilt*. New York: 1982.

Mack, Hananel. *The Aggadic Midrash Literature*. Tel Aviv: 1989.

Maitlis, Jacob. *The Ma'aseh in the Yiddish Ethical Literature*. London: 1958.

Manger, Itzik. *The Book of Paradise*. New York: 1965.

Marcus, Ivan G. "The Recensions and Structure of *Sefer Hasidim*." *Proceedings of the American Academy for Jewish Research*, 45 (1978), 131–53.

Marcus, Jacob R. *The Jew in the Medieval World*. Philadelphia: 1960.

Matt, Daniel Chanan, ed. *Zohar: The Book of Enlightenment*. New York: 1983.

Melito, Saint, Bishop of Sardis. *On Pashcha and Fragments*. Oxford: 1979.

Meltzer, David, ed. *The Path of the Names, Writings by Abraham ben Samuel Abulafia*. Berkeley, Calif.: 1976.

Meltzer, David. *The Secret Garden: An Anthology in the Kabbalah*. New York: 1976.

Metzger, Bruce M., ed. *The Apocrypha of the Old Testament*. New York: 1965.

Millgram, Abraham E. *Sabbath: The Day of Delight*. Philadelphia: 1944.

Millgram, Abraham E. *An Anthology of Medieval Hebrew Literature*. New York and London: 1961.

Millgram, Abraham E. *Jewish Worship*. Philadelphia: 1971.

Millgram, Abraham E. *Jerusalem Curiosities*. Philadelphia: 1990.

Mintz, Jerome R., ed. *Legends of the Hasidim: An Introduction to Hasidic Culture and Oral Tradition in the New World*. Chicago: 1968.

Mordell, Phineas. *The Origin of Letters and Numerals According to the Sefer Yetzirah*. New York: 1975.

Muller, Ernst. *History of Jewish Mysticism*. Oxford: 1946.

Musaph-Andriesse, R. C. *From Torah to Kabbalah: A Basic Introduction to the Writings of Judaism*. New York: 1982.

Mykoff, Moshe, ed. *The Breslov Haggadah*. Jerusalem: 1989.

Mykoff, Moshe, trans. *Once Upon a Tzaddik: Tales of Rebbe Nachman of Breslov*. Jerusalem: 1989.

Mykoff, Moshe, and Ozer Bergman, eds. *Likutey Moharan*. Jerusalem: 1886–1990. Four volumes to date.

Nachman of Bratslav. *Restore My Soul! (Meshivat Nefesh)*. Jerusalem: 1980.

Nachman of Bratslav. *Azambra!* Jerusalem: 1984.

Nachman of Bratslav. *Tsohar*. Jerusalem: 1986.

Nachman of Bratslav. *Mayim*. Jerusalem: 1987.

Nachman of Breslov. *The Aleph-Bet Book: Rabbi Nachman's Aphorisms on Jewish Living (Sefer Hamiddot.)*. Jerusalem: 1986.

Nadich, Judah, ed. *Jewish Legends of the Second Commonwealth*. Philadelphia: 1983.

Nahmad, H. M. *A Portion in Paradise and Other Jewish Folktales*. New York: 1970.

Nathan of Breslov. *Advice (Likutey Etzot)*. Jerusalem: 1983.

Nathan of Breslov. *Tzaddik (Chayey Moharan): A Portrait of Rabbi Nachman*. Jerusalem: 1987.

Neubauer, A., and A. Cowley, eds. *Catalogue of the Hebrew Manuscripts in the Bodleian Library*. Oxford: 1886–1906. Two volumes.

Neugroschel, Joachim, ed. *Yenne Velt: The Great Works of Jewish Fantasy and Occult*. New York: 1976. Two volumes.

Neusner, Jacob. *First Century Judaism in Crisis: Yohanan ben Zakkai and the Renaissance of Torah*. New York: 1982.

Neusner, Jacob, and William Scott Green, eds. *Origins of Judaism: Religion, History, and Literature in Late Antiquity*. New York: 1990. Twenty volumes.

Newman, Louis I., and Samuel Spitz. *The Talmudic Anthology: Tales and Teachings of the Rabbis*. New York: 1945.

Newman, Louis I., and Samuel Spitz. *Maggidim and Hasidim: Their Wisdom*. New York: 1962.

Newman, Louis, and Samuel Spitz. *The Hasidic Anthology: Tales and Teachings of the Hasidism*. New York: 1963.

Noah, Mordecai Manuel, trans. *The Book of Yashar (Sefer ha-Yashar)*. New York: 1972.

Noy, Dov. "Motif Index of Talmudic-Midrashic Literature." Ph.D. diss. Indiana University, 1954.

Noy, Dov, ed. *Folktales of Israel*. Chicago: 1963.

Noy, Dov, ed. *Moroccan Jewish Folktales*. New York: 1966.

Noy, Dov. "Is There a Jewish Folk Religion?" In *Studies in Jewish Folklore* ed. Frank Talmage (Cambridge, Mass.: 1980), 273–86.

Noy, Dov. "What is Jewish About the Jewish Folktale?" Foreword to *Miriam's Tambourine: Jewish Folktales from Around the World*, ed. Howard Schwartz (New York: 1986), xi–xix.

Oesterley, William O. E., and George H. Box. *A Short Survey of the Literature of Rabbinical and Mediaeval Judaism*. London and New York: 1920.

O'Hara, John. *Appointment in Samarra*. New York: 1953.

Patai, Raphael. *Man and Temple in Ancient Jewish Myth and Ritual*. New York: 1967.

Patai, Raphael. "Exorcism and Xenoglossia Among the Safed Kabbalists." *Journal of American Folklore*, 91 (1978), 823–35.

Patai, Raphael, ed. *The Messiah Texts*. Detroit: 1979.

Patai, Raphael, ed. *Gates to the New City: A Book of Jewish Legends*. Detroit: 1981.

Patai, Raphael. *On Jewish Folklore*. Detroit: 1983.

Patai, Raphael. *The Hebrew Goddess*, third ed. Detroit: 1991.

Patai, Raphael, Francis Lee Utley, and Dov Noy, eds. *Studies in Biblical and Jewish Folklore*. Bloomington, Ind.: 1960.

Pearl, Chaim, trans. *Sefer Ha-Aggadah*. Tel Aviv: 1989.

Pearl, Chaim, trans. *Stories of the Sages*. Tel Aviv: 1991.

Peretz, I. L. *The Book of Fire*. New York: 1959.

Peretz, I. L. *In This World and the Next*. New York: 1975.

Peretz, I. L. *Selected Stories*. Edited by Irving Howe and Eliezer Greenberg. New York: 1982.

Petuchowski, Jakob J. *Our Masters Taught: Rabbinic Stories and Sayings*. New York: 1982.

Pick, Bernard. *The Cabala: Its Influence on Judaism and Christianity*. La Salle, Ill.: 1974.

Piontac, Nechemiah, ed. *The Arizal: The Life and Times of Rabbi Yitzchak Luria*. New York: 1969.

Prager, Moshe. *Rabbi Yisroel Baal-Shem-Tov*. New York: 1976.

Prose, Francine. *Judah the Pious*. New York: 1973.

Pye, Faye. "A Brief Study of an Hasidic Fairy Tale." *Harvest: Journal for Jungian Studies of the Analytical Psychology Club*, 21 (London, 1975), 94–104.

Rabinowicz, Harry M. *A Guide to Hassidism*. New York: 1960.

Rabinowicz, Harry M. *The Slave Who Saved the City and Other Hasidic Tales*. New York: 1960.

Rabinowicz, Harry M. *Hasidism: The Movement and Its Masters*. Northvale, N.J.: 1988.

Rabinowitsch, Wolf Zeev. *Lithuanian Hasidism*. New York: 1971.

Rader, Benzion, ed. *To Touch the Divine: A Jewish Mysticism Primer*. Brooklyn, N.Y.: 1989.

Rapaport, Samuel. *A Treasury of the Midrash*. New York: 1988.

Rapoport-Albert, Ada. "On Women in Hasidism." In *Jewish History: Essays in Honor of Chimen Abramsky*, ed. Ada Rapoport-Albert and Steven Zipperstein (London: 1988), 495–525.

Rappoport, Angelo S. *The Folklore of the Jews.* London: 1937.

Rappoport, Angelo S. *Myth and Legend of Ancient Israel.* New York: 1966. Three volumes.

Reimer, Jack. "Franz Kafka and Rabbi Nachman." *Jewish Frontier*, 28, 4 (1961), 16–20.

Reps, Paul. *Zen Flesh, Zen Bones.* Garden City, N.Y.: 1961.

Robinson, James M. *The Nag Hammadi Library*, third ed. San Francisco: 1988.

Rosenberg, Roy A., trans. *The Anatomy of God.* New York: 1973.

Rossoff, Dovid. *Safed: The Mystical City.* Jerusalem: 1991.

Roth, Cecil, ed. *The Dark Ages: Jews in Christian Europe 711–1096.* Volume II of *World History of the Jewish People.* New Brunswick, N.J.: 1966.

Roth, Cecil, and G. Wigoder, eds. *Encyclopedia Judaica.* Jerusalem: 1972. Sixteen volumes.

Rothenberg, Jerome, Harris Lenowitz, and Charles Doria, eds. *A Big Jewish Book.* Garden City, N.Y.: 1978.

Rowland, Christopher. "The Vision of God in Apocalyptic Literature." *Journal for the Study of Judaism in the Persian, Hellenistic and Roman Period*, 10 (1979), 137–54.

Rudavsky, David. *Modern Jewish Religious Movements*, third ed. New York: 1979.

Ruderman, David B. *Kabbalah, Magic and Science: The Cultural Universe of a Sixteenth-Century Jewish Physician.* Cambridge, Mass.: 1988.

Ruderman, David B. *A Valley of Vision: The Heavenly Journey of Abraham ben Hananiah Yagel.* Philadelphia: 1990.

Runes, Dagobert D., ed. *The Talmud of Jerusalem.* New York: 1956.

Runes, Dagobert D. *The Wisdom of the Kabbalah.* New York: 1967.

Rush, Barbara, and Eliezer Marcus, eds. *Seventy and One Tales.* New York: 1980.

Sabar, Yona. *The Folk Literature of the Kurdistani Jews: An Anthology.* New Haven, Conn., and London: 1982.

Safran, Alexandre. *The Kabbalah: Laws and Mysticism in the Jewish Tradition.* New York and Jerusalem: 1975.

Safran, Bezalel, ed. *Hasidism: Continuity or Innovation?* Cambridge, Mass., and London: 1988.

Saperstein, Marc. *Decoding the Rabbis: A Thirteenth-century Commentary on the Aggadeh.* Cambridge: 1980.

Saperstein, Marc. "The Simpleton's Prayer: Transformation of a Motif in Hebrew Literature." *Judaism* 29, 3 (1980), pp. 295–304.

Saperstein, Marc. *Jewish Preaching 1200–1800: An Anthology.* New Haven, Conn., and London: 1989.

Sarachek, Joseph. *The Doctrine of the Messiah in Medieval Jewish Literature.* New York: 1932.

Schachter, Zalman M. "Some Recent Mystical Literature: The Dimensions of Devoutness in Jewish Mysticism." *Judaism* 11 (1962), 271–82.

Schachter, Zalman. *Fragments of a Future Scroll.* Germantown, Pa.: 1975.

Schachter, Zalman M., and Edward Hofman. *Sparks of Light: Counseling in the Hasidic Tradition.* Boulder, Colo.: 1983.

Schachter-Shalomi, Zalman Meshullam. *Spiritual Intimacy: A Study of Counseling in Hasidism.* Northvale, N.J.: 1991.

Schäfer, Peter. *The Hidden and Manifest God: Some Major Themes in Early Jewish Mysticism.* Albany, N.Y.: 1992.

Schaya, Leo. *The Universal Meaning of the Kabbalah.* Baltimore: 1972.

Schechter, Solomon. *Studies in Judaism: Essays on Persons, Concepts, and Movements of Thought in Jewish Tradition.* New York: 1970.

Schochet, Elijah Judah. *Animal Life in Jewish Tradition: Attitudes and Relationships.* New York: 1984.

Schochet, Jacob Immanuel. *Rabbi Israel Baal Shem Tov.* Toronto: 1961.

Schochet, Jacob Immanuel. *The Great Maggid: The Life and Teachings of Rabbi Dov Ber of Mezhirech.* Brooklyn, N.Y.: 1974.

Schochet, Jacob Immanuel. *Mystical Concepts in Chassidism.* Brooklyn, N.Y.: 1979.

Schochet, Jacob Immanuel. *The Mystical Dimension.* Brooklyn, N.Y.: 1990. Three volumes.

Scholem, Gershom. *Jewish Gnosticism, Merkabah Mysticism and Talmudic Tradition.* New York: 1960.

Scholem, Gershom. *Zohar: The Book of Splendor.* New York: 1963.

Scholem, Gershom. *Major Trends in Jewish Mysticism.* New York: 1964.

Scholem, Gershom. *On the Kabbalah and Its Symbolism.* New York: 1965.

Scholem, Gershom. *The Messianic Idea in Judaism and Other Essays on Jewish Spirituality.* New York: 1971.

Scholem, Gershom. *Shabbatai Zevi: The Mystical Messiah.* Princeton, N.J.: 1973.

Scholem, Gershom. *Kabbalah.* Jerusalem and New York: 1974.

Scholem, Gershom. *On Jews and Judaism in Crisis: Selected Essays.* New York: 1976.

Scholem, Gershom. *Origins of the Kabbalah.* Philadelphia: 1987.

Scholem, Gershom. *On the Mystical Shape of the Godhead: Basic Concepts in Kabbalah.* New York: 1991.

Schram, Peninnah. *Jewish Stories One Generation Tells Another.* Northvale, N.J.: 1987.

Schram, Peninnah. *Tales of Elijah the Prophet.* Northvale, N.J.: 1991.

Schrire, T. *Hebrew Magic Amulets: Their Decipherment and Interpretation.* London: 1966.

Schurer, Emil. *The Literature of the Jewish People in the Time of Jesus.* New York: 1972.

Schwartz, Howard. "Rabbi Nachman of Bratslav: Forerunner of Modern Jewish Literature." *Judaism,* 31 (1982), 211–24.

Schwartz, Howard. "The Aggadic Tradition." *Judaism,* 32 (1983), 85–101.

Schwartz, Howard, ed. *Elijah's Violin and Other Jewish Fairy Tales.* New York: 1983.

Schwartz, Howard, ed. *Gates to the New City: A Treasury of Modern Jewish Tales.* New York: 1983.

Schwartz, Howard. "Reimagining the Bible." *Response* (1983), 35–46.

Schwartz, Howard. "Tools of Interpretation." *Agada,* 2 (1983), 27–38.

Schwartz, Howard, ed. *Miriam's Tambourine: Jewish Folktales from Around the World.* New York: 1986.

Schwartz, Howard. "Jewish Tales of the Supernatural." *Judaism,* 36 (1987), 339–351.

Schwartz, Howard, ed. *Lilith's Cave: Jewish Tales of the Supernatural.* San Francisco: 1988.

Schwartz, Howard. *The Dream Assembly: Tales of Rabbi Zalman Schachter-Shalomi.* Nevada City, Calif.: 1989.

Schwarzbaum, Haim. *Studies in Jewish and World Folklore.* Berlin: 1968.

Segal, Alan F. *Two Powers in Heaven: Early Rabbinic Reports About Christianity and Gnosticism.* Leiden: 1977.

Segal, Alan F. *Rebecca's Children: Judaism and Christianity in the Roman World.* Cambridge, Mass.: 1986.

Segal, Alan F. *The Other Judaisms of Late Antiquity.* Atlanta, Ga.: 1987.

Segal, Alan F. *Paul the Convert: The Apostolate and Apostasy of Saul the Pharisee.* New Haven, Conn., and London: 1990.

Segal, S. M. *Elijah: A Study in Jewish Folklore.* New York: 1935.

Seymour, St. John D. *Tales of King Solomon.* London: 1924.

Shah, Idries. *Tales of the Dervishes: Teaching-stories of the Sufi Masters.* New York: 1969.

Sharot, Stephen. *Messianism, Mysticism and Magic: A Sociological Analysis of Jewish Religious Movements.* Chapel Hill, N.C.: 1982.

Shenhar, Aliza. "Concerning the Nature of the Motif 'Death by a Kiss' (Motif A185.6.11)." *Fabula,* 19 (1978), 62–73.

Sherwin, Byron L. "The Exorcist's Role in Jewish Tradition." *Occult,* (1975).

Sherwin, Byron L. *Mystical Theology and Social Dissent: The Life and Works of Judah Loew of Prague.* Rutherford, N.J.: 1982.

Sherwin, Byron L. *The Golem Legend: Origins and Implications.* New York: 1985.

Shulman, Yaacov Dovid, trans. *The Return to G-d: Based on the Works of Rabbi Nachman of Breslov and His Holy Disciples (Derech Hatshuvah).* Brooklyn: no date.

Shulman, Yaacov David. *The Chambers of the Palace: The Teachings of Rabbi Nachman.* Northvale, N.J.: 1993.

Silver, Daniel Jeremy. *The Story of Scripture: From Oral Tradition to the Written Word.* New York: 1990.

Silverman, Dov. *Legends of Safed.* Jerusalem: 1991.

Singer, Isaac Bashevis. *The Collected Stories.* New York: 1982.

Singer, Isadore, ed. *The Jewish Encyclopedia.* New York: 1901. Twelve volumes.

Singer, Sholom Alchanan. *Medieval Jewish Mysticism: Book of the Pious (Sefer Hasidim).* Wheeling, Ill: 1971.

Smith, Morton. "Observations on Hekhalot Rabbati." In Altmann, Alexander, ed. *Biblical and Other Studies.* Cambridge, Mass.: 1963.

Soloveitchik, Hayim. "Three Themes in the Sefer Hasidim." *AJS Review,* I (1976), 311–57.

Spector, Sheila A. *Jewish Mysticism: An Annotated Bibliography on the Kabbalah in English.* New York and London: 1984.

Sperber, Daniel. "On Sealing the Abysses" in *Journal for Semitic Studies* 11 (1966), 168ff.

Sperling, Harry, and Maurice Simon, eds. *The Zohar.* London: 1931–34. Five volumes.

Spiegel, Shalom. *The Last Trial.* Philadelphia: 1967.

Steinman, Eliezer. *The Garden of Hasidism.* Jerusalem: 1961.

Steinsaltz, Adin. *The Essential Talmud.* New York: 1976.

Steinsaltz, Adin. "The Imagery Concept in Jewish Thought." *Shefa Quarterly,* 1, 3 (April 1978), 56–62.

Steinsaltz, Adin. *Beggars and Prayers.* New York: 1979.

Steinsaltz, Adin. *The Thirteen Petalled Rose.* New York: 1980.

Steinschneider, Moritz. *Jewish Literature from the Eighth to the Eighteenth Century with an Introduction on Talmud and Midrash.* New York: 1965.

Stern, David, and Mark Jay Mirsky, eds. *Rabbinic Fantasies: Imaginative Narratives from Classical Hebrew Literature.* Philadelphia: 1990.

Stern, David. *Parables in Midrash.* Cambridge, Mass.: 1991.

Stone, Michael E. *Scriptures, Sects and Visions: A Profile of Judaism from Ezra to the Jewish Revolts.* Philadelphia: 1980.

Stone, Michael E., trans. *The Testament of Abraham: The Greek Recensions*. Missoula, Mont.: 1972.

Strack, Hermann L. and G. Sternberger, *Introduction to the Talmud and Midrash*. Minneapolis, Minn.: 1992.

Talmage, Frank, ed. *Studies in Jewish Folklore*. Cambridge, Mass.: 1980.

Tanakh: A New Translation of the Scriptures. Philadelphia: 1985.

Thieberger, Frederic. *The Great Rabbi Loew of Prague: His Life and Work and the Legend of the Golem*. London: 1955.

Thompson, R. Campbell. *Semitic Magic: Its Origins and Development*. New York: 1971.

Tishby, Isaiah. "Gnostic Doctrines in Sixteenth-Century Jewish Mysticism." *Journal of Jewish Studies*, 6 (1955), 146–52.

Tishby, Isaiah, ed. *The Wisdom of the Zohar: An Anthology of Texts*. New York: 1989. Three volumes.

Tolkien, J. R. R. *The Silmarillion*. Boston: 1977.

Townsend, John T. *Midrash Tanhuma*. Hoboken, N.J.: 1989.

The Torah: The Five Books of Moses. Philadelphia: 1962.

Trachtenberg, Joshua. "The Folk Element in Judaism." *The Journal of Religion*, 22 (1942), 173–86.

Trachtenberg, Joshua. *The Devil and the Jews*. New Haven, Conn.: 1943.

Trachtenberg, Joshua. *Jewish Magic and Superstition: A Study in Folk Religion*. New York: 1961.

Twersky, Isadore, ed. *Rabbi Moses Nahmanides (Ramban): Explorations in His Religious and Literary Virtuosity*. Cambridge, Mass.: 1983.

Twersky, Isadore, and Bernard Septimus, eds. *Jewish Thought in the Seventeenth Century*. Cambridge, Mass., and London: 1987.

Unterman, Alan, ed. *The Wisdom of the Jewish Mystics*. New York: 1976.

Unterman, Alan. *Dictionary of Jewish Lore and Legend*. London: 1991.

Unterman, Isaac. *The Talmud: An Analytical Guide to Its History and Teaching*. New York: 1952.

Urbach, Ephraim. *The Sages: Their Concepts and Beliefs*. Jerusalem: 1975. Two volumes.

Van der Horst, Pieter. "Moses' Throne Vision in Ezekiel the Dramatist." *Journal of Jewish Studies*, 34,1 (Spring 1983), 21–29.

Verman, Mark. *The Books of Contemplation: Medieval Jewish Mystical Sources*. Albany, N.Y.: 1992.

Vermes, Geza. *Scripture and Tradition in Judaism*. Leiden: 1961.

Vermes, Geza. *Post-biblical Jewish Studies*. Leiden: 1975.

Vilnay, Zev. *Legends of Jerusalem*. Philadelphia: 1973.

Vilnay, Zev. *Legends of Judea and Samaria*. Philadelphia: 1973.

Vilnay, Zev. *Legends of Galilee, Jordan and Sinai*. Philadelphia: 1978.

Visotzky, Burton I. *Reading the Book: Making the Bible a Timeless Text*. New York: 1991.

Wallach, Shalom Meir. *Haggadah of the Chassidic Masters*. Brooklyn, N.Y.: 1990.

Waxman, Meyer. *A History of Jewish Literature from the Close of the Bible to Our Own Days*. New York: 1960. Six volumes.

Weiner, Herbert. *9 1/2 Mystics: The Kabbala Today*. New York: 1969.

Weinreich, Beatrice Silverman. "The Prophet Elijah in Modern Yiddish Folktales." M.A. thesis, Columbia University, 1957.

Weinreich, Beatrice Silverman, ed. *Yiddish Folktales*. New York: 1988.

Weinreich, Uriel, and Beatrice Silverman Weinreich. *Yiddish Language and Folklore: A Selective Bibliography for Research*. The Hague: 1959.

Weiss, Joseph. *Studies in Eastern European Jewish Mysticism*. London and New York: 1985.

Werblowsky, R. J. Zwi. "Some Psychological Aspects of the Kabbalah." Harvest: *Journal of the Analytical Psychology Club of London*, 3 (London, 1956), 77–96.

Werblowsky, R. J. Zwi. "Mystical and Magical Contemplation: The Kabbalists in Sixteenth-Century Safed." *History of Religions*, 1 (1961), 9–36.

Werblowsky, R. J. Zwi, and Geoffrey Wigoder. *The Encyclopedia of the Jewish Religion*. New York: 1965.

Werblowsky, R. J. Zwi. *Joseph Karo: Lawyer and Mystic*. Philadelphia: 1977.

Werthheim, Aaron. *Law and Custom in Hasidism*. Hoboken, N.J.: 1992.

Westcott, Wm. Wynn, trans. *Sepher Yetzirah: The Book of Formation and the Thirty Two Paths of Wisdom*. New York: 1975.

Wiesel, Elie. *Souls on Fire: Portraits and Legends of Hasidic Masters*. New York: 1972.

Wiesel, Elie. *Somewhere a Master: Further Hasidic Portraits and Legends*. New York: 1981.

Wiesel, Elie. *Sages and Dreamers: Biblical, Talmudic, and Hasidic Portraits and Legends*. New York: 1991.

Wineman, Aryeh. *Beyond Appearances: Stories from the Kabbalistic Ethical Writings*. Philadelphia: 1988.

Winkler, Gershon. *Dybbuk*. York: 1980.

Winkler, Gershon. *The Golem of Prague*. New York: 1982.

Winkler, Gershon. *They Called Her Rebbe*. New York: 1992.

Yassif, Eli. *The Sacrifice of Isaac: Studies in the Development of a Literary Tradition*. Jerusalem: 1979.

Yassif, Eli. *Jewish Folklore: An Annotated Bibliography*. New York: 1986.

Youncenar, Marguerite. *Oriental Tales*. New York: 1985.

Zangwell, Israel. *The Master*. New York: 1897.

Zayis, Shimon, ed. *The Holy Candelabrum: Tales of the Talmud*. Jerusalem: 1988.

Zeitlin, Solomon. "Dreams and Their Interpretation from the Biblical Period to the Tannaitic Time: A Historical Study." *Jewish Quarterly Review*, 66 (1975), 1–18.

Zenner, Walter P. "Saints and Piecemeal Supernaturalism Among the Jerusalem Sephardim." *Anthropological Quarterly*, 38 (1965), 201–217.

Zevin, S. Y. *A Treasury of Chassidic Tales on the Torah*. New York: 1980. Two volumes.

Zimmels, H. J. *Magicians, Theologians and Doctors*. New York: 1952.

Zimmer, Heinrich. *Myths and Symbols in Indian Art and Civilization*. New York: 1946.

Zimmer, Heinrich. *Philosophies of India*. New York: 1951.

Zinberg, Israel. *A History of Jewish Literature*. New York: 1972–78. Twelve volumes.

INDEX

Aaron
  "The Young Man without a Soul" and,
    145–148, 314–315
Aaron (brother of Moses), sons of, 187–189,
  326
Abandoned wives, "Rabbi Naftali's Trance"
  and, 152–154, 316–317
Abba, "The Golden Scepter" and, 73–74,
  291–292
Abbadi, Mordecai, "Interpreting the Zohar"
  and, 154, 317
Abraham, 102, 186, 287, 292, 310, 312, 336
  Angel of Death and, 320
  "Isaac's Ascent" and, 43, 278
  "Miriam's Tambourine" and, 311
  precious stone of, 287
  ram sacrificed by, 69, 127, 201, 312, 313
  tallis of, 136
  "The Tenth Man" and, 135, 312
  the Tzohar and, 60
Abulafia, Abraham, 13
Abulafia, Jacob, 307
Adam, 11, 59, 333
  book given by Raziel to, 74–75, 292–293
  Book of Mysteries and, 185–186
  Fall of, 282
  garments of, 326
  giving of the Tzohar to Seth, 59
  King David's life span and, 114, 306
Adam (Rabbi)
Adam Baal Shem, 328
  "The Book in the Cave" and, 183–187,
    325–326
  "The Prince of Fire" and, 187–189, 326
  tradition linked to, 326
Adultery, 174, 338
Af, 339
Affirmation of God, "A Vision of Light"
  and, 341
Age forty, 293

Aggadah, 8
Agunot, 316
Aher, "The Four Who Entered Paradise"
  and, 29, 51–52, 280–281. See also
  Elisha ben Abuyah
Ahijah the Shilonite, 332, 333
Ahimaaz, 147, 148
Ahitophel, 54, 55
Ahizat Enayim, 330
Akatriel Yah, 55, 284
Akedah, 278
Akiba ben Joseph, 3, 6, 8, 9, 33n, 46, 28,
  29, 103, 283
  death of, 53
  "The Four Who Entered Paradise" and,
    51–52, 280–281
  parallel with Baal Shem Tov, 328
  spirit of, 113
Albuv, Yehoshua, "The Angel in the Mir-
  ror" and, 102, 103, 302–303
Alchemists, 281
Alexander the Great, 24
  "The Gates of Eden" and, 62, 288
Algiers, 309
Alkabetz, Shlomo (Solomon), 112, 300
Alshich, Moshe, "Greeting the Sabbath
  Queen" and, 93–94, 299–300
Amnon of Magence, 171
Amram, 333
Amsterdam, 317
Amulet, 176
Angel(s), 4, 23, 344. See also Maggid
  birth of, 213
  for Children of Israel, 47
  encounters with, 24–25
  evil, 15, 143–145, 314, 336
  God's Name written on forehead of, 144
  good, 336
  human, 336
  imperfect, 260, 336, 352

life span of, 213–214
names of, 13
"Reading of the Lips of the Ari" and, 89–90, 298–299
rebirth of, 214
types of, 144
"Angel in the Mirror, The," 102–103, 302–303
"Angel of Conception, The," 57–58, 286
Angel of Death, 42, 278, 308, 320, 336
bridegroom and, 162–164, 319–320
Reb Pinhas' visit to, 219–221, 337
Angel(s) of destruction, "The Ascent of Moses" and, 45, 279
"Angel of Forgetfulness, The," 81–83, 295–296, 348
"Angel of Friendship, The," 213–214, 336
"Angel of Losses, The," 238, 343–344
"Angel of the Mishnah, The," 25, 112–113, 305–306
Angel of the Sea, 185
Angel of the Torah, 137
"Angel of the Zohar, The," 10, 212, 335–336
"Angel's Daughter, The," 160–161, 319
"Angel's Sword, The," 189–191, 326–327
Anger of God, 267
Anima, 25, 26, 298
Animal, soul entering of, 177
Ankawa, Ephraim ben Yisrael, 309–310
Annopol, 247
Ansky, S., 317, 339
Apocrypha, 24
"Appointment with Death, An," 42, 277–278
Arabian Nights, The, 276–277
Arabot, 23
Aramaic, 79
Archangels, 13
Ari (Isaac Luria), 5, 6, 7, 8, 10, 12, 16, 20, 186, 256, 282, 290, 336
"The Angel in the Mirror" and, 102–103, 302–303
"The Angel of Forgetfulness" and, 81–83, 295–296, 348
Angel of Losses and, 344
"The Blessing of the Kohanim" and, 84–85, 297
"The Body of Moses" and, 100, 302
"The Book of Adam" and, 293
book of tales about, 331
central teachings of, 16
"The Chains of the Messiah" and, 109
"The Dancing of the Ari" and, 83–84, 296–297

death of, *yahrtzeit* of, 103
"Delivering a Message" and, 95–97, 300–301, 309
"Gathering Sparks" and, 94–95, 300
gilgul and, 27
"Greeting the Sabbath Queen" and, 93–94, 299–300
"The Handwriting of the Messiah" and, 31, 103–104, 303
"The Journey to Jerusalem" and, 86, 297, 328
meeting of the Sabbath Queen, 19
mystical power of, 299
myths related to, 16–17
"The Pillar of Cloud" and, 80–81, 295
"The Precious Prayer" and, 86–87, 297–298
"Reading of the Lips of the Ari" and, 89–90, 298–299
Sefirot and, 16–17
Shimon bar Yohai and, 9
soul of, 258–259, 351
ascent of, 299
"The Speaking Flame" and, 90–92, 299
"A Stone in the Wall" and, 97, 301
true teachings of, 96
"A Vision at the Wailing Wall" and, 87–89, 298
"A Visit to the City of the Dead" and, 101–102, 302
"The Widow of Safed" and, 98–99, 301
Ark, 49, 60
building of, *Tzohar* and, 288
"Gabriel's Palace" and, 123
Ark of the Tabernacle, 49
Arsin, Joseph, 98
Aryeh Leib of Shpola (Saba Kadisha, Shpola Zeide), 248–249, 347
link to Reb Pinhas and Baal Shem Tov, 348
Ascent, 3, 12, 28, 38
"The Boy Who Blew the Shofar" and, 127–130, 310
"Rabbi Ishmael's Ascent, 32–53, 281–283
"Reading the Lips of the Ari" and, 298–299
"The Sword of the Messiah" and, 234–236, 342–343
"Ascent of Moses, The," 45–47, 279
"Asenath's Dove," 148–149, 315
Asher, 48, 279, 280
Ashkelon, 142
Ashkenazi, Yosef, "The Speaking Flame" and, 90–92, 299

Asmodeus, 20, 107, 108, 305
Assi, death of, 294
Astral body, 340
Astral projection, 31, 35n–36n, 317, 340
  "A Vision" and, 354
Authority, 288
Avihu, 326
Azazel, 319
Azriel of Gerona, 37n

Baal Shem(s), 315, 328–329
  Adam Baal Shem, 328
  Yoel Baal Shem, 329
Baal Shem Tov (Israel ben Eliezer), 6, 7, 9,
    10, 32, 188, 287, 326, 347
  "The Angel's Sword" and, 189–191, 326–
    327
  ascent of the ladder of prayers, 13
  ascent to paradise, 332
  barred from going into the Holy Land,
    307
  "The Book in the Cave" and, 183–187,
    325–326
  "The Circle of Fire" and, 14, 202–203,
    331
  "A Crown of Shoes" and, 24, 194–195,
    328
  disciples of, 329
  "The Enchanted Island" and, 199–201,
    329–330
  "The Field of Souls" and, 204–205, 332
  "The Flaming Tree" and, 195, 328–329
  gabbai of, 202
  "The Healing Spring" and, 207–208, 333
  Hayim ben Attar's death and, 307
  "The Ladder of Prayers" and, 191, 327
  letter from, 333
  "Lighting a Fire" and, 209–210, 333–334
  link of Reb Pinhas and Saba Kadisha to,
    348
  "The Master Key" and, 198–199, 329
  "The Tale of the Frog" and, 203–204,
    331–332
  parables attributed to, 330
  parallel with Rabbi Akiba, 328
  powers of, 328
  "The Prince of Fire" and, 187–189, 293,
    326
  "The Saba Kadisha in the Upper World"
    and, 249
  shofar blower of. *See* Kitzes, Wolf
  "The Tree of Life" and, 24, 192–193,
    327–328
  "Unlocking the Gates of Heaven" and,
    15, 205–207, 332–333

"A Visitor from the Other World" and,
    196–197, 329
Baal Tekiah, 198
Ba'al Teshuvah, 346
Babylon, 4, 56
Baer, Dov. *See Maggid* of Mezhirich
Baker, dreams of, 61
Barking dog, 175, 323–324
Baruch of Kameda, 195
Baruch of Medzibozh, 256, 350
  death of, 350
  return from the Other World, 256
Barzani, Samuel, 148–149, 315
Bat kol, 63, 239, 297
Bedouins (Sons of the Desert), 17, 115,
    306
"Beggar King, The," 336
Beit Midrash, 64, 278. *See also* House of
    Study
Belz, 264
  Hasidim of, 27, 353–354
  tzaddik of, 264–265, 354
Ben-Zvi, Itzhak, 306
Ber, Issacher, 257
Berditchev, 245
Beruchim, Abraham, vision of *Shekhinah*,
    87–89, 298
  "A Vision at the Wailing Wall" and, 353
"Besht." *See* Baal Shem Tov
Betza, 19
Biblical figures, portrayed as alive, 353
Bill of divorcement, 153, 316. *See also* Get
Bimah, 127, 265
"Bird's Nest," 23, 41, 191, 207, 327
  "The Golden Dove and, 41, 276
Birkat Kohanim, 297
Birkat ha-Mazon, 277
Black dog
  Joseph della Reina and, 107, 108, 109
  "The Ruin" and, 175, 323–324
"Blessing of the Kohanim, The," 84–85,
    297
"Blind Angel, The," 26, 259–261, 352
Blood Libel, 209–210, 323
Bodily ascent, 343, *See also* Ascent
Body, binding to soul, 74
"Body of Moses, The," 100, 302
"Book in the Cave, The," 183–187, 293,
    325–326
"Book of Adam, The," 74–75, 292–293
Book of Daniel, 313
Book of Ezekiel, 28
"Book of Flying Letters, The," 14, 77–78,
    294
Book of Life, 10, 87, 141

Book of Mysteries, 183–187, 326
Book of Raziel, 74, 292, 293, 325
Book of Ruth, 112
Book of the future, 114
"Book that was Burned, The," 239–240, 344
"Bowl of Soup, A," 21, 222, 338, 340
"Boy Who Blew the Shofar, The," 22, 127–130, 310
Bratslav, 236, 237, 242, 344
Bread, soul entering of, 177
Bride, Levi Yitzhak's vision of, 245–246, 347
"Bridegroom and the Angel of Death, The," 162–164, 319–330
Bridegroom of blood, 339
Bridegrooms of the Law, 116
Bridges of Rome, collapse of, 285
Brit (circumcision), 253
Broken heart, 199, 329, 355
Bruria, 315
Burning Bush, 45, 193, 328, 333
Butler, dreams of, 61

Caesar, 285, 286
Cain
    death of, 282
    punishment of, 318
Campfires, 296
Candle(s)
    affixing to tree, 334
    cottage of, 124–126, 308–309
    joining of, 262
    "The Enchanted Inn" and, 132, 133, 311
    lighting of, 333
    western, 307
"Candles in the Synagogue," 78–79, 294–295
Caro, Joseph, 25, 26n, 81, 212
    "The Angel of the Mishnah" and, 112–113, 305–306
    maggid and, 143
    "A New Lease on Life" and, 114
Carob tree, 63
Cave
    enchanted, leading to Holy Land, 189–191, 320, 326–327
    of Machpelah, 310, 312
"Cave of King David, The," 139–141, 312–313
"Cave of Mattathias, The" 31, 261–262, 352–353
"Cave of Shimon Bar Yohai, The," 69–70, 290
"Cave of Temptations, The," 166–168, 320–321

"Cave to the Holy Land, The," 164–166, 320
"Celestial Academy, The," 76–77, 293–294
Celestial academy of Eber, 43, 278
Celestial temple, 42
Celestial world, 23
Chain midrash, 280, 293, 325
    the *Tzohar* and, 287
"Chains of the Messiah, The," 106–109, 304–305
Chair, Reb Nachman's, 241–242, 345
Challas, crumbs of, 116
Chambers of the Chariot, 43, 51
Chariot
    Chambers of, 43, 51
    fiery, 49
    mysteries of, 4, 12, 18, 50–51, 280–281
Chernobyl, 353
Childless woman, divorce of, 269
Children of Israel, 193
    angels for, 47
    crossing of Red Sea, 48, 49
Christians, Blood Libel and, 323
Chronicle of Abimaaz (Megillat Abimaaz), 314
"Chronicle of Serah Bat Asher, The," 47–50, 279–280
"Circle of Fire, The," 14, 202–203, 331
"City of Luz, The," 278
City of the dead, 246
    visit to, 101–102, 302
Classic rabbinic tales, 8
Cleaving to God, 13
Clock(s), meditation on, 257–258, 351
"Clock of the Seer of Lublin, The," 257–258, 351
Coat of many colors, 61
Code of Jewish Law, 25
Coffin, of Joseph, 279
Coleridge, Samuel Taylor, 311
Collective unconscious, 25, 36n–37n
Commandments of Israel, 115
Condemnation, 311
Congregation of Israel, 205
Contemplative Kabbalah, 13
Cordovero, Moshe, 80, 81, 295
    "The Pillar of Cloud" and, 295
    "A Visit to the City of the Dead" and, 101, 302
"Cottage of Candles, The," 27, 124–126
"Count Who Wanted to Study Kabbalah, The," 172–173, 322–323
Cow, 320
Craftsman, 352
Creation, 16
    myths, 16

primary forces of, 283
of the World, 300
Crops, soul entering of, 177, 178
"Crown of Shoes, A," 24, 194–195, 328
"Curse, The," 157–158, 313
"Curtain of Fire, The," 71–72, 291

Damascus, 82
"Dancing of the Ari, The," 83–84, 296–297
Daniel, 33n, 313
Danube (river), 171, 322
David (King), 20, 49
cave of, 139–141, 312–313
general of, 253
harp of, 137
legends related to, 312–313
life span of, 114, 306
soul of, ascent of, 54
"The Waters of the Abyss" and, 54, 283
Days of Awe, 115, 199, 254
de Leon, Moshe, 5, 25, 34n, 290
Dead
blessing of, 214
bones of, rolling through enchanted caves
to Holy Land, 320
living, 147
reviving of, 213
"Dead Hasidim," 10
Death, 311
"An Appointment with Death," 42, 277–
278
Jaws of, 146, 147, 315
punishment after, 340
Deborah, 280, 315
"Decree, The," 70–71, 290–291
"Delivering A Message," 95–97, 300–301,
309
della Reina, Joseph, 5, 20
"The Chains of the Messiah" and, 106–
109, 304–305
reincarnation of, 27, 37n, 109
purification of soul, 106
Demon(s), 4, 26
"The Chains of the Messiah" and, 107,
108
human marrying of, 319
Dervish, 101
Devekut, 13
Diaspora, 17, 165, 320
Din, Dovid, "Trying to Pray" and, 267, 355
Divination, 343
method of, 27–28
Divine, 4
Divine Chariot, 12, 15, 18
Divine Presence, 12, 21, 25

Divine tests
"The Cottage of Candles," 124–126, 308–
309
"The Enchanted Inn," 130–134, 310–311
"The Enchanted Island," 199–201, 329–
331
"The Journey to Jerusalem," 86, 297
Divine Throne, 13, *See also* Throne of
Glory
"Divining from the Zohar," 27, 237, 343
Divinity, 18
Divorce, 268
bill of divorcement, 153, 316, *See also Get*
of childless woman, 269
Dolphina (Queen), 304
Dove, 104
Asenath's, 148–149, 315
golden, 41–42, 191, 235, 276–277, 327
Drash, 35n, 197, *See also PaRDeS*
Dream(s), 31
essential number for, 324
"The Garden of the Torah" and, 229–
231, 341
gateway to, 341
of Jacob, 341
Joseph's interpretation of, 61
prophetic, 31
Reb Nachman and, 341
solving problems with, 323
transmitting object through, "The Mira-
cle of the Ring" and, 158–160, 318–
319
"Dream Questions of the Maharal, The,"
174, 323
D'var Torah, 298
Dybbuk, 8, 34n, 307
defined, 324
exorcising of, 295
"The Fishhead" and, 342
"The Voice in The Attic" and, 289
"The Widow of Safed" and, 98–99, 301
Dybbuk, The (Ansky), 311, 317, 339
Dying, "Isaac's Ascent" and, 278

Eber, celestial academy of, 43, 278
Ecclesiastes Rabbah, 295, 325
Eden, Gates of, 24, 62, 197, 288, *See also*
Garden of Eden
Egypt, 48, 266
Ein Sof, 35n
Ein Tov, 312
Eizek of Kallo, 6, 14
"The Sabbath Guests" and, 20
"The Wandering Well" and, 250–251,
348

Eleazar (son of Shimon bar Yohai), 69
  "The Curtain of Fire" and, 71
  "The Decree" and, 70, 290–291
  "A Saint from the Other World" and, 72,
    291
  "The Shining Robe" and, 141–143, 313–
    314
Eleazar ben Arakh, "Mysteries of the Char-
    iot" and, 50–51, 280–281
Eleazar ben Shammua, 283
Eliakim, "The Blind Angel" and, 259–261,
    352
Eliezer of Mayence, "The Words in the
    Sand" and, 171–172, 322
Eliezer ben Hyrcanos, 279
  "The Law is Not in Heaven", and, 63,
    288–289
Eliezer ben Shimon, "The Voice in the At-
    tic" and, 64–65, 289
Eliezer ha-Levi, 304
Elijah, 6, 7, 34n, 47, 81, 133, 160, 234,
    264, 291, 303, 311, 312, 331
  "The Bridegroom and the Angel of
    Death" and, 162–164, 319–320
  "The Cave of Shimon Bar Yohai" and, 69
  "Forcing the End" and, 65–66, 289–290,
    350
  Hibbur Yafeh me-bay Yeshuah and, 319
  horn blown by, 137
  Joseph della Reina and, 106, 107
  "The Law is not in Heaven" and, 63, 288
  mantle of, 137
  portrayed as alive, 353
  roles of, 7
Elijah (Rabbi), 202
Elimelech of Lizensk, 6, 9, 11, 313, 335
  "A Bowl of Soup" and, 21, 222, 338
  "The Garden of the Torah" and, 229–
    231, 341
  "Reb Shmelke's Whip" and, 226, 339
  "The Shadow on the Wall," and, 228–
    229, 340
  "Three Stars" and, 227–228, 339–340
  "The Wine of Paradise" and, 223–224,
    338
  "The Woman in the Forest" and, 221–
    222, 337–338
  "The Young Magician" and, 224–225,
    339
Elisha, "The Golden Dove" and, 277
Elisha ben Abuyah, 29. *See also* Aher
Eliyahu, "The Boy Who Blew the Shofar"
    and, 127–130, 310
Enchanted caves, 320
"Enchanted Inn, The," 130–134, 310–
    311

"Enchanted Island, The," 28
Enchanted jewel, 216, 217
Enchanted journey, 12
End of Days, 43, 47, 137, 189–190, 191,
    256, 320, 349
  announcement of, 262
  forcing of, 264
Endor, witch of, 350
Enoch, 6, 13, 23–24, 47, 106, 107, 287,
    292, 331. *See also* Metatron
  ascent of, 24
  Book of Mysteries and, 186
  three books of, 331
  Tzohar and, 59–60
Ephraim, Shlomo, 239
Esau, 11, 45, 60
  guardian angel of, 11, 44. *See also* Samael
  Jacob's encounter with, 44, 278
Eternal light *(Ner Tamid)*, 62, 287
Etrog, 265–266, 354
Etz Hayim, 296
Eve, 59
  Fall of, 282
  garments of, 326
Evil, 15, 26
  elements of, control of, 339
  fully explored, 26
  in kabbalistic literature, 26
Evil angel(s), 15, 314, 336
"Evil Angel, The," 25, 143–145, 314
Evil Inclination *(Yetzer ha-Ra)*, 285, 286,
    338
Evil spirits, 4
Executions, 52
Exile of *Shekhinah*, 12, 18, 35n
Exiled and the Redeemed, The, 306
Existence, kabbalistic view of, 26,
    37n
Exodus, 52
Exorcisms, 323
Extra Soul, 20, 231. *See also* Neshamah
    yeterah
  departure of, 117
Ezekiel, 4, 15, 28
  vision of, 12, 18, 30, 291, 331
Ezra, 157

Faith, absence of, 333
Fall (cosmic), 16
False messiahs, 20, 333
  Shabbati Sevi, 5
Famine, 48
Fast day, 240
Fasting, 76–77, 106, 293
Father
  death of, vow taken by son at, "The

Words in the Sand" and, 171–172, 322

son's disobeying of, "The Words in the Sand" and, 171–172, 322

Female
disguised as a man, 159–160, 319
inner being, fusion of male to, 349

"Field of Souls, The," 22, 204–205, 332

Fiery chariot, 49

Fiery everturning sword, 189–191, 326

"Finger, The," 305

Fire, 45
in Temple of Jerusalem, 56

Firmament
creation of, 29, 37n
gates of, 45
opening of, 47

Fish, soul entering body of, 177

Fish, Yaakov, 255, 348
"The Wandering Well" and, 250–251, 348

Fish seller, 233–234

"Fishhead, The," 342

Flame, speaking, 90–92, 299

"Flaming Letters, The," 22, 247–248, 347

"Flaming Tree, The," 195, 328–329

Flying letters, book of, 77–78, 294

"Flying Letters, The," 156–157, 318

Folk origin, tales of, 6, 31–32

Forbidden fruit, 59

"Forcing the End," 4, 65–66, 289–290, 350

Forest, *tzaddik* of, 109–112, 305

"Formation of the Child, The," 286

Foundation Stone, 49, 54, 283

"Four Who entered Paradise, The," 3, 30, 51–52, 280–281, 305

Friends, meeting of, angel's life span and, 213–214

Frog, soul of scholar as, 203–204, 331–332

"From the Beyond," 253–254, 349–350

Future, book of, 114

Future visions, *See* Prophetic visions

Gabbai, 136, 202, 306

Gabriel, 13, 25, 53, 283, 287, 302
feeding of Abraham by, 60
making crowns out of shoes by, 195
palace of, 25, 61, 121–123, 308

"Gabriel's Palace," 25, 121–123, 308

Gadiel, 75–76, 293

Gaeta, 146

Gan Eden, *See* Garden of Eden

Garden of Eden (*Gan Eden*), 24, 28, 57, 178, 326
ascent of soul to, 177
"A Crown of Shoes" and, 194–195, 328

leaves from, 134–135, 311
linkage of Israel to, 320
location of, 328
"The Saba Kadisha in the Upper World" and, 248
water from, 139

"Garden of the Torah, The," 229–231, 341

Garland(s)
of flowers, 13
of prayer, 209
weaving of, from prayers of Israel, 328

Garments of light, 288

"Gates of Eden, The," 24, 62, 288

Gates of heaven, Luz and, 277

"Gathering Sparks," 17, 94–95, 300

Gehenna, 21, 26, 57, 133, 153, 211, 243, 266, 314, 321, 332
gates of, 98
Korah followers falling into, 354
path to, 220
punishments of, 85; sparing of, during Sabbath, 227–228
"Reb Pinhas and the Angel of Death" and, 219, 220, 337
water from, 139

Gematria, 220, 321, 335

Generation gap, 334–335

Generations, simultaneous existence of, 289

Genesis, 16, 52, 278

German Jewry, 308

Gershom of Kittov, 192, 333

Gershon, 192

Get, 269, 270, (*See also* Divorce)
"Rabbi Naftali's Trance" and, 152–154, 316–317

Gihon (river), 185

Gilgul, 9, 26–27, 317, 346
Ari's belief in, 301
holy child and, 293
process of, 342
"The Sabbath Fish" and, 342
"A Stone in the Wall" and, 301
"The Tale of the Frog" and, 331
"The Voice in the Tree" and, 177, 324

Glossary of terms, 367–376

Glowing stone, "The Soul of the Ari" and, 258–259, 351. See also *Tzohar*

Goat, 310, 312
"The Cave of the Holy Land" and, 320

God, 12. See also Akatriel Yah
affirmation of, 341
anger of, 267
authority of, 288
bride of. See Shekhinah
cleaving to, 13
feminine aspect of, 298. See also Shekhinah

garments of light, 288
messengers of, 13
Serah's looking upon, 48
sovereignty of, 47
transmitting of Torah to Moses, 46–47
visions of, 4, 279
voice of, 46, 279
God of Mercy, 163–164
God's Name(s), 55, 75, 246, 284, 309. *See
    also* Tetragrammaton
combining of letters from, 22–23, 26n
"The Evil Angel" and, 144–145
pronunciation by dead, 147, 314–315
written on forehead of angels, 144
Golden dove, 41–42, 235
attempt to capture, 191, 327
"The Ladder of Prayers" and, 191, 327
"Golden Dove, The," 41–42, 276–277
"Golden Feather, The," 313
Golden horn, 200, 201
"Golden Scepter, The," 73–74, 291–292,
    304
"Golden Table, The," 4, 58–59, 286–287
Golem, 174, 323
legends related to, 323
"Golem, The," 315
Good, 15, 26
Good angels, 336
Good deed, 260, 336
Good inclination *(Yetzerha-Tov)*, 285, 338
"Greeting the Sabbath Queen," 93–94, 299–
    300
Guardian angel, 193
Guf, 23, 36n

Hadarniel, 183, 185
Hagigah, 4, 324, 335
defined, 325
spirit of, 179–180, 324–325
Halachah, Kabbalah and, 36n
Halachic debate, 277
Halevi, Abraham, "Reading of the Lips of
    the Ari" and, 89–90, 298–299
Hallel prayer, 265
Halperin, David, 324
Hamnuna Sava, 72, 291, 293
Hand washing, before Sabbath, 307
"Handwriting of the Messiah, The," 31,
    103–104, 303
Haninah ben Hakhinai, 283
Haninah ben Dosa, "The Golden Table"
    and, 58–59, 286–287
Haninah ben Teradion, 282–283
death of, 53, 294
Hanipol, 228, 229

Hanukah
"The Blind Angel" and, 260, 352
first candle of, oil for, 261
lighting of candles, "The Cave of Mat-
    tathias" and, 261–262, 352–353
Hanukiah, 352
Harp, David's, 137
Hashmal, 28–29
Hasidic masters, linking to figures of past,
    353
Hasidic movement, 321, 325
Hasidic period, 5
Hasidic rabbis, 6
Hasidic tales, 3, 4, 8
Hasidim
"The Cave of Mattathias" and, 261–262,
    353
dead, 10
mystical masters among, 9
opponents of, 339–340
Havdalah, 20, 90, 227, 340
delay in saying, 340
Hayey Moharan, 348
Hayim, 134
Hayim ben Attar, *See* Or Hayim
Hayim the Vinekeeper (hidden saint), 18,
    305
"From the Beyond" and, 254, 350
"The Prayer Leader" and, 254–255
Rabbi of Kallo and, 350
Hayon, Gedaliah, 306
Healing potion, 320
"Healing Spring, The," 207–208, 333
Heaven, 23, 330, *See also* Paradise
journeying into, 23
palaces of, 281; hidden, 333
Heavenly ascents, 28
Heavenly journeys, visions of, 343
Heavenly rewards, "The Golden Table"
    and, 58–59, 286–287
Heavenly voice, 239
Hebrew alphabet, letters of, 32
Hebron, 106, 135, 312
Hekhalot, 331
Hekhaloth, defined, 30
palaces of heaven, 281
Hekhaloth Rabbati, 331, 332
"Hekhaloth texts," 3, 18, 30–31, 38n, 281,
    332
Helen of Troy, 304
Hell, 21, *See also* Gehenna
names for, 321
Hemah, 339
Herzog, Haim, 345
Hibbur Yafeh me-hay Yeshuah, 319

Hidden saint. *See* Hayim the Vinekeeper; Saint, hidden
Hideckel (river), 294
Himnona, death of, 294
Hindu, 342
Hirsch, Zevi, "The Soul of the Ari" and, 258–259, 351
Hiyya, 65, 256, 289, 312
  "The Celestial Academy" and, 76–77, 293–294
  "The Curtain of Fire" and, 71–72, 291
  death of, 294
  "Forcing the End" and, 350
  return to the world, 77
Holland, Jewish population of, 317
"Hollow of the Sling, The," 168–169, 321
Holy book, opening of, 343
Holy child, "Rabbi Gadiel the Child" and, 75–76, 293
Holy Land (Israel), 4, 131
  Baal Shem Tov and, 190–191
  cave leading to, 164–168, 189–191, 320–321, 326–327
  children of, 45
  linkage to Garden of Eden, 320
  Maid of Ludomir's move to, 263
  messianic longings in, 20–21
  Nachman of Bratslav setting foot on, 327
Holy messenger, 353
Holy name(s), 13, 155, 313, 315–316, *See also* God's name
  "The Flying Letters" and, 248
  "Reb Pinhas and the Angel of Death" and, 220, 337
  written in the sand, 171–172
Holy of Holies of the Temple, 55, 284
Holy Spirit, *See Ruach ha-kodesh*
Horn, 137, *See also* Shofar
Horn of Plenty, 201
House of Israel, pillar of, 249
House of Jacob, 48
House of Study, 49, 87, 246, 278, 347
  collapse of walls, 63, 289
House of the World, 73–74, 292
"How Rabbi Judah the Pious Became a Great Scholar," 170, 321–322
Human angel, 336
Huppah, 168
Hutzapit, 283

Ibur, 7–8, 25, 34n, 298, 306, 346
  "A Kiss from the Master" and, 295
  "Soul of Reb Nachman" and, 244–245
Idel, Moshe, 334, 347
Idolatry, spirit of, 56–57, 285

IFA, 21, 35n
Ilai (forest), 285, 286
Illusion tales, 11
  "The Enchanted Inn", 130–134, 310–311
  "The Enchanted Island," 199–201, 329–330
  "The Magic Flock," 44–45, 278–279
  "Opening a Verse", 210–211, 335
  "The Palace of Illusions," 330
  "The Tale of the Kugel," 268–271, 355
  "The Young Magician," 224–225, 339
Imperfect angel, 260, 336, 352
Imrey Noam, 340
Incantation, 22
Individuation, 25
Inquisition, "Rabbi Shimon's Escape" and, 126–127, 309–310
"Interpreting the Zohar," 154, 317
Isaac, 60, 135, 186, 336
  ascent of, 43, 278
  binding of, 43, 278
  ram sacrificed in place of, 43, 69, 137, 201
Isaiah, 33n
"Isaac's Ascent," 43, 278
Isfahan, 49
Ishmael the High Priest (Ishmael ben Elisha), 7, 8, 202, 283
  ascent of soul, 38
  return to world, 53
  "Rabbi Ishmael's Ascent" and, 52–53, 281–283
  "The Vision of the High Priest" and, 55, 284
Ishmael ben Elisha, *See* Ishmael the High Priest
Ishmaelites, 237
Israel, 44, *See also* Holy Land
  commandments of, 115
  mother of, 19, *See also* Shekhinah
  prayers of, 13, 209, 328
Israel ben Eliezer, *See* Baal Shem Tov
Israel of Rizhin, 210, 333
Israel Folktale Archives (IFA), 6, 276
Israelites, 295
  enslavement of, 48
  Miriam's well following of, 250
Issachar of Radoshitz, 257
Issachar Dov the First, "A Vision" and, 10–11, 265–266, 354
Itzhak Ben-Zvi, 306

Jabbok (Yabbok) (River), 44, 279
Jacob, 135, 186, 266, 333, 336
  dream of, 234–235, 341

ladder of, 234–235, 241
Luz and, 277
"The Magic Flock" and, 44–45, 278–279
sons of, 48, 280
the *Tzohar* and, 60–61
Jacob of Annapol, 202
Jaws of Death, 146, 147, 315
Jeremiah, 292
exile of the *Shekhinah* and, 18
Jerico, 116
Jerusalem, 241, 242
Ari's journey to, 86, 297
Bratslaver synagogue in, 242
celestial, 23
Mount of Olives in, 264
Temple in, 186; destruction of, 56, 257,
285, 349; keys of, 56, 284–285; ruins
of. *See* Wailing Wall
Jesus, death and resurrection of, 278
Jewel, enchanted, 216, 217
Jews, decree against. *See* Pogrom
Joav ben Tsrouya, 253, 350
Joppa, 146
Joseph, 31, 287, 292
Book of Mysteries buried with, 186
brothers of, 52, 53, 282
"Chronicle of Serah Bat Asher" and, 48,
279, 280
coat of many colors and, 61
coffin of, 48–49, 61, 279, 280
interpretation of dreams by, 61
sale into slavery, 53, 61
the *Tzohar* and, 60–62
Joseph of Torchin, 257
Joseph the Gardener, "The Shining Robe"
and, 142–143
Joshua ben Haninah. *See* Yehoshua ben
Haninah
Joshua ben Levi. *See* Yehoshua ben Levi
Journey, enchanted, 12
"Journey to Jerusalem, The," 20, 86, 297,
328
Judah, "The Book of the Flying Letters"
and, 77–78, 294
Judah-ha-Nasi, 312
Judah the Pious, 7, 170, 315
"The Words in the Sand" and, 171–172,
322
Jung, C.G., 25–26, 37n
Just men, 350
Justice, "The Cottage of Candles" and,
124–126, 308–309

Kabbalah, 33
age to begin study of, 293

biblical roots of, 33n
central text of, 8
Contemplative, 13
count who wanted to study, 172–173,
322–323
dangers of, 314
defined, 5–6, 32
halachah and, 36n
Lurianic, 300
meaning of words in, 347
Practical, 13
primary focus of, 14
secrets of, 155–156, 317–318
Speculative, 13
study of, 322; by non-Jews, 322
Theosophical, 13
Kabbalat Shabbat, 19, 84, 297, 300
Kabbalistic
defined, 33n
distinguished from mystical, 5–6
Kabbalistic era, beginning of, 5
Kabbalistic myths, 15–21, 35n
Kabbalistic tales, 3, 4, 5, 8
Kaddish, 263, 269, 270, 332
orphan's, 244
Kadi, son of, kidnapping of, 237, 343
Kafka, Franz, 309
Kallo, 245
Rabbi of
hidden saint and, 350
"The Prayer Leader" and, 254–255,
350
"The Sabbath Guests" and, 251–252,
348–349
successor to, 350
Kamionka, Rabbi of, 266
"The Tale of the Etrog" and, 265–266,
354
Kaph Kela, 321
Karaites, 156, 158, 318
Karaster, 253
Karma, 342
law of, 27
Katz, Naftali, 10, 21, 354
trance of, 152–154, 316–317
Kavanah, 22, 194, 248, 297, 329, 307, 335
Kazimir (King), 157
Kemuel, 45
Ketubot, 347
"Keys of the Temple, The," 56, 284–285
Kfitsat ha-Derech ("Leaping of the Way"),
12, 327–329
Kiddish cup, tale of, 149–150, 315–316
Kiddush Levanah. *See* Moon
Kidnapping, 52, 237, 343

Kiev, 243
King of Demons, 107
King of Kings, 163
"King Who Loved Music, The" (Levi
    Yitzhak of Berditchev), 334–335
Kinneret, 348
"Kiss from the Master, A," 8, 79–80, 295
Kitzes, Wolf, 341
    "The Enchanted Island" and, 199–201,
        329–330
    "The Master Key" and, 198–199, 329
    "A Visitor from the Other World" and,
        196–197, 329, 348
Knowledge, 297
Kohanim, blessing of, 84–85, 297
Kohen, 297
Kol Nidre, 136, 205, 250
Kook, Abraham Isaac "The Soul of Reb
    Nachman" and, 244–245, 346
Korah, 27, 210, 266, 354
    followers of, 354
Kotel, 267, 298, 355
    woman mourning at, *Shekhinah* as, 88,
        325
Kurdish legends and tales, 315
Kushta, 117
Kvittel, 219, 336, 337

Laban, 44, 266
Ladder, Nathan's attempt at climbing, 232
Ladder of light, 234–235
"Ladder of Prayers, The," 13, 191, 327
Lag ba-Omer, 78, 79, 294, 296
    dancing of the Ari and his students at the
        grave of Shimon bar Yohai during,
        83–84, 296
Lailah, 267
    "The Angel of Conception" and, 57–58,
        286
Lamech, 60, 287
Lamed Vav Tzaddikim, 309, 350
Land of Israel, *See* Holy Land
Langer, Jiri, "A Vision" and, 264–265
Law, 132
"Law is Not in Heaven, The," 63, 288–289
Leah, 134, 135
"Leaping of the Way," (*Kfitsat ha-Derech*),
    12, 327–328
"Leaves from the Garden of Eden," 134–
    135, 311
Lecha Dodi (Alkabetz), 19, 112, 251, 300
Leib, Moshe, 209–210
Lekutei Moharan, 284
Letter(s)
    combining of, 22–23, 26n

of Hebrew alphabet, 32
of the Torah, flying of, 156–157, 318
"Letter, The," 303–304
"Letter from Beyond, A," 240–241, 244–245
Letter from the Messiah, 103–104, 303
Levi Yitzhak of Berditchev, 6, 334–335
    "A Vision of the Bride" and, 245–246,
        347
Light, 45, 214, *See also* Primordial light
    garments of, 288
    ladder of, 234–235
    loss of, 59
    "The Young Magician" and, 224–225,
        339
Light of the soul, 238
"Lighting a Fire," 209–210, 333–334
Lilith, 20, 107, 304, 305, 321, 338, 339
Lion, 310
"Lion of Ilai, The," 285–286
Living dead, 147
Lizensk, 224, 228
Locks, 199, 329, *See also* "Master Key, The"
Loew, Judah, *See* Maharal
Looking back, "The Flaming Tree" and,
    195, 328–329
Lord of Hosts, 55
"Lost Princess, The," 26, 349
Lost souls, redemption of, 115–116,
    306
Lot, wife of, 328
Love, 336
Lublin, 114, 306
    seer of, 337
Ludomir, 134
Luria, Isaac. *See* Ari
Luria, Shlomo. *See* Maharashal
Lurianic Kabbalah, 300
Lust, 338
Luz, 42, 139, 277–278, 312
    histories of, 139

Ma'aseh Bereshith, 15, 16, 29, 280
    study of, 30
Ma'aseh Merkavah, 15, 18, 29, 37n, 202,
    280, 331. *See also* "Mysteries of the
    Chariot"
    study of, 30, 281
Ma'aysiot Noraim ve-Niflaim, 314, 336
Maccabees, 262, 253
Machpelah, cave of, 310, 312
Maggid (Maggidim), 25, 114, 212, 317,
    336
    appearance of, 305, 306
    Joseph Caro and, 112–113
    "The Evil Angel" and, 143–145

Maggid Mesharim (Joseph Caro), 25, 112, 306
Maggid of Mezhirich (Dov Baer), 202, 203
  Blood Libel and, 209, 210
  "A Crown of Shoes" and, 194–195, 328
  "The Flaming Letters" and, 247–248, 347
Maggid of the Mishnah, 112–113, 305–306
Magic, kabbalistic, 14, 224
"Magic Flock, The," 44–45, 278–279
Magic Herd, 11
"Magic Mirror of Rabbi Adam, The," 338
Magic ring, 283
Maharal (Judah Loew), 309, 315
  "The Count Who Wanted to Study Kab-
    balah" and, 172–173, 322–323
  dream questions of, 174–323
  Golem and, 174, 323
  legends related to, 323
  "The Ruin" and, 175, 176, 323–324
Maharam (Meir of Rothenburg)
  "Gabriel's Palace" and, 121–122, 308
  imprisonment of, 121, 308
Maharshal (Shlomo Luria), 300
  as follower of the Ari, 96–97, 300
Maid of Ludomir (Hannah Rochel Werber-
    macher), 6, 315
  "A New Soul" and, 263–264, 353
Majorca, 126, 309
Malachha-Moves, 336, *See also* Angel of
    Death
Male
  girl disguised as, 159–160, 319
  inner beings, 349
Man of clay. *See* Golem
Mantle, Elijah's, 137
Marriage, unwillingness for, 157–158, 318
Marriage contracts (*ketubot*), 347
Martyrs. *See* Ten martyrs
Mashal, 329
"Master Key, The," 198–199, 329
Master of Prayer, 254, 255
Master of the Good Name. *See* Baal Shem
    Tov
Master of the Name, 315. *See also* Baal
    Shem
Mattesdorf, 178
Matzohs, making of, Blood Libel and, 323
Mayence, 171, 172
Meaning, levels of, 15
Medianites, 61
Meditation
  on clocks, 257–258, 351
  kabbalistic, 25
Megillat Abimaaz (The Chronicle of Abimaaz),
    314
Meir of Rothenburg. *See* Maharam

Meir Baal ha-Ness, 83, 296
Melamed, 253, 254. *See also* Mordecai
Menachem ben Benjamin Recanati,
    295
Menachem Mendel of Kotzk, 312
  "The Ram Whose Horns Reached to
    Heaven" and, 137–139, 312
Menachem Mendel I of Lubavitch, 11
  "The Tale of the Kugel" and, 268–271,
    355
Menachem Mendel of Riminov, 222, 256,
    312, 350, 353
  "The Cave of Mattathias" and, 261–262,
    352–353
Menorah
  "The Blind Angel" and, 261
  modified, *Hanukiah*, 352
  mystical aspects of, 261, 352
"Menorah of Defects, The," 352
Merkavah, 12, 18, 30, 291, 324. *See also* Di-
    vine Chariot
  descending of, 29, 30, 37n
Meron, 79, 294
  Shimon bar Yohai's grave in, 83, 296
Meshullam, 115
Messiah, 16
  age of, 190
  chains of, 106–109, 304–305
  coming of, 4, 20–21, 22, 144, 258, 349
    "The Book of Adam" and, 75, 292
    "The Clock of the Seer of Lublin"
      and, 257–258, 351
    "The Golden Dove" and, 42, 277
    hastening of, 65–66, 289–290, 350–351
    "The Pact" and, 256–257, 350–351
    "A Visit to the City of the Dead" and,
      302
  false, 5, 20, 333
  footsteps of, 138, 201, 256, 258, 264
  golden dove of, 41, 191, 235
  "The Golden Scepter" and, 292
  handwriting of, 103–104, 303
  Hayim Vital and, 303
  heavenly, 35n
  identification of the golden bird with, 41,
    276
  longing for, 353
  myth of, 20
  palace of. *See* Bird's Nest
  return of Rabbi Hiyya to the world and,
    77
  seeing of, "Journey to Jerusalem" and, 86,
    297
  soul of, 106
  wedding of, 252, 349
Messiah ben David, 20, 35n

Messiah ben Joseph, 20, 35n
Messianic era, 303, 353
Messianic longings, 20–21
Messianic movement, 33n
Metatron (Prince of the Presence), 13, 24, 59, 106, 107, 186, 202, 220, 331. *See also* Enoch
  "The Chains of the Messiah" and, 106, 107
  "The Four Who Entered Paradise" and, 51, 52, 281
Methusaleh, 60, 287, 333
  Book of Mysteries and, 186
Mezzuzah, 347
  Elimelech's hand placed on, 230
  new style of letters for, 247–248, 347
  "The Widow of Safed" and, 99, 301
Michael, 13, 45, 278
Midnight, 14
  vision taking place at, 179, 324
Midrash, 37n, 38n, 64, 263, 333
  Primal Serpent in, 339
Midrash Eleh Ezkerah, 283
Midrashic literature, 4, 8
Midwife of souls, 57. *See also* Lailah
Mikveh, 11, 85, 110, 139, 176, 188
  "The Underground Forest" and, 215, 218
Minhagim, 340
Minyan, 138, 146, 311, 312
Miracle(s), 4
"Miracle of the Ring, The," 158–160, 318–319
"Miracle of the Sukkah, The," 151, 316
Mirage, 330
Miriam, 47, 315, 336
  Chronicle of "Serah Bat Asher" and, 48
  virtues of, 348
  well of, 83
  "The Wandering Well" and, 250–251, 348
"Miriam's Tambourine," 311
Mishnah, 29, 30, 90, 299
  angel of, 112–113, 305–306
Mishnah Avot, 336
Mitnagdid, Mitnagdim, 227, 339–340
Mitzvah, 12
Mitzvot, 16
Monotheism, 282
Moon
  creation of, 59
  sanctification of (*Kidush Levanah*), 312
Mor Uktsia, 294
Mordecai the melamed
  "From the Beyond" and, 253–254, 349–350

Mordecai of Chernobyl, 26
  "The Blind Angel" and, 259–261, 352
Mortification, 106
Moses, 6, 47, 137, 186, 279, 287, 295, 312
  Akiba and, 46
  "The Ascent of Moses" and, 45–47, 279
  Baal Shem Tov and, 333
  body of, 100
  "Chronicle of Serah Bat Asher" and, 48, 279
  death of, 100, 142
  dictation of Torah to, 22
  followers of, 266
  Kiss of the *Shekhinah* and, 142, 336
  portrayed as alive, 353
  rebellion against, 354
  receiving of the Torah, 45, 46–47, 100, 293–295, 279
  as the Redeemer, 48
  search for Joseph's coffin, 48
  soul of, 100
  staff of, 326
  Tablets of Law thrown down by, 294
  vision of, 193
  "The Vision of the High Priest" and, 284
  writing of thirteen Torahs, 308
Mother Zion, 18, 19, 35n. *See also* Shekhinah, 18
  personification of, 325
Mount Ararat, 60
Mount Moriah, sacrifice of ram at, 23, 69, 137, 201, 312, 313
Mount of Olives, 264
Mount Seir, 107
Mount Sinai, 9, 15, 100, 137
  dictation of Torah to Moses at, 22
  Moses ascent of, 45–47, 279
Moyshe of Ihel, "A Wandering Soul" and, 266–267, 354
Mysteries, 204
"Mysteries of the Chariot," 4, 12, 18, 50–51, 280–281, 304. *See also* Ma'aseh Merkavah
"Mysteries of the Frog, The," 203–204, 331–332
Mystical, distinguished from kabbalistic, 5–6
Mystical contemplation, 30
  dangers of, 28–29
Mystical powers, use of, 21
  improper, "From the Beyond" and, 253–254, 349–350
Mystical states, 332
Mystical tales, emergence of, 12
Mystical traditions, "The Circle of Fire" and, 331

Mystical transformation, *See* Transformation
Mystical union, 13
  "The Curtain of Fire" and, 71–72, 291
  "The Golden Scepter" and, 73–74, 291–
    292
Mystical visions, tales about, 4

Nachman of Bratslav, 6, 9, 26, 27, 32–33,
    27, 284, 306, 314, 321, 341
  "The Angel of Losses" and, 238, 343–344
  "The Book that was Burned" and, 239–
    240, 344
  burial place of, 345
  "Divining from the Zohar" and, 237, 343
  leadership after death, 240–242, 344–345
  "The Letter" and, 303–304
  "A Letter from the Beyond" and, 240–
    241, 344–345
  "The Menorah of Defects" and, 352
  raising of souls in Uman cemetary, 21–
    22, 35n
  reaching of Holy Land, 327
  "Reb Nachman's Chair" and, 241–242,
    345
  "Reb Nachman's Tomb" and, 242–245,
    346
  "The Sabbath Fish" and, 233–234, 342
  scribe of, *See* Nathan of Nemirov
  "The Scribe" and, 232–233, 341
  "The Soul of Reb Nachman" and, 244–
    245, 346
  "The Souls of Trees" and, 236, 343
  spirit of, 9–10, 11, 241
  "The Sword of the Messiah" and, 234–
    236, 342–343
  "A Vision of Light" and, 231–232,
    341
Nachmanides, 34n
Nachshon, 131, 132
Nadav, 326
Nahash ha-Kadmoni, 339, *See also* Primal
    Serpent
Name. *See also* God's name; Holy name
  power of, 53
Narshiya, death of, 294
Nathan, "A Vision in the Cemetery," 178–
    179, 334
Nathan of Gaza, 333
Nathan of Nemirov, 63, 344, 348
  ascent of father's soul, 234
  "The Book that was Burned" and, 240,
    344
  "The Field of Souls" and, 204–205,
    332
  "The Hollow of the Sling" and, 321
  "The Sabbath Fish" and, 233–234, 342

  as scribe of Nachman of Bratslav, 232–
    234, 341, 342
Navarro, Shlomo, 304
Nazis, 242
Nebuchadnezzar, 313
Neilah prayer, 206
Ner Tamid, 62. *See also* Eternal light
Neshamah yeterah, 20. *See also* Extra soul
"New Lease on Life, A," 114–115, 306
"New Soul, A," 263–264, 353
Nifla'ot Maharal, 323
Nile (river), 186
Nimrod (King), decree of, 60
Nimshal, 329
Ninth of Av, 257
Nirvana, 324, 342
Nissim, "The Shining Robe" and, 313
Noah, 23, 292
  dove of, 277
  rainbow of, 137
  Tzohar and, 60, 287
Non-Jews, study of Kabbalah by, 322
Noy, Dov, 275–334

Ocean, soul crossing of, 177
Odesser, Yisrael Dov, 240, 344
  "A Letter from Beyond" and, 240–241,
    244–245
Oil, "The Cottage of Candles" and, 125,
    308, 311
Okup, 187, 188
Olam Haba, 23
Omer, 245, 347
"Opening a Verse," 210–212
Or Hayim, (Hayim ben Attar), 17, 116,
    306, 307, 326
  death of, 117, 307
  tefillin of, 117–118, 307
Orchard, sages who entered, 28
Orphan's Kaddish, 244
Other Side, 26
  angels from, 144
Out of body experiences, 4, 12
Out of time experiences, 4

Palace of Hagigah, 180
Palace(s) of heaven, 281
  hidden, 333
Palace of Illusion, 169, 330
"Palace of Illusion, The," 330
Palace of the Messiah, 41, 191, 235
Palace(s) in Paradise, 332
"Palace of the Vanities, The," 104–105, 304
Paradise, 24, 193
  celestial, temple in, 54, 55
  earthly, 28, *See also* Garden of Eden

four sages who entered, 3, 4, 28, 51–52, 326, 328
human entering of, "The Celestial Academy" and, 77–78, 293–294
Isaac's ascent to, 278
ladder of prayers leading to, 191, 327
Moses ascent to, 45–47, 279
palaces in, 332
path to, 220
quest to reach, 327–328
Reb Pinhas in, 220
Serah bat Asher's ascent to, 49
Parasha of Mishpatim, 237, 343
Pardes (PaRDeS), 15, 35n, 37n
defined, 28
four sages who entered, 28–29, 37, 281
Pargod, 25, 53, 185, 197, 219, 291
Passover (Pesach), 171
Blood Libel and, 323
pogroms following, 174
"The Tale of the Kiddish Cup" and, 149–150, 315–316
Pastech, Moshe, "A New Lease on Life" and, 114
Peki'in, 69
synagogue of, candles in, 78–79
Persia, 158
Pesach. *See* Passover
Peshat, 35n. *See also* PaRDeS
Pesikta de Rav Kahana, 314
Pesikta Rabbati, 279, 340
Pharaoh, 280
dreams of, 61
Pilam, Shimon, 17–18
"The *Tzaddik* of the Forest" and, 109–112, 305
"Pillar of Cloud, The," 80–81, 295
Pillar of salt, 328
Pinhas of Koretz, 6, 9, 10, 11, 248, 249, 260
"The Angel of Friendship" and, 213–214, 336
"The Angel of the Zohar" and, 212, 335–336
link to Baal Shem Tov and Saba Kadish, 348
"Opening a Verse" and, 210–212, 335
"Reb Pinhas and the Angel of Death" and, 219–221, 337
"The Underground Forest" and, 214–218, 336–337, 338
Pinto, Hayim, "The Tale of the Kiddish Cup" and, 149–150, 315–316

Pinto, Moshe, "The Secrets of the Kabbalah" and, 156, 317
Pogrom(s), 174
"A Bowl of Soup" and, 222, 338
of 1768, 243
Poland, 96
Karaites of, 157, 158, 318
Posen, 152, 153
Possession, 346
"The Ruin" and, 175, 323–324
Power of the Name, 309
Practical Kabbalah, 13
Prague, 264, 354, 265, 309
Golem and, 174, 323
Prayer(s), 12
allegory of, 335
failure to ascend to heaven, 206–207, 332
freeing of soul by, 97, 301
inner depths of, 297
kavanah in, 297
key to, broken heart as, 355
Master of, 254, 255
"The Precious Prayer," 86–87, 297–298
time for, interpretations of, 340
treasury of, 43
"Unlocking the Gates of Heaven," 205–207, 332–333
Prayers of Israel, 13
refusal of, 205–207, 209
weaving of garlands from, 328
"Prayer Leader, The," 14, 18, 254–255, 350
"Precious Prayer, The," 86–87, 297–298
Primal Serpent (*Nahash ha-Kadmoni*), 226, 339
Primordial light, 38n, 59–62, 287–288
flowing stone containing, 351
"Prince of Fire, The," 187–189, 193, 326
Prince of the Presence. *See* Metatron
Prince of the Sea. *See* Rahab
Prince of the Torah, 23, 188, 264, 326
"Princess and the Slave, The," 313
Prophetic visions
essential number for, 324
tales of, "The Blind Angel," 259–260, 352
Psalms, 244, 276
Pseudoepigrapha, 24
Psychic unity, 349
Punishment
of Gehenna, 85, 227–228
period of, 332
reincarnation as, 354
Purification, 106

Rabbah bar bar Hannah, 317, 354
  "The Golden Dove" and, 41–42, 276–277
  "Interpreting the Zohar" and, 134, 315
  reincarnation of, 154
Rabbi(s)
  description of the Law, 289
  wandering, 317
"Rabbi Gadiel the Child," 75–76, 293
"Rabbi Ishmael's Ascent," 24, 28, 31, 52–53,
  281–283
"Rabbi Joshua and the Witch," 316
"Rabbi Naftali's Trance," 21, 152–154,
  316–317
"Rabbi Shimon's Escape," 14, 126–127,
  309–310
Rabbinic models, 4
Rahab, 13, 150, 315, 316
Rainbow of Noah, 137
Ram
  Abraham's sacrifice of, 23, 312, 313
  horn made from, 201
"Ram Whose Horns Reached to Heaven,
  The," 137–139
Ramak, 80, 81
Raphael, 213
Rashbi, *See* Shimon bar Yohai
Raziel, 13, 59, 185, 325
  "The Book of Adam" and, 74, 292, 293
"Reading of the Lips of the Ari," 89–90,
  298–299
"Reb Nachman's Chair," 10, 241–242, 345
"Reb Nachman's Tomb," 242–245, 346
"Reb Pinhas and the Angel of Death," 219–
  221, 337
"Reb Shmelke's Whip," 226, 339
Rebbe(s)
  conflict between, 348
  role in Hasidic tales, 9
Rebecca, 60, 315
Recanti, Rafael, 313
  "The Cave of King David" and, 139–141,
  312–313
Red Sea, 193
  crossing of, 48, 231, 301
  parting of, 48, 49
  walls of, 49
Redeemer, Moses as, 48
Redemption, announcement of, 262
"Redemption of the Lost Souls," 17, 115–
  116, 306
Regensburg, 170
Reincarnation, 9, 109, 317
  cycle of, freedom from, 324
  as punishment, 354
  "The Sabbath Fish" and, 233–234, 342

stages of, 177, 324, 342. *See also Gilgul*
  "The Voice in the Tree" and, 177, 324
Remarriage, "Rabbi Naftali's Trance" and,
  152–154, 316–317
Remez, 35n. *See also PaRDeS*
Repair of the world, 305, 306–307
"Repairing Souls," 17, 116, 306–307
Resurrection, 47
  "Isaac's Ascent" and, 278
Reuven, 214
Rhodes, 237
Rigyon (river), 45
Riminov, 222, 256, 350
Ring, miracle of, 158–160, 318–319
Ritual murder, 323
Rizhin, 210
Robbers, 189
Romans, 69
Rome, bridges of, collapse of, 285
Rosh Hashanah, 127, 128, 241, 243, 256
  "The Golden Dove" and, 41
Rosh Hodesh, 214
Rosh Yeshivah, 143, 144
Rothenburg, 121
"Royal Garments, The," 313
Ruach, 289
Ruach ha-Kodesh (Holy Spirit), 27, 232, 307
Rudolf I (Emperor), 308
"Ruin, The," 175–176, 323–324

Saag, 254
Saba Kadisha, *See* Aryeh Leib of Shpola
"Saba Kadisha in the Upper World, The,"
  248–249, 347–348
Sabbath, 117, 231
  beginning of, delaying of, 251
  desecration of, 251
  end of, 227, 340
  extension of, "Three Stars" and, 227–228,
  339–340
  punishment after death and, 227–228,
  340
  washing of hands before, 307
"Sabbath Fish, The," 233–234, 342
"Sabbath Guests, The," 19, 20
Sabbath Queen, 19, 20, 251. *See also
  Shekhinah*
  greeting of, 93–94, 251, 264, 299–300
  Hayim Vital's, 84–85
  wedding of, 252, 349
Sacred tales, distinguished from secular
  tales, 31–32
Sacred text, 248
Safed, 5, 19, 81, 87, 93, 95, 108, 299
  Ari's position as leader in, 296

rabbi of, 100
sages of, 305
widow of, 98–99, 301
Sages, 256. *See also* Three sages
spirit of, possession of, 307. *See also Ibur*
Sagis, Moshe "A Visit to the City of the Dead" and, 101, 302
Saint(s), hidden, 143, 280, 305, 309. *See also* Hayim the Vinekeeper
"Saint from the Other World," 72, 291
Samael, 16, 44, 303
Samaritans, 151, 316
Samuel, 350
Samuel the Pious, 170
Sand, holy names written in, 171–172
Sandalphon, 13, 46, 138, 284
weaving prayers of Israel, 194, 209, 328
Sanhedrin, Saba Kadisha's ascent to, 248–249, 347–348
Sarah, 311, 315
Sarug, Israel, 256, 350
"Delivering A Message" and, 95–97, 300–301
Satan, 165
Saul (King), 350
Scholem, Gershom, 5, 317
Scribe *(sopher)*, 347, 348
of new letters of the Torah, 347
"Scribe, The," 232–233, 341, 348
Scroll, hidden, 204
Second soul, 340
Second World War, 242
"Secrets of Vabbalah, The," 155–156, 317–318
Secular tales, distinguished from sacred tales, 31–32
Seer of Lublin, 256, 257, 337, 350
clock of, 257–258, 351
Sefer Bahir, 5
Sefer ha-Hezyonot, 302, 303
Sefer-ha-Nisraf, 344
Sefer ha-Razim, 26, 325
Sefer Yetsirah, 5
Sefirot, 13, 15–16, 25, 312
Ari and, 16–17
Sendril, 192, 193
Sephardim, 307
Serah bat Asher, 61, 326
"The Chronicle of Serah Bat Asher" and, 47–50, 279–280
Serpent, 216
Primal, 226, 339
Seth, 59, 287
Sexual fantasy, "The Woman in the Forest" and, 221–222, 337–338

Sha'ar Kvod Adonai (Ephraim ben Yisrael Ankawa), 309
Shabazi, Shalom, 264
Shabbatian movement, 6, 34n
Shadow of Death, 321
"Shadow on the Wall, The," 228–229, 340
Shammash, 78
"Redemption of the Lost Souls" and, 115–116
Shape, sending of, 354
Sharabi, Shalom, 5, 17
"Redemption of the Lost Souls" and, 115–116, 306
Shattering of the Vessels, 16–17, 35n, 95, 300
Shavuoth, 14, 100, 107
Shebreshin, 164, 165, 166
Sheep, 266
soul entering of, 178
Sheilat Sefer, 27, 299, 343
Shekhinah, 12, 13, 16, 19, 20, 25, 28, 73
Abraham Beruchim's vision of, 353
anima and, 25, 298
basic forms of, 298
defined, 18
Divine Presence and, 21
exile of, 18, 35n, 349
face of, viewing of, by Hayim Vital, 84–85, 297
"The Flying Letters" and, 247–248, 347
grief over destruction of Solomon's Temple, 88
kiss of, 30, 142, 281, 336
"Mysteries of the Chariot" and, 50
myths of, 349
personification of, 325
robe of, 288
"The Sabbath Guests" and, 349
as second soul, 340
visions of, 245–246, 298, 347
at the Wailing Wall, 87–89, 298
Shem, 333
celestial academy of, 43, 278
tents of, 278
Shema, 73, 151, 304
Shemhazai, 319
Sheol, 158, 321
Shepsel, 134, 135
Shilge, Moshe, "Reb Nachman's Tomb" and, 242–245, 346
Shimon, 346
"The Book that was Burned" and, 239–240, 344
"The Sword of The Messiah" and, 234–236, 342–343

Shimon bar Yohai (Rashbi), 5, 6–9, 34n, 186, 209–210, 294, 304
  "The Book of Adam" and, 74–75, 292–293
  "The Book of the Flying Letters" and, 77–78, 294
  "Candles in the Synagogue" and, 78–79, 294–295
  cave of, 79, 169–170, 290
  "The Celestial Academy" and, 76–77, 293–294
  "The Curtain of Fire" and, 71–72, 291
  death of, 76, 77–78, 294
  "The Decree" and, 70–71, 290–291
  followers of, 9, 14
  "The Golden Scepter" and, 73–74, 291–292
  grave of, 79
    dancing of the Ari and his students at, 83–84, 296–297
  Isaac Luria and, 9
  "A Kiss from the Master" and, 79–80, 295
  "Rabbi Gadiel the Child" and, 73–74, 293
  reappearance of, 7–8, 11, 34n
  "A Saint from the Other World" and, 72, 291
  soul of, 82
  tomb of, 94, 300
  wall of synagogue of, 301
Shimon ben Azzai, 14, 29–30, 37n, 326
  "The Four Who Entered Paradise" and, 51–52, 280–281
Shimon ben Lakish, 19
Shimon ben Tsemah Duran, 126
Shimon ben Zoma, 29, 37n
  "The Four Who Entered Paradise" and, 51–52, 280–281
"Shining Robe, The," 141–143, 313–314
Shiva, 169
Shivhei ha-Ari, 331
Shivhei ha-Besht, 287, 331
Shivhei ha-Ran, 346
Shmelke, whip of, 226, 339
  "The Garden of the Torah" and, 229–231, 341
  "Three Stars" and, 227–228, 339–340
Shmuel Isaac
  ascent of Jacob's ladder, 342
  "The Sword of the Messiah" and, 234–236, 342–343
Shoes, flying off dancing feet, *See* "Crown of Shoes, A"

Shofar
  blasts of, "The Master Key" and, 198–199
  boy who blew, 127–130, 310
  "The Enchanted Island" and, 199, 200–201
Shofar blower, of Baal Shem, *See* Kitzes, Wolf
Shohet of Teplik, 241
Shpola, 347
  Saba Kadisha of, 248–249, 347–348
Shpola Zeida, *See* Aryeh, Leib of Shpola
Shulhan Aruch (Caro), 25, 114
Sick, lighting of candles for, 334
Siddur Sha'ar Shamayim, 303
Side of Holiness, angels from, 144
Silhouette (*tsel*), 340
Simeon ben Gamaliel, 283
Simhat Torah, 116, 328
  "The Pact" and, 256–257, 350–351
  shoes falling from dancing feet, crowns made from, 24, 194–195, 328
Sins
  "The Evil Angel" and, 144
  repair of, 205
Sipphoris, 73
Sippurim Mishekvar, 317
Sitre Abre, 26, 314. *See also* Other side
  angels from, 144
Sixth heaven, 53
Sky, opening of, 14
Slavery, Joseph's sale into, 53
Snuffbox, 138
Sod, 35n. *See also* PaRDeS
Sofer, 118
Sofer, Moshe, Rabbi Nathan's vision in the cemetery and, 178–179, 324
Solomon (King), 292
  "An Appointment with Death" and, 42, 277–278
  "The Beggar King" and, 336
  Book of Mysteries and, 186
  illusion tale about, 11, 279
  magic ring, 283
  miraculous throne of, 277
  "The Water of the Abyss" and, 54, 283
Solomon's Temple, 88. *See also* Wailing Wall
  destruction of, 88
Song of Songs, 112, 116, 231
Sons of God, 314, 319
Sons of the Desert, *See* Bedouins
Sopher, 248, 341, 348, *See also* Scribe
Sopher, Moshe, 247, 248, 347

Sorcerer, "The Book in the Cave" and, 183
Soul(s), 224
  ascent of, 12, 21–22, 298–299, 343. *See also* Ascent
  assisting of, 337
  binding to body, 74
  divine origin of, 286
  extra, 231. *See also Neshamah yeterah*
  freeing of, "The Stone in the Wall" and, 97, 301
  history of, 266–267, 354
  images, projection of, 21. *See also Tselm*
  Kaddish and, 332
  light of, 238
  of the living, 27
  midwife of, 57. *See also* Lailah
  purification of, 106
  repair of, 116, 306–307
  second, 340
  shape of, 73–74
  sparks of, 9
  transformations of, 26, 177–178
  transmigration of, 21, 27, 342. *See also Gilgul*
  Treasury of, 23, 36n
  visiting of living by, 196–197, 329
  wandering, 211
Soul-candle, 27, 125, 309
  "The Cottage of Candles" and, 125, 309
  "The Enchanted Inn" and, 133, 311
"Soul of Reb Nachman, The," 244–245, 346
"Soul of the Ari, The," 258–259, 351
"Souls of Trees, The," 236, 343
Soviet regime, 346
Spain, expulsion of Jews from, 17
Sparks, gathering of, 94–95, 300
Sparks of soul, 9
"Speaking Flame, The," 90–92, 299
Speculative Kabbalah, 13
Spirit(s), 25. *See also* Maggid
  calling forth of, 254, 350
"Spirit of Idolatry, The," 56–57, 285
"Spirit of the Hagigah, The," 179–180, 324–325
Spirit possession, 346
Spiritual renewal, 333
Spring, holy, 207–208, 333
Stars, creation of, 59
Stone
  containing primordial light, 351
  reincarnation of soul into, 97, 301
  "The Soul of the Ari" and, 258–259, 351
"Stone in the Wall, A," 27, 97, 300

Sufi masters, tales about, 3, 33n
Sukkah, 312
  indoor, 151
Sukkot, 265
  etrog for, 265–266, 354
Sultan (Turkish), "The Cave of King David" and, 139–141, 312–313
Sun, creation of, 59
"Supernal House," 286, 292
Supernatural tales, "The Shadow on the Wall," 228–229, 340
Sword, fiery everturning, 189–191, 326
"Sword of the Messiah, The," 31, 234–236, 342–343
Sympathetic magic, "A Bowl of Soup" and, 222, 338, 340
Synagogue of Serah bat Asher, 49

Table leg, "The Golden Table" and, 58–59, 286–287
Tablets of Law, 294
"Tale of the Etrog, The," 265–266, 354
"Tale of the Kiddish Cup, The," 149–150, 315–316
"Tale of the Kugel, The," 11, 268–271, 355
"Tale of the Millstone, The," 345
Tallis, 53, 118, 176, 205, 244, 263
  of Abraham, 136
  Seer of Lublin's landing on, 256
  tying of knots of, 264
Talmud, 4, 8, 276, 343, 354
  gates of heaven and, Luz and, 277
  "The Golden Table" and, 286
  mystical folktales originating from, 32, 324
  tractate Hagigah of, *See* Hagigah
  use of tetragrammaton in, 283
Tammuz, 240
Tehom, 283
Tefillin, 8, 53, 176, 244, 263, 307, 347
  "The Angel of the Mishnah" and, 306
  "The Golden Dove" and, 277
  new style of letters for, 247–248, 347
  "The Speaking Flame" and, 91–92, 299
"*Tefillin* of the Or Hayim, The," 8, 117–118, 307
Temple in Jerusalem, 186
  destruction of, 349
Temptations, cave of, 166–168, 320–321
Ten Commandments, 312
Ten martyrs, 31, 38n
  deaths of, 282
"Tenth Man, The," 135–136, 311–312
Tents of Shem, 278

Teplik, 241
Test tales. *See* Divine tests
Testament of Abraham, The, 320
Tetragrammaton, 13, 32, 309, 339
    angels and, 314
    secret pronunciation of, 315, 329, 335
    use in Talmud, 283
Theosophical Kabbalah, 13
Thirty-six Hidden Saints (Thirty-six Just
        Men), 309, 350. *See also Lamed Vav
        Tzaddikim*
"Thirty-Two Paths," 15
Thoughts, God's reading of, 215
Three sages, downfall of, 3
"Three Stars," 227–228, 339–340
Throne of Glory, 13, 18, 24, 73, 138,
        195
    "The Ascent of Moses" and, 46, 279
Throne of King Solomon, 277
Tiberias, 73, 86, 87, 97
Tibetan Book of the Dead, 3
Tikkun, 327, 336, 346
Tikkun olam, 17, 305, 306–307
Tlemcen, 310
Torah, 52, 136, 263, 282, 304, 333
    Angel of, 137
    body of Moses and, 100
    celestial, 59, 308
        receiving of, by Rabbi Meier ben
            Baruch of Rothenburg, 308
    dictation of, 5
    end of, Hayim Vital sitting closest to,
        301
    giving of, 15, 33n, 193
    "A Kiss from the Master" and, 79–80
    legend of the thirteen Torahs, 308
    letters of, 46
        flight of, 14, 156–157, 318
        meaning of, 22–23, 36n
        new style for, 247–248, 347
    Moses' receiving of, 45, 46–47, 100, 279,
        293–294
    Moses' writing of, 308
    mysteries of, 11–12
    "The Palace of Illusions" and, 330
    as possession of Jews, 63, 288
    Prince of, 188, 264, 326
    Rabbi Meier of Rothenburg's transcribing
        of, 121–123, 308
    Samaritans and, 316
    scrolls of, dropping of, 174
    Tzohar and, 288
    water of, 133
    way of, 132
    wisdom of, 132

words of
    Ben Azzai and, 51
    manipulation of, 22–23, 26n
    in Worms, 121–123
"Torah of the Flying Letters," 156–157,
        318
Torchin, 257
Tosefet Shabbat, 340
Tradition, original, retaining of, 334
Transformation, "The Tale of the Etrog"
        and, 265–266, 354
Transgression, 336
Treasury of prayers, 43
Treasury of souls, 23, 36n
Tree(s)
    affixing of candle to, 334
    flaming, 195, 328–329
    soul entering of, 177
    souls of, 27, 236, 343
Tree of Life, 15, 190
    branches of, blast of shofar and, 198
    "Tree of Life, The," 24, 192–193, 327–328
Tree of Souls, 334
Trial, The (Kafka), 309
"Truth," 56
"Trying to Pray," 267, 355
Tsadkiel, "The Angel in the Mirror" and,
        102, 302–303
Tsedaka, Abraham, "The Miracle in the
        Sukkah" and, 151, 316
Tsel, 340. *See also* Silhouette
Tselem (Astral Body), 317, 340
Tsura (shape or figure), 316
Turkey, 140
Twelve tribes, 122
Twersky dynasty, 352
Tzaddik, 20, 103, 232, 344
    crumbs of, 116
    doctrine of, 10, 34n
    hidden, 350
    Rabbi Adam, 187
    as servant of Yodea, 238
Tzaddik ha-dor, 10
Tzaddik of Belz, 264–265, 353–354
Tzaddik of Kallo, "The Sabbath Guests"
        and, 251–252, 348–349
"*Tzaddik* of the Forest, The," 18, 109–112,
        305
Tzaddikim, 122
    golden coaches of, 135
Tzimtzum, 16
Tzohar, 33
    midrashim about, 38n
    "The Soul of the Ari" and, 351
"*Tzohar*, The," 24, 33, 59–62, 287–288

Uman
  cemetery in, 21, 35n, 243
  Reb Nachman's tomb in, 242–245, 346
"Underground Forest, The," 11, 214–218,
  336–337, 338
Unification, prayers of, 21
Unio mystica, 13
"Unlocking the Gates of Heaven," 15, 205–
  207, 332–333
Uriel, 13

"Vanity of Vanities," 105
Vessels, shattering of, 16–17, 95, 300
Vision(s)
  of God, 279
  prophetic, *See* Prophetic visions
"Vision, A," 264–265, 353–354
"Vision at the Wailing Wall, A," 19, 28,
  87–89, 298, 353
"Vision in the Cemetery, A," 178–179, 324
"Vision of Light, A," 231–232, 341
"Vision of the Bride, A," 19, 28, 245–246,
  347
"Vision of the High Priest, The," 4, 28, 55,
  284
"Visit to the City of the Dead," 101–102,
  302
"Visitor from the Other World, A," 196–
  197, 329, 348
Vital, Hayim, 7, 9, 256, 302, 336, 350
  "The Angel in the Mirror" and, 102–103,
    302–303
  "The Angel of Forgetfulness" and, 81–83,
    295–296, 348
  deprivation of memory, 82–83
  dreams and visions of
    of the Ari, 102, 103
    record of, 303
    "A Visit to the City of the Dead" and,
      101–102, 302
  "The Handwriting of the Messiah" and,
    31, 103–104, 303
  Miriam's well and, 348
  Sefer ha-Hezyonot and, 302, 303
  viewing of face of *Shekhinah* by, 84–85,
    297
  "The Widow of Safed" and, 99, 301
"Voice in the Attic, The," 64–65, 289
"Voice in the Tree, The," 26, 177–178, 324
Voice of God, 46, 279

Wailing Wall, 267
  tales set at, 355
  vision of *Shekhinah* at, 87–89, 298
  Western Wall, *See Kotel*

Wandering Jew, 318
Wandering rabbis, 317
Wandering soul, falling of, 211
"Wandering Soul, A," 27, 266–267, 354
"Wandering Well, The," 250–251, 348
Water(s)
  dividing of, 29, 37n
  enchanted, "The Cave of King David"
    and, 140–141
Water carrier, 317
Water of the Torah, 133
"Waters of the Abyss," 54–55, 283–284
Way of the Torah, 132
Weddings, 251
Well
  creation of, by Baal Shem Tov, "The
    Healing Spring" and, 207–208, 333
  Miriam's, *See* Miriam's well
  "The Wandering Well" and, 250–251,
    348
Werbermacher, Hannah Rochel. *See* Maid
  of Ludomir
Western candle, 307
Western Wall. *See Kotel*
Wheat, soul entering of, 177
Whip, 310
  "Reb Shmelke's Whip" and, 226, 339
"Widow of Safed, The," 8, 98–99, 301
"Wine of Paradise, The," 223–224, 338
Wisdom of the Torah, 132
Witch, "The Young Man without a Soul"
  and, 146–147, 148
Witch of Endor, 350
Wives, abandoned, "Rabbi Naftali's Trance"
  and, 152–154, 316–317
Wolf, Ze'ev, 213
"Woman in the Forest, The," 221–222,
  337–338
Wonder Child, 299
Word(s)
  manipulation of, 22–23, 26n
  mysteries of, 12
"Words in the Sand, The," 171–172, 322
Work of the Chariot, 18
World
  creation of, 16, 137, 300
  destruction of, 70
  repair of, 305, 306–307
World of Truth, 133
World to Come, 23, 123, 161. *See also*
  Olam Haba
  "Rabbi Naftali's Trance" and, 316
Worms, Torah in, 121–123

Yahrtzeit candle, lighting of, 334

Yakov bar Acha, death of, 294
Yalkut Shimoni, 319
Yannai, 300
Yehezkel of Prague, 314, 336
Yehiel Mikhal, 192
Yehoshua (Joshua) ben Hananiah, 152,
     285–286
   "The Lion of Ilai" and, 285–286
Yehoshua (Joshua) ben Levi, 336
   "Law is Not in Heaven, The" and, 63,
     289
   "Shining Robe, The" and, 141–143, 313–
     314
Yehudim, 16
Yermiyahu (rabbi), 63
Yeshivah, 283
Yetzer ha-Ra, 285, 286, 338. *See also* Evil in-
     clination
Yetzer-ha-Tov, 285, 338. *See also* Good in-
     clination
Yihudim, 12, 22, 23
Yismach Moyshe of Ihel, 266
Yitzhak of Vorki, 312
YIVO, 6
Yocheved, 280
Yodea, 238, 344
Yodea, defined, 344
Yoel Baal Shem, 329
Yoezzer ben Yaakov, "The Golden Scepter"
     and, 73–74, 291–292
Yohanan ben Zakkai, 8, 97, 103, 220, 337
   "Chronicle of Serah Bat Asher" and, 49
   "Mysteries of the Chariot" and, 50–51,
     280–281
Yom Kippur, 136
   appearance of the wandering well and,
     250–251, 348
   Baal Shem Tov's ascent to paradise dur-
     ing, 332
   dropping of the Torah during, 174
   Master of Prayer on, 255
Yosef, death of, 294

Yosef David, 260, 352
Yosse, "The Book of Adam" and, 74–75,
     292–293
Yossi Ha-Kohen, "Mysteries of the Chariot"
     and, 51
"Young Magician, The," 11, 224–225, 339
"Young Man without a Soul, The," 145–
     148, 314–315
Yuda ben Baba, 283
Yuda ben Dema, 283

Zalman, Schneur, "The Flaming Letters"
     and, 247–248, 347
Zemach Tzaddik. See Mendel, Menachem
Zen masters, tales about, 3, 33n
Zevi, Shabbatai, 5, 6, 33n, 34n, 333
Zipporah, 339
Zohar, 5, 25, 34n, 155, 210, 237, 276, 280,
     343
   angel of, 10, 212, 335–336
   appearance of, 33n, 287
   author of, 5, 34n
   book of
     in the cave of Shimon bar Yohai, 69
     discovery of, 106
     interpreting of, 154, 317
     "A Kiss from the Master" and, 79
   Divining from the Zohar, 343
   esteem of, 317
   golden dove and, 327
   heavenly palace presided over by four
     women in, 280
   mythical commentary in, 8
   "The Soul of the Ari" and, 259
   writing of Torah and, 22
Zoma, Ben, 29, 37n
   "The Four Who Entered Paradise" and,
     51–52, 280–281
Zushya of Hanipol, "The Shadow on the
     Wall" and, 228–229, 340
   "The Flaming Letters" and, 247, 248,
     347